Social Psychology

Social Psychology

Stephen Worchel
University of Southern Maine

Joel Cooper
Princeton University

George R. Goethals
Williams College

James M. Olson
University of Western Ontario

Wadsworth
Thomson Learning

Australia • Canada • Denmark • Japan • Mexico • New Zealand • Philippines • Puerto Rico
Singapore • South Africa • Spain • United Kingdom • United States

Psychology Editor: *Marianne Taflinger*
Editorial Assistant: *Suzanne Wood*
Marketing Manager: *Jenna Opp*
Project Editor: *Marlene Vasilieff*
Print Buyer: *Stacey Weinberger*
Permissions Editor: *Bob Kauser*
Text Designer: *Jane Rae Brown*

Photo Researcher: *Randall Nicholas*
Illustrator: *Corasue Nicholas*
Cover Designer: *Stephen Rapley*
Cover Image: *"Arena in Arles" by van Gogh/SuperStock*
Compositor: *E. T. Lowe*
Printer/Binder: *Courier*

Printed in the United States of America

1 2 3 4 5 6 03 02 01 00 99

Library of Congress Cataloging-in-Publication Data

Social psychology / Stephen Worchel . . . [et al.].
    p.   cm.
Includes bibliographical references and index.
ISBN 0-8304-1470-3 (alk. paper)
1. Social psychology. I. Worchel, Stephen.
HM251 .U56 2000.
302—dc21
                                    98-14914
                                       CIP

For more information, contact
Wadsworth/Thomson Learning
10 Davis Drive
Belmont, CA 94022-3098
USA
www.wadsworth.com

International Headquarters
Thomson Learning
290 Harbor Drive, 2nd Floor
Stamford, CT 06902-7477
USA

UK/Europe/Middle East
Thomson Learning
Berkshire House
168-173 High Holborn
London WC1V 7AA
United Kingdom

Asia
Thomson Learning
60 Albert Street #15-01
Albert Complex
Singapore 189969

Canada
Nelson/Thomson Learning
1120 Birchmount Road
Scarborough, Ontario M1K 5G4
Canada

Contents

Chapter 1

"Tony Sheehan" by Brian Counihan

Chapter 2

"Bench Philosophers" by Hannah Messinger

Chapter 3

"Take Five" by Dianni-Kaleel

Chapter 4

"Denial" by Bruce Cegur

Chapter 5

"The Dance Continues" by Mary Hatch

Chapter 6

"Three Ages of Women" by Pat Olson

Chapter 7

"Bag Lady" by Geoffrey Bent

Chapter 8

"Cathy's Dream" by Nancy Wieting

Chapter 9

"Commemoration" by Gabriella Boros

Chapter 10

"Ruby Guns Down Oswald" by Edward Karl Fresa

Chapter 11

"New Arrival" by Bruce Cegur

Chapter 12

"The Rowers" by Edward Karl Fresa

Chapter 13

"Battery Park" by Pat Olson

Chapter 14

"Exodus" by Dianni-Kaleel

Preface

The new millennium brings with it a whole package of questions, paradoxes, and opportunities. We hear promises of a new generation of drugs that will prolong our lives. The advent of cloning hints that it will not be long before we can duplicate ourselves. And the advances in space travel offer possibilities that we may be able to carry on our lives in different worlds. As enticing as it is to focus attention on the future, it is equally important that we not lose sight of the present. For, as we stand on the brink of a new beginning, the condition of our present lives suggests that we must still address issues that have confronted humankind during the previous millennium.

In the last years of the twentieth century within the United States, the impeachment of President Clinton raised issues that were as old as human politics and the search for justice. Although few people disputed the "facts" of the case that were laid open to the world, there was great disagreement over the interpretation of these "facts." Debate swirled over whether Clinton intended to mislead the grand jury. Basic questions were asked about the character of President Clinton. The air was filled with accusations that members of Congress were casting their votes to conform to a party line rather than to the information that was presented. Many commentators took time to change their focus from politics to personal relationships as they openly marveled at the support Hillary Clinton continued to give her husband. While this drama played out in the United States, Canadians in Quebec held another election on whether or not Canada should be split into separate groups along ethnic and cultural lines. In the Middle East, rockets filled the air as simmering conflicts between Israelis and Palestinians turned violent and the United States and its allies grew tired of Saddam Hussein's reneging on promises of open arms inspections. Against this dark background,

the plight of people in Honduras and Guatemala who faced floods and mudslides touched the heart of the world, and help poured into Central America.

These and other current events pointedly demonsrate that even as humankind stands on the edge of a new millennium, the need to understand basic human behavior is as important as it ever was. Whether that behavior involves determining the intentions behind the act of a single individual or the massive destruction of a group of people acting in unison, efforts to understand and explain human interaction fall under the domain of *social psychology*. It seems somewhat fitting that as humankind prepares for the new millennium, social psychology celebrates its one hundredth birthday, marking its beginning with Triplett's study in 1898.

The present volume is designed to capture this hundred years of development of the field of social psychology. In this effort, we have attempted to present the "classic" studies and theories on which social psychology has been built. Our aim has been to demonstrate how early work served as the foundation for the current emphasis in social psychology. To this end, the reader will find ample discussion of early work in such areas as attribution (chapter 2), social comparison (chapter 3), attitude formation and change (chapters 5 and 6), cognitive dissonance (chapter 6), social influence (chapter 11), and group dynamics (chapter 13).

But our aim is not only to invite old friends to the table. We also want to show the current state of the field and how new directions developed from earlier topics of interest. For example, current social psychology has embraced the cognitive revolution that has influenced many areas of psychology. However, the emphasis on information processing and cognition is not the result of simply jumping on a passing bandwagon. The cognitive approach, so pronounced in such areas as the self and social identity (chapter 3), perceiving others (chapter 2), stereotyping (chapter 7), and intergroup relations (chapter 12), has a long history in social psychology. It has, however, begun to reach its potential during the last two decades. Today's social psychology also boasts of new methods (for example, physiological measures of attitudes, chapter 5), new approaches (for example, evolutionary psychology, chapter 8), and new applications (for example, aggression and video games, chapter 10; AIDS and safe-sex, chapter 5).

And no presentation of social psychology would be complete without a peek at the future of the field. Although social psychology was largely developed in North America, it has attracted the interest of investigators throughout the world. We have recognized this growing interest by making an effort to include research from investigators in all parts of the world. Likewise, social psychologists have become more aware of the role of culture in influencing human behavior. Culture is not merely a passive observer; rather, it is an active partner that affects all aspects of behavior. Chapter 14 recognizes this development and examines its implications for the field of social psychology.

The book builds on the previous editions of *Understanding Social Psychology*. It embraces the aim of combining basic theory and research with application. It accepts the premise of bringing together classic and new theories and research. And it retains the collaboration of the three authors of the earlier editions. Yet, the present book is also very different. A new author, James Olson, has been added. Jim brings a new perspective and a new emphasis to the team. He not only adds the cognitive perspective of social psychology but also helps expand the focus beyond the boundaries of the United States. The addition of a new perspective and a new expertise allows us to present a more complete picture of the field of social psychology. An aside on the author team arose when we began discussing our background, and figured that between us, we represented one hundred years of experience in teaching social psychology! Although we were not sure whether this was a very comforting or very disturbing discovery from a personal perspective, it did give us a certain sense of confidence as we developed a plan for the book.

The book begins at the micro level and moves through human interaction to the more macro level.

Accordingly, we introduce social psychology by focusing on the self and the processing of social information (chapters 2, 3, and 4). Still within this framework we move into an examination of attitudes and persuasion (chapters 5 and 6). The relationship between information processing and attitudes is explored within the specific framework of prejudice and stereotypes (chapter 7). From this focus on the self, we move into the realm of interpersonal relations, beginning with attraction (chapter 8) and altruism (chapter 9) before moving to the darker side to explore aggression (chapter 10). The next three chapters expand the arena of social interactions by examining group behavior. Chapter 11 deals with influence within social settings, and chapter 12 addresses conflict that can result when groups are formed. From the focus on the relationship between groups, we next examine the processes that arise within groups (chapter 13). And we conclude our examination of social psychology by exploring how social behavior is affected by the culture in which it takes place (chapter 14).

Social psychology is a field that has often marched to two simultaneous drumbeats. On one hand, the field has paid close attention to social issues of the day, drawing on these issues for ideas and applying theories and the results of research to better understand and deal with issues. On the other hand, social psychology has remained devoted to Kurt Lewin's admonishment that the field adhere to the guideposts of the scientific approach. The combination of these two goals has resulted in social psychology's claim for both relevance and respect. Our aim has been to fairly represent these two principles throughout this volume. Therefore, the reader will find discussion of theory, research, and methodology intertwined with application.

Supplements and Additional Features

Given our hundred years of experience, one might suspect that we should be able to go it alone at this point. However, time has taught us the value of the support and advice offered by others. We have, indeed, been fortunate in this respect. We gratefully acknowledge the help of many people who have contributed to this volume. Dawna Coutant, Hank Rothgerber, Manuela Ivaldi, John Iuzzini, Dora Capoza, Anne Maass, Paco

Morales, William Webb, Vicki Esses, Bill Fisher, Carolyn Hafer, and Dick Sorrentino helped us develop ideas and guided us to material that was included in this volume. The folks at Nelson Hall, Inc. were the glue that kept the team together and their support helped maintain our enthusiasm for the project. Thanks to Richard Meade and Dorothy Anderson. Thanks to Jane Brown for her engaging design for the text. And our appreciation to the reviewers—Karen L. Horner, Jack L. Powell, Brian W. Schrader, and Peter Miene—who gave us valuable feedback. Sharmon Toner and Joan Boggis helped prepare the manuscript and meet deadlines that brought us across the finish line to the final product. Finally, the wonderful support of our families who put aside their needs, listened to our ranting and raving, and kept us sane at the most insane moments is finally recognized. It is you who made this project possible and enjoyable.

Every effort has been made to make this text attractive and usable. The text includes an extensive test bank, prepared by Dawna Coutant. It contains approximately 75 test items per chapter, consisting of approximately 35 multiple choice, 35 true/false, and 5 essay questions. The test bank is available to instructors both as a printed document and on disk (please contact your local Thompson Learning representative for a copy of these items).

1 Social Psychology: What, Why, and How

Chapter 1

Social Psychology: What, Why, and How

On Halloween eve, 1938, a radio program of Spanish music was interrupted by a "newscast" reporting explosions on Mars. Sometime later, Roman Raquello and his orchestra were again interrupted, this time with the information that a huge flaming object had landed in the small town of Grover's Mill, near Princeton, New Jersey. The radio network sent reporter Carl Phillips to the scene. This is part of the report heard by millions of listeners on the CBS network:

> [Phillips] Well, I . . . I hardly know where to begin, to paint for you a word picture of the strange scene before my eyes, like something out of a modern *Arabian Nights*. Well, I just got here. I haven't had a chance to look around yet. I guess that's it. Yes, I guess that's the . . . thing, directly in front of me, half buried in a vast pit. Must have struck with terrific force. The ground is covered with splinters of a tree it must have struck on its way town. What I can see of the . . . object itself doesn't look very much like a meteor, at least not the meteors I've seen. It looks more like a huge cylinder. . . . (Hadley Cantril in Koch, 1940/1968).

After Philips had gone into a more detailed description, he said:

> [Phillips] Just a minute! Something's happening! Ladies and gentlemen, this is terrific! This end of the thing is beginning to flake off! The top is beginning to rotate like a screw! The thing must be hollow! . . . Ladies and gentlemen, this is the most terrifying thing I have ever witnessed. . . . Wait a minute! Someone's crawling out of the hollow top. Someone or . . . something. I can see peering out of that black hole two luminous disks . . . are they eyes? It might be a face. It might be . . . Good heavens, something's wriggling out of the shadow like a gray snake. Now it's another one, and another. They look like tentacles to me. There, I can see the thing's body. It's large as a bear and it glistens like wet leather. But that face. It . . . it's indescribable. I can hardly force myself to keep looking at it. The eyes are black and gleam like a serpent. The mouth is V-shaped with saliva dripping from its rimless lips that seem to quiver and pulsate. . . .

Phillips then moved to find a better position from which to view the strange happenings. Once in position, he reported:

> [Phillips] A humped shape is rising out of the pit. I can make out a small beam of light against a mirror. What's that? There's a jet of flame springing from that mirror, and it leaps right at the advancing men. It strikes them head on! Good Lord, they're turning into flame! Now the whole field's caught fire. [Explosion] The woods . . . the barns . . . the gas tanks of automobiles . . . it's spreading everywhere. It's coming this way. About 20 yards to my right. . . .

> [Announcer Two] Ladies and gentlemen, due to circumstances beyond our control, we are unable to continue the broadcast from Grover's Mill. Evidently there's some difficulty with our field transmission. (Koch, 1940/1968)

When communication with the scene was restored, forty people, including six troopers, were reported dead, burned beyond all recognition. Martial law was declared in central New Jersey. Captain Lansing of the armed forces took to the air to announce that the feared object was surrounded by eight infantry battalions.

A few seconds later, the radio audience was exposed to sounds of gunfire, the shouting of orders, and general pandemonium. Silence fell, only to be broken by a bulletin read by a newsman in the New York studio:

> [Announcer Two] Ladies and gentlemen, I have a grave announcement to make. Incredible as it may seem, both the observations of science and the evidence of our eyes lead to the inescapable assumption that those strange beings who landed in the Jersey farmlands tonight are the vanguard of an invading army from the planet Mars. The battle which took place tonight at Grover's Mill has ended in one of the most startling defeats ever suffered by an army in modern times; seven thousand men armed with rifles and machine guns pitted against a single fighting machine of the invaders from Mars. One hundred and twenty known survivors. The rest strewn over the battle area from Grover's Mill to Plainsboro, crushed and trampled to death under the metal feet of the monster, or burned to cinders by its heat ray. The monster is now in control of the middle section of New Jersey and has effectively cut the state through its center. (Koch, 1940/1968)

As the drama continued, the listeners were addressed by the U.S. secretary of the interior, whose advice to the worried citizens was that they should place their faith in God. Residents of New York were urged to evacuate and were told which routes to take and which to avoid. It was reported that communication with New Jersey had been broken and that the smoke was descending upon New York as reports were being received of Martian landings in Buffalo, Chicago, and St. Louis. "This is the end now," explained the reporter. "People are trying to run from it, but it's no use. They're falling like flies. Now the smoke's crossing Sixth Avenue . . . Fifth Avenue . . . one hundred yards away . . . it's 50 feet. . . . "

It is estimated that at least six million people heard Orson Welles's Mercury Theater broadcast based on H. G. Wells's *War of the Worlds* and that well over one million people believed that it was a legitimate newscast and that the Earth was being invaded by Martians. Before the hour-long program had ended, hundreds of thousands of Americans were seized with panic as they tried to flee the monsters from the planet Mars. People cried, screamed, gathered loved ones, huddled together or drove to flee the attacking onslaught. A male college student reported:

> One of the first things I did was to try to phone my girl but the lines were all busy, so that just confirmed my impression that the thing was true. We just started driving. We had heard that Princeton was wiped out and gas was spreading over New Jersey . . . we figured our friends and families were all dead. . . . (Cantril, 1940/1968)

The "invasion from Mars" stimulated a variety of responses and created a fertile ground for the study of numerous social phenomena. Hadley Cantril, a Princeton social psychologist, conducted 135 interviews in an effort to catalog people's reactions. One that occurred with regularity was a tendency to seek the company of other people to confront the stressful situation as a member of a group. People huddled in stores, storm cellars, apartments, and houses, and groups crowded into cars. One hysterical New Jersey woman phoned her local police department, which informed her that the danger was probably not "immediate." "We all kissed one another," she reported, "and felt we would all die. When I heard the gas was in the streets of Newark, I called my brother and his wife and told them to get in their car and come right over so we could all be together." Another of Cantril's respondents spoke of "gathering her friends and driving as far as she could," and coeds recalled that "the girls in the sorority houses and dormitories huddled around their radios, trembling and weeping in each other's arms."

Defining Social Psychology

The *War of the Worlds* broadcast had a profound and far-reaching effect on the people who turned on their radios that Halloween eve. Assume for the moment that you are part of a group whose class project is to describe and explain the effects of the broadcast. This is clearly a mammoth task; six million people heard the broadcast. How would your group go about working on this project?

One way would be for each group member to take a slightly different approach in examining the audience and its reactions. For example, you could examine the impact on individuals who heard the broadcast and on those who did not. You could then compare the attitudes, behaviors, and emotions of the people in these two categories. Another member of your group could focus on the effects of the broadcast

Orson Welles stands in the studio with arms raised in a rehearsal of one of his radio plays. His broadcast of H. G. Wells' War of the Worlds, *October 31, 1938, was intended as an entertainment special but led millions of listeners to fear for their lives and seek out social support from friends.*

on groups. This person could investigate how families or social groups were influenced by the events of that evening. Still a third member of your group might focus on specific individuals. This student might identify four people who heard the broadcast and compare each person's reaction to the reactions of the other three. Each of these perspectives would add to our understanding of the event by taking a slightly different approach.

In laying out these approaches, we have roughly identified the focuses of social psychology, sociology, and personality psychology. **Social psychology** can be defined as a discipline that uses scientific methods to "understand and explain how the thought, feeling, and

behavior of individuals are influenced by the actual, imagined, or implied presence of others" (Allport, 1985, p. 3).

An important point to remember is that the focus of social psychology is on the *individual* rather than on the group or some other unit. It is individuals who think, feel, and behave. As social psychologists we want to learn how the individual is affected by social events. It is this concern with the individual that ties social psychology to the family of psychology rather than to some other branch of social science. Having said this, we need to take one additional step to capture the flavor of social psychology. While the focus is on the individual, the goal is to understand how *most* peo-

TABLE 1.1   REACTIONS OF PEOPLE TO VARIOUS SOCIAL SITUATIONS

	Meeting a friend at dinner	Listening to a frightening broadcast	Encountering two friends arguing
Mary	Ignores him	Seeks a friend	Ignores them
John	Acts politely	Seeks a friend	Breaks up argument
Sue	Gets into argument	Seeks a friend to argue with	Joins argument
George	Races to cafeteria line	Seeks a friend	Listens to argument

Social psychology approach:
Identify the most likely responses within the situation and examine how the situation affects the most likely response.
Personality approach: Compare each person with the others to identify how each is unique.

ple act in a given situation. We are not so concerned about the unique personal characteristics of individuals that may cause them to act differently from each other. Our aim is to understand the general tendencies in the actions, feelings, and thoughts of individuals.

If you took this approach to your class project, you might ask whether most people were frightened by the broadcast (emotions), whether most people tried to be with others or stayed alone (behavior), and whether most people believed the Martians were coming to their area (attitudes). Carrying your role as a social psychologist further, you would be interested in explaining why people reacted as they did: Was it fear that caused people to want to be with others, and if so, why? And you might conclude your presentation with predictions about how people would respond in similar situations.

Your classmate who was interested in the effects of the broadcast on groups would be taking the sociological perspective. In general, sociologists are interested in the structure and functioning of groups. The groups can be small (a family), of moderate size (a sorority or fraternity), or large (a society). The focus here might be on the rules that the group has developed to deal with the crisis created by the *War of the Worlds*; or on what groups (social or work) were most strongly affected by the broadcast.

The student who researched a single individual represents the approach of personality psychologists. The interest here is in identifying *individual differences* that guide behavior. In this case, we would be concerned with how a single individual (Mary) reacted to various situations and how Mary's response differed from that of another person (John). To illustrate this approach, consider table 1.1. The personality

psychologist, who is interested primarily in identifying consistencies within people, will be most concerned with the horizontal axis. How does Mary (John, Sue, or George) act across situations? The social psychologist, who considers the effects of situations on persons, is interested in investigating the vertical consistencies in table 1.1. We know that Mary, John, Sue, and George differ in many ways. They will react to situations with some differences, and we may come to recognize them as having different personalities. But personality differences are not what concern social psychologists; they are interested in determining the way *most* people react.

From the table, it appears that being frightened causes most people to affiliate—to seek other persons. Though Mary generally seems to be more reclusive than John and less argumentative than Sue, this does not alter the fact that all of the individuals in the sample react to the social situation of the frightening broadcast by wanting to affiliate. As social psychologists, we know that if we continue to sample individuals, we will find someone who will not affiliate when afraid; differences among people will lead some to behave differently from the way the majority act.

Having examined these differences, we must point out that we are referring to the *emphasis* of the fields and not to clear disciplinary boundaries: while these distinctions may help us understand the focus of social psychology, personality, and sociology, they do not exclude considerable overlap. No sharp boundaries separate these fields; instead, interest and approach overlap among these and other fields (figure 1.1).

Serge Moscovici, a French social psychologist, characterizes social psychology as a "bridge" between

FIGURE 1.1   **SOCIAL PSYCHOLOGY AND ITS RELATIVES**

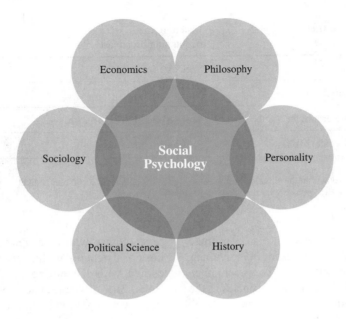

Note:
In addition to these disciplines, social psychology is developing close relationships with business, education, architecture, medicine, and law.

other branches of knowledge (Moscovici, 1989). The field recognizes the importance of the individual in a larger social system and therefore draws on sociology, political science, anthropology, and economics. It acknowledges the wide range of human activities and the influence of culture and of the past on human behavior. In taking this focus, social psychology intersects with philosophy, history, art, and music. In addition to this broad perspective, social psychology understands the relevance of internal human activities to social behavior. Social psychologists may ask, for example, how being with other people after a frightening incident affects levels of physiological arousal, such as blood pressure and heart rate. Because of this perspective, you will find us discussing such issues as perception, cognition, and physiological responses in our descriptions of research in social psychology. Therefore, although social psychology has its own exciting, unique identity, it is fair to characterize it as a close cousin of many other disciplines in the humanities, social sciences, and natural sciences. Indeed, our hope is that, after reading this text, you not only will be motivated to learn more about social psychology, but also will develop a greater interest in learning about human social behavior from other perspectives.

The Goal of Social Psychology: More Than Meets the Eye

As we will see, the field of social psychology has undergone some interesting transformations since its beginning. But none of the changes is more dramatic than the "behaviors" that social psychologists put under their microscope. If we look at the Cantril study, we find that the investigator was most interested in learning how people behaved when they heard that the "Martians were coming." Whom did they telephone? Whom did they visit? What did they talk about? Even, what did they pack into their automobiles when they fled their homes? In this case, Cantril (1940/1968) was examining how a social situation (the *War of the Worlds* program) affected both personal and interpersonal behaviors that could, for the most part, be observed and reported. This approach characterized many of the early studies in social psychology.

It was not long before social psychologists expanded their definition of "behaviors" that deserved their attention. They began examining responses beyond directly observable behaviors. These first included attitudes and emotions, and later embraced perceptions and interpretations. With this focus, Cantril may have examined how people felt while hearing the program or what their thoughts were. The aim, in this case, would still be how social stimuli affected responses, but the category of "response" was broadened.

Once research encompassed thoughts, perceptions, and emotions, the horizon expanded even further. Now social psychologists could explore the relationship between actions, attitudes, feelings, and perceptions. The focus now centered on the *process* involved in human social behavior, and some surprising findings began to unfold. We might be tempted to assume that an event occurring in the environment triggers a combination of feelings and actions in those affected. But as we will see, research shows that different people perceive and interpret the event differently, and their responses are often guided by their interpretations. Further, feelings and attitudes may

pave the way for behavior, or people's behaviors may influence their feelings and attitudes. And rather than the social event occurring as a stimulus outside the individual's control, we will see that an individual's attitudes and behaviors may, in fact, shape the nature of the social stimulus. In other words, the examination of the process uncovered some interesting relationships between social events, attitudes, feelings, interpretations, and actions.

But even this venture into processing was not the end of the realm of social psychology. Social life is not a series of discrete events, one beginning after the preceding one has closed. Just as we can remember a tune long after the band has packed its instruments and headed home, we store information about social interactions. And this warehouse of past information affects our expectations about current situations, our interpretation of them, and the way we categorize people and events in the setting. In recognition of these issues, social psychology's domain has also expanded

A social psychologist might view this family's looking at a personal picture album as a process of recalling social interactions and experiences, which may serve to influence present behavior.

to include the examination of how people store information about their past social interactions and experiences, and how this information influences their behavior in present situations. For example, Kelly (1997) discusses how our past experiences shape our language and beliefs about interpersonal relationships, and how these factors, in turn, influence our reaction to present relationships.

The point of this discussion is to help you appreciate and understand the extent of social psychology's grasp. As we examine many of the areas in greater depth, you may find yourself wondering why certain studies seem to focus more on cognitive issues such as information processing and mental representations of situations than on explicit social interactions. Indeed, the field of social psychology embraces many issues that fall under the heading of cognitive psychology, but this expansion is based on the premise that many of our cognitions are both a product of, and a force behind, our social behavior. In light of this view, it is interesting to speculate how Cantril's study would have expanded if it were run today rather than nearly sixty years ago! With an understanding of how social psychology has evolved to include an increasingly large sample of human behavior, let's take a brief look at its history to understand how the field has come to focus on specific topics.

The History of Social Psychology

Now that we have identified social psychology and its next of kin, let us take a quick look at its roots. This is actually a rather easy task because social psychology is really a child of the twentieth century. In fact, it has been estimated that 90 percent of all social psychologists who ever lived were alive in 1979 (Cartwright, 1979)!

In addition to being localized in time, social psychology is rather localized in place. The field has been largely a product of the Western world. Although modern social psychology had some early European architects, the field was confined to North America until fairly recently (Jones 1985; Graumann, 1988).

As we read the history of the field, let us keep one interesting point in mind. Possibly more than any other science, social psychology has been shaped by world events, political currents, and social issues (Harris, 1986). Important events of the day have been the im-

petus for many of its themes and areas of study. And, of equal importance, the findings of this young science can be used to influence the course of social events.

The year 1897 is generally celebrated as the year of the first social psychology experiment. Norman Triplett (1897) examined official records of bicycle races and noticed that a rider's maximum speed was approximately 20 percent faster when he raced in the presence of other riders than when he raced alone. Triplett then devised a laboratory study to demonstrate this effect further. In that study, children were given the task of winding line on a fishing reel either alone or in the presence of other children performing the same task. The effect of the presence of others on individual task performance was essentially the only issue studied experimentally for the first three decades of social psychology (Allport, 1985).

Soon after the turn of the century, two social psychology textbooks were published. One, titled *Social Psychology*, was written by E. A. Ross (1908), a sociologist, who argued that social behavior was caused by imitation or suggestion. Ross was interested in crowd psychology and the behavior of collectives. His work set the tone for the development of the study of social psychology within sociology (Pepitone, 1981). A second text, by William McDougall (1908), suggested that much of human behavior resulted from instincts. Instincts are innate, unlearned behavior tendencies that are common to members of a species. Hence McDougall viewed much of human social behavior as internally derived or motivated. McDougall focused more squarely on the individual than Ross did; this is the focus of social psychology. Although the two decades that followed the publication of McDougall's book were a time of growth for social psychology, it remained a discipline devoid of its own theoretical approach. Its methodology was also derivative, its techniques borrowed from the study of memory, learning, and education.

In 1929 Louis L. Thurstone and E. J. Chave published *The Measurement of Attitudes*. With this work an entire new field was born. Thurstone and Chave's work meant that attitudes could be conceptualized and measured. Soon new techniques were added (by Rensis Likert [1932], among others) and the 1930s became an era for measuring and studying the functions of attitudes. The first public opinion polling institute was founded in 1934 and spawned the giant industry that today tells us what we think about everything from toothpaste to presidential candidates.

The events of the 1930s played an important role in setting the stage for social psychology in the United States. The Great Depression found many young psychologists out of work. These psychologists banded together and found that unemployment was not their only common bond; they believed that psychologists should study important social issues, such as the fascism that was developing in Europe and the labor problems that were common in the United States (Finison, 1986; Stagner, 1986). This group of psychologists, which included such people as Ross Stagner, David Krech, Gordon Allport, Ernest Hilgard, and Gardner Murphy, formed the Society for the Psychological Study of Social Issues (SPSSI) in 1936. Although the society included psychologists from all areas of the discipline, a large proportion of the members were social psychologists.

Research in social psychology was still very different from what it is today until Kurt Lewin came on the scene. Lewin came from a tradition of applied psychology. During World War I he developed a test for wireless operators in Germany and his interests were on means for increasing group productivity (John, Eckardt, and Hiebsch, 1989). While this interest clearly fit the focus of those psychologists in SPSSI, Lewin had a broader agenda that established him as the founder of modern social psychology. Lewin, who emigrated from Hitler's Germany in 1933, introduced theory into social psychology. An unabashed proponent of the deductive method in science, he believed that general propositions that linked human behavior with social situations could and should be developed (Lewin, 1935). Moreover, he felt that these general propositions could be tested with the aid of experimentation. Under the influence of Lewin and his colleagues, social psychology began to view research not just as investigations into separate and unconnected phenomena but also as a way of testing general theories on human behavior (Lewin, 1935). With this new outlook, social psychology entered its modern age.

Lewin was also noteworthy for setting the tone for social psychology as a science that investigated social phenomena of the time and that then used its data to influence those social issues. For example, the beginning of World War II raised the issue of how people in the United States could be persuaded to conserve materials and food that were needed for the war effort. Lewin (1943) conducted a study on the effectiveness of various methods of social influence in getting homemakers to serve different and readily available foods. The war also created increased interest in the United States in what type of government

Modern bicyclists in the Tour de Houston race. One hundred years ago, Norman Triplett's observation that a rider's maximum speed significantly increased in the company of others during a race led to what is considered the first social psychology experiment.

was most effective: dictatorship or democracy. Lewin (Lewin, Lippitt, and White, 1939) took advantage of the war climate to compare the effects of different styles of leadership on group performance and dynamics. Lewin and his students also initiated a series of studies on group dynamics that served as one of the foundations for industrial/organizational psychology. In an effort to study group development, Lewin developed the participant-observation method, which gave rise to the use of T-groups in research and industry.

World War II was also the stimulus for the development of the Yale Communication Research Program. National leaders' concerns about the effects of propaganda and their desire to construct effective, persuasive propaganda campaigns led this group of researchers to apply learning theory to the area of attitude change (Lott and Lott, 1985). These investigators conducted dozens of studies to find out who should say what and how in order to persuade an audience to believe a message or adopt a position (see chapters 5 and 6).

The 1950s and early 1960s saw social psychology leave the starting gate and enter the race with a vengeance. The atrocities of the war created concern about the extent to which people would obey the orders of authority figures and conform to group patterns. Social psychologists initiated studies on conformity (Asch, 1956; see chapter 11) and obedience (Milgram, 1965; see chapter 11). Growing world tension, the arms race, and a war of words and nerve between Eastern and Western powers that was known as the Cold War focused attention on the issues of conflict and conflict resolution. Social psychologists combined their talents with those of sociologists, mathematicians, political scientists, and economists to develop theories and research methodologies for the study of conflict and decision making (Deutsch and Krauss, 1960).

While these efforts focused on the *relationship* between individuals, the theory that fanned the glowing embers of social psychology into a blaze emphasized the effect of *social situations* on individuals. Leon Festinger began his work by questioning how people evaluate themselves, including their efforts, attitudes, appearances, and behavior. He argued that in the absence of objective measures, people compare themselves with others (Festinger, 1954; see chapter 3). The concern with the evaluation process led Festinger to examine what happened when people were faced with inconsistencies between their behaviors, their attitudes

and behaviors, and their attitudes. He proposed the theory of cognitive dissonance (Festinger, 1957; see chapter 6), in which he argued that people strive for consistency in their cognitions (beliefs, attitudes, and information about their behaviors and those of others). The discovery of inconsistency creates a state of cognitive dissonance and motivates individuals to restore consistency. Research on cognitive dissonance filled

Adolf Eichmann, Lt. Colonel in the Nazi Security Service (S.S.), was charged in a 1961 trial in Jerusalem with crimes against humanity, including the deportation of 3 million Jews and others to death camps. He was found guilty and executed. Crimes such as this led to the social psychological study of obedience to authority.

the social psychology journals for the next fifteen years, and the theory was used to improve understanding of such issues as consumer behavior, interpersonal attraction, school desegregation, and learning.

The ten years from the mid-1960s to the mid-1970s found social psychology increasingly concerned with the way the individual perceived and interpreted social events. The attribution process (Kelly, 1967; Jones and Davis, 1965; see chapter 2) captured the imagination of social psychologists and was applied to further explain emotions, self-evaluation, and the perception of other people. This period also witnessed another change in emphasis in social psychology. If the field was truly to be taken seriously as a science, it had to develop methods that could be replicated and reported, and that could stand the rigorous scrutiny demanded by other sciences. Hence social psychologists turned their attention to refining their research methods, embracing new techniques for recording and observing human behavior, and applying more advanced statistical tools for analyzing and interpreting their data (Kenny, 1985). Technological advances allowed researchers to incorporate physiological measures and precise video recordings in their studies and to use increasingly sophisticated computer software to conduct research and analyze data. In addition to refining their methodology, social scientists were able to refine their theories, thanks to the new vistas that the technological advances opened up to them. For example, Cacioppo and his colleagues (Cacioppo, 1997; Cacioppo, 1993) pioneered the use of sophisticated neural recording techniques to measure attitudes. This method would not have been possible without the technological advances in computers and psychophysiology that have occurred in the last twenty years.

This concern with housekeeping was viewed with alarm by some social psychologists (Elms, 1975). Was social psychology losing its dedication to social issues and was it destined to become a science preoccupied with minutiae and irrelevant details? Indeed, this was not a new concern; it had been expressed by J. F. Brown, one of Lewin's students, in the early 1930s (Minton, 1984). The alarm was unfounded, however, as the 1970s saw social psychology incorporate its more sophisticated methodologies and theories into the study of women's issues, the environment, the law and legal process, and peace and conflict resolution. And with their unique training in behavioral theories and methodology, social psychologists have been sought for positions in government, law firms, and industry.

And the field expanded its geographical boundaries. The European Association of Experimental Social Psychology was founded and important European research in such areas as social influence and group behavior became widely known. And in 1996, an Asian Society of Social Psychology was launched to recognize the activities in the field in the Pacific Rim countries.

The 1980s also saw a change in the emphasis of social psychological theory and research. There was an increasing fascination with the way people perceive and process social information (cognition). Emphasis on the cognitive approach (Markus and Zajonc, 1985; see chapter 2) has shown that people are not merely passive pawns who react to their social environment; rather, they organize and interpret events. The work on social cognition is directed at identifying how people process this information and at making more precise predictions about the relationship between people and their social world.

The drumbeat of progress and change continued into the 1990s as social psychology remained sensitive to social issues. For a number of years, social psychologists had realized that culture has profound effects on people's behavior, and if the discipline wished to present itself as one concerned with general theories of social behavior, it would be necessary to include studies in other cultures. Several investigators (for example, Berry, 1979; Bond and Yang, 1982; Brislin, 1980; Lonner, 1980; Triandis, 1975) stood as stalwart proponents of the need to study culture's influence on social behavior. However, their efforts were not initially considered central in social psychology. But increasing globalization in the political, business, and entertainment arenas of the world and the growing contribution from social psychologists outside the Western countries have brought about increasing interest in cross-cultural studies. The 1990s saw the introduction of several influential books on culture's role in social behavior (Kitayama and Markus, 1994; Matsumoto, 1996; Triandis, 1994).

In the 1990s social psychology expanded its horizons to deal with other important social issues. In response to the persistent increase of AIDS throughout the world, the use of social influence techniques to change human sexual behavior has generated increased interest (Fisher and Fisher, 1992b). And the tragic outbreaks of ethnic violence in Yugoslavia, Central Africa, and the former Soviet Union excited new research on self-identity and the importance of ethnicity in this identity (Ethier and Deaux, 1994;

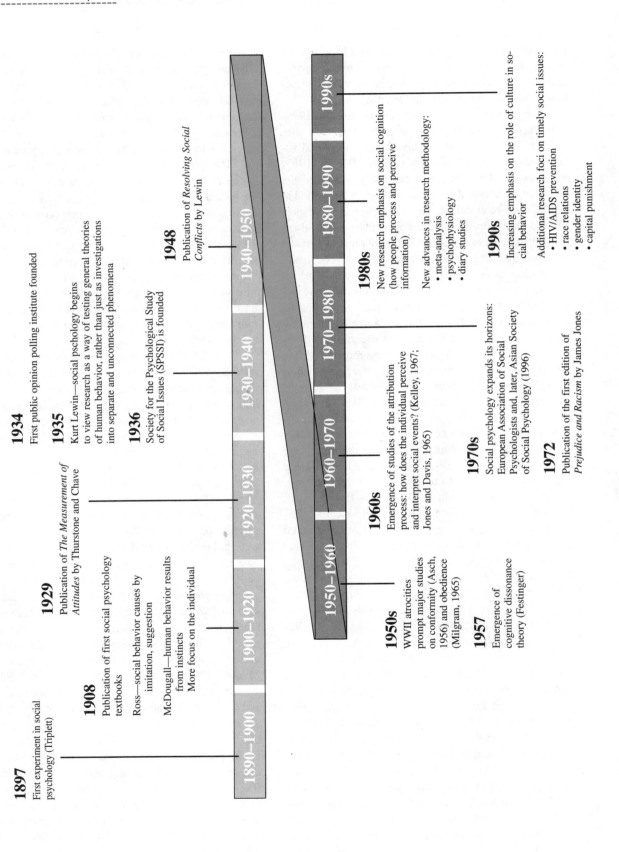

FIGURE 1.2   HIGHLIGHTS IN THE HISTORY OF SOCIAL PSYCHOLOGY

1897
First experiment in social psychology (Triplett)

1908
Publication of first social psychology textbooks

Ross—social behavior causes by imitation, suggestion

McDougall—human behavior results from instincts
More focus on the individual

1929
Publication of *The Measurement of Attitudes* by Thurstone and Chave

1934
First public opinion polling institute founded

1935
Kurt Lewin—social pschology begins to view research as a way of testing general theories of human behavior, rather than just as investigations into separate and unconnected phenomena

1936
Society for the Psychological Study of Social Issues (SPSSI) is founded

1948
Publication of *Resolving Social Conflicts* by Lewin

1950s
WWII atrocities prompt major studies on conformity (Asch, 1956) and obedience (Milgram, 1965)

1957
Emergence of cognitive dissonance theory (Festinger)

1960s
Emergence of studies of the attribution process: how does the individual perceive and interpret social events? (Kelley, 1967; Jones and Davis, 1965)

1970s
Social psychology expands its horizons: European Association of Social Psychologists and, later, Asian Society of Social Psychology (1996)

1972
Publication of the first edition of *Prejudice and Racism* by James Jones

1980s
New research emphasis on social cognition (how people process and perceive information)

New advances in research methodology:
• meta-analysis
• psychophysiology
• diary studies

1990s
Increasing emphasis on the role of culture in social behavior

Additional research foci on timely social issues:
• HIV/AIDS prevention
• race relations
• gender identity
• capital punishment

1890–1900   1900–1920   1920–1930   1930–1940   1940–1950

1950–1960   1960–1970   1970–1980   1980–1990   1990s

Sidanius, 1993; Turner, 1987). Although we are not suggesting that social psychology is a field driven solely by current social issues, it is important to recognize that throughout its history, it has stood ready to apply its theories and methods to better understanding pressing social problems of the time. These issues have often helped define new directions for the field and have maintained its vitality and importance. Thus, present-day social psychology is neither myopically focused on practical issues nor concerned solely with basic theoretical ones. Rather, the social psychology of today represents the coexistence of the applied and basic approaches—and a new excitement characterizes both. Although debates—sometimes heated—rage about which approach is the true social psychology (Gergen, 1989; Zajonc, 1989), a new, more vigorous field may grow out of this philosophical conflict. The basic research is gleaning new ideas and areas of study from the virgin territory being opened by investigators in the areas of applied research. And conversely, the psychologist whose interest is carrying the torch of social psychology into the arena of social issues is able to draw on a rapidly expanding store of knowledge. As we will see throughout this text, social psychology today is represented by a diversity of concerns, approaches, and methods, each with the potential to complement and strengthen the other.

Elliot Aronson (1989) likened the field of social psychology to

> a large circus tent, where a lot of different acts are going on simultaneously, and the acts occasionally cross, intermingle, and overlap. In this circus-tent world, we frequently bump into one another, challenge one another, influence one another, and sharpen one another's thinking to the overall betterment of the final product. (P. 510)

Methods of Social Psychology

Now that we have clearly identified the field of social psychology, let us turn from the question of *what* to that of *how*. We can begin by returning to the panic created by the *War of the Worlds* broadcast.

Hadley Cantril's account of the events following the broadcast provides us with detailed illustrations of human behavior during a crisis. Our first response to the 135 interviews, however, might be dismay and confusion. We would find that some people screamed, some wept, some gathered their families together, and some ran to be with friends. We would find that some people panicked while others calmly stood their ground and waited for the Martian onslaught. Still others did not believe the broadcast and went on with their normal routine. This is quite an array of events, and we would be hard pressed to give an accurate description of human behavior in crisis after a cursory glance at Cantril's interviews.

Investigators in almost every field of knowledge are often faced with similarly imposing tasks: they must make sense of vast amounts of data and communicate their conclusions to other investigators. In an effort to achieve consistency in the investigating and report-

Jud Kopicki (left), a PWA (Person with AIDS), uses social influence techniques in speaking to participants in an educational conference on HIV and AIDS.

BOX 1.1

The Changing Face of Social Psychology

There are many ways to follow the development of an area of study like social psychology. Obviously, the best would be to carefully read all the literature in the field. But this would be a task well outside the limits of our time, tolerance, and ability. Another approach might be to compare the content of textbooks in the field throughout its history. We mentioned the focus on crowd behavior by Ross's text (*Social Psychology,* 1908) and McDougall's interest in instincts (1908). We can compare these books to modern-day books, such as the present textbook, to see how much the field has changed. Although our book discusses both instincts and crowd behavior, these topics are of very little concern to today's social psychologist. Textbooks are generally written to introduce students to a field or area. As such, they often present broad overviews rather than in-depth examinations of specific topics.

As areas mature and develop growing bodies of literature, individuals within the discipline often like to get a snapshot of current issues of importance to other researchers in their field. Books entitled *Handbook* or *Sourcebook* attempt to meet this need and are generally designed to give an up-to-date view of a field to professionals. To capture the development of social psychology, compare the contents of the first *Handbook of Social Psychology* (Allee et al., 1935) with the fourth edition published over sixty years later (Gilbert, Fiske, and Lindzey, 1997). Although the two books claim to represent the field of social psychology, the differences are astounding. Examine the two contents lists and form your own impressions. Indeed, we might lament the passing of the study of the social psychology of bacteria, plants, insects, birds, and mammalian herds from the field, yet we can also see common threads such as language and attitudes that have stood the test of time and remain concerns of presentday social psychologists.

A Handbook of Social Psychology

Edited by Carl Murchison
Clark University Press, Worcester, Massachusetts, 1935

TABLE OF CONTENTS

PART I
SOCIAL PHENOMENA IN SELECTED POPULATIONS
1. Population Behavior of Bacteria
   R.E. Buchanan, Iowa State College
2. Social Origins and Processes among Plants
   Frederic E. Clements, Carnegie Institution of Washington
3. Human Populations
   Warren S. Thompson, Scripps Foundation for Research in Population Problems

PART II
SOCIAL PHENOMENA IN INFRAHUMAN SOCIETIES
4. Insect Societies
   O.E. Plath, Boston University
5. Bird Societies
   Herbert Friedmann, United States National Museum
6. The Behavior of Mammalian Herds and Packs
   Frederich Alverdes, Zoological Institute, Marburg

PART III
HISTORICAL SEQUENCES OF HUMAN SOCIAL PHENOMENA
7. Social History of the Negro
   Melville J. Herskovits, Northwestern University
8. Social History of the Red Man
   Clark Wissler, Yale University
9. Social History of the White Man
   W.D. Wallis, University of Minnesota
10. Social History of the Yellow Man
    Edwin Deeks Harvey, Dartmouth College

PART IV
ANALYSES OF RECURRING PATTERNS IN SOCIAL PHENOMENA
11. Language
    Erwin A. Esper, University of Washington

Continued

BOX 1.1
Continued

The Handbook of Social Psychology, Fourth Edition

Edited by
    Daniel T. Gilbert, Harvard University
    Susan T. Fiske, University of
        Massachusetts at Amherst
    Gardner Lindzey, Center for Advanced
        Study in the Behavioral Sciences
The McGraw-Hill Companies, Inc., 1997

TABLE OF CONTENTS

Continued

BOX 1.1

Continued

Continued

BOX 1.1

Continued

Chapter 27
Social Conflict
> Dean G. Pruitt, State University of New York at Buffalo

Chapter 28
Social Stigma
> Jennifer Crocker, University of Michigan
> Brenda Major, Univeristy of California at Santa Barbara
> Claude Steele, Stanford University

Chapter 29
Intergroup Relations
> Marilynn B. Brewer, The Ohio State University
> Rupert J. Brown, University of Kent at Canterbury

Chapter 30
Social Justice and Social Movements
> Tom R. Tyler, University of California, Berkeley
> Heather J. Smith, Sonoma State University

PART SEVEN

INTERDISCIPLINARY PERSPECTIVES

Chapter 31
Health Behavior
> Peter Salovey, Yale University
> Alexander J. Rothman, University of Minnesota
> Judith Rodin, University of Pennsylvania

Chapter 32
Psychology and Law
> Phoebe C. Ellsworth, University of Michigan
> Robert Mauro, University of Oregon

Chapter 33
Understanding Organizations: Concepts and Controversies
> Jeffrey Pfeffer, Stanford University

Chapter 34
Opinion and Action in the Realm of Politics
> Donald R. Kinder, University of Michigan

Chapter 35
Social Psychology and World Politics
> Philip E. Tetlock, The Ohio State University

PART EIGHT

EMERGING PERSPECTIVES

Chapter 36
The Cultural Matrix of Social Psychology
> Alan Page Fiske, Univeristy of California, Los Angeles
> Shinobu Kitayama, Kyoto University
> Hazel Rose Markus, Stanford University
> Richard E. Nisbett, University of Michigan

Chapter 37
Evolutionary Social Psychology
> David M. Buss, University of Texas, Austin
> Douglas T. Kenrick, Arizona State University

ing of events, researchers develop a standardized set of rules governing these procedures. It is this set of rules for inquiry that constitutes a **science.** Whether we talk about the study of chemistry, physics, or social behavior, the common ground that leads each of these fields of inquiry to be labeled a science is adherence to the scientific method—a standardized set of rules for investigating events and communicating findings.

Many of us are intimidated by the term *science.* The word sends chills down our spine as we think of a gang of bespectacled individuals in laboratory coats working on some complex, almost mysterious problem and speaking in long, incomprehensible sentences. There is, however, nothing mysterious about science. It is a process that aims to (1) describe, (2) predict, and

(3) explain events. Achieving these objectives allows the scientist to control conditions so the desired event can be produced. In a sense, we can view science as a never-ending quest for understanding in accordance with an agreed-upon set of rules. The excitement for many people, and the frustration for others, is that each answer we find raises new questions and challenges for scientific inquiry. The philosopher George Santayana captured this process in his description of William James:

> I think it would have depressed him if he had to confess that any important question was finally settled. He would still have hoped that something might turn up on the other side, and that, just as the

scientific hangman was about to dispatch the poor convicted prisoner, an unexpected witness would ride up in hot haste, and prove him innocent. (Santayana, 1920, p. 84; see also Viney, 1989)

In an effort to expedite these goals and to guide inquiry, scientists develop theories and hypotheses. A **theory** is a systematic statement that seeks to explain *why* two or more events are related. Theories may be of broad scope, such as Copernicus's theory of the heliocentric motion of the planets, or they may be more focused, seeking to explain, for example, why people become fearful in a given situation, why particular attitudes are formed, or why people act aggressively toward others.

Scientists also develop **hypotheses,** which express educated guesses about the relationship between events. Unlike theories, hypotheses do not attempt to explain why two events are related; they express *what* the relationship between two events will be. Hypotheses can be derived from theories, or they can be formed from existing data. One hypothesis suggested by Cantril's interview data, for example, is that people tend to affiliate when they are anxious, nervous, or afraid. This statement is a hypothesis rather than a theory because it simply states a relationship and does not attempt to explain why this relationship exists. The hypothesis may be correct or incorrect; testing hypotheses is a major task of science. Social psychology, like other sciences, is involved in explaining, predicting, understanding, and verifying the relationships between events.

In using the scientific method, the social psychologist may have a theory or a hypothesis about a certain type of human behavior, just as a detective may have a hunch about the perpetrator of a certain crime. The task of both is to track down information that will verify or refute the theory or hunch. Just as a detective must collect information that is clear enough to convince a judge or a jury that a hunch is correct "beyond a reasonable doubt," so the social psychologist must obtain enough clear support for a theory to convince critics and other social psychologists of its correctness. Carrying the analogy one step farther, just as detectives have developed methods for tracking down leads, so social psychologists have devised procedures for following through on their hunches and testing their theories.

Social psychologists use a variety of methods to test theories and follow leads. Hence part of the social psychologist's detective work is to select the best strategy for investigating a particular problem. With this point in mind, we will examine the methodologies of social psychology. In order to illustrate their use, we will focus on the reactions of people to the *War of the Worlds* broadcast. If we want to pursue the hypothesis that fear, such as that aroused by the broadcast, causes people to affiliate with others, how can we go about obtaining evidence to support the hypothesis?

Case History

One method of testing hypotheses, the **case history,** uses a few respondents and analyzes their reactions in depth. In one part of Cantril's work, for example, people who admitted that they had been scared by the broadcast were interviewed at length about their reactions; several excerpts from those interviews have been presented in this chapter. Such testimony is valuable, but are we certain that we have learned much that is reliable about the way most people behave? We do not know whether the reports are representative of the population at large or are unique to the few individuals whose statements were recorded. Most of Cantril's reports were gathered in the state of New Jersey, the reputed site of the Martians' landing. The imminent disaster may have led people there to behave very differently from people in more distant areas. Other case histories were obtained from people who learned of Cantril's investigation and took the trouble to write to him. Such reports are interesting, but they represent a very select portion of the population, those who felt the desire or need to relate their stories. Consequently, we tend to use case histories as ways of generating, not testing, hypotheses.

Archival Search

Rather than focus on one incident, as in the case history method, one could, by engaging in **archival research,** examine historical accounts of a broad variety of incidents that had one or more features in common and try to identify common responses to these events. If we were interested in studying the effects of fear on behavior, we could search through newspapers, magazines, and books to identify instances when groups faced fearful situations. Our search would uncover natural disasters, such as volcanic eruptions and hurricanes; industrial catastrophes, such as the nuclear accident at Chernobyl and the chemical leak at Bhopal, India; and the crisis of a community that learned that its food supply had been poisoned. We would study these reports to map out people's reactions under the various circumstances and to see if we could identify behavior patterns common to all the incidents. This approach would yield rich information because we would not be dealing with only one type of fear-arousing situation. If we found common behavior patterns, we could **generalize** beyond a specific case—that is, use the information collected from our sample of situations to predict and explain behavior in similar situations. In other words, we could be more confident that people's responses were due to fear rather than to concern about a Martian invasion. However, we would still be faced with many nagging doubts. How accurate were these random accounts of the incident and people's responses? Were people experiencing fear or reacting to some other emotion? Were the reports of the incident tainted by the reporters' own feelings and interpretations? These types of issues limit the value of the archival method for developing precise theories and testing hypotheses.

Survey

One way of getting into people's heads and making a better determination of what they thought and felt would be to devise a questionnaire; select a large sample that represents the geographical, socioeconomic, and educational background of the population; and ask questions of persons in the sample about their fear and their desire to affiliate. This is the **survey method**.

The survey is useful because it attempts to uncover how people react to a real situation. In addition, a representative sample of respondents can be chosen to participate. A survey is used to describe people's attitudes, feelings, and reported behaviors in regard to a particular event. There are problems with a survey, however. First, people often do not remember exactly what they did in a particular situation. Second, respondents may try to slant their answers to a survey in order to appear in a better light. A man who panicked and ran screaming from his house when he heard that the Martians were coming may tell the interviewer that he quickly ran outside to see whether he could help his neighbors. In short, the responses on a survey questionnaire may not be completely accurate. Finally, some people are not willing to be interviewed.

A Point in Common: Relation, Not Causation

As you look over the three methods we have discussed—case history, archival search, survey—what do you think they have in common? Indeed, they seem very different: one involves reading newspaper accounts, while another requires us to ask people questions. The common point is that each method gives us information about the *relationship* between events, but none of them tells us clearly which event is the cause and which is the effect. In statistical terms, we are dealing with a **correlation,** which is a statistical measure of the degree of association between events. A correlation can range between 1.00 and −1.00. If we found a positive correlation between fear and affiliation, it would mean that an increase in fear was associated with an increase in affiliation. Conversely, a negative correlation would indicate that an increase in fear was accompanied by a decrease in affiliation.

The degree of relationship between two variables is a valuable piece of information. If we know that two events are positively correlated, we know that when one of the two events occurs, the other is also likely to occur. However, we probably also want to know which event *caused* the other; that is, does fear *cause* people to affiliate, or does affiliation *cause* people to become fearful? A correlation does not provide this answer. A correlation between two variables can have one of three meanings:

1. A difference in the first variable causes a difference in the second variable.
2. A difference in the second variable causes a difference in the first variable.
3. A third, unspecified variable causes differences in both the first and the second variables.

Suppose that Cantril found the following data:

1. Seventy-five percent of the people who reported feeling a great deal of fear after hearing the broadcast spent time with other people after the broadcast.
2. Fifteen percent of the people who reported feeling little fear after hearing the broadcast spent time with other people after the broadcast.

What do these data mean with regard to the hypothesis that fear causes people to affiliate? One possible meaning is the one suggested by the hypothesis—fear causes people to affiliate. However, a second possible interpretation is that affiliation leads to fear. This is a plausible explanation, since we can easily imagine that people may have congregated and discussed the *War of the Worlds* program and that this discussion may have generated fear. Finally, it is also possible that a third variable that is not even measured in the correlation could be responsible for the results. For example, we might find that individuals who score high on some personality dimension, say gregariousness, are motivated to be with other people and also tend to frighten easily. Thus the correlation may not mean that fear leads to affiliation or that affiliation leads to fear. It may simply result from the fact that the third variable, the personality trait, was responsible for both fear and affiliation.

Thus surveys, case studies, and archival research can be used to achieve the aim of prediction since they tell how closely related two variables are. In most cases, however, they do not enable the researcher to achieve the second scientific goal of understanding or explanation. That is, they do not enable the researcher to uncover a cause-and-effect relationship between variables.

Experiment

To examine cause-and-effect relationships, the researcher must have some control over the variables he or she wishes to study and must be able to eliminate the possibility that some unspecified variable is systematically affecting the results. The method that is designed to allow the necessary control so that cause-and-effect relationships can be uncovered is the experiment.

The **experiment** is a procedure for testing the validity or correctness of a hypothesis. The basic design of an experiment is quite simple. The experimenter manipulates the **independent variable** and studies the effects of the manipulation on the **dependent variable.** The independent variable gets its name from the fact that it is not under the control of the subject. The experimenter determines which level of the independent variable the subject will receive. The dependent variable is the subject's response. The hypothesis is stated in terms of the independent variable causing the dependent variable (fear causes affiliation). Thus the aim of the experiment is to investigate the causal relationship between the independent variable and the dependent variable.

To be able to say that a particular independent variable did cause the dependent variable, the experimenter must be sure that no **extraneous variables** were present in the experiment. An extraneous variable is a factor that may influence people's reactions in a systematic way, although it has nothing to do with the relationship between the independent and dependent variables. Let us assume that you set up an experiment to test whether fear causes people to affiliate. You decide to use two levels of fear (high and low). You manipulate high fear by running into a room and telling people that the building is on fire. In the low-fear condition, you run into a room and tell people that a building in the next town is on fire. Hence the degree of fear is your independent variable and you have control over it. Your dependent variable is affiliation, which is measured by how often people in the room talk to one another after they hear the news. So far, so good. You run the experiment, and you find that high fear leads to greater affiliation than does low fear. Can you be confident that you have obtained evidence that fear causes affiliation?

It is possible that in reviewing your procedure you may find that all of your efforts were for naught. Even though you manipulated and controlled your independent variable and carefully observed your dependent variable, extraneous variables may have affected your results. For example, you may discover that the people who happened to be in the rooms where you manipulated high fear were all friends, whereas the people in the low-fear rooms were strangers to one another. Thus the extraneous variable of prior acquaintance may have "caused" your affiliation results. Further, you may find that all of your high-fear conditions were run after lunch, when people naturally wanted to affiliate, whereas the low-fear conditions were run just before lunch, when people tended to be grumpy and wished isolation. Thus, even though you manipulated your independent variable and found the predicted results, the existence of these extraneous variables would not allow you to believe that your study demonstrated that fear causes affiliation.

A "clean" experiment must eliminate or control the extraneous variables. To ensure that the extraneous variable of preexisting subject characteristics is not the cause of the results in an experiment, subjects are randomly assigned to the various conditions. By **random assignment** we mean that each subject has an equal opportunity of being in each experimental condition. Through random assignment, the experimenter ensures that the characteristics of the subjects assigned to any particular experimental condition are the same as those of subjects in the other experimental conditions. One way to illustrate the procedure of random assignment is to imagine a blindfolded individual whose task is to divide one hundred pennies, half of which are colored red and half green, into two equal piles. The chances are that when the task is finished, each pile will have a similar distribution of red and green pennies. Thus the reason for randomly assigning participants to conditions is to get similar groups of subjects into the different experimental conditions so that preexisting subject characteristics cannot be the cause of differences in the results. In addition to randomly assigning participants to conditions, we can eliminate other extraneous variables by randomly assigning the order of conditions. In the earlier example, we could eliminate the alternative explanation based on hunger by not running all high-fear conditions after lunch and all low-fear conditions just before lunch. This can be done by randomly choosing a condition to run at a particular time.

As you can see, much of experimentation is an exercise in control. We must have control to determine when and how the independent variable will be manipulated, and we must have control to eliminate extraneous variables. Campbell and Stanley (1963) have used the term **internal validity** to describe an experimental design that is free from contamination by extraneous variables. As they phrase it, "Internal validity is the basic ingredient without which an experiment is uninterpretable" (p. 5).

Constructing an Experiment

We have discussed the aims and some of the possible pitfalls of experimentation. You may be able to think of a way to conduct an experiment to test the hypothesis that fear leads to affiliation. The important points to remember are:

1. You must create at least two levels of the independent variable (that is, conditions of high fear and low fear).
2. Participants must be randomly assigned to the conditions (that is, you would not want to assign all smart people or all poor people or all Northerners to one condition).
3. The dependent variable (affiliation) must be measured.

An experiment that was designed to demonstrate that high fear causes people to affiliate was reported by Stanley Schachter (1959). Suppose that you are a volunteer who has been randomly assigned to the high-fear condition. You will encounter a serious-looking man in horn-rimmed glasses who is intent on giving you a good scare. For effect, he is dressed in a white lab coat with a stethoscope dribbling conspicuously from his pocket, and he is standing in front of an array of elaborate-looking electrical equipment. He introduces himself to you as Dr. Gregor Zilstein, and he informs you that you are in an experiment that is concerned with the effects of electric shock. Pausing slightly, so that his words will have maximum impact. Zilstein says:

> We would like to give each of you a series of electric shocks. Now, I feel I must be completely honest with you and tell you exactly what you are in for. These shocks will hurt, they will be painful. As you can guess, it is necessary that our shocks be intense. What we will do is put an electrode on your hand, hook you into apparatus such as this, give you a series of shocks, and take various measures. . . . Again, I do want to be honest with you and tell you that these shocks will be quite painful but, of course, they will do no permanent damage. (Schachter, 1959, p. 13)

You probably would have been more fortunate, or at least less frightened, if you had been randomly assigned to the low-fear condition. You would still have been greeted by Dr. Zilstein, but the pile of electrical equipment would not have been displayed. With a much more pleasant demeanor, Dr. Zilstein would tell you (as he does in the high-fear condition) that this is an experiment involving the effects of electric shock. But this time he would qualify this statement by saying, "I hasten to add, do not let the word *shock* trouble you; I am sure that you will enjoy this experiment." He would continue:

> We would like to give each of you a series of very mild electric shocks. I assure you that what you will feel will not in any way be painful. It will resemble more a tickle than anything unpleasant. We will put an electrode on your hand, give you a series of very mild shocks and measure such things as your pulse rate . . . which I am sure you are all familiar with from visits to your family doctor. (Pp. 13–14)

In this manner Schachter manipulated the independent variable into two levels; low fear and high fear. Did he successfully create two levels of fear in the minds and feelings of his subjects? One way to find out is to ask. So Schachter gave each participant a printed form to be filled out that asked: "How do you feel about taking part in this experiment and being shocked?" The participant was asked to respond along a five-point scale ranging from "I dislike the idea very much" to "I enjoy the idea very much." When the questionnaires were examined, subjects who had met the stern Dr. Zilstein in the high-fear condition were much less inclined to be shocked than were those who had met the benign and reassuring Dr. Zilstein. This procedure, which is known as a **check on the manipulation,** allows investigators to feel secure that the variable they thought they were manipulating with elaborate staging was accurately perceived by the participants.

Schachter's experiment was designed to test the hypothesis that fear leads to affiliation. Once he had successfully induced two levels of fear, the next step was to get a measure of the desire to affiliate (dependent variable). Schachter decided to solve this problem by giving the participants a choice of waiting together or alone for the shock portion of the study. In both fear conditions, Dr. Zilstein stated:

> Before we begin with the shocking proper there will be about a 10-minute delay while we get this room in order. We have several pieces of equipment to bring in and get set up. . . . Here is what we will ask you to do for this 10-minute period of waiting. We have on this floor a number of additional rooms so that each of you, if you would like, can wait alone in your own room. These rooms are comfortable and spacious; they all have armchairs and there are books and magazines in each room. It did occur to us, however, that some of you might want to wait for these 10 minutes together with some of the other girls here. If you would prefer this, of course, just let us know. We'll take one of the empty classrooms on the floor and you can wait together with some of the other girls there. (Pp. 13–14)

Participants were then given a chance to state whether they preferred waiting alone or waiting with others or had no preference. This constituted the measurement of the dependent variable. What Schachter hoped to find was that women assigned to the high-fear condition would want to wait together more than women in the low-fear condition. Schachter's results are presented in table 1.2.

The table makes it quite clear that subjects in the high-fear condition wanted to wait together much more than subjects in the low-fear condition did. Thus the hypothesis was supported by the data.

The Advantages of Experiments

As you can see, Schachter expended a great deal of time and effort to test the rather simple hypothesis that fear leads to affiliation. Was it worth it? Why go to such lengths to set up an experiment? The answer is that there are many important advantages to experiments that justify their use. In fact, the vast majority of data collected in social psychology come from laboratory research.

A number of advantages of experimentation should be clear. First and most important, experimentation provides a way of determining the direction of causation. Because the experimenter controls the independent variable and assigns people to different levels of that variable on a random basis, the question of which variable is cause and which is effect can be answered.

Another advantage of experimentation is that extraneous elements that might otherwise influence the results can be well controlled. For example, some of the people in Cantril's survey may have listened during a thunderstorm, tuned in late, or heard the program on a crackling radio. It is unknown whether any of these factors could have influenced fear or affiliation.

TABLE 1.2 RELATIONSHIP OF FEAR TO THE AFFILIATIVE TENDENCY

	Number Choosing		
	Waiting together	Don't care	Waiting alone
High fear	20	9	3
Low fear	10	18	2

Source: Adapted from Schachter (1959)

We do know, though, that such factors are extraneous to the relationship in question. Some individuals were exposed to one or more of them; others to none. The factors remain uncontrolled. By contrast, the experiment controls for such events. The variables are usually manipulated in the confines of a small unit of space and time. All subjects are generally treated identically, with the exception of the one event that serves as the independent variable.

Yet another advantage of experimentation is that the experimenter can devise *numerous levels* of an independent variable and study trends in the data. For example, Schachter used only two levels of fear arousal (high and low). The experimenter might hold the hypothesis that very fearful subjects would not want to affiliate. An experiment could then be developed so that there were three conditions of fear (low, high, and very high). Such systematic variation of the fear variable would present a clear relationship between fear and affiliation.

Issues of Concern in Experimentation

Mark Twain once remarked that a common characteristic of everything developed by humans is imperfection. This statement clearly describes experimentation: while the experiment represents an excellent method for collecting data and determining cause and effect, it is not perfect. You have probably already identified many problems with the experimental method.

One of the basic problems that plagues research is generalization beyond the laboratory: How far can we go in applying the results we collect in an experiment? For example, we would like to be able to argue that the Schachter study supported the position that *fear* causes *people* to *affiliate*. This desire to generalize raises a number of questions. One is that we want to describe the behavior of people in general, while the study used only college students as subjects. In raising this issue, we do not wish to imply that college students are not people: rather, college students may be special people in that they possess characteristics that are not common to the population as a whole. For example, Schachter's subjects were white, female, mostly from the Northeast, most probably from middle-class families, and had some years of college education. Would respondents of different backgrounds or educational levels behave as Schachter's subjects did? We can take this question of generalization further by asking whether (1) studies of females can predict males' behavior, (2) studies of

whites can predict the behavior of blacks or Hispanics, (3) studies of eighteen- to twenty-two-year-olds can predict the behavior of older or younger people, (4) studies of college students can predict the behavior of less-educated people, and so on. If these generalizations are to be made with some degree of confidence, additional experiments with different subjects must be conducted.

Another generalization question concerns the setting and specific manipulations that we use in the experiment. Are people who are afraid of having a university scientist place electrodes on them experiencing the same kind of fear that people experience in a natural ongoing situation? Is the fear of Schachter's laboratory the same as the fear we would experience if we encountered a burglar in our house, a lion in the jungle, or a Martian in the New Jersey meadowland? When we raise these questions, we are referring to the **external validity** of an experiment (Carlsmith, Ellsworth, and Aronson, 1976).

The best way to deal with questions of external validity is to test the relationship in a series of similar but not identical ways. If Schachter's participants were really scared and if fear leads to affiliation, then other studies using different fear manipulations should yield the same result. Indeed, several other studies that use different methods of fear arousal and affiliation measurement have produced very similar results (Darley and Aronson, 1966; Gerard, 1963). This fact makes us more confident that we can generalize from our experimental results to fear and affiliation as they occur in the natural environment.

Another concern with experimentation is that of realism. We must actually consider two types of realism. The first, **experimental realism,** concerns the impact the experiment has on subjects. "An experiment is realistic if the situation is involving to the subjects, if they are forced to take it seriously, if it has impact on them" (Aronson, Brewer, and Carlsmith, 1985, p. 482). It is vital for a study to have high experimental realism if we wish to argue that the independent variable caused the dependent response. It is not hard to see that Schachter's study had a high degree of experimental realism; the ominous-looking Dr. Zilstein who gravely explained the painful shocks certainly captured the subjects' attention. The second type of realism is **mundane realism.** An experiment is high in mundane realism to the extent that the situation that subjects encounter is similar to situations they face in the normal course of their lives. While a high degree of mundane realism may increase a study's impact, its presence is not a necessary research requirement. For example, Schachter's study was quite low in mundane realism. (How often are we approached in our everyday lives by a Dr. Zilstein who threatens to shock us?) Yet Schachter's study did manipulate the fear that subjects experienced, as well as allowing him to study the relationship between fear and affiliation. Having high mundane realism in our study gives us greater latitude to generalize beyond the specific experimental setting.

The Social Psychology of the Subject and the Experimenter

Thus far our concern has been the design and manipulation of the experimental setting. Experiments, however, involve more than just a setting; they are also the stage for the interaction of the subjects and the experimenter. Let us quickly examine how the psychology of subject and experimenter can influence the results of a study. The subject's role in a study is unique. Martin Orne (1962) has demonstrated people's willingness to do the "right thing" in an experiment, that is, to do what they think the experimenter wants them to do. You do not want to appear silly, obstinate, or recalcitrant. You want to be cooperative and to be seen as a "good subject." In some of his demonstrations, Orne showed that people will use a variety of bizarre behaviors to be good subjects. For example, Orne asked people whether they would be willing to copy numbers in the school library, although he told them that doing so would not be very useful to anyone. Not only were subjects willing to comply with the request, but they stayed after the investigator and librarian had left and after the library was closed and locked!

The implication of such behavior is clear. If people who want to be good subjects can know the purpose of an experiment or if they have a notion about what the experimenter wants them to do, they are likely to cooperate. If the subjects in Schachter's study had known that he hoped they would affiliate in the high-fear condition and remain alone in the low-fear condition, they might have cooperated. When people act in a particular way not because it is their typical reaction to the situation but because they are trying to do what the experimenter desires, we say that they are acting in accord with the experiment's **demand characteristics.**

Several methods can be used to guard against demand characteristics in an experiment. A popular method, though not necessarily the most effective one,

is **deception**. In this case, the experimenter gives the subject a false but plausible hypothesis, so that if the subject's behavior is affected by this hypothesis, the effects will not be in any way systematic. Further, through this deception or cover story the experimenter prevents subjects from discovering the true hypothesis. Schachter used deception in his study. He told subjects that he was interested in studying the effects of actual electric shocks on his subjects, when in fact he was interested only in the effects of fear on affiliation.

Another way to reduce the problem of demand characteristics is to measure the dependent variable in a context apart from the independent variable and to use **unobtrusive measures.** In fact, one group of investigators (Morris et al., 1976) employed unobtrusive measures in a study on fear and affiliation. In their study, some subjects arrived at the experiment room to find a table piled with shock apparatus and medical supplies (high fear) whereas other subjects found a table filled with books and other nonthreatening materials (low fear). A note on the door suggested that the experimenter would soon return. There were no chairs or other furniture in the room, so subjects were left to occupy themselves until the experimenter returned. Actually, the experimenter and his aids were seated behind a one-way mirror noting how often (and how close) the subjects interacted with each other. Subjects did not know that they were being observed. The results indicated that subjects interacted more often and at closer distances when fear-arousing items were on the table than when no such items were present. Because the subjects did not know that they were being observed, it is unlikely that they were responding to demand characteristics or harbored concerns about being evaluated.

A final problem involves the unique psychology of the experimenter in a research effort. Experimenters have hypotheses: They think that they *know* what a subject will do; they know what they *want* a subject to do to confirm their hypotheses. Robert Rosenthal and his colleagues have shown that such expectations may actually influence the behavior of subjects in experiments. In one study, Rosenthal and Fode (1963) used photographs of faces that had previously been rated as neutral with regard to success and failure. They gave these pictures to students who were serving as assistant experimenters and asked the students to obtain ratings from subjects as to whether the people in the pictures appeared successful or unsuccessful. Rosenthal and Fode told half of the assistant experimenters that they were trying to duplicate a "well-established" finding that people generally rated the persons photographed as successful. The other half of the experimenters were told that the "well-established" finding was that people generally rated the persons photographed as unsuccessful.

Armed with identical photographs, two sets of assistant experimenters set out to collect evidence. They were instructed about what to say and how to collect the ratings. Both groups were supposed to behave in precisely the same fashion. Yet the results were dramatically different. Every experimenter who was led to expect that people generally rated the persons photographed as successful obtained higher success ratings than the experimenters who expected to obtain failure ratings. Most assuredly the experimenters' influence on the subjects' ratings was unintentional, yet the experimenters' expectations were somehow communicated to the subjects, who behaved accordingly. The influence of a subject's performance as a function of an investigator's expectation has been called **experimenter bias.**

Experimenter bias is a troublesome problem, and investigators are now more careful to make certain that their hypotheses do not become self-fulfilling prophecies because of bias. The best way to keep an experimenter's expectancy from influencing people's behavior is to keep the experimenter unaware of the experimental treatment to which the subject has been exposed. Often two experimenters are used to obtain this result. In Schachter's research, for example, any possibility of experimenter bias could have been eliminated if someone other than Dr. Zilstein had asked the subjects whether they wished to wait together or alone. Only Zilstein would know whether a particular participant had been subjected to high-fear or low-fear treatment. Therefore, only his expectations could affect the final measure. Anyone else who collected that final measure would not know what to expect on the measure of affiliation.

The Field Experiment

One common criticism of laboratory experiments is that because the setting is unlike anything experienced in the real world, it is difficult to create an impactful experience for subjects. While we could successfully argue that the Schachter study certainly made an impact on its subjects, it could equally well be argued that the manipulation was not as successful as it could have been because the subjects knew they were in an

experiment; they may have reduced their fear by telling themselves that Dr. Zilstein couldn't really do anything too terrible because this was only an experiment. To achieve a real-world effect, we might want to run a field experiment.

In theory, the **field experiment** is similar to the laboratory experiment except that the location has changed. The field experiment is run in a natural setting, and subjects often do not know that they are in an experiment. The experimenter varies the independent variables and examines the effects of the manipulation on the dependent variable. The added realism of the setting should allow greater generalization of results from the field experiment.

For example, Freedman and Fraser (1966) wished to test the hypothesis that people will comply with a large request if they are first asked to perform a small favor. Their ultimate aim was to get people to agree to place a large billboard in their front yard that read Drive Carefully. In some cases, the experimenter ap-

"I tell you, Mr. Arthur, this survey has no way of registering a non-verbal response!"

proached randomly selected houses in a neighborhood and asked residents to display a three-inch-square sign in their window that stated Be a Safe Driver. Almost everyone agreed to this small request. Two weeks later a different experimenter approached the residents and asked them to agree to put the large billboard in front of their home. Of those residents who had agreed to put the small sign in their window, 76 percent agreed to put the monstrous billboard in their yard. However, only 17 percent of the residents who had not been asked to display the small sign agreed to allow the larger one in their yard.

As you can see, this field study included randomization of subjects to conditions. It had the advantage of studying people, in their natural settings, agreeing to actions that clearly affected them. Obviously, the situation was impactful and important to the subjects, and the study was able to employ some vital controls.

However before we rush to adopt this method, let's consider some of its possible weaknesses. One problem is the lack of control over extraneous variables. Although the experimenters wished to argue that the act of complying with a small request increases the chance that people will comply with larger requests, other interpretations are possible. For example, we do not know what happened to residents who displayed the small sign during the two-week interval before the larger request. It's possible that their neighbors commented on the sign and began characterizing the residents as "experts" on safe driving. Therefore, feeling they were experts on an issue predisposed the residents to take large steps to support the cause. The response of neighbors in this case would be an extraneous variable that was not controlled in the situation.

Another drawback to field experimentation is that in the field it is often difficult to manipulate complex variables or to manipulate a number of variables simultaneously. For example, it would be difficult to conduct a field experiment that tests the hypothesis that tired people have a stronger desire than well-rested people to affiliate when they are fearful. To test this hypothesis we would have to manipulate both fear and tiredness. In the field it would be nearly impossible to assign people randomly to a restful or tired condition. We could, however, do this in the laboratory, where before manipulating fear we could have some subjects go one night without sleep while providing other subjects with a restful night.

Hence the field experiment has the advantage of generalization of results but may achieve this advantage at the sacrifice of control over extraneous variables. Further, some hypotheses are difficult to test in a field setting because of the complexity of the required manipulations.

Choosing a Method

Earlier we pointed out that social psychology often requires a great deal of detective work. Not only must social psychologists observe behavior and develop theories to explain that behavior, they must also determine the best method for testing their theories. As you can see in table 1.3, there is no single right or wrong method; each method offers both advantages and disadvantages. The researcher must determine the goal of his or her investigation and select the method that will best fit that goal. In most cases, the social psychologist is interested in establishing a cause-and-effect relationship and therefore uses the laboratory experiment.

The ideal modus operandi, however, would be to use a mix of methods to study a problem. That is, the same hypothesis could be tested by means of a survey, a laboratory experiment, and a field experiment. If the hypothesis were tested and supported by each of these methods, a great deal more confidence could be placed in its correctness than if it were tested and supported by only one method. This multiple-method approach requires considerable time, and it is rarely used by a single investigator. Later in this book, however, we will examine instances in which a hypothesis has been tested by several investigators who used a variety of methods.

One other point should be made clear: an experiment, whether it is carried out in the laboratory or in the field, can be no better than the idea it is testing. As Leon Festinger (1980) points out: "Precision of measurement and precision of experimental control are a means to an end—the discovery of new knowledge. Too much emphasis on precision can lead to research which is barren" (p. 252). Like a hammer used to build a house, experimental methods are only tools used to expand knowledge. The success of an experiment is measured less by the precision of its execution than by the knowledge that results from it. Therefore, careful planning and thought about the idea to be tested are vital steps to be taken before a method is chosen.

TABLE 1.3   RESEARCH METHODS: STRENGTHS AND WEAKNESSES

Method	Strengths	Weaknesses
Case history	Involves a real event; high mundane realism; in-depth study of a single event; generates hypotheses	Cannot determine cause and effect; no control over independent variables; no randomization of subjects; relies on recall, which may be faulty
Archival research	Involves real events; high mundane realism; involves many incidents, so increases generalizability; easy and cheap to collect data; generates hypotheses	Cannot determine cause and effect; no control over independent variables; no randomization of subjects; relies on secondhand reports; possible bias in reports; often very incomplete accounts of events and responses
Survey	Collects much information from a wide variety of subjects; can deal with a variety of events; easy to collect data	Cannot determine cause and effect; no control over independent variables; relies on people's memory, which may be faulty
Experiment	Allows determination of cause and effect; random assignment of subjects to condition; maximum control over independent variables; high control over extraneous variables	Often low mundane realism; difficult to achieve high generalizability; time-consuming; limits type and intensity of independent variables
Field experiment	Allows cause and effect to be determined; high mundane realism; some control over independent variables; permits study of wide range of subjects	Difficult to control extraneous variables; may be impossible to test some complex hypotheses in such settings

Beyond a Reasonable Doubt: Statistical Significance

To obtain a guilty verdict, a prosecuting attorney must convince the members of the jury that a defendant is guilty beyond a reasonable doubt. This does not mean that the prosecutor must positively prove guilt—it only means that the jury must believe it highly probable that the defendant is guilty. The social psychologist, too, works with probabilities. The aim of an experiment is not to prove that a hypothesis is correct. Rather, the aim is to demonstrate that it is highly probable that the hypothesis is correct. Researchers ask the question in the following way: "What is the probability that the results I have obtained could have been found by chance alone?" Hence social psychology, like most other sciences, deals with probabilities rather than absolutes.

As a means of demonstrating this point, let us reexamine the Schachter experiment. Schachter found that approximately 63 percent of the high-fear subjects wanted to wait together, whereas only 33 percent

of the low-fear subjects wanted to do so. What does this difference mean? Is it reliable, or is it simply a chance finding? With the Schachter study we must ask whether highly fearful people really want to affiliate more than low-fear people do. Is the difference large enough to make us believe that if more and more people participated in the study, the same connection between fear and affiliation would be found? Or would we discover that the difference was found only by chance and that the addition of more people washes out the difference?

To answer these questions, investigators apply statistical tests that are designed to estimate the likelihood that a difference found in the data would continue to be manifested if everyone in the population participated in the study. By convention, we agree that we will accept a difference as **statistically significant** (reliable) if the likelihood of its having occurred by chance (that is, the likelihood that the difference would disappear if the entire population were tested) is less than one in twenty. In other words, the result could have occurred by chance less than 5 percent of the time. The difference reported in the Schachter study was tested with one statistical procedure, and it was found that the likelihood that the difference had occurred by chance was less than one in twenty. We therefore refer to the result as statistically significant. Thus social psychologists assume that a finding that could have occurred by chance less than 5 percent of the time is reliable beyond a reasonable doubt.

Without confusing the issue or going into great detail, we should point out that psychologists are actively exploring other approaches to analyzing data and determining what the results "tell us" (Abelson, 1995; Loftus, 1996). These efforts should open new avenues to understanding information collected in our research.

Of all the aspects of experimentation, students probably loath statistics the most. There is nothing magical or mysterious about statistics. If we ask subjects in an experiment to indicate on a scale how much they want to be with other subjects, our data will have two properties of major concern to us. First, we will have a **mean,** or average, of all the scores. Second, we will have a measure of **variability** around the mean. For example, if our scores averaged 5 on a 7-point scale, we might find that all our subjects checked point 4, 5, or 6. This would indicate rather low variability. On the other hand, we could have gotten our mean of 5 if various numbers of subjects checked each of the points on the scale. This would indicate high variability. The **analysis of variance test,** a popular statistical procedure used to analyze experimental data, takes into account both the mean and the variability to determine the statistical significance of our results. This is not the place to enter into an extended discussion of statistical procedures. We simply want to point out that these procedures are tools that allow scientists to examine their data and communicate their findings.

Questions of Ethics

We have discussed some of the methods that are used in social psychology and have examined how the hypothesis that fear leads to affiliation could be tested. The suggestion that we could test the hypothesis by telling people that the building they are in is burning may have made you uncomfortable. You may even have winced as you thought about the fear experienced by the subjects in Schachter's high-fear condition. Finally, you may have felt that we were a little callous when we suggested that the method used in a study should be chosen on the grounds of how well it fits the goals of the experimenter. In all of these cases

we seem to have been overlooking one important ingredient in the experiment—the subject.

Shouldn't some concern be shown for the subject who is terribly frightened? Shouldn't some attention be given to choosing a method that will protect the subject? The answer to both of these questions is an emphatic yes. Almost from the time social psychologists began conducting experiments, they expressed deep concern for the physical and psychological safety of their subjects. Before our newspapers reported secret CIA experiments with LSD and before the Kennedy Committee on Human Experimentation began its hearings, social psychologists were discussing the problems of ethics in research and developing guidelines to protect subjects in psychological experimentation. The American Psychological Association (1982) published a comprehensive guideline outlining ethical precautions that should be taken when research is conducted.

Let us review quickly some of the ethical problems that social psychologists have identified. The first problem is *invasion of privacy*. Although this may not have been a serious problem in the Schachter study because little "sensitive" information was asked, it does become a problem when sensitive information is requested. Some studies ask subjects questions about their sex lives or about criminal activities they may have participated in. Other studies give subjects personality and intelligence tests. In all of these cases, the experimenter is obtaining private information from the subject. Is this ethical? This is a difficult question to answer. Psychologists have attempted to safeguard the privacy of subjects by keeping responses anonymous or by letting no one but the experimenter have access to them. Further, they attempt to follow the principle of **informed consent:** subjects are given the choice of participating or not participating in an experiment after they have been told of the procedures that will be used. In practice, however, this principle is often difficult to follow because some experiments require the subject to be unaware of what is really being studied.

A second problem is the *use of deception*. Deception is practiced when the experimenter tells subjects something other than the truth. In the Schachter study, the subjects were deceived about the purpose of the study and they were told that they would receive an electric shock even though they were never actually shocked. Such deception is often necessary to prevent the subjects from focusing on the true nature of the interaction being studied. In an effort to make the deception only temporary, experimenters carry out elaborate debriefing sessions at the conclusion of studies. At these sessions, subjects are told exactly what did happen in the study, what problem was being investigated, and why they had been deceived. In this way, the experiment and debriefing become an educational experience for the subjects.

A third problem is the *harmful consequences* that the subject may suffer in the course of the study. Subjects may be given drugs that have unpleasant side effects or may have to suffer painful shocks. Other harmful consequences may be psychological rather than physical. In the Schachter study, the subjects suffered stress and fear. In other studies, the subjects may be degraded or insulted and suffer depression. Again the question can be asked: Is this ethical? There has been a great deal of discussion about this matter. The answer is to try to find procedures that do not create negative consequences for the subject.

Another ethical problem is that *subjects may be taught something about themselves that they do not wish to know*. For example, a subject in the Schachter study could become so fearful that she cries and begs to be let out of the study. In this case, the subject is being shown that she has little tolerance for stress. One might argue that the experimenter is only showing the subject something true about herself. However, the subject did not come to the experiment asking to learn about herself. She came to be a subject in an experiment.

The question of ethics is a difficult and controversial one; what is ethical to one person may not be ethical to another. And while it is important to consider ethical issues in every experiment, it is also important not to become paralyzed by these issues. A valuable experiment must be both involving for the subject and considerate of ethical issues. An experiment that slights either of these concerns in favor of the other loses value for the subject, the experimenter, and our store of knowledge on human behavior.

Social psychologists are well aware of the ethical problems connected with research and have spent a great deal of time pondering those problems. Despite the value of social-psychological research, such research will have a bitter taste if it is achieved at the expense of the subjects involved in it. In an effort to protect the rights of subjects, universities and many psychology departments have set up **institutional review boards (IRBs),** committees in which a cross section of professionals considers the risks and benefits of research to participants.

These IRBs review proposed experimental procedures before psychologists are allowed to proceed with their studies. The IRBs determine whether subjects' rights will be protected. The boards may not allow an experimenter to run a study, or they may suggest alternative methods that offer better safeguards for the subjects. The system is not perfect, however, because ethics is a very subjective concept. One study asked IRBs at several universities to review a research proposal (Ceci, Peters, and Plotkin, 1985). Although all the IRBs reviewed the same proposal, their responses varied widely. This finding may be disturbing, but other researchers who had subjects and psychologists evaluate research proposals found that psychologists were more likely than subjects to declare a study ethically unacceptable (Sullivan and Deiker, 1973). In other words, psychologists may be their own harshest critics.

The bottom line, then, is that research is actually guided by three principles: the desire for maximum control, the desire to create impactful situations, and the desire to protect the subjects in the study. As you read the remainder of this text, you will see how these three guidelines have been skillfully combined to create settings that yield valuable knowledge about human social behavior.

Learning about Social Psychology

We are now ready to guide you through the halls of social psychology. Our aim in this text is to introduce you to the variety of areas studied by social psychologists and to show you some of the more important theories and research findings. We've included the older classic studies as well as the newer findings. There is a great deal of material here, but it should be viewed as only the beginning chapter in your lesson on social psychology.

Our students often ask us, "How can I really get to know the field of social psychology?" A first step is to take a class on the subject and read the text and other books in the area. However, there are many other things you can do to supplement your understanding of the field. One is simply to *observe* other people in their day-to-day activities. Whom do these people talk to? What do they talk about? How do they interpret events? How do they justify their actions? What are the similarities and differences in people's behavior? In conducting your observations, don't forget to look at yourself. The beauty of social psychology is that the world is its storehouse of information and its source of ideas. Your observations should encourage you to develop your own hypotheses and stimulate you to seek out research on the topics you find interesting.

A second step is to *become part of social psychology research*. At most universities you can volunteer to be a subject in ongoing research. But your involvement shouldn't stop there. Talk to professors to learn about the research they are conducting. When you find a professor studying a topic of interest to you, volunteer to work with him or her as a research assistant. You will find that many faculty members are delighted to have you participate in planning and conducting research. At many universities you can receive course credit for this activity. You may even find a professor willing to hire you as a research assistant. This experience will help you appreciate the time, effort, and thought that goes into research. You'll experience the excitement of obtaining significant results and the frustration associated with nonsignificant results. But above all, you'll leave with a better understanding of the science of social psychology. Learn social psychology by doing social psychology.

Finally, *take a broad range of courses*, both in psychology and in other fields. Courses in history, philosophy, political science, sociology, economics, and anthropology not only will show you exciting areas to study but also will reveal how other disciplines approach and study human behavior. Learning about social psychology should increase your appreciation of these other disciplines. Likewise, the information you get from these other disciplines should help you better understand the value of social psychology and its approach to human behavior.

With this introduction, we will return to Aronson's metaphor of the circus and invite you into the big tent of social psychology.

So What Can I Do with Social Psychology?

Hardly a semester goes by that we are not approached by a student who confesses, "I really enjoy this social psychology, but I'm reluctant to go on with my studies because I'm not sure what I can do with a degree in the area." This is a fair enough question, but fortunately we can give the student an encouraging response. Although we don't wish to create a general panic by suggesting that "social psychologists are everywhere," the opportunities for social psychologists are surprisingly broad and widespread.

Many social psychologists are attracted to academic positions within universities where they teach and conduct research. Within the university setting, most social psychologists will be found in departments of psychology, but this is not their only home. Because social psychology covers so many areas, you will likely find them on the faculty in schools of business (possibly studying group performance), architecture (examining the influence of environment on behavior), medicine, law, engineering (helping design environments to facilitate human interaction and performance), education (for example, studying the dynamics of the student-teacher relationship), and even agriculture (possibly working to develop plans for resolving community disputes over land use).

But the university is not the only setting in which social psychologists work. The applications offered by the field are useful in almost every situation involving human interaction. Advertising, for example, is concerned with attitude change and social influence, and advertising agencies often employ social psychologists. If we boil down a trial to its basic elements, we find a situation where lawyers for the two sides are engaged in a struggle to entice a judge or jury to adopt a particular position. Questions of how to present the most convincing case and who to choose on the jury are issues of social influence. Hence, social psychologists are in increasing demand by law firms and legal consulting firms. It is easy to look in awe as astronauts rocket into space to spend weeks or months circling the earth or working in a space station. Of all the daunting tasks facing the crews, one of the most basic concerns is how to get along with each other and how to work in confined quarters. Social psychologists can be found in almost every type of organization concerned with developing effective work teams; these organizations range from NASA to airline companies to automobile manufacturers. We could continue with these examples, but our point should be clear. Opportunities exist for social psychologists to work in a wide variety of settings on an equally diverse fare of issues and problems.

Throughout this book, we will give examples of the comfortable relationship between basic social psychology and its applications. We will draw on research conducted in a variety of settings and applied to a host of issues. As you read about the field, challenge yourself to find additional applications of social psychology in areas that interest you.

Summary

Social psychology is a discipline that employs scientific methods to understand and explain how the thoughts, feelings, and behaviors of individuals are influenced by the actual, imagined, or implied presence of others. Social psychologists are interested in discovering how most people behave most of the time. Sociologists generally focus on the structure and functioning of groups, while personality psychologists are most concerned with differences between individuals.

Social psychology is a twentieth-century science that developed in the United States and has recently been expanding in Western Europe. World and social events have played a major role in influencing the themes and issues studied by its practitioners. The first social psychology study, in 1897, examined the effects of performing alone and performing in front of a group. The first social psychology textbooks were published in 1908.

In the 1930s, social psychology was concerned with measuring and studying the functions of attitudes. During that decade, Kurt Lewin (1935) presented his field theory and demonstrated the importance of conducting controlled research on social phenomena. World War II influenced the direction of Lewin's research; Lewin examined social influence, leadership, and group dynamics. The war also gave rise to the study of attitude and attitude change by the Yale Communication Research Program. The post-war period of the 1950s and 1960s found social psychologists studying conformity, obedience, and conflict. Leon Festinger introduced the theory of cognitive dissonance in 1957, a theory that captured the attention of social psychologists for the next fifteen years.

In the late 1960s and early 1970s, attribution theory was a much-researched topic. In addition, social psychologists developed new methods for gathering and analyzing data. The 1980s were the heyday of research on social cognition, work that focused on how individuals store and process information about their social setting and how this information affects their interpretation of events and their behavior. During the 1990s, interest in social cognition continued although the field began to more directly embrace studies of the impact of culture on behavior. As in other periods, social psychology continued to be influenced by social issues of the period—for example, the spread of AIDS and the need to influence people's choice of sexual behavior.

Science is a set of rules for investigating events and communicating findings. The goals of any science include (1) the description of events, (2) the prediction of events, and (3) the explanation of why events occur. Scientists generally work with theories, which explain why events are related, and with hypotheses, which are educated guesses about the nature of the relationship between events.

Social psychologists use numerous methods in conducting their inquiry into human behavior. The case history, archival search, and survey are correlational methods for making predictions about the relationship between events. The laboratory experiment and the field experiment are methods for determining cause-and-effect relationships. In an experiment, the experimenter controls the independent variable and examines changes in the dependent variable. Extraneous variables must be eliminated if the experimenter is to be able to determine that the manipulation of the independent variable caused the observed changes in the dependent variable. The experiment is a valuable scientific tool because it allows the experimenter to randomly assign subjects to conditions and hence to arrive at the cause-and-effect relationship between variables. Laboratory experiments are often criticized because it is sometimes difficult to generalize beyond the laboratory, because they may lack external validity and mundane realism, and because they may allow demand characteristics and experimenter bias to affect the results. The field experiment generally has more external validity and mundane realism than the laboratory experiment. The field experiment's major drawback is that the experimenter loses some control over extraneous variables. Each method has advantages and disadvantages. The research method chosen must fit the experimental question and the aims of the experimenter.

Statistical tests are used to determine whether the results obtained in a study are reliable. Social psychologists have adopted the 5 percent chance level as the acceptable measure of significance of results. An important consideration in all research is the protection of subjects' psychological and physical safety. Ethical concerns in research center on invasion of privacy, the use of deception, potential harmful consequences, and the fact that subjects are often the unwilling recipients of a lesson about themselves. Strict guidelines have been developed to protect human subjects in social psychology research studies. Most institutions have institutional review boards that examine research proposals to ensure protection of subjects.

You can learn about social psychology by taking classes on the subject, observing people in their day-to-day activities, getting involved in experimentation, and taking a broad range of courses in the social sciences, the natural sciences, and the humanities.

Key Terms

analysis of variance test	external validity	mundane realism
archival research	extraneous variables	random assignment
case history	field experiment	science
check on the manipulation	generalize	social psychology
correlation	hypotheses	statistically significant
deception	independent variable	survey method
demand characteristics	informed consent	theory
dependent variable	institutional review boards	unobtrusive measures
experiment	(IRBs)	variability
experimental realism	internal validity	
experimenter bias	mean	

Suggested Readings

Campbell, D., and Stanley, J.C. (1963). *Experimental and quasi-experimental designs for research.* Chicago: Rand McNally.

Collier, G., Minton, H., and Reynolds, G. (1991). *Current thoughts in American social psychology.* New York: Oxford University Press.

Festinger, L. (1980). *Retrospections on social psychology.* New York: Basic Books.

Gilbert, D., Fiske, S., and Lindzey, G. (Eds.). (1997). *The handbook of social psychology* (4th ed.). New York: Random House.

Higgins, E.T., and Kruglanski, A. W. (Eds.). (1996). *Social psychology: Handbook of basic principals.* New York: Guilford.

Chapter 2

Social Cognition

In late September 1960, millions of people across North America tuned in to hear the first of four debates between John F. Kennedy and Richard M. Nixon, the Democratic and Republican nominees for president of the United States. Not since the historic Lincoln-Douglas debates of 1858 had there been such a momentous confrontation between two candidates. With the election six weeks away, interest in the two candidates was growing intense. Dwight "Ike" Eisenhower was finishing his second term and had become the oldest man to serve as president. Both Nixon and Kennedy were much younger men of considerable promise, and though Nixon had an early lead in the campaign, it looked like the race might be very close. People wanted to get to know the candidates and form their own impressions of each one. Kennedy in particular was an unknown. While Nixon had been Ike's vice-president for eight years, Kennedy was only the junior senator from Massachusetts.

After opening statements by both men, the first question was directed to Senator Kennedy. Not surprisingly it dealt with a central concern of the campaign, Kennedy's youth and inexperience, and the question of leadership. Bob Fleming of ABC news asked, "On this issue, why should people vote for you rather than the vice-president?" Kennedy made a mistake: he began answering the question from his chair. Nixon became quite agitated and called Kennedy's error to the attention of the moderator, Howard K. Smith. Smith also looked agitated, reached for his gavel to stop Kennedy, and then quietly caught Kennedy's attention and pointed toward the podium. With barely a pause, Kennedy calmly walked to the podium in midsentence and continued his answer. Despite the fact that Kennedy erred, it was Smith and Nixon who looked uncomfortable and confused. Kennedy himself seemed completely at ease and self-assured.

That pattern continued. Throughout the debate,

Kennedy exuded calm self-assurance while Nixon seemed tense and uncertain. Nixon was campaigning on the slogan "Experience Counts," but his edge in that department didn't seem to make any difference. He looked tired and he perspired freely. Kennedy was relaxed and seemed to embody "cool." Indeed, after the debate studies showed that Kennedy was perceived as the more experienced of the two. Furthermore, among the crucial group of independent voters, Kennedy's image moved consistently in the direction of the "ideal president," whereas Nixon's did not systematically change (Tannenbaum, Greenberg, and Silverman, 1962). Although the next three debates were fairly even, Kennedy's more effective performance in the first one had redefined the race for the presidency.

When voters went to the polls on November 8, Kennedy won in one of the closest elections in U.S. history. Although there were many pivotal events during the campaign, surely the debates played a crucial role (White, 1961). Voters formed impressions or changed impressions based on what they saw, particularly in the first debate.

In recent years, debates have become a regular part of presidential campaigns. And in many elections they have once again played a central role. Ronald Reagan's calm, polished, and reassuring tone in his debate with Jimmy Carter in 1980 convinced voters that he was not too reckless or militaristic to be trusted with the nuclear arsenal of the United States. His performance turned a close election into a landslide. In 1984 Reagan again used the debates to win a resounding re-election over Walter Mondale. After performing poorly in the first debate, Reagan had to show in the second that he was not too old to continue as president. Many wondered whether he was losing the intellectual control that most voters feel is necessary to govern effectively. Because the issue was potentially so explosive, the press did not know quite how to handle it.

In the second debate someone finally popped the question. Henry Trewhitt of the *Baltimore Sun* asked, "You already are the oldest president in history, and some of your staff say you were tired after your most recent encounter with Mr. Mondale. I recall yet that President Kennedy . . . had to go for days on end with very little sleep during the Cuban missile crisis. Is there any doubt that you would be able to function in such circumstances?" Reagan looked supremely confident when he heard the question. He began, "Not at all, Mr. Trewhitt." Then looking very serious, he added, "And I want you to know that also I will not make age an issue of this campaign. I am not going to exploit for political purposes my opponent's youth and inexperience." The response to Reagan's one-liner was immediate and intense. A distinctly audible

"whoop" was followed by loud laughter and applause. Reagan, Mondale, Trewhitt, and the audience all enjoyed Reagan's mastery and dismissal of the age issue. He went on to a forty-nine-state landslide.

Social Cognition: Making Sense of People

Throughout a presidential campaign, citizens try to understand and make sense of the candidates' behavior. They try to interpret specific behaviors, remember who said and did what, and form a general impression of each candidate's character and qualifications. This

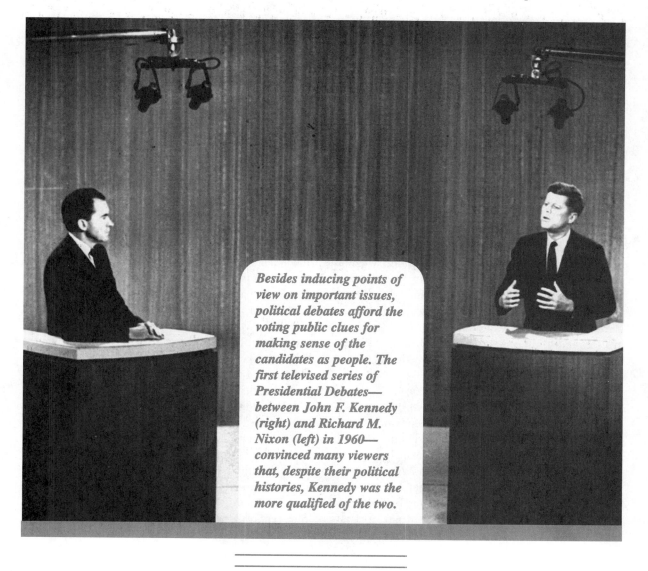

Besides inducing points of view on important issues, political debates afford the voting public clues for making sense of the candidates as people. The first televised series of Presidential Debates— between John F. Kennedy (right) and Richard M. Nixon (left) in 1960— convinced many viewers that, despite their political histories, Kennedy was the more qualified of the two.

complex social understanding process goes into high gear during a presidential debate. We watch the candidates behave, we hear what they say, and we form opinions about their competence, their decisiveness, their energy, and how much we like them. Debates give voters a chance to see the candidates in action in a competitive, stressful situation and thereby make important inferences about whether the candidates will be good leaders. In this chapter we will consider just how people come to understand others. In chapter 3 we will consider the closely related topics of self-perception and self-understanding.

We call the process of understanding or making sense of people **social cognition.** Two key components of social cognition are (1) making attributions about why people act as they do and (2) building an overall impression on the basis of what we know, or think we know, about them as individuals and as members of groups. We will consider attribution processes first.

Attribution Processes

In our everyday experience we encounter a wide range of behaviors in other people. First thing in the morning we may run into grumpy, sour, barely conscious roommates who grunt more than talk but still manage to act unhappy and unfriendly. An hour or so later we may meet people in class who seem much cheerier and much more pulled together. They've obviously had a shower and a cup of coffee. As we proceed through the afternoon and evening, we will have to interact with people who are friendly and helpful, rude and incompetent, or funny and energetic. During the evening we may watch a political debate and see one candidate seem cool and controlled and another seem flustered and confused. How do we sort out all of this information about the way people act?

Psychologists who study the way we form impressions of other people have shown that one way we make sense of the vast array of behaviors we observe is by trying to determine what qualities in each person explain their actions and make them act as they do. What is it that makes one individual act optimistic and extraverted and another behave cautiously and industriously? The personal qualities or traits that distinguish one person or group from an-

other are called **dispositions,** and we infer their existence by making **attributions** about the causes of people's actions. Basically, we make attributions by inferring whether a particular behavior is caused by a personal disposition or by something in the situation. If we decide that a personal disposition caused a behavior, we are making an **internal attribution.** If we decide that the behavior reflects something in the environment or the situation, we are making an **external attribution.** For example, when Richard Nixon appeared nervous and tense in debating John Kennedy, voters had to decide whether Nixon was a naturally nervous person (internal attribution) or whether the highly charged televised debate situation created a lot of tension (external attribution). Voters' attributions likely had a significant impact on their votes on election day.

Attribution theory in social psychology originated with the work of Fritz Heider (1944, 1958) and classic papers by Jones and Davis (1965) and Kelley (1967). Heider pointed out that people attribute behavior to either internal or external causes but prefer to make internal attributions because a person's dispositions are likely to guide his or her behavior over time and thus serve as useful reference points. Attributing Richard Nixon's discomfort to a tense disposition not only permitted us to explain one particular incident but told us how he was likely to act in other situations. If we can identify people's dispositions, we can predict and perhaps control their behavior in the future. Thus, knowing a person's dispositions or personal traits not only helps us understand the social environment, it also allows us, through prediction and control, to act effectively in it.

How do people make attributions? How would we have decided whether Ronald Reagan was really in control or was too old to manage his job as president? Here we will discuss the main theories concerning the principles people typically follow in making such attributions. First we discuss how we make internal or external attributions on the basis of observing various samples of behavior. Later we outline the ways people violate some of the basic principles of attribution. We begin by considering several important approaches to the attribution process, the process people use when analyzing the behavior of someone else and making decisions about what that other person is like. We also consider modifications of theories that have grown out of recent research.

Discounting, Augmentation, and the Subtractive Rule

Suppose you go to a party and meet a fellow student named Carole. You and Carole chat for a while and then, seeing a nearby Ping-Pong table, the two of you pick up a pair of paddles and begin to hit the ball back and forth. You aren't sure whether Carole will just try to keep the ball in play or start to hit hard shots that you can't return. That is, will her play be cooperative or competitive? You would just as soon hit the ball casually and try to keep it in play, and it turns out that that is what Carole does. Her behavior is clearly cooperative. But you want to go beyond categorizing Carole's behavior. You want to make an attribution and see if you can infer a personal disposition. Her behavior may reflect a cooperative disposition or it may be caused by something in the situation. Perhaps Carole is just following your lead, perhaps she thinks it's more appropriate to play casually rather than competitively at a party, or perhaps she is following a traditional norm that tells her that women should be cooperative and supportive rather than competitive and assertive.

A number of principles have been developed to explain how you might interpret Carole's behavior. First, Harold Kelley (1972) developed the closely related principles of discounting and augmentation. The **discounting principle** holds that "the role of a given cause in producing a given effect is discounted if other plausible causes are also present" (Kelley, 1972, p. 8). For example, behavior that is in accord with what's expected in a situation could be attributed to "other plausible causes," such as social norms or a person's effort simply to act appropriately, rather than to a personal disposition. Therefore, a perceiver is likely to discount (which means reduce, not eliminate) internal causes as explanations of behavior. Let's return to Carole playing Ping-Pong. If the party situation is a plausible cause in producing Carole's cooperative behavior, you would discount her disposition as the cause. You would not make a correspondent inference. Thus, you won't know whether Carole is a truly cooperative person. She may be, but maybe not.

The **augmentation principle** sounds more complicated, but it is really just the reverse of the discounting principle: "if for a given effect both a plausible inhibitory cause and a plausible facilitative cause are present, the role of the facilitative cause in producing the effect will be judged greater than if it alone were present as a plausible cause for the effect" (Kelley, 1972, p. 12). Again consider Carole. Suppose that at the friendly, low-key party Carole begins to overwhelm you with an assortment of slams, spinning backhands, and unreturnable drop shots. Her behavior is competitive but the party is an inhibitory force toward competitiveness; that is, the party calls for easygoing cooperation and inhibits competitiveness. Therefore you would judge the role of the facilitative cause, the cause that facilitates or produces Carole's competitive behavior, to be greater. That facilitative cause can only be Carole's competitive disposition. You infer more of it than you would if the party did not inhibit competitiveness. In other words, you make a strong internal attribution and decide that Carole must be highly competitive if she competes at a friendly party.

One study showing the operation of the augmentation principle looked at people's ratings of the funniness of a five-minute humor monologue filled with one-liners such as, "If you're at a picnic and a thunderstorm strikes, . . . try to lie as flat on the ground as possible, and be sure to make someone else hold the weenie fork." People who laughed at the monologue but were told that the laboratory setting, where in fact the study was conducted, inhibits laughter rated the monologue as particularly funny. They apparently reasoned that since they laughed in the inhibiting laboratory setting, the monologue must really have been pretty funny. Its power to cause laughter was augmented (Olson and Roese, 1995).

More recently, the discounting and augmentation principles have been combined in what is called the **subtractive rule:** "The contribution of situational inducements should be subtracted from the personal disposition implied by the behavior itself" (Trope, Cohen, and Moaz, 1988). Thus, in the example above if the party situation provides an inducement for Carole to be cooperative, that inducement should be subtracted from the cooperative disposition that may be inferred from her behavior. That is, you should follow the discounting principle and discount a cooperative disposition as the cause of Carole's behavior if the party situation is also a plausible cause for it. Again, you won't know whether Carole is really a cooperative person.

But suppose situational inducements toward competitive behavior are negative, as they are at the party. Again you follow the subtractive rule and subtract these negative inducements. As you may remember

---

FIGURE 2.1   **THE SUBTRACTIVE RULE: DISCOUNTING AND AUGMENTATION IN ATTRIBUTION**

Example 1:   **Positive inducement for behavior and discounting:**

A person behaves in a cooperative manner in a situation that calls for cooperative behavior.

Behavior: Cooperative

Disposition implied by the behavior: Cooperativeness

Situational inducement: Positive for cooperation

Application of subtractive rule: The subtractive rule says that the contribution of situational inducements should be subtracted from the personal disposition implied by the behavior. Since the inducement is positive for the disposition implied by the behavior, cooperativeness, the attribution of cooperativeness should be reduced.

Attribution: The situation caused the behavior. The person may not have a cooperative disposition. Cooperativeness is discounted as a cause of the behavior.

Example 2:   **Negative inducement for behavior and augmentation:**

A person behaves in a competitive manner in a situation that calls for cooperative behavior.

Behavior: Competitive

Disposition implied by the behavior: Competitiveness

Situational inducement: Negative for competition

Application of subtractive rule: The subtractive rule says that the contribution of situational inducements should be subtracted from the personal disposition implied by the behavior. Since the inducement is negative for the disposition implied by the behavior, competitiveness, the attribution of competitiveness should be increased. That is, the negative inducement is subtracted, with the effect that it is added to the attribution of competitiveness.

Attribution: The disposition caused the behavior. The person probably has a strongly competitive disposition. Competitiveness is augmented as a cause of the behavior.

---

from elementary algebra, when you subtract a negative you actually add. You thus augment your perception of Carole's competitiveness because you figure she must be a competitive person indeed to play so hard when the situation really calls for cooperation. In short, the subtractive rule sometimes leads you to discount the role of a disposition and sometimes it leads you to augment your perception of its strength (see figure 2.1).

Research shows that people can and do follow the logic of the subtractive rule. In one study, subjects judged Dan, who behaved in an angry fashion, in one of two situations (Trope, Cohen, and Moaz, 1988). In one situation subjects read: "When Dan came to the city hall and was told by the clerk he couldn't be helped because of a strike, Dan was very itchy and almost screamed at the clerk." In the other situation subjects read: "As Dan came home, his little son jumped on him and hung onto his neck. Dan was very itchy and almost screamed at him." In the first situation the subtractive rule says that we should discount the angry disposition implied by Dan's behavior. His behavior can be attributed to a frustrating situation. In accord with this principle, Dan is seen as having a personality that is only slightly more angry than average. In the

latter situation the subtractive rule says that we should augment the angry disposition implied by Dan's behavior. The situation calls for Dan to be happy, not angry, and in accordance with the subtractive rule, Dan is seen as having a personality that is much more angry than average in this situation.

In sum, subjects do follow the subtractive rule in discounting dispositions as causes for behaviors that the situation can explain and augmenting dispositional attributions for behaviors that do seem to be called for by the situation. So the next time a politician shakes your hand at a rally and acts as though he or she is your close friend, remember to apply the discounting principle and the subtractive rule in deciding whether her disposition toward you is really one of high regard and affection.

The Covariation Principle

Thus far we have considered attribution questions that arise when people perform a specific behavior, such as Richard Nixon acting nervously in a presidential debate, but we don't know how the person has performed in other circumstances or how other people would have responded in the same circumstance. Very often, however, we know about more than just a single instance of behavior. We can interpret an action by our roommate in the context of his or her behavior in a variety of situations, the behavior of a brother or sister in the context of years of experience, and the reactions of a boyfriend or girlfriend in the context of many dates in many places. And very important, we know how other people in general react in many of the same situations in which we have seen the behavior of our roommate, brother, or date.

Harold Kelley (1967, 1972) identified several key variables we consider when we have such information in deciding whether someone is acting as a result of an internal disposition (a **person attribution**) or as a response to some external person, object, or situation in the environment (an **entity attribution**).

Kelley suggested we consider three such factors: consistency—whether the person's response is consistent in that situation; distinctiveness—whether it is unusual for the person to behave as he or she did in that situation; and consensus—whether other people respond the same way in that situation (Kelley, 1967, 1972). Suppose your friend Paul came home from his physics class in a gloomy, frustrated mood. Should you make an internal attribution and infer that Paul's blue mood is attributable to a depressive or gloomy personal disposition, or should you make an external attribution and decide that physics class is a bad entity responsible for Paul's bad humor?

Let's consider how you might use information about consistency, distinctiveness, and consensus to make the attribution. Of first importance is *consistency*. If Paul's response to the class is not consistent on different days, we can't really attribute it to either Paul or the physics course. If Paul likes the physics class on some days but not on others, we can't say that Paul has a gloomy disposition or that the course is frustrating. Paul's gloomy reaction can be attributable only to specific circumstances, perhaps the winter weather or a particular topic in physics. This circumstance attribution doesn't tell us much about Paul or about the course.

If Paul's response is high in consistency, we may then think about its uniqueness or *distinctiveness*. Is Paul generally gloomy or is his response to the physics course unusual and distinctive? If Paul responds in a gloomy way to many things, the response has low distinctiveness. If it is unusual—that is, Paul is generally quite upbeat—we refer to his response as having high distinctiveness. In the case of a low-distinctiveness response (Paul is often gloomy), we

should attribute his gloominess to his personal disposition. In the case of a high-distinctiveness response (it's unusual for Paul to be gloomy), we may suspect the physics class.

The final variable we need to consider is *consensus*. How do other people react to the physics class? If Paul's response has low consensus—that is, it makes few people as gloomy as Paul—we tend to attribute the response to Paul's disposition. If consensus is high (most people get frustrated and depressed by the class), we tend to think there is something wrong with the class.

Putting consistency, distinctiveness, and consensus information together, we can predict the following attributions. When consistency is high but distinctiveness and consensus are low we can make a person attribution and infer that Paul is a gloomy person. He consistently reacts that way to the physics class, it's not just the physics class that makes him feel that way, and no one else is bothered by the class. On the other hand, when consistency is high and distinctiveness and consensus are also high, we suspect the entity. Something's wrong with the class. It almost always puts Paul in a funk, though he reacts to most things in a cheerful, easygoing manner, and almost everyone else gets upset by it as well.

Do people really use information about consistency, distinctiveness, and consensus in making internal and external attributions? When the question was put to an experimental test, the answer was clearly yes. Participants in a study by McArthur (1972) were given information about a fictitious person. They were told about a particular behavior and then read three pieces of information designed to manipulate the degrees of consensus, distinctiveness, and consistency. For example, subjects may have learned that "John laughed at the comedian." They were then told that:

Consensus:
a. almost everyone who hears the comedian laughs at him; or
b. hardly anyone who hears the comedian laughs at him.

Distinctiveness:
a. John does not laugh at almost any other comedian; or
b. John also laughs at almost any other comedian.

Consistency:
a. in the past, John has almost always laughed at the same comedian; or

b. in the past, John has almost never laughed at the same comedian.

In the end, subjects were asked how much they attributed John's laughter to something about John or to something about the comedian. The results of the study were generally supportive of Kelley's model. Internal attributions (something about John) were facilitated by low distinctiveness, low consensus, and high consistency. External attributions (something about the comedian) were facilitated by high distinctiveness, high consensus, and high consistency.

Evidence also shows that consistency, distinctiveness, and consensus information affect not only our attributions but also the way we interact with other people. Experimental subjects watched a videotape of a young woman who behaved rudely in an interview. A female interviewer asked her how often she took the initiative in her interactions with men and whether she was willing to be the aggressor in relationships, "even in the sexual domain." The woman refused to answer. She said, "Do I really have to go through this again? It's none of your business about my sex life. I'm not answering that question. Go on to the next one." Some subjects were given attributional information implying an internal cause. They were told that the woman had refused to answer that question in a previous interview (high consistency), that she didn't answer several other questions either (low distinctiveness), and that all the other women who were asked that question answered it (low consensus). These subjects rated the woman as dispositionally rude and during a meeting with her they kept at a distance and didn't talk to her very much. In contrast, other subjects were given information that implied an external cause. They were told that the woman had not answered that question in a previous interview (high consistency) but that she had answered all other questions (high distinctiveness) and that a lot of other women had refused to answer the question (high consensus). The subjects with this information attributed the woman's response to the question, they did not perceive her as rude, and they were much friendlier when they interacted with her (Hazelwood and Olson, 1986).

Recent research has questioned the extent to which people actually go through the kind of complex causal calculus described by Kelley in making attributions. One theory has argued that people only use Kelley's covariation principle when they are explaining an unusual event and have to identify the abnormal condition that produced it (Hilton, 1990; Hilton and Sugolski, 1986). For example, if a person gets sick from eating a meal at a popular restaurant, this unusual event requires explanation. Perceivers might ask if others got sick too (consensus), in which case the restaurant is to blame. If not, they would ask if other food made the person sick (distinctiveness), in which case the person may be having a digestive illness (Fiske and Taylor, 1991). But it is the unusual event of illness after eating that engages the attribution process. Similarly, recent research also suggests that people only use Kelley's covariation principle to explain behavior that is rare. For example, if someone gets angry or makes charitable contributions, people use the covariation principle only if that behavior is rare for the individual. In the same way, if someone does something that only few other people do, only then do perceivers think in terms of covariation (Johnson, Boyd, and Magnani, 1994). In short, people do the detective work involved in using the covariation principle only when they feel that they have a mystery to solve.

Attributions for Success and Failure

Thus far we have seen the complex ways that perceivers decide whether someone's behavior is internally or externally caused. Attributions affect not only the judgments we make about other people but how we interact with them as well. But in many cases attribution goes further than deciding whether behavior is caused by something in a person or something in the situation, particularly when we judge success and failure. Consider the following example. We turn on the television on a Sunday in November and see a football player make a diving catch in the end zone. "Lucky!" shouts someone in the room. "Whaddaya mean?" another responds angrily. "He's the best receiver in the league." A third, more intellectual-looking viewer explains that the success was due not to the player's luck or skill but to the unusual amount of effort that he expended to catch this particular pass. The fourth person in the room responds, "Aw, it was easy anyway."

What these people are arguing about is both whether the cause of the catch was internal or external and whether it was stable or unstable; that is, whether the football player could make that kind of catch again or is likely to do so infrequently. Only when attributions of internality/externality *and* attributions of stability/

TABLE 2.1   CLASSIFICATION SCHEME FOR THE
PERCEIVED DETERMINANTS OF
ACHIEVEMENT BEHAVIOR

Stability	Locus of Control	
	Internal	External
Stable	Ability	Task difficulty
Unstable	Effort	Luck

Source: Weiner, Frieze, Kukla, Reed, Rest, and Rosenbaum (1971)

instability are made can a final attribution for the success or failure be made.

Table 2.1 summarizes the view of Weiner and his colleagues (1971) as to how the factors are combined to form a final attribution. We can judge that the football player made his catch because he is good (a stable, internal attribution); because making such a catch is easy (a stable, external attribution—he could do it again and again; anyone could; it has to do with the kind of catch, not his ability); because he tried hard (an unstable, internal attribution—he couldn't do that again and again; it was his tremendous effort); or because of luck (an unstable, external attribution—he couldn't do it that many times; it was lucky that his hands and the ball happened to wind up in the same place).

An interesting study that provides data relevant to the football player's situation was conducted by Frieze and Weiner (1971). They told subjects about the success or failure that a hypothetical person had experienced at a task. They then told the subjects about the success or failure that person had at similar tasks and the percentage of other people who had succeeded or failed at that task. In this way, Frieze and Weiner established the basic conditions that would enable an attribution of internality or externality. Then the subjects were informed that the actor had done the task one more time, and some subjects were told that he had succeeded, whereas other subjects were told that he had failed.

To what did subjects attribute the most recent success or failure? The answers generally confirmed the predictions of Weiner and his colleagues' model. Performance that was inconsistent with the person's past performance (whether he succeeded or failed) and different from the performance of other persons was attributed to effort (he tried extra hard in the case of success; he

didn't try very hard in the case of failure). Performance that was consistent with the person's past performance and similar to the performance of other persons was attributed to task difficulty (success = easy task; failure = hard task). Performance that was consistent with the person's past performance and different from the performance of other persons was attributed to ability (success = high ability; failure = low ability).

Thus the questions we would have to ask about the football player in order to make an attribution for the success we observed on TV become clear. First, was it a catch that anyone could make—that is, was consensus high or low? Second, was the success a stable phenomenon—that is, was it something that was consistent or inconsistent with the player's past behavior as a pass receiver? We would conclude that he is a player of high ability if we rated catching the pass to be internal and his success in receiving to be stable.

Attributions that we make first to internal or external factors and then to stable or unstable factors have important consequences. Typically our evaluation of a person depends on whether we make internal or external attributions. We evaluate people positively when we make internal attributions for their successes (high ability or effort) and external attributions for their failures (a difficult task or bad luck). Negative evaluations follow from internal attributions for failure (low ability or effort) and external attributions for success (an easy task or good luck). Whereas internal and external attributions affect evaluation, stable and unstable attributions affect expectancies. If the cause of a success or failure is stable (ability or task difficulty), we expect to see more of it in the future. If the cause is unstable (effort or luck), we aren't as likely to expect the same success or failure in the future.

Weiner has modified his original theory to include causal dimensions beyond internality and stability, which also have important consequences. One such dimension is *controllability* (Weiner, 1985, 1986). Suppose a person failed a test because she hadn't put effort into studying. Lack of effort is an internal-unstable cause, and we might evaluate the person negatively and expect that her future performance might improve. But our reaction will be affected by whether the lack of effort was due to something the person could control, such as choosing to go sailing on Sunday afternoon, versus one that she could not control, such as being required to serve on a jury.

In general, if people fail because of causes beyond their control, we feel pity rather than anger, and

"I don't get it. They run, but they're not chasing anything."

we are inclined to try to help them. We have the opposite reactions when someone fails because of factors he or she can control. These reactions were shown in a study of people with a stigma—some characteristic that marks them as "deviant, flawed, limited, spoiled or generally undesirable" (Jones, Farina, Hastorf, Markus, Miller, and Scott, 1984, p. 6). People with stigmas that were perceived to be uncontrollable, such as blindness, cancer, or delayed stress reactions to fighting in Vietnam, elicited feelings of pity and inclinations to help. People with stigmas that were seen as controllable, such as obesity, AIDS, and drug addiction, elicited reactions of anger and inclinations toward neglect (Weiner, Perry, and Magnusson, 1988). A key factor here seems to be that we hold people responsible for stigmas or failures that are controllable and could have been prevented, and we react to them with anger. When people cannot control their stigmas or failures, they are not held responsible. Consequently, we feel pity and we want to help them.

A final dimension of attribution is *globality*. We often judge whether causes are very specific in their effects or are global; that is, whether they affect just a few outcomes or a wide range of them (Abramson, Seligman, and Teasdale, 1978). If Tom failed a math test, for example, we might think he had some kind of ability deficit. On the one hand, we might infer that he cannot take timed multiple-choice math tests, a very specific shortcoming, but that he is generally competent in math and is basically quite intelligent. A more global attribution would be that Tom just doesn't have any math aptitude, although he is com-

petent in other areas. An even more global attribution is that Tom has a deficit that will affect a great many performances and a wide range of experiences—he just isn't very bright.

A series of studies on attributions and marital happiness show the importance of the globality dimension as well as the internal/external and stable/unstable dimensions. All couples have to deal with disappointments, disagreements, and difficulties in their marriage. The attributions they attach to their partner's negative behavior make a big difference in the success of their marriage (Fincham, 1985; Bradbury and Fincham, 1992). People who attribute their marital problems and their spouse's negative behavior to internal causes ("My wife intentionally picked a fight about our vacation") and to stable and global characteristics ("My husband always makes trouble about everything") are more likely to create unhappiness in their marriages, and they are more likely to engage in destructive behavior themselves (Karney, Bradbury, Fincham, and Sullivan, 1994). Their maladaptive attributions generally come from "negative affect," that is, a tendency to report "distress, discomfort, and dissatisfaction over time" (Watson and Clark, 1984, p. 483), and they subsequently lead to unhappiness in marriage.

In sum, when we make attributions, we identify causes that are internal or external and that vary in their stability, controllability, and globality. In chapter 3 we will see that people make attributions about their own behaviors and their own successes and failures as well as about other people's. We will also see that people's feelings and expectations about their behaviors and performances are strongly affected by these self-attributions.

Biases in Attribution

We have seen that people can follow several essentially rational principles of attribution in forming impressions of others. All that these principles require is a little elementary logic. People can use the subtractive rule either to discount or to augment the dispositional attribution implied by a behavior, and they can use information about an action's consistency, distinctiveness, and consensus to infer whether the behavior is attributable to the person or the entity.

Consider, for example, people watching the 1984 Mondale-Reagan debate who were trying to decide whether Ronald Reagan was really quick and witty on the basis of his adept one-line response to the question about his age. They might have followed the subtractive rule and decided that the wit implied by Reagan's quip should be discounted because it was planned and well rehearsed. Or they might have applied the principles of consistency, distinctiveness, and consensus. Then they would ask whether Reagan was consistently cool and witty in debates, whether he was quick in other situations, and how witty other candidates are when they are dealing with such questions in debates. They *might* use these principles, but *do* they?

In fact, attribution theorists have shown that in many instances people do not follow the simple logic of basic attributional principles. Indeed, there are a number of pitfalls in applying these principles and a number of biases that can sidetrack logical attribution. Some of these biases are due to our shortcomings in processing information and some of them come from motives that lead us to prefer to make a particular kind of attribution that may not be implied by the available information. We don't want to imply that people are either rational or irrational. They are clearly both, and it depends on the person and on the situation whether they will be rational in any given instance. Here we will consider three specific obstacles to accurate attribution: the correspondence bias, the saliency bias, and defensive attribution.

The Correspondence Bias

The psychologist Fritz Heider (1944, 1958), as noted earlier, was the first to write about the processes of attribution. He explained that although it is perfectly possible to attribute behavior to external factors, we tend to be more comfortable with internal attributions. We prefer to know the dispositions of the people with whom we interact because this knowledge help us to predict and perhaps control their behavior. As a result of our preference for knowing dispositions, we often underestimate the role of situational forces in causing behavior when we make attributions. We overestimate the role of personal dispositions and assume that people's behavior simply reflects their dispositions. For example, we might decide that a political figure is cold and unemotional because that's how he behaved. We ignore the forces in the situation that made him act that way. Because a dispositional attribution requires us to decide that

an action corresponds directly to a disposition, the bias toward making dispositional attributions is called the **correspondence bias** (Gilbert and Jones, 1986; Gilbert and Malone, 1995). For example, we are falling prey to the correspondence bias when we decide that a person who behaves angrily when provoked is an angry person. Ignoring the provocation, we assume the angry behavior corresponds to an angry disposition. Because it is such a pervasive and important phenomenon, the correspondence bias has also been called the **fundamental attribution error** (Ross, 1977).

The correspondence bias can be seen at work in an experiment in which subjects had to present information about a case study to a woman who was described as a graduate student in clinical psychology. The subjects were told that the woman was practicing techniques for helping people such as teachers and nurses discuss case study information. In some cases the subjects were told that the woman was practicing a technique that called for her to be as open and spontaneous as possible; thus her behavior was freely chosen. Other subjects were told either that the graduate student was practicing a technique that required her to be distant and unfriendly to help teachers and nurses develop independence or that she was practicing a technique that required her to be as friendly and supportive as possible to help her clients feel comfortable. Thus the woman's behavior in these cases was forced, either forced unfriendly behavior or forced friendly behavior. After being given this information about the woman's freely chosen or constrained behavior, the subjects actually read a case study and discussed it with her. The woman's behavior in the discussions was either very friendly or very unfriendly.

How did the subjects perceive the graduate student's personality? The results showed that information about the woman's forced friendly or unfriendly behavior was never taken into account. Subjects thought she was a friendly person when her behavior was friendly, whether that behavior was freely chosen or forced. When her behavior was unfriendly, she was seen as being extremely cold and hostile even when she was just practicing a technique that required her to be unfriendly. In short, subjects showed a strong correspondence bias. They simply did not consider situational inducements when they judged the woman's personality (Napolitan and Goethals, 1979). A direct application of the subtractive rule would not have produced the attributions made in the forced behavior conditions. Thus, we see that the correspondence bias essentially involves the failure to use the subtractive rule—the failure to discount personal disposition when there are situational inducements for behavior.

The correspondence bias not only operates in perceiving individuals, it also affects the way we perceive groups (Allison, Mackie, and Messick, 1996). Whenever a group makes a decision, we assume that individual members of the group have attitudes corespondent with that decision even when we know that many individuals disagreed with it. For example, Allison, Mackie, and Messick point out that news magazines in the United States emphasized the American people's great support for Ronald Reagan after he won the election of 1980 with less than 51 percent of the popular vote. The magazines assumed that individual Americans supported Reagan even though nearly half voted for one of his opponents.

In one study on the "group correspondence bias," subjects judged members of a group as either successful or unsuccessful in making a cooperative decision. In both groups four of seven members chose to make the cooperative decision while three chose not to. However, one group was successful in making the cooperative decision because only three cooperative members were needed to make that decision whereas the other group was unsuccessful because five cooperative members were required to make the cooperative decision. Subjects judged the typical group member to be more cooperative in the successful group than in the unsuccessful group even though in both groups four of seven individuals cooperated (Allison and Kerr, 1994). The outcome of the group's decision was used to infer attitudes of individual group members despite the actual attitudes of individual members.

It is also the case that the correspondence bias governs predictions of future behavior. Once people make correspondent inferences on the basis of behavior, they often assume others will behave consistently with the disposition they attribute to them even when the situation calls for quite different behavior (Newman, 1996). If Ronald Reagan is witty in a situation where humor is required, we might see him as a genuinely witty person because of correspondence bias and expect him to make humorous remarks even when a serious response is called for.

What causes the correspondence bias? Why do people fail to apply the subtractive rule? A number of factors are critical in determining just how much people show the correspondence bias.

As Heider suggested, one important factor in this determination may simply be people's desire to identify dispositions and predict behavior. Therefore we take behavior as an indicator of a disposition and overlook the fact that doing so may not be logical. Heider also suggested another important reason when he said that "behavior in particular has such salient properties it tends to engulf the total field" (Heider, 1958, p. 54). By that Heider meant that sometimes behavior is so vivid, and environmental constraints so subtle in comparison, that we attribute a good sense of humor, for example, to Ronald Reagan just because he fired off a few well-timed one liners. Certainly subjects in the study with the clinical psychology graduate student encountered behavior that was vivid in its friendliness or unfriendliness.

Several recent experiments have told us a great deal more about the correspondence bias—both what makes it appear and what makes it go away. One important factor is simply that people are busy and have only so much time and energy to think through the logical implications of behavior and situational inducements. Therefore, it may be true that the busier people are, the more they demonstrate the correspondence bias. This is exactly what was shown in an experiment conducted by Gilbert, Pelham, and Krull (1988).

In this experiment subjects watched seven silent videotape segments of a woman who was having a discussion with another woman she had just met. The first woman's behavior appeared to be extremely anxious. Some subjects were told that many of the topics the first woman was discussing on the taped segments were in fact anxiety producing, such as embarrassing moments, personal failures, hidden secrets, and sexual fantasies. Other subjects were told that all of the topics were relaxing, such as fashion trends, world travel, ideal vacations, and best restaurants. In addition, half of the subjects in each group were given a task that made them cognitively busy—they had to memorize the list of topics the woman was discussing. The other half of the subjects in each were not busy; they didn't have to memorize the topics. After watching the tape, all subjects were asked to infer to what extent the woman actually had an anxious disposition.

The results showed that the not-busy subjects used the subtractive rule perfectly well and avoided the correspondence bias. Nonbusy subjects who were told that the woman was discussing relaxing topics augmented their dispositional attribution and saw her as highly anxious. She had behaved in an anxious way even though the situation should have made her relaxed. And subjects who thought she was discussing anxiety-provoking topics thought she was a much less anxious person. They subtracted the situational inducement toward anxiety and discounted the anxious disposition implied by her behavior. On the other hand, busy subjects, who had to memorize the discussion topics, showed the correspondence bias. They thought the woman was relatively anxious whether she was discussing anxious or relaxing topics. The situational inducement was not factored into their attributions. It's important to note that the busy subjects didn't forget the situational inducements. In fact, they were busy memorizing what they were. But memorizing the topics made subjects unable to think through their logical attributional implications.

Other research shows that when we are interacting with someone, the demands of interacting effectively often keep our minds so busy that we can't apply the subtractive rule as we should, and as a result we fall prey to the correspondence bias. For example, in one study subjects had their hands full trying to be friendly to an unfriendly confederate. The subjects knew that some of the attitudes the confederate expressed were dictated by the experimenter, but they attributed those attitudes to her anyway. Subjects didn't do this when they were being friendly to someone who was friendly in return. They didn't have to work as hard, and they were able to think about the situational inducements that caused her to express the attitudes she did. They did not think she believed what she was saying (Gilbert, Krull, and Pelham, 1988). A similar result was found in an experiment in which subjects had to present themselves to another person in a favorable way. Their positive self-presentations elicited similar positive self-presentations from the other person. From these reciprocated positive self-presentations the subjects inferred that the other person had very high self-esteem. Devising their own positive self-presentations kept subjects too busy to think about the fact that the other person's self-presentations were induced by their own behavior and should not have been taken as an indication of high self-esteem (Baumeister, Hutton, and Tice, 1989).

Time is not the only factor that affects whether people think through the logical attributional implications of situational inducements. Inclination is another. Some people are more motivated and inclined to be thoughtful. One recent study shows that depressed people, because they are trying to regain a sense of control, will take the time and effort, if they can, to think logically about attributions. As a result they are often less likely to show the correspondence bias. Their thoughtfulness makes them more accurate (Yost and Weary, 1996).

Several other studies have shown that nonverbal behavior can be key in helping us to overcome the correspondence bias and apply the subtractive rule. For example, when subjects watch a videotape of someone reading an essay, they tend to think the reader agrees with the attitude expressed in the essay even though they know he was randomly assigned to read that particular essay rather than one expressing the opposite point of view. But if subjects see the person nonverbally express disappointment when he is assigned to read a particular essay—a pro-choice essay, say, rather than an antiabortion essay—they don't infer a pro-choice attitude corresponding to the pro-choice essay. The nonverbal expression of disappointment reminds subjects to think about the situational constraint. When they do, they avoid the correspondence bias (Fleming and Darley, 1989).

Spontaneous Trait Inferences (STIs)

Closely related to Heider's idea that "behavior engulfs the field" is the concept of **spontaneous trait inferences (STIs)** (Uleman, Newman, and Moskowitz, 1996), which holds that when people observe behavior they automatically make trait inferences. What does it mean to say people make trait inferences automatically? Automatic processes in social cognition are unintentional, involuntary, effortless, and take place outside of awareness (Fiske and Taylor, 1991). They just happen without any effort to exert control. Support for the idea of spontaneous trait inferences, or STIs, comes from a number of clever experiments that subtly reveal that people automatically and unconsciously make trait inferences when they learn about the behavior of an actor. For example, when people read, "The reporter steps on his girlfriend's feet during the foxtrot," they spontaneously infer that the reporter is clumsy, and when they read, "The child tells his mother that he ate the chocolates," they infer that the child is honest. How do we know people make such spontaneous trait inferences?

Several types of relevant data inform us. We'll mention three. First, in a procedure called *cued recall* subjects are asked to memorize a number of sentences like the one about the reporter stepping on his girlfriend's feet. If subjects are given words such as *clumsy* as cues or hints to the sentences, they are more likely to recall them than if they are not given cues. The world *clumsy* serves as a cue or hint to the sentence because subjects have already spontaneously linked the trait clumsy to the behavior described in the sentence (Winter and Uleman, 1984).

Second, in several studies subjects were asked to look at photos of people accompanied by self-descriptive statements that implied traits. Subsequently they were told the persons' traits and were asked to learn them. They learned the traits faster if they had read the self-descriptions than when they had not. For example, if subjects saw a photo of a woman who said, "Tonight is my anniversary. I have fixed a candlelight dinner for my husband. I'm going to serve dinner on a table that I have set up in our bedroom," they learned more rapidly that she was "romantic" than if they had not read her statement. They apparently had already learned that she was romantic by spontaneously making that trait inference from her statement. As a result, when they subsequently were asked to learn that she was romantic, it was simpler to do (Carlston and Skowronski, 1994; Carlston, Skowronski, and Sparks, 1995).

Finally, in another procedure people were asked to judge as quickly as they could whether a statement, such as "He took fifteen minutes to find his car in the parking lot," contained the word *forgetful*. They took longer to answer the question and made more mistakes than if they had to judge whether the sentence "He took fifteen minutes to find a place for his car in the parking lot" contained the word *forgetful*. The first sentence brings the trait forgetful to mind as a result of spontaneous trait inferences, and subjects have a harder time being sure that the sentence did not contain it (Uleman, Hon, Roman, and Moscowitz, 1996).

In sum, the research on STIs along with the research on the correspondence bias suggests that people automatically make trait inferences from behavior. Thus, the correspondence bias may be something that occurs routinely unless substantial thought is given to the causes of the observed behavior and people are able to apply the subtractive rule.

The Saliency Bias

When Heider wrote that behavior engulfs the field, he implied that we may fall prey to the correspondence bias simply because behavior is so salient and vivid in comparison with subtle environmental pressures. Tak-

ing this idea one step further, Taylor and Fiske (1975) argued that any stimulus that is vivid or salient in a situation will be seen as the cause of behavior in that situation. They showed that if the attention of perceivers was focused on a particular member of a dyad during a conversation, that member was perceived as more central and causative in directing the course of the conversation. Observers thus fell prey to the **saliency bias.** McArthur and Post (1977) demonstrated that making an actor's environment salient increased the number of attributions that were made to the environment. Taylor, Fiske, Etcoff, and Ruderman (1978) showed that a novel member of a group, by being more salient, was perceived as greatly influential. Perceivers rated the only black person in a group of whites, for example, as having talked more frequently and as having been more influential in affecting the discussion. His salience affected his availability in perceivers' memories, which in turn affected their memory of how frequently he contributed to the group.

The Impact of Schemas

One of the most important concepts in social cognition is that of **schema**. A schema is cognitive structure that contains our general knowledge about any person, object, or event (Fiske and Taylor, 1991). We have many kinds of schemas stored in our memory, including social schemas, which contain our knowledge of particular individuals and of certain kinds of people. The word *schema* is the Greek word for "shape"; it refers to the shape or general outline of what we know about somebody or something (Crider, Goethals, Kavanaugh, and Solomon, 1993). Because we use what we know to make guesses about what will happen in the future, our schemas can also be thought of as general expectations or preconceptions about other people (Myers, 1983). During the 1960 presidential campaign, for example, many people were generally aware that John Kennedy was young and inexperienced in comparison with Richard Nixon. This schema (or general image) of Kennedy led many voters to the expectation that he would be overmatched in his first debate with Nixon. The fact that Kennedy violated this clear expectation made his performance that much more impressive.

A concept closely related to the concept of schema is that of scripts. A **script** is our knowledge of

These restaurant customers are following a common script that tells them the way events in the public dining situation unfold. For example, the party in the left foreground knows that when they finish their main course they will be asked if they want dessert. The party to the right knows to expect a bill soon.

a particular situation and the way events in that situation unfold (Abelson, 1981; Schank and Abelson, 1977); it can be thought of as an event schema. For example, we know that when people go into a restaurant, they will be seated, given a menu, asked if they would like a cocktail, and so on. Similarly, in recent debates candidates follow a clear script. They walk over and shake each other's hands, turn to kiss their wives, chat with political commentators and their advisers, and so on. The most distinctive characteristic of a script is that it includes knowledge of the sequence of events that characterize situations.

How do schemas work? Generally, they provide us with expectations or preconceptions about how people will behave. Consequently, we notice information that is consistent with our schemas, we interpret information that may be ambiguous as fitting our schemas, and we recall information that is related to our schemas better than information that is unrelated to them. Furthermore, we tend to recall information that we interpreted as fitting a schema as being even more consistent with that schema as time passes (Hig-

gins and McCann, 1984). Let us consider how schemas affect our impressions of other people and how they affect our memory of their behavior.

Schemas and Impressions

Schemas provide us with expectations and a tendency to perceive people's behavior as fitting those expectations. One interesting example comes from the world of sports. Baseball expert Bill James has noted that hard-hitting shortstops, such as former Chicago Cubs player Ernie Banks, are usually thought—often wrongly—to be poor fielders because of the schemas people use to understand the game. "People have trouble reconciling the image of the power hitter—the slow, strong muscleman . . . —with the image of the shortstop, who is lithe, quick, and agile" (James, 1988, p. 377). Therefore they tend to push aside the image of Banks the shortstop to accommodate the stronger image of Banks the slugger. The record shows that Banks was an excellent fielder, but, because of the slugger schema, he seldom gets the credit he deserves.

The impact of expectations on our perceptions of people can be seen in a classic experiment known as the "warm-cold" study (Kelly, 1950). The subjects in this study were undergraduates taking an introductory economics course at MIT. They were all told that they were to have a guest instructor for a specific class and were then given a little bit of information about the visitor. Students in half the sections were told that the visitor was twenty-nine years old, that he was married, and that people considered him "a rather cold person, industrious, critical, practical, and determined." Students in the other sections were given the same information except that they were told he was said to be "a rather warm person, industrious, critical, practical, and determined." In short, the only difference was that one-half of the subjects were told that the guest lecturer was cold and the other half were told that he was warm. Because warm versus cold is an important "central trait" in the perception of a person (Asch, 1946), this one-word difference created strong expectancy differences in the two subject groups. The impact of this expectancy difference was dramatic. The subjects who were told that the guest was warm had much more positive impressions of him than those who were told the opposite. Both groups of subjects saw the same guest giving the same lecture, and both groups spent a full class period with him. Yet their impressions of him, based on that hour of instruction, were strongly affected by the one-word difference: they interpreted the man's behavior according to their "knowledge" that he was warm or cold.

How can a schema have such a strong effect? As noted, we interpret ambiguous information to fit our schemas. For example, when subjects were told that the guest lecturer was a determined person, they probably envisioned his determination as ruthlessness if they thought he was cold but as dedication when they thought he was warm. Also, we remember information that fits our schemas better than information that is unrelated to them. In short, we see things as fitting our schemas and we remember those things.

When do we use schemas? Do we always let our expectations exert such strong control over our impressions? Does the evidence always get pushed aside, as with former Chicago Cubs shortstop Ernie Banks? Research suggests that people can and do use the evidence in a variety of circumstances, such as when they will be held accountable for their judgments (Pendry and Macrae, 1996). One influential treatment of this issue concludes, "In short, people are

In 1959, Ernie Banks, as shortstop, begins a double play by forcing a runner at second base. Banks gained fame as a power hitter but was also an excellent fielder. What schemas attached to these two roles made fans remember him primarily as a slugger?

no fools" (Fiske and Taylor, 1991, p. 136). In accord with this view, a dual process of impression formation suggests that when another person is relevant and we are motivated to be thoughtful about that person, we pay attention to his or her individual characteristics (Brewer, 1988). A similar model of schema use suggests that people move along a continuum from using schemas to form impressions to ignoring schemas and using each individual piece of data (Fiske and Neuberg, 1990). People give up using their schemas when they are interested in a person and when the information they have just doesn't fit their schemas (Hilton and Fein, 1989). For example, a study of social class schemas showed that when people had no information about a girl's academic performance, they assumed she did poorly if she came from a lower social class and did well if she came from a higher social class. However, when subjects were given unequivocal information showing how well the little girl performed in an IQ test, they ignored their social class schemas and judged the girl on the basis of her performance (Baron, Albright, and Malloy, 1995).

Schemas and Memory

Schemas affect not only what we remember but how we remember. If we have some general knowledge of a person and form an impression as a result, we will often remember the person's behavior as fitting that impression more than it actually does. For example, if we watched John Kennedy debate Richard Nixon with the preconception that Kennedy was young and inexperienced, we might slightly misrecall what he said in the debate to fit that impression. We might forget his saying that he had fourteen years of experience in government, the same as Nixon. An interesting experiment on memory for conversations shows precisely this kind of error.

In the memory experiment subjects read or actually observed a conversation between two businessmen, Robert and Michael. Sometimes they were told that Robert was the boss of a company and that Michael was his employee and sometimes they were told that Robert and Michael were executives of equal status in the company. Two days after reading or listening to the conversation, subjects had to recall what Robert had said in the conversation. If they thought Robert was the boss, they remembered what he said as being considerably more assertive than they did if they thought Robert and Michael had equal status.

Subjects' memory of what Robert said fitted their impression of him as the boss or as just another executive (Holtgraves, Srull, and Socall, 1989).

While we often remember people as behaving in ways that fit our schemas, at times we also recall very clearly incongruent behaviors that don't fit our schemas (Belmore and Hubbard, 1987). For example, an old Cubs fan might remember vividly a few sparkling plays that Ernie Banks made at shortstop because good fielding doesn't fit her slugger schema. Our attention is drawn to novel and unexpected behaviors, and as a result they stick in our minds (Hastie, 1980).

One interesting study of memory for information that is inconsistent with a schema took advantage of gender schemas (Bardach and Park, 1996). Both men and women subjects read about a number of behaviors performed by a woman, Marcia, or by a man, Mark. The behaviors were stereotypically masculine or feminine, or they were neutral. For example, a masculine behavior was "went whitewater rafting on the Snake River," while a feminine behavior was "helped care for her ailing grandmother." Subjects read that either Mark or Marcia performed twelve masculine, twelve feminine, and twelve neutral behaviors and were asked to remember as many behaviors as they could. Subjects remembered schema-inconsistent behaviors more but only under some circumstances. Women recalled Mark performing feminine behaviors more than masculine behaviors, but they remembered Marcia's masculine and feminine behaviors equally. In contrast, men recalled Marcia's masculine behavior more than her feminine behavior, but they recalled both kinds of Mark's behavior equally. It seems that we have strong schemas about the behavior of those of the opposite sex, and we remember people of the other sex performing schema-inconsistent behavior.

Key factors in determining whether we have superior recall for incongruent information is what attributions we make about the causes of inconsistent behavior and whether we take the time and make the effort to understand it and build it into a coherent impression (Fiske and Taylor, 1991). One clear demonstration that attributions about incongruent information make a difference in what we remember and how we change our impressions comes from a study by Crocker, Hannah, and Weber (1983). Subjects were led to form a schema that someone named John was friendly. They were then given the incongruent information that John had cut in front of a line at the bank. The subjects were also given information indicating that John's unexpected behavior was attributable to something external (John was being paged for an emergency) or that it was attributable to John's personal characteristics (he didn't care what the other people in line thought about his behavior). When subjects attributed John's incongruous behavior to the emergency, they forgot about it and didn't change their opinion of John. However, if they attributed John's rude behavior to his personality, they remembered it well, and the better they remembered it the worse they thought of John.

In short, we typically interpret information as consistent with our schemas or expectations; we also recall information that is consistent with them. However, we sometimes recall highly incongruent information if we think about its meaning. When we do recall the new information, we change our schemas to accommodate it.

Priming: The Impact of What's on Your Mind

As people watch presidential debates, a variety of things can determine the dispositions they attribute to the candidates, the impressions they form of them, and what they recall about the candidates' performances. Attributions are important determinants, whether they are true to the logic of attribution principles or are undermined by attribution biases. Our schemas exert a significant role as well. Another, often more subtle, influence on the impressions we form and the memories we construct is what just happens to be on our minds as we turn on the television to watch a debate.

Suppose, for example, that before watching the debate between Michael Dukakis and George Bush, a college student was thinking about the importance of dealing with a romantic problem calmly, rationally, and maturely. When Dukakis responded unemotionally to the question about a mandatory death penalty for his wife's killer, the student might have perceived Dukakis's response as calm, thoughtful, and mature. Simply because those traits were on her mind and because Dukakis's behavior could potentially have been perceived in that way, she might have attributed these dispositions to Dukakis and recalled his behavior as reflecting them. She might also have inferred that he would be a very rational, deliberative, and perhaps effective president. A person who did not have those

traits in mind might have perceived Dukakis very differently, perhaps as cold, unemotional, and uncaring.

The person who has the attributes of calmness, thoughtfulness, and maturity in mind is said to be *primed* to perceive those traits in others. Ambiguous behavior that might be perceived as reflecting those traits is much more likely to be perceived as in fact indicating them if the observer has been primed for them. **Priming** is the process of somehow bringing certain attributes, typically behaviors or personal characteristics, to mind, that is, *activating* them. In some instances priming is done subconsciously so that the primed person is unaware that the ideas have been activated.

Psychologists have done a number of studies to demonstrate the impact of priming on perception, behavior, and memory. In one study subjects were primed by having to find four names embedded in a puzzle. For some subjects the four names were of figures thought of as moderately nonhostile (Daniel Boone, Robin Hood, tennis champion Billie Jean King, and former Secretary of State Henry Kissinger), while for others the names were of figures thought of as relatively hostile (Israeli Prime Minister Menachem Begin, acid rock singer Alice Cooper, heavyweight boxing champion Joe Frazier, and Indiana basketball coach Bobby Knight). Then subjects read an ambiguous description of Donald, a person whose behavior could be characterized as either hostile or nonhostile. When subjects indicated their impressions of Donald, those who had been primed with the list of nonhostile names perceived Donald as less hostile than those who had been primed with the hostile names. When subjects later played a bargaining game with a person they thought was Donald, they played more competitively if they had been primed with hostile names. Thus, both their impression of Donald and their behavior toward him were affected by priming (Herr, 1986). They assimilated their impressions to the "primes." A similar study showed that people primed to think of kidnapping by reading a real missing-child poster were more likely to think that an ambiguous videotaped interaction between an adult and a child, which could have been a kidnapping, was actually an emergency situation (James, 1986).

Priming can also affect memory. Primed traits act like a schema and influence the way we recall incoming information that is related to them. In one experiment, subjects read a list of dispositional labels and were urged to hold those labels in memory as part of a

If primed to view this episode of whitewater rafting as "adventurous," you would probably recall it in a more positive light than if you associated it with the word "reckless."

study on "information processing." Next, as part of what the subjects thought was a second study, they were asked to read descriptions of behavior that could be interpreted either positively or negatively. If subjects had been primed with a positive label—for example, "adventurous"—they recalled a related behavior, shooting rapids, more positively than they did if they had been primed with the negative label "reckless" (Higgins, Rholes, and Jones, 1977). In short, what we are thinking about when we receive information about people can have a dramatic effect on what we remember about them and how we evaluate them.

In the studies of priming we have mentioned thus far, subjects were primed with information that was brought into conscious awareness. It is probably the case that the subjects were not actually aware of the primed information when they judged Donald or the kidnapping videotape, though they had previously been made consciously aware of the priming information. Later studies have suggested that sometimes people can be primed without being consciously aware of the information at any time. This is done through the technique of subliminal perception, in which experimenters present trait or behavior words to subjects on a screen in very brief flashes. The subjects cannot read the words, cannot recall them, and cannot recognize whether they have seen them when the words are presented to them later. Yet those words clearly prime them for certain trait or behavior concepts and affect their impressions.

In one study words related to kindness (*considerate, caring, thoughtful*) were flashed subliminally on a television screen. Then subjects read a twelve-sentence description of a person (named Donald again!) whose behavior was ambiguous but could have been perceived as reflecting a kind disposition. Subjects who had been

BOX 2.1

Issues in Thought Suppression

Have you ever tried not to think of something—a former girlfriend or boyfriend, a large peanut butter and jelly sandwich, or an insulting remark that your roommate made? How successful were you? Do you think most people can successfully suppress thoughts? Some fascinating research on this question suggests that people are not very good at suppressing thoughts, and that trying to suppress them might not be healthy, psychologically or physically (Wegner and Pennebaker, 1993).

Daniel Wegner of the University of Virginia has done compelling research on this question (Wegner, 1992). In one study, subjects were asked to think out loud but not to think of a white bear. They were also told that if they did think of a white bear, they should ring a bell to report it. Two findings were very clear. First, subjects could not keep the thought of a white bear out of their minds. They did ring the bell, and they did report thoughts of a white bear. Second, later on, when subjects were told that they could and should think out loud about a white bear, those who had been suppressing generated more white bear thoughts than people who had not been suppressing. This "rebound" in white bear thoughts suggests that during the time those thoughts had been suppressed, they were gathering below the surface, ready to pour out when the constraint was lifted (Wegner, Schneider, Carter, and White, 1987).

How does the process of suppression produce rebounds? Wegner (1992) suggests that a dual-process suppression cycle is responsible. On the conscious level there is a *controlled distracter search* through which people try to think of something else, anything other than white bears. At the same time there is a largely unconscious, and effortless, *automatic target search* in which the person stays on the alert for any sign of the suppressed thought. The person trying to suppress the thought of a white bear might consciously think of shopping to get away from bears. But then the fun begins. Shopping brings to mind grocery stores, which brings to mind milk, which brings to mind white, and then the white bears are back. It is the job of the automatic target search to see this chain of associations coming and to signal to the controlled distracter search that something other than shopping is needed to keep white bears at bay. The irony is that the automatic target search's vigilance for thoughts related to white bears actually makes such thoughts highly accessible and likely to spring to mind. They can be avoided, but they will return.

Generally, people don't care if white bears come to mind, but there are other thoughts that they do want strongly to suppress. For example, people "coming off" painful romantic episodes might want to suppress thoughts of their old flames. Those thoughts simply stir up unpleasant emotions. Several studies looking at people's attempts to suppress thoughts of old flames that they still desired showed that these emotionally charged thoughts work differently from thoughts about white bears or the Statue of Liberty (Wegner and Gold, 1995). When people who had been suppressing thoughts of their hot old flames were told to go ahead and think of them, the usual rebound effect did not take place. Why? Probably because people are highly practiced at suppressing such unpleasant thoughts and don't experience a flood of them when they are unconstrained. However, physiological measures showed that being released to think about old flames caused emotional arousal. Unpleasant thoughts about old flames were suppressed enough so that they did not come to mind consciously, but they did cause strong emotional reactions.

Trying to suppress unwanted thoughts seems to create lots of mental and emotional turmoil. Suppression is necessary so that we can control our behavior, control what we say, and control our feelings. However, even if we are successful, the costs are high (Wegner and Pennebaker, 1993).

primed with the kindness words thought Donald was kinder than subjects who had been primed with neutral words. The same was true if words related to shyness (*timid, meek, bashful*) were presented before an ambiguously shy behavioral description (Bargh, Bond, Lombardi, and Tota, 1986). Another study showed similar results with subjects subliminally primed with words related to honesty and meanness (Erdley and D'Agostino, 1988). In short, studies of priming show that what is on our minds when we receive information about a person can have a dramatic impact on our impressions, our behavior, and our memory.

Recent studies have explored in more detail the effects of priming. When do subjects judging the ubiquitous Donald assimilate their impressions of him to primed concepts? In one study subjects were primed with the negative words *conceited, arrogant, stubborn,* and *bullheaded* or with the positive words *confident, self-assured, determined*, and *persistent*. Later they read that Donald "had already climbed Mt. McKinley, shot the Colorado in a kayak, driven in a demolition derby, and piloted a jet-powered boat—without knowing very much about boats. . . . Now he was in search of new excitement. . . . By the way he acted one could readily guess that Donald was well aware of his ability to do many things well. . . . Once Donald made up his mind to do something it was as good as done. . . . Only rarely did he change his mind even when it might have been better if he had (Thompson, Roman, Moskowitz, Chaiken, and Bargh, 1994, p. 489).

Whether subjects' impressions of Donald were affected by the primes depended first on whether they were given strong motivation to be accurate. Those who tried hard to be accurate did not assimilate their impression to the primes. Those who were not trying to be accurate did. Also, if subjects tried to be accurate only after forming an impression that was affected by the primes, they could shake the effects of the prime, but only if they could remember the information about Donald and were given the opportunity to think hard about him (Thompson et al., 1994).

A similar study also shows that when accuracy is stressed, the effect of priming is less, and it also shows that priming has greater effects if people are cognitively busy (Ford and Kruglanski, 1995). Together these two studies show that priming often affects impressions, but not always. When subjects have both the motivation to be accurate and the time to think carefully, they do not assimilate their impressions to primed concepts.

Social Inference: Making Judgments about People

Millions of people watch the nationally televised presidential debates every four years. For many, these debates are their major source of information about the candidates and the issues. On the basis of what they perceive and remember about the debates and any information they get from other sources, people must decide for whom to vote. How do they put together the various bits and pieces of information they have and arrive at a judgment about the two candidates? Social cognition research that focuses on inferences attempts to understand these judgment processes. What we have learned from this research is that human beings are not perfect in their judgments and inferences. Whether this imperfection means that people are basically irrational and thus make flawed judgments or that they are pretty sound in their thinking, given the difficulties of meeting perfect standards, has been a matter of considerable debate (Fiske and Taylor, 1991; Nisbett and Ross, 1980; Markus and Zajonc, 1985). Most of the research that we will describe illustrates people's mistakes and the shortcuts they take in making inferences. These mistakes result from following modes of thinking that work well in most instances; unfortunately, sometimes these modes are inappropriate, and then the results can be serious.

Underusing Base-Rate Information

Imagine an individual, Bob, deciding what kind of car to buy. Because reliability is important to him, Bob has carefully gone through all the data on frequency of repair in consumer magazines and decides that he will buy a Toyota; it has the best repair record. Shortly before Bob makes a final decision, a friend tells him about his neighbor's cousin who bought a 1980 four-door Toyota Tercel that was always in the shop. Bob is impressed by this story and decides he'd better not get tangled up with a Toyota. In this situation, a person ignores the available **base-rate information** on auto repairs and makes a judgment about the most reliable car on the basis of a single, albeit impressive, example.

Studies suggest that people make this error frequently. They ignore available general information and pay attention to concrete instances. In one study, for

BOX 2.2

What Might Have Been:
The Psychology of Counterfactual Thinking

Often people evaluate their experiences by thinking about how events might have turned out differently. Sometimes they think about how things might have been worse, and they feel good. At other times they think about how things might have been better, and they feel bad. Thinking about "what might have been" is called counterfactual thinking (Miller, Turnbull, and McFarland, 1990). In one early study of this phenomenon, subjects were asked to think of missing a scheduled airplane flight by five minutes or thirty minutes. Which situation would make you feel worse? The results show that missing a flight by five minutes creates more distress (Kahneman and Tversky, 1982). It is easier in this case to do counterfactual thinking about little things that might have been changed to arrive at the gate on time. When people think of how things could easily have been better, they feel distinctly worse.

An interesting field study of counterfactual thinking looked at silver and bronze medal winners at the Winter Olympics. The first part of the study analyzed videotapes of these athletes at two times: when the outcomes of their events were announced and when they received their medals on the reviewing stand. Subjects' ratings of an athlete's happiness were higher for bronze medal winners than silver medal winners. The second part of the study analyzed network interviews and found that silver medal winners had counterfactual thoughts about how they might have

won. They tended to think about almost finishing first and how they might have done things differently to win the gold medal. They felt bad about just missing. In contrast, bronze medal winners had counterfactual thoughts about how they almost missed winning a medal altogether. They were glad to walk away with something (Medvec, Madey, and Gilovich, 1995). Again, when people

During the 1998 Olympics award ceremony for women's figure skating in Nagano, Japan, gold and bronze medalists Tara Lipinsky (center) and Chen Lu (right) appear happier than silver medalist Michelle Kwan (left).

Continued

BOX 2.2

Continued

think about better alternatives to their experiences, they feel bad. When the alternatives they imagine are worse, they feel good (Markman, Gavanski, Sherman, and McMullen, 1995).

Recent laboratory studies suggest that people are likely to think of how things might have been better after failure and how they might have been worse after success (Olson and Roese, 1995). Thinking about how things might have been better after failure makes people feel bad, but it may well be functional. If people can be led to think about how they might handle future situations differently, they can plan behaviors that will increase the probability of success and will experience less negative affect (Boninger, Gleicher, and Strathman, 1994; Roese, 1994).

Counterfactual thinking has also been studied among people who have experienced wrenching real-life tragedies. For ex-

ample, when people who have accidents that lead to spinal cord injuries and paralysis, they often think about how the accident might have been avoided. The more they think about these positive counterfactuals, the more they blame themselves for the accident (Davis, Lehman, Silver, Wortman, and Ellard, 1996). Similarly, people who have lost a spouse or a child in an automobile accident, or a baby to sudden infant death syndrome, often think about ways that things might have turned out differently. Specifically, they engage in "undoing" thoughts, thoughts about how they might have changed the outcome. When people think of things that they *could* have done to "undo" the tragedy, they feel that they *should* have done them. Even though undoing thoughts cause great distress, they may give people some sense of control over life events (Davis et al., 1995).

example, subjects were told about a taxi that was involved in a nighttime accident. One of the eyewitnesses said the cab could have been blue. Subjects were also told that 85 percent of the cabs in the city were green and 15 percent were blue. Most subjects went with the eyewitness's testimony and guessed that the cab was blue, thereby ignoring the base-rate information, which indicated that the cab was probably green (Ginosar and Trope, 1980).

Although people often underweigh base-rate information, there are clearly times when they use it. For example, in the study reported above, when the subjects were told that 85 percent of the cars involved in the city's accidents were green, they did use that base-rate information (Ginosar and Trope, 1980). Another study shows that people use base-rate information if they are induced to think scientifically or if they realize the relevance of such information to their goals (Zukier and Pepitone, 1984). In addition, more recent research suggests that people will use base-rate information if it is made salient or if it is the only information available (Beckett and Park, 1995). Thus people

do use base-rate information. Very often, however, they make the mistake of ignoring its relevance.

The Dilution Effect

Imagine a voter in 1960 who missed the first debate between John Kennedy and Richard Nixon but heard from a friend that Kennedy looked surprisingly cool and competent. That voter might infer that Kennedy did have the experience and ability to be president. Now suppose the voter was told not only that Kennedy looked cool and competent but also that he arrived on time, that he had shrimp scampi for dinner, and that Jackie Kennedy was wearing a green dress. Would the voter's impression of John Kennedy be any different? Perhaps you think not, but several studies have shown that an impression can be softened if it is relevant or if *diagnostic information* (in this case about Kennedy's performance) is diluted with irrelevant, nondiagnostic information (such as what John Kennedy had for dinner or what Jackie Kennedy was wearing). You might actually have a less positive view of Kennedy's perfor-

TABLE 2.2   **COMPARISON OF STATEMENTS DESCRIBING AND LATER ATTRIBUTED TO GROUPS IN HAMILTON AND GIFFORD'S STUDY OF STEREOTYPING**

Groups and Types of Behaviors	Number of Statements Describing Each Type of Behavior	Number of Statements Attributed to Each Group
Variation I		
Group A		
Desirable behaviors	8	5.87
Undesirable behaviors	16	15.71
Group B (minority)		
Desirable behaviors	4	6.13
Undesirable behaviors	8	8.29
Variation II		
Group A		
Desirable behaviors	18	17.52
Undesirable behaviors	8	5.79
Group B (minority)		
Desirable behaviors	9	9.48
Undesirable behaviors	4	6.21

Source: After Hamilton and Gifford (1976)

mance in the second case (Nisbett, Zukier, and Lemley, 1981; Zukier, 1982). The tendency to be influenced or distracted by such irrelevant information is called the **dilution effect.** Politicians seem to understand it; they often give out cheerful but irrelevant information to soften the impact of bad news.

Illusory Correlation

Another of the errors that we make in perceiving the world around us is to conclude that a relationship exists between two things when that conclusion simply isn't supported by the available data. For example, a person may believe that "politicians are dishonest" when the available data actually show otherwise. To accurately conclude that there is a unique association between dishonesty and politicians, the person would have to list honest and dishonest politicians and honest and dishonest physicians, bankers, and college professors, and then show that dishonesty occurs more frequently among politicians than among members of other occupational groups. A belief that is held even when the data right in front of you don't support that belief is called **illusory correlation** (Chapman, 1967). People seem to make this error because confirming instances (in this case, examples of dishonest politicians)

can be highly salient and can obscure all the data that show numerous honest politicians and crooked bankers.

Some important research suggests that illusory correlations can have a strong impact on perceptions of groups and can ultimately contribute to stereotypes (Hamilton and Sherman, 1996). In one classic study of illusory correlations and perceptions of groups, subjects were told about positive and negative acts performed by members of Group A and Group B. For example, subjects heard that "John, a member of Group A, visited a sick friend in the hospital." While Group A always had more members than Group B, the proportion of positive and negative behaviors of the members of the two groups was constant. Sometimes both groups performed more desirable behaviors and sometimes they performed more undesirable behaviors. However, the results showed that Group B members, who were always in the minority, were recalled to have performed more desirable behaviors than they actually did when desirable behaviors were performed less often and more undesirable behaviors when undesirable behaviors were performed less often (Hamilton and Gifford, 1976). (See table 2.2.) It seems that a person from an underrepresented group performing an unusual behavior is especially salient and memorable—the combination of a rare person with a rare behavior is highly distinctive and highly accessible in memory (Johnson and Mullen, 1994).

Think of how illusory correlations could contribute to stereotypes. For a white person being raised in the suburbs and attending predominantly white schools, blacks may be uncommon. Further, displays of aggressive behavior in such an environment might be unusual. In these circumstances a black person behaving aggressively would be especially distinctive and salient and therefore overrecalled, leading to the illusory correlation that blacks are aggressive.

Several studies show that we are likely to form illusory correlations about the performances—both successes and failures—of salient individuals, including ourselves. In particular, we see the salient person as more closely associated with the predominant behavior, success or failure, than other people are even though that simply isn't true. As a result of this tendency, if several individuals, some salient and some nonsalient, are performing well in a particular situation, we will recall the salient person as performing better even if all are doing equally well. If the individuals are all doing poorly, we will recall the salient one as doing worse than the others. Again, we see the salient person as more closely associated with the predominant behavior than he or she actually is.

There is one exception to this pattern. If the salient person is you, and the predominant performance level is low, you won't see yourself as performing more poorly than others. In this case, a bias toward perceiving ourselves positively (see chapter 3) counteracts the typical illusory correlation (Sanbonmatsu, Shavitt, Sherman, and Roskos-Ewoldsen, 1987).

The Availability Bias

Suppose a voter who watched George Bush and Michael Dukakis debate in 1988 had been asked how

For this predominantly white audience, Rep. (D) Bennie Thompson, a black man, would be considered distinctive and salient.

Dukakis performed. What came to mind most readily was Dukakis' unemotional "iceman" response to the question about Kitty Dukakis's hypothetical rape and murder. Because the debate was so available or accessible in memory, the voter may have judged Dukakis's coldness as a frequent feature of the debate. Making judgments about the frequency or probability of events on the basis of the instances that come easily or quickly to mind is called the **availability bias** (Tversky and Kahneman, 1973). If you think back to illusory correlations, you can see that the availability bias is implicated there as well. Watergate and other instances of political corruption are so readily available to you that you overestimate the frequency of dishonest politicians, thereby inferring an illusory correlation.

The Representativeness Bias

A common rule of thumb used to judge whether a person belongs to a group is called the **representativeness bias.** We tend to leap to the conclusion that a person who shares some characteristics with typical members of a group probably belongs to that group. For example, people reading that Tom is intelligent but not creative, that he is orderly with a corny sense of humor, and that he has little interest in interacting with others are likely to see him as an engineer or computer scientist even if they know that engineers and computer scientists are relatively rare (Kahneman and Tversky, 1973); Tom seems representative of the category. To use the representativeness bias to make this judgment, when engineers and computer scientists are rare, is to make the error of underusing the base-rate information that we discussed earlier. Thus, as you can see from the last two examples, biases in inference often work together.

Some Consequences of Forming Impressions: The Self-Fulfilling Prophecy

When we form impressions of people, we tend to act in ways that perpetuate those impressions. In Kelley's (1950) study of warm and cold guest lecturers, students tended to act in a distant fashion to the instructor who they believed would be cold. Undoubtedly, in a situation in which the instructor was not a confederate, the distant manner of the student would have encouraged behavior in the teacher that would confirm the student's impression that the teacher was a cold person.

Some interesting research has been done on the consequences of believing information about others. In a famous study, Rosenthal and Jacobson (1968) told elementary school teachers that some of the children in their classrooms could be expected to show dramatic spurts in academic performance during the school year. It was alleged that such information was based on the reliable Harvard Test of Inflected Acquisition. In truth, there was no such test, and approximately one-third of the students were chosen at random to be designated as "spurters." At the end of the school year, the children's IQs were measured. Figure 2.2 depicts the results for the children in the first and second grades. Those students who had been designated as spurters actually showed a marked gain in their IQ scores over the year even though their designation as spurters bore no relation to any legitimate test.

Like Henry Higgins in George Bernard Shaw's play *Pygmalion*, the teachers apparently created the person they expected to find. The possible implications of this research were startling. Is long-term academic achievement largely a function of biased expectations? The Rosenthal and Jacobson study thus drew the attention of many social psychologists and policymakers.

Rosenthal and Jacobson's study drew considerable criticism because, as one might expect, there were deficiencies in this pioneering study. Nevertheless, Rosenthal and Jacobson's main finding has withstood the test of time. Within fifteen years, hundreds of studies had examined the effects of teacher expectations (Brophy, 1982; Rosenthal and Rubin, 1978). Among the early studies, systematic **expectancy effects,** or **self-fulfilling prophecies,** were found in middle-class schools in the East and West (Conn, Edwards, Rosenthal, and Crowne, 1968; Rosenthal and Evans, 1968). Also, Anderson and Rosenthal (1968) observed the expectancy effect in a class of mentally retarded boys, while Michenbaum, Bowers, and Ross (1969) reported it in a study that systematically varied behavioral and academic expectancies in an Ontario training school for female offenders. More recent research suggests that even though these effects are present, they are generally not very powerful. However, it appears that low-status and stigmatized groups do show powerful effects of negative expectations (Jussim, Eccles, and Madon, 1996). Specifically, expectancy effects are stronger for girls than they are for boys, for people who are poor, and

FIGURE 2.2   GAINS IN TOTAL IQ FOR CHILDREN IN FIRST AND SECOND GRADES

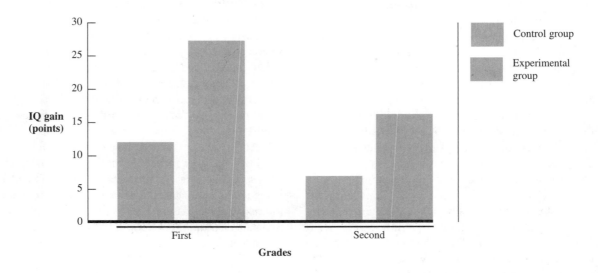

Source: Rosenthal and Jacobson (1968)

for African-Americans. It may be that individuals in these groups feel devalued in school and are therefore more likely to be affected by teachers' expectations.

What produces expectancy effects? It appears that four factors are important: *climate, feedback, input,* and *output* (Harris and Rosenthal, 1985; Rosenthal, 1973). According to the theory that explains research findings, teachers provide a warmer climate for students whom they expect to do well. The warmth is conveyed both verbally and nonverbally. Second, teachers give more careful, detailed feedback to students for whom they have high expectations. These students are given more guidance about what they should and should not do. Third, teachers give these students more input—more instruction and explanation about learning materials. Finally, high-expectancy students are given more opportunity for output. They have more time to ask and answer questions and more opportunities to learn how to produce.

The characteristics of people who hold either positive or negative expectations are critical in determining whether these expectations become self-fulfilling prophecies. Teachers who are biased against students because of negative expectations tend to "leak" nonverbal negative feelings about such children through face and body signals at the same time that they are communicating positive feelings verbally (Babad,

Bernieri, and Rosenthal, 1989). In general, people who create self-fulfilling prophecies are highly expressive nonverbally, and, not surprisingly, students who are most sensitive to nonverbal communications are the most affected by them (Cooper and Hazelrigg, 1988).

Other studies have shown that the impact of expectations is not felt only in the classroom. They also play an important role in everyday interpersonal relationships, and they affect not only the behavior of the people who hold the expectancies but also the behavior of the targets of the expectancies. For example, male and female college students who had been led to believe that another person liked them behaved in a way that led them to be liked. They expressed less dissimilarity, disagreed less, spoke in a more positive tone of voice, and expressed overall a more positive attitude than students who thought the other person disliked them. In short, people who thought that others had positive or negative impressions of them behaved in ways that confirmed those impressions (Curtis and Miller, 1986). Another study has shown that some people who initially believe they rank low in sociability improve their self-perception if they interact with someone who thinks they are high in sociability and acts accordingly. They respond to the other person's sociable behavior and behave sociably themselves, with the eventual result that their self-perception improves (Major, Cozzarelli, Test, and McFarlin, 1988).

What determines whether expectations become self-fulfilling prophecies? Both the goals of the perceiver and the goals of the target make a difference. If we are the perceivers with the goal of discovering whether the people we are interacting with actually have the characteristics we expect, we will often find that our expectations are incorrect and we change them (Darley, Fleming, Hilton, and Swann, 1988). We are thus less likely to make our expectations self-fulfilling. Also, if we simply interact with the goal of forming an accurate impression even if we have a negative expectation, we are less likely to behave in ways that elicit negative performances from the other person. When we are open-minded and objective ourselves, we are less likely to convey a negative bias and disrupt the other person's behavior (Neuberg, 1989).

The goals of the target make a difference as well. Targets who are trying to establish a smooth interaction with the perceiver are more likely to accede to and confirm the perceiver's expectations. On the other hand, targets who are trying to get the perceiver to form accurate impressions or who are concerned with finding out what the perceiver is really like are less likely to behave in ways that confirm the perceiver's expectancies (Neuberg, 1994; Snyder and Haugen, 1995).

As Darley and Fazio (1980) have noted, the self-fulfilling prophecy is just one of the possible outcomes of our day-to-day social interactions. It is a particularly intriguing phenomenon, however, because the individuals involved are seldom aware that the expectancy of one has substantially influenced the behavior of the other. As the research we have discussed indicates, the potential for misunderstanding and perpetuation of bias among social participants is great.

Summary

Attribution is the process of deciding whether behavior was caused by a personal disposition of the actor or external situational forces. One of the principles we follow in making attributions is the subtractive rule, which states that we should subtract the situational inducements from the personal disposition implied by the behavior. If the situational inducement may have contributed to the behavior, the role of disposition should be discounted. If the situational inducement actually inhibits the behavior, the role of disposition should be augmented. Other factors considered in making internal (person) or external (entity) attributions for behaviors include the distinctiveness, the consensus, and the consistency of that behavior. Low distinctiveness, low consensus, and high consistency lead to internal attributions.

Psychologists have stressed the importance of considering factors beyond internal or external causes. In judging success and failure, for example, we often judge whether a cause is stable, controllable, and global. When we consider whether success or failure is caused by internal or external factors, we attribute performance to ability, luck, effort, or the difficulty of the task.

Attribution researchers have discovered a number of biases in the way people make attributions. The correspondence bias, or fundamental attribution error, is the tendency to attribute behavior to corresponding internal dispositions rather than to external factors. Spontaneous trait inferences (STIs) are the automatic inferences made about the traits of a person on the basis of knowing his or her behavior. The saliency bias is the tendency to attribute behavior to salient or easily noticeable possible causes.

A schema is a general body of knowledge about a person, object, or event. A closely related concept is that of script, the sequence of events we have come to expect in a given situation. We tend to interpret information consistently with our schemas and scripts, and to recall information that is consistent with them. Incongruent information is also well recalled when people take the time to think about its meaning.

Priming occurs when specific ideas are activated through recent or frequent use. When we have been primed by information so that it is on our minds, it can affect our memory for people's behavior. In making inferences about other people, individuals make many errors. They underuse or ignore base-rate data, let irrelevant information affect an inference (dilution effect), and perceive illusory correlations. In addition, people are prey to the availability bias, judging the likelihood of events by the ease with which they come to mind; and the representativeness bias, assuming that people belong to a group if they have characteristics similar to those of typical members of the group.

The impressions that people form of others have implications for the way those others act. Rosenthal and Jacobson are among researchers who have demonstrated the effect of the expectancy effect, or the self-fulfilling prophecy. In their research, school children whose teachers expected them to perform well actually performed better than did students for whom teachers had no favorable expectation.

Key Terms

attributions	entity attribution	representativeness bias
augmentation principle	expectancy effects	saliency bias
availability bias	external attribution	schema
base-rate information	fundamental attribution error	script
correspondence bias	illusory correlation	self-fulfilling prophecies
dilution effect	internal attribution	social cognition
discounting principle	person attribution	spontaneous trait inferences (STIs)
dispositions	priming	subtractive rule

Suggested Readings

Fiske, S. T., and Taylor, S. E. (1991). *Social cognition*. New York: McGraw-Hill.

Gilbert, D. T. (1998). Ordinary personality. In P. T. Gilbert, S. T. Fiske, and G. Lindzey (Eds.), *The handbook of social psychology* (Vol. 2, pp. 89–150).

Heider, F. (1958). *The psychology of interpersonal relations*. New York: Wiley.

Jones, E. E., and David, K. E. (1965). From acts to dispositions: The attribution process in person perception. In L. Berkowitz (Ed.), *Advances in experimental social psychology* (Vol. 22, pp. 219–266). New York: Academic Press.

Kelley, H. H. (1972). Attribution in social interaction. In E. E. Jones, et al., *Attribution: Perceiving the causes of behavior*. Morristown, NJ: General Learning.

Smith, E. R. (1998). Mental representation and memory. In A. T. Gilbert, S. T. Fiske, and G. Lindzey (Eds.), *The handbook of social psychology* (Vol. 1, pp. 391–445). New York: McGraw-Hill.

Chapter 3

Knowing the Self

At age thirty-four, it just wasn't going to happen. In the 1996 Olympics in Atlanta, Jackie Joyner-Kersee's attempts to win the heptathlon and long jump fell short. Still, on an injured leg she won the bronze medal in the long jump, making 1996 the fourth Olympics in which she had won a medal. Jackie's career has been spectacular. She just missed a gold medal in 1984 but then won a total of three of them while setting world records in 1988 and 1992. Before the 1996 games began, she knew that even though she was still America's best female athlete, it was time to leave sports behind. But the Atlanta Olympiad was being held in her home country, and she had to be a part of it. Then she would retire and move on to the next phase of life—children, the community, and trying to give back.

Jackie's coach, Bob Kersee, is also her husband. Like Jackie, he wanted to proceed to a world beyond sports: "It's time for us to start a family" (Deford, 1996, p. 72). But he also knew it would be impossible not to participate in an American Olympics. Especially with her gritty winning of the bronze in 1996, Jackie's achievements won her an honored place in athletic history, not to mention endorsements from McDonald's, Honda, and Nike. Now with the Olympics and competition behind her, she will develop her plans to be a model for many others who began life as she did.

Jackie Joyner was born in 1962 in the ghetto of East St. Louis. She was named after the First Lady of the United States, Jacqueline Kennedy. Her parents were very young when they were married, her father only fourteen and her mother sixteen. They were barely able to provide for Jackie's older brother, Al, and then for her. Jackie's father worked for the railroad and traveled a great deal. When he was home he gave most of his attention to the athletic career of his son. Without involvement from her father, Jackie

looked to her mother for emotional support and to her brother for guidance in sports. Jackie knew she could run and jump with the very best. But she would have to succeed on her own with what help she could get from Al and her mother.

Succeed she did. Jackie was admitted to UCLA on a basketball scholarship. She was an instant star and became an All-American. However, early in her UCLA career she suffered a devastating setback. Her mother died suddenly at the age of thirty-eight, when Jackie was still eighteen. Pouring herself into her athletic career, she began to work out on the track. In a way, track had always been her first love in sports. Quickly she came to the attention of one of the UCLA coaches, Bob Kersee. He could see that her tremendous versatility made her a likely candidate to succeed in one of the most difficult and prestigious track and field competitions, the heptathlon.

The heptathlon is a variation on the better-known men's decathlon; both are referred to as "multi-events." The heptathlon consists of seven events in comparison with the ten of the decathlon. On the first day of heptathlon competition, women do the 100-meter hurdles, the high jump, the shot put, and the 200-meter dash. In essence, they run, they jump, and they throw. On the second day it's more of the same: the long jump, the javelin, and the 800-meter run. The final challenge, the 800-meter, is a middle-distance event that severely tests already exhausted athletes. As a whole, the heptathlon is a grueling, challenging multievent that only the best athletes can survive. Jackie did in fact succeed in the heptathlon. She was also a world champion in one of the events that comprise it, the long jump. At age twenty-two, Jackie came close to winning her first gold medal in the 1984 Olympics in Los Angeles but had to be satisfied with the silver medal, having been edged out by the slightest of margins for the gold. Still, she had something to celebrate. Her brother Al became the first member of the Joyner family to win an Olympic gold medal, in the triple jump. Jackie's narrow defeat gave her and her coach the strongest incentive to win in 1988. Along the way, Jackie's relationship with her coach got complicated: they fell in love.

While watching a baseball game together in Houston, Bob Kersee initiated the inevitable conversation, asking Jackie whether he might be a good marital prospect. It took a while before Jackie realized that this discussion was not just academic. He was, in a way, proposing. Bob says that after Jackie understood, they "stopped paying a lot of attention to the game" (Deford, 1996, p. 75). They were married in 1986 and

then started to get serious about the Olympics in Seoul two years later.

Their goals were two gold medals, in the heptathlon and the long jump, and two world records. They succeeded. In spite of these achievements, Jackie was actually overshadowed by another member of the family, Al's wife, sprinter Florence Griffith-Joyner, or Flo-Jo, who won several gold medals and set world records in 1988. But only Jackie managed to repeat as an Olympic champion in 1992 in Barcelona, again winning the heptathlon and long jump.

As Jackie and Bob worked together, there was a clearly defined partnership. Jackie was the stunningly talented athlete. Bob was the coach, serving both as

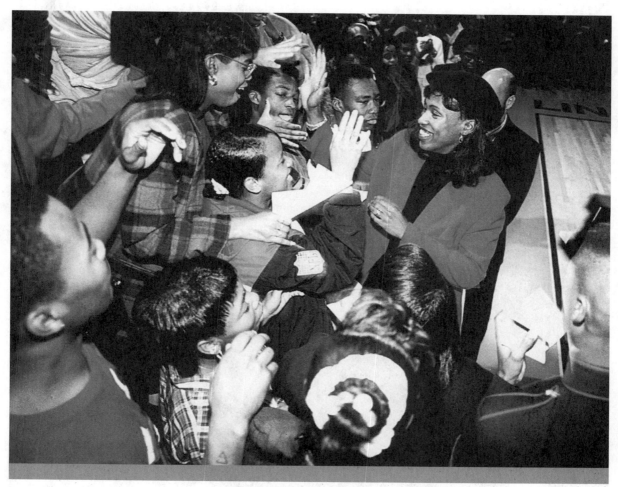

The founder of the Jackie Joyner-Kersee Youth Center mobbed by supporters. The 37–acre East St. Louis facility, which comprises basketball courts, ball fields, indoor and outdoor tracks, a library, computer lab, and other educational resources, revived the community center that nurtured Jackie when she was growing up. "I know how much it will mean to those kids," she said, "because I know what it meant to me."

Jackie's assistant and her guide. In her post-athletic phase of life, Jackie's talent, her winning personality, and her "megawatt smile" (*Newsweek,* 1996) will give her the opportunity to translate her athletic success into something positive for the dismal East St. Louis world where she grew up. She will begin by opening a community center and she will maintain a home and office in the area. She will work as hard to give back to those on the bottom as she worked to rise to the top. Jackie Joyner-Kersee will take her gold medals and think of the golden rule. She'll give to others as she wished others could have given to her. The world is richer for her presence.

Knowing the Self

In many respects, Jackie Joyner-Kersee has a clear idea of who she is. She is an athlete, a wife, an Olympian, a concerned citizen, and much more. Yet she is now on the verge of considering how she will cope with life after competitive athletics and how she will combine public demand with her desire to have a normal, private family life. She will make these decisions in terms of her own self-concept and how her personal goals relate to her aspirations for her family and community. Where does an individual acquire a sense of self; how do we know what we believe, how well we can perform, and, generally speaking, what

kind of person we are? In this chapter on knowing the self, we will start to answer these questions.

Social psychologists have discovered a great deal about both our self-concept, that is, the content of our knowledge and beliefs about our personal attributes, and our self-esteem, how we evaluate ourselves. We will begin by considering how our self-concept emerges from our interactions with other people. Then we will consider the way we make attributions about ourselves on the basis of our behavior. We will also consider important applications of research on self-perception and the ways in which self-perception can be biased.

Social Interaction and Self-Conception

We learn who we are through all our experiences in the world, especially our interactions with other people. One of the founders of psychology, William James (1890), wrote over a century ago that our sense of who we are, of "me," is derived from our experiences with others. For example, we learn that we are polite when an uncle or aunt compliments our behavior, or that we are a good speller by finding out that we got the highest score in the class. One way we learn about ourselves from social interaction is by finding out what other people think of us. Throughout our lives, we are influenced by other people's opinions about everything from how cold it is outside to whether our national government should allow prayer in the schools. Our self-concepts are no exception. We are impressed by what other people think of us. The process of perceiving what we are like

Pals who can share a good time and show appreciation for one another help build a positive sense of self through reflected appraisal.

and feeling that we are good or bad on the basis of what other people think of us has been called reflected appraisal (Gergen, 1971). It is one of the most important processes affecting our self-concept.

Reflected Appraisal

The term **reflected appraisal** refers to the idea that how we appraise ourselves reflects, or mirrors, how others appraise us. Charles Horton Cooley (1902) talked about this concept many years ago; he called it the "looking-glass self." Cooley said that we always imagine what others think of us, and what we think they think about us affects our own self-evaluation. A few years later, George Herbert Mead (1934) used the same idea. He said that we pay close attention to the opinion of us that is implied in the behavior of "significant others," that is, important other people such as parents and friends. Furthermore, we come to think of ourselves in terms of the opinion that the behavior of significant others implies. Again, our self-concept reflects what others seem to think of us.

Some important evidence exists that reflected appraisals have an influence on children. A study of fourth- through eighth-grade children shows that imagined appraisals of parents do affect self-appraisals even though these imagined or reflected appraisals are frequently inaccurate (Felson, 1989). In short, what we imagine our parents or other significant people in our lives think of us may not be what they actually think. But that reflected appraisal has an impact nevertheless. What about adults? Are they affected by reflected appraisals? Several recent studies show that they are. College students studied over a semester changed their self-views in line with their roommates' initial impressions of them (McNulty and Swann, 1994). Also, a study of students falling in love shows that their self-esteem and their assessment of their personal effectiveness improves when they fall in love. A key part of their self-concept change seems to be the positive appraisals they receive from the person who loves them (Aron, Paris, and Aron, 1995).

Although among adults the process of reflected appraisal is real, the relation between what other people think of us and what we think of ourselves is complex. First, this relation is a two-way street. In the study of students and their roommates mentioned above, the roommates' opinions affected the students' self-concepts, but the students' self-concepts also affected the roommate's opinions (McNulty and Swann,

1994). In general, other people's views of us affect our self-concepts, but out self-concepts also affect what others think of us. As a result of this mutual influence, the views that people have of themselves and the views that others have of them are often very similar (Fuhrman and Funder, 1995). Second, we carefully appraise what other people think of us. Our reaction to their appraisal of us depends on their credibility (Eisenstadt and Lieppe, 1994).

Finally, another person's appraisal, or the way we imagine it to be, can affect our feelings as well as our self-concept. This is shown in a study in which college women were asked to visualize the faces of either two fellow students or two older members of their families. Then they read a sexually explicit piece of fiction and indicated how much they enjoyed it. The students who had been asked to visualize older members of their families, and presumably imagining how those family members would react to their enjoyment of pornographic material, rated the fiction as much less enjoyable than those who were imagining their peers (Baldwin and Holmes, 1987).

The research on reflected appraisal shows how much we can be affected by our social interactions with others. Perhaps, though, we would do well to remember that we know a great deal about ourselves that others do not know, and that we shouldn't let ourselves be too greatly affected by what others think. Reflected appraisal is powerful, but it should not be all-powerful.

Social Comparison

Another way we learn about ourselves during social interaction is through a process called **social comparison.** We can evaluate our ability in math or tennis, for example, by comparing our performances with those of other people, and we can evaluate our opinion of a movie or a presidential candidate by comparing our opinions with those of other people. Jackie Joyner-Kersee uses social comparison in assessing some aspects of her track and field ability. On the one hand, she evaluates her ability in the long jump by comparing it with others. She feels the event is a competition with other jumpers. On the other hand, she feels that her performance in the heptathlon, scored using an abstract and complex scoring system, is more about competing with herself.

Leon Festinger, one of our most distinguished social psychologists, developed a theory of social comparison processes that outlines how and when comparison with other people affects our self-evaluations (Festinger, 1954). Inspired by Festinger's original theory, other researchers have explored social comparison in detail (Goethals and Darley, 1987; Suls and Wills, 1990).

When and Why People Compare

The original idea behind Festinger's social comparison theory was that people engage in social comparison because they have a strong need to evaluate themselves and sometimes they must compare themselves with other people in order to do it (Festinger, 1954). Social comparison was something people decided to do or decided not to do in a controlled and rational way in order to arrive at objective assessments of their personal qualities. Now we realize that the situation is more complicated, and that people are less objective about social comparison. People compare themselves with each other for a variety of reasons and very often interpret information about others in a biased way so that they can feel good about themselves. On the other hand, they sometimes try to avoid social comparison and self-assessment. In a word, social comparison is complicated, and we will try to give you a sense of its intricacies.

What are the motives for social comparison? Why do we compare our opinions, our abilities, our behaviors, our performances, our looks, and our health with other people's? Recent studies of social comparison suggest many motives (Helgeson and Mickelson, 1995). First, as originally proposed, we compare ourselves with other people to *evaluate* ourselves. Jackie Joyner-Kersee compares her long jumping with other women's to find out—to evaluate—how good she is. We also make comparisons so that we can *improve*. By learning how others perform well or cope with difficult circumstances, we stand a better chance of doing better ourselves. Third, we compare ourselves with others so we can *enhance* ourselves. In other words, by comparing ourselves with people who have performed poorly, we can sometimes make ourselves seem better by comparison. There are several other motives that can lead to comparison, such as sharing a common bond with others, but evaluating, improving, and enhancing ourselves are the most important.

Because there are so many motives for comparison, we might think that people compare all the time. Actually, many times people have no interest in com-

parison—maybe they're busy doing something more important—and other times they try hard to avoid comparison because they anticipate they won't "score" well (Brickman and Bulman, 1977; Gibbons, Benbow, and Gerrard, 1994). But people often make comparisons much more than they want to because comparison can be an automatic or spontaneous process that happens whether we want it to or not.

"Why am I always the bad guy?"

A recent study on automatic comparison looked at how people were affected by their knowledge of another person's performance even when they knew that the other person's performance was not comparable to their own (Gilbert, Giesler, and Morris, 1995). Subjects took a test of their ability to pick out which of two photographs showed someone who was schizophrenic. They also watched a videotape of another person performing the same task. Sometimes the other person did better than the subject, and sometimes she did worse. Furthermore, the subjects knew that the performance of the other person had been made easier or made harder so that her relative performance didn't mean very much—it wasn't comparable. When the subjects had time to think about the meaning of the confederate's performance, their evaluation of their own ability was not much influenced by it. But if the subjects were kept cognitively busy with a digit-rehearsal task, the comparison did affect them. They downgraded their ability when the confederate performed better than themselves and upgraded it when the confederate did worse.

These results suggest that we make comparisons spontaneously and effortlessly when we see how someone else performs. Then, if we have the time and inclination, we can think more carefully about the other's performance and decide what it means and whether it provides useful information for self-evaluation. But the key point is that comparison sometimes takes place automatically even if it doesn't always serve our motives. We compare first and ask questions later.

Although comparisons can happen spontaneously, we also have some control over how much we compare. While it's hard to ignore the implications of comparison, we can choose to avoid people and duck the comparison process altogether. Recent research has shown that people either seek out or avoid comparisons depending on how they think it's going to make them feel. For example, people with low self-esteem are more likely to seek out comparisons after they have succeeded, when they feel it's safe. When they fail they avoid comparisons because they feel it will reflect poorly on them. In contrast, people with high self-esteem are more likely to compare after they have failed to compensate for that failure by finding that they actually compare well with others (Wood, Giordano-Beach, Taylor, Michela, and Gaus, 1994).

Social Comparison, Self-Definition, and Self-Esteem

Social comparison can provide information that affects both how we define ourselves and how we evaluate ourselves. Research on the way people describe themselves illustrates the importance of societal comparison in self-definition. When they are asked to respond to the question, Who am I? people answer by mentioning ways in which they differ from others, ways in which they are unique. For example, fourth-grade children who were asked to describe themselves mentioned whether they were male or female more often if they came from homes where their gender was in the minority (McGuire and McGuire, 1981). So if you are the only boy in your family, being male makes you distinctive and becomes part of your self-concept. Similarly, people are likely to mention their race or ethnicity if that characteristic makes them distinctive; or they are apt to mention being tall or heavy if those qualities are distinctive (McGuire, McGuire, Child, and Fujioka, 1978; McGuire and Padawer-

Singer, 1976). In short, people's sense of who they are depends on the ways they are distinctive in comparison with others.

Social comparison also affects our overall self-evaluation and sense of worth. This was shown in a study in which students who came to apply for a job as a research assistant in a college research center encountered someone, actually a confederate of the researchers, who posed as another job applicant: the confederate presented himself as either Mr. Clean or Mr. Dirty. Mr. Clean was immaculately dressed, seemed serious and well prepared, and acted sophisticated and well read. Mr. Dirty seemed sloppy, confused, and uninterested. Subjects filled out questionnaires that measured their self-esteem both before and after meeting Mr. Clean or Mr. Dirty. The results showed that people evaluated themselves in comparison with the other applicant. Their self-esteem rose when the other was Mr. Dirty, who seemed less well qualified, and it fell if the other was Mr. Clean, who seemed better qualified (Morse and Gergen, 1970). Both the traits or characteristics that we feel define us and how favorably we evaluate ourselves are affected by comparison with other people.

The Similarity and Related Attributes Hypotheses

One of the central hypotheses of social comparison theory is the **similarity hypothesis,** which suggests that we choose to compare ourselves with people who are similar to us. For example, if we want to evaluate our tennis-playing ability, we need to compete against people whose performance level is about the same as our own to find out just how good we are. Research shows that we usually compare ourselves either with similar others or with people who are slightly better than we are. We strive to become better and better (Festinger, 1954, called this the *unidirectional drive upward*), so we want to see how well we compare with those whose performance level is slightly above ours (Wheeler, 1966; Wheeler, Koestner, and Driver, 1982). In her early days as an athlete before she became the best herself, Jackie Joyner-Kersee compared herself with champions and worked as hard as she could to improve herself to their level.

There is an important exception to the tendency to compare ourselves with similar people. When we evaluate *opinions* we sometimes compare our opinions with those of people who are very different from us (Gorenflo and Crano, 1989). We sometimes feel that if people who do not share our biases agree with us, we must be correct, and we find their agreement extremely gratifying (Goethals, 1972; Orive, 1988).

The **related attributes hypothesis** holds that we compare ourselves not only with those whose performance is similar to ours but also with those whose performance level *should* be similar to ours, given their standing on performance-related attributes (Goethals and Darley, 1977). By comparing ourselves with people who are similar in respect to related attributes, we can most accurately assess our own ability. For example, if you wanted to compare your basketball-playing ability, you would learn the most by comparing your playing with that of others of the same sex, of roughly the same age, and with about the same amount of recent practice. In that way if your performance is better, you know that the reason is your greater ability rather than the fact that you are in better shape or have been working like mad to improve your game.

The related attributes hypothesis also applies to opinion evaluation. Americans should compare their opinions about President Clinton's performance in office with the opinions of other Americans, and especially with Americans who share our political philosophy, rather than with those of Europeans. Knowing that you disagree with a European only tells you that the two of you have dissimilar points of view. You need to know how your opinion compares with that of someone whose opinion should be similar to yours.

A great deal of research supports the related attributes hypothesis (Suls, Gaes, and Gastorf, 1979; Wheeler and Koestner, 1984). One study showed that when people felt that sex was related to performance on a test, they wanted to compare their performance with that of other people of the same sex (Zanna, Goethals, and Hill, 1975). Men sought to learn the scores of men to assess the adequacy of their performance whereas women wanted to compare themselves with women.

Although the related attributes hypothesis has strong support, research also shows that we want to compare ourselves with people who are similar to us on such salient characteristics as physical attractiveness and sex even when those characteristics are not specifically related to the ability or opinion being evaluated (Miller, 1982, 1984). Furthermore, we like to compare ourselves with those with whom we share an identity or bond, or those who are similar to us in ways that nonetheless make us distinctive (Miller, Turnbull, and McFarland, 1988). For example, in the 1980s Jackie Joyner-Kersee often compared herself to sprinter Florence Griffith-Joyner. They were both gold medalists, and they were sisters-in-law. Their bond was strong even though they did not always put the same priority on athletics.

One consequence of the importance of similarity is that people do not always judge it objectively or accurately. For example, as a consequence of the unidirectional drive upward, people want to see themselves as similar to people who perform a little better than they do and as very different from people who perform just a little worse. Or people will want to distance themselves from people who seem threatening to them. For example, people perceive themselves as highly dissimilar to people who are HIV-positive and might have AIDS. They then can perceive these people as noncomparable and believe that the fate of these people has no implications for their own (Gump and Kulik, 1995).

Similar related attributes of gender, age, and practice help these two karate black belts to accurately assess their ability levels.

Downward Comparison and Self-Evaluation Maintenance

Although we generally compare ourselves with people who are similar or slightly superior to us, at times we engage in downward comparison: we compare ourselves with people who are inferior to us or worse off than we are. Downward comparison makes us feel better about ourselves because it allows us to feel that even if we have negative traits, others have them to a far greater degree (Wills, 1981). Research shows that when depressed people are feeling especially blue, they compare themselves with people who are suffering and feel better after they have done so (Gibbons, 1986). Downward comparison is most likely to occur after we have failed or if we have low self-esteem (Smith and Insko, 1987). But we don't always compare ourselves with people whose fate is worse than our own when we want to feel better. One study showed that people facing coronary bypass surgery preferred to have a hospital roommate who had been through the operation rather than one who was waiting for it (Kulik and Mahler, 1989). In a case like this, our desire to believe that we will survive the trauma leads us to compare ourselves with people who have already survived it.

The principle of downward comparison reminds us that the desire for accurate self-knowledge is not always paramount in the way we think about ourselves (Brown and Dutton, 1995a). Thus, not all of our social comparison choices are designed for objective self-evaluation; often we make comparisons to validate ourselves as well (Gruder, 1977). Efforts to show that we are as good as people who are superior and very different from people who are inferior demonstrate a self-validating or self-serving bias. They reflect our desire to evaluate ourselves positively. Sometimes that desire leads us to engage in "active" downward comparison, actually denigrating or harming others so that we can feel good in comparison with them (Wills, 1981).

Our desire to evaluate ourselves positively sometimes leads to more constructive behavior than does a downward comparison. The theory of self-evaluation maintenance suggests that people are upset when close friends outperform them on tasks that are important for their self-definitions (Tesser, 1988; Tesser, Millar, and Moore, 1988). If your piano-playing ability is less than that of a friend and you pride yourself on that ability, you may try to improve your performance level to maintain your self-evaluation. You want to compare favorably on characteristics that are important to your self-definition. On the other hand, if piano playing isn't important to your self-definition, you won't care about comparing favorably. Instead, you will maintain your self-evaluation by closely associating with your talented friend and basking in his or her reflected glory. Consistent with the principles of downward comparison, studies on self-evaluation maintenance also show that people don't always try to improve their performance level to maintain their self-evaluation. Sometimes they denigrate the other person's performance or actually try to interfere with it. Thus the desire to compare favorably can lead to both constructive efforts at self-improvement and destructive efforts to undermine others.

False Consensus Estimates

We sometimes make estimates about how other people's opinions or behaviors compare with our own in ways that make us feel good about ourselves, and we then ignore social comparison information that shows perhaps we are wrong. For example, several studies demonstrate what is known as the false consensus effect. **False consensus** refers to a tendency to overestimate the number of people who agree with our opinions or behave as we do (Ross, 1977; Mullen, Atkins, Champion, Edwards, Hardy, Story, and Vanderklok, 1985). If we overestimate the number of people who agree with us, we can evaluate our opinion as correct. And if we overestimate the number of people who do what we do, we can feel that our actions are appropriate. One study of false consensus judgments asked college students whether they would be willing to walk around campus wearing a sign that said "Eat at Joe's." Those who agreed to wear the sign thought that most other people would wear it, specifically 67 percent of the others. Those who said they wouldn't wear it thought that only 33 percent would wear the sign and that 67 percent would say no (Ross, Greene, and House, 1977). Each group felt that it had made the appropriate choice and assumed that others had done the same.

Other research shows that the false consensus bias is truly strong, perhaps even "ineradicable," and that it is equally strong for important and unimportant attitudes (Fabrigar and Krosnick, 1995; Krueger and Clement, 1994). For example, when people are given comparison information showing that their consensus estimates are wrong and that other people don't agree as much as they thought, they ignore this information unless it is very clear and simple (Goethals, 1986). Furthermore, when people are instructed in ways that they might consider information other than their own ideas and actions in judging others, they still show strong false consensus effects (Krueger and Clement, 1994). These and other studies suggest that nonmotivational factors, such as our tendency to interact with other people who think and act like we do and our tendency to simply anchor our judgments about others in our knowledge of others, also contribute to the false consensus effect (Fiske and Taylor, 1991; Marks and Miller, 1987).

While nonmotivational factors surely play a role, the force of motivational concerns is shown in the fact that not all self-serving consensus estimates inflate the number of people who act as we do. If we do something that isn't clearly good or bad, such as wearing a sign saying "Eat at Joe's," we may be prompted to believe that most other people will do the same. Further, if we do something negative, we may want to think that most others will do the same so that we can feel we aren't so bad. On the other hand, if we do something positive, we may want to think that our behavior is distinctive (Mullen and Goethals, 1990). Hence we may underestimate the number of people who would do the same thing.

Several studies show that if people make a desirable choice, such as helping someone in trouble, giving blood, or leaving the larger piece of pizza for a friend, they underestimate the number of others who would do the same (Goethals, 1986). In general, when it comes to positive traits, people show a uniqueness bias, seeing their own strengths and abilities as being unusual (Campbell, 1986; Goethals, Messick, and Allison, 1990). This tendency to see ourselves as better than average is stronger when we compare ourselves with other people in general rather than with specific people (Alicke, Klotz, Breitenbecher, Yurak, and Vredenburg, 1995). When we think of another flesh and blood individual rather than people in the abstract, we are a little more realistic. It turns out that we have a general tendency to see ourselves as better than average, and we therefore are often unrealistically optimistic about future events (Weinstein, 1980). For example, sexually active college women see themselves as less likely than similar women to have an unwanted pregnancy. Consequently, they tend not to use effective methods of birth control (Burger and Burns, 1988).

Self-Attribution

Having considered how the processes of reflected appraisal and social comparison affect our self-concept, we now explore the important role that attribution processes play in self-knowledge and self-perception. The basic notion behind theories of self-attribution is that we can and often do make attributions about our own behavior in the same ways we make them about other people's behavior. For example, a person might use the criteria of distinctiveness, consistency, and consensus (see chapter 2) to decide whether a roommate's interest in chemistry is attributable to the roommate's personality or to chemistry itself. You could use the same principle to decide whether your admiration for the movie *Air Force One* is attributable to your own unique taste and interests (you like tense, exciting movies) or to the fact that the movie really is good. You would use the same criteria of distinctiveness (Do you like other movies?), consistency (Did you like the movie as much the second time?), and consensus (Did other people enjoy the movie?).

Another attribution theory that can be applied to your own behavior as well as that of other people is Weiner's theory of attributions of success and failure. People make attributions about their own successes and failures just as they do in regard to others'. They decide that their own success is due to great ability, extra effort, or good luck. Jackie Joyner-Kersee attributed her gold medals in the Olympics in 1988 and 1992 to her own hard work but also to the support of her coach and husband, Bob Kersee. As we shall see, a range of attribution theories have been applied to the self.

Self-Perception Theory

One of the most provocative theories of self-attribution is known as **self-perception theory** (Bem, 1972), which considers the way we perceive our own attitudes and preferences. It argues that just as we would infer that our friend likes rock music because he listens to it whenever he has a chance, so we infer that we like country music from our own behavior. We notice that when we are in the car we are most likely to push the button that brings in the local country station. All this sounds reasonable enough—but isn't something missing? Don't we just *know* whether we like country music? Must we infer that we do? Self-perception theory says we don't "just know," that we don't have a very good idea of how we feel about things on the basis of our feelings alone. We *really* learn what we like or dislike from our behavior.

The basic principles of self-perception theory follow. First, self-perception is simply a special case of social cognition in which we, rather than others, are the objects of perception. That is, we perceive ourselves in exactly the same way we perceive others. Second, we learn about our attitudes, preferences, and feelings by considering two things: our behavior and the situation in which it took place. The most important aspect of the situation that must be taken into account is whether there are situational constraints that explain the behavior. For example, if you listen to the country station because your sister begs you to turn it on, you wouldn't infer that you like country music; your sister's pressure explains your behavior. The discounting principle, discussed in chapter 2, leads you to discount your own attitude as a cause of your behavior because your sister's begging explains why you listened. Only when our behavior is freely chosen do we infer that it reflects our attitudes or feelings. But the basic idea is the most important one. We infer our attitudes and feelings, internal characteristics, from external information, our behavior, which we consider along with the forces in the situation. As the British novelist E. M. Forster said many years ago, "How can I tell what I think 'til I see what I say?"

Considerable evidence supports self-perception theory. First, we know that people internalize roles. The fact that people actually do define themselves in accordance with the behavior specified by their roles supports self-perception theory. One interesting and subtle example of role internalization is the finding that members of professional football and ice hockey teams who wear black uniforms actually play more aggressively as measured by numbers of penalties (Frank and Gilovich, 1988). Black is associated with evil and death in many cultures, and black uniforms become a cue for athletes to adopt an aggressive role and thereby see themselves as aggressive persons.

Second, several experiments illustrate important aspects of inferring feelings and attitudes from behavior. For example, in one study subjects listening to a tape recording were distracted by noises that were too low to notice. They observed that they were not paying attention to the recording and actually experienced boredom (Damrad-Frye and Laird, 1989). Because they didn't realize that their inattention was due to an external distraction, they inferred that it must be due to bore-

dom. In another study subjects had to summarize a description of one individual's personality for a second person who either liked or disliked that individual. Not surprisingly, subjects responded to the second person's expectations and made their summary more positive or more negative depending on that person's feelings about the first individual. What is surprising is that subjects reported liking the person more if they had described him positively than if they had described him negatively (Higgins and Rholes, 1978). Further, they felt that they had freely chosen to describe the person somewhat positively or negatively and they perceived their attitudes by inferring them from their behavior.

There is also evidence that our descriptions of ourselves can be a basis for inferring what we actually think of ourselves. In one study subjects were induced to describe themselves to an interviewer in either very modest or very flattering terms. On a later test of self-esteem, subjects who had described themselves positively actually felt more positive about themselves while those who had been modest felt more negative. Consistent with self-perception theory, these effects on self-esteem were stronger when subjects felt they had freely chosen the way they described themselves (Jones, Rhodewalt, Berglas, and Skelton, 1981). Similar research shows that people who present themselves as sociable in one situation actually come to see themselves as more sociable and subsequently behave more sociably in later situations. For example, they begin to speak sooner and talk longer than they did before (Schlenker, Dlugolecki, and Doherty, 1994). The change in self-concept induced by the way we present ourselves can affect both how we see ourselves and how we behave.

Other studies showed fascinating self-perception effects. If subjects were asked to hold the end of a pencil in their teeth, they configured their faces in a manner that resembled a smile. If they held the end of the pencil in their lips, they configured their faces in a manner that resembled a frown. If they were then told to rate the humorousness of cartoons, people with the forced smiles rated the cartoons as funnier than did people with the forced frowns. It may be that subjects actually inferred their enjoyment of the cartoon from the expressions on their faces (Strack, Martin, and Stepper, 1988). Similarly, if subjects were induced to adopt facial expressions of fear, anger, disgust, or sadness, or postures typical of feelings of fear, anger, or sadness, they actually felt these emotions (Duclos, Laird, Schneider, Sexter, Stern, and Van Lighten, 1989). In another study, subjects were asked to nod their heads up and down or from side to side to test their headphones while they listened to a speech. Those who nodded up and down (the usual yes gesture), agreed with the speech they had heard more often than those who shook their heads in the usual negative fashion. This was true even though subjects were not consciously aware of their head movements (Wells and Petty, 1980).

Even though self-perception effects are remarkably strong and remarkably pervasive, they are not without limits. For example, when people have clearly defined internal attitudes about an issue, they are less likely to infer how they feel about the issue from a single instance of a particular behavior (Chaiken and Baldwin, 1981). Still, self-perception theory has shown interesting and impressive effects. In the remainder of the book, we will see that it has wide applicability. One particularly important application is in the area of what are called **overjustification effects** (see Box 3.1).

The Attribution of Emotions

The research on self-perception and overjustification suggests that people often infer their attitudes, their feelings, and even why they didn't cheat from their behavior and the situation in which it took place. Research also suggests that we infer our emotions from external information: we are often unsure about how we feel, and when this is the case, we make attributions about our emotions rather than just experiencing them directly.

Considerable thought about the attribution of emotions has grown out of the work of Stanley Schachter. His classic studies of anxiety and affiliation (discussed in chapter 1) demonstrated that anxious subjects who had been threatened with electric shock wanted to wait with other people (Schachter, 1959). Follow-up research has shown that they wanted to wait with other people only when those people were also waiting to be shocked. The threatened subjects were somewhat unsure about their own reactions and wanted help from others in understanding and interpreting what they were feeling. They needed to compare their emotions with those of people who were in the same threatening situation as they were.

Schachter (1964) took this insight and ran with it. He proposed that if people are emotionally aroused but aren't sure what they are feeling, they will look for cues in the environment, including the behavior of other peo-

ple, in an effort to find the correct interpretation for their ambiguous feelings. Schachter's theory emphasizes not only self-attribution but also social comparison. We clarify our emotions by comparing our reactions with those of others, especially with reactions of those people who are similar on related attributes in that they face the same situations we face. We then attribute to ourselves the same emotions that the others are feeling.

What evidence is there that people experience emotions on the basis of the reactions of other people? In a classic experiment, Schachter and Singer (1962) were the first to demonstrate this phenomenon. Subjects were given injections of epinephrine, or adrenaline, which makes people feel highly physiologically aroused. Some subjects were informed of the drug's effects; they were told that they would experience an increase in heart rate, a flushed face, and occasional trembling. Because they had an explanation, or attribution, for the arousal they would experience later, they should not have had to compare their reactions with those of others to figure out what they were feeling. Other subjects were misinformed; they were told that they would experience headaches or numb feet. These subjects would need an explanation for the unexpected effects of the epinephrine. And still other subjects were uninformed; they too would need an explanation for their arousal. Finally, for control purposes some subjects were given a placebo, which does not cause arousal. None of the subjects who received the placebo should have had to compare themselves with others because they would not have had any arousal to explain.

After the subjects were given the injections and were informed, misinformed, or given no information, they were asked to wait with another person who presumably had had the same injection. The other person was a confederate of the experimenters who acted in one of two ways during the waiting period. In some cases, he acted euphoric, throwing paper airplanes, shooting crumpled balls of paper into the wastebasket, and twirling a hula hoop. In other cases, the confederate became angry. He and the subject had to complete a questionnaire that asked extremely intimate and inappropriate questions (With how many men has your mother had extramarital affairs: four and under, five to nine, or ten and over?); the confederate became angrier and angrier and finally ripped up his questionnaire in a fit of rage. After a few moments, the experimenter returned and asked the subjects to complete a questionnaire about their feelings.

BOX 3.1

Overjustification: Killing a Good Thing

We are often deluged by offers of bonuses for buying a brand of popcorn, double coupons at a particular supermarket, and special cups and glasses for eating at a fast-food store. In the advertising trade these are known as "come-ons"; their purpose is to get you to come into the store or to try a product. But if you already like the product and do not need a come-on to enter the store, what effect will the added inducement have on your attitude toward the store or the product? An attributional analysis suggests that the come-ons, or the "overjustification," may have the reverse effect of the one intended.

After behavior is committed, the actor asks himself why he acted that way. A review of the context surrounding the behavior suggests an answer: "I bought Poppy brand popcorn because they offered me a Mickey Mouse ring inside the package." In other words, the behavior is attributed *not* to the actor's preference for that kind of popcorn but rather to the bonus—or to the overjustification. However, popcorn brands outlive the bonus come-ons they offer. When the person who has already bought Poppy popcorn returns to the supermarket to restock his popcorn supply, he recalls that he purchased that particular brand before because of the extra bonus. With the bonus removed, there is no reason to purchase the brand anymore. Indeed, after examining consumer behavior in Chicago, Dodson, Tybout, and Sternthal (1978) found an **overjustification effect:** advertisements featuring come-ons actually resulted in reduced loyalty to the brand offering the come-on.

Because of overjustification, the last laugh may be on Madison Avenue's advertising and gimmick people. But a moment's reflection will conjure up less laughable situations in which needless overjustifications can ruin the intrinsic value that an important behavior might hold. In a first-grade classroom, children know that they will receive one gold star for picking up a book and two gold stars for reading it. In a mental hospital, patients know that they will receive better food if they successfully make their beds and put on their clothing (see Ayllon and Azrin, 1968). But adding an attractive inducement may cause the behavior to be attributed not to an interest in reading or in taking care of oneself but rather to the gold stars and other external rewards. When the rewards are no longer available, when the children are no longer being awarded stars, when the mental patients leave the hospital and try to return to their natural environment, the overjustifications for their original behaviors may result in a lack of interest in continuing those behaviors.

A fascinating study was conducted at Horizon House, a psychiatric rehabilitation center in Philadelphia (Bogart, Loeb, and Rittman, 1969). To achieve better attendance at group therapy sessions, the institution offered prizes for good monthly attendance. In one condition, the value of the prizes could reach approximately $8. In a second condition, patients were offered prizes that could reach only $2 in value. During the month in which prizes were offered, attendance increased. In the $8 condition, it rose from 90 percent before the reward period to 95 percent during the reward period. After a month, the reward was withdrawn and attendance fell sharply—to 75 percent. In the small-reward condition, attendance improved from 82 percent to 88 percent during the reward period and stayed about there after the reward period ended (90 percent). A number of technical difficulties with this study make it less than definitive in demonstrating the detrimental effect of overjustification, but it does suggest that the effects of large rewards may often be counterproductive.

Lepper, Greene, and Nisbett (1973) undertook a direct test of the overjustification hypothesis with nursery school children in California. The children were asked to play

Continued

BOX 3.1

Continued

with new drawing equipment that was so attractive that any child would welcome the opportunity to play with it. Some of the children were told that they were drawing to obtain a "Good Player award," which included a certificate with colored ribbons. Two other groups of children were offered no extrinsic reward for playing with the equipment. Of the last groups, one served as an "unexpected reward" treatment in which a Good Player award was given at the end, although it had not been anticipated. The other group served as a control with no reward given or anticipated. Several days later, the children from all groups were allowed to use the drawing materials if they wished or to play with a variety of other toys. Observers, who watched from behind a one-way mirror, noticed that the children who had originally anticipated and received an external reward for playing with the drawing material played with it only about half as much as the children from the other two groups: it appeared that their interest in the art activity had been diminished by the award offer.

Because of its theoretical and practical implications, the concept of overjustification received considerable attention following its discovery (Fazio, 1981). It has been both extended and qualified by more recent research. One interesting extension shows that if people are asked not to cheat in an exam and are thus given "superfluous deterrence"—that is, more pressure not to cheat than they need—they attribute their noncheating to the deterrence rather than to their own honesty. Hence they are not af-

forded the opportunity to see themselves as behaving with voluntary honesty. Consequently, they are more likely to cheat in the future (Wilson and Lassiter, 1982).

The overjustification effect presents a serious problem to parents, educators, and others trying to encourage behaviors that they hope will become intrinsically motivated. We should be careful, therefore, not to do for a reward something in which we otherwise have no interest or to encourage others to do so.

We should also realize that there are exceptions to the overjustification effect. If rewards are seen as signs of competence rather than efforts to control behavior, they can increase intrinsic interest (Sansone, 1986, 1989). Of interest, such rewards as praise can either increase or decrease intrinsic motivation, depending on several other variables. For example, there are gender differences in response to various kinds of praise. A study of fifth- and sixth-grade children showed that for boys praise based on ability increased intrinsic motivation more than praise based on effort. For girls the opposite was true. Their intrinsic motivation increased more after praise based on effort than after praise based on ability (Koestner, Zuckerman, and Koestner, 1989). How can this pattern of results be explained? Perhaps boys are socialized to become competent and develop interest in activities in which they can feel competent. Girls may be socialized to try hard and may like activities at which they feel they will be rewarded for effort.

Table 3.1 summarizes the conditions of the Schachter and Singer experiment and the predictions for each condition. Basically, the results were consistent with the predictions. Subjects took on the mood of the confederate when they had received an injection of epinephrine and were either misinformed or unin-

formed of its effects. The informed subjects, who already had an explanation of the drug's effects, and subjects who had received the placebo and were thus not aroused did not experience the confederate's emotions to the same degree.

On the basis of these findings, Schachter and

TABLE 3.1   CONDITIONS OF SCHACHTER AND SINGER'S EXPERIMENT

	Confederate's Behavior	
Arousal Information	Angry	Euphoric
Subjects informed	Subjects should not become angry	Subjects should not become euphoric
Subjects uninformed	Subjects should become angry	Subjects should become euphoric
Subjects misinformed	Subjects should become angry	Subjects should become euphoric
No arousal control (placebo)	Subjects should not become angry	Subjects should not become euphoric

Singer developed a **two-factor theory of emotions** that postulates our emotions are based on two components: physiological arousal and cognitions about what that arousal means. Stated as a formula, E (emotion) = A (arousal) x C (cognition). Both the arousal and the interpretation or cognition are necessary for a specific emotion to be experienced. In their experiment, Schachter and Singer gave subjects the arousal, but in some cases (uninformed and misinformed conditions) they gave them no cognitions to explain the arousal. The subjects who did not have an explanation for their arousal compared themselves with those experiencing the same arousal and attributed the emotion the others were obviously experiencing to themselves.

Schachter and Singer's provocative research has not gone unchallenged. Reviews of the research on Schachter and Singer's theory caution us that the support for the theory is still "soft" (Cotton, 1981). On the other hand, there is enough evidence for us to conclude that in many situations in which feelings are ambiguous, people will use the information in the situation, especially the reactions of other people, to attribute emotions to themselves.

Excitation Transfer: From One Emotion to Another

Schachter and Singer's theory and later work by Schachter (1964, 1971) show that arousal needs to be understood before we can experience an emotion. If the cause of arousal is ambiguous, we look to the environment, including other people's feelings, for an explanation. A more recent theory extends Schachter's

work and shows that arousal generated by one emotion or experience can be transferred or channeled into another emotion (Zillmann, 1978, 1983, 1984, 1996). For example, if you become aroused because you ran to the top of a hill, your arousal could be interpreted as romantic feelings if you had met someone really attractive at the top; or it could be interpreted as anger if a passing motorist had honked at you. In the latter case, your anger could have been fueled by the arousal from running and might therefore have been more intense than otherwise. This theory of **excitation transfer** holds that emotions consist of an excitatory component, in which arousal occurs, and an experiential component, in which the excitation is interpreted and an emotion is attributed. Arousal can be transferred if a person makes a misattribution. If you attribute your arousal from running to the beautiful person you have just met or to the motorist you have just cursed, that arousal increases your emotional reaction of romance or anger as the case may be. In later chapters, we will see how sexual arousal can be transferred to aggression and how arousal caused by fear can be transferred to sexual attraction. In short, Zilman's theory explains how we attribute and sometimes misattribute feelings to ourselves in ways suggested by Schachter and Singer.

Attributions to Self and Others: The Actor-Observer Bias

We noted earlier that attribution principles discussed in chapter 2, such as those of Kelley and Weiner, could be applied to the self. At times we make attributions about the self just as we make them about other people. Bem's (1972) self-perception theory makes an even stronger claim. He argues that self-perception is just like other-people perception; it's simply the special case in which the actor and the perceiver are the same person. Jones and Nisbett (1971) disagree, holding that actors and observers view the world quite differently.

Let us consider the following clinical case. Betty and George Barnes seek psychotherapy for problems in their marriage. Both of them agree that Betty often flies into fits of rage, throws dishes, and makes life very difficult for the two of them. Betty claims that her actions are caused by her husband's stupidity. She asserts that she becomes enraged when George forgets to put enough money into the checking account, loses his keys, is unable to get a raise. George asserts that his wife becomes enraged because she is unpleasant, illogical, and irascible.

No doubt there is motivation to this madness. Betty attributes her behavior to George's actions, and George attributes Betty's behavior to Betty. He blames her; she blames him. But the analysis must go deeper. Betty, the actor, blames the *situations* that George allegedly causes. George, the observer, blames Betty's *disposition*. Jones and Nisbett (1971) have argued that this **actor-observer bias** is a common tendency. In their terms, "there is a pervasive tendency for actors to attribute their actions to situational requirements whereas observers tend to attribute the actions to stable dispositions" (p. 80). In effect, observers show the correspondence bias—they attribute behavior in others to internal dispositions, whereas actors do not.

A study reported by McArthur (1972) supports this proposition. The procedure was elegantly simple. She asked subjects to volunteer for a survey about interpersonal relationships and then asked the subjects why they had agreed to participate. Written accounts of the request and the consent were given to observers. Like the involved subjects, the observers were asked why they thought the subjects had agreed to participate. The results showed that the involved subjects attributed their participation to the importance of the survey (situational attribution). The observers, on the other hand, attributed the actors' participation to a disposition to take part in surveys.

Consistent with the actor-observer hypothesis, a more recent study of letters written to advice columns "Ann Landers" and "Dear Abby" showed that in describing the sources of their own difficulties, writers blamed the behavior of other people, that is, external

factors. They did not show this tendency in explaining other people's difficulties (Fischer, Schoeneman, and Rubanowitz, 1987). Similarly, studies of attributions for negative emotions show that people attribute their own negative emotions more to situations than dispositions, that is, external factors, whereas observers make more balanced attributions (Karasawa, 1995).

Actors and Observers: Why Are They Different?

Jones and Nisbett contended that several factors combine to produce the different attributions of actors and observers. The first is that the actor has access to a greater history of behaviors than the observer. The actor knows that he or she behaved one way today, a different way yesterday, and yet another way last week. Therefore, the actor looks to the environment for an explanation. The observer, on the other hand, has but one act of behavior with which to judge the actor. The observer is apt to generalize and to assume that the actor's behavior is consistent across situations. Consequently, the observer is more prepared to attribute the cause of a behavior to the disposition of the actor.

Second, Jones and Nisbett reasoned that the actor and the observer approach an act from different perspectives. Each has a different focus, and different information is salient to each. As we noted in chapter 2, people tend to attribute causality to whatever is salient in their environment or whatever they are focusing their attention on (Taylor and Fiske, 1978). Because the actor's attention is focused on the environment, he or she is more likely to attribute causality to things in the environment. The observer's attention is focused on the actor, an important aspect of his or her environment, so the observer is likely to attribute causality to the actor. Thus, the observer will make more internal dispositional attributions for the actor's behavior than the actor will.

There is considerable support for this differential focus-of-attention explanation of the actor-observer bias (Ross and Fletcher, 1985). For example, one study showed that attributions to internal versus external causes made by actors and observers could be changed if each was given a different perspective. Two actors, A and B, had a conversation and were watched by two observers, one looking at each actor. After the conversation, A and B and the two observers made attributions consistent with the focus-

FIGURE 3.1 TESTING THE PERCEPTUAL EXPLANATION FOR THE ACTOR-OBSERVER EFFECT

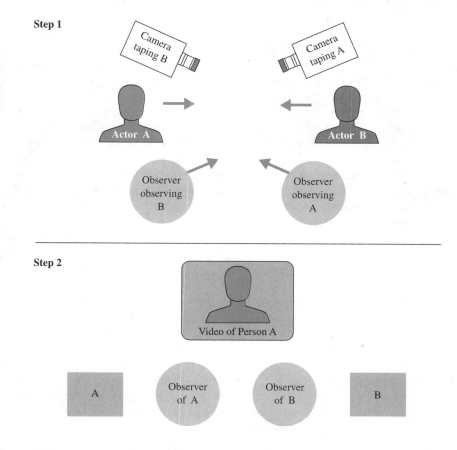

Step 1

Camera taping B

Camera taping A

Actor A

Actor B

Observer observing B

Observer observing A

Step 2

Video of Person A

A

Observer of A

Observer of B

B

Source: After Storms (1973)

of-attention explanation. Each actor attributed his own behavior to the situation and the other actor's behavior to his disposition, while each observer attributed the behavior of the actor he watched to that actor and the behavior of the other actor to the situation. In short, all four subjects attributed causality to the person on whom they were focused. Later in the experiment, the subjects were shown a videotape of actor A participating in the conversation. The subjects who had not paid attention to actor A before—that is, actor A himself and the observer watching actor B—now made more dispositional attributions to actor A; they saw him more as the locus of causality. The subjects who had been paying attention to actor A previously—that is, actor B and the observer watching A—did not change their attributions. As before (see figure 3.1), they made dispositional attributions for the behavior of actor A (Storms, 1973).

Another factor may be influencing the attributions of actors and observers, one that is closely tied to the way we view ourselves in comparison with others. We like to see ourselves as having the ability to respond appropriately to external circumstances. Thus we typically say that our behavior was caused by an external circumstance and was the appropriate response to it. Furthermore, we believe that we have the ability to respond appropriately to a wide range of external circumstances because we have many traits. We are multifaceted (Sande, Goethals, and Radloff, 1988). We can show an angry side if the situation calls for it and a gentle side if that is required. We are variable, flexible, and adaptive (Baxter and Goldberg, 1987). But we don't see others this way. As observers of their behavior, we see their actions as caused by the specific traits that dominate their personalities. Again, our own behavior is caused by external factors and reflects a flexibility and adaptiveness that come from having a wide range of traits. Consistent with this idea is a recent study in which actors and observers were asked to describe what features of an actor best described his or her "authentic self." Actors were much more likely to mention specific behaviors, such as things they have done for adventure rather than a general tendency to be adventurous. Observers, who were friends of the actor, were more likely to see the authentic self of the actor as being revealed in the traits rather than the behaviors (Johnson and Boyd, 1995). We think of ourselves in terms of what we have done in response to the environment, we think of others in terms of their specific traits.

Why do people think of themselves and others in such different ways? One possible explanation may be *linguistic norms.* Studies of the rules that people follow in using language suggest that these rules may not allow people to describe themselves in brief, abstract terms, such as trait labels, but encourage them to speak that way about others. In talking about ourselves, we are expected to be specific about how we behaved and what made us behave that way. This expectation may lead us to account for our behavior in terms of specific environmental causes (Fiedler, Semin, Finkenauer, and Berkel, 1995).

Biases In Self-Perception: The Totalitarian Ego

In chapter 2 we discussed several biases, such as the correspondence bias, that affect our perceptions of other people. What biases, if any, distort our perceptions of ourselves? Jones and Nisbett's actor-observer concept shows that we don't make attributions about ourselves in exactly the same way we make them about others. It's not surprising, then, to learn that several biases are unique to self-perception. Taken together, they make up what is known as the totalitarian ego (Greenwald, 1980).

The **totalitarian ego,** or self, is described as an organization of knowledge characterized by cognitive biases. These biases function to preserve our organization of social information and our positive views of ourselves. Greenwald noticed a similarity between the way the ego controls and biases information and the

way totalitarian governments control and bias information. Two of the biases by which the totalitarian ego manages information are called egocentricity and beneffectance. We consider them here.

Egocentricity: Self as the Focus of Knowledge and Attribution

Much of our knowledge about the world around us is autobiographical—we remember people and events in accordance with our role in interacting with them and in influencing them or being influenced by them. Our memory of a city that we visited, for example, centers on where we went and what we saw. Our memory of what happened when we participated in a softball game centers on the hits or outs we made and the balls we caught or missed. This tendency to recall information better if it is related to the self is called **egocentricity.**

One of the consequences of egocentricity is the tendency to exaggerate the importance of one's role in shaping events. Ross (1981) provides numerous examples of this tendency. People who have collaborated on a research project, a newspaper story, or a musical composition may try to recall their contributions to the joint product. When order of authorship implies level of contribution, many collaborators sit in disbelief as their partners indicate that they believe they should be named first. Each person, however, tends to remember events through his or her own eyes. A meeting that the authors may have had will be remembered differently by each participant, because each views it with egocentricity. None of the participants may be lying when they all claim that they were the primary contributor to the meeting. Each recalls that part of the event to which he or she contributed and remembers less well those parts to which others contributed.

Consider husbands and wives who are asked how much they contribute to various household chores. Ross and Sicoly (1979) interviewed married couples and asked them how much each contributed to cleaning house, caring for children, making important decisions, and causing conflicts. Both husbands and wives claimed to have made the major contribution about 70 percent of the time. Of course, it is impossible for an activity to be the wife's responsibility 70 percent of the time and the husband's responsibility 70 percent of the time. It is not that the partners wish to lie about their roles. The fact is their judgments of responsibility for everyday activities are self-centered: the bias in processing and recalling information results in the egocentric judgment.

Due to egocentricity, the husband shown here may believe that he is more involved in the preparation of his and his wife's meals.

Beneffectance: The Self-Serving Bias

People are motivated to see themselves in a good light. We tend to take credit for success and deny responsibility for failure. This bias is referred to as **beneffectance.** The term comes from the fact that we tend to view ourselves positively in two ways: (1) as beneficent, that is, helpful and moral, and (2) as competent, that is, as having "effectance." Beneffectance combines beneficence with effectance. Although this bias is not inconsistent with the actor-observer bias, it does qualify it. We generally attribute our behavior to the environment, and this tendency is much greater when our negative actions are at issue than when our positive actions are under consideration. The beneffectance bias is illustrated in a study in which women college students were made to succeed or fail on an intellectual task after which they were asked to indicate what causes they thought best explained their success or failure. After success they chose internal causes. After failure they chose external causes that constituted excuses for poor performance (DeJong, Koomen, and Mellenbergh, 1988).

Observers are not likely to share the actor's bias. Johnson, Feigenbaum, and Weiby (1964) asked women taking educational psychology classes to participate in an experiment teaching mathematics to nine-year-old boys. Each teacher taught two boys. During the first part of the learning sequence, boy A did well and boy B did poorly. During the second half, A continued to do well. For half of the teachers, B showed improvement so that he was doing as well as A; for the other half, B continued to do poorly. When the teachers were asked to what they attributed the performance of the students, teachers who had an improving B saw themselves as responsible for the performance. The teachers whose B continued to do poorly blamed the performance on the student (see figure 3.2). In a replication of this study, Beckman (1970) found precisely the same effect. However, she also asked observers to make attributions for students' performance. In marked contrast to the teachers, the observers saw the teachers as more responsible for B's poor performance and B as more responsible for his own good performance.

Consistent with these studies of the actor's bias is research showing that people tend to inflate their performance in managerial group discussion tasks (John and Robins, 1994). Although subjects generally gave more positive evaluations of their contribution than trained, objective observers, not everybody showed this

FIGURE 3.2   TEACHERS' ATTRIBUTIONS OF THE SUCCESS AND FAILURE OF STUDENTS

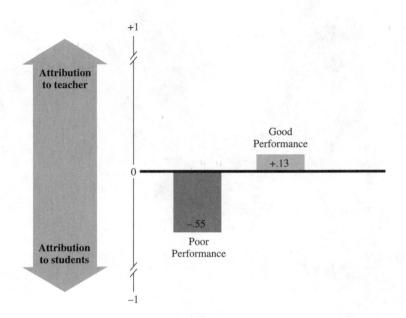

Note: A score of +1 equals total attribution to the teacher's effort; a score of -1 equals total attribution to the student.
Source: Johnson, Feigenbaum, and Weiby (1964)

self-serving bias. Some were fairly objective in evaluating themselves while some actually underestimated their performance. The people who were most unrealistically positive tended to be narcissistic, that is, they had an exaggerated view of their own importance and saw themselves as "special" without any justification.

Reviews of the literature on the self-serving bias generally support it (Fiske and Taylor, 1984; Riess, Rosenfeld, Melburg, and Tedeschi, 1981; Ross and Fletcher, 1985). A review by Bradley (1978) specified that both types of beneffectance biases—taking credit for success and denying responsibility for failure—are most likely to occur under the following conditions: (1) when the actor is highly *involved* in an activity; (2) when the actor has *choice* in engaging in the activity; and (3) when the actor's performance in the activity is *public.*

This last condition of a public activity has been explored carefully. Is beneffectance simply a public claim or do people really believe in private that they are responsible for their success but not their failure? Several studies seem to suggest that people genuinely believe in their own beneffectance. For example, in one study (Greenberg, Pyszcynski, and Solomon,

1982), subjects took what they believed to be a test of intelligence. In half of the cases, the test results were private. Subjects graded their own tests, they did not put names on their answer sheets, and they were told the tests would not be collected. The other subjects had their tests scored by the instructor with their names attached. All of the subjects learned that they had answered twelve of twenty items correctly, but half were led to believe this was a good score; the other half believed this was a bad score.

After receiving their scores, the subjects were asked to attribute their performance to their ability, their effort, or luck. Consistent with the self-serving bias, subjects who believed they had done well indicated that their performance was due to their effort and ability, whereas subjects who thought they had done poorly attributed their results to bad luck. And it made no difference whether the test performance was public or private.

Riess and his colleagues (1981) also explored whether beneffectance is a private, self-serving bias designed to bolster self-esteem or a public display of impression management. They used a technique known as the *bogus pipeline* to measure attributions. With this technique, subjects are convinced that their true attributions are being measured by electronic gadgetry, and their job is to predict what the machine is saying about their real attributions. Their predictions are taken as the subjects' attributions. The results showed that the self-serving bias held up under the scrutiny of the bogus pipeline. Subjects took credit for good performance and avoided blame for poor performance even if they believed that their private perceptions were being measured accurately by the machinery.

Research has also shown what is known as *vicarious beneffectance.* Married people evidence the beneffectance bias when explaining their spouse's behavior (Hall and Taylor, 1976). People also tend to be unrealistically optimistic about those who are close to them as well as themselves but not about people in general (Regan, Snyder, and Kassin, 1995). People also evidence the beneffectance bias in explaining poor debate performances by their preferred presidential candidates (Winkler and Taylor, 1979). Similarly, people strengthen their identification with groups to which they belong when a group is doing well. People are thus more likely to wear their college's sweatshirts following a football victory than after a football loss, reporting "We won" and "They lost" after victory and defeat (Cialdini, Borden, Thorne, Walker, Freman, and Sloan, 1976).

In summary, beneffectance seems to be a distortion of information that is designed at least partly to protect self-esteem. We protect ourselves and those with whom we identify, although we may identify with people or groups less after they fail.

Wearing "Making LA Sparkle" T-shirts helps project these teenaged volunteers' self-esteem and the value they place on their group's efforts.

Self-Perception and Psychological Well-Being

Obviously our psychological well-being is closely tied to our self-perception. Reflected appraisal, social comparison, and self-attribution all affect the way we feel about ourselves. They directly influence whether we evaluate ourselves positively or negatively and whether we feel good about the person that we are. But beyond their direct impact on self-esteem, self-perception processes play an important role in producing depression, anxiety, and feelings of helplessness. At the same time, these self-perception processes can be used to alleviate such problems. Here we will consider how a variety of self-perception processes, particularly self-attribution, affect our psychological well-being and how they offer ways to improve it.

Self-Attribution, Feelings of Control, and Learned Helplessness

We have seen that people make many self-attributions, including those explaining why they succeeded or failed. Generally, they attribute their actions or the outcomes of these actions to either internal or external causes. These attributions are often affected by the

beneffectance bias, and this bias undoubtedly protects self-esteem. But not all people are protected by the beneffectance bias to the same degree. We vary considerably in our thinking about what causes our successes and failures, and more generally about what causes the outcomes, both good and bad, that we experience in day-to-day living.

Research has shown that different people have consistently different perceptions of the causes of the outcomes of their behavior (Rotter, 1966; Phares, 1984; Lefcourt, 1982). Some individuals perceive an internal locus of control; they believe that they are the masters of their own destiny and are in control of their own fate. Others believe that what happens to them is determined by external factors—luck, fate, or chance. Rotter argued that people's experiences lead them to develop generalized expectancies that outcomes are internally or externally controlled. He went on to develop a scale that measures whether people perceive an internal or external locus of control. Answer the questions in figure 3.3 to see if you tend to perceive an internal or external locus of control.

People who perceive an **internal locus of control,** referred to as "internals," believe that what happens in their lives depends on how hard they work and that nobody is going to give them anything, but anything is within their reach if they exert the effort. Thus internals work. They are aptly characterized by the slogan "We try harder." Jackie Joyner-Kersee is typi-

---

FIGURE 3.3   SAMPLE ITEMS FROM AN EARLY VERSION OF ROTTER'S TEST OF INTERNAL-EXTERNAL LOCUS OF CONTROL

I more strongly believe that:

1. a. Many people can be described as victims of circumstance.
   b. What happens to other people is pretty much of their own making.

2. a. The world is so complicated that I just cannot figure things out.
   b. The world is really complicated all right, but I can usually work things out by effort and persistence.

3. a. Most students would be amazed at how much grades are determined by capricious events.
   b. The marks I get in class are completely my own responsibility.

4. a. Promotions are earned through hard work and persistence.
   b. Making a lot of money is largely a matter of getting the right breaks.

5. a. In my case, the grades I make are the results of my own efforts; luck has little or nothing to do with it.
   b. Sometimes I feel that I have little to do with the grades I get.

6. a. Getting along with people is a skill that must be practiced.
   b. It is almost impossible to figure out how to please some people.

Source: Adapted from Rotter (1971)

cal of many internals. She believes that she is largely in control of her success in running, and she works hard to make success happen. People with an **external locus of control,** on the other hand, perceive their fate as controlled by factors outside themselves. Because they believe that they have no control over what happens to them, they don't put much effort into their lives. In one study, for example, hospitalized tuberculosis patients' attitudes differed dramatically depending on their perceived locus of control. Internals made efforts to find out what caused their disease and what they could do about it, while externals were more passive (Seeman and Evans, 1962). Langer (1981) has argued that many elderly people are passive not because they are senile but because their life difficulties cause them to perceive an external locus of control.

Research on learned helplessness shows that you don't have to be elderly to begin to perceive that your outcomes are beyond your control and thus to become passive and helpless. It also shows that whether people become helpless or not after they have had difficult life experiences depends on the attributions they make about the causes of their difficulties. **Learned helplessness** is a phenomenon first discovered in animal research by Martin Seligman and his colleagues (Overmier and Seligman, 1967; Maier, Seligman, and Solomon, 1969). It turns out that animals, after being exposed to inescapable shock when they are learning a task, later fail to learn a second task. Not only do animals in this situation fail to learn the second task, they usually cease behaving entirely. Seligman has labeled this state learned helplessness because the animal is learning that there is no relationship between its responding and its reinforcement, and thus it simply stops responding.

The state of learned helplessness has been experimentally produced in humans as well as animals by exposing people to such experiences as inescapable aversive stimuli (electric shocks and loud noise) or insoluble problem tasks (Hiroto and Seligman, 1975; Thornton and Jacobs, 1971; Roth and Kubal, 1975). In all of these studies, experience with uncontrollability produced deficits in learning, whether the later task was learning to make an avoidance response or solving a cognitive problem. The common occurrence is that subjects with helplessness pretraining make significantly fewer attempts to respond and adopt a general state of passivity resembling depression.

In what way do attributions relate to this research? The attributions people make about the causes

of their failure on the first task are extremely important. If people attribute failure to their inability to cope with difficult situations, then there is little reason for them to try again in the future. However, if people attribute failure to the task, then that failure may not lead to a state of helplessness and a subsequent unwillingness to try again.

The importance of attributions was shown in a study by Tennen and Eller (1977). Subjects thought that they were participating in two separate experiments. In the first experiment (the pretreatment stage), they were given either ability (self) or task difficulty (external) explanations for their apparent inability to solve a discrimination problem. The subjects in one insoluble condition were told that the task was becoming more difficult, whereas the subjects in another insoluble condition were told that the task was becoming easier. As you can see, the potential was created for the subjects in one group to attribute failure to task difficulty (the harder task condition), whereas the subjects in the other group should have attributed failure to their own lack of ability (the easier task condition). The measure of helplessness was a subject's success at solving anagrams in the second experiment. Subjects in the ability attribution condition solved significantly fewer anagrams than did either subjects without prior helplessness training or subjects who could attribute their previous poor performance to task difficulty. This finding provides strong support for the role of self-attribution in learned helplessness. It is not simply the expectation that responding is unrelated to outcome that is critical. Rather, it is the self-attribution that failure reflects the lack of an ability that causes people to carry the helplessness expectation into other situations.

Let's be more specific about what kinds of attributions lead to learned helplessness. A classic paper by Abramson, Seligman, and Teasdale (1978) presents what is known as the **revised learned helplessness (RLH) model.** It suggests that people become helpless when they attribute their failures and other negative outcomes to causes that are internal, stable, and global. Psychologists measure these attributions by asking people what kind of attributions they make for events, evoking such statements as "You can't get all the work done that others expect of you" (Horneffer and Fincham, 1996). Or suppose you ask someone to go to a dance with you and are turned down. What attributions might you make for this situation? If you make an internal rather than external attribution, you decide it's something about you, perhaps your appearance or your voice, rather than the fact that the person is busy or doesn't like to dance. If you make a stable rather than unstable attribution, you further decide you were turned down because of something that won't change, such as your height or hair color, rather than the way you asked the question, which can be changed. Finally, if you make a global rather than specific attribution, you decide that whatever caused you to be turned down this one time is going to affect lots of other interpersonal interactions too. You might, for example, decide that your high-pitched voice put the other person off and is likely to cause trouble with many other people as well, including future prospective dates, casual acquaintances, and employers. Why bother? These attributions are enough to make anyone stop trying. Obviously, then, they can lead to passivity and lack of effort or what we call learned helplessness.

How much support does this theory have? A great deal of research has shown that the pattern of internal, stable, and global attributions for setbacks can have devastating effects on future performance. A study of college freshmen looked at students' responses to upsetting academic events encountered early in the year. Those who attributed their problems to internal, stable, and global causes ended up with lower grades despite the fact that they were just as bright. Their lower grades were tied to setting vague academic goals and not taking advantage of academic advisers. In other words, they responded to their problems passively and got into academic difficulties (Peterson and Barrett, 1987).

Other research shows that the global dimension may be particularly important in learned helplessness. If people fail in one situation and make global attributions (there's something about me that won't change, *and* it will affect everything I try to do) they are likely to perform poorly in a broad range of situations, not just situations similar to the one in which they initially failed (Mikulincer, 1986). Furthermore, subjects who make global attributions for failures are likely to experience cognitive interference from irrelevant thoughts when they try to work on a task (Mikulincer and Nizan, 1988).

Self-attribution has effects on psychological well-being beyond its impact on learned helplessness. It also affects anxiety and psychological "hardiness" (Kobasa, 1979). For example, anxious people don't take personal credit for success the way their nonanxious counterparts do (Alden, 1987); that is, they don't show the beneffectance bias that protects most people. And research shows that psychologically hardy people—people who get highly involved, who like challenges, and who feel

in control—tend to make less internal, stable, and global attributions for negative events than do their nonhardy counterparts (Hull, Van Treuren, and Propsom, 1988). In short, patterns of self-attribution have a significant impact on a range of psychological problems.

Whether people are active or helpless in addressing their problems is affected by more than just attribution processes. One key variable is **perceived self-efficacy** (Bandura, 1977), one's confidence in one's ability to produce a positive outcome. People who are high in perceived self-efficacy are likely to take action to solve or get out of stressful or painful situations. They feel they have control and they exercise it (Litt, 1988). Similarly, people who view themselves as effective problem solvers feel they can solve their personal problems by exerting effort (Baumgardner, Heppner, and Arkin, 1986). In short, when you have problems to deal with, seeing yourself as having the capacity to cope and be effective may be half the battle.

Self-Attribution and Depression

One of the first applications of the learned helplessness concept was to the psychological disorder of depression. The passivity observed in the early studies of learned helplessness reminded many researchers of depression. More specifically, the revised learned helplessness model, emphasizing self-attribution, has been extended to suggest that people who make internal, stable, and global attributions for failures and other negative outcomes become depressed. A great deal of research has been done to test this hypothesis in recent years. In general, there is considerable evidence that these kinds of attributions are "depressogenic," that is, they contribute significantly to being depressed (Horneffer and Fincham, 1996). However, research has also suggested further revisions.

A study that is typical of those supporting the RLH model looked at depressive symptoms and attributional style in school children, who were studied over the course of a year. It was found that those who explained negative events in terms of internal, stable, and global causes were more likely to show depressive symptoms throughout the year and to have lower levels of school achievement (Nolen-Hoeksema, Seligman, and Girgus, 1986). Another study of college students' responses to low grades on midterm exams showed that immediately after the exams, students' depressive moods were explained simply by their grades. However, their long-term depressive reactions were determined both by the grades and by their internal, stable, and global attributions (Metalsky, Halberstadt, and Abramson, 1987). A recent study showed that depressed people make pessimistic attributions just for themselves, not for positive or negative events that happen to close friends or other people in general. They do not differ in their overall approach to attribution, just in the way they interpret their own behavior and outcomes (Schlenker and Britt, 1996). Although some studies do not support the revised learned helplessness model (Follette and Jacobson, 1987, for example), a meta-analytic review of more than one hundred studies with nearly fifteen thousand subjects showed clear support for it (Sweeney, Anderson, and Bailey, 1986).

Even though the revised learned helplessness model has clear support, it has undergone some fine-tuning over the years. One modification argues that attributing negative events to stable and global causes is key in creating "hopelessness" and therefore depression, whereas also attributing such events to internal causes adds the consequence of low self-esteem. The argument suggests that depression is more likely when negative events are considered important (Abramson, Alloy, and Metalsky, 1986). Another addition to the model suggests that depression is likely only when the internal, stable, and global causes for negative events are also seen as uncontrollable (Brown and Siegel, 1988).

One important question in this research on attributions and depression is how people initially develop the depressive attributional style—seeing negative events as the result of internal, stable, and global causes. A recent study suggests that low self-esteem may be a key factor in producing the depressive attributional style (Tennen and Herzberger, 1987). This study is important in tying together the three broad aspects of self-perception we have considered in this chapter—reflected appraisal, social comparison, and self attribution. The first two processes, reflected appraisal and social comparison, may be critical in establishing high or low self-esteem. Level of self-esteem may, in turn, exert a strong impact on an individual's attributional style. Consistent with this hypothesis is a study showing that, for emotions like pride and humiliation that relate to the self, low self-esteem people have stronger emotional reactions to failure than high self-esteem people, and, more important, that they tend to overgeneralize the meaning of their failures (Brown and Dutton, 1995b).

Two other aspects of self-perception are involved in depression. One is pessimism. Depressed people see negative outcomes as much more likely than positive outcomes. Not that depressed people are biased toward pessimism; it would be truer to say that nondepressed people are biased toward optimism. Nondepressed people see themselves as more likely to experience positive events than do similar others and are less likely to experience negative events—a bias that depressed people do not show (Alloy and Ahrens, 1987). These and other findings suggest the existence of a phenomenon that has been called **depressive realism.** It may be that depressed people view themselves and the world quite realistically. Nondepressed people are protected by a range of biases, such as the beneffectance and optimism biases, which support high self-esteem and an active approach to living. Perhaps it isn't good for you to be too honest with yourself or completely accurate in perceiving both yourself and others. A little self-deception can be protective and adaptive.

A final aspect of self-perception involved in depression is the quickness with which negative thoughts about the self come to mind. When depressed people are busy with a memory task, they can still do another task very quickly—deciding whether negative adjectives apply to them. It takes them more time, however, to decide whether those adjectives apply to other people (Bargh and Tota, 1988). It seems that depressed people find it very easy—nearly automatic—to think of themselves in negative terms. Negative thoughts about the self are highly available and accessible in their memory. The easy accessibility of these negative thoughts about the self may be a key contributor to depression.

Self-Complexity, Self-Discrepancies, and Psychological Well-Being

In recent years social psychologists have discovered a number of other aspects of self-perception that have a large impact on both physical and psychological well-being. One of the most interesting is **self-complexity** (Linville, 1987), the condition of perceiving oneself as having many aspects, each of which differs greatly from the others. A noncomplex woman, for example, may perceive herself to be simply a woman, an athlete, and a champion. Jackie Joyner-Kersee, in contrast, has a highly complex view of herself. She is well aware that she is all of those things and many more: a loyal family member, an involved citizen of her hometown of East St. Louis, someone who wants to have a family and move beyond athletic competition, and so on. She is a person of high self-complexity.

What difference does self-complexity make? It seems to buffer us against stress-related illness and depression. We all have to deal with stressful life events, but the effects of such events vary with the degree of our self-complexity.

Low-complexity individuals respond to high levels of stress with feelings of depression and high rates of flu and other physical illnesses. High-complexity people are buffered or protected from these unhealthy consequences of stress.

How does this work? The key may be that individuals who have high levels of self-complexity can throw themselves into other activities or concerns when stress interrupts one part of their lives. People who are low in self-complexity suffer both physically and psychologically when stress disrupts one of the few aspects of their lives. They have little else to turn to, and their well-being is impaired. The concept of evaluative differentiation discussed in Box 3.2 is closely related to self-complexity and seems to work in the same manner.

Another aspect of self-perception that affects psychological well-being consists of self-discrepancies (Higgins, 1989). According to **self-discrepancy theory,** people's psychological well-being is affected not only by their self-concepts or their actual selves but also by the way their self-concepts match or mismatch various "self-guides." There are two kinds of self-guides. One is an *ideal self,* what you hope or aspire to be, or what someone else hopes you will be. The other kind of self-guide is an *ought self,* what you feel duty-bound or obligated to be, or what someone else believes you ought to be.

Self-discrepancy theory predicts that if people have a mismatch or discrepancy between their actual self and their ideal self, and thereby feel that they aren't being all that they *could* be, they will suffer from sadness and dejection, feelings that might lead eventually to depression. On the other hand, the theory predicts that if there is a discrepancy between the actual self and the ought self, so that one feels that one isn't what one *ought* to be, one will suffer agitation and anxiety. Several recent studies have supported these predictions (Strauman and Higgins, 1987; Higgins, Bond, Klein, and Strauman, 1986; Higgins, Roney, Crowe, and Hymes, 1994). In addition, they have shown that people with discrepant self-guides show signs of being in chronic conflict about how to

behave and are muddled, indecisive, distracted, and confused about their identity (Van Hook and Higgins, 1988). Finally, an important study shows that self-esteem is correlated with the discrepancy between actual self and ideal self, just as the theory predicts (Moretti and Higgins, 1990).

Summary

As a result of social interaction, we learn a great deal about ourselves. Our view of ourselves is affected by both reflected appraisal—what others think of us—and social comparison—the ways in which we appraise ourselves in comparison with others. Usually we compare ourselves with people who are similar to us on related attributes, though we may compare ourselves with people who are worse (or more negative) than we are to enhance our feelings of well-being. Sometimes people "make up" social comparison information in self-serving ways: they overestimate consensus for many behaviors but underestimate consensus for socially desirable behaviors.

Bem's self-perception theory argues that we make attributions about ourselves just as we do for others; that is, we consider our own behavior and the situation in which it takes place. We do not attribute attitudes to ourselves from things we were forced or pressured to do. One application of self-perception theory is understanding the overjustification effect, in which high external justification leads to the possibily mistaken attribution that a behavior was engaged in not for its own intrinsic merit but rather for its high external reward.

Schachter and Singer have suggested that emotions are subject to a type of attribution process. In their view, emotions are a function of physiological arousal and cognitive labeling. Schachter and Singer demonstrated that people who were physiologically aroused by a drug but had no adequate explanation for their arousal used the behavior of another person in the same situation to infer their emotion. Zillman has shown that arousal from one source can be transferred to another emotion and can make that emotion more intense.

Jones and Nisbett have shown that we do not make attributions about ourselves in exactly the same way as we make them about others. They have demonstrated the actor-observer bias: as actors, we attribute our own behavior to external causes, while as observers, we attribute other people's behavior to internal personal causes.

BOX 3.2

Subjective Well-Being

Recent research suggests a complex set of relations between life events, the self-concept, and psychological well-being. Life events make a difference in our self-concept and feelings of well-being, but in turn aspects of our self-concept strongly affect how we handle those events and how they affect our well-being. Subjective well-being can be thought of as a mix of life-satisfaction, positive affect, and the absence of negative affect (Diener and Larsen, 1993). The experience of well-being tends to be stable over time but can be affected by recent events (Suh, Diener, and Fujita, 1996). Many different kinds of life events can make a difference.

One of the most prominent elements affecting well-being is a person's physical attractiveness (Diener, Wolsic, and Fujita, 1995). Our appearance is not really a life event, but it is a significant personal charac-teristic that we experience in life. How does being physically attractive or unattractive affect our subjective well-being? Not surprisingly, attractive people tend to have higher levels of subjective well-being. As we might expect, being beautiful helps people be happy. But it's not that simple. In one study, when appearance enhancers, such as hair style, clothing, and jewelry were removed, there was a much lower correlation between physical attractiveness and well-being. This finding suggests that happy people take action to make themselves look as attractive as possible so that for them, at least in part, well-being causes attractiveness. Attractive-ness doesn't just happen to us. We can make it happen to some degree if we are happy and try to enhance our beauty.

The relationship between life events and well-being is also affected by the way our self-concept is organized. Individuals differ

Making ourselves attractive increases our subjective well-being.

Continued

BOX 3.2

Continued

according to whether they have a high or low degree of *evaluative differentiation* in their self-concept organization (Showers and Ryff, 1996). People with a high degree of evaluative differentiation assess different aspects of their self-concept distinctly. They may evaluate some aspects of their self positively and other aspects negatively. Of course, these people have a high level of self-esteem if the aspects of themselves that they evaluate positively are also deemed to be important (Pelham, 1995). In contrast, people with a low degree of evaluative differentiation tend to have an average level of self-evaluation across almost all of the different aspects of self. Their selves are not as compartmentalized (Showers and Kling, 1996a).

How does evaluative differentiation affect responses to life events? First, when people encounter events that make them sad, those with high degrees of evaluative differentiation can think about the important and highly positive aspects of their self-concept and lift themselves out of their negative mood. This will not automatically happen, but it is one way to get over the negative feelings caused by unpleasant events. People with lower degrees of evaluative differentiation don't have those highly positive, though somewhat isolated, aspects of self to draw on for good feeling (Showers and Kling, 1996b). Second, when people make major life transitions, such

as moving to a different home, those with a highly differentiated self-concept often have greater well-being. Important and highly positive elements of their self-concept seem to provide a buffer against stress and make them more resilient to the difficulties of making a major life change. It seems to be helpful to have some very positive areas of the self, along with negative ones, rather than having an undifferentiated average evaluation.

Another perspective on self-concept organization and reaction to life events comes from a study on the aspects of the self that are affected by mood. When life events cause either a happy or sad mood, is the self-concept affected? Do we evaluate ourselves positively when events put us in a good mood, or negatively when they put us in a bad mood? Research indicates that only peripheral, but not central, aspects of our self-concept are affected by mood. The central, important aspects of our self-concept that are generally held with certainty do not change with variations in mood. However, those less well-defined and less important peripheral aspects of the self-concept are affected by mood (Sedikides, 1995).

In short, life events affect our mood, our sense of well-being, and our self-concept. However, the relations among these aspects of our experience are complex.

A number of other biases affect our perceptions of ourselves. They operate much like the biases encountered in our discussion of attributions to others. However, the operation of biases in self-perception leads to different outcomes than that of biases in perceiving others. Many of the biases that affect the self have been characterized as part of the totalitarian ego—the organization of information in a manner that enables us to form a favorable impression of ourselves. Among these biases are egocentricity, or the tendency to process and recall information that is self-relevant,

and beneffectance, or the tendency to see ourselves as responsible for good rather than bad outcomes.

Different individuals perceive different loci of control for their outcomes. People with an internal locus of control perceive what happens to them as a result of their own behavior, and they generally "try harder." People with an external locus of control believe that chance controls what happens to them, and they are more passive. Learned helplessness is a phenomenon whereby people cease to behave adaptively after experiencing uncontrollable events. Learned helplessness is a function of the attributions people make about their failures as well as a function of their perceptions about their degree of control over their fate in general. People who attribute their failures and negative outcomes to internal, stable, and global causes are likely to become helpless and depressed.

Key Terms

actor-observer bias
beneffectance
depressive realism
egocentricity
excitation transfer
external locus of control
false consensus
internal locus of control

learned helplessness
overjustification effects
perceived self-efficacy
reflected appraisal
related attributes hypothesis
revised learned helplessness
    (RLH) model
self-complexity

self-discrepancy theory
self-perception theory
similarity hypothesis
social comparison
totalitarian ego
two-factor theory of
    emotions

Suggested Readings

Baumeister, R. F. (1998). The self. In D. T. Gilbert, S. T. Fiske, and G. Lindzey (Eds.), *The handbook of social psychology* (Vol. 1, pp. 680–740). New York: McGraw-Hill.

Berkowitz, L. (1988). *Advances in experimental social psychology* (Vol. 21). San Diego, CA: Academic Press.

Cotton, J. L. (1981). A review of research on Schachter's theory of emotion and the misattribution of arousal. *European Journal of Social Psychology, 11,* 365–397.

Festinger, L. (1954). A theory of social comparison processes. *Human Relations, 7,* 117–140.

Gergen, K. J. (1971). *The concept of self.* New York: Holt, Rinehart and Winston.

Jones, E. E., and Nisbett, R. (1971). *The actor and the observer: Divergent perceptions of the causes of behavior.* Morristown, NJ: General Learning Press.

Nisbett, R., and Ross, L. (1980). *Human inference: Strategies and shortcomings of social judgment.* Englewood Cliffs, NJ: Prentice-Hall.

Schachter, S., and Singer, J. E. (1962). Cognitive, social, and physiological determinants of emotional state. *Psychological Review, 69,* 379–399.

Suls, J., and Miller, R. J. (Eds.). (1977). *Social comparison processes: Theoretical and empirical perspectives.* Washington, DC: Hemisphere/Halsted.

Wegner, D. M., and Vallacher, R. R. (1980). *The self in social psychology.* New York: Oxford University Press.

Chapter 4

Presenting the Self

Perhaps Ira Gershwin said it best. Speaking of the music he composed with his brother George, he remarked, "I never knew how good our songs were until I heard Ella Fitzgerald sing them." (Holden, 1996, p. 33). When Ella Fitzgerald died in 1996, America knew that it had lost one of its finest entertainment and artistic talents. She was a cultural treasure. Ella worked hard and recorded prodigiously for five decades, always wanting to keep developing. Once a naive interviewer asked a music critic who was America's finest female jazz vocalist. Puzzled, he responded, "You mean . . . besides Ella?"

Ella Fitzgeralds's music was so sweet and pure that it not only helped her listeners escape pain and bitterness, it hid her own. She was born in 1917 in Newport News, Virginia. Her parents separated within a year of her birth, and her mother married another man. Ella, her mother, and her stepfather then moved to Yonkers, New York. The years in Yonkers were good ones. Ella excelled in school and, from her mother, acquired her love for the arts and performance. First she wanted to be a dancer. Then she listened to Louis Armstrong and Bing Crosby records and began to sing herself. Maybe she could be a singer.

As a young teenager, Ella performed a dance routine with a friend in local clubs and seemed headed toward a career in music. But things changed radically in 1932, when she was fifteen. Her mother died and she found herself in an abusive relationship with her stepfather. She went to live with an aunt in Harlem, but life quickly unraveled for her. She dropped out of school and began to live on the streets. She became involved in small-time crime and even served as a lookout at a house of illegal gambling and prostitution, signalling when the police came around.

Not long after, Ella Fitzgerald was apprehended by the authorities and placed in the Colored Orphan Asylum in the Riverdale section of the Bronx. Because of overcrowding during the economic depression of the 1930s, she was then placed in one of the few other institutions that accepted "wayward" black girls, the New York State Training School for Girls in Hudson, New York. The black girls were segregated into the most rundown of the school's buildings where they were frequently beaten by male staff members and disciplined by being shackled and fed on bread and water (Newman, 1996). She was not allowed to sing with the school's noted choir: it was all white.

Eventually Ella was released and left reform school behind forever. Back in Harlem she tried again to find a life in music, making her first formal stage appearance in an amateur contest at the Apollo Theater, singing two songs, and winning first prize. Then Fitzgerald was technically "paroled" by the state of New York to Chick Webb's band after she persuaded Webb to let her sing for his group. She was seventeen at the time. She quickly became a star attraction in Harlem and made her first recordings in 1935 when she was eighteen.

Ella Fitzgerald's early records were successful but not distinguished. Mostly pop songs, they revealed the beauty of her voice but not the feeling she brought to her nightclub performances. During this formative part of her career, she married a shipyard worker but ended the relationship after two years. Then, at twenty-two, she married Ray Brown, a bass player in the noted Dizzy Gillespie band. Ella and Ray adopted the son of Ella's half sister. The boy was named Ray Brown, Jr., and was Ella's only child. Ella continued to work, while her aunt Virginia took care of Ray, Jr.

During World War II, when Ella was in her twenties, she began experimenting with singing to the inventive musical styles of musicians such as Gillespie and Charlie Parker. During this time she perfected a new singing technique known as "scat," in which performers sing improvised meaningless syllables such as "de-de-dum" or "dooby-doo," mimicking jazz instruments. Ella became an enormously successful and popular singer but over the years grew tired of singing pop "be-bop" songs.

Her career took a turn in 1955 when she signed a contract with Verve records and did a number of *Songbook* albums in which she recorded the songs of a noted composer backed up by either a small band or an orchestra. Her first was the notable *Cole Porter Songbook* in which she recorded some of her finest music, including a ringingly clear and joyful version of the hit show song, "Anything Goes." Ella herself recalled that

Ella Fitzgerald performing on stage at the Pla-Mor, Kansas City, Missouri, in 1936. Her singing, which captivated millions, also liberated her from early personal misfortune.

the Cole Porter work "was a turning point in my life" (Holden, 1996). Perhaps her finest work was the fifty-three-song *Ella Fitzgerald Sings the George and Ira Gershwin Songbook,* recorded in 1959.

During these years of peak achievement and recognition, Ella worked with great energy and persistence. She toured more than forty weeks a year all over the world and continued a highly productive recording career. She teamed up with such stars as Louis Armstrong, Count Basie, and Frank Sinatra. She was widely regarded as the queen of jazz vocalists.

In her later years Ella's health began to fail. She suffered from eye problems and diabetes, and required heart surgery. But she kept performing until the early 1990s when working on stage became impossible. Ella Fitzgerald had always lived a private life surrounded by close friends who spoke for her. She loved to perform in public, but she wanted to sing, not talk about herself; in fact, she never talked about the early reform school years.

Fortunately, Ella's contributions were recognized before her death. This remarkable, disciplined, and simply beautiful singer was given a number of awards for the work of a lifetime, including the Kennedy Center Award in 1959. She was also given several honorary degrees from colleges and universities, including Dartmouth and Yale. When she received her doctorate from Yale, she commented modestly, "Not bad for someone who only studied music to get that half-credit in high school" (Holden, 1996, p. 34).

Ella Fitzgerald's life was often exceedingly difficult. She was chained in solitary confinement in reform school. Two marriages failed, and she bore no children of her own. Both legs were amputated below the knees a few years before she died. But she loved working and relating to people through her music. And her music is truly a gift to the cultural history of North America that enriches us all.

Presenting the Self

In his famous play *As You Like It,* William Shakespeare wrote, "All the world's a stage," implying that the way people behave in everyday life is like playing different parts in the theater. Ella Fitzgerald's life—and our own lives as well—shows that there is a big difference between private life and public performance. Nevertheless, the *real* joy that Ella's singing brought both her and her audiences demon-

strates the degree to which we become the way we act. Much of the way we interact with our fellow human beings involves presenting ourselves in ways that we hope will leave a positive impression on them, just as singers, dancers, actors, and musicians do. In fact, as we shall see, many have argued that Shakespeare's comparison of life and the stage is highly instructive, and that we need to understand how much of our everyday behavior involves presenting ourselves as people in the theater do. In this chapter we consider how people present themselves and how concerns with the self affect the way they behave in face-to-face interaction.

Self-Awareness and Behavior

Much of our everyday behavior is fairly routine and automatic. We get up, get dressed, eat breakfast, and read the newspaper in a fairly habitual manner without giving a lot of thought to what we are doing. Some of this behavior is referred to as mindless (Langer, 1989). Generally, we do not think about ourselves very much when we are performing automatic behaviors, nor do we think about what others may be thinking of us (Wicklund and Frey, 1980)—we just go about our business. On the other hand, events in the environment may focus our attention on ourselves and put us in a state that has been called self-awareness, self-focused attention, self-directed attention, or simply self-attention. Then we are no longer mindless but very self-conscious and self-aware. For performers such as Ella Fitzgerald, self-awareness is a part of doing business. She had to be aware of the impact she had on others, how others judged her, and how she judged herself. As we shall see, when we are self-aware we can behave with a great deal of deliberation and thought. We will also see that self-awareness is often unpleasant. Actresses like Meryl Streep make plain that one of the most difficult parts of a performing career is losing anonymity and dealing with the "intrusion of extreme self-consciousness" that is part of the celebrity role. Whether or not performers enjoy being the focus of attention, they typically understand that being in the spotlight is inevitable. What happens when people become self-aware, and why is self-awareness so often unpleasant?

Self-Awareness and Self-Assessment

Recent theories of self-awareness, or self-attention, suggest that people can become self-aware whenever they are asked to talk about themselves, when they are in unfamiliar or unstructured settings, when they can see themselves in the mirror or hear themselves on a tape recorder, when television cameras or microphones are pointing at them or people are looking at them, or when they are in a minority status in a group and thus stand out. Obviously, being on stage or recording produces self-awareness, so self-awareness was a large part of Ella Fitzgerald's life. But it is something we *all* deal with at times, so what are its consequences?

Self-attention theorists (Carver and Scheier, 1990; Duval and Wicklund, 1972; Gibbons, 1990; Mullen, 1987; Wicklund and Frey, 1980) argue that when people become self-focused, two things happen. First, our overall self-concept and the various parts of it are brought into consciousness. Second, when the self-concept is on our mind, "self-assessment is inevitable" (Gibbons, 1990, p. 286); that is, we begin to evaluate ourselves by comparing some aspect of ourselves with standards that the situation makes salient.

Any of four aspects of the self can become the focus of attention. First, we may simply focus on our appearance and evaluate the way we look in comparison with other people or in comparison with the way we ourselves look at other times. Second, we may focus our attention on our physiological or psychological experience. This often happens when we are in a strong mood or have been aroused by exercise, anger, passion, anxiety, disgust, or some other strong emotion (Hansen, Hansen, and Crano, 1989). Then we compare our experience with our normal levels of mood or arousal and precisely assess our emotion. Third, we may focus on the "self" as a whole and form an overall evaluation of ourselves. Usually this overall evaluation is made with respect to our ideal self, although it may involve comparison with others. Fourth, and most common, we may focus our attention on our specific behavior and compare our actions with relevant rules, norms, or other behavioral standards. In some cases, we may focus attention on more than one of these aspects of self.

Consider, for example, what happens when we see ourselves in the mirror. We are likely to compare the way we look or the way we are acting with ideal standards of appearance or conduct. When we make this comparison, we often find that our behavior falls short of what we perceive as ideal. We may feel that our performance is not as good as we would like it to be, that our appearance isn't as pleasing as that of attractive people we see on television, or that we aren't being as helpful or cooperative as we feel we ought to be. In other words, comparing behavior with standards is apt to be an unpleasant and painful experience because in all likelihood we will discover that we fall short of *our ideal standards*. What happens when people experience the unpleasant feelings that accompany the self-aware state of mind?

Escaping from Self-Awareness

One obvious method of dealing with an unpleasant situation is simply to try to get out of it. For example, Ella Fitzgerald and other celebrities tried to avoid or escape self-focused attention by attempting to blend into a crowd and remain anonymous. What coping methods do people in psychological experiments on self-awareness use? If they face the unpleasant combination of self-awareness and falling short of standards, they too will escape as soon as they feel they can. In one study, subjects took a test that measured "cleverness," a combination of intelligence and creativity. Some subjects were told that they had done very well (in the upper 10 percent), and others were told that they had scored very poorly (in the bottom 10 percent). The subjects were then told to wait in another room for a different experimenter to arrive but that if the experimenter did not arrive within five minutes, they should leave. For some subjects, the other room had a mirror and a television camera pointed at them, which, of course, induced self-awareness. Others went to a room that had no mirror or camera. According to self-awareness theory, the subjects who were not made self-focused by the mirror and camera should not have wanted to escape; they didn't need to think about themselves or their performance. But the situation was different for subjects who were made self-aware. Those who had scored at the top on the cleverness scale should not have minded being self-aware as they would have felt they had done well in meeting ideal standards. The subjects who scored poorly, however, should have felt extremely uncomfortable when they were self-aware and compared their performance with ideal standards; they should have wanted to get out of the situation, to escape. And they did! Subjects in the low-performance/self-aware condition stopped waiting for the absent experimenter and left significantly sooner than subjects under the other three conditions. Recently, psychologists have found some evidence that many unhealthy, puzzling, or bizarre behaviors may have their roots in the desire to escape self-awareness, including erroneous memories of being picked up by flying saucers, sexual masochism, and excessive drinking and binge eating (Baumeister, 1989; Heatherton and Baumeister, 1991; Hull, Young, and Jouriles, 1986; Newman and Baumeister, 1996).

Although people typically avoid self-focused attention, several studies indicate there are exceptions. If we expect to compare well with standards and to achieve a desired identity, we may welcome self-focused attention; we may even seek it out (Greenberg and Musham, 1981).

Matching to Standards

Sometimes people cannot run away from self-awareness; escape is impossible. What typically happens here is that people try to change their behavior so that it more nearly meets ideal standards. These attempts are referred to as **matching to standards** (Carver and Scheier, 1981; Mullen, 1983). However, whether or not people attempt to match to standards is influenced by their sense of whether or not they will be successful, their *outcome expectancy*. If people have a positive outcome expectancy, if they think they will succeed in matching to standards, they will attempt to do so. This process is called **self-regulation.** For example, people who are self-aware are more likely to help others. In one study, subjects who had seen a videotape about a venereal disease epidemic and were made self-aware were more likely to volunteer their services in a prevention program than were control group subjects. The self-aware group attempted to match to social responsibility standards (Duval, Duval, and Neely, 1979).

Another interesting instance of self-regulation occurred in a study of Halloween trick-or-treaters (Beaman, Klentz, Diener, and Svanum, 1979). The trick-or-treaters were told by the owner of a house (actually an experimenter) not to take more than one piece of candy. The candy was put in a bowl and the children were left alone to take what they wanted. Self-awareness was created with a mirror behind the candy bowl. The results showed that without the mir-

ror, well over half the children took more than one piece of candy. But when the mirror stood behind the bowl and the children watched themselves taking candy, the cheating (taking more than one piece of candy) dropped to less than 10 percent. In general, when people are made self-aware, their efforts to match to standards lead them to socially desirable behavior that matches to social standards.

Other interesting instances of self-regulation include findings that self-aware individuals are more likely to behave according to their own personal values. College women who were rated either high or low on guilt about sex were required to read pornographic passages and to rate how much they enjoyed them. Some of the subjects were made self-aware when they participated in the experiment and some were not. For self-aware subjects, there was a much higher correlation between sex-guilt scores and dislike of the passages. In short, when made self-aware, the subjects thought about the extent to which they had negative feelings about sex and reacted to the pornography accordingly (Gibbons, 1978).

While self-regulation or matching to standards is a common response to self-awareness or self-focused attention, people will not self-regulate if they have a low outcome expectancy. If they expect to fail, they will simply demonstrate *withdrawal*, a breakdown of normal self-regulation and matching to standards.

A Self-Attention Perspective on Group Behavior

We noted earlier that having a minority status in a group can generate self-awareness (Wicklund and Frey, 1980). One theory has taken this insight and considered the consequences of being self-attentive in a group setting (Mullen, 1983, 1987). The application of self-attention theory to groups holds that self-attention and matching to standards increases in a group as an individual and his or her subgroup become outnumbered by people belonging to another subgroup. More specifically, self-attention is proportional to what is known as the *other-total ratio*. For a performer like Ella Fitzgerald, this ratio translates to the number of people in the audience (other subgroup) divided by the total number of people in the situation—singers, musicians, and the audience. Mullen (1983) has shown that self-attention and self-regulation increase precisely according to increases in the other-total ratio. Stated simply, the more you

BOX 4.1

Self-Attention and Depression

Self-attention is a fact of life, but recent research suggests that its consequences can be severe. Generally, though not always, self-attention is not pleasant. People typically find that they do not completely match relevant standards, such as their ideal selves or their standards of ideal behavior in specific situations. When this happens, as noted, two responses are to try to escape from self-awareness or to try to behave in a more desirable way. Either of these courses of action reduces self-awareness and its unpleasantness. However, some individuals may consistently focus attention on themselves with the result that they are consistently unhappy. They may continue thinking about and evaluating themselves, finding that they are not all that they might be. They may feel that they don't measure up to relevant standards and they may be continually aware of that. What is the likely consequence of this chronic self-evaluation and sense of falling short? Several studies suggest that the consequence is depression.

A number of findings implicate a high degree of self-attention as a factor in depression. We know, for example, that depressed people have a **negative memory bias** (Blaney, 1986), that is, they typically recall more of the negative things that happen to them than positive things. This tendency to recall the negative can, of course, contribute to depression. What would cause people to have a negative memory bias? One possibility is that it comes from self-attention. When people spend lots of time focusing their attention on themselves, negative personal qualities and events can become salient. In other words, focusing too much attention on yourself can make you depressed! If this is true, one way of reducing the negative memory bias and consequent depression is by distracting people from thinking about themselves. A recent study showed that when they were self-focused, depressed people remembered more negative things that happened to them during a previous two-week period than did nondepressed people. However, when they were paying attention to external objects, depressed people did not show the negative memory bias (Pyszczynski, Hamilton, Herring, and Greenberg, 1989). In other words, it is possible to break the cycle of self-attention leading to negative self-evaluation that in turn leads to depression by getting people to avoid self-attention.

Other research suggests that women tend to have higher levels of self-attention than men, and that these high levels of self-attention may contribute to the well-established finding that women are more frequently depressed than men (Ingram, Cruet, Johnson, and Wisnicki, 1988). Furthermore, very strong arguments have been made that self-attention can lead to depression and a series of steps that culminate in suicide (Baumeister, 1990).

feel that you or your group is outnumbered, the more self-attentive you become and the more you match the majority's standards.

A number of interesting studies demonstrate this effect. For example, in classrooms students are more likely to participate in discussions (matching standards for classroom behavior) as the ratio of teachers (other subgroup) to the teacher-plus-student total increases. As the number of students increases and that ratio decreases, students spend less time participating.

Similarly, reports of lynchings in the South showed that when the lynch mob is large, the atrocity of the lynching, as measured by shooting, burning, dismemberment of the victim, and so on, increases. Engaging in these kinds of behaviors represents an absence of self-regulation, which is what self-awareness theory predicts will occur when self-attention is low. When mob members vastly outnumber victims, the other-total ratio (number of victims divided by number of victims plus mob members) is low and the predicted absence of self-regulation occurs (Mullen, 1986). As we shall see in chapter 13, when the other-total ratio is low and self-regulation diminishes greatly, people are "deindividuated."

Self-awareness theory is like a theory of the superego or conscience in that people who are a majority in a group have a low other-total ratio, are less self-aware, and show less evidence of being regulated by a conscience. Individuals in a large mob provide an excellent example of lack of self-regulation. Fortunately, self-awareness is generally a civilizing state (Wicklund and Frey, 1980).

The Presentation of Self in Everyday Life

Self-awareness often leads us to try to match other people's expectations. Our knowledge that others judge us, just as we judge them, makes us very concerned with presenting ourselves in a favorable light. For Ella Fitzgerald, this was a constant fact of life, but she relished trying to present herself as effectively as possible and winning over every audience. We have learned a great deal about self-presentation from a number of scholars, and what we have learned about self-presentation has in turn unlocked many secrets about the overall nature of interpersonal behavior.

Goffman's Dramaturgical Approach

The sociologist Erving Goffman (1959, 1967) was one of the keenest observers of human interaction in general and of self-presentation in particular. His approach is often referred to as the *dramaturgical approach* because, like Shakespeare, he compared the way we present ourselves with the way people on the stage present themselves. Goffman wrote that when people interact, each person acts out a "line" much like a part in a play. By a line Goffman meant all the verbal and nonverbal expressions that people use to convey their view of a situation, the people they are interacting with, and themselves. An important part of an individual's line is what Goffman called **face,** which he defined as the positive social value one claims about him- or herself when interacting with others. For example, when a woman walks into a party, her line may convey that she thinks this is a good place to have a good time, that the people are

friendly and interesting, and that she is looking forward to the evening. The face she presents is that of one who enjoys a good time and knows how to have one. *Acting out certain lines and claiming a certain face are the heart of self-presentation.*

One important way in which people claim face is through the acting out of what Goffman calls **idealized performance.** When we give an idealized performance, we act as though we support and live up to ideal social values and behavioral standards more than in fact we do. At least publicly, we engage in matching to standards. For example, we may act as though we have more interest in culture and education than we really do by letting people see our copy of *War and Peace* (largely unread though it may be) but keeping our *People* magazine hidden. This idealized performance is part of our line that claims face—that is, positive social value—in the realm of history and literature.

Goffman makes it very clear why people act out lines and present certain faces. One of the realities of social life that we saw in Chapter 2 is that people are constantly forming impressions of each other and making attributions. We need to understand our world, particularly our fellow human beings. In so doing, we quickly realize that just as we are judging others, they are judging us. It then becomes apparent that it is in our interest to control, if we can, other people's impressions of us so that they will treat us as we would like them to. Thus, the basic reason for engaging in self-presentation is to control other people's impressions of us. Trying to control these impressions is referred to as **impression management.** As we shall see, more must be said about the motives behind self-presentation, but the heart of the phenomenon is trying to control what others think of us.

Once an individual has claimed a certain face by acting out a line, how do other people respond? For example, when someone drops hints that he is experienced in dancing and is pretty good at it, what is the reaction from others likely to be? Goffman argues that at least publicly people go along with other people's claims of face, thereby achieving a working consensus or the "veneer of consensus." Recent research suggests that Goffman was right. Just as people lie to some degree in their self-presentations, they lie a little in responding to other people's self-presentations, largely to protect other people's feelings (DePaulo, Kashy, Kirkendol, Wyer, and Epstein, 1996). Thus we would act as though we were impressed by, and interested in, the person's dancing experience.

The agreement may not be genuine but it is carefully maintained by everyone.

Goffman also suggests that others expect us to claim good things about ourselves just as they expect us to openly agree with the good things they claim about themselves. Furthermore, not only do we initially support other people's faces, but we do all we can to help them when subsequent events embarrass or contradict their claims. For example, if a friend who has presented himself as good in biology gets a poor grade on a test, not only will we go along with his excuses but also we are likely to offer our own ("you really didn't have enough time to study properly with all the noise in the dorm the night before the exam"). In fact, if we think our friend did poorly, we will avoid even asking about his grade to prevent embarrassing him. We expect the same treatment from other people. These efforts either to prevent embarrassment or to correct it and to restore face when someone has lost it are referred to as **face work.**

Why are we so often expected to present ourselves positively and to put so much effort into maintaining faces—our own and others'? Goffman thinks that face work and other "interaction rituals," such as the "How-are-you-fine-thanks" exchange, are necessary conditions for social life to work. They allow people to interact smoothly, if somewhat superficially, and to avoid having to worry about hurt feelings or discomfort. Interaction rituals allow us to transact our business with people in a relatively safe and predictable environment. If something is lost in honesty and authenticity, something is gained in security, simplicity, and efficiency. As you might imagine, psychologists and sociologists have argued at length about whether face work is desirable; but there is considerable agreement that it is necessary and even more agreement that it is pervasive.

Audience Pleasing, Self-Construction, and Situated Identities

Goffman's theories have inspired much thinking and research about how and why people engage in self-presentation. One general theory of self-presentation by Baumeister (1982; Baumeister and Hutton, 1987) suggests two major motives. The first is **audience pleasing.** We want to please other people either because we have a generally high need for approval (Crowne and Marlowe, 1964) or because we want

them to behave in certain ways (Arkin, 1980). Thus, in general, we try to conform to others' expectations and preferences. The second important motive in self-presentation is **self-construction** (Baumeister, 1996). Here we have an ideal image of the kind of person we would like to be, and we want to come as close to the ideal in our actual behavior as we can; in many respects, however, we are unsure about how close we really come. Therefore, we act as if we have certain desired traits and then see if others view our behavior as supporting our self-image. When others validate our self-presentation, the process of self-construction has occurred. For example, a young woman may want to see herself as effective in leading a group. In a review session for an exam, she takes the initiative in organizing the discussion. When others go along, the woman has advanced the construction of her identity as a leader.

An important distinction between audience pleasing and self-construction rests on *whose* ideas and preferences determine self-presentation—the audience's or the actor's. Often these preferences can conflict, such as when a student back home from college on vacation doesn't know if he should reveal his new values and tastes—in the hope that they will be accepted—or conform to his parents' expectations.

When we engage in self-construction, we may do so in particular settings. For instance, the young woman who wants to be identified as a leader by her peers may want to be seen as an aspiring musician by her parents and as a witty humorist by her boyfriend. We attempt to get others to accept our view of ourselves in each of these settings, thereby "negotiating" a **situated identity** for each (Alexander and Rudd, 1981). Ella Fitzgerald tried to maintain an identity as an upbeat, outgoing, and confident performer in her professional life and as a somewhat retiring, publicity-avoiding person in her private life. We try to negotiate the most positive and satisfying situated identity we can in each setting that is important to us.

An interesting study of the difficulties of achieving desired identities indicates that professional sports teams on the verge of winning a championship are more likely to "choke" if they have to win at home (Baumeister, 1985; Baumeister and Steinhilber, 1984). Data from seven games played in baseball's World Series and basketball's NBA Finals show that the home team often loses in the final game. The pressure of achieving the desired identity plus the presence and distraction of supportive home-town fans can lead to more fielding errors and missed free throws for the home team. Ironically, home-town support acts to distract players from concentrating on effective performance.

Self-Presentation and the Self-Concept

When Ella Fitzgerald sang joyfully, she appeared to feel joyful. Do our self-presentations often lead to changes in attitude or feeling? Goffman (1959) argued that we are often "taken in by our own act" and hence begin to feel like the person we are portraying. Further, research suggests that self-presentation can cause us to adopt attitudes consistent with the way we have presented ourselves (Baumeister and Tice, 1984). Once we act as though we believe or feel something, we often internalize our behavior and come to genuinely feel the way we act. Just as we internalize the roles we play (recall chapter 3), we internalize many of our self-presentations (Baumeister, 1986).

Power and Ingratiation

Implicit in Goffman's self-presentation theory is the idea that in everyday life, power is important. We want to be able to control other people's impressions of us and ultimately the way they treat us, which is why we engage in various forms of impression management. The idea that power is important in social life is much more explicit in Edward E. Jones's theory of ingratiation and self-presentation, a theory heavily influenced by Goffman.

The Principles of Ingratiation

Jones's theory of ingratiation and strategic self-presentation (Jones, 1964; Jones and Wortman, 1973; Jones and Pittman, 1982) begins by considering the plight of the person in a low-power position. Power is one person's ability to reward or punish, help or hurt another person. The person in the low-power position in a relationship is the one who has less power to reward or punish the other. A factory foreman, for example, may have the power to give a worker a raise or to fire the worker. The worker, on the other hand, has relatively little ability to affect the actions of the foreman and thus has less power. In contrast, a performer like Ella Fitzgerald gained considerable power in negotiating her contracts: she could affect potential em-

ployers' profits by recording with one company or by taking her services elsewhere. From the perspective of the low-power individual, Jones suggests that motivation exists to modify the power relationship.

How can a person in a low-power position modify the relationship and thereby reduce the power differential? The answer: If the low-power person can ingratiate him- or herself with the high-power person and induce that person to like him or her, the power differential can be reduced. What does liking have to do with relative power? Let's consider a student and a professor. Assume that the professor, by virtue of the ability to give grades, has more power than the student, who, whether friendly or unfriendly, has little real impact. If the student can make the professor like him or her, two things will happen. First, the professor will be less likely to punish a student by giving a bad grade, thus reducing the professor's power over the student. Second, the professor will be more affected by a student's friendliness or unfriendliness and will care more about what the student thinks of the professor's teaching, thus increasing the student's ability to reward or punish the professor. In these two ways, the professor's power advantage is reduced—though the professor can still flunk the student if necessary!

On the basis of the above analysis, Jones (1964) predicted that low-power people will try to curry favor or attempt to ingratiate themselves with those in power and make themselves liked. A great deal of research has been conducted on the various ways in which people try to ingratiate themselves. Most of this research recognizes the difficulty of successful **ingratiation** and how those difficulties can be overcome. Some of these difficulties are summarized in the concept of the **ingratiator's dilemma,** which has two aspects. The first is that the less power one person has in a relationship, the more he or she will want to ingratiate. At the same time, the more powerful person will be increasingly alert to possible ingratiation attempts. The less powerful person's attempts to win the approval of the more powerful person may be seen as ingratiating and thus backfire. For example, the manager of a fast-food restaurant may be aware that certain employees act friendly in an effort to influence their chances for promotion. The dilemma for these employees is that the less power they have, the more they want to ingratiate, but the manager's awareness of the ingratiating behavior makes it harder for them to succeed.

The second aspect of the ingratiator's dilemma is that low-power persons, such as employees interacting with a manager or local managers interacting with a regional manager, do not want to view themselves as ingratiating, because ingratiation is considered somewhat demeaning behavior. Ideal behavioral standards dictate that we don't try to get someone to like us for ulterior motives, so we typically give idealized performances, indicating that we concur with that standard. But, as with other idealized performances, we sometimes violate the standard; that is, we ingratiate more than we admit. But the fact remains that people don't like to see themselves as ingratiating, as being a "brownie," and this too is part of the ingratiator's dilemma.

One phenomenon that lessens the ingratiator's dilemma is known as the **autistic conspiracy.** As we have mentioned, the potential ingratiator, the low-power individual, does not want to view her- or himself as such. Furthermore, the target person, the more powerful person toward whom ingratiating behavior is directed, does not want to view the low-power person as an ingratiator. In our example, the manager doesn't want to think that the employees are being nice for ulterior motives. The manager prefers to see the ingratiators' behavior as genuine. If the employees compliment the manager's decision, the manager wants to believe that the decision is really a good one and that the compliments are therefore well deserved. Similarly, if a student agrees with a professor's point in class, the professor wants to believe that he or she was really persuasive and insightful, not that the student was "brown-nosing." In short, both persons, the high-power and the low-power individuals, prefer to look the other way and believe that ingratiation is not taking place. This mutual self-deception about what's really happening is what is meant by autistic conspiracy, a phenomenon that not only lessens the ingratiator's dilemma but also makes it much easier for ingratiation to be successful.

Another way people try to cope with the ingratiator's dilemma is by being subtle. While there are a variety of ingratiation tactics, the general subtlety principle applies to all of them. Since people want their behavior to be believed, ingratiation cannot be so blatant that it arouses suspicions of ulterior motives. We will discuss three behaviors that can be ingratiation tactics, all of which require subtlety.

Ingratiation Tactics

One ingratiation tactic is conformity to the opinions and values of the high-power person. You can easily imagine a student nodding his head and saying yes when the professor makes a point. You have probably also heard of presidential aides doing the same thing when they talk to the chief executive. Several studies of conformity by Jones and his colleagues indicate how frequently and subtly people conform when they have an opportunity to agree or disagree with the opinions of a high-powered person who can control their outcomes. These studies show that lower power leads to both more conformity and more subtlety—just as the ingratiator's dilemma would lead us to predict.

In one study, naval ROTC freshmen conformed a good deal to the opinions expressed by high-status ROTC seniors. However, they seemed to "pick their spots"; that is, they would conform on issues that concerned the ROTC program, but maintained independence on such issues as music and the movies, which had nothing to do with ROTC. In this way the freshmen showed that they could think for themselves without challenging the authority of their senior officers (Jones, Gergen, and Jones, 1964). In another study, low-power subjects who conformed indicated that they were extremely confident about their opinions, as if to show that the views they were mirroring were their own. When they disagreed, they qualified what they said by indicating that they were not very confident about their opinions (Jones and Jones, 1964). In still another study, subjects who were low in power showed a tendency to conform more on the target person's basic values than on the person's specific opinions (Davis and Florquist, 1965). In all cases, people tried to indicate that their conformity was not total and that they really meant it when they agreed.

Sometimes conformity is nonverbal. In one study, women subjects who came for a job interview were given information about the opinions of the male interviewer. Some were told that the interviewer valued the traditional emotional and deferential female, while others were told that the interviewer preferred more liberated women. When the subjects came to the interview, they actually dressed and behaved differently in addition to saying the things they thought the interviewer wanted to hear depending on what they had been told about the interviewer. When the interviewer allegedly preferred traditional women, the subjects wore more makeup and a lot of feminine jewelry; they also behaved more passively in general. The women who were interviewed by the man who allegedly preferred liberated women talked more and made more eye contact with the interviewer and generally acted more assertively (Von Baeyer, Sherk, and Zanna,

1981). In short, ingratiating conformity can be both verbal and nonverbal, and it is usually highly subtle.

Another ingratiation tactic is flattery, or other enhancement. If we say nice things to other people, indicating that we like or admire them, there is a good chance that they will like us in return. Subtlety is important here as well. Our flattery, or building up, of the other person must be perceived as sincere and credible. For example, research indicates that we like people who like us—especially if they appear discerning and discriminating in their judgments. People who are *always* positive aren't liked as much; their enhancing comments about us aren't perceived as especially significant (Mettee and Aronson, 1974). Other research shows that it is important that the person who says nice things about us doesn't seem to have anything to gain. In general, the more people like us, the more we like them, but this isn't true if the other person has an ulterior motive and is obviously ingratiating (Jones and Wortman, 1973).

There are a number of interesting ways to flatter others. In his famous book *How to Win Friends and Influence People,* Dale Carnegie (1936) discussed ways of showing that others are significant to you. One way is simply to call them by name. Army officers sometimes find that soldiers generally respond more favorably when they are called by name. As Carnegie said, our names are the "sweetest sound" we can hear.

We noted earlier that the behavior of "self-construction" (Baumeister and Hutton, 1987) often occurs around personal characteristics that we value highly but are unsure that we possess. For example, a male who values being athletic will see if he can impress others in a game of volleyball. Gaining others' approval results in self-construction. It's not surprising that flattery often works best when we flatter other people in areas in which they are unsure of themselves (Schlenker, 1980). Complimenting a statistics professor on her facility with mathematical expressions won't have much impact; she already knows she's good with numbers. But telling her that you like her witty examples, which she is very insecure about, should lead her to appreciate your discerning appraisal.

Ella Fitzgerald's remarkable career shows that a third form of ingratiation is often successful—simply presenting oneself as positively as possible. Often this means using self-enhancement, revealing positive information about ourselves. When people tell little white lies in self-presentation, it is often to present themselves as favorably as they can (DePaulo, Kashy, Kirkendal, Wyer, and Epstein, 1996). Research shows, however, that people often present themselves very positively, or sometimes modestly, depending on what they consider appropriate to the occasion or audience (Gergen and Taylor, 1969). For example, people habitually present themselves much more modestly to friends than to strangers and have difficulty being modest with strangers and self-enhancing with friends (Tice, Butler, Muraven, and Stillwell, 1995). There's a time and place for both positive and modest self-presentations. In short, self-presentation, in the direction of either modesty or self-enhancement, is a third ingratiation tactic, along with conformity and flattery.

Do these ingratiation tactics work? A recent review of several decades of research on ingratiation suggests that they do. One study found that flattery seemed to be a good way for ingratiators to get targets to like them (Gordon, 1996). Other methods worked but less reliably. Also, ingratiation seemed to be more likely to work with women, who were more likely than men to take ingratiating behavior at face value; men were more skeptical than women (Gordon, 1996). These are useful generalizations to some extent, but the main conclusion is that ingratiation is a highly complex form of social interaction that works sometimes.

Other Self-Presentation Tactics

Thus far, we have considered self-presentation tactics designed for ingratiation—making other people like us. Making others like us gives us more power in our relationships. However, several other important self-presentation strategies (Jones and Pittman, 1982) are used to try to control the way other people view and treat us. While ingratiation aims at getting people to like us, the other strategies are designed to elicit somewhat different perceptions in others and to induce them to act accordingly. The four we will consider— intimidation, self-promotion, exemplification, and supplication—are used to induce others to fear us, respect our abilities, respect our morals, and feel sorry for us, respectively.

In the case of **intimidation,** a person tries to influence someone else's behavior through fear. The intimidator attempts to appear powerful and willing to use power and often uses threats of punishment. Jones and Pittman give street robbers or muggers as examples of intimidators who use threats and fear to gain compliance; for example, to force their victims to hand over money. Intimidation is frequently seen in sports. During the introductions and instructions before a boxing match, the fighters glare at each other as menacingly as possible, each trying to strike fear in the other. In football games, the players frequently shout in threatening ways at each other, especially at quarterbacks who have just been tackled. One former football player, Jack Tatum of the Oakland Raiders, wrote a book called *They Call Me Assassin* to discuss the intimidating reputation he had while playing in the NFL, a reputation he carefully cultivated to frighten his opponents and disrupt their play. The word *intimidation* is now used frequently to describe a tactic for dominating other players in hockey and basketball as well as in football.

Intimidation can also be used in other domains. When Lyndon Johnson was president of the United States, he often intimidated members of Congress and his aides to gain their compliance. Jones and Pittman note that self-presentation strategies can be combined, and Johnson provides a good example of such mixing. He often mixed intimidation with sweet cajolery and ingratiation. He wanted to be liked as well as feared, so he presented himself as both likable and formidable.

The person who uses **self-promotion** wants to be respected more than liked. Specifically, self-promoters want to be respected for their intelligence and competence. To enhance the credibility of claims that they make about their abilities, self-promoters may acknowledge certain of their minor flaws or shortcomings (Baumeister and Jones, 1978). In so doing, they acknowledge that they have both strengths and weaknesses but are generally confident about their competencies. Admitting a flaw in fact can enhance claims of competence.

Related to the idea of enhancing the credibility of competence claims by admitting weaknesses is the notion of enhancement (Schlenker, 1980). When we have done something competently, we may try to enhance the amount of ability that went into our successful performance by emphasizing how difficult it was (Quat-

trone and Jones, 1978). Self-promoters may try to take advantage of the enhancement phenomenon by suggesting, for example, that their performance would have been more effective had they not been ill when they gave it. In some ways, Ella Fitzgerald was the opposite of a self-promoter. She made very difficult performances look and sound easy, and she liked to present a casual air. In fact, she impressed people, probably unintentionally, by seeming to have so much ability that she could sing beautifully without much effort.

Another method of self-promotion relies on the principle of association (Cialdini, 1993; Schlenker, 1980): we present ourselves as part of, or connected to, what is successful or competent. One form of self-promotion by association is "basking in reflected glory" (Cialdini, 1993), which is similar to the idea of

vicarious beneffectance discussed in chapter 3. One way of basking in reflected glory is to wear college sweatshirts after the school's football team has won (Cialdini, Borden, Thorne, Walker, Freman, and Sloan, 1976). Another is for the president of the United States to telephone Olympic athletes who have won a gold medal or space shuttle astronauts after they have safely landed to enjoy being associated with the medal winner or the astronauts' successful flight. By getting as close as they can to the winning team or the successful astronauts, students and presidents bask in and share the glory.

Another picture of self-promotion by association comes from a study of students who had an opportunity to link themselves to another person by revealing that they had the same birth date (Cialdini and De Nicholas, 1989). Depending both on how the subjects performed on a test themselves and how the other person, Douglas, performed on the test, subjects either hid or revealed the fact that Douglas had the same birthday. By linking themselves to Douglas or denying the link, subjects attempted to create a favorable impression.

A third self-presentation strategy is **exemplification.** Here individuals try to present themselves as being moral and worthy and as having integrity. The person who works late at the office or gives a great deal to charity is being exemplary in ways that might influence other people to behave in the same manner. Such individuals provide a clear and worthy model for others to follow. Like other self-presentation strategies, exemplification is used to influence both other people's impressions and their behavior.

A final self-presentation strategy, which can be viewed almost as a last resort, is one that Jones and Pittman term **supplication.** In this case, people play on others' sympathies by acting weak and helpless. The goal of the supplicator, quite simply, is to get help. Children who want to stay home from school may act ill or otherwise helpless to get their parents to relent and allow them to stay home. Supplication works best when people convey the fact that their helpless or weak position is not their fault. For example, college students faced with accumulating paper deadlines may ask for help from professors or deans by pleading the overwhelming pressures of assignments that are beyond their control. In short, we often present ourselves as being likable. But we also try to appear threatening, competent, morally exemplary, and needy, all of which can affect people's behavior as effectively as ingratiation.

The Psychology of Self-Handicapping

Others often judge us by the way we perform. For this reason, people use the self-promotion strategy of conveying as much information as possible about their competence. Of course, what people claim about their abilities eventually must be put to the test. People often do things that put obstacles in the way of effective performances. For example, actors may skip key rehearsals or drink too much on opening night. And college students frequently stay up all night before exams, sometimes studying but often partying. Why would people put obstacles in the way of successful performance? Why would they engage in behavior that has come to be known as **self-handicapping**?

Self-handicapping can easily be seen as a self-presentational strategy that makes clever use of some of the basic principles of attribution. It is premised on the idea that putting obstacles in our own way provides an excuse for failure (Jones and Berglas, 1978). If we fail in the face of obstacles, an attribution of low ability can be discounted. The failure can be attributed to the obstacles; they provide the excuse (Rhodewalt and Hill, 1995). For example, the student who fails a test after partying can blame the poor grade on being unprepared, not on low ability. Research on self-handicapping suggests that drinking and underachieving are specific strategies that people use to give themselves and others excuses for failure. Thus, having a problem with alcohol and having trouble working to capacity are personal problems that can explain poor performance (Jones and Berglas, 1978).

Self-handicapping may have another beneficial effect. In a study of self-handicapping, people who handicapped themselves by not practicing in a game of pinball actually enjoyed the game more. When people self-handicap, they remove the pressure they feel to do well in an activity and thus can enjoy it more (Deppe and Harakiewicz, 1996). They allow themselves some "breathing room" in exploring the activity. Thus, not practicing hard to prepare for a tennis game may actually let people enjoy the tennis more and focus less on winning.

Studies of self-handicapping have helped to make us aware of the circumstances in which it is most likely to be used. One such circumstance is when people do not have confidence in their abilities; they are therefore likely to be worried about failure and are more apt to engage in excuse-generating self-handicapping. In a study designed to test this hypothesis, subjects participated in an experiment described as a study of the effects of two drugs on performance. One of the drugs was expected to lower performance, and the other was expected to raise it. Before taking the drugs, one group of subjects was given an intelligence test. For some, the test was easy, and they were told that they did well. Other subjects were given insoluble problems, but they also were told that they had done well. The first group felt that they had performed well, were told that they had, and felt confident about future success. The second group did well but didn't know why. They were *not* confident about doing well in the future as they did not feel that they had been in control of the situation.

After receiving the feedback, subjects had the option of taking one of the two drugs before another form of the same intelligence test was administered. As the researchers predicted, those subjects who did not feel they had been in control of the situation but were told that they had answered the insoluble questions correctly chose the drug that lowered performance; that is, they handicapped themselves. Those who were confident tried to do even better on the second part of the test; they took the performance-enhancing drug (Berglas and Jones, 1978). These findings suggest that people are likely to handicap themselves when they are unsure of their abilities because then at least they can avoid being blamed for failure should it occur.

Self-handicapping takes many forms. One of the most interesting is presenting oneself as ill or actually feeling ill (Smith, Snyder, and Perkins, 1983). Similarly, people can present themselves as handicapped by claiming low effort, anxiety, or the effects of medication. However, people do run the risk of having others evaluate their performances more negatively if they claim low effort (Rhodewalt, Sanbonmatsu, Tschanz, Feick, and Waller, 1995). One study showed that people will use—and possibly abuse—alcohol to handicap themselves. Students at Vanderbilt University, in Nashville, were told that they would be taking part in a study of the effects of self-determined quantities of alcohol on intellectual performance. Some students were given insoluble problems and either told or not told that they had done well. Subjects who were told that they had done well on the insoluble problems drank more alcohol before taking a second test than subjects who were not told that they had done well. Thus, in a situation where people succeeded but did not have confidence about future success, people used drinking as a means of self-handicapping (Tucker, Vucinish, and Sobell, 1981).

Self-handicapping strategies are not only ways of managing impressions that others form of you. They also provide solutions for the attributions that you make about yourself. Self-handicappers never have to face their own negative attributions about themselves. By self-handicapping, they can always discount the possibility that their abilities are too limited (Smith, Snyder, and Handelsman, 1982). Even though self-

handicapping can be done for oneself as well as for others, research suggests that it is primarily a self-presentational tactic (Baumeister and Tice, 1985; Baumeister and Hutton, 1987). Self-handicapping is particularly likely to be used when other people expect future success from you on the basis of your past success, and it is less likely to occur when people can't observe your self-handicapping actions (Kolditz and Arkin, 1982). It is also most likely to occur when people feel that their performances are important and they have no other obvious or salient excuse for not performing well (Sheppard and Arkin, 1989).

Self-Monitoring

People differ in the way they present themselves. We are not all alike. One of the most interesting and important differences between people that is related to self-presentation is the extent to which people engage in self-monitoring (Snyder, 1974, 1979, 1987). **Self-monitoring** is adjusting one's behavior to situational norms or to the expectations of others. If you are self-monitoring, you control both your verbal and nonverbal self-presentation so that you can respond to those expectations. High self-monitoring individuals are concerned about and aware of the way others react to them, but they are more concerned about actively and effectively changing their behavior to adjust to others' reactions and expectations.

Snyder and Gangestad (1986) developed a scale to measure the extent to which people self-monitor. It contains such items as "I may deceive people by being friendly when I really dislike them," "I'm not always the person I appear to be," and "I would not change my opinions (or the way I do things) in order to please someone or win his favor." Other items on the self-monitoring scale are shown in figure 4.1. Although recent research suggests that there are not just high and low self-monitors—people may be high, low, or anywhere in the middle (Miller and Thayer, 1989)—it is useful to identify some characteristics of both high and low self-monitors.

High self-monitors have been shown to be extroverted, good actors, and willing to change their behavior to suit others (Briggs and Cheek, 1988; Briggs, Cheek, and Buss, 1980). They will initiate drinking alcohol if they perceive that as effective in managing other people's impressions (Sharp and Getz, 1996). High self-monitors have been described as having a "pragmatic self" (Snyder, 1987). They have also been shown to (1)

FIGURE 4.1   **SAMPLE ITEMS MEASURING SELF-MONITORING**

Answer the following items *true* or *false*.

1. I find it hard to imitate the behavior of other people.

2. In a group of people, I am rarely the center of attention.

3. I may deceive people by being friendly when I really dislike them.

4. I can argue only for ideas that I already believe.

5. I can make impromptu speeches even on topics about which I have almost no information.

6. I am not always the person I appear to be.

7. In different situations and with different people, I often act like very different persons.

Source: Adapted from Snyder (1974)

---

have a concern for the appropriateness of behavior; (2) give careful attention to others for cues as to what is appropriate; (3) be skillful in presenting many different behaviors in different situations; and (4) be able to change the manner of self-presentation (Gabrenya and Arkin, 1980). In short, high self-monitors are interested in adapting to the situation, are skillful in sensing others' wishes and expectations, and are able to modify their behavior to meet others' expectations.

Because they perceive themselves as successful in impressing other people, high self-monitors tend to have higher self-esteem (Sharp and Getz, 1996). They are also socially skilled in the way they test hypotheses about other people's personalities. They ask questions that are likely to generate information that will confirm their hypotheses (Dardenne and Leyens, 1995). One interesting example of adapting behavior to the situation is shown in a study in which subjects either did or did not anticipate future interaction with a fellow subject. High self-monitors were more cooperative when they anticipated future interaction than when they did not. Low self-monitors were equally cooperative whether they anticipated future interaction or not (Danheiser and Graziano, 1982).

Low self-monitors are marked by consistency in behavior across situations. They have a clearer self-image and are truer to that self-image than high self-monitors. They are referred to as having a "principled self" rather than the "pragmatic self" of the high self-monitor (Snyder, 1987). They are more likely to enter situations that are consistent with their attitudes, especially if they attach importance to low self-monitoring (Mellema and Bassili, 1995; Snyder and Gangestad, 1982). One reason that their behavior is more consis-

tent with their attitudes is that they can access their attitudes from memory more quickly than high self-monitors (Kardes, Sanbonmatsu, Voss, and Fazio, 1986). Values and principles seem more important to low self-monitors than to high self-monitors and they come to mind faster. In one study, for example, low self-monitors supported a woman suing a university for sex discrimination to a degree that was predictable from their attitudes about affirmative action. The support of high self-monitors, on the other hand, was not consistent with their affirmative action attitudes (Snyder and Swann, 1976). High self-monitors show their adaptability and flexibility by acting more in accordance with their attitudes when the importance of being consistent is made salient (Snyder and Kendzierski, 1982). That is, they can demonstrate the same consistency of low self-monitors if that's what's expected.

Some interesting differences exist between the ways high and low self-monitors process social information. High self-monitors remember more information about other people and make more confident and extreme inferences about them (Berscheid, Graziano, Manson, and Dermer, 1976). The ability to remember other people's actions better has been associated with a capacity on the part of high self-monitors to make more accurate eyewitness identifications (Hosch and Platz, 1984). While this is generally true, some research suggests that leading questions by a lawyer can interfere with the accuracy of the memories of high self-monitors more than with those of low self-monitors (Lassiter, Stone, and Weigold, 1987). Because they are more sensitive to the lawyer's expectations and beliefs, high self-monitors may be more misled by false information that the lawyer suggests.

Another area of difference between high and low self-monitors lies in the area of intimate and romantic relationships. As we will see in chapter 8, high self-monitors put more emphasis on physical attractiveness than on personal qualities when they choose romantic partners (Snyder, 1987). Not surprisingly, then, high self-monitors believe compatibility between a man and a woman is determined more by similarity in physical attractiveness than by similarity in personality traits. Low self-monitoring individuals believe the opposite. They predict greater compatibility for couples matched on personality and interests than for those matched on physical attractiveness (Glick, DeMorest, and Hotze, 1988).

Finally, a field study of people in organizations shows that high self-monitoring individuals function better than low self-monitors in what are known as boundary-spanning positions (Caldwell and O'Reilly, 1982; Snyder, 1987. *Boundary spanning* means working at the intersection between organizations or with people in several different organizations outside one's own. Such behavior requires flexibility and being open to other people's desires and expectations. This is where the high self-monitor excels.

A century ago William James (1890) wrote about the many different social selves an individual shows to different audiences: "Many a youth who is demure enough before his parents and teachers swears and swaggers like a pirate among his 'tough' friends. We do not show ourselves to our children as to our club companions, to our customers as to the laborers we employ, to our own masters and employers as to our intimate friends" (p. 282). The kind of variability in behavior that James suggests is more often found in some individuals than in others. The high self-monitor has the ability and inclination to behave differently with different people in different situations. Low self-monitors are on a straighter track: they know who they are and they act that way without being unduly influenced by the social situation.

Interpersonal Communication in Relationships

Self-presentation and self-monitoring seem to be a large part of a great deal of social behavior. Certainly,

Ella Fitzgerald presented herself in a way that created a public "persona" that was important in winning over audiences around the world. But in much of our dealing with other people we want to go beyond self-presentation and communicate more fully and openly in the context of a relationship. In this section we discuss some basic principles of communication in relationships, how different people behave and coordinate in relationships, and how we use nonverbal communication and self-disclosure to communicate our feelings and our views of relationships.

Principles of Communication

Some basic principles of communication have been outlined in *The Pragmatics of Human Communication* by Watzlawick, Beavin, and Jackson (1967). A first principle is that every behavior in a relationship is a communication and that it is impossible to *not* communicate. A second principle is that all communications carry messages at two levels, the *content* level and the *relationship* level. Communication at the content level is about tasks that people are working on, situations that they are facing together, or problems they are trying to solve. It concerns matters outside the relationship itself, such as whether it's a good idea to go to the library, whether it is likely to rain, or how to get the car fixed. Communication at the relationship level is about how one person views himself or herself in relation to the other person.

Communication at the content level is typically done verbally, that is, with words. Communication at the relationship level is typically done nonverbally through tone of voice, gestures, facial expressions, and general demeanor. If content communication is the words, relationship communication is the music. We often convey how we view our relationship with another person by the way we say things rather than what we say. In many cases it isn't easy to talk about our feelings so they are communicated through nonverbal channels. In fact, our view of our relationship with another person is usually conveyed by our overall manner or *interpersonal style*. Let us consider the varieties of interpersonal styles and what each one conveys about our view of a relationship.

Varieties of Interpersonal Behavior and Styles

Goffman (1955) noted that during self-presentation an individual acts out a line, a total pattern of verbal and

nonverbal expression that conveys his or her definition of the situation, other people in the situation, and
him- or herself. It might seem that there is an endless
set of lines that different people could enact and that
the varieties of interpersonal behavior would be infinite. Certainly, if you imagine how different people
are, you are impressed with the great variety in human
behavior. However, psychologists who have studied
the varieties and classifications of interpersonal behavior have found that they fall into a surprisingly
small number of categories (Bales, 1958; Carson,
1969; Leary, 1957).

Leary's research showed that if the correlations
between diverse sets of ratings of interpersonal style
are subjected to factor analysis (a statistical technique for determining the basic dimensions that describe the ratings), the basic dimensions number only
two. One is a positive versus negative or friendly
versus hostile dimension and the other a dominant
versus submissive dimension. That is, even though
people can be rated on numerous scales, many of the
ratings are correlated with each other. There seem to
be only two basic sets of correlations, one indicating
that behavior is classified according to how friendly
or hostile it is and the other indicating that it is classified according to how dominant or submissive it is.
From these findings, Leary developed the **circumplex,** the depiction of the varieties of interpersonal
behavior shown in figure 4.2. Each variety differs
from others in terms of how friendly it is—anywhere
from very friendly to very hostile—and how dominant or submissive it is—from highly dominant
through partly dominant and from partly submissive
to highly submissive.

Subsequent research has supported Leary's representation of interpersonal behaviors in three important
ways. First, research shows that Leary's dimensions
really do characterize interpersonal behavior. Scales
have been developed to measure eight of the major
classes of behavior depicted in the circumplex; studies
have been done to show that there are two dimensions
of interpersonal behaviors; and still other research
shows that actual interpersonal behavior does in fact
vary from one individual to another along the dimensions of dominance and friendliness (Gifford and
O'Connor, 1987; McCrae and Costa, 1989; Wagner,
Kiesler, and Schmidt, 1995; Wiggins, 1979).

Second, research shows that people are highly
consistent in their friendliness from one situation to
another but somewhat less consistent in their domi-

nance (Hoyt, 1994). When individuals interact with
people with whom they are familiar, they are consistent in their dominance. If you are a dominant person,
you are likely to be that way consistently with friends,
family, teammates, or other people you are well acquainted with. However, you are not so likely to be
consistently dominant when you interact with
strangers or when you are in business rather than informal situations (Moskowitz, 1988, 1994). People's
interaction in romantic relationships is also often quite
distinct (Moskowitz, 1994). We may depart from usual
modes of interpersonal behavior when we are with those
with whom we are intimate. Interpersonal behaviors
may show high degrees of consistency because they reflect personality traits as well as the external situation.
Friendliness is quite closely linked to the fundamental
personality traits of extraversion and agreeableness, and
dominance is closely related to a combination of dis-
agreeableness and extraversion (McCrae, Zonderman,
Costa, Bond, and Paunonen, 1996).

Third, research shows that each kind of interpersonal behavior provokes a complementary kind, just
as Leary predicted (and as figure 4.2 shows). Leary
proposed that friendly behavior would provoke or invite complementary friendly behavior in return and
that unfriendly behavior would elicit complementary
unfriendliness. That is, friendliness or unfriendliness
would invite similar behavior from others. He also
suggested that dominance and submissiveness invite
their opposites. Dominant behavior provokes complementary submissiveness while submissiveness, in
turn, invites dominance. Research supports this part of
Leary's theory as well (Strong, Hills, Kilmartin, De-
Vries, Lanier, Nelson, Strickland, and Meyer, 1988).
However, friendly behavior shows more complementarity than does unfriendly behavior (Tracey, 1994).
We do not reciprocate unfriendly behavior as reliably
as we reciprocate friendly behavior.

Since people tend to behave consistently within
and to some extent across situations, we can talk about
interpersonal styles in terms of whether people's characteristic interpersonal behaviors are of the friendly
versus unfriendly variety and of the dominant versus
submissive variety.

As suggested earlier, interpersonal behavior and
styles are closely related to relationships. In relationships a person acts out a line that is—both verbally
and nonverbally—to some degree friendly or hostile
and to some degree dominant or submissive. In this
way people convey what they think of themselves and

FIGURE 4.2   LEARY INTERPERSONAL BEHAVIOR CLASSIFICATION SYSTEM

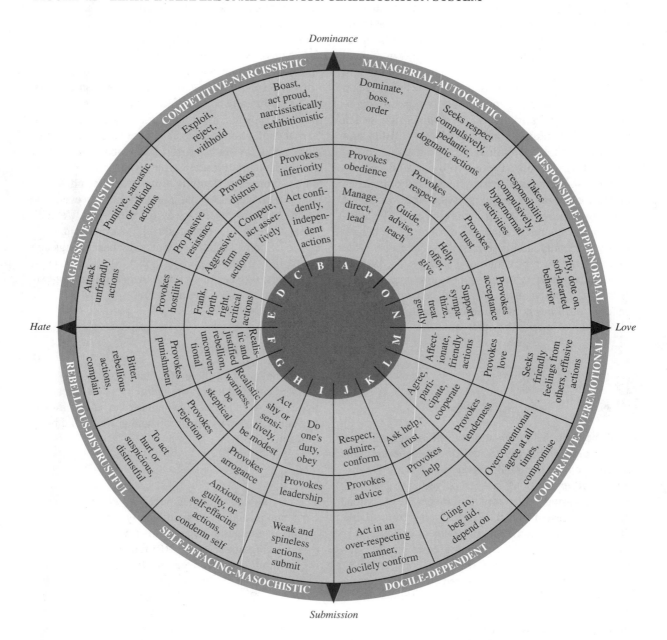

Classification of interpersonal behavior into sixteen mechanisms or reflexes. Each of the sixteen interpersonal variables is illustrated by sample behaviors. The inner circle presents adaptive reflexes; for the variable *A*, for example, *manage.* The center ring indicates the type of behavior that this interpersonal reflex tends to "pull" from the other one. Thus we see that the person who uses the reflex *A* tends to provoke others to *obedience,* and so on. These findings involve two-way interpersonal phenomena (what the subject does and what the "other" does back) and are therefore less reliable than the other interpersonal codes presented in this figure. The next circle illustrates extreme or rigid reflexes; for example, *dominates.* The perimeter of the circle is divided into eight general categories employed in *interpersonal diagnosis.* Each category has a moderate (adaptive) and an extreme (pathological) intensity, such as *managerial-autocratic.*

Source: Adapted from Leary (1957)

how they feel about their relationships with others. For example, by acting friendly, we indicate that we see a relationship as a friendly one. By acting submissive, we indicate that we see the relationship as one of unequal status in which the other person is dominant. When we behave in these ways we invite the other to complement our behavior. In this way we can agree on how the relationship stands on the two basic dimensions of relationships, the *solidarity* dimension, which runs from friendliness and warmth to hostility and coldness, and *status,* which runs from equal to unequal (Brown, 1965). These two dimensions are essentially the same as the friendliness and dominance dimensions of interpersonal behavior. Thus, when one person in a relationship behaves in a friendly-dominant way and the other complements that behavior with friendly submissive behavior, the two agree that the relationship is high on solidarity but marked by unequal status, with the first person having higher rank. The quality of interpersonal behavior that we enact in our lines conveys how we see the quality of our relationship with the other person.

Nonverbal Communication

In his book on the presentation of self in everyday life, Erving Goffman (1959) noted that self-presentation involves both verbal and nonverbal behavior. He distinguished expression "given," or verbal expression, from expression "given off," or nonverbal expression, and he suggested that the latter is less controllable than the former. Nonverbal behavior or expression is especially powerful in conveying emotion, and because it is less controllable, it conveys our true feelings about relationships even when we wish we could hide them. Of course, people vary in the extent to which they express their feelings and in how much they can control them (Kring, Smith, and Neale, 1994). Actors are an interesting case because they work hard to control their nonverbal expression so as to convey feelings that are ordinarily expressed uncontrollably. For example, in the movie *Sophie's Choice,* Meryl Streep, who plays Sophie, is ordered by an officer at a Nazi concentration camp to choose which of her two children will be sent to immediate death and which will survive. The horror of the situation and the emotional wrenching it causes are por-

trayed with genius. Meryl Streep must control her nonverbal expressions to make it look as though Sophie's feelings are spilling out despite her attempts to contain them. It's a stunning performance.

Nonverbal behavior communicates a great deal of information about feelings, moods, and attitudes. Information about these internal states comes from voice quality, eye contact, facial expressions, gestures, body movements, and touching (Brown, 1986). Nonverbal expression is often called the language of emotion, and many studies report that verbal behavior, by comparison, contributes relatively little to our inferences about a person's feelings (Archer and Aliert, 1977). Brown (1986) has pointed out, however, that words certainly can convey a lot of what we feel. When we hear Ella Fitzgerald sing, the words and the music combine seamlessly to convey her feelings and the feelings of the composer. In fact, Ella's genius was to take the words and combine them with the nonverbal expression that gave them life.

Some Elements of Nonverbal Communication

As we have noted, there are many nonverbal behaviors that communicate. Among the most significant of these behaviors are gaze (which is often referred to as eye contact), facial expression, and gestures and body movements.

The Effects of Gaze

The way we look at a person says a great deal about our feelings, and it can significantly affect the quality of social interaction. People in love spend a lot of time looking at each other (Rubin, 1970), and looking at another person generally conveys positive feelings and leads to positive reactions (Imada and Hakel, 1977). In addition, gaze is associated with status. Lower-status people tend to gaze more at upper-status people (Exline, Ellyson, and Long, 1975). One important exception here is staring, or **visual dominance behavior.** Staring or looking at someone while speaking is assertive, dominating behavior. It can be an effective aspect of leadership behavior (Exline, Ellyson, and Long, 1975). But staring can also generate uncomfortable feelings and undermine attempts to be persuasive (Carli, LeFleur, and Loeber, 1995; Strom and Buck, 1979). In short, looking into someone's eyes can convey extremely

Rep. (D) Xavier Becerra (right) speaks to his campaign organizer. Based on their nonverbal behavior, what do you think they are communicating emotionally to one another?

warm feelings, but staring also conveys feelings of dominance. Thus, a high degree of eye contact can intensify any feeling, positive or negative (Ellsworth and Carlsmith, 1968).

Facial Expressions

Scientists have been studying facial expressions for more than a century. In 1873, Charles Darwin argued, in *The Expression of the Emotions in Man and Animals,* that particular facial expressions may convey the same emotions in all human societies and in animals as well as people. Subsequent research provides support for the idea that the same facial expressions are distinguished across cultures and that people in one culture can identify the videotaped emotions of a person in a culture with which they

have had no visual contact (Ekman, Friesen, and Ellsworth, 1982).

Some emotions are particularly clearly expressed in the human face. One is pain. In one study, a woman received a high level of shock and experienced a great deal of pain, which she successfully tolerated. The woman fooled herself but not observers about how much pain she felt. Actions such as brow lowering, narrowing of the opening of the eyes, and blinking clearly revealed pain the woman reported not feeling (Patrick, Craig, and Prkachin, 1986). Another emotion clearly identifiable by facial expression is anger. Human beings seem to be very sensitive to anger in other people's faces, and hostile, threatening faces are much more likely to "pop out" of crowds than happy, benign faces (Hansen and Hansen, 1988). We are extremely alert to signs of threat, and we respond quickly to anger in people's faces.

Gestures and Body Movements

Gestures and body movements are key in communicating how we define our relationship with other people. They express not only how positive we feel about someone else but also how much relative power or status we feel we have in the relationship. People who like each other lean forward, face each other directly, and assume a relaxed position. Dislike is conveyed by leaning away, looking away, and visible tenseness. High status or dominance is conveyed by relaxing and leaning back; low status is shown by physical rigidity—arms drawn in, feet together, and standing or sitting straight, more or less as if at attention (Mehrabian, 1972).

Deception and Detection

Earlier we noted that self-presentation and ingratiation can be somewhat demeaning. Ingratiation, for example, may involve flattering someone when you don't mean it or pretending to agree with someone's opinions. Goffman (1959) recognized the exaggerated or downright deceitful side of self-presentation and suggested that people constantly try to check up on others' self-presentations by observing whether the less controllable aspects of self-presentation, the nonverbal, are congruent with what is being said. A good deal of research has been done on the nonverbal aspects of deception and its detection (Zuckerman, DePaulo, and Rosenthal, 1981).

Central to this research are studies that deal with nonverbal sensitivity (Hall, 1984; Rosenthal and Benowitz, 1985). When no deception is taking place, people looking at videotaped nonverbal behavior, with voice quality but not actual words preserved, make the most accurate judgments about other people's emotions when they pay attention to those aspects or *channels* of nonverbal behavior that are the most controllable. The most controllable nonverbal channel is facial expression, which is followed by body movement; the least controllable is voice quality. Words—that is, verbal expressions—are the most controllable channel and, if added to the videotapes, convey the most information, as long as they are congruent or consistent with the nonverbal behaviors and the nonverbal behaviors are congruent with each other (Blanck and Rosenthal, 1982).

The nonverbal behaviors that are the least controllable, voice quality and body movement, have the most "leakage"; that is, they reveal or leak the individual's real feelings, feelings that he or she may be trying to conceal. Therefore, these are the behaviors that are important to note in attempting to detect deception. One can construct a controllability-leakage continuum with controllable behaviors on one end and uncontrollable leaky behaviors on the other (Brown, 1986; Ekman and Friesen, 1969; see figure 4.3). When the various verbal and nonverbal channels of expression are congruent, as noted, the controllable behaviors generally convey the most precise information. Thus, when we are being truthful, words followed by facial expression say the most about our feelings. However, when one person is deceiving another, incongruent messages are likely to be coming through the other channels. This incongruity can alert the target to the deception. Or the person toward whom deception is aimed may be alerted by specific cues associated with deception, such as slow speech, speech slips, and avoidance of eye contact (Zuckerman, DePaulo, and Rosenthal, 1981).

When deception is occurring, it is the leakier rather than the more controllable nonverbal channels that are apt to be most informative, and those are the channels to which people look when they try to detect the deceiver's real thoughts or feelings. Parents can often tell, for example, if their child is lying about a mess in the kitchen by paying attention to voice quality and body movement, as those chan-

---

FIGURE 4.3   **THE CONTROLLABILITY-LEAKAGE CONTINUUM**

Controllable channels of communication   Leaky channels of communication

Verbal expression, words	Facial expression	Body movement	Voice quality

Note: The communication channels at the left of the continuum are relatively controllable. The ones at the right are relatively leaky.
Source: Adapted from Brown (1986)

BOX 4.2

Situational Influences on Nonverbal Communication

Although considerable research suggests that nonverbal behaviors are universal and largely controlled by biology, and other research shows that culture also has a strong impact, recently psychologists have begun to study how the immediate social situation affects nonverbal behavior. For example, new research has revealed a distinctive nonverbal display of embarrassment comprised of a unique set of gaze shifts, smiles, smile controls, head movements, and face touches. It has been shown that this display has a clear social function, which is to indicate appeasement to people in higher-status groups. In the United States it is a particularly clear display among women and blacks, who have had a long history of having to show appeasement to men and whites through expressions of embarrassment (Keltner, 1995).

The importance of status is also shown in a study of nonverbal accommodation in the voices of talk-show hosts and their guests. Analyses of low-frequency nonverbal signals in computerized voice spectra show that both host and guest adjust their speech patterns to each other, with the lower-status person accommodating his or her voice signal to that of the higher-status person (Gregory and Webster, 1996). Listen carefully when two people of unequal status talk to each other. You should notice that the speech of the lower-status person will begin to sound something like the speech of the higher-status person.

Finally, there are several important recent studies on the expression and perception of emotions. One new theory proposes that the intensity of facial expressions is better determined by the social situation that people are in rather than by the strength of the emotion that they are actually feeling (Fridlund,

1991). A test of the theory supports it in part but shows that three factors combine to determine the intensity of facial expressions: the situation, the intensity of the emotion, and the relationship between the person experiencing the emotion and that person's audience (Hess, Banse, and Kappas, 1995). All three factors are important.

Just as facial expressions differ according to the social situation, so too do people's perceptions of facial expressions. For example, if subjects in an experiment are shown a photograph of a man's face that ordinarily would seem to express fear but are told a story that suggests the man was angry because some young kids ran off with the hubcaps of his new car, the subjects are likely to perceive the photograph as expressing anger rather than fear (Carroll and Russell, 1996). People do not automatically judge someone's emotions on the basis of their nonverbal expression. They carefully consider the person's situation as well.

Finally, some recent research on the facial expression of amusement suggests that people so habitually inhibit the expression of their feelings in a wide range of social situations that they believe that they are expressing much more feeling than others actually perceive them to be expressing (Barr and Kleck, 1995). The suppression of emotional expression seems to be overlearned and spontaneous in North American culture, and many of us express less than we think we do.

In short, there are strong situational influences on how we behave nonverbally and how we perceive other people's nonverbal expressions. Nonverbal behavior is influenced by a complex set of biological, cultural, and situational forces.

nels can leak the truth and disconfirm the child's denial. Young children are often able to mask their deception by using the highly controllable facial expression of smiling (Keating and Heltman, 1994). It seems odd that smiling can be used so easily and effectively. Though it often masks deception, smiling leads people to treat others leniently, probably because it is associated with trustworthiness (LaFrance and Hecht, 1995). The implication is that when there is a concern about deception, the controllable and generally informative verbal and facial expressions must be taken with a grain of salt. Although the less controllable channels—voice quality and body movement—are less precise and informative when they are congruent with the other channels because they leak what is being hidden, they are crucial in detecting deception.

Recent research has started to explore how even the relatively controllable channel of facial expression can be penetrated to detect deceit. For example, people often smile when they are not happy. They tend to smile particularly when they are engaging in face work. But are the smiles of a person who is not really happy the same as the genuine article? It seems not. Muscular activity around the eyes and lips is more frequent when people are truly happy than when they are faking. The facial muscles can reveal disgust, fear, contempt, or sadness to the trained observer, although the muscular activity is difficult for most people to detect (Ekman, Friesen, and O'Sullivan, 1988).

You may wonder what kinds of people are most adept at deception. Not surprisingly, socially skilled people lead the way (Riggio, Tucker, and Throckmorton, 1987). People who are expressive and socially tactful are the best at deceiving. Those who are socially anxious are the worst. Apparently, socially skilled people convey a much more honest demeanor, while socially anxious people convey a deceptive demeanor. Dominance is strongly associated with deceptive success. As just noted, deception is a social skill, and people with the social skill to deceive are able to achieve and maintain higher social status (Keating and Heltman, 1994).

Gender Differences in Nonverbal Communication

Throughout the history of research on nonverbal communication, a number of gender differences have been observed. These differences help us to understand the ways in which men and women differ and the relationships between the sexes.

Gender Differences in Nonverbal Behavior

One difference between men and women is that their nonverbal behaviors are not the same (Henley, 1977). Women typically gaze when someone else is speaking, especially a man, while men typically do not look at women speaking. Women are generally apt to be more tense and formal in their posture and demeanor, while men are generally relaxed and informal. Women are more likely to smile. Henley has argued that these differences between men and women are associated with the high-status, high-power position of men in our society and the lower status and power of women. Men's nonverbal behaviors are those that are performed by people with power. Women's nonverbal behaviors are those of submission. Henley argues that by engaging in these inconspicuous, small behaviors many times each day, men and women maintain the power difference between them. Although women may behave ingratiatingly, their behavior is so clearly a product of the power difference that it thus reinforces rather than reduces that difference.

Another particularly pervasive difference between men and women has to do with touching. Men touch but do not generally like being touched (Whitcher and Fisher, 1979). Women generally respond positively to touch but do not usually initiate touching. In short, in day-to-day interactions, men touch women but women do not touch men (Henley, 1977; Major, 1981). In noting that men assert the right to touch and women acknowledge that right but do not claim it for themselves, we see another example of differences in nonverbal behavior that perpetuate power differences between the sexes.

Gender Differences in Expressiveness and Sensitivity

The difference between men and women in nonverbal expressiveness and sensitivity can be stated succinctly: women are superior both in accurately sending and in understanding nonverbal communication (Hall, 1984; Mayo and Henley, 1981; Rosenthal and Benowitz, 1985). Although there are occasional exceptions to these generalizations, such as the finding in one study

In general, men are comparatively more relaxed and informal in their posture and demeanor than women.

of a tendency for men to be more accurate at recognizing anger (Wagner, MacDonald, and Manstead, 1986), the generalizations have been very clearly established. One study suggests that women's superiority in conveying nonverbal messages may, in fact, be related more to the masculinity versus femininity phenomenon than to their actual gender. The term *masculinity versus femininity* refers to people's psychological tendencies (measured by a questionnaire) to behave in either a typically masculine or typically feminine manner. Subjects higher on femininity, whether male or female, were superior in using both facial expressions and tone of voice to convey their feelings (Zuckerman, Amidon, Bishop, and Pomerantz, 1982). Women's superiority in understanding nonverbal communication is especially evident in their ability to identify negative feelings, with the possible exception, as we have noted, of anger. This heightened ability may be a function of women's less-powerful position in relation to men; they may have to develop sensitivity to the leakage of negative feelings (Brown, 1986).

Nonverbal communication of feelings, whether affection, dominance, or a temporary mood, is impor-

tant in relationships. We know, for example, that nonverbal expressiveness, independent of physical attractiveness, contributes to initial likability (Friedman, Riggio, and Casella, 1988). Such expressiveness contributes to an individual's personal charisma (Friedman and Riggio, 1981). We may not be able to see personal charisma in a photograph, but we know it when we interact with a charismatic person and feel the charm of that nonverbal expressiveness.

Research has also shown that nonverbal communication of feelings is important in marriage. One study showed that the nonverbal skill of a wife in both conveying and interpreting nonverbal information was significantly related to marital satisfaction (Sabatelli, Buck, and Dreyer, 1982). Another study showed again that women's nonverbal skills were superior to men's, and husbands' and wives' ability to communicate with each other nonverbally was related to marital adjustment (Noller, 1980).

Nonverbal communication is an important element of both self-presentation and mutual understanding. Its subtlety and pervasiveness make it a subject worthy of continued research.

Self-Disclosure

One of the more important forms of self-presentation is self-construction (Baumeister, 1982; Baumeister, and Hutton, 1987). Self-construction entails presenting ourselves as the person we would like to be and hope we are. We want our audience, the person or people we are interacting with, to accept that definition of who we are. One of the kinds of behavior involved in self-construction is self-disclosure. **Self-disclosure** can be defined as talking to another person about private matters; for example, your needs, values, attitudes, background, worries, and aspirations (Archer, 1980). Several items from a scale measuring self-disclosure are shown in figure 4.4, in which people are asked to indicate how much they have talked to their parents, their male and female friends, and their spouses about each topic. Ella Fitzgerald would probably have scored low on this scale. She was a very private person, who kept a great deal to herself.

We generally find self-disclosure highly rewarding: it offers the possibility of both self-construction and self-realization. We also generally like it when others disclose to us, thereby communicating liking and trust. Self-disclosure can also reduce loneliness, although lonely people may be less likely to disclose themselves in the first place (Davis and Franzoni, 1986). In addition, self-disclosure often leads to intimacy with the person with whom we are sharing personal information (Jourard, 1971; Rubin and Schlenker, 1978). In intimate relationships, including marriage, mutual self-disclosure enhances the quality of the relationship (Hendrick, 1981).

One important determinant of self-disclosure is **reciprocity** (Cohn and Strassberg, 1983; Cozby, 1972). The more someone discloses to us, the more we disclose to him or her. Reciprocity can produce relationships marked by a high degree of mutual self-disclosure even though the individuals in it are not generally high self-disclosers (Miller and Kenny, 1986). We don't always like a person who discloses a great deal to us—sometimes it's too much too soon—

**FIGURE 4.4   SAMPLE ITEMS FROM
JOURARD'S SELF-DISCLOSURE QUESTIONNAIRE**

Instructions: The answer sheet you have been given has columns with the headings "Mother," "Father," "Male Friend," "Female Friend," and "Spouse." You are to read each item on the questionnaire and then indicate on the answer sheet the extent that you have talked about that item to each person; that is, the extent that you have made yourself known to that person. Use the rating scale that you see on the answer sheet to describe the extent that you have talked about each item.

1. My personal views on sexual morality—how I feel that I and others ought to behave in sexual matters:

2. What I would appreciate most for a present:

3. What I enjoy most and get the most satisfaction from in my present work:

4. How I really feel about the people that I work for or work with:

5. All of my present sources of income—wages, fees, allowance, dividends, etc.:

6. The facts of my present sex life—including knowledge of how I get sexual gratification; any problems that I might have; with whom I have relations, if anybody:

7. Things in the past or present that I feel guilty or ashamed and guilty about:

8. My present physical measurements, for example, height, weight, waist, etc.:

Source: Jourard (1971)

Women in conversation tend to freely discuss personal matters and express emotions.

but even here we follow the reciprocity principle and disclose more in return (Kleinke and Kahn, 1980). We may not match the other's degree of self-disclosure exactly if it doesn't seem appropriate to do so in the situation; instead, we will compromise between the reciprocity principle and a desire to follow the situational norms for appropriate self-disclosure.

If mutual self-disclosure often leads to intimacy but sometimes, if it happens too soon, produces negative reactions, what is the right amount at the right time? We prefer people who warm up to us slowly—in that their self-disclosures come at the end of a conversation (Jones and Gordon, 1972; Jones and Archer, 1976). One exception to this rule is that we like being told very early in our interaction with someone about a negative event for which that person was responsible (Archer and Burleson, 1980). This seems to clear the air and lead to greater liking. We also like it when someone who is ordinarily reserved opens up to us and discloses something that seems to signify that he

or she feels unusually open with us (Taylor, Gould, and Brounstein, 1981).

Research on self-disclosure shows consistent differences between men and women in both their degree of self-disclosure and what they actually reveal (Shaffer, Pegalis, and Bazzini, 1996). Women generally disclose more than men, especially about emotions, relationships, and other personal matters (Cozby, 1972; Davidson and Duberman, 1982). One instance in which men, especially highly masculine men, disclose somewhat more is when they are talking to women with whom they anticipate future interaction. These men seem to want to take the lead in exploring possibilities for a future romantic relationship with the women (Shaffer, Pegalis, and Bazzini, 1996). Henley (1977) has also pointed out that men disclose only to women with whom they are intimate, or wish to become intimate, which puts women in the position of being an "emotional service station." She argues that such a pattern is not good for either men or women.

Gender-role stereotypes can also govern self-disclosure. Both men and women who are insecure and socially anxious are likely to disclose themselves in a way that is consistent with gender-role stereotypes, and thus they may reinforce and perpetuate those stereotypes (Snell, 1989). Times may be changing, but research shows that men are still evaluated more negatively than women for personal self-disclosure, perhaps because men see disclosing as a sign of weakness (Cunningham, 1981). If this is the case, no wonder men don't self-disclose as much! Jourard (1971) has argued that men's lack of self-disclosure, their tendency to hold everything in, adds stress to their lives.

Summary

When people are not self-aware, their behavior is generally fairly routine and automatic. People can be made self-aware by a variety of external stimuli, such as tape recordings of their own voices and mirrors. Self-aware people compare their behavior with ideal standards and generally find themselves falling short. Therefore, self-awareness is usually unpleasant and people will escape it if they can. If they cannot escape, people will respond to self-awareness by attempting to match their behavior to salient standards. In a group, people become more self-attentive if there is a proportionally large number of people in subgroups other than their own.

Erving Goffman argued that self-presentation is pervasive in everyday life because we try to control other people's impressions of us by presenting ourselves positively. We do this by claiming face. When we claim face, other people generally go along with our claim to form a working consensus that facilitates efficient social interaction. We try to support each other's faces by preventing or ignoring embarrassments or explaining them in a positive way. These mutually supportive behaviors are called face work.

Jones's theory of ingratiation and strategic self-presentation holds that we ingratiate, or try to get other people to like us, to enhance our power in a relationship. We must do this subtly to avoid alerting the other person to our attempts to ingratiate. We can ingratiate by con-forming, flattering the other person, or presenting ourselves positively. Other self-presentation strategies include intimidation, self-promotion, exemplification, and supplication.

Sometimes individuals put obstacles to successful performance in their own way. This behavior, known as self-handicapping, is most likely to happen when people are unsure of their abilities in an area. They handicap themselves so that they can have an excuse for failure and so that failure cannot be attributed to low ability.

People who are high self-monitors are extremely sensitive to other people's expectations and are skilled in modifying their behavior to respond to those expectations. Low self-monitors are consistent across situations and their behavior reflects their clear self-concept.

Interpersonal behaviors can be classified along the dimensions of friendliness versus hostility and dominance versus submissiveness. Individuals' interpersonal styles vary along these same two dimensions.

Nonverbal behaviors convey a great deal about our emotions and our feelings about others. Channels of nonverbal communication include gaze or eye contact, facial expression, body movements and gestures, touch, and voice quality. Much of our nonverbal communication conveys our liking for other people and our feelings of relative power or status in relation to them. Nonverbal channels vary along a controllability-leakage continuum, with facial expression the most controllable and voice quality the most leaky. Men and women differ in their nonverbal behaviors and abilities. In general, men assert their power in nonverbal behavior whereas women are submissive in theirs. Women are superior to men in conveying feelings nonverbally and in interpreting nonverbal communications.

Self-disclosure is extremely rewarding and can lead to the forming of intimate relationships. Even though people generally like others who self-disclose, self-disclosure must be timed and limited carefully. Self-disclosure follows a reciprocity principle; that is, we generally disclose as much as others disclose, although we also observe norms about the appropriate degree of self-disclosure in different situations. Women disclose more than men; and men are evaluated less positively when they self-disclose.

Key Terms

audience pleasing
autistic conspiracy
circumplex
exemplification
face
face work
idealized performance
impression management

ingratiation
ingratiator's dilemma
intimidation
matching to standards
negative memory bias
reciprocity
self-construction situated identity
self-disclosure

self-handicapping
self-monitoring
self-promotion
self-regulation
situated identity
supplication
visual dominance behavior

Suggested Readings

Bales, R. F. (1970). *Personality and interpersonal behavior.* New York: Holt, Rinehart and Winston.

Chaikin, A. L., & Derlega, V. L. (1974). *Self-disclosure.* Morristown, NJ: General Learning Press.

DePaulo, B. M., and Friedman, H. S. (1998). Nonverbal communication. In D. T. Gilbert, S. T. Fiske, and G. Lindzey (Eds.), *The handbook of social psychology* (Vol 2, pp. 3–40). New York: McGraw-Hill.

Duval, S., and Wicklund, R. A. (1972). *A theory of objective self-awareness.* New York: Academic Press.

Ekman, P. (Ed.). (1982). *Emotion in the human face* (2nd ed.). Cambridge, England: Cambridge University Press.

Goffman, E. (1959). *The presentation of self in everyday life.* Garden City, NY: Doubleday.

Jones, E. E. (1964). *Ingratiation: A social psychological analysis.* New York: Appleton-Century-Crofts.

Schlenker, B. R. (1980). *Impression management: The self-concept, social identity, and interpersonal behavior.* Pacific Grove, CA: Brooks/Cole.

Snyder, M. (1987). *Public appearances/private realities.* The psychology of self-monitoring. New York: Freeman.

Chapter 5

Attitudes

Excerpted from *People Like Us* (Fisher and Fisher, 1992a):

KERRY:
I come from a pretty small home town, in Maine, and not much goes on there. . . . I grew up in an upper-middle-class family. I had a lot of friends. We'd have slumber parties and go shopping and play dolls. I really loved dolls. . . . I was into field hockey and horseback riding and all kinds of things like that, and the whole social part of it. I've had about a thousand jobs since age fifteen. . . . I worked in pet stores. I like animals. I've always had a lot of animals around. They're really good company, especially now, they're real good company for me. . . . The most important thing to me, which is really hard, was that I always wanted a family.

PAUL:
You know, I had so many dreams, so many things I wanted to do. I just love people, and there's so much, you couldn't do it all in your lifetime. . . . I grew up in Connecticut. I was in horse shows, water ski, snow ski. I was an outside kid. We had a beautiful house with a pool in the backyard. . . . It was hard for me when I was in high school. I was not sure if I was gay or straight. I played around a little, both sides. I wanted to work with the disabled, mentally disabled, helping them walk, eat correctly, not hurt people. . . . I've always wanted to take care of people and still do. You lose everything, you know, you lose everything when you have this disease. You can't work. I can never work again.

KERRY:
I'm eighteen years old. I was fifteen when I found out that I was HIV positive. No one ever told me that, as a fifteen year old kid, I could end up with someone who was infected. "They" were other people. "They" were gay men and that is what I was told. Before I contracted HIV, I had never used a condom. I don't think I thought about them much at

all. I don't think I ever talked with a partner about birth control or condom use or anything. I was not comfortable with negotiating skills as far as those subjects are concerned.

PAUL:
I'm twenty-eight years old. I have AIDS, full-blown AIDS. . . . I hate to tell you the honest truth. Abstinence never entered my mind, period. At all. When I heard about AIDS in 1980, I thought to myself, I'll never get it. Condoms were not foremost in my mind. The sex was. We discussed condoms. I just said, well, fine, I am not going to use a condom. Not me, I'll never get it. And then I did.

KERRY:
I slept with a guy when I was fifteen. . . . We didn't discuss condom use. I found out a week after being exposed to the virus by him that he was infected. I was told by many people, including my aunt who is a registered nurse, that the chances were one in a million through three or four encounters that I would become infected. . . . So I didn't expect a positive result, I really didn't. We all have that whole immortality wall that we put up. I remember feeling, when I first found out, I'm fifteen years old and I don't want to die. I remember screaming it to my parents—I'm only fifteen, I'm only fifteen. . . . I just felt so tiny. I felt so small. It was devastating to say the least, absolutely crushed my world.

PAUL:
Bladder infections, herpes. Bladder infections after bladder infections after bladder infections. I had an infection in my mouth, and that was pretty bad for me. Growing 104, 105 degree fevers. Had 106 degree fever and my eyes, my head just wanted to burst open. I could not get out of my bed. I could not see. I could not open my eyes I was so hot. . . . I have had about thirty-five transfusions. They could not figure out why I was so anemic. I could not tolerate any more. I had no veins left. I would not let them stick

me in the leg or the feet, so basically I said I want to get off AZT. That was causing the problem but helps build up your immune system, so either way you are losing out. . . . After that, he put me on DDI. DDI is something that increases the immune system also. I took it for three days and could not walk. . . . At this point in time, I have nothing to protect me.

KERRY:

I am very afraid of becoming sick. The types of medication I take are AZT. I take 500 milligrams of that a day. I give myself daily injections of Interferon, which I am in a clinical trial of. Most women I know who have been on DDI have lost the use of their legs. Paralysis is very frightening for me, losing the use of my legs.

PAUL:

They have me on Tylox, which is one step down from morphine, for the pain I go through. Because what is happening is my body is totally deteriorating. . . . I cannot eat. It hurts too much. Makes me sick. I try as hard as I can to eat, but I can't. Being twenty-eight years old is too young to die. . . . It is scary because I don't want to die. . . . My mother comes over and checks on me, but she always wears gloves now. It makes me feel like I'm a disease. I have the disease, but you're not going to catch it by hugging me, you're not going to get it from my tears. The only thing I want is a hug.

KERRY:

There's no way of telling whether someone has HIV disease or not. No one would ever think by looking at me that I was HIV infected. People are not always monogamous like we think they are. Girls are always saying, well, the guys don't like them, and they'll feel like a raincoat, and I don't want to make him feel uncomfortable. . . . There is nothing in this world that is worth your life being compromised for. Nothing. No guy, no girl, no matter how cute they may be, is worth waking up to this every day.

PAUL:

You also have to really think. Is this person being straight with me, or are they out there screwing around behind my back? Who cares about being embarrassed? You're saving your own life, and the other person's, possibly. Is sex worth catching AIDS? Is sex worth not using a condom? You may not get the same sensation, but you're safe. Think of it.

Paul died in March 1994.
Kerry died early in 1995.

Acquired immunodeficiency syndrome (AIDS) has become one of the most serious health threats of the century. Worldwide, approximately 5 million persons have been diagnosed with full-blown AIDS, and an estimated 18.5 million have been infected with *human immunodeficiency virus* (HIV), the virus that causes AIDS (Bureau of HIV/AIDS and STD Laboratory, Centre for Disease Control, Health Canada, 1995; Cox, 1996). In the United States, more than 500,000 people have been diagnosed with AIDS, and an estimated 2 million people have been infected with HIV (Centers for Disease Control, 1994).

These participants in the interview study **Just Like Us** *and video* **People Like Us** *all had either HIV+ or full-blown AIDS. Their interviews are poignant discussions combining youthful memories and aspirations with present-day remorse for the naive, often unconsidered attitudes they held about sex.*

HIV is transmitted by the exchange of infected blood and bodily fluids. Therefore, certain behaviors are associated with increased risk for becoming infected with HIV, such as sexual intercourse without condoms and sharing intravenous needles. Certain populations have already been devastated by AIDS, including hemophiliacs, gay men, and intravenous drug users (Fisher and Fisher, 1992b), and there is increasing evidence that the general heterosexually active public is also at risk (Ickovics and Rodin, 1992). Yet preventive actions, such as condom use, are only inconsistently taken by sexually active young people, whether heterosexual or homosexual (Catania, Coates, Stall, Turner, Peterson, Hearst, Dolcini, Hudes, Gagnon, Wiley, and Groves, 1992; McCusker, Stoddard, McDonald, Zapka, and Mayer, 1992).

Why do people put themselves at risk by engaging in unprotected sex? One potentially important factor is people's attitudes. People may have negative attitudes toward using condoms or toward instigating other protective strategies (for example, abstinence) because they believe that these behaviors will have undesirable consequences. A young woman, for example, might think that her boyfriend will be insulted if she asks him to use a condom, or a young man might think that condoms reduce pleasure and, besides, his girlfriend looks perfectly healthy. Yet, the sad reality is that HIV has infiltrated into the general public, and any amount of unprotected sex is risky.

In this chapter, we describe social psychological research and theorizing about attitudes. We begin by defining the concept of attitudes, then discuss the process of attitude formation. Following that, we describe how attitudes affect information processing and, finally, turn to the impact of attitudes on behavior. Throughout the chapter, we focus on important, socially relevant attitude domains, including sexual behavior and sexually transmitted diseases.

Definition of Attitudes

The term *attitude* is common in everyday life, so almost everyone has some idea of its meaning. "He loves the Maple Leafs," "She thinks that capital punishment for murder is a good idea," "He is a prejudiced bigot," and "They support the president's policy in Bosnia" are all everyday examples of the concept of attitudes.

How do social psychologists define attitudes? Many definitions have been offered over the years, ranging from simple ones (such as "likes and dislikes," Bem, 1970) to complex ones (such as "a mental or neural state of readiness, organized through experience, exerting a directive or dynamic influence upon the individual's response to all objects and situations with which it is related," Allport, 1935). The definition that we adopt in this chapter is that an **attitude** is *an evaluative (good-bad) judgment of a target.* Thus, an attitude represents the perceiver's favorability or unfavorability toward the target.

Zanna and Rempel (1988) identified four core features of the concept of attitudes. First, attitudes refer to a stimulus object; that is, they always have a *referent.* Attitudes are always directed *at* a target (an issue, a behavior, a person, a group, or any other identifiable aspect of the environment). Thus, people have attitudes *toward* things, ranging from concrete or specific targets like "Bruce Springsteen" and "using condoms" to abstract and general targets like "freedom" and "health." The phrase "He's got a bad attitude"

Attitudes can be very strong, like the love between sisters.

would not be used by social psychologists because it does not specify the target of the attitude.

Second, attitudes refer to individuals' *evaluations* of targets. Attitudes are judgments along an evaluative dimension (a good-bad continuum) that reflect the perceiver's favorability or unfavorability toward the target. Thus, attitudes are often measured by asking people to rate the target (for example, "Bruce Springsteen" or "Using a condom every time I have sex") on several evaluative dimensions, such as good-bad, favorable-unfavorable, wise-foolish, and like-dislike (Osgood, Suci, and Tannenbaum, 1957). Another way to measure attitudes is by asking people to rate their agreement-disagreement with several statements that reflect evaluations of the target (Likert, 1932), such as "Condoms protect against sexually transmitted diseases," "Bringing up the issue of condoms will insult my partner," and "Condoms reduce the man's sexual enjoyment."

Third, attitudes are *represented in memory*. Thus, they fit into our network or structure of representations in memory (Pratkanis and Greenwald, 1989). For example, thinking about your attitude toward doctors will also activate your attitudes toward closely related objects like hospitals, nurses, and needles. Attitudes also differ in the ease or speed with which they can be retrieved from memory—a concept that has been labeled the **accessibility** of the attitude (Fazio, 1990). As we shall see later in this chapter, highly accessible attitudes are more "consequential" than inaccessible attitudes—that is, they have more impact on information processing and behavior.

The fourth and final core feature of attitudes is that they can be *developed from cognitive, affective, and/or behavioral information*. This means that evaluations of objects can be based on knowledge and beliefs about the objects (cognitive information), feelings and emotional reactions toward the objects (affective information), and/or previous behaviors and responses to the objects (behavioral information). For example, Susan might develop a favorable attitude toward George, a man in one of her classes, because she believes that he is honest and friendly (knowledge), because she feels a strong attraction to him (affect), or because she takes the time to explain an assignment to him when he looks confused in class (behavior). Often, attitudes will be based on all three of these sources (for example, if all three of the preceding things were true about Susan). The sources will not always or necessar-

ily be consistent with one another, however. For example, you might love the taste of chocolate cake (positive affect) but know that it is unhealthy (negative beliefs). Or you might know that you should exercise (positive beliefs) but find physical exertion unpleasant (negative affect). Notwithstanding possible inconsistencies among the three sources, attitudes represent a concept that truly integrates cognition and affect—a "synergistic" perspective (a perspective that assumes reciprocal influence between components) that has been labeled the "Warm Look" by Sorrentino and Higgins (1986), who argued that this perspective is an important one for social psychologists. When we discuss attitude formation in the next section, we address the three possible sources of attitudes separately.

Of course, it is the *consequences* of attitudes that account for the centrality of the concept in social psychological theories and research. As early as 1935, Allport described attitudes as "the most distinctive and indispensable concept in contemporary American social psychology," and this statement is arguably still true today (see Petty, Wegener, and Fabrigar, 1997). Social psychologists have directed so much attention to attitudes because evaluations of objects have significant effects on perceptions, emotions, and behavior. If we want to understand why young people fail to practice safer sex, why racial and ethnic conflict is common, why some people are careful to conserve energy while others are wasteful, and why issues like abortion evoke such strong emotions, then we must study and understand attitudes.

Why Do People Have Attitudes?

People can form attitudes rapidly and effortlessly; they are able to develop evaluations of objects based on relatively little information and without consciously intending to do so. Think about your first class of the year. You probably developed an initial attitude toward the professor (like, dislike; interesting, boring) within the first few minutes of the class. Your attitude was tentative, of course, but it was there nonetheless. Why are attitudes formed so apparently "automatically"? Zajonc (1980) has argued that evaluative or affective responses are more "primitive" than cognitive responses (many species besides humans experience affect, but few species "think" in ways that even approach human cognition). Thus, in an evolutionary sense, affective reactions may be older or more elementary than cognitive reactions. Indeed, Zajonc argued that basic affective responses (like-dislike) can occur even before perceivers are consciously aware of what an object is (prior to categorization and recognition).

Not only can attitudes form quickly and easily, but once formed, they are usually defended strongly. In short, people protect their attitudes from change through such mechanisms as counterarguing, ignoring information, and rationalization. Although attitudes can and do change, psychological resistance is working against change. It is easier to convince someone that a movie is good or bad if they do not possess an existing attitude (for example, if they haven't seen the movie) than if they already have a clear evaluation.

These qualities of attitudes—rapid and effortless formation with subsequent resistance to change—suggest that attitudes may serve important psychological *functions* for individuals. Why have humans evolved to make rapid evaluative judgments? What are the benefits of attitudes? In fact, attitudes serve a crucial survival function. Because attitudes motivate behavior consistent with the evaluation, people will typically approach things they evaluate favorably and avoid things they evaluate unfavorably. Assuming that favorable attitudes develop when people are rewarded by objects, whereas unfavorable attitudes develop when people are punished by objects, subsequent approach/avoidance based on an attitude will serve to increase rewards and minimize punishments. It is imperative for organisms to quickly identify threats

Though disposed in attitude to pursue the new and strange, tourists in foreign courntries may become threatened by the unfamiliar and feel punished by the stimulus objects in their environment.

in the environment as well as possible sources of rewards. Attitudes serve these goals by storing in memory summary evaluations of stimulus objects.

Several theorists have speculated about the functions of attitudes. Perhaps the best-known functional analysis was provided by Katz (1960), who identified four possible functions of attitudes. First, attitudes serve to maximize rewards and minimize punishments, as discussed above, which Katz called the **utilitarian function.** Second, attitudes help perceivers to understand their environments by providing summary evaluations of objects and groups of objects, which Katz called the **knowledge function.** Third, attitudes sometimes communicate individuals' values and identities to other people (for example, adolescents' attitudes toward music and clothing), which Katz called the **value-expressive function.** In this context, social psychologists differentiate between attitudes and values, the latter concept referring to broad standards or goals that people consider to be important, such as equality, freedom, and health (see Seligman, Olson, and Zanna, 1996). Finally, attitudes might occasionally protect people from admitting to themselves an uncomplimentary truth. A professor who is a poor teacher, for example, might protect his or her ego by forming an unfavorable attitude toward students ("They can't keep up with my brilliant thinking"). Katz called this the **ego-defensive function.** Since Katz's work appeared, many researchers have investigated the characteristics of attitudes that fulfill different functions (e.g., Herek, 1986; Maio and Olson, 1995; Shavitt, 1990).

Thus, it is easy to understand why humans have learned to evaluate objects quickly and effortlessly. Of course, this propensity to form attitudes can have undesirable consequences, such as when unfavorable evaluations of a person or a group of people are made prematurely. But the fact remains that, for the most part, attitudes effectively fulfill important psychological functions.

Attitude Formation

When we defined attitudes, we pointed out that they can be based on three kinds of information: cognitive, affective, and behavioral. Most attitudes probably represent a combination of more than one of these categories. In this section we describe more precisely how attitudes can develop from each type of information.

Attitudes Based on Cognitive Information

It may seem intuitively obvious that the way people evaluate an object (their attitude toward the object) will be influenced by what they know or believe about it (cognitive information). But how, exactly, will knowledge and evaluations be related?

Perhaps the best-known model of attitudes that connects beliefs and evaluations is the **theory of reasoned action** (Fishbein and Ajzen, 1975). In this model, people are assumed to be rational, deliberate thinkers who act on the basis of what they know (hence, the name "reasoned action"). This theory is actually a comprehensive model of the relations among attitudes, beliefs, social pressure, intentions, and behavior, but for now we focus only on its implications for attitude formation (we will return to the model later in this chapter when we discuss attitude-behavior consistency). Fishbein and Ajzen hypothesized that attitudes are determined by the characteristics that perceivers associate with an object (their **beliefs** about the object); that is, an attitude is determined by whatever features of the object are salient to the individual (come to mind easily and quickly when thinking about the object), weighted by whether the features are good or bad. Imagine that Susan was asked about her attitude toward dogs. She might report a moderately positive attitude, say +2 on a scale from –3 to +3. Another individual, William, might report a slightly negative attitude, say –1 on the same scale. Fishbein and Ajzen would predict that Susan's beliefs about dogs are more positive than William's beliefs. Table 5.1 presents hypothetical beliefs that might be reported by these two individuals. If Susan were asked to list the first things to come into her mind when she thinks about dogs, she might say, "Friendly, cute, noisy, and playful." William, on the other hand, might list as his first thoughts, "Vicious, loud, and loyal." Clearly, these different beliefs might explain the different overall attitudes.

Fishbein and Ajzen (1975) present a formula that specifies how an individual's salient beliefs are integrated to form an overall attitude. The formula is:

$$A_o = \sum_{i=1}^{n} b_i e_i$$

where A_o is the attitude toward the object, $\sum$ means "sum of all," b_i is the belief i about the object, e_i is the evaluation of the feature involved in belief i, and n is the number of salient beliefs. Each belief (b) is a prob-

---

TABLE 5.1   ATTITUDES BASED ON BELIEFS ABOUT THE TARGET

Susan's overall attitude rating toward dogs is +2
Susan's salient beliefs about dogs:

	Strength (b)	Evaluation (e)	b × e
Friendly	.9	+3	+2.7
Cute	.7	+1	+0.7
Noisy	.4	−1	−0.4
Playful	.8	+2	+1.6
			Sum: +4.6

William's overall attitude rating toward dogs is −1
William's salient beliefs about dogs:

	Strength (b)	Evaluation (e)	b × e
Vicious	.7	−3	−2.1
Loud	.8	−1	−0.8
Loyal	.6	+2	+1.2
			Sum: −1.7

ability from 0 to 1, reflecting the certainty with which the feature is associated with the object (the *strength* of the belief). Each evaluation (*e*) is a rating from −3 to +3, reflecting the positive or negative value of the feature. To return to the dog example, Susan might be very certain that dogs are friendly (*b* = .9), moderately confident that dogs are cute (*b* = .7), slightly confident that dogs are noisy (*b* = .4), and very confident that dogs are playful (*b* = .8). Further, she might evaluate friendliness very positively (*e* = +3), cuteness slightly positively (*e* = +1), noisiness slightly negatively (*e* = −1), and playfulness moderately positively (*e* = +2). To get an estimate of Susan's overall attitude from these constituent beliefs, Fishbein and Ajzen would multiply .9 × +3 (friendliness), .7 × +1 (cuteness), .4 × −1 (noisiness), and .8 × +2 (playfulness), and then add up the products (2.7 + 0.7 − 0.4 + 1.6 = +4.6). Thus, Susan's overall attitude would be favorable, which makes sense because she has mostly positive beliefs about dogs. Note that "scores" derived in this manner will not correspond exactly to people's ratings on an eval-

uative attitude scale (for example, the +2 attitude toward dogs reported above for Susan) because the belief scores are not limited to a range from −3 to +3. Rather, scores derived from combining beliefs should correlate with (predict) scores on the overall attitude scale. Thus, for example, the score derived from William's beliefs should be less positive than Susan's belief score, as illustrated in table 5.1.

It might seem implausible that people "calculate" their attitudes in this manner. Certainly, if the mental arithmetic occurs at all, it is not conscious. But people can integrate information in surprisingly complex ways without being aware of the combinatorial rules (for example, see Anderson, 1981). Moreover, the notion that a large proportion of positive (or negative) beliefs translates into a positive (or negative) attitude is not far-fetched. And, indeed, researchers who have tested the theory of reasoned action have found good support for the hypothesized relation between beliefs and attitudes in many different domains, including attitudes toward birth control methods, political candidates, and racial groups (for reviews, see Ajzen and Fishbein, 1980; Eagly and Chaiken, 1993).

In a recent set of studies on safer sex behaviors, Fisher, Fisher, and Rye (1995) tested the usefulness of the theory of reasoned action. They obtained three diverse samples consisting of gay men, heterosexual university students, and heterosexual high school students. Participants' attitudes toward a range of safer sex behaviors (for example, using condoms, refusing to have unsafe sex, asking a partner to have an HIV test) were measured, as were their salient beliefs about each behavior—that is, the salient features or conse-

Sources of Beliefs

If attitudes are often based on beliefs, then understanding attitude formation requires us to go back a step and consider the sources of beliefs. Where do we get our knowledge about the features of objects, groups, and so on? There are two primary categories of beliefs—those based on direct, personal experience with the object and those based on indirect information obtained from other people.

With regard to direct experience, many of our beliefs come from personal exposure to objects and peo-

Speculate upon the attitudes and beliefs this father may be cultivating in his son.

quences of the behaviors (for example, for using condoms, common salient beliefs were reducing the risk of AIDS, reducing the risk of other sexually transmitted diseases, and reducing fear about getting AIDS). Across samples, twenty-five of the thirty attitudes were significantly correlated with scores derived from beliefs (multiplying beliefs times evaluations and summing the products). For these sexual behaviors, then, individuals who believed that the actions would bring mostly positive consequences also expressed positive evaluations of the behaviors, and thus the theory of reasoned action held up very well in this real-life test.

ple. We learn firsthand that our mother comforts us, that bananas taste good, that the lake water at Algonquin Park is cold, that getting stuck with a needle hurts, that jogging makes us tired, and that social psychology is interesting to study. Each of these beliefs involves associating a specific feature or characteristic, such as good-tasting, with a target, such as bananas.

It turns out that attitudes based on direct experience with an object are more accessible (easily brought to mind), more confidently held, and more clear than attitudes based on indirect experience (see Fazio and Zanna, 1981). Not surprisingly, attitudes based on direct experience also predict future behavior better than attitudes based on indirect information. We trust our own senses more than we trust information from other people.

Of course, for many objects (for example, Russians, cocaine, the NASA space program) and many issues (such as abortion and capital punishment), most people have had no personal experience with the relevant objects and must rely on information gleaned from other sources. Who or what are the most important sources of indirect information about the world?

Our first exposure is to our parents, who have a profound influence on us. Children share many of their parents' beliefs. To take just a couple of examples, children tend to support the same political party as their parents (Jessop, 1982) and exhibit similar levels of racial prejudice as their parents (Epstein and Komorita, 1966). It is difficult to overstate the impact that parents have on their children's developing attitudes and beliefs.

We are also influenced by our friends and peers. Schoolmates exert important effects on our attitudes, ranging from innocuous attitudes like clothing and music to more substantive attitudes like racial and religious beliefs. Peers often serve as an important **reference group**—a group whose beliefs, attitudes, and behaviors provide a standard against which individuals compare themselves. A famous study of reference groups was conducted by Newcomb (1943), who studied an incoming class of students at Bennington College, at that time a small liberal arts college for women in New England. Most of the faculty and senior students at Bennington were quite liberal, whereas the families of most of the students were quite conservative. Newcomb followed a class for four years at the college and found a clear shift toward more liberal attitudes over the years. Moreover, the degree of liberalism that students expressed was correlated with their popularity and prestige on campus. Also, many of the women who remained conservative expressed strong feelings of closeness and identification with their families. Thus, it appeared that the faculty and senior students served as a reference group for most students, resulting in more liberal attitudes, whereas the family remained the central reference group for a minority of students, resulting in stable conservative attitudes. Finally, it is interesting that Newcomb did a follow-up study twenty years later (Newcomb, 1963) and found that the sample of Bennington College graduates expressed more liberal attitudes and had more liberal husbands than a comparable group of women from a similar socioeconomic background. The Bennington peer group would seem to have had an enduring impact on the women's attitudes and lives.

Another source of indirect information is societal institutions. For example, schools are an important source of general knowledge, but they also present information about important social values like honesty, democracy, and freedom. Religious institutions also teach us about both religious issues (prophets, life after death) and nonreligious topics (the role of women, the importance of work).

Finally, the mass media are an important source of information. Television, radio, movies, newspapers, and magazines are so central to our lives that it is difficult to imagine what life would be like without them (yet most of these media have existed for less than one hundred years). The media are often the only source of information about far-off events, but even personal or local issues like crime, health care, and taxes are shaped by the media (see Haney and Manzolati, 1984; Oskamp, 1991; Roberts and Maccoby, 1985).

Attitudes Based on Affective Information

To this point, we have focused on how people's knowledge about objects can influence their evaluations of the objects. Of course, knowledge can also induce affective responses, such as feeling affection for a friend who possesses desirable characteristics or feeling angry because we know that someone benefited from dishonesty. In these instances, cognitive information and affective information are interdependent.

But can affect also become linked with objects independently of knowledge? Can people, in other words, feel good or bad about a target for reasons that have nothing to do with their beliefs? The answer to this question is yes. In this section, we describe two psychological processes through which affect can become linked with objects without cognitive mediation: **mere exposure** and **classical conditioning.**

Mere Exposure

In 1968, Zajonc (the same psychologist who argued that affective responses can precede cognition, as described earlier) proposed that repeated exposure to an object leads to a more favorable attitude toward the object—that is, "familiarity breeds content" (rather

FIGURE 5.1
FAVORABILITY OF RATED MEANINGS OF CHINESE CHARACTERS AS A FUNCTION OF FREQUENCY OF EXPOSURE

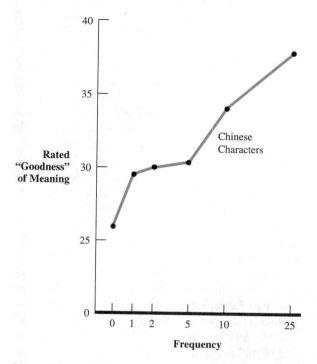

Source: Zajonec (1968), p. 14

about the stimuli; participants did not learn anything new or important about the Chinese characters as they were exposed repeatedly to them. The effects of exposure seem not to have been mediated by cognitive information (at least, not *conscious* cognition) but rather reflected some basic affective process that linked positive affect with familiar objects.

There are some limitations to the mere exposure effect (see Bornstein, 1989). For example, after a large number of repetitions, liking plateaus and sometimes actually decreases. Presumably, this down-turn in liking reflects satiation and boredom. In addition, the mere exposure effect does not consistently occur when a stimulus is already disliked to begin with, which means that repeated exposure to a disliked stimulus does not generally result in enhanced liking and can even lead to greater dislike (Perlman and Oskamp, 1971). It seems that if a stimulus is disliked, exposure to it is unpleasant, which serves as a punishment and results in even more negative affect being associated with the object.

Notwithstanding these limitations, the mere exposure effect is a reliable and generalizable phenomenon, as we will describe in more detail in chapter 9 on interpersonal attraction. Simple exposure, without any gain of knowledge or information, results in more favorable feelings toward an object; and such affect can translate into more positive evaluations of the object.

Classical Conditioning

Classical conditioning occurs when a stimulus comes to evoke a response that it did not previously evoke, simply by being paired with another stimulus that "naturally" evokes the response. If a dog is hit every time its owner clenches his fists, then after a few such episodes, clenched fists will produce fear and cowering from the dog. Alternatively, if an animal is given a food treat every time its owner says "treat," then this word alone will come to cause salivation and excitement.

Many of our attitudes probably contain some classically conditioned affect. We feel affection for people and places associated with happy experiences but feel dislike for things associated with negative experiences. An interesting study by Griffitt and Veitch (1971) illustrated this process. Participants in this experiment completed several tasks in a small room. Two variables were manipulated to influence participants' affect: heat and density. For half of the participants, the temperature in the room was uncomfortably

than contempt). He documented this phenomenon in several fascinating experiments in which participants were exposed different numbers of times to novel stimuli and then reported their evaluations of the stimuli. In one study, for example, the experimenter told participants that he was investigating the learning of a foreign language. Participants were shown Chinese characters various numbers of times (never, once, twice, five times, ten times, or twenty-five times) for two seconds each time and were then asked to guess whether the word had a favorable or an unfavorable meaning (they were told that all characters were adjectives with evaluative connotations). Figure 5.1 presents the results of this study. As predicted, the more often participants had seen a character, the more favorable they estimated its meaning to be. Thus, repeated exposure to the characters led participants to like them significantly more.

One reason this study is interesting is that repeated exposure did not give participants added knowledge hot (94 degrees F), whereas the room was comfortable for the other participants (73 degrees F). In addition, half of the participants were exposed to "crowded" conditions with twelve to sixteen people jammed into the room, whereas the other participants completed the study in groups of three to five. After working on the tasks, participants rated how much they liked an anonymous stranger, who allegedly agreed with them either on eighteen out of twenty-four or on six out of twenty-four attitude items. Figure 5.2 presents the results of the study. The attitudinally similar stranger was always better liked than the attitudinally dissimilar stranger. As depicted in the left panel of figure 5.2, hot conditions produced significantly less liking for either stranger than did normal temperatures. As depicted in the right panel of figure 5.2, high density (crowded) conditions produced significantly less liking than did low density (uncrowded) conditions. Thus, negative feelings aroused by environmental conditions (heat and crowding) transferred to judgments about another person. It seems unlikely that beliefs mediated these findings, because the target person had nothing to do with the conditions in the room.

Several experimenters have used words as the targets of classical conditioning. In this paradigm, positive or negative stimuli are paired with particular words and then liking for the words is measured. For example, Zanna, Kiesler, and Pilkonis (1970) delivered electric shocks to participants, allegedly for the purpose of testing physiological measures. One word was always used to signal the onset of shock (either "light" or "dark"), and the antonym always signaled the offset of shock ("dark" or "light"). After the shock trials, participants took part in what they believed to be an unrelated study. Their evaluations of the critical words were assessed. Table 5.2 presents the results for those participants who exhibited physiological evidence of conditioning during the learning trials. There was a general tendency for people to rate "light" more positively than "dark" (see the control group in table 5.2). When "light" signaled the onset and "dark" signaled the offset of shock, however, this preference for "light" was eliminated. And when "dark" signaled the onset and "light" signaled the offset of shock, the preference for "light" was enhanced. Thus, affect produced by the shock trials influenced participants' evaluations of the words. Words that were semantically related to the critical words showed similar effects of conditioning. When "light" signaled the onset and "dark" signaled the offset of shock, people's preference for the word "white" over the word "black" was reduced, whereas when "dark" signaled the onset and "light" signaled the offset of shock, the preference for "white" was enhanced.

Zanna, Kiesler, and Pilkonis (1970) showed that attitudes toward meaningful words can be influenced by classical conditioning. Of course, to the extent that people already possess attitudes toward meaningful words, conditioning effects might be "watered down" by preexisting evaluative associations. To test this idea, Cacioppo, Goodell, Tassinary, and Petty (1992) paired electric shocks either with meaningful words (such as "master," "permit," "finger," "mother") or with nonwords consisting of the same letters (such as "trames," "primet," "fering," "thomer"). After the shock trials, participants rated the pleasantness of each word and nonword. Compared to a condition where shocks were randomly paired with words (where shocks sometimes followed meaningful words and sometimes followed nonwords), whichever set of words was linked to the shocks was rated as less pleasant. More important, this conditioning effect was stronger for the nonwords than for the meaningful words, presumably because the meaningful words already evoked some evaluative reactions prior to the experiment.

FIGURE 5.2   **EVALUATIONS OF A STRANGER AS A FUNCTION OF HEAT, CROWDING, AND ATTITUDINAL SIMILARITY**

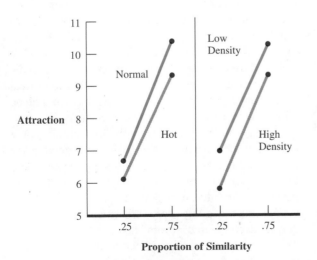

Source: Griffitt and Veitch (1971), p. 95

TABLE 5.2 **EVALUATIONS OF WORDS PAIRED WITH ONSET OR OFFSET OF ELECTRIC SHOCK**

Condition	Word			
	Light	Dark	White	Black
Light = shock onset, Dark = shock offset	25.08	25.15	24.23	21.77
Control	26.22	22.00	25.78	19.00
Dark = shock onset, Light = shock offset	27.21	19.57	25.50	16.21

Note: Higher numbers mean more favorable evaluations.
Source: Zanna, Kiesler, and Pilkonis (1970), p. 326

Attitudes Based on Behavioral Information

We have discussed how attitudes can be based on beliefs about an object's characteristics (cognitive information) and on feelings that the object evokes (affective information). In this section, we describe a third way that attitudes can form: inferences from past behaviors.

In chapter 3, Bem's (1967, 1972) **self-perception theory** was outlined. Bem proposed that we make judgments about the self in much the same way as we make judgments about other people; that is, we infer internal states from freely chosen behaviors. If we see someone voluntarily giving money to a charity, we infer that they are generous. Similarly, if we think back over our own actions in a certain domain or toward a certain object, we will infer an internal state consistent with our behavior ("I voluntarily give money to charities, so I am generous").

Self-perception of attitudes from behavior is most likely when attitudes are newly formed, weak, or ambiguous. Once an individual has developed a strong, accessible evaluation (for example, of NFL football), he or she will not have to analyze relevant behaviors to know his or her attitude (such as, "Do I watch the NFL on television?", "Do I talk about football with other people?"). But when attitudes are weak, self-perception processes may indeed be used to infer one's position.

A study by Chaiken and Baldwin (1981) nicely illustrates how self-perception occurs only for weak attitudes. These authors identified groups of people with "well-defined" or "poorly defined" attitudes toward environmental issues based on whether people's cognitions and feelings in this domain were consistent or inconsistent ("well-defined" attitudes were those that were comprised of either favorable beliefs and favorable feelings or unfavorable beliefs and unfavorable feelings). Participants were given a questionnaire to complete that was designed to make them review their past behaviors in a biased way. Some participants completed a "pro-ecology" questionnaire, which made their previous pro-ecology behaviors salient, whereas other participants completed an "anti-ecology" questionnaire, which made their previous anti-ecology behaviors salient. Participants then rated their attitudes toward environmental issues. Table 5.3 presents the results of the attitude ratings. For those individuals with poorly defined attitudes, the biased review of past behaviors influenced their attitudes: Those persons for whom pro-ecology behaviors were made salient rated themselves as significantly more pro-environment than did those individuals for whom anti-ecology behaviors were made salient. In contrast, the salience manipulation did not influence the attitude ratings of individuals who possessed well-defined attitudes. In sum, only those individuals whose attitudes were weak or ambiguous used their past actions (as made salient by the researchers' biased questions) to infer their environmental attitudes.

As we will see in chapter 6 on persuasion, self-perception theory was originally proposed as an alternative to dissonance theory. It turns out that self-perception processes cannot easily explain the full range of dissonance phenomena, so its original goal was not achieved. Nevertheless, self-perception theory has stimulated its own literature distinct from dissonance effects and has provided useful information about self-inference mechanisms.

TABLE 5.3   **SELF-RATING OF ENVIRONMENTAL ATTITUDES AS A FUNCTION OF SALIENT PAST BEHAVIORS**

	Poorly Defined Attitudes	Well-Defined Attitudes
Pro-environmental behaviors salient	11.33	8.25
Anti-environmental behaviors salient	9.00	9.68

Note: Higher numbers indicate a greater tendency to rate oneself as pro-environment.
Source: Adapted from Chaiken and Baldwin (1981), p. 6

Biological Factors in Attitude Formation

One of the universal assumptions in the social psychology of attitudes is that attitudes are learned—that is, they develop from people's direct and indirect experiences. We are not born loving basketball or opposing capital punishment; these evaluations develop from our experiences as children and adults.

The assumption that attitudes are learned has led social psychologists to focus on external, environmental determinants of attitudes rather than on internal, biological ones. Some attitude theorists have speculated about the role of biology (McGuire, 1985; Olson and Zanna, 1993; Oskamp, 1991), but few have collected relevant data. How might biological characteristics affect attitudes? The most likely sequence is that physical factors determine predispositions toward particular attitudes, which may or may not develop depending on environmental factors. For example, hormones may play a role in some classes of behaviors (for example, testosterone in aggressive behavior), and people's hormone levels could make it more likely that particular attitudes will develop. High levels of testosterone might predispose positive attitudes toward aggressive sports because people with lots of testosterone might be naturally aggressive themselves.

Drugs and Attitudes

One type of study that underscores humans' biological nature is pharmacological research. Abundant evidence exists that various drugs influence moods, emotions, behavior, and attitudes.

Probably the most researched drug is alcohol. Bostrom and White (1979) found that alcohol reduced recipients' attitude change to a counterattitudinal message (arguing for a position different than the recipient's attitude). They speculated that alcohol, a central nervous system depressant, lessened the discomfort caused by the counterattitudinal message and thereby reduced individuals' motivation to change their attitudes.

Steele and Josephs (1990) coined the term **alcohol myopia** to refer to the fact that alcohol intoxication reduces cognitive capacity, which leads to a focus on only the most salient cues in the environment. Thus, for example, if salient cues suggest aggression is appropriate, then alcohol intoxication will increase aggressive behavior, whereas if salient cues suggest helpfulness is appropriate, then alcohol intoxication can actually increase helpful behavior (Steele, Critchlow, and Liu, 1985). Consistent with this reasoning, MacDonald, Zanna, and Fong (1995) found that intoxicated individuals expressed more favorable attitudes than did sober individuals toward drinking and driving when salient cues suggested that such behavior might be reasonable (for example, when they needed to go only a short distance).

In the domain of sexual attitudes and behavior, there has been considerable interest in the role of alcohol both in initiating sex and in reducing sexual precautions. Evidence suggests that alcohol and sex often co-occur (Temple and Leigh, 1992), which may reflect the fact that alcohol can reduce inhibitions when situational cues are favorable for sexual contact. Some correlational evidence indicates that alcohol use is associated with factors that indicate increased risk for transmission of HIV, the virus responsible for AIDS (Kelly, St. Lawrence, and Brasfield, 1991). Although

As a social occasion involving drinking proceeds, its participants tend to focus on the most salient cues from the group and respond with expressions of the appropriate attitudes.

the young people whose stories opened this chapter did not implicate alcohol in their acquisition of HIV, many other infected people do report that alcohol impaired their judgment about practicing safer sex (Fisher and Fisher, 1992b). MacDonald, Zanna, and Fong (1996) surveyed university students and identified more than one thousand who had been sexually active in the last six months and who reported that they were regular users of condoms. Participants were asked to think back to the most recent time they had sexual intercourse and report whether or not they used a condom and how intoxicated (if at all) they were. Among men (but not women), greater intoxication was associated with less condom use. For example, 84 percent of the male regular condom users who reported consuming little or no alcohol prior to their last sexual liason also reported using a condom, whereas only 68 percent of the male regular condom users who reported being moderately or heavily intoxicated when they last had sex also reported using a condom.

In a laboratory experiment, Gordon and Carey (1996) found that alcohol intoxication led men to express more negative attitudes toward condoms and less confidence that they would be able to engage in safer sex behaviors, such as initiating a discussion of condom use with a new partner. In three experiments (two in the laboratory and one in a campus pub), Mac-

Donald, Zanna, and Fong (1996) showed a videotape to men who were regular condom users. The videotape portrayed a man and a woman who both wanted to have sexual intercourse but did not have any condoms. Participants were asked whether they would have sex if they were in this situation. Alcohol intoxication increased men's reported likelihood of engaging in this unprotected sex. Alcohol also increased men's agreement with justifications for the unprotected sex (for example, the woman looked healthy and was on the pill). Thus, alcohol use appears to be causally connected to internal mediators (beliefs, attitudes, and intentions) of risky sexual behavior.

Genetic Factors and Attitudes

Perhaps the most provocative biological perspective on attitudes concerns the role of genetic factors. The main idea underlying behavioral genetics is that individuals' genotypes (genetic makeups) determine, in part, their phenotypes (observable characteristics). The statistic usually calculated to estimate genetic influence is the **heritability coefficient,** which represents an estimate of the amount of variance in a particular characteristic within a sample that is attributable to genetic factors. By comparing the similarity between different kinds of relatives, estimates of genetic influence are possible. For example, if identical twins (who share 100 percent of their genes) are more similar to one another than fraternal twins (who share approximately 50 percent of their genes), then a genetic influence on the characteristic is suggested (assuming that the environments of identical and fraternal twins are equally similar to one another, which is an important and sometimes questionable assumption). Of course, to the extent that identical twins differ between themselves at all on a characteristic, environmental factors are necessarily implicated (because the twins are genetically identical). Heritability coefficients estimate the extent to which differences between people in a sample are due to genetic factors (thus, heritability coefficients depend, in part, on the diversity or variability of the sample). But heritability coefficients do *not* tell us whether a feature can be changed. To take a simple example, hair color, which is genetically determined, is totally malleable.

With these caveats in mind, let us review some behavioral genetics research on attitudes. In a sample of more than three thousand pairs of British twins, Martin, Eaves, Jardine, Heath, Feingold, and Eysenck (1986) calculated heritability coefficients for fifty items relating to political and social attitudes. These authors obtained heritabilities ranging from 7 percent to 51 percent, with twenty-three of the fifty items revealing significant genetic effects. In a sample of more than eight hundred pairs of British twins, Eaves, Eysenck, and Martin (1989) obtained heritability coefficients ranging from 1 percent to 63 percent on sixty attitude items. Finally, Olson, Vernon, Harris, and Jang (in press) surveyed more than three hundred pairs of Canadian twins and obtained measures of thirty attitudes. The authors performed a factor analysis of the attitude items—a procedure that looks for similarity in how items are answered. This analysis identified nine underlying factors (including attitudes toward equality, preservation of life, athletics, intellectual activities, treatment of criminals). Six of the nine factors yielded significant heritability coefficients, which went as high as 66 percent. For example, attitudes toward athletic activities (exercise, organized sports) exhibited a significant genetic component. Perhaps individuals' natural (inherited) athletic abilities (such as coordination, strength, speed) predisposed them to form either favorable or unfavorable attitudes toward sports.

In a fascinating set of studies, Tesser (1993) tested the implications of this idea that attitudes may have a genetic component. He reasoned that if some attitudes are biologically based, people may not want (or be able) to change them. Thus, people might build up psychological defenses around their genetically based attitudes, which would serve to make those attitudes stronger and more resistant to change. Tesser selected for his studies several attitude issues that had been shown to yield high heritabilities in earlier research on twins (such as attitudes toward the death penalty) and several issues that had yielded low heritabilities (such as attitudes toward capitalism). He found that the highly heritable attitudes were more accessible in people's minds (people were able to report them more quickly) and were more resistant to influence than low heritability attitudes. He also found that similarity between two people on highly heritable attitudes increased liking to a greater extent than did similarity between two people on low heritability attitudes. These data are consistent with the idea that highly heritable attitudes may be more "important" or "strong," perhaps because they have a biological substrate that makes change difficult.

Attitudes and Information Processing

One of the functions of attitudes mentioned earlier was the knowledge function, which refers to the fact that attitudes facilitate the identification of objects— they constitute one of the factors guiding the perception and interpretation of objects. In a sense, then, attitudes serve as a psychological "lens" through which information is processed and the world is viewed. In this section, we discuss the impact of attitudes on information processing. The theme of this section is *selectivity*: attitudes bias information processing so that information consistent with attitudes is more likely to be processed. Selectivity can operate at all stages of information processing, including attention (what gets noticed), perception (how stimuli are interpreted), and memory (what gets recalled). The effects of attitudes on information processing should be greater when attitudes are highly accessible (that is, when attitudes come to mind quickly; Fazio, 1990) because accessible attitudes are automatically activated in the presence of the object and therefore influence perception.

"Women and children first. I mean, come on."

Selective Attention

One of the oldest ideas in the attitudes literature is that people are more likely to pay attention to things that support, or are consistent with, their attitudes, values, and decisions. This hypothesis of **selective attention** received its clearest statement in Leon Festinger's (1957, 1964) dissonance theory, which is discussed in detail in chapter 6. For the present purposes, we need only know that Festinger proposed two patterns of motivated attention based on the assumption that people want to believe that their attitudes and decisions are correct. First, people selectively seek out or pay attention to information that is consistent with their attitudes. Second, people selectively avoid or ignore information that is inconsistent with their attitudes. Together, these components make up the **selective exposure hypothesis:** perceivers actively control their exposure to information so that consistent information is approached and inconsistent information is avoided.

Early tests of the selective exposure hypothesis yielded inconsistent results (see Freedman and Sears, 1965). Some studies indicated that perceivers preferred consistent over inconsistent information, but other studies actually uncovered a preference for inconsistent information. Gradually, boundary conditions for selective exposure were identified (see Frey, 1986; Wicklund and Brehm, 1976). Most important, people approach and avoid information for many reasons, only one of which is the information's consistency or inconsistency with existing attitudes. These other factors must be controlled in order to test the selective exposure hypothesis fairly. Information that is useful will often be approached even if it is inconsistent with attitudes (for example, a magazine article that questions the safety of something you own will be read carefully because this information might protect you). Also, situational norms often demand that people pay attention to information on both sides of an issue irrespective of their opinions (for example, jurors in a trial are expected to pay close attention to all evidence).

When these complicating factors are controlled, evidence supports the selective exposure hypothesis as in an interesting field study reported by Sweeney and Gruber (1984). During the Watergate scandal in 1973, people were contacted and interviewed about the affair. Watergate was presumably attitudinally inconsistent for voters who had supported President Nixon in the 1972 election; in contrast, voters who had supported the Democratic candidate McGovern might have found the affair attitudinally consistent. As this logic would imply, the researchers found that McGovern supporters reported significantly *more* attention to and discussion of Watergate than did a group of undecided citizens (selective approach of consistent information), whereas Nixon supporters reported significantly *less* attention to Watergate than the undecided group (selective avoidance of inconsistent information). Table 5.4 presents these results.

Selective Perception

Not only do attitudes guide attention, but they also influence how stimuli are perceived, or interpreted. That is, assuming that information gets noticed in the first place (which will depend, in part, on its attitudinal consistency), individuals' processing of the information will be further biased by selective interpretation, or **selective perception.** In general, perceivers tend to interpret information as being more supportive of their attitudes than it really is. This effect should be particularly pronounced when the information is ambiguous because such circumstances allow the greatest flexibility in perception (just like schemas guide

TABLE 5.4   SELECTIVE EXPOSURE TO WATERGATE NEWS AS A FUNCTION OF POLITICAL ATTITUDES

	Attention to Watergate	Discussion of Watergate
Nixon supporters	2.11	1.70
Undecided	2.41	1.73
McGovern supporters	2.68	2.25

Note: Higher numbers indicate greater reported attention to Watergate and more frequent reported discussion of Watergate.
Source: Sweeney and Guber (1984), pp. 1211–12

perceptions of ambiguous stimuli, as discussed in chapter 2).

Many researchers have documented the effects of attitudes on interpretations of information. For example, Vidmar and Rokeach (1974) found that viewers' perceptions of the television show *All in the Family* were related to their racial attitudes. Low-prejudice viewers said that the bigoted character of Archie Bunker was the principal target of humor and sarcasm in the show, whereas high-prejudice viewers saw Archie more sympathetically and thought that he won most of his arguments with his liberal son-in-law Mike (the "meathead," in Archie's words).

Fazio and Williams (1986) telephoned people during the 1984 U.S. presidential election campaign and asked them to evaluate the candidates, Ronald Reagan and Walter Mondale. They recorded both the direction of participants' attitudes (for or against each candidate) and the latency of the responses. The researchers assumed that response speeds indicated the accessibility of the attitudes. Subsequently, participants were contacted again and asked to evaluate the performances of the candidates in televised presidential and vice-presidential debates. Evaluations of the candidates were correlated with participants' attitudes. For example, pro-Reagan participants evaluated Reagan's and Bush's performances more favorably than did anti-Reagan participants. Of importance was that when the analyses were limited to participants who actually watched the debates, the correlations were significantly *stronger* for participants whose attitudes toward Reagan were highly accessible (those who had expressed their original evaluation of Reagan quickly) than for participants whose attitudes toward Reagan were not accessible. Thus, selective perception was more pronounced when individuals' attitudes were highly accessible. We will return to this study in the section on attitude-behavior consistency.

In an interesting extension of selective perception to a population where it might not be expected to occur, Mahoney (1977) showed that research scientists' evaluations of other scientists' work was influenced by their theoretical orientations. Specifically, when a study purported to find results consistent with the reviewer's favored theoretical perspective, it was judged more favorably than when it purported to find results contradicting the reviewer's favored perspective.

If interpretations of information are biased so that the amount of attitude-consistent information is overestimated, there may be a general tendency toward attitude polarization over time, because everyone is interpreting the available information as supporting their own view. But what about cases where the information is clearly *mixed*—that is, some evidence supports one position and other evidence supports a different position? Box 5.1 describes two studies suggesting that attitude polarization may also occur in such a setting.

Selective Memory

The final source of attitudinal selectivity to be discussed is the impact of attitudes on memory—**selective memory.** There are several reasons to expect that information consistent with attitudes will be overrepresented in memory relative to inconsistent information. First, information that is consistent with attitudes may be easier to encode in long-term memory because it fits or matches existing structures and schemas (see chapter 2). Thus, such information is more likely to be there when perceivers subsequently search their memory. Second, people may intentionally try to repress or forget inconsistent information, which, over time, will increase the proportion of supportive material in memory. Third, people may use their attitudes as clues for searching memory, which will direct them toward supportive material.

BOX 5.1

Seeing What You Want to See: Selective Perception of Mixed Information

Selective perception refers to biased interpretations of information based on existing attitudes. In general, people tend to see information as being more supportive of their attitudes than is warranted. But what about situations in which some information supports one view and other information supports another view? Cases of mixed information are very common—indeed, they may be the norm rather than the exception when it comes to controversial issues like abortion, capital punishment, political ideologies, and so on. Ideally, one might hope that mixed information will result in attitudes becoming more moderate. After all, if there is supportive information available for competing views, then perceivers should be less confident that their own position is "correct."

Evidence from social psychology, however, suggests that mixed information has less magnanimous effects. In a well-known study, Lord, Ross, and Lepper (1979) recruited participants who had preexisting favorable or unfavorable attitudes toward capital punishment. All participants were given descriptions of two (alleged) studies of the deterrent effects of capital punishment. These two studies constituted a clear "mix" of evidence in that one study concluded that capital punishment *is* a deterrent to murder and the other concluded that capital punishment *is not* a deterrent. Each description included information about the procedures and results of the study along with some criticisms of the research and the authors' rebuttals to the criticisms.

How did participants react to this mixed bag of evidence? Did they moderate their positions, realizing that the issue is not open-and-shut? No. In fact, after reading the descriptions of the two studies, pro-capital punishment participants became significantly more pro, and anti-capital punishment participants became significantly more anti. In short, attitude *polarization* occurred following exposure to mixed information! Participants were also asked to evaluate the quality of the two studies, and these data indicated that the source of the polarization effect may have been selective perceptions of the relevant data. Specifically, participants evaluated the study that supported their position more favorably than the study that opposed their position. Thus, the *objectively* mixed evidence did not *seem* mixed to participants in the study. Rather, participants believed that there was one high-quality study that supported their views and one low-quality study that opposed their views; it may not be surprising that they consequently became even more confident in their original position.

Houston and Fazio (1989) replicated this study but also measured how quickly participants reported their attitudes toward capital punishment before reading the articles. Results showed that, like the earlier study, participants evaluated the two alleged studies in a biased manner, rating the study that supported their position more favorably than the study that opposed their position. This pattern was statistically reliable, however, only for participants whose attitudes were highly accessible; that is, when respondents reported their initial attitudes relatively quickly, their subsequent perceptions of the studies were biased toward consistency with their attitudes. These data suggest that selective perception is a consequence primarily of accessible attitudes.

Ross (1989) reviewed a number of studies showing that people use their attitudes as clues for searching memory and/or reconstructing past events. For example, Ross, McFarland, and Fletcher (1981) exposed respondents to a message arguing either for or against frequent toothbrushing (the "anti" message argued for flossing instead). Some participants then completed measures of attitudes, which showed that the messages were effective in producing divergent attitudes. Of more interest was that other participants completed a questionnaire (in what they thought was a different experiment) assessing the frequency with which they had performed a number of behaviors in the last month, including toothbrushing. Participants who had been exposed to a negative toothbrushing message reported brushing their teeth less often in the past month than did participants exposed to a positive toothbrushing message. The authors argued that subjects used their newly formed attitudes to reconstruct their behaviors in the previous month.

Other researchers have shown that, when people are exposed to information on an issue, they subsequently recall material that supports their attitudes better than nonsupportive material. For example, Roberts (1984) exposed smokers, ex-smokers, and nonsmokers to favorable and unfavorable statements about smoking. Participants were then unexpectedly tested for recall of the statements. The results are presented in table 5.5. Nonsmokers and ex-smokers recalled significantly more antismoking statements than prosmoking statements, whereas smokers showed a nonsignificant tendency in the opposite direction, recalling slightly more prosmoking than antismoking statements. In a second

According to the Roberts study, would the statements from this American Lung Association poster tend to be recalled more by nonsmokers and ex-smokers or by smokers?

TABLE 5.5   **RECALL OF SMOKING STATEMENTS AS A FUNCTION OF SMOKING STATUS**

	Statement Category	
	Antismoking (8)[a]	Prosmoking (5)
Smokers (15)[b]	1.26	1.53
Ex-smokers (24)	1.83	1.08
Nonsmokers (36)	2.56	1.50

a. Number of statements in communication.
b. Number of subjects per group.

Source: Roberts (1984), p. 210

TABLE 5.6   **RECALL OF SEAT BELT STATEMENTS AS A FUNCTION OF SEAT BELT USAGE**

	Statement Category	
Seat Belt Behavior	Pro–Seat Belt (5)[a]	Anti–Seat Belt (5)
Always wear (28)[b]	2.29	1.61
Sometimes wear (18)	1.72	1.78
Never wear (15)	1.60	2.07

a. Number of statements in communication.
b. Number of subjects per group.

Source: Roberts (1984), p. 212

study, Roberts (1984) exposed people to statements about seat belts, both favorable and unfavorable. Again, an unexpected recall test yielded evidence of selective memory (see table 5.6). Participants who reported they always wore seat belts recalled significantly more pro–seat belt than anti–seat belt statements, whereas participants who reported they never wore seat belts recalled significantly more anti–seat belt than pro–seat belt statements. Participants who reported that they "sometimes" wore seat belts were right in the middle, recalling approximately equal numbers of pro– and anti–seat belt statements. These and other data suggest that attitudes exert a selective effect on memory, making supportive information more likely to be stored and retrieved than nonsupportive information.

Attitudes and Behavior

People's attitudes are presumed to determine, at least in part, their actions. If we like someone, we act differently than if we dislike someone; an individual with favorable attitudes toward social welfare programs will behave differently (for example, voting, talking with others) than will an individual with unfavorable attitudes.

This assumed attitude-behavior relation is both intuitively plausible and critically important for continued interest in the attitudes concept. Yet, attitude-behavior consistency has not always proved easy to document, which has led some theorists to question whether attitudes are significant determinants of action. An early and famous example of apparent inconsistency between attitudes and actions was reported by LaPiere (1934). At the time his study was conducted, anti-Chinese feelings were quite prevalent in North America. LaPiere took a well-dressed Chinese couple on a tour of the United States, covering more than ten-thousand miles and visiting over two hundred fifty restaurants, hotels, and autocamps. Only one establishment (a "rather inferior autocamp") refused to serve the Chinese couple. After the tour was completed, LaPiere sent a letter to every place they had visited, asking the proprietors whether they served members of the Chinese race at their establishment. Almost exactly 50 percent of the establishments replied: Incredibly, only one answered yes to the question about accepting Chinese guests, whereas more than 90 percent answered no (the remaining responses were "it depends"). It is difficult to imagine a more extreme example of apparently nonoverlapping attitudes and behaviors.

Some methodological problems marred LaPiere's study, however. For example, it is possible that some of the people who answered the questionnaires were not the same ones who served the Chinese couple. Also, the questionnaire asked about the rather ambiguous target of "members of the Chinese race," whereas the Chinese couple that arrived at the establishments was young, well dressed, and often accompanied by a Caucasian. Thus, there were reasons to doubt that LaPiere's study really showed that attitudes do not predict behavior. However, in 1969, Wicker published a review of more than thirty studies that examined attitude-behavior consistency. He found that the correlation between measures of attitudes and measures of behaviors rarely exceeded .30, which is a fairly weak relation (it implies that attitudes account for less than 10 percent of the variance in behaviors). Wicker concluded that there was "little evidence to support the postulated existence of stable, underlying attitudes within the individual which influence both his verbal expressions and his actions" (1969, p. 75).

This pessimistic conclusion served as a challenge to researchers in the attitudes literature, who continued to believe that the attitudes concept was useful for understanding and explaining behavior but who recognized that compelling evidence was lacking. Fortunately, in the years since 1969, several factors have been identified as influencing attitude-behavior consistency to show that attitudes and behaviors are closely related in some circumstances but not in others. In the following sections, we discuss several factors that influence attitude-behavior consistency.

Compatibility of Attitude and Behavior Measures

An important conceptual advance came from Fishbein and Ajzen's (1975) theory of reasoned action (which we mentioned earlier when discussing how attitudes can be based on cognitive beliefs). Fishbein and Ajzen argued that because "general" attitudes will predict only "general" behaviors and "specific" attitudes will predict only "specific" behaviors, measures of attitudes and behaviors must be *compatible* (both general or both specific). This issue of the **compatibility of attitude and behavior measures** has been shown to be critical for understanding attitude-behavior consistency.

General Attitudes and General Behaviors

By general attitudes, Fishbein and Ajzen meant attitudes toward objects, people, and issues. By general behaviors, they meant measures of the entire *class* of actions toward the target. They argued that an individual's attitude toward an issue will predict the favorability of the overall set of behaviors relevant to the issue, but the attitude will not predict single, specific behaviors very well. For example, your attitude toward energy conservation will predict the overall degree to which you exhibit conservation behaviors across many different situations and over a long period of time. However, your attitude will not predict (at least, not nearly as well) specific conservation behaviors, such as whether you recycle newspapers next week, ride the bus to work tomorrow, or turn down the

thermostat in your house tonight. The reason is that each of these single behaviors will be determined in part by factors unrelated to conservation attitudes, such as whether a recycling program is available where you live, whether you need to keep the house warm tonight for a visitor, and so on. Also, unexpected events sometimes interfere with specific behaviors (for example, you may be sick and fail to put the recycling box outside to be picked up). Presumably, these individual, idiosyncratic circumstances and events should "even out" across the whole set of behaviors that are relevant to the attitude object. Therefore, general attitudes will predict the favorability of an entire class or set of activities even if they don't predict individual actions.

When the studies reviewed by Wicker (1969) are examined, it turns out that many of them used measures of general attitudes to predict measures of specific behaviors. For example, a measure of prejudicial attitudes of whites toward blacks might be used to predict how close white participants sit to a specific black person in a particular setting. According to Fishbein and Ajzen, strong correlations should not be expected in these circumstances.

Measures that include a wide variety of behaviors related to an attitude (general behavior measures) are called **multiple-act behavioral criteria.** Several researchers have shown that measures of general attitudes correlate highly (typically, .50 or even higher) with multiple-act behavioral criteria, whereas the typical correlation between measures of general attitudes and specific behaviors is much lower (often at or below the .30 level noted by Wicker, 1969). For example, Zanna, Olson, and Fazio (1980) measured participants' attitudes toward religion and found that these general attitudes correlated weakly (.09 to .38) with participants' reports of specific religious behaviors, such as attending religious services and praying in private. A multiple-act behavioral criterion, however, consisting of a questionnaire that assessed ninety actions relevant to religion, correlated much more highly (.54) with participants' attitudes. Box 5.2 describes another study that nicely demonstrated the importance of multiple-act behavioral criteria for testing the predictive utility of general attitudes.

Specific Attitudes and Specific Behaviors

A specific attitude is an attitude toward a particular behavior, such as drinking coffee, attending a psy-

BOX 5.2

Multiple-Act Behavioral Criteria: Forming General Measures of Behavior

An attitude toward an object or issue should predict the favorability of the overall class of actions relevant to the target rather than the favorability of single, specific actions toward the target. Thus, to test attitude-behavior consistency fairly, measures of behaviors must sample widely from the set of behaviors related to the target across time and circumstances. Such measures of behavior are called "multiple-act behavioral criteria."

Weigel and Newman (1976) conducted an interesting study of attitude-behavior consistency, which documented the importance of multiple-act behavioral criteria. One of the outstanding features of this study was that the behavioral measures assessed "real," objective behavior rather than self-reported behavior or behavioral intentions (which are much easier to obtain and therefore more common than measures of actual behavior).

In Weigel and Newman's study, forty-four residents of a town in New England completed a survey of attitudes toward a variety of social issues, including their concern about the environment (measured by sixteen items). An overall measure of attitudes toward the environment was calculated by summing respondents' answers to the sixteen items.

Three months later, an experimental assistant went door-to-door to each of the residents and presented three petitions protesting environmental issues (the assistant claimed to be a member of an environmental protection organization comprised of local citizens). The petitions opposed off-shore drilling along the New England coast, opposed construction of nuclear power plants, and proposed tougher laws to keep people from removing air pollution devices from cars' exhaust sytems. Participants could sign or not sign each petition; they were also

asked whether they would be willing to circulate the petitions to family or friends.

Six weeks after the petition request, residents were contacted by a second experimental assistant, who asked them to participate in a roadside litter pick-up program in the town. Three possible times were specified, and residents were encouraged to bring a friend or family member to participate as well. The behavioral measures were whether residents attended one of the litter pick-up sessions and whether or not they brought another person along with them.

Two months after the litter pick-up request, residents were contacted by a third experimental assistant, who asked them to participate in a recycling program for newspapers and glass, in which they would put these materials outside to be picked up on a regular weekly route. A behavioral measure was then obtained for each of eight weeks, reflecting whether or not residents put out materials for recycling that week.

Weigel and Newman computed the correlations between environmental attitudes and various measures of behavior. First, they computed correlations between attitudes and each *specific,* individual behavior measure; second, they computed correlations between attitudes and each *category* of behaviors (petitions, litter pick-up, and recycling); and, finally, they computed the correlation between attitudes and a comprehensive behavioral index that summed across *all* behavior items. The table presents the results of these analyses. As the table shows, general attitudes toward the environment were only weakly related to specific environmental behaviors, with an average correlation of .29. When behaviors were summed across a category, the attitude-behavior relations were

Continued

BOX 5.2

Continued

much stronger, with an average correlation of .42. And when the broadest possible multiple-act criterion was computed, attitude-behavior consistency was very high, with a correlation of .62.

These data show that general attitudes do indeed predict behavior so long as the behavior measure is also a general one (a multiple-act behavioral criterion). Compatibility between measures of attitudes and behaviors is a critical moderating variable for attitude-behavior consistency.

CORRELATIONS BETWEEN ENVIRONMENTAL ATTITUDES AND VARIOUS BEHAVIORAL CRITERIA

Single Behaviors	r^a	Categories of Behavior	r^b	Behavioral Index	r^b
Offshore oil	.41**				
Nuclear power	.36*	Petitioning behavior	.50**		
Auto exhaust	.39**	scale (0–4)			
Circulate petitions	.27				
Individual participation	.34*	Litter pick-up	.36*		
Recruit friend	.22	scale (0–2)		Comprehensive behavioral index	.62***
Week 1	.34*				
Week 2	.57***				
Week 3	.34*				
Week 4	.33*	Recycling behavior	.39**		
Week 5	.12	scale (0–8)			
Week 6	.20				
Week 7	.20				
Week 8	.34*				

Note: N = 44
a. Point-biserial correlations are reported in this column.
b. Pearson product-moment correlations are reported in this column.
 * $p < .05$
 ** $p < .01$
 *** $p < .001$
Source: Weigel and Newman (1976)

chology class, or abstaining from sex. A specific measure of behavior is a measure of an action toward a target in a particular place at a particular time. As this latter definition implies, behaviors can be specified along four dimensions, or components: action (what the behavior is—drinking, attending, abstaining), target (what the action is directed at—coffee, a psychology class, sex), context (the place where the act occurs), and time (when the act occurs). A measure of a single, specific behavior will always be limited in these ways (action, target, context, time). For example, a researcher might measure whether students attend class on a given day or whether people in a shopping mall on a particular day stop to help a woman who drops her groceries.

If the goal is to predict a specific behavior, then the measure of attitudes should be compatible—that is, it should consist of participants' attitudes toward performing the specific act. The more components (action, target, context, time) that match, the higher the attitude-behavior correlation should be (attitudes toward attending a class on a specific day should yield the highest correlation). The most important matches, though, are action and target. Thus, attitudes toward behavior X will normally provide a good prediction of any specific measure of behavior X, irrespective of the action's context or time.

Davidson and Jaccard (1979) conducted a study that demonstrated the importance of using compatible measures of attitudes and behaviors. Their interest was in predicting whether women would use birth control pills during a two-year period following an attitude survey. Attitudes were measured at various degrees of specificity, ranging from general attitudes (for example, attitudes toward birth control) to specific ones (for example, attitudes toward using birth control pills during the next two years). Table 5.7 shows that as the attitude measure matched the behavior measure more closely, the correlation steadily increased. Attitudes *do* predict behavior so long as the measures of attitudes and behaviors are compatible.

Fishbein and Ajzen (1975) proposed a full model of the causes of specific behaviors. Their theory of reasoned action is diagrammed in figure 5.3. As the figure shows, the immediate, proximal cause of a specific behavior is assumed to be the individual's intention to perform or not perform the act because people normally do what they intend to do. But where do behavioral intentions come from? Fishbein and Ajzen hypothesized that intentions are based on two things: attitudes toward performing the behavior and subjective norms concerning the behavior. We have already discussed attitudes toward behaviors—they are the specific attitudes in our preceding discussion (which will be based on people's beliefs about the consequences of the behaviors). **Subjective norms** refer to perceived social pressure to act in a certain way. They result from our beliefs about what other people want us to do (called **normative beliefs**). If we believe that our mother wants us go to church on Sundays, we will feel some pressure to do so (assuming that we care about what our mother wants).

The theory of reasoned action postulates that people's actions in a particular situation are jointly determined by how they evaluate possible behaviors in the situation (attitudes) and the social pressures they feel concerning the possible behaviors (subjective norms). This model of the causes of behavior has received

---

TABLE 5.7 **CORRELATIONS BETWEEN ATTITUDE MEASURES AND USE OF BIRTH CONTROL PILLS DURING TWO-YEAR PERIOD**

Attitudinal Variable	*r*
Attitude toward birth control	.083
Attitude toward birth control pills	.323*
Attitude toward using birth control pills	.525*
Attitude toward using birth control pills during the next 2 years	.572*

*$p < .01$.
Source: Davidson and Jaccard (1979), p. 1372

FIGURE 5.3   THE THEORY OF REASONED ACTION.

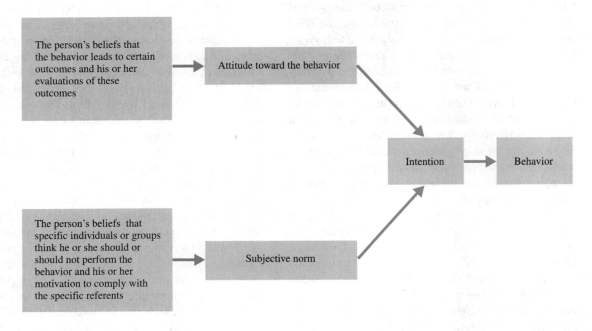

Note: Arrows indicate the direction of influence.
Source: Ajzen and Fishbein (1980), p. 8

good support in many studies where the focal behaviors have included voting, smoking, using birth control, drinking alcohol, donating blood, using a seat belt, and buying various products (for reviews, see Ajzen and Fishbein, 1980; Eagly and Chaiken, 1993). The theory of reasoned action has been the dominant theoretical framework in the attitude-behavior consistency literature for the last twenty years.

Nature of the Behavior

A second factor that influences attitude-behavior consistency is the nature of the behavior. Certain kinds of behaviors are more likely to be consistent with individuals' attitudes than are other kinds of behaviors. What aspects influence whether behaviors will be consistent with attitudes? The theory of reasoned action gives us one clue. Fishbein and Ajzen (1975) argued that subjective norms (social pressures) are independent from attitudes as determinants of behavior. Therefore, if the norms concerning a behavior are very strong, it is *un*likely that the individual's attitudes will influence the behavior

(rather, the powerful norms will carry the day). For example, social customs and politeness norms prescribe many behaviors, which we perform automatically without considering our attitudes. Saying hello to coworkers even if we don't like them, leaving a tip for the waiter even when the service was mediocre, and saying a friend's new haircut is nice even when we think it is ghastly are examples of behaviors guided by social norms. Attitudes will predict behavior only when the actions are not highly controlled by norms and social pressures.

Normatively controlled behavior is just one example of a broader category of actions that will be relatively independent of attitudes. Why don't attitudes predict normatively prescribed behavior? *Because such behaviors are not fully under volitional control.* Attitudes (personal preferences) can influence behavior only when the individual has personal choice about whether to perform the action. Many factors can make an action relatively involuntary, of which social norms are but one example. Extreme threats or large rewards can supplant volition, such as when children do not play with matches (though they want to) because their parents have threatened punishment, or when children practice the piano (though they don't want to) because their parents have bribed them with a reward. In these circumstances, the behaviors are externally controlled, so individuals' internal characteristics (such as attitudes) make little difference. For other actions, people will simply *believe* that they cannot perform a behavior, which will effectively eliminate attitudes as a cause of action. For example, a drug addict might desperately want to stop using drugs but believe that he is incapable of stopping, or a university student might have a positive attitude toward exercising but believe that she is so busy that she cannot possibly fit exercise into her schedule at this time. For these persons, the focal behaviors (quitting drugs, starting ex-ercise) are perceived as being outside their personal control, so attitudes are irrelevant.

When the theory of reasoned action was proposed, Fishbein and Ajzen (1975) explicitly limited their model to volitional behavior. Subsequently, however, Ajzen (1985) expanded the model to incorporate behavior not fully under volitional control by adding a third determinant of behavioral intentions. This **theory of planned behavior** is displayed in figure 5.4. Ajzen proposed that **perceived behavioral control** influences behavioral intentions independently of attitudes and subjective norms. He meant that people take into account whether they are capable of performing a behavior when they formulate their intentions. If a behavior seems beyond their personal control, then people will simply not intend

FIGURE 5.4   **THE THEORY OF PLANNED BEHAVIOR**

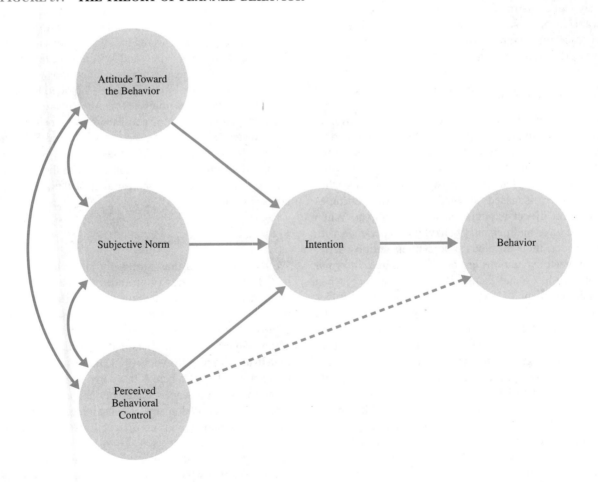

Note: The broken line indicates that perceived behavioral control can sometimes have a direct effect on behavior, not mediated by intentions.
Source: Ajzen and Madden (1986), p. 458

to perform it. This concept of perceived behavioral control is very similar to the notion of **self-efficacy** (Bandura, 1977), which refers to the extent to which individuals believe they have the skills and opportunities necessary to perform an action. Several studies have suggested that the theory of planned behavior may have better predictive power in some domains than the theory of reasoned action (see Ajzen, 1991).

The failure to use condoms to protect against AIDS and other sexually transmitted diseases (STDs) may often reflect, at least in part, perceptions of low self-efficacy or low volitional control. For example, individuals may believe that if they want to hold on to their partner, they simply cannot question his or her health status by insisting on the use of condoms. Thus, safer sex behavior is not an option in these individuals' minds. Alternatively, people may feel incapable of discussing safer sex behaviors in advance because they feel embarrassed or would be admitting that they want to have sex. Thus, perceptions of low self-efficacy might inhibit these persons from acting the way they know they should.

Nature of the Attitude

Not only are certain behaviors (namely, volitional ones) more likely to depend on attitudes, but certain attitudes are also more likely to predict behaviors. What kinds of attitudes strongly predict behavior? One relevant characteristic was mentioned earlier when we discussed attitude formation—attitudes based on **direct experience** with the object. When people have had personal behavioral experience with an object, their attitudes predict their actions better than when evaluations are based on indirect information (see Fazio and Zanna, 1981). For instance, when Fazio and Zanna (1978) measured students' attitudes toward participating in psychological experiments, some respondents had taken part in experiments before, whereas others had not. Subsequently, all participants were given the opportunity to volunteer for future studies. The researchers divided participants into three groups based on the extent of their direct experience with psychological experiments: high, moderate, or low direct experience. Individuals who had participated in many experiments before acted in accordance with their expressed attitudes (that is, they volunteered for future studies if they had favorable attitudes but did not volunteer if they had unfavorable attitudes) to a greater extent than did those who had

little or no previous experience. The correlations between attitudes and behavior were .42, .36, and −.03 for participants who had high, moderate, and low direct experience, respectively.

Why does direct experience produce attitudes that predict behavior better? Fazio (1990) has suggested that attitude accessibility is the critical factor. Accessibility refers to the ease with which an attitude comes to mind; highly accessible attitudes are activated automatically when the object is encountered. Recall that the effects of attitudes on perceptions depend on accessibility: accessible attitudes bias interpretations more than do inaccessible attitudes. In the study by Fazio and Williams (1986) described earlier, voters who reported their attitudes of Ronald Reagan quickly (high accessibility) evaluated the candidates' performances in the televised debates in a manner consistent with their attitudes to a greater extent than did slow reporters (low accessibility). If accessible attitudes guide individuals' perceptions of the situation, then they are likely to serve as the basis for actions as well. This is exactly what Fazio and Williams (1986) also found: In a subsequent follow-up interview with respondents after the election, people who rated Reagan quickly in the initial interview (either positively or negatively) reported voting consistently with their rating to a greater extent than did people who rated Reagan slowly. Response times in the initial interview therefore predicted whether people voted in line with their initial ratings—an impressive demonstration of the power of accessible attitudes.

Personality Factors

We have suggested that attitudes will predict behavior when the measures of attitudes and behavior are compatible, when the behavior is volitional, and when the attitude is accessible. Let us close the issue of attitude-behavior consistency with consideration of one final factor—the personality variable known as **self-monitoring** (Snyder, 1974) that was discussed in chapter 4. The idea here is that some people may behave more in accordance with (all of) their attitudes than other people across domains of behaviors and attitudes; that is, attitude-behavior consistency may be truer of some people than of others.

As described in chapter 4, self-monitoring refers to the extent to which people rely on internal versus external cues for behavior. People who are low in self-monitoring make their behavioral choices based on relevant internal states, such as attitudes, values, and beliefs. These individuals would therefore be expected to manifest substantial attitude-behavior consistency. People who are high in self-monitoring, on the other hand, use external cues, such as norms and the behavior of other people, to guide their behavioral choices. Thus, high self-monitors would not be expected to show much attitude-behavior consistency. Several studies have yielded results supportive of these predictions (Snyder and Swann, 1976; Zanna, Olson, and Fazio, 1980).

In an interesting exploration of the mechanisms underlying the finding that low self-monitors exhibit more attitude-behavior consistency than high self-monitors, Kardes, Sanbonmatsu, Voss, and Fazio (1986) found that the attitudes of low self-monitors were more accessible than the attitudes of high self-monitors. Presumably, low self-monitors think about their attitudes more often than do high self-monitors, which should make the attitudes more accessible. Perhaps this greater accessibility explains why the attitudes of low self-monitors are more likely to guide behavior.

Postscript: How Can We Increase Safer-Sex Behavior in the Era of AIDS?

We began this chapter with the tragic stories of two young people who died of AIDS-related causes. At various points, we have mentioned factors that might explain why sexually active young persons engage so often in behaviors that put them at risk for contracting the AIDS virus (and other sexually transmitted diseases). Such factors include beliefs about the negative consequences of using or discussing condoms, the effects of alcohol, and perceptions that discussing or insisting on condoms is beyond one's control. Let us close the chapter with an explicit consideration of what we can learn from social psychology about encouraging safer sex behavior.

Perhaps the most detailed model of the psychological determinants of AIDS-related behaviors has been proposed by Jeffrey and William Fisher, who are at the University of Connecticut and the University of Western Ontario, respectively. Fisher and Fisher (1992b) have proposed the **IMB model of AIDS-preventive behaviors,** in which *information, motivation,* and *behavioral skills* are considered to be joint determinants of safer sex behaviors. Figure 5.5 presents the IMB model.

Fisher and Fisher argued that information about AIDS and AIDS-preventive behaviors is one prerequisite for safer sex behaviors. Unless people know how the AIDS virus is transmitted and what they can do to reduce their risk, they will not take preventive actions. Most educational campaigns directed at young people have emphasized this informational component. But information is only one part of the successful avoidance of risk. A second prerequisite is the motivation to engage in AIDS-risk-reduction behaviors. Fisher and Fisher borrowed from the theory of reasoned action (see figure 5.3) to conceptualize motivation, proposing

FIGURE 5.5　**THE IMB MODEL**

Source: Fisher, Fisher, Misovich, Kimble, and Malloy (1996)

that people's motivation to perform preventive behaviors (such as using condoms, refusing to engage in unprotected sex) will depend on their attitudes toward these behaviors and their subjective norms (perceived social pressure) concerning the behaviors. Finally, Fisher and Fisher hypothesized that behavioral skills for performing specific AIDS-preventive behaviors are critical. Even knowledgeable, highly motivated people must possess some basic skills for negotiating safer sex, using condoms effectively, and so on in order for them to benefit from their knowledge and motivation.

The accuracy of the IMB model has been tested in several samples. For example, Fisher, Fisher, Williams, and Malloy (1994) recruited 126 gay men from various gay organizations in New Haven and Hartford. Participants completed measures of information, motivation, behavioral skills, and behavior pertaining to AIDS prevention. Results showed that information and motivation were related to behavioral skills, and motivation and behavioral skills were related to reported behavior at two points in time (including a follow-up measure obtained two months after the initial survey). Another test of the model with heterosexual university students also yielded supportive results (Fisher, Fisher, Williams, and Malloy, 1994).

Based on these results, Fisher, Fisher, Misovich, Kimble, and Malloy (in press) developed an intervention procedure designed to encourage safer sex behaviors (for other promising interventions to encourage safer sex behaviors, see Jemmott, Jemmott, and Fong, 1992; Jemmott, Jemmott, Spears, Hewitt, and Cruz-Collins, 1992). The intervention consisted of three, two-hour sessions held one week apart in several dormitories at the University of Connecticut, involving more than five hundred students. The intervention included elements that were aimed at each component of the IMB model. For example, a slide show on HIV transmission and prevention was used to expand participants' information and knowledge about AIDS. To increase motivation, small group discussions were led by peer educators (other students), who tried to make participants' attitudes toward AIDS-preventive behaviors more favorable. Motivation was also addressed by having participants watch *People Like Us* (Fisher and Fisher, 1992a), the video from which the stories that opened this chapter were taken. Learning that AIDS victims are typical young people was expected to enhance perceptions of personal vulnerability to HIV. Finally, behavioral skills were taught to participants in several ways, in-cluding video and live portrayals of negotiating safer sex and using condoms.

All of the components of the IMB model were measured one month after the intervention, and AIDS-preventive behaviors were measured one and two months after intervention. Scores for participants who completed the intervention were compared with scores for control students who lived on dormitory floors where the intervention was not available. The results were clear: the intervention increased AIDS-prevention information, led to more favorable attitudes toward AIDS-risk-reduction behaviors, produced stronger intentions to practice AIDS-risk-reduction behaviors, and improved participants' perceptions of their behavioral skills related to AIDS prevention. Most important, the intervention resulted in sustained (one and two months after the intervention) increases in (1) buying condoms and keeping them accessible and (2) using condoms during intercourse. Thus, critical AIDS-risk-reduction behaviors occurred with greater frequency after the intervention.

Summary

An attitude is an evaluative (good-bad) judgment of a target. An attitude represents the perceiver's favorability or unfavorability toward the target. Attitudes fulfill important functions for the individual. The primary function of attitudes is a utilitarian one: attitudes serve to maximize rewards and minimize punishments. Other functions that attitudes can fulfill include facilitating the identification of objects (the knowledge function), communicating the individual's identity and values (the value-expressive function), and protecting the individual from admitting an uncomplimentary truth about himself or herself (the ego-defensive function).

Attitudes can be based on any or all of three kinds of information: cognitive, affective, and behavioral information. Cognitive information refers to beliefs about the object. Attitudes are often based on the individual's knowledge about the object. The theory of reasoned action assumes that people are rational, deliberate thinkers, who form attitudes toward objects based on their salient beliefs about the features of the objects. People develop beliefs about objects from direct experience with the objects and from indirect information, including parents, peers, social institutions, and the mass media.

Affective information can also influence attitudes. People often evaluate an object based on how they feel about it. The mere exposure effect refers to the finding that simple exposure to a stimulus increases liking for it. A second process by which affect can become linked to an object is classical conditioning. Classical conditioning occurs when a stimulus comes to evoke a response that it did not previously evoke simply by being paired with another stimulus that "naturally" evokes the response.

Behavioral information can also influence attitudes. Self-perception theory proposes that perceivers sometimes infer their own internal states (including attitudes) in the same way that they infer other people's internal states—by looking at overt behavior. In other words, people may infer that they are favorable (or unfavorable) toward an object because they have behaved favorably (or unfavorably) toward the object in the past. Such inferences are most likely when attitudes are newly formed, weak, or ambiguous.

Biological factors also play a role in attitude formation. The most likely role of biology is to create a predisposition toward particular attitudes, which may or may not develop depending on the individual's experiences. The impact of drugs and alcohol on attitudes is consistent with a biological perspective. Alcohol myopia refers to the fact that alcohol intoxication reduces cognitive capacity, which leads to a focus on only salient cues in the environment. There is some evidence that attitudes have a genetic component. Specifically, heritability coefficients, which represent the percentage of variance in a sample that is attributable to genetic factors, are often significantly greater than zero for attitudes.

Attitudes influence the processing of information. In general, attitudes bias processing in such a way that information consistent with attitudes is more likely to be perceived and recalled. The selective exposure hypothesis proposes that perceivers seek out information that supports their attitudes and avoid information that contradicts their attitudes. Attitudes also guide the interpretation of information, especially ambiguous information. Perceivers are likely to interpret ambiguous information as supporting their attitudes. Finally, information that is consistent with an individual's attitudes is more likely to be recalled than inconsistent information.

Attitude-behavior consistency has been an issue of debate in social psychology. Several factors have been identified that moderate the attitude-behavior relation. First, the measures of attitudes and behaviors must be compatible. That is, if the attitude measure assesses a general attitude (toward an object, person, or issue), then the behavior measure must also be general. A general measure of behavior is called a multiple-act behavioral criterion and samples widely from all behaviors related to the target. In contrast, if the attitude measure assesses a specific attitude (toward a behavior), then the behavior measure must also be specific. A specific measure of behavior is a measure of an action toward a target in a particular place at a particular time. The theory of reasoned action proposes that specific behaviors are caused by intentions, which, in turn, are caused by attitudes toward the behavior and subjective norms. Subjective norms refer to perceived social pressure to perform or not perform the behavior.

A second factor that influences attitude-behavior consistency is the nature of the behavior. Attitudes predict behavior only when the behavior is under volitional control. The theory of planned behavior recognizes this point and extends the theory of reasoned action by adding perceived behavioral control as a third determinant of intentions.

A third factor that influences attitude-behavior consistency is the nature of the attitude. Attitudes that are based on direct experience with the object predict behavior better than attitudes based on indirect experience.

A fourth factor that influences attitude-behavior consistency is the personality dimension of self-monitoring. Low self-monitors exhibit greater attitude-behavior consistency than do high self-monitors.

The IMB model of AIDS-preventive behaviors hypothesizes that information, motivation, and behavioral skills are joint determinants of safer sex behavior. People must know how to reduce their risk, must be motivated enough to engage in such behaviors, and must have the necessary skills to complete the behaviors effectively before preventive behavior can occur.

Key Terms

accessibility
alcohol myopia
attitude
belief
classical conditioning
compatibility of attitude
  and behavior measures
direct experience
ego-defensive function
heritability coefficient

IMB model of AIDS-
  preventive behavior
knowledge function
mere exposure
multiple-act behavioral
  criterion
normative beliefs
perceived behavioral control
reference group
selective attention

selective exposure hypothesis
selective memory
selective perception
self-efficacy
self-monitoring
self-perception theory
subjective norms
theory of planned behavior
theory of reasoned action
utilitarian function
value-expressive function

Suggested Readings

Ajzen, I. (1991). The theory of planned behavior. *Organizational Behavior and Human Decision Processes, 50,* 179–211.

Ajzen, I., and Fishbein, M. (1980). *Understanding attitudes and predicting social behavior.* Englewood Cliffs, NJ: Prentice-Hall.

Eagly, A. H., and Chaiken, S. (1993). *The psychology of attitudes.* Fort Worth, TX: Harcourt Brace Jovanovich.

Fazio, R. H. (1990). Multiple processes by which attitudes guide behavior: The MODE model as an integrative framework. In M. P. Zanna (Ed.), *Advances in experimental social psychology* (Vol. 23, pp. 75–109). San Diego, CA: Academic Press.

Fisher, J. D., and Fisher, W. A. (1992). Changing AIDS-risk behavior. *Psychological Bulletin, 111,* 455–474.

Oskamp, S. (1991). *Attitudes and opinions* (2nd ed.). Englewood Cliffs, NJ: Prentice-Hall.

Petty, R. E., Wegener, D. T., and Fabrigar, L. R. (1997). Attitudes and attitude change. *Annual Review of Psychology, 48,* 609–642.

Tesser, A. (1993). The importance of heritability in psychological research: The case of attitudes. *Psychological Review, 100,* 129–142.

Zanna, M. P., and Rempel, J. K. (1988). Attitudes: A new look at an old concept. In D. Bar-Tal and A. W. Kruglanski (Eds.), *The social psychology of knowledge* (pp. 315–334). Cambridge, England: Cambridge University Press.

Chapter 6

Persuasion

Suzanne Marquette was eighteen years old and living at home in Minneapolis (see Levine, 1984). She had completed one year of junior college, but her heart was set on a career in figure skating. She was extremely talented and had participated in many shows and competitions. She was also a thoughtful and helpful person, both around the house and in volunteer activities at a nursing home.

It was summer, and a well-known professional ice show was conducting auditions for its autumn tour. Suzanne had flown from Minneapolis to Santa Monica to audition for a position in the troupe. She traveled alone, but her parents were not worried because she was responsible and mature.

Suzanne was lying on the beach near her hotel in Santa Monica on a Friday morning, soaking up the sun before her 2:00 P.M. audition. She heard voices and looked up to see John, Rich, and Anna. She thought they looked quite beautiful—well dressed, happy, and peaceful. They asked if they could join her, and Suzanne quickly agreed because they seemed safe and nonthreatening. They spread a blanket, poured juice, and softly played a guitar. They smiled, always smiled. The four young people sang and talked and laughed together for several hours.

When it was time for Suzanne to go for her audition, Anna invited her to rejoin them in the evening when she could meet their friends. Suzanne was noncommital but took the information about where their house was located.

The audition went extremely well, and Suzanne knew that she was about to assume an adult role in the professional world. She felt excited and decided to take her new friends up on their invitation. When she arrived at their house, she was greeted by Anna and John. There were many other young people at the house, and everyone seemed so happy that Suzanne soon felt as comfortable and relaxed as she had earlier in the day on the beach. Abundant fresh fruit and salads were on a table and music wafted through the house. Both the music and people's conversations focused on love and hope and caring. The evening seemed wonderful, almost magical.

Suzanne was sad when it was time for her to go back to her hotel. Her new friends said she could return the next morning and accompany them to their country retreat in northern California for a long three-day weekend and she agreed.

The following Monday evening, Suzanne phoned her parents in Minneapolis. The audition had gone well, she told them. But she was not going to pursue a career in skating. And she was not coming home. She had joined the Unification Church. She was a Moonie.

Steven Hassan was nineteen years old and attending college in Queens, New York (see Hassan, 1988). He was bright and hardworking, and felt an abiding concern about social injustice and environmental issues. He was proud of his Jewish heritage but was not deeply religious. He loved poetry; in fact, he had written hundreds of poems and prized this collection above all else.

While he was reading a book in the student union cafeteria one Monday, three young women and one young man approached him; they were carrying books and looked like students. They asked if they could join him and, on his acquiescence, began a friendly conversation. They said they were part of a small community of "young people from all over the world" and invited him to visit them at their house. The semester had just started, so Steven wanted to make new friends. He drove to their house that evening, where he found a lively group of about thirty people from many different countries. He asked if they were a religious group, to which they laughed and said no. They told him they were part of the "One World Crusade," dedicated to promoting cultural exchanges and fighting social injustice. Steven enjoyed the conversation and was impressed by how happy everyone seemed.

Steven returned to the house on Wednesday and heard a lecture about the "principles of life," which had a decidedly religious tone, focusing on Adam and Eve and Satan. Steven was confused by the religious theme and said that he probably wouldn't be coming back. Immediately, a dozen people surrounded him and made him *promise* to come back the following night. When Steven returned the next evening, he was showered with compliments from many different people telling him how smart he was, how dynamic he was, and how happy they were that he was here. They convinced him to accompany them to a weekend retreat in upstate New York.

The entire weekend was structured. Newcomers were assigned to small groups in which members outnumbered them three to one. Lectures, discussion groups, singing, and praying filled the hours. Sleep was restricted to a few hours a night. Steven learned about God's plan for the world, which had been revealed to mankind by the coming of the second Messiah—a humble Korean man named Sun Myung Moon. Moon had survived severe hardships to spread God's word and to fight Satan. The Unification Church was the organization performing these duties. Steven was skeptical about the lectures but had difficulty dismissing them, partly because he was physically and mentally exhausted.

Steven returned home and spent several days thinking and praying about what he had experienced. He talked to his rabbi, who had never heard of the Unification Church. Steven eventually decided that he had to learn more about the group. He contacted them again and agreed to attend another weekend retreat. The second retreat was similar to the first, but the lecture topics were new. Steven kept an open mind, having decided that he had been too cynical the previous weekend. He learned that communism was Satan's religion and must be opposed. He learned that members of the Unification Church were God's chosen people and were working to bring about the Garden of Eden. By the end of the weekend, again physically exhausted, Steven nevertheless felt exhilarated. He felt honored to have been chosen by God and was excited that he could work to achieve love, truth, and beauty.

When he returned to the city, Steven moved into the One World Crusade house in Queens. He dropped out of college and quit his part-time job. He donated all of his money to the center. He agreed not to contact his family or friends for forty days. And he learned that he should show his commitment to God by "sacrificing" something that was very important to him. Steven threw out all of the poetry he had ever written.

Who are the Moonies? They are led by Sun Myung Moon, who was born in North Korea in 1920 (see Clay, 1987; Hassan, 1988; Swenson, 1987). His family converted to Christianity when he was nine or ten. Moon claims to have had a vision at age sixteen of Jesus, who told him that he was chosen to carry on God's work. In 1950, Moon moved to Seoul, the capital of South Korea, where he established the Unification Church in 1954. In 1957, Moon published *The Divine Principle,* which became the "bible" of his movement. Shortly thereafter, Moon said that he had found the "perfect wife" (his fourth) and had established the "perfect family," which was destined to produce "perfect children" and become the nucleus of God's family on earth. The Unification Church grew rapidly in South Korea over the next ten years and became involved in many business ventures that reaped large profits.

In 1972, Moon moved to the United States. He purchased a $625,000 estate in upstate New York as his personal home as well as numerous other real estate properties. In North America, the Unification Church invested in many businesses, including hotels, newspapers, exporting companies, fish and lobster processing plants, and even an elk farm. The church also expanded to many other countries, including Canada, Japan, Honduras, Uruguay, South Africa, Ghana, Nigeria, and Zimbabwe (Clay, 1987).

In 1982, Moon was convicted of conspiracy, obstruction of justice, and perjury involving his failure to pay taxes on interest income from a $1.6 million bank account. He spent thirteen months in the Danbury federal prison in Connecticut. His followers regarded this imprisonment as unjust, the result of racial and religious prejudice.

The Unification Church has an estimated membership of two million worldwide, with approximately thirty-thousand members in the United States (Swenson, 1987). Its income is probably in the hundreds of millions of dollars annually (Hassan, 1988; Swenson, 1987), much of this money being tax-free because of the organization's religious status. The typical "Moonie" in the United States and Canada is a young (between eighteen and thirty), intelligent man or woman, who dresses conservatively and is clean-cut and courteous. Members sell flowers and other items to raise money and are continually involved in recruiting new members; all income goes to the church. Members receive only food and shelter and they live in communal groups, segregated by sex. Marriage is allowed only by decision of Moon himself, who matches partners.

Is the Unification Church a "cult"? MacHovec (1989) provides an excellent definition of what he calls a **destructive cult:**

> A destructive cult is a rigidly structured absolutist group, usually under an authoritarian, charismatic leader, which isolates itself from established societal traditions, values, and norms, recruits members deceptively without informed consent, and retains them by continually reinforced direct and indirect manipulative techniques, which cause personality and behavior change, deny freedom of choice, and interrupt and obstruct optimal personality development. (P. 10)

On the basis of this definition, it seems reasonable to argue that the Unification Church is indeed a destructive cult. It is rigidly structured and led by an authoritarian leader. It espouses unusual and extreme values and norms. It recruits members deceptively (for instance, potential recruits are not told that the organization is religious). It socializes and retains members through manipulative means. Techniques are employed that knowingly deny true freedom of choice (they are designed to induce recruits to join even if they don't really want to).

A recent, rather horrifying example of a destructive cult was provided by the so-called Heaven's Gate group. In March 1997, thirty-nine men and women committed mass suicide in Rancho Sante Fe, California (near San Diego). In successive groups of three or four, members sedated themselves with barbituates mixed in pudding or applesauce and washed down with vodka. Plastic bags were then placed over the heads of the sedated individuals, causing death by suffocation. The leader of this bizarre group was sixty-five-year-old Marshall Applewhite, who, along with several other male members of the cult, had been castrated in pursuit of "androgenous immortality." The group members believed that the passage of the Hale-Bopp comet near the earth in March 1997 was a sign that it was time for them to leave their "earthly vehicles or containers" (their bodies). They believed that a spaceship carrying

In 1997, twenty-eight thousand couples participated in a marriage affirmation ceremony at the Washington, D.C., RFK Stadium, officiated by the Reverend and Mrs. Sun Myung Moon, founders of the Unification Church.

aliens was hiding behind the comet. Once released from their earthly containers, members believed that their spirits would be picked up by the spaceship and transported to heaven. Where these beliefs originated is rather unclear, but the members (many of whom came from very ordinary backgrounds) believed strongly enough to take their own lives. Investigations after the mass suicide indicated that at least some members had initially learned about the group from information posted on the Internet by Applewhite.

How do cults recruit members? Would everyone fall prey to their propaganda if exposed to their techniques? In chapter 5 we pointed out that people defend their attitudes (resist attempts at influence), yet cults seem to induce radical attitude change. Is persuasion really so easy? In this chapter, we describe social psychological research on attitude change. We cover both motivational and cognitive models of persuasion. At the end of the chapter, we identify some of the persuasive techniques used by cults to recruit and retain members.

Cognitive Dissonance Theory: Motivated Attitude Change

Probably the most famous theory of attitude change (indeed, perhaps the most famous theory in all of social psychology) is Leon Festinger's (1957, 1964) **cognitive dissonance theory.** Dissonance theory has stimulated hundreds of experiments and has been variously praised and damned since it appeared forty years ago. The major premise of dissonance theory is that people are motivated to achieve and maintain consistency among their many cognitions. A *cognition* is a thought, a piece of knowledge, or a belief. Cognitions encompass knowledge about attitudes, values, behavior, other people, ourselves, general knowledge, or any other target. For example, "Today is Tuesday" is a cognition; "I like coffee" is a cognition; "Elizabeth hurt Tom's feelings" is a cognition; and "University education is worthwhile" is a cognition.

Festinger proposed that any two cognitions can be related to one another in three different ways. First, most cognitions are irrelevant to one another; that is, the two cognitions are independent or unrelated. For example, the four cognitions listed in the previous paragraph could exist simultaneously in someone's head without having any implications for one another.

More important to Festinger's theory are cognitions that *do* have implications for one another. **Consonant cognitions** are consistent with one another; they are compatible, or support each other. For example, the cognitions "I drink milk" and "Milk is good for me" are consonant, as are the cognitions "Children are starving in the Third World" and "I donated money to UNICEF." Festinger argued that people like consonance between their cognitions. It "feels good" to have cognitions that support one another.

Dissonant cognitions are inconsistent or incompatible with each other; they psychologically contradict one another. For example, the cognitions "I like Judy" and "I hurt Judy's feelings" are dissonant, as are the cognitions "I worked hard on my psychology assignment" and "I received a D on my assignment." (You may have noticed that all of our examples of pairs of cognitions have included one cognition about the perceiver's personal actions; it turns out that cognitions about one's own behaviors are typically very important in research on dissonance theory.) Festinger proposed that being aware of dissonant cognitions is unpleasant or aversive; people are motivated to reduce dissonance. As we will see, reducing dissonance often involves changing attitudes; thus, dissonance theory is an important motivational perspective on attitude change.

Reducing Dissonance

How can dissonance be reduced? First, people can *change one of the dissonant cognitions.* Dissonance produced by the cognitions "I like Judy" and "I hurt Judy's feelings" could be reduced by changing "I like Judy" to "I don't like Judy." This would be an example of dissonance-induced attitude change. Of course, someone could also decide that he or she didn't really hurt Judy's feelings (and thereby reduce dissonance while maintaining the cognition that he or she likes Judy). Festinger proposed that people will change whichever cognition is easier to change, remembering that cognitions about one's public behaviors are often difficult to deny. Notice also that cognitions do not have to change completely to reduce dissonance. "I like Judy" doesn't have to change to "I hate Judy"; the change might be from "I like Judy a lot" to "I like Judy a little bit," which will also reduce dissonance because the negative behavior is less dissonant with the new attitude toward Judy.

A second way to reduce dissonance is to *add consonant cognitions.* Consonant cognitions justify or rationalize the inconsistency between the two focal dissonant cognitions. Dissonance produced by the cognitions "I never exercise" and "Exercise is good for me" might be reduced by adding such cognitions as "My schoolwork is so demanding that I cannot afford the time to exercise" and "I will start exercising after I graduate." Notice that these cognitions do not deny either the lack of exercise or the benefits of exercise; they simply provide justifications or reasons for the inconsistency.

Paradigms Used to Study Dissonance

Many different situations occur in which people might experience inconsistency among their cognitions. Social psychologists have employed several paradigms to study the effects of dissonant cognitions. In science, a paradigm is a method or model used to test a theory. It is always desirable to test a theory using several different paradigms, because such diversity establishes the breadth and generality of the theory. Thus, the use of multiple paradigms is one of dissonance theory's strengths.

One application of dissonance theory was mentioned in chapter 5, namely selective exposure. Recall that Festinger proposed the **selective exposure hypothesis,** which states that people are motivated to seek out information that is consistent with their attitudes (consonant information) and to avoid information that is inconsistent with their attitudes (dissonant information). Researchers have found support for the selective exposure hypothesis when additional factors that affect information seeking are taken into account (for example, the usefulness of the information).

In this chapter, we describe three other paradigms that have been used to test dissonance theory. These paradigms involve dissonance that occurs after making a choice or decision, after behaving counterattitudinally, and after exerting a lot of effort.

The Free Choice Paradigm: Postdecisional Dissonance

In the **free choice paradigm,** people are given a choice between two or more alternatives. When people freely make a choice, they will often feel some dissonance. Why? Because the chosen alternative will usually have at least one or two negative features, and

the rejected alternative will usually have some positive features. Imagine that you are trying to decide whether to buy a new small car or a used midsize car. The small car is more economical to run and shouldn't require much maintenance for several years. The midsize car is more comfortable, safer in the event of an accident, and more powerful for highway driving. You eventually choose the new car because you don't want to risk having to invest more money in repairs. After making this choice, you might experience **postdecisional dissonance** when you think about driving the small car on the highway or when you contemplate how comfortable the midsize car would have been.

As in all cases of dissonance, postdecisional dissonance is unpleasant, and people are motivated to reduce it. How can this be achieved? The most common way to reduce dissonance after a decision is by adding

Whether this customer decides to buy this car or another, she will probably experience dissonance due to the positive and negative features of each choice.

TABLE 6.1 EVALUATION OF ALTERNATIVES.

Condition	Changes from First to Second Rating for		
	Chosen Item	Nonchosen Item	Net Change
Low dissonance (items of disparate value)	+0.11	0.00	+0.11
High dissonance (items of close value)	+0.38	–0.41	+0.79
Gift (control)	0.00		

Note: A positive sign indicates an increase in attractiveness; a negative sign indicates a decrease. The "net change" represents the degree of "spreading apart" of the alternatives following a choice.
Source: Adapted from Brehm (1956)

consonant cognitions—thoughts that support the decision. Usually, such thoughts will involve convincing yourself how good the chosen alternative is and how bad the rejected alternative is. In the car example, you might think about how the small car will be easy to maneuver and park or about how the midsize car was ugly and dated. These rationalizations typically result in the evaluation of the chosen alternative becoming more favorable and the evaluation of the rejected alternative becoming less favorable.

The first study to document this postdecisional reevaluation of alternatives was conducted by Brehm (1956). College women were asked to help a marketing firm evaluate several consumer items, such as a toaster, an electric coffeepot, and a silk-screen print. The women rated each item on a scale. They were then allowed to choose one of two items to take home with them in appreciation for their participation. Some participants (the *high-dissonance condition*) were asked to choose between two items that they had rated very closely on the rating scale. Other participants (the *low-dissonance condition*) were asked to choose between two items that they had rated quite far apart on the scale. Clearly, there will be little dissonance when one alternative is much more attractive than the other alternative right from the start. Finally, in a *control condition* the experimenter simply selected one item and gave it to the women as a gift. The women were then asked to read some research reports written by the manufacturers of the items and then to rerate all of the items.

Table 6.1 presents the results, which strongly supported dissonance theory. First, there was no reevaluation at all in the control condition, where women were simply given one of the items. Second, in the high-dissonance condition, participants significantly increased their rating of the chosen item and significantly decreased their rating of the nonchosen item. This pattern of reevaluation is called "spreading of alternatives"—the two items were spread farther apart in evaluation than they were before the choice. Finally, in the low-dissonance condition there was little change in the evaluations of either the chosen or the nonchosen alternatives.

People who join cults have made a decision that will have enormous effects on their lives. Postdecisional dissonance should lead to increasingly positive evaluations of their chosen path. Having made a dramatic public commitment to an unusual lifestyle, people will feel considerable pressure to rationalize their decision to themselves and to others. Postdecisional dissonance might be one mechanism that explains why people remain in cults.

The Induced Compliance Paradigm: Counterattitudinal Behavior

Sometimes people behave in ways that are inconsistent with their attitudes. For example, an employee might express support for a decision by his boss even though he privately disagrees. In the **induced compliance paradigm,** such inconsistencies are experimentally created: individuals are induced to behave in ways that are inconsistent with their private attitudes. For example, a student who opposes a tuition increase might be asked to write an essay arguing in favor of a tuition increase. If he or she agrees to do so, the behavior will produce two dissonant cognitions, namely, "I believe X" and "I acted not-X." How can the uncomfortable state of tension produced by these cognitions be reduced? As mentioned earlier, it is often difficult to change cognitions about past behavior. Unless the student is particularly adept at outright denial, it will be difficult to change the cognition "I acted not-*X*." Privately held attitudes, on the other hand, are often easier to change. Thus, the student might decide that a tuition increase is acceptable ("I believe not-*X*"). If, however, individuals have *good reasons* for their counterattitudinal behavior (such as, they were paid a lot of money, or they were threatened with severe punishments), then they will have a consonant cognition that should reduce dissonance even without attitude change. For example, if the student is paid $25 for writing the pro–tuition-increase essay, the cognition "I was paid $25" will reduce the dissonance between "I believe *X*" and "I acted not-*X*," which might eliminate the need to change "I believe *X*" to "I believe not-*X*."

In one of the most famous experiments in social psychology, Festinger and Carlsmith (1959) had participants work for an hour on two *very* boring tasks—turning pegs on a board and placing spools on (and off) another board. When the session was done, participants were told that they were in a control condition where people perform the tasks without any advance expectations. Participants were further told that other subjects were being led to expect that the tasks would be exciting and fun, and the experimenter was testing whether these positive expectations improved performance compared to the control condition. The experimenter explained that positive expectancies were being induced by having a paid confederate sit beside a subject in the waiting room, pretend that he had just completed the study, and tell the waiting subject that the session would be fun and exciting. The experimenter then made an unexpected request of participants. He said that the confederate who usually gave the spiel was not here, and there was a subject in the waiting room who was supposed to be in the positive expectancies condition. Therefore, the experimenter wondered if the participant would be willing to serve as the paid confederate for the next subject only. That is, would the participant go into the next room and tell the waiting subject that the experiment was fun and exciting? Only three of fifty-one participants refused to tell this lie; the remaining participants went into the waiting room and sat beside the prospective subject (actually a confederate), who, after learning from the real participant that the tasks were fun, expressed enthusiasm about the upcoming session.

Participants were thus left with dissonant cognitions: "The tasks were boring" and "I convinced some-

one that the tasks were fun." According to dissonance theory, this circumstance might lead participants to rationalize that the tasks weren't so bad after all, because changing cognitions about the deceitful behavior would be difficult. However, there was another manipulation in the experiment that was expected to influence the amount of dissonance experienced by participants. Specifically, some participants were told they would be paid $1 for telling the lie, whereas other participants were told they would be paid $20 for telling the lie. In the 1950s, $20 was a large payment, so the latter participants had a strong, consonant cognition that justified their behavior ("I was paid a great deal of money for saying the tasks were fun"). Thus, the $20 participants were not expected to have to convince themselves that the tasks were fun.

After telling the lie, participants thought the experiment was finished. They were asked to visit a secretary in the psychology department before they left, and the secretary would give them a questionnaire being completed by all participants in all experiments. This questionnaire asked participants to rate how enjoyable and interesting the tasks in their experiment had been. Figure 6.1 presents the results of the study for the $1 and $20 conditions as well as for a control

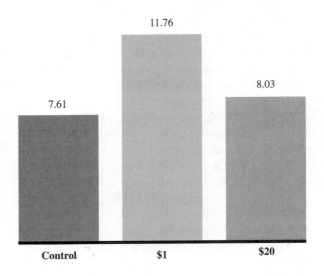

FIGURE 6.1   EVALUATION OF BORING TASKS: DEGREE OF POSITIVE FEELING TOWARD TASK

Note: The higher the mean, the more favorable the evaluation of the tasks.
Source: Festinger and Carlsmith (1959)

condition where participants completed the tasks but did not tell anyone that the session was fun.

As predicted, participants who were paid a lot of money to tell the lie did not rate the tasks as any more enjoyable than did participants in the control condition. It would seem that the $20 payment served as a consonant cognition that reduced dissonance between people's attitudes and behavior. Participants who were paid only $1, however, rated the tasks as significantly more enjoyable than did participants in the $20 and control conditions. It would seem that the $1 payment was not enough to justify the deceitful behavior to these participants, so they reduced dissonance by deciding that the tasks were tolerable.

Festinger and Carlsmith's experiment had a huge impact on social psychology. First, it showed that behavior could affect attitudes (rather than the common assumption that attitudes affect behavior). Second, it uncovered a paradoxical effect of rewards: counterattitudinal behavior had more effect on attitudes when rewards were small (rather than the common assumption that larger rewards for a behavior will produce more positive attitudes toward the behavior). Many researchers followed up Festinger and Carlsmith's study using other variations of the induced compliance paradigm.

One subsequent study that produced particularly clear results was conducted by Cohen (1962) at Yale University. The New Haven police had recently been involved in a disturbance on campus, where they had used more force than was probably necessary, and Yale students were virtually unanimous in their condemnation of the police's actions. Cohen contacted students in their dormitories and told them that a research institute wanted them to write forceful essays taking the police side of this incident. Further, the students were offered money for the essay, either $.50, $1, $5, or $10. According to dissonance theory, the more money they were paid, the less dissonance the students should have felt because larger amounts of money provided better reasons (stronger consonant cognitions) for their counterattitudinal essay writing. To measure dissonance, participants were asked to report their attitudes toward the police. Figure 6.2 presents the results for each of the payment conditions as well as for a control condition where students simply reported their attitudes toward the police without writing a pro-police essay. Exactly as would be predicted from dissonance theory, attitudes toward the police were most favorable when participants wrote a pro-police essay for very little money ($.50), and attitudes became more negative (and

FIGURE 6.2 **ATTITUDES TOWARD POLICE ACTIONS**

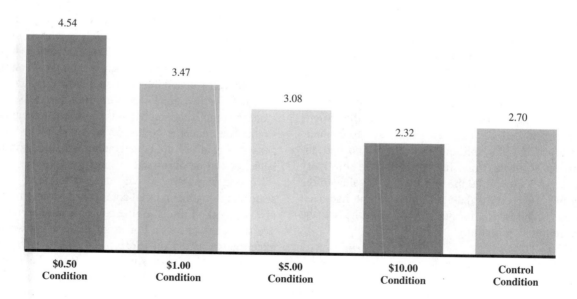

Note: The higher the mean, the more positive the attitudes toward the New Haven police.
Source: Adapted from Cohen (1962)

more similar to the control condition) as the size of the payment increased.

Money Isn't Everything

Dissonance theorists predict that *any* good reason for behaving inconsistently with our attitudes will serve as a consonant cognition and therefore reduce dissonance. Although both studies described so far used money as an external justification, other studies have involved different incentives. For example, strong threats of punishment can also justify counterattitudinal behavior. In a version of the induced compliance paradigm that has been called the **forbidden toy paradigm,** Aronson and Carlsmith (1963) produced counterattitudinal behavior by telling five-year-old children that they should *not* play with a very attractive toy. Such behavior was expected to result in the dissonant cognitions "I like the toy" and "I didn't play with the toy." Assuming that cognitions about behavior are difficult to change, the researchers predicted that dissonance would be reduced by attitude change toward the toy ("I don't like the toy"). However, half of the children were given a powerful external justification for their behavior: the experimenter threatened them severely if they disobeyed ("I would be very angry; I would take all the toys away and never come back"). These children were expected to feel little dissonance and to continue rating the toy as very attractive. The remaining children were given only a mild threat ("I would be a little angry with you if you played with this toy"). These children were expected to decide that the toy was not very attractive.

The experimenter left the room after communicating the mild or severe threat. None of the children in either condition played with the forbidden toy while the experimenter was gone. After the experimenter returned, the children were asked to evaluate the toy again. As predicted, children who had abstained from playing with the toy for a relatively weak reason (the mild threat condition) evaluated the toy more negatively than did children who had been given a good reason for not playing with the toy (the severe threat condition).

Critical Factors in Induced Compliance

In the years since Festinger and Carlsmith introduced the induced compliance paradigm, researchers have identified four factors that are necessary for counter-

attitudinal behavior to produce dissonance: choice, commitment, aversive consequences, and personal responsibility (see Cooper and Fazio, 1984).

Choice. If individuals are not given freedom of choice to perform or not perform a counterattitudinal behavior, dissonance will not be aroused. Lack of choice means that the person was forced to behave counterattitudinally, so there is no reason to feel bad about violating one's private views. In many dissonance studies, a no-dissonance control condition is included by not giving some participants any choice about the behavior; for example, participants are simply instructed to write a counterattitudinal essay without having any opportunity to refuse. In the high-dissonance conditions of induced compliance experiments, participants are always asked whether they "would be willing" to comply with the request (for example, "It's completely up to you, but I'd sure appreciate it if you would . . ."). Thus, researchers are careful to produce the perception of free choice. (Of course, given that very few participants refuse to do the counterattitudinal behavior, the situational pressures are actually quite strong; participants must simply *believe* that they had freedom of choice.)

Commitment. Counterattitudinal behavior is more likely to produce dissonance if the individual is psychologically committed to the action. Thus public behavior induces more dissonance than private behavior. If no one knows that you wrote a counterattitudinal essay, dissonance will be minimal. Similarly, if you know that you will be able to retract your counterattitudinal advocacy later, dissonance will be minimal even when the behavior was public. These conditions—privacy, revocability—weaken the psychological connection between you and the counterattitudinal behavior.

Aversive consequences. An important element in induced compliance settings is the need for some undesirable consequences of the action. If nothing bad happens as a result of the counterattitudinal behavior, the behavior can be dismissed as having caused no harm ("No one was hurt, so why does it matter?"). Researchers using the induced compliance paradigm have always worked into the procedures some degree of aversive consequences. For example, in essay writing experiments, participants are typically told that their essays will be used for some purpose in the future, thereby raising the possibility that other people will be convinced by the counterattitudinal essay (an undesirable consequence). In the Festinger and Carlsmith (1959) $1/$20 lie-telling experiment, the aversive consequence was that an unsuspecting participant was misled into expecting an enjoyable study.

The importance of aversive consequences was clearly documented in a study by Cooper and Worchel (1970). These authors replicated the Festinger and Carlsmith (1959) lie-telling experiment but added another manipulation. Participants completed the dull peg-turning task and were asked, in return for either a low or a high inducement, to mislead a waiting confederate into thinking that the task was exciting. After trying to convince the confederate, half of the subjects heard him say, "You are entitled to your opinion, but every experiment I have ever been in has been dull, and I expect this one to be dull as well." The confederate thus remained unconvinced by the participant's lie in this condition, which eliminated the principal aversive consequence of the counterattitudinal behavior because he did *not* expect an enjoyable task. The remaining participants saw the confederate become enthusiastic and excited about participating in an interesting study (paralleling the aversive consequences in the original study).

Participants' evaluations of the boring tasks are presented in figure 6.3, including a control condition where people simply performed the dull tasks and did

not tell a lie to anyone. When participants believed that the confederate was unconvinced by their lie, they evaluated the tasks just as negatively as did control participants, irrespective of whether they were given a small or large incentive for the lie. Thus, the absence of aversive consequences eliminated dissonance. On the other hand, when participants believed that the confederate was convinced by their lie, the incentive manipulation had a substantial impact on evaluations of the task; those who received little incentive evaluated the tasks significantly more positively than did those who received a large incentive.

Recently, some researchers have argued that although aversive consequences increase dissonance, they may not be absolutely necessary for dissonance to occur. For example, Harmon-Jones, Brehm, Greenberg, Simon, and Nelson (1996) induced some participants to drink an unpleasant-tasting beverage. Next, in private these participants agreed voluntarily (choice condition) to write on a piece of paper that they liked the beverage and they then threw away the paper. The authors argued that no aversive consequences occurred in this condition. Nevertheless, these participants evaluated the unpleasant drink significantly more favorably than did participants in a no-choice

FIGURE 6.3 EVALUATION OF BORING TASKS: DEGREE OF ENJOYMENT

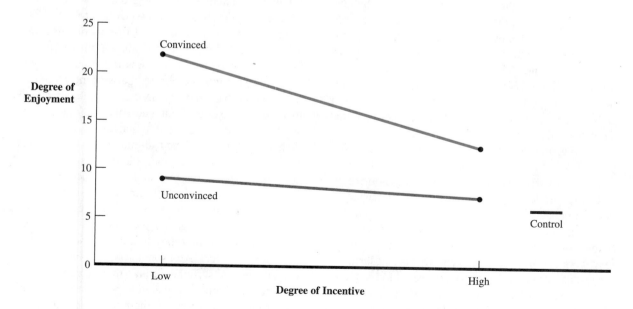

Note: Higher numbers represent greater enjoyableness.
Source: Cooper and Worchel (1970)

control condition—a finding that suggests dissonance was aroused in the choice condition. It seems likely that the role of aversive consequences in dissonance effects will continue to receive attention from social psychologists over the next few years.

Personal responsibility. Finally, in order for dissonance to occur, people must feel personally responsible for their behavior and for any aversive consequences it produced. Freedom of choice is one component of responsibility because, obviously, people will not feel responsible for things they were forced to do. But responsibility for aversive consequences implies not only that the behavior was freely performed but also that the aversive consequences were foreseeable. That is, the actor must say to himself or herself, "I should have known that my behavior could produce this negative outcome." Personal responsibility thus involves the individual's accepting the blame for the negative things that occurred because of his or her behavior.

The Effort Justification Paradigm: To Suffer Is to Love

The **effort justification paradigm** rests on the assumption that we do not like to exert undue effort; we do not like to suffer. When individuals exert a lot of effort (or endure a lot of pain or spend a lot of money) to achieve a goal, they will be motivated to believe that the goal is important and worthwhile. It is unpleasant to think that one has exerted a lot of effort for a silly cause. The dissonant cognitions are "I exerted a lot of effort" and "The goal is not worthwhile." The first cognition refers to past behavior and, thus, is difficult to change. The second cognition offers an easier path to dissonance reduction—convincing oneself that the goal really is important.

In the first demonstration of the effects of effort justification, Aronson and Mills (1959) invited women students to participate in a sexual discussion group. Before the students could join the group, they were required to undergo a "screening test" to be certain they would be able to contribute openly to the discussion. Some women were assigned to a severe test in which they were given a list of obscene words and lurid descriptions of sexual activity to read aloud. Other women were assigned to a mild test in which they read ordinary words such as *petting* and *prostitute*.

After their screening tests, all participants (plus a control group that received no screening test) listened

An aversive consequence of an act, coupled with the actor's feeling of personal responsibility for it, creates cognitive dissonance that might promote a change in attitude.

to a discussion being held by the group. It was explained that because the participants had not done the reading for this week's discussion, it would be better if they did not actually join the group now but instead listened to the week's discussion over earphones. The discussion the women listened to was dreadful. As Aronson and Mills (1959) described it, the discussion concerned "secondary sex behavior in the lower animals. [The group members] inadvertently contradicted themselves and one another, mumbled several non sequiturs, started sentences that they never finished, hemmed, hawed, and in general conducted one of the most worthless and uninteresting discussions imaginable" (p. 179). In fact, the discussion that the subjects overheard was actually a tape recording that had been designed to be as boring as possible.

After listening to the tape, the prospective group members (the experimental participants) were asked to rate how interesting they found the discussion and the group members. Aronson and Mills predicted that women who had suffered through the severe screening test would be highly motivated to perceive the discussion group as interesting so their suffering would not have been wasted. Table 6.2 presents the mean ratings of the discussion and of the discussion group members

TABLE 6.2 **EVALUATIONS OF BORING DISCUSSION AND PARTICIPANTS**

Rating scales	Control	Mild	Severe
Discussion	80.2	81.8	97.6
Participants	89.9	89.3	97.7

Source: Adapted from Aronson and Mills (1959)

by women in the control, mild, and severe conditions. The results conformed nicely to dissonance theory: women in the severe screening-test condition were significantly more favorable toward the discussion and the group members than were women in the mild or no screening-test conditions.

Cooper and Axsom (1982) applied the logic of effort justification to a weight loss program. Overweight women who wanted to lose weight were recruited. At the first session, the women were weighed and informed about a "new experimental procedure" that was being developed to aid weight loss. Allegedly, this procedure involved cognitive tasks that were designed specifically to produce "neurophysiological arousal," which could in turn lead to weight loss. The women learned about a series of tasks they would perform. For some women, these tasks were very effortful. One task, for example, involved reading tongue twisters and nursery rhymes into a microphone while hearing one's own voice fed back to the earphones with a 0.3 second delay. None of the tasks involved any physical exercise, but each was difficult. The tasks lasted about forty minutes. Two additional conditions were also run. In a low-effort condition, the same tasks were introduced, but each one was easier and shorter than the parallel tasks in the high-effort condition. Finally, women in a control group were weighed during the initial session but were not contacted again until it was time to collect the dependent measures.

Participants in the high- and low-effort conditions returned to the laboratory for five sessions during a three-week period. At the end of the fifth session, they returned to the scale and were weighed. The prediction of the researchers was that women in the high effort condition would lose more weight than women in either the low effort or control conditions. The first column of table 6.3 presents the results at the end of the three-week period. As expected, the high-effort condition produced more weight loss than

the low-effort and control conditions, although differences were understandably small in such a short period of time. The second and third columns show the results on delayed measures. Without having been informed of this possibility at the outset of the research, each participant was called in to be weighed after intervals of six months and one year. After six months, 94 percent of the women in the high-effort condition had lost weight for an average loss of nearly nine pounds. Presumably, these women justified their effortful participation by deciding that weight loss was very important to them (and then worked to achieve this goal). In contrast, only 39 percent of the women in the low-effort condition had lost weight, and the average outcome was no change in weight. Women in the control condition had actually gained a small amount of weight after six months. The results after one year paralleled those for the six-month period.

When young people join a cult, they willingly undertake effortful and costly changes in lifestyle. For example, they typically give all of their money to the group and begin working full time on whatever tasks are assigned by the leaders of the movement. Such commitments will produce substantial motivation to see the movement as important and worthy of these investments. Perhaps effort justification underlies, at least in part, the devotion and remarkable commitment of many cult members to "the cause."

Alternative Perspectives on Dissonance Findings

In the years since cognitive dissonance theory was introduced, several theorists have suggested alternative explanations for the effects of dissonance manipulations.

TABLE 6.3 **WEIGHT CHANGES IN POUNDS**

Effort Condition	After Three Weeks	After Six Months	After One Year
High	−1.76	−8.55	−6.70
Low	− .82	− .07	− .34
Control	+ .17	+ .94	+1.86

Source: Cooper and Axsom (1982)

Self-Perception Theory

The first clear alternative to dissonance theory was Bem's (1967, 1972) **self-perception theory** discussed in chapters 3 and 5. Bem proposed that people sometimes infer their attitudes from their freely performed behaviors. For example, if people willingly tell someone else that tasks were fun, they might infer that they enjoyed the tasks (Festinger and Carlsmith, 1959). Or if people willingly write an essay in favor of police actions during a student uprising, they might infer that they support the police (Cohen, 1962). Of course, if people are paid a great deal of money to do these things (for example, the $20 condition in Festinger and Carlsmith, 1959), they will not infer corresponding attitudes (just as they would not infer that someone else who was paid a lot of money to do a task necessarily liked it).

Self-perception inferences undoubtedly occur in some circumstances, as discussed in previous chapters. But it seems unlikely that most dissonance findings actually reflected self-perception processes. The most compelling evidence against self-perception theory comes from experiments that have documented the *arousal properties* of dissonance. Self-perception theory would not predict that people feel negatively aroused in dissonance settings because the attitude change is assumed to result from simple, logical inferences. But dissonance theory *does* predict that people feel aversive arousal when exposed to a dissonance manipulation. Several researchers have tested this assumption.

In one of the first such experiments, Zanna and Cooper (1974) reasoned that if attitude change in dissonance experiments is motivated by arousal, then it should be possible to eliminate attitude change by misleading participants about *why* they feel aroused. Specifically, if people who perform a counterattitudinal behavior believe that their arousal is due to a drug they have taken, they should not be "motivated" to reduce dissonance. In this study, participants believed that the study was testing the effects of various drugs on memory. Participants ingested a pill that, unknown to them, was actually milk powder. But some participants were led to believe that there was a "side effect" to the pill—they would become aroused and feel tense. Other participants were told that the pill would make them feel relaxed, and still others were told that the pill would have no side effects at all.

After taking the pill, participants were told that they had to wait a few minutes for the pill to be absorbed before completing the memory test. In the meantime, they were asked to participate in "an-

---

FIGURE 6.4   ATTITUDE CHANGE TOWARD POSITION ADVOCATED IN MESSAGE

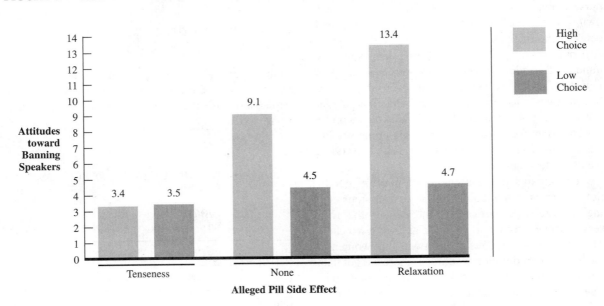

Source: Adapted from Zanna and Cooper (1974)

FIGURE 6.5 **ATTITUDES TOWARD TUITION INCREASE**

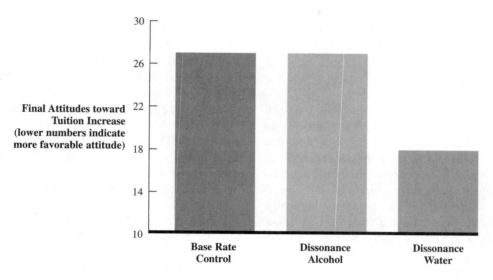

Source: Adapted from Steele, Southwick, and Critchlow (1981)

other experiment unrelated to the memory project." They wrote an essay advocating a ban on controversial speakers at their college—a position that Zanna and Cooper knew was discrepant with participants' true attitudes. Half of the participants wrote the essay under high-choice conditions, which should arouse dissonance. The other half wrote their essays without having a choice, which should eliminate dissonance.

After writing the essay, participants' attitudes toward the issue were assessed. Zanna and Cooper predicted that a typical induced compliance effect should occur in conditions where no side effects were expected from the drug. The middle panel of figure 6.4 shows that, as predicted, the high-choice condition resulted in significantly more favorable attitudes toward the position advocated in the essay than did the low-choice condition. More important, Zanna and Cooper predicted that when participants believed they were aroused because of the pill, they would not change their attitudes. The left-hand panel of figure 6.4 shows that, as predicted, the high- and low-choice conditions did not differ when the pill was expected to produce arousal. Finally, the right-hand panel of figure 6.4 shows that when participants believed that the pill would make them feel relaxed, the high-choice condition resulted in even more attitude change than usual. It is as if these latter participants reasoned, "I took a

relaxing pill and I still feel aroused—I must *really* be upset about writing the essay."

If attitude change occurs in order to reduce unpleasant arousal, then any technique that reduces arousal should reduce attitude change as well. In an interesting demonstration of this idea, Steele, Southwick, and Critchlow (1981) first induced participants to write a counterattitudinal essay advocating a tuition increase. Then, under the guise of performing a taste discrimination test between different brands of vodka, participants sipped alcoholic drinks for ten minutes (the dissonance alcohol condition). After reporting their preferences for the vodka brands, participants were given a questionnaire that assessed their attitudes toward a tuition increase (the topic of their previous essay). Other participants completed a similar procedure but sipped brands of water rather than vodka (the dissonance water condition). Finally, a third group sipped vodka for ten minutes but never wrote a counterattitudinal essay (base-rate control condition).

The results are presented in figure 6.5. Participants who drank alcohol after writing the essay reported virtually identical attitudes to participants in the control condition, whereas participants who drank water after writing the essay reported significantly more favorable attitudes toward a tuition increase. Thus, alcohol—a central nervous system depressant—eliminated the motivation to reduce dissonance.

Steele, Southwick, and Critchlow (1981) speculated that chronic dissonance arousal (for example, in people whose roles force them to behave in ways that go against their private attitudes) could potentially result in alcohol abuse, designed to reduce the aversive state.

Impression Management Theory

In another alternative to dissonance theory, Tedeschi, Schlenker, and Bonama (1971) proposed **impression management theory.** These authors argued that people are socialized to want to appear consistent to others. As a result, participants in dissonance experiments experience *evaluation apprehension* (an aversive tension) when they behave counterattitudinally, because they are worried about what the high-status experimenter will think of them after they have behaved inconsistently with their attitudes. To avoid negative evaluations by the experimenter, participants make themselves appear consistent by reporting attitudes that are in accordance with their actions. Thus, these authors suggested that induced compliance does not produce real attitude change at all. Instead, participants lie about their attitudes in order to appear consistent.

Impression management motives probably contributed to some dissonance findings. Research participants are concerned about the experimenter's impressions of them, and public conditions do increase attitude change (recall our discussion of public commitment as a factor in induced compliance). But some attitude change usually occurs even when counterattitudinal behavior is private, which argues against a lying explanation. Also, impression management theory has difficulty accounting for the full range of dissonance findings (for example, selective exposure effects). It seems likely that dissonance and impression management motives both operate in situations involving counterattitudinal behavior.

Self-Affirmation Theory

Steele (1988; Steele and Liu, 1981) proposed that people are not generally concerned about consistency between their cognitions. He suggested that they are very concerned, however, about their status as good, competent persons (their self-worth). In dissonance situations, according to Steele, counterattitudinal behavior threatens individuals' views of themselves as rational or honest, so people affirm their self-worth

by changing their attitudes to be consistent with their actions. Steele argued, however, that people can reduce dissonance by affirming their worth in any way at all—his **self-affirmation theory.** From this perspective, people do not need to change one of the dissonant cognitions but can do anything that shows they are good people. This logic implies that giving participants some other way of affirming their self-worth should eliminate attitude change even if it does not deal with the inconsistency. In one study (Steele and Liu, 1981), participants were induced to write an essay opposing state funding for facilities serving the handicapped. Before writing the essay, some participants were told that they would later be asked to help a blind student, whereas other participants were not given this expectation. When attitudes were measured after the essay, attitude change occurred only for the participants who did *not* expect a chance to help. Presumably, participants who expected to help a blind person were undisturbed by their counterattitudinal behavior because they knew that their self-worth would be reaffirmed.

Self-Concept Theory

A similar model has been proposed by Aronson (1968; 1992), who suggested that any threat to the self-concept induces dissonance regardless of whether it involves counterattitudinal behavior. Aronson argued that dissonance experiments produce attitude change because people are disturbed by the implications of their actions for their self-concept. Aronson would argue that participants in Festinger and Carlsmith's (1959) experiment were not disturbed by the cognitions "The tasks were boring" and "I told someone the tasks were fun" but rather by the cognitions "I am an honest person" and "I have misled someone." In most circumstances, **self-concept theory** makes similar predictions to dissonance theory, but there are some differences. For example, self-concept theory would predict that if an individual's self-concept does not include the notion that the individual is always honest (such as someone who believes that it's okay to mislead other people in order to achieve his or her goals), the individual will not experience dissonance from telling a lie. Self-concept theory also predicts that even *pro*attitudinal behavior can produce dissonance if the actor's self-concept is threatened. Box 6.1 describes an interesting example of such an effect—hypocritical behavior.

BOX 6.1

Hypocrisy: Dissonance from Proattitudinal Behavior

Aronson and his students (Aronson, Fried, and Stone, 1991; Stone, Aronson, Crain, Winslow, and Fried, 1994) have identified a source of dissonance arousal that does not involve counterattitudinal behavior. **Hypocrisy** occurs when people realize they have publicly advocated behavior that they do not practice personally. Aronson's self-concept theory (1968; 1992) predicts that realizing that one has behaved hypocritically produces dissonance between the cognitions "I publicly recommended behavior *X*" and "I do not perform behavior *X*." This is an intriguing case of dissonance because the public behavior is completely *pro*attitudinal— the individual calls for a socially desirable behavior like conserving energy or using

condoms. Also, the behavior does not have any aversive consequences, which some theorists have argued are necessary for dissonance to occur (Cooper and Fazio, 1984). Thus, hypocritical behavior extends dissonance theory in a new direction.

In one experiment, Stone, Aronson, Crain, Winslow, and Fried (1994) recruited university students who had been sexually active in the last three months and asked them to develop a persuasive message about AIDS and safer sex (everyone was given some standard information to prepare the message). Half of the participants then delivered their message in front of a video camera, allegedly so that the experimenter could use the speeches to create a videotape of university students talking about safer sex to show to high school students. The remaining participants did not read their messages in front of a camera and, therefore, did not make a public commitment to safer sex behaviors. In each of these groups, half of the participants then completed a questionnaire that was designed to make them aware of their own failures to practice safer sex

If this father were reminded that he had repeatedly condemned smoking to his son, his resulting feelings of hypocrisy might motivate him to stop.

Continued

BOX 6.1

Continued

behaviors in the past (the "mindful" manipulation). The questionnaire listed ten common reasons why people do not use condoms, and participants were asked to prepare a separate list of the circumstances surrounding their own past failures to use condoms (using the ten reasons or any others that they could think of). The remaining participants did not complete this questionnaire.

Thus, four conditions were created. Participants in the *hypocrisy* condition made a public commitment and then were reminded of their own past failures to use condoms. Participants in the *commitment-only* condition made a public commitment but were not made mindful of their own past failures. Participants in the *mindful-only* condition did not make a public commitment but were reminded of their own past failures to use condoms. Participants in the *control* condition did not make a public commitment and were not reminded of their past actions.

All participants then answered some questions in an interview and were told that the session was complete. They were given four $1 bills as payment for their participation. The experimenter then explained that when the campus health center heard about this study looking at safer sex behaviors, it made available a supply of condoms at the price of 10 cents apiece. The experimenter pointed to a desk in the room where a clear plastic container was filled with 140 condoms, ten each of fourteen brands. A bowl of loose change and an envelope with $1 bills were beside the plastic container. The experimenter said that if any of the participants wanted to buy any condoms, they could put some money in the envelope and take the necessary change from the bowl. The experimenter thanked the participants for taking part in the study and left to go to another room to prepare for the next subject. Thus, participants believed that whether or not they purchased condoms was private and anonymous.

The figure shows the percentage of participants in each condition who purchased condoms. The results supported the authors' prediction that participants in the hypocrisy condition would purchase more condoms than participants in any other condition. When participants made a public commitment and were reminded of their own past failures to live up to their advocated standards, 83 percent of them bought at least one condom compared with 50 percent or less in the other three conditions. Notice that simply making a public commitment or simply being reminded of past failures to use condoms did not result in more condom purchasing than the control condition. People had to advocate condom use *and* think about their past failures in order to show a heightened propensity to buy condoms.

Stone and associates (1994) suggested that hypocrisy induction might provide an effective way to encourage desirable but frequently ignored behaviors. If people publicly discuss why a certain behavior is desirable and then think about their own past inaction, they should be motivated to change their behaviors to match their public position. This technique could be applied to a wide range of desirable behaviors, such as exercising regularly, avoiding foods that are high in fat, and using sunscreen.

Continued

Conclusions:
Cognitive Dissonance Theory

Dissonance theory has had a controversial but productive history. It was the first formulation to focus explicitly on how behavior can change attitudes. Researchers have identified limiting conditions for dissonance effects, and some data suggest that threats to the self-concept may be involved rather than cognitive inconsistencies per se. Nevertheless, dissonance theory

BOX 6.1

Continued

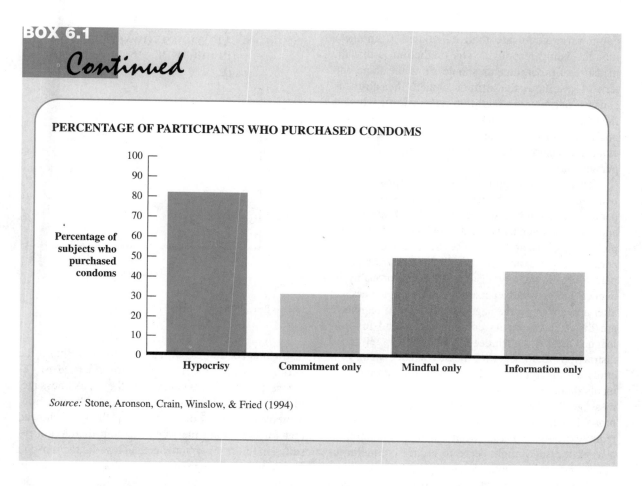

PERCENTAGE OF PARTICIPANTS WHO PURCHASED CONDOMS

Source: Stone, Aronson, Crain, Winslow, & Fried (1994)

remains intuitively compelling and provides explanations for interesting phenomena that would otherwise be hard to understand. Even today, dissonance theory is probably the clearest example of a motivational model of attitude change.

The Cognitive Response Approach: Thought-Based Attitude Change

A perspective on persuasion that is very different from dissonance theory is provided by the **cognitive response approach.** This approach (for reviews, see Eagly and Chaiken, 1984, 1993; Petty and Cacioppo, 1981, 1986) evolved from earlier work by Hovland, Janis, and Kelley (1953), Greenwald (1968), and McGuire (1968a, 1972). The basic assumption of the cognitive response

approach is that the effectiveness of a message depends on the thoughts, or cognitive responses, generated by the recipients as they anticipate, receive, or reflect on the persuasive communication. In other words, the major determinant of the success of a message is whether it leads recipients to generate mostly positive, supportive thoughts (termed *proarguments*) or mostly negative, critical thoughts (termed *counterarguments*). These thoughts can refer to the communicator, the issue, or the message itself. When favorable thoughts predominate, persuasion occurs in the direction of the message, whereas when unfavorable thoughts predominate, little or no persuasion occurs.

Because cognitive responses are viewed as the primary determinant of attitude change, a common procedure in studies conducted within this framework is to obtain measures of participants' thoughts. Typically, research participants are exposed to a message, asked to indicate their attitudes, and then asked to list any thoughts that occurred to them while they read the message. The numbers of proarguments and counterarguments are then calculated from these thought-listing responses. The prediction is that the measure of proarguments should show the same pattern of results as the attitude change measure (because proarguments facilitate persuasion), whereas the measure of counterarguments should show the opposite (mirror image) pattern of results as the attitude change measure (because counterarguments inhibit persuasion).

Tests of the cognitive response approach have been supportive for numerous variables that affect persuasion, including source credibility, forewarning, and one-sided versus two-sided messages. For example, Petty, Wells, and Brock (1976) conducted two experiments that examined the effect of *distraction* on persuasion. Intuitively, distraction would probably be expected to reduce the persuasive impact of a message; after all, how can a message be persuasive if recipients are distracted from its content? Petty and his colleagues argued that, indeed, this inhibitory effect of distraction would occur for messages that contain generally strong arguments. Distraction from strong arguments should reduce their impact. But what about weak messages? In this case, undistracted recipients will probably generate mostly unfavorable thoughts, which reduce persuasion. Paradoxically, then, distraction from a weak message might serve to reduce counterarguments and increase attitude change. Thus, distraction may interfere with the "dominant" response to a message, either acceptance of a strong message or rejection of a weak message.

In one study, Petty and his colleagues exposed students to an oral message over headphones arguing for a reduction in tuition (a proattitudinal position for most students). The message contained either strong or weak arguments in support of tuition reductions. In addition, participants were required to perform another task while processing the message. This distraction task required participants to record on a sheet the quadrant in which Xs appeared on a screen in front of them. In the low distraction condition, the Xs appeared at fifteen-second intervals, whereas in the medium distraction condition, the Xs appeared at five-second intervals. After hearing the message over the headphones, participants indicated their attitude toward reduced tuition and then listed any thoughts that occurred to them during the message.

Figure 6.6 presents the results on the attitude measure. The weak message produced less persuasion than the strong message under both low- and medium-

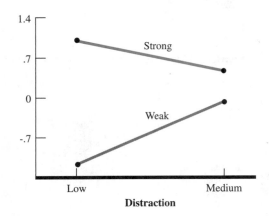

FIGURE 6.6   **ATTITUDES TOWARD TUITION REDUCTION**

Source: Petty, Wells, and Brock (1976)

distraction conditions, which makes sense. But for the strong message, medium distraction served to decrease persuasion, whereas for the weak message, medium distraction actually increased persuasion. Moreover, analysis of participants' thoughts showed that for the strong message, medium distraction resulted in fewer proarguments than low distraction, and for the weak message, medium distraction resulted in fewer counterarguments than low distraction. Thus, the attitude and thought-listing measures both supported the cognitive response approach.

If distraction serves to interfere with the "dominant" response to a message, then *repetition* should serve to heighten the dominant response. Repeatedly hearing a strong message allows recipients more opportunities to recognize that the arguments are compelling, which should produce more proarguments and more persuasion. In contrast, repeatedly hearing a weak message allows recipients more opportunities to recognize that the arguments are unconvincing, which should produce more counterarguments and less persuasion.

In an experiment testing the effects of repetition, Cacioppo and Petty (1985) exposed students to a message arguing that seniors at their university should be required to pass a comprehensive exam in their major area as a requirement for graduation. Naturally, this idea was counterattitudinal for most participants. Half of the participants heard a message containing strong arguments for the institution of the exam (such as,

FIGURE 6.7 ATTITUDES TOWARD COMPREHENSIVE EXAMS

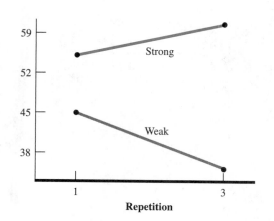

Source: Petty and Cacioppo (1986), p. 142

graduates from universities with comprehensive exams are recruited more heavily by employers), whereas half heard a message containing weak arguments (such as, comprehensive exams maintain a tradition dating back to the ancient Greeks). In addition, participants heard the message either once or three times. After hearing the message, participants indicated their attitude toward comprehensive exams for undergraduates, and their memory for the message was tested.

Figure 6.7 presents the results on the attitude measure. Again the weak message produced less persuasion than the strong message in both repetition conditions. More important, repetition served to increase attitude change for the strong message but to decrease persuasion for the weak message. Participants also exhibited better recall of the message when they heard it three times rather than just once. Although cognitive responses were not directly assessed, the memory data suggest that repetition allowed participants to analyze the message more thoroughly.

The cognitive response approach also provides a nice framework for understanding instances of *self-persuasion,* where people appear to convince themselves that a certain position is valid. For example, Tesser (1978) identified a self-persuasion phenomenon that he labelled **attitude polarization via mere thought.** Tesser showed that merely thinking about an issue often makes attitudes more extreme (polarized) because people usually generate thoughts that are con-

sistent with their original position. Imagine that the midterm exam in your psychology course was difficult and, in your view, unfair. Tesser's work suggests that if you took this exam in the afternoon and then thought about it later in the evening, you might find yourself becoming angrier and angrier about the unfairness of the exam because you would tend to generate thoughts that supported your initial position.

In an empirical test of this reasoning, Sadler and Tesser (1973) recruited participants for a study of how people form impressions. Participants heard someone who they thought was another participant describing himself for two minutes. Half of the participants listened to a likable partner, who complimented the participant and described himself positively without appearing to brag. The remaining participants listened to a dislikable partner, who criticized the participant and was smug and arrogant. Some participants were then asked to think about this partner for a few minutes, whereas other participants were given an irrelevant task to distract them from thinking about their partner. All participants then reported their impressions of the partner. As expected, participants reported more liking for the likable than the dislikable partner. More important, thinking about the likable partner served to increase liking but thinking about the dislikable partner served to decrease liking compared to the condition where participants completed an irrelevant task to distract them from thinking about their partner. Thus, "mere thought" polarized participants' attitudes, making positive attitudes more positive and negative attitudes more negative.

Comprehensive Theories of Attitude Change: The Systematic-Heuristic and Elaboration Likelihood Models

In the last ten or fifteen years, a number of broad, comprehensive theories of persuasion have appeared in social psychology. Two of these theories, the **systematic-heuristic model** (Chaiken, 1980, 1987) and the **elaboration likelihood model** (Petty and

Pope John Paul II blesses a crowd during his 1998 visit to Cuba. Do you think his Christian message to this audience of young people who have known only life under secular socialism would be primarily processed by them systematically and centrally or heuristically and peripherally?

Cacioppo, 1981, 1986), have been particularly influential. These models postulate that there are two qualitatively different ways that messages can produce attitude change. On the one hand, the arguments in the message can be strong and convincing, which produces attitude change via the merits of the position. On the other hand, people can adopt a message's recommendations without carefully analyzing the arguments simply because there is some clue or feature suggesting that the advocated position is probably valid. The first kind of attitude change is what most people mean when they say "persuasion"; the cognitive response approach typifies this type of rational, argument-based persuasion. The latter kind of attitude change is somewhat harder to understand; a prototypical example would be when dedicated sports fans adopt the attitudes of their athletic heroes without carefully considering the pros and cons of the issues.

In the systematic-heuristic model, Chaiken (1980, 1987) distinguishes between **systematic processing** and **heuristic processing.** Systematic processing in persuasion settings reflects a careful, thoughtful analysis of the relevant information. Heuristic processing occurs when people adopt or reject attitude positions on the basis of cognitive **heuristics**—simple rules of thumb—rather than by carefully analyzing the relevant information. Heuristics simplify our world by providing assumptions or rules that allow us to make rapid judgments. Heuris-

tics will often be accurate and effective short-cuts, but they can also lead to errors. In the domain of persuasion, common heuristics include "Experts are usually right" and "I usually agree with people I like."

In the elaboration likelihood model, Cacioppo and Petty (1981, 1986) distinguish between the **central route to persuasion** and the **peripheral route to persuasion.** The central route occurs when attitude change results from rational, information-based reasoning (paralleling systematic processing), whereas the peripheral route occurs when attitude change results from noncognitive factors (including heuristic cues as well as such processes as mere exposure and classical conditioning). Obviously, there are many parallels between the systematic-heuristic and elaboration likelihood models, which developed independently and simultaneously. There are also some important differences (see Eagly and Chaiken, 1993), but we will discuss these two theories jointly.

In both models, systematic/central processing is hypothesized to be more effortful than heuristic/peripheral processing. Therefore, systematic/central processing is postulated to occur only when people are both (1) *motivated* enough to process the arguments carefully and (2) *able* to process the arguments carefully. Careful message processing, for example, will occur when the issue is important to the perceiver (high motivation) and when the arguments are simple enough for the perceiver to understand (high ability). If either motivation or ability is lacking, then heuristic/peripheral processing will occur, which will not focus on the arguments in the message.

These models predict that different factors produce attitude change in the two processes/routes. Specifically, if systematic/central processing occurs, then attitude change will depend primarily on the strength of the arguments because people are paying close attention to the message. If heuristic/peripheral processing occurs, however, then attitude change will depend on whether heuristics, or **peripheral cues,** are present because people are not analyzing the message thoughtfully. Common peripheral cues include the expertise, attractiveness, and likability of the source (with greater acceptance of recommendations from experts, attractive sources, and likable sources) and the number of arguments in the message (with greater acceptance of long messages).

Many experiments have shown that when people are highly motivated to process a message carefully, the strength of the arguments determines persuasion, whereas when people are not highly motivated, persuasion depends on heuristics, or peripheral cues. For example, Petty and Cacioppo (1984) gave students a message that seniors at their university should be required to pass a comprehensive exam in their major in order to graduate (the same topic as in a study de-

scribed earlier). High motivation to process the message carefully was aroused in half of the participants by telling them that the issue of comprehensive exams was being considered for possible adoption at their university in the coming year (thus the issue might affect them personally). The remaining participants were told that the issue was being considered for possible adoption only in ten years' time (low motivation). High motivation was expected to activate systematic/central processing, whereas low motivation was expected to activate heuristic/peripheral processing. Participants received one of four messages: the message was either long (nine arguments) or short (three arguments) and either strong (all good arguments) or weak (all poor arguments). The length of the message (nine versus three arguments) served as a heuristic/peripheral cue, which was expected to be influential only when heuristic/peripheral processing was activated. After reading the message, participants reported their attitude toward instituting comprehensive exams.

Figure 6.8 presents the results of the study. In the low-involvement (low motivation) condition, where heuristic/peripheral processing should occur, participants reported more favorable attitudes toward comprehensive exams when they were exposed to a long message than to a short message irrespective of the quality of the arguments. These low-motivation participants seemed to adopt the heuristic "When there

---

FIGURE 6.8   ATTITUDES TOWARD COMPREHENSIVE EXAMS

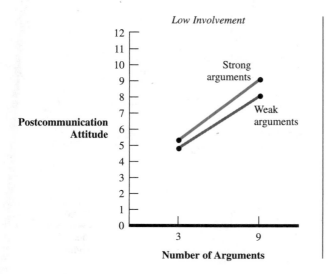
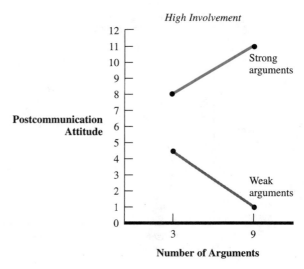

Source: Petty and Cacioppo (1984)

are lots of arguments for a position, it is usually valid." In contrast, participants in the high-involvement (high motivation) condition were much more persuaded by strong arguments than by weak arguments, and long messages simply exaggerated this difference (nine strong arguments were significantly *more* convincing than three strong arguments, whereas nine weak arguments were significantly *less* convincing than three weak arguments). The powerful impact of argument strength suggests that these high-involvement participants were processing the message systematically (the central route was activated).

In another study, Petty, Cacioppo, and Schumann (1983) asked university students to look at several magazine advertisements. One ad was for a new brand of disposable razor. High motivation to process the ad carefully was aroused in half of the participants by telling them two things. First, the product would soon be available in their town, and second, they would later be choosing a free gift for taking part in the study from among several disposable razors. Participants in the low-motivation condition were told that the product would soon be test marketed in some distant cities, and they would be choosing a free gift from among several brands of toothpaste. High motivation was expected to activate systematic/central processing, whereas low motivation was expected to activate heuristic/peripheral processing. Four different versions of the razor advertisement were prepared. Two ads used famous sports celebrities as the endorsers, and the other two ads used unknown middle-aged citizens as the endorsers. The famous endorsers were expected to constitute a heuristic/peripheral cue that would be used if heuristic/peripheral processing was activated. One sports ad and one citizen ad contained six "strong arguments" in favor of the razor (such as its handle is ribbed to prevent slipping), whereas the other sports ad and citizen ad contained six "weak arguments" about the razor (such as it is designed with the bathroom in mind). After reading the advertisement, participants reported their attitudes toward the disposable razor.

Figure 6.9 presents the results. In the high-involvement (high motivation) condition, the only determinant of persuasion was the quality of the arguments in the ad. Strong arguments produced significantly more positive attitudes than weak arguments, and whether the endorser was famous or not made no difference. This pattern exactly conformed to the expectation that the high-motivation condition would activate systematic/central processing. In the low-involvement (low-motivation) condition, both argument strength and, more important, fame of the endorser significantly affected attitudes. Strong arguments led to more positive attitudes than weak arguments, and the celebrity endorser led to more positive attitudes than the unknown endorser. The impact of the latter variable (fame of the endorser) suggests that heuristic/peripheral processing was activated in the low-motivation condition.

FIGURE 6.9   ATTITUDES TOWARD DISPOSABLE RAZOR

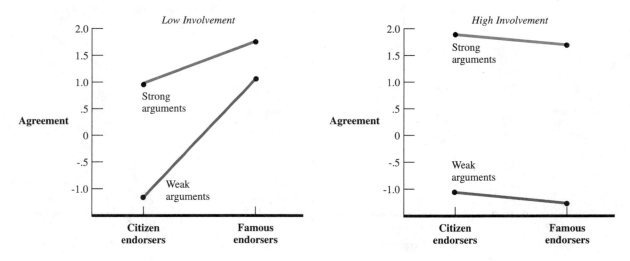

Source: Petty, Cacioppo and Schumann (1983)

It seems likely that cults exert influence on recruits primarily via the peripheral route. Charismatic leaders and emotional appeals provide strong cues to adopt the advocated beliefs even if the arguments supporting them are neither strong nor clear. One common characteristic of cults is that they discourage rational thought (Rudin and Rudin, 1980; Swenson, 1987); instead, members are told to "go with their feelings" and to fight critical thoughts, which are typically attributed to evil influences. If cults induce peripheral processing, then the weakness of their arguments may not impair their persuasive success.

"I think it's your cap, Slim.
The cows don't see you as an authority figure."

Factors in the Persuasion Setting

In all persuasion settings (that is, whenever a persuasive communication is delivered), it is possible to identify a *source,* a *message,* and a *recipient* (target or audience). Various characteristics of each of these components influence the effectiveness of the persuasion attempt. That is, some people are more effective communicators than others; certain characteristics of messages enhance persuasion; and some people or audiences are more easily persuaded than others. In the remainder of this chapter, we discuss the impact of several specific factors in the persuasion setting, using the systematic/central versus heuristic/peripheral framework to understand the findings.

Source Characteristics

The advertising industry subscribes to the belief that the person who delivers a message is important: companies spend millions of dollars every year hiring spokespersons for products. Most source characteristics exert their influence via the heuristic, or peripheral, route to persuasion. That is, they serve as cues suggesting that the recommendations are probably good ones. Thus, source characteristics should be particularly influential when recipients are either unmotivated or unable to process the message arguments carefully.

Likability, Fame, and Attractiveness

Sources who are well liked are generally more effective than disliked sources. Liking can be based on the source's fame, pleasant personality, physical attrac-

tiveness, or anything else that appeals to the perceiver. This liking effect is probably mediated by several processes, including identification with the source, wanting to please the source, and adhering to the heuristic rule "I usually agree with people I like."

We already described an experiment by Petty, Cacioppo, and Schumann (1983) in which famous endorsers were more effective than nonfamous endorsers in generating favorable evaluations of a disposable razor, but only in a low-motivation condition (see figure 6.9). Thus, the positive reactions that were produced by fame (such as liking or admiration) influenced recipients' attitudes toward the product only when heuristic processing was activated. In another pair of studies, Chaiken (1980) showed that the likability of a communicator was more important in low-involvement than in high-involvement conditions.

Physical attractiveness is another factor that might induce liking. Several researchers have found that messages presented by very attractive sources are effective even when the arguments are weak, whereas less attractive sources need to present compelling arguments to be persuasive (Norman, 1976; Pallak, 1983). Again this pattern suggests that liked (attractive) sources can be influential via nonmessage, peripheral means.

Credibility

The most researched source characteristic has been **credibility.** Credible sources are those who can be taken seriously, who can be believed. Credibility is usually conceptualized as consisting of two components:

expertise and *trustworthiness.* Expertise refers to the possession of relevant knowledge and experience. Trustworthiness refers to the lack of ulterior motives—communicators are expressing their honest beliefs based on the evidence as they know it. Credible sources generally produce more attitude change than noncredible sources, whether the credibility derives from expertise, from trustworthiness, or from both components (see Eagly, Wood, and Chaiken, 1978).

Credibility can increase persuasion whether the recipient is processing information systematically or heuristically. With regard to systematic/central processing, people pay more attention to arguments from credible sources, so arguments are more likely to have an impact. With regard to heuristic/peripheral processing, source credibility offers a powerful cue that the message is valid (for example, we follow our doctor's advice).

Petty, Cacioppo, and Goldman (1981) nicely documented the possible heuristic cue value of source credibility. Students were exposed to a message arguing that comprehensive exams should be required for graduating seniors (a topic we have seen before). Half of the participants were told that exams were being considered for possible implementation at their university next year (*high motivation* to process carefully), whereas the remaining participants were told that the policy would only start in ten years (*low motivation*). In addition, half of the participants heard eight strong arguments in favor of exams, and half heard eight weak arguments. Finally, half of the participants were told that the message was prepared by a local high school class, and half were told that the message was prepared by the Carnegie Commission on Higher Education, chaired by a Princeton University professor. After reading the message, participants reported their attitudes toward comprehensive exams.

Figure 6.10 presents the results of the experiment. As shown in the right-hand side of the figure, when students were highly motivated to process the message carefully, the strength of the arguments was the only factor that made any difference. Recipients were more persuaded by strong arguments than by weak arguments irrespective of whether the source was high or low in expertise. As shown in the left-hand side of figure 6.10, however, source expertise made a big difference when participants were not motivated to process the message carefully. Low-motivation participants agreed significantly more with a high-expertise than with a low-expertise source for both strong and weak arguments (and they also agreed more with strong than with weak arguments). Thus, source expertise served as a heuristic, or peripheral, cue that influenced recipients who were not highly motivated to engage in careful processing.

The Sleeper Effect

An early experiment on source credibility by Hovland and Weiss (1951) uncovered evidence of a fascinating

FIGURE 6.10   ATTITUDES TOWARD COMPREHENSIVE EXAMS

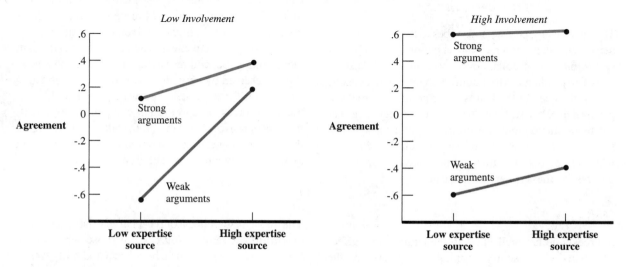

Source: Petty, Cacioppo and Goldman (1981)

interaction between source credibility and the passage of time on measures of attitude change. Specifically, these researchers found that measures of attitudes taken immediately after a message yielded the typical effect of more attitude change from a high-credibility than a low-credibility source, whereas measures of attitudes taken several weeks after the message revealed little difference between the high- and low-credibility sources. More important, whereas the amount of attitude change produced by a high-credibility source decreased over time (as would be expected because of forgetting), the amount of attitude change produced by a low-credibility source actually *increased* significantly over time. This latter effect for the low-credibility source was labeled the **sleeper effect:** attitude change increased as recipients "slept" on the message. The sleeper effect is interesting because the notion that attitude change will increase over time, even after a message has been removed, seems paradoxical.

The explanations that have been proposed for the sleeper effect involve three processes: **discounting, dissociation,** and **differential decay** (Gruder, Cook, Hennigan, Flay, Alessis, and Halamaj, 1978; Pratkanis, Greenwald, Leippe, and Baumgardner, 1988). Initially, recipients discount the message when it comes from a low-credibility source, thereby suppressing any attitude change that might have occurred from the message itself. As time passes, however, the message becomes dissociated (separated) in memory from information about the source (i.e., recipients forget the source of the information). Thus, the message can influence attitudes because it is no longer being discounted. Also, both the message and source information decay in memory over time, and source information often decays faster than message information (differential decay). Again, then, the message can influence attitudes without being restrained by the fact that it came from a noncredible source. Of course, delaying attitude measurement too much will not reveal a sleeper effect because even the message information will have been forgotten. Most experiments that have found a significant sleeper effect have involved delays of less than a month between exposure to the message and measurement of attitudes.

Message Characteristics

Another component of persuasion settings is the message. Obviously, the content of a message affects whether or not attitude change occurs. Characteristics of the message can influence both systematic and heuristic processing. Three message features that have yielded interesting results are described in the following sections. Box 6.2 provides a detailed example of an experiment on the effects of message comprehensibility.

Argument Strength

We have already referred to several experiments in which argument strength was manipulated (Petty and Cacioppo, 1984; Petty, Cacioppo, and Goldman, 1981; Petty, Cacioppo, and Schumann, 1983). In these studies, strong arguments produced more persuasion than did weak arguments, and this finding was especially clear when recipients were processing systematically, or centrally (that is, when both motivation and ability were high).

Message Length

We have also referred to an experiment in which the number of arguments in a message (message length) was manipulated (Petty and Cacioppo, 1984). Long messages produced more attitude change than short messages *only* when recipients were processing heuristically (see figure 6.8). Thus, message length served as a peripheral cue that was used to infer the validity of the message when people were not motivated to pay close attention to the quality of the arguments.

Fear Appeals

Media messages that are aimed at convincing people to stop unhealthy behaviors (e.g., smoking, unprotected sex) often present fear-provoking pictures and statistics, hoping to scare people into changing their bad habits. Are fear appeals an effective way to produce attitude and behavior change?

This question has been examined in many studies in social psychology. The results of early studies were inconsistent, with some researchers finding that high fear led to more persuasion (Chu, 1966) and others finding no effect or even the opposite effect (Janis and Feshbach, 1953). McGuire (1969) suggested that the inconsistent results might be attributable to the fact that fear-provoking messages have two competing effects. First, they increase the audience's willingness to accept the speaker's recommendations because the audience doesn't want to suffer the negative consequences that are described in the message. But they

BOX 6.2

Message Comprehensibility and Persuasion

A group of researchers at Brock University in St. Catharines, Ontario, recently tested the effects of message comprehensibility on persuasion. Hafer, Reynolds, and Obertynski (1996) exposed students to a message arguing that *plea bargaining* is an effective tool that prosecutors should use. Plea bargaining involves having an accused person plead guilty in return for either a reduced charge (such as manslaughter instead of first-degree murder) or some other special treatment (such as a reduced sentence). At the time the study was conducted, a highly publicized plea bargain had recently been negotiated in St. Catharines—Karla Homolka's guilty plea to manslaughter in the sexual abuse and murder of two local teenage girls. Homolka received a sentence of twelve years in return for testifying against her former husband, Paul Bernardo, who was eventually convicted of first-degree murder and sentenced to life imprisonment. Plea bargaining was controversial in Canada because of the publicity surrounding the Homolka deal; shortly after the deal was completed, new evidence in the form of videotapes was uncovered, which rendered Homolka's testimony far less critical and provided graphic evidence of her involvement in the crimes. Thus, most people considered her plea bargain to be unjust. A pretest conducted by Hafer and her coauthors confirmed that most students had unfavorable attitudes toward plea bargaining.

Participants listened to a taped speech arguing in favor of plea bargaining. The speech was either high or low in comprehensibility. The easy-to-understand speech used common words and simple grammatical constructions. The hard-to-understand speech used legal jargon and complex grammatical constructions. The researchers assumed that plea bargaining would be an involving issue for their St. Catharines students, so participants would be highly motivated to process the message carefully, but the comprehensibility of the message was expected to determine whether participants were *able* to process carefully. When the message was easy to comprehend, participants were expected to be both motivated and able to engage in systematic processing. When the message was difficult to comprehend, participants were expected to be unable to process systematically (even though they would be motivated to do so).

Two other message factors were manipulated to document and test the implications of the expected processing effects. First, the message contained either five strong arguments or five weak arguments in favor of plea bargaining. Strong arguments included: "Plea bargaining may make a charge more appropriate to the circumstances of the crime" (easy-to-understand condition) and "Plea bargaining can acquire a conviction by obtaining a guilty plea in a weak case that may otherwise yield an acquittal, should the case be held over for trial" (hard-to-understand condition). Weak arguments included: "Plea bargaining benefits the public because there is a conviction to a crime and the criminal gets a record" (easy-to-understand condition) and "Negotiated dispositions in a properly constructed system of plea bargaining will approximate the probable results of a trial" (difficult-to-understand condition). Second, the message was attributed to a speaker who was either high or low in status. In the high-status source condition, participants were told before listening to the taped speech that the speaker was His Honor Judge William Grovestead, a summa cum laude graduate of Harvard Law School, who had been sitting on the bench for fifteen years, was an expert on plea bargaining, and had written numerous learned papers on the topic. In the low-status source condition, the speaker was introduced as William Grovestead, a second-year law

Continued

BOX 6.2

Continued

student at Rockway University, who had recently become interested in plea bargaining. After the speech, participants reported their attitudes toward plea bargaining.

The table presents the results on the attitude measure for each condition. The pattern was exactly what would be expected if systematic processing occurred in the easy-to-understand condition and heuristic processing occurred in the hard-to-understand condition. When the message was easy to comprehend (the top half of the table), participants expressed significantly more favorable attitudes toward plea bargaining when the arguments were strong rather than weak (4.69 versus 3.65) regardless of whether the source was high or low status. In fact, there was a nonsignificant tendency for the easy message to produce more agreement when the source was low rather than high status (4.35 versus 4.00). When the message was difficult to understand, however (the bottom half of the table), participants expressed significantly more favorable attitudes toward plea bargaining when the source was high rather than low status (4.96 versus 3.27) regardless of whether the arguments were strong or weak. In fact, there was a nonsignificant tendency for the difficult message to produce more agreement when the arguments were weak rather than strong (4.38 versus 3.85).

Thus, when the message was simple, participants exhibited systematic processing and were strongly influenced by the quality of the arguments. But when the message was com-

ATTITUDES TOWARD PLEA BARGAINING

Source Condition	Argument Strength		
	Strong	Weak	*M*
Easy Comprehension			
High Status	4.31	3.69	4.00
Low Status	5.08	3.62	4.35
M	4.69	3.65	
Difficult Comprehension			
High Status	4.69	5.23	4.96
Low Status	3.00	3.54	3.27
M	3.85	4.38	

Note: Attitudes were measured on a 7-point scale (1 = completely opposed, 7 = completely in favor). $n = 13$ per cell (total = 104)
Source: Hafer, Reynolds, and Obertynski (1996)

plex, participants exhibited heuristic processing and were strongly influenced by the status of the source. Message comprehensibility influenced the type of processing that occurred through its effects on recipients' *ability* to process the persuasive message carefully. For another experiment on message complexity and source expertise that yielded similar results, see Cooper, Bennett, and Sukel (1996).

also reduce the audience's desire to pay attention to the message because the fear-provoking details are gruesome or threatening.

Over the last two decades, the results of studies on threatening messages have been consistent enough to lead most theorists to conclude that the arousal of fear typically *increases* the impact of messages on attitudes and behavioral intentions (Eagly and Chaiken, 1993; Perloff, 1993). There have also been important conceptual advances in that the mechanisms through which fear exerts its effects have been identified.

The most comprehensive theory of fear appeals is **protection motivation theory** by Rogers and his colleagues (Maddux and Rogers, 1983; Rogers, 1983; Rogers and Mewborn, 1976). Rogers argued that threatening messages produce attitude change by motivating the listener to protect himself or herself from the dangers described in the message. Rogers identified four ways that threatening messages can arouse protection motivation:

1. *Severity of the problem.* If listeners believe that the problem described in the message is serious

Cuba's President Fidel Castro promised to limit his welcome of Pope John Paul II to no longer than fifteen minutes. Could Castro, notorious for speeches lasting an hour or more, have intended the shortening of his message as a peripheral cue?

(for example, lung cancer, AIDS), they will be more motivated to avoid it.

2. *Susceptibility to the problem.* If listeners believe that the problem can occur to them personally, they will be more motivated to avoid it.

3. *Effectiveness of behavior change in avoiding the problem.* If listeners believe that by changing their behavior they can greatly reduce their likelihood of developing the problem, they will be more motivated to follow the recommendations.

4. *Self-efficacy.* If listeners believe that they can easily or effectively perform the recommended behaviors, they will be more willing to do so.

Rogers argued that these cognitive perceptions rather than the emotion of fear per se determine the impact of a threatening message on attitudes and behavior. Several experiments have supported this model. For example, Rogers and Mewborn (1976) exposed smokers to messages about smoking. Each of the first three components of fear appeals was manipulated. Messages were produced that depicted the effects of smoking as either moderately or extremely severe (with graphic pictures of lung cancer surgery in the high-severity condition), that presented statistics implying that typical smokers are either somewhat or very susceptible to lung cancer, and that argued that quitting smoking would either slightly or greatly reduce the likelihood of developing lung cancer. Participants' intentions to quit smoking were then measured. The results generally supported protection motivation theory; for example, participants expressed significantly stronger intentions of quitting smoking when they believed that doing so would greatly reduce their likelihood of developing lung cancer.

Recipient Characteristics

A third component of persuasion settings is the recipient of the message. Are some people more easily persuaded than others? The evidence on this question is mixed. What seems very clear is that when people have strong, accessible attitudes, they are more resistant to persuasion (see Bassili, 1996). There is also evidence that some people prefer to process information systematically rather than heuristically, whereas other people show the opposite preference. Given that the type of processing affects which variables influence persuasion (for example, argument strength versus source characteristics), this processing preference is important. Below we discuss three recipient characteristics that influence the type of processing people engage in.

Need for Cognition

Some people enjoy thinking and thus engage in effortful cognitive tasks more often than do other people. Cacioppo, Petty, and Kao (1984) developed a scale to measure this individual difference, which they labelled the **need for cognition.** Individuals who are high in the need for cognition habitually engage in effortful thinking and enjoy cognitive tasks more than do individuals who are low in the need for cognition. It might be expected from this description that high-need-for-cognition individuals will be more likely to use systematic/central processing than low-need-for-cognition individuals. Consistent with this reasoning, Cacioppo, Petty, and Morris (1983) exposed participants to a set of either strong or weak arguments on a counterattitudinal issue. As revealed in figure 6.11, the strength of the arguments had more impact on the final attitudes of high-need-for-cognition participants, who were more persuaded by the strong message and less persuaded by the weak message than were low-need-for-cognition participants. High-need-for-cognition participants seemed to process the message more systematically than low-need-for-cognition partici-

pants. Other research has shown that low-need-for-cognition persons are more influenced by heuristic cues than are high-need-for-cognition persons, which supports the idea that low-need-for-cognition individuals more often employ heuristic/peripheral processing (Axsom, Yates, and Chaiken, 1987).

Uncertainty Orientation

Both comprehensive models of persuasion predict that when an issue is important or personally relevant to an individual, he or she is more likely to engage in systematic/central processing. Thus, the strength of the relevant arguments will be more influential for personally important topics. Sorrentino, Bobocel, Gitta, Olson, and Hewitt (1988), however, found that this prediction was confirmed for individuals labeled "uncertainty-oriented" but not for individuals labeled "certainty-oriented." This dimension relates to individuals' interest in new information about themselves and their environment. Persons with an **uncertainty orientation** seek out new information and approach uncertain situations, whereas certainty-oriented persons strive to maintain existing perceptions and avoid uncertainty (Sorrentino, Short, and Raynor, 1984). In contrast to predictions of the comprehensive models, certainty-oriented individuals actually engaged in heuristic/peripheral processing more when an attitude issue was personally relevant than when it was irrelevant (Sorrentino, Bobocel, Gitta, Olson, and Hewitt, 1988). This tendency in certainty-oriented persons presumably reflects their inclination to rely on others (such as experts) when an issue is important.

Positive Mood

We talked earlier about how fear can motivate attitude change through a threatening message. What about *positive* emotions—can they persuade? Advertisers clearly think so; most ads try to evoke positive feelings toward the product by presenting attractive models, pleasing music, humor, or happy settings. Several early studies suggested that, indeed, positive moods enhance persuasion. For example, Janis, Kaye, and Kirschner (1965) induced positive moods by giving some participants food while they read persuasive messages. Participants read persuasive messages about a series of controversial topics, such as the wisdom of reducing the size of the armed forces. Some

FIGURE 6.11 INDIVIDUAL DIFFERENCES IN RESPONSES TO STRONG AND WEAK ARGUMENTS

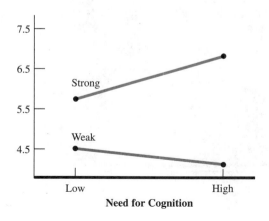

Source: Cacioppo, Petty, and Morris (1983)

participants merely read the messages in a typical laboratory room. Others were provided with a snack and soda while they read the messages. As shown in figure 6.12, those participants who were given food exhibited more attitude change on a variety of issues than did those participants who did not receive food.

Worth and Mackie (1987) obtained evidence that mood influences whether systematic or heuristic processing occurs. A positive mood was induced in some participants by giving them a dollar, whereas other participants did not receive any money. All participants then read a message on acid rain, which consisted of either nine strong or nine weak arguments and was attributed to either an expert or a nonexpert source. Compared with participants in a neutral mood, individuals who were placed in a positive mood were less influenced by the strength of the arguments and more influenced by the expertise of the source; that is, the positive-mood participants exhibited heuristic/ peripheral processing. There are at least two reasons why positive moods might induce heuristic processing (see Mackie and Worth, 1991). First, systematic processing is effortful, and persons in a good mood might want to maintain their mood by avoiding difficult thinking. Second, good moods might reduce the ca-

pacity to process carefully because they activate a lot of positively valenced material in memory.

These studies on the effects of positive mood provide yet another way that cults can influence recruits without strong arguments to support their case. Potential members are often exposed to **"love-bombing"** at recruitment meetings, which refers to expressions of unconditional love and caring from everyone around. For lonely people, such tactics can be very powerful and often produce a sense of exhilaration. The positive mood so induced will encourage heuristic processing. Thus, argument strength will be largely irrelevant with attitude change depending instead on heuristic cues like source expertise. Under such conditions, a charismatic leader can be very influential.

Postscript: How Do Cults Recruit and Retain Members?

We began the chapter with the stories of Suzanne and Steven, two young people who joined the Moonies,

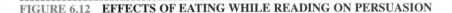

FIGURE 6.12 EFFECTS OF EATING WHILE READING ON PERSUASION

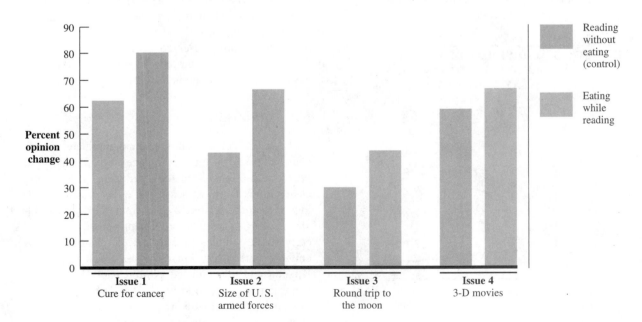

Source: Janis, Kaye, and Kirschner (1965)

much to the surprise of their friends and parents. How can cults recruit "normal" young people who are not actively looking for an alternative lifestyle? How powerful are the techniques of cults?

It has been estimated that the Moonies successfully recruit something like 10 percent of the individuals who attend one of their weekend retreats (Galanter, 1989). Of course, those who attend a weekend retreat have been highly selected both by recruiters (who pinpointed them) and by themselves (they agreed to attend the retreat). Perhaps 1 percent or even less would be a better estimate of how many "randomly selected" young people would join the cult if they attended a weekend retreat.

Whom do the cults choose for possible recruitment? They look for young people between the ages of approximately eighteen and thirty (Clay, 1987). They avoid people who are deeply troubled, whether the problems are psychological or drug related; such persons cannot benefit the cult sufficiently (Hassan, 1988). Individuals with a strong commitment to social justice are preferred, because such persons will be susceptible to promises of "improving the world." A recent loss or crisis, such as the death of a loved one, the breakup of a relationship, or a significant failure at school (Clay, 1987; Lofland and Stark, 1965), also seems to characterize many people who join cults or undergo ideological conversions. Losses induce a sense of loneliness that makes people more vulnerable to emotional appeals.

What are the persuasive techniques used by cults? We briefly describe some of their strategies in the following sections (see Clay, 1987; Hassan, 1988; Mac-Hovec, 1989; Pratkanis and Aronson, 1992; Rudin and Rudin, 1980; Swenson, 1987). Note that these techniques are neither unusual nor extremely powerful in isolation. In fact, many of the techniques are used routinely by other religious and nonreligious groups that we would not consider to be cults, as well as by salespersons, recruiters, and advertisers. But cults use the techniques simultaneously and forcefully; in concert, the techniques can be quite powerful.

Love-Bombing

Potential recruits are showered with love, flattery, and affection, always offered unconditionally ("We love you for just being you!"). This is a powerful reinforcement for young people uncertain about their popularity and attractiveness.

Foot-in-the-Door

Initially, recruits are given only small requests—come to the meeting, listen to the lecture. Next, somewhat larger requests occur—sing along with the members, talk about your hopes and wishes. Even larger requests follow—give money to the group, tell other people about the movement. Finally, requests become extreme—quit your job, move into the commune, and dedicate your life to the cult! When requests increase slowly in size, individuals can find themselves complying with substantial requests to which they would never have agreed at the outset—called the **foot-in-the-door effect** (see Cialdini, 1993; Freedman and Fraser, 1966; Gorassini and Olson, 1995). Compliance with the small initial requests produces public commitment to the cult that increases the likelihood of subsequent compliance with larger requests.

Repetition

Recruits are typically exposed to repeated lectures presenting the doctrine of the cult. When information is heard repeatedly, it develops an aura of legitimacy. Through such mechanisms as mere exposure (see chapter 5), familiarity leads to positive attitudes toward the material as well as toward the leader and members.

Altered States of Consciousness

At weekend recruitment "retreats," cults often employ techniques that are designed to produce mental confusion and an altered state of consciousness. Sleep deprivation and minimal provision of food can reduce mental alertness. Group chanting and singing can also produce a sense of unreality. The goal is to reduce logical processing and counterarguing, thereby increasing susceptibility to the cult's messages. Also, these techniques can induce an altered time perspective where both the past and the future fade away, and the present becomes all that matters. When the past and the future are forgotten, people make decisions and commitments that they would never make if they thought about the implications for their friends, family, and future.

Denial of Privacy

At recruitment meetings, potential recruits are denied privacy. When not engaged in group activities, they are almost always accompanied by at least one member of the cult. Thus, they never have a chance to sit quietly and think about what they are doing nor to talk to other nonmembers. Rather, pressure to join the cult is maintained at a constant, intense level.

Structured Activities

Closely related to denial of privacy is strict regimentation of activities for recruits. The entire weekend at Moonie retreats is filled with structured activities—lectures, discussion groups, singing. Again the primary goal is to deny any opportunity for quiet reflection about what is happening. And the structure serves to remove decision-making power from individuals and transfer it to the cult. Thus, recruits may feel that it is not up to them whether to join the group ("It is God's will").

Reciprocity

In our society, there is a strong reciprocity norm—we return favors to those who help us. Cults take advantage of this norm to pressure potential recruits to join. Recruits are subtly and not so subtly reminded that they are guests of the cult, are receiving free meals and accommodation while at the retreat, and have been treated with respect and affection by everyone. Cult members react with sadness and hurt feelings (not anger) when potential recruits resist participating fully in the activities, which serves to arouse further guilt about being an ungrateful guest. Cults know full well that idealistic, naive young people will want to show their appreciation for "everything that has been done for them."

Simple Solutions

In their lectures, cult leaders typically offer simplistic, vague solutions to complex problems. Poverty is blamed on godlessness, war is blamed on communism, and drugs are blamed on capitalism. For young people faced with a sometimes intimidating world, simplistic answers can be very appealing.

Fear Mongering

As well as offering simplistic solutions, cults also appeal to fears about the future. Nuclear war, financial collapse, and social anarchy are described as real possibilities if the cult's recommendations are ignored. The government is typically portrayed as persecuting the group and its leaders, and society is described as evil and under Satan's control. Accepting the group's doctrine serves to reduce these fears.

Nine techniques used by cults have been described (and there are many more). Not all of the techniques are used by every cult, of course. But the simultaneous application of numerous strategies can be very effective, especially when the recruits' environment is completely controlled (as at weekend retreats). There is nothing magical in what cults do. Rather, their success is understandable from a social psychological perspective. Cults show the power of a concerted, sophisticated application of the principles of persuasion.

Summary

Dissonance theory proposes that people are motivated to achieve and maintain consistency among their cognitions. Cognitions are bits of knowledge. Two cognitions can be irrelevant, consonant, or dissonant with each other: they can have no implications for one another, support one another, or contradict one another. Awareness of dissonant cognitions is aversive, and people try to reduce dissonance by changing one of the dissonant cognitions or by adding new consonant cognitions.

Dissonance theory has been tested in several ways by social psychologists. In the free choice paradigm, people choose between two or more alternatives. Dissonance is aroused by the negative features of the chosen alternative and the positive features of the rejected alternative. Such postdecisional dissonance is typically reduced by increasing the attractiveness of the chosen alternative and decreasing the attractiveness of the rejected alternative. In the induced compliance paradigm, individuals are induced to behave in ways that are inconsistent with their private attitudes. If people do not have good reasons (such as a large monetary payment) for behaving inconsistently, they will often change their attitudes to be more consistent with their public behavior. Researchers have identified several factors that are necessary for counterattitudinal behavior to arouse dissonance. First, people must believe that they had free choice to perform or not perform the behavior. Second, there must be some public commitment to the behavior. Third, the behavior must create some aversive consequences. Finally, people must feel some personal responsibility for their behavior, which includes the notion that the aversive consequences were foreseeable. In the effort justification paradigm, people are induced to exert some effort or incur some costs in pursuit of a goal. To rationalize their effort, people often increase the perceived importance or attractiveness of the goal.

Several alternative interpretations of dissonance findings have been proposed. Self-perception theory proposes that induced compliance might produce attitude change because individuals use their behaviors to infer their attitudes. Impression management theory proposes that attitude change in dissonance settings is simply faked in order to make the individual appear more consistent. Self-affirmation theory suggests that counterattitudinal behavior threatens individuals' perceptions of themselves as good, competent persons. Thus, people can reduce dissonance by performing any action that reaffirms their worth irrespective of whether it addresses the actual inconsistency between cognitions. Similarly, self-concept theory argues that dissonance settings produce attitude change by threatening individuals' self-concepts as good, honest people. Thus, even proattitudinal behavior can arouse dissonance if it threatens the actor's self-concept.

The cognitive response approach is based on the idea that persuasion results from the thoughts that are generated in response to a message. Proarguments are favorable thoughts about the message or speaker and lead to attitude change. Counterarguments are unfavorable thoughts about the message or speaker and inhibit attitude change. For a strong message, distraction reduces persuasion whereas repetition increases persuasion. For a weak message, distraction increases persuasion whereas repetition reduces persuasion.

The cognitive response approach provides a nice framework for understanding self-persuasion. For example, thinking about an issue generally makes people more extreme in their position, which has been labelled attitude polarization via mere thought.

The systematic-heuristic model and the elaboration likelihood model both hypothesize that attitude change can result in two ways. First, careful consideration of the merits of a position can lead to persuasion. This "rational" form of persuasion is labelled systematic processing by the heuristic-systematic model and the central route to persuasion by the elaboration likelihood model. Second, people sometimes adopt positions recommended in a message simply because of a clue or feature suggesting that the advocated position is valid. This relatively "mindless" form of persuasion is labelled heuristic processing by the heuristic-systematic model and the peripheral route to persuasion by the elaboration likelihood model.

Both models suggest that systematic/central processing is effortful and will occur only when people are both motivated and able to process the message carefully, in which case persuasion will depend on the strength of the arguments in the message. However, if the recipient of a message is either unmotivated or unable to process carefully, then persuasion will depend on the presence or absence of heuristics or peripheral cues suggesting that the recommendation is valid.

Several characteristics of the *source* of a message influence persuasion. Likable, famous, attractive, and credible sources are more effective than unlikable, unknown, unattractive, and noncredible sources. The sleeper effect refers to the finding that attitude change following a message from a low credibility source sometimes increases over time.

Message characteristics also determine persuasion. For example, strong arguments and long messages are generally more effective than weak arguments and short messages. Fear arousal is another message characteristic that has been studied. Protection motivation theory is a comprehensive model of fear appeals. From this perspective, a threatening message will be effective at producing attitude and behavior change when it convinces recipients that a problem is serious, that the recipients are susceptible to the problem, that behavior change will effectively avoid the problem, and that the recipients are capable of performing the recommended behaviors.

Recipient characteristics constitute a third component of persuasion settings. People high in the need for cognition are more likely to engage in systematic/central processing of messages than are people low in the need for cognition. Uncertainty orientation refers to individuals' interest in new information about themselves and the environment and influences when systematic/central processing is likely to occur. There is also evidence that moods affect message processing, such that systematic/central processing is less likely when people are in a positive, rather than neutral, mood.

Key Terms

attitude polarization via
  mere thought
central route to persuasion
cognitive dissonance theory
cognitive response approach
consonant cognitions
credibility
destructive cult
differential decay
discounting
dissociation
dissonant cognitions
effort justification paradigm

elaboration likelihood model
foot-in-the-door effect
forbidden toy paradigm
free choice paradigm
heuristic processing
heuristics
hypocrisy
impression management
  theory
induced compliance paradigm
love-bombing
need for cognition
peripheral cues

peripheral route to
  persuasion
postdecisional dissonance
protection motivation theory
selective exposure hypothesis
self-affirmation theory
self-concept theory
self-perception theory
sleeper effect
systematic-heuristic model
systematic processing
uncertainty orientation

Suggested Readings

Chaiken, S. (1987). The heuristic model of persuasion. In M. P. Zanna, J. M. Olson, and C. P. Herman (Eds.), *Social influence: The Ontario symposium* (Vol. 5, pp. 3-39). Hillsdale, NJ: Erlbaum.

Cooper, J., and Fazio, R. H. (1984). A new look at dissonance theory. In L. Berkowitz (Ed.), *Advances in experimental social psychology* (Vol. 17, pp. 229–266). San Diego, CA: Academic Press.

Perloff, M. (1993). *The dynamics of persuasion.* Hillsdale, NJ: Erlbaum.

Petty, R. E., and Cacioppo, J. T. (1986). The elaboration likelihood model of persuasion. In L. Berkowitz (Ed.), *Advances in experimental social psychology* (Vol. 19, pp. 123–205). San Diego, CA: Academic Press.

Petty, R. E., Wegener, D. T., and Fabrigar, L. R. (1997). Attitudes and attitude change. *Annual Review of Psychology, 48,* 609–647.

Pratkanis, A. R., and Aronson, E. (1991). *Age of propaganda: The everyday use and abuse of persuasion.* New York: Freeman.

Rogers, R. W. (1983). Cognitive and physiological processes in fear appeals and attitude change: A revised theory of protection motivation. In J. T. Cacioppo and R. E. Petty (Eds.), *Social psychophysiology: A sourcebook* (pp. 153–176). New York: Guilford.

Steele, C. M. (1988). The psychology of self-affirmation: Sustaining the integrity of the self. In L. Berkowitz (Ed.), *Advances in experimental social psychology* (Vol. 21, pp. 261–302). San Diego, CA: Academic Press.

Zimbardo, P. G., and Leippe, M. R. (1991). *The psychology of attitude change and social influence.* New York: McGraw-Hill.

Chapter 7

Prejudice and Stereotypes

Dead silence—not a sound to be heard in the town. The lamps in the street, the lights in the shops and in the houses are out. It is 3:30 A.M. All of a sudden noises in the street break into my sleep, a wild medley of shouts and shrieks. I listen, frightened and alarmed, until I distinguish words: "Get out, Jews! Death to the Jews!" . . . Fists are hammering at the door. The shutters are broken open. . . . I run out of my room, and down the stairs . . . my eyes looked straight into the guns. . . . "I am hit," stammers my father, before he breaks down on the stairs. I am forced to go on, but I can see blood on the stairs and a dark stain on my father's back. (Bentwich, 1981, p. 84)

These words describe the experience of a sixteen-year-old Jewish boy in Emden, Germany, on the night of November 9–10, 1938. Similar attacks on Jews were repeated that evening all over Germany, Austria, and parts of Czechoslovakia. The dark hours of that night have come to be called *Kristallnacht,* or the Night of the Broken Glass. During those hours, Adolf Hitler's Nazis went on a rampage against Jews throughout the Third Reich. By the morning of November 11, the dimensions of the attacks were clear. Approximately "100 Jews had been killed, 7,500 Jewish businesses had been destroyed, 275 synagogues had been razed or burned, and 30,000 Jews had been arrested" (U.S. Holocaust Memorial Council, 1989). Streets were blanketed with broken glass from businesses, homes, and synagogues. Most of the people who were arrested were eventually taken to prison camps.

Although worse things were to come, *Kristall-nacht* marked a crucial turning point in the Nazis' persecution of the Jews. It was the first instance of widespread, organized physical violence against Jews—a signal that the government approved of lawless behavior toward law-abiding citizens who happened to be Jewish. It had been designed to look like a spontaneous outbreak of anti-Semitic feeling. In re-

ality, the attacks were carefully organized by two of Hitler's top lieutenants, Josef Goebbels and Reinhard Heydrich, and carried out by Nazi soldiers disguised as citizens.

Why did *Kristallnacht* occur? How can we understand the events of that night and the Holocaust that took place during the next six and a half years? We need to recognize the madness of Nazi anti-Semitism and Hitler's obsession with the "Jewish problem." Adolf Hitler controlled Germany for twelve years, from 1933 to 1945. Hitler's reign began and ended on nearly the same dates as Franklin Roosevelt's terms as president of the United States. Hitler came to power during the Depression, and he committed suicide just before Germany finally surrendered at the end of World War II. Hitler exploited a deep anti-Semitism that had been part of German history and culture for centuries. Though Jews made up not more than 1 percent of the German population, they were often blamed for Germany's problems. As a distinct group whose achievements often aroused envy, they were convenient targets for smoldering frustrations. For years a "Jewish conspiracy" was held responsible for problems ranging from rampant inflation to defeat in World War I. Hitler himself had a deep hatred for Jews and gained political support for his Nazi party by fanning the flames of anti-Semitism among a substantial portion of the German population, many of whom were frustrated and angry about their financial difficulties during the Depression. Although the Nazis were reviled by many Germans and never received a majority vote in any election, they were able to take power in a badly crippled and divided nation in 1933.

As soon as Hitler became chancellor of Germany, he moved against the Jews. "Non-Aryans" were excluded from the civil service within months. By 1935, Jews had lost their German citizenship, and marriage between Jews and German "subjects of the state" was forbidden. Soon Jews were forbidden to fly the German flag. Within a short time, they were excluded from all aspects of German economic and cultural life. Concentration camps were established, and many Jews were simply locked up. And then, when a seventeen-year-old Jewish boy shot a Nazi official in Paris, Hitler and his lieutenants had the pretext they needed to organize *Kristallnacht,* and the attack on Jewish synagogues, businesses, and homes soon followed. Nazi leaders subsequently claimed the attacks reflected the nation's "healthy instincts."

After *Kristallnacht,* many Jews committed suicide, and many more tried to escape from Germany. Only about a third of those who attempted to leave ever succeeded. One ten-year-old boy got out only after being separated from both of his parents. It was a typical story: his mother left him at a friend's home in Berlin until he could be transported out of the country. Later he recalled: "My mother had to leave me there, and the last I ever saw of her was in the Berlin street, outside the friend's house, walking backward along the pavement to get a last look at me, until she rounded the corner and we were parted" (Eisenberg, 1981).

World reaction to *Kristallnacht* was swift and harsh. In the United States, President Roosevelt said he could "scarcely believe that such things could occur in a twentieth century civilization." But although many nations deplored the actions of the German government, none did anything to punish Germany or to stop further persecution of the Jews. Within two days, Cabinet Minister Herman Goering declared that Jews had to pay $400 million for the damage done to their properties by Nazi thugs. Three days later, Jewish children were forbidden to attend German schools. In a month, ownership of Jewish businesses was transferred to non-Jews. Nothing was done by the international community in response to these developments. In January 1939, less than three months after *Kristallnacht,* Hitler predicted the destruction of Jews in Europe in the event of a war.

In the war that soon followed, Hitler did his worst to translate his prediction into reality. Nearly 6 million Jews in Europe were killed by the Nazis, 3.5 million in Poland alone. Men, women, and children were herded into gas chambers and killed mercilessly. At some camps, ovens burned twenty-four hours a day to dispose of the bodies of murdered Jews.

Kristallnacht, or the Night of the Broken Glass, was a singular manifestation of prejudice. During a few dark hours in 1938, Nazis arrested Jews and destroyed their property throughout the Third Reich, leaving in their wake a multitude of shattered glass and lives.

The Holocaust is probably the most extreme example of genocide in history. But anti-Semitism is still a problem in many countries today. Indeed, it sometimes seems that humans have made little progress in eradicating racial and religious prejudice toward many different groups. Ethnic conflict, racism, and prejudice are endemic throughout the world today, from Bosnia to Northern Ireland to Russia to the United States. How can we understand intergroup hatred? What can we do to address the problem? In this chapter, we discuss what social psychologists have taught us about prejudice and stereotypes. Although this chapter opened with the horrific example of the Holocaust, we do not mean to imply that social psychologists are interested only in extreme forms of prejudice nor that only "monsters" like Nazis are prejudiced, whereas "normal" people aren't. In fact, most of us possess some group prejudices, and one important message of social psychological research is that prejudice and stereotypes often result from naturally occurring cognitive processes.

Definitions

To begin, we need to be clear about what we mean by prejudice and related concepts. **Prejudice** can be defined as an attitude, usually negative, toward members of a group. It is an evaluation of someone based solely on that person's race, gender, religion, or membership in some other group. Social psychologists have focused on understanding negative prejudice (dislike for a group), although positive prejudice also exists (for instance, most people evaluate members of their own group positively). Our goal in this chapter is to try to understand why people evaluate others negatively (often *very* negatively) simply because they belong to a group without necessarily knowing anything else about them.

Whereas prejudice is an attitude, **stereotypes** are beliefs—specifically, perceivers' beliefs that members of a group share a particular characteristic: old people are feeble, African Americans are aggressive, French Canadians are religious, and so on. Stereotypes are cognitive, whereas prejudice incorporates emotional feelings. Like prejudice, stereotypes can be either negative or positive, although social psychologists have been most interested in negative stereotypes. Stereotypes can be thought of as essentially similar to the concept of schema discussed in chapter 2—stereotypes are schemas about groups. They represent our knowledge of people in particular groups (although what we "know" may be false).

Stereotypes and prejudice can lead to **discrimination,** which is behavior directed at someone based solely on his or her group membership. Like prejudice and stereotypes, discrimination can be positive (such as favoritism to members of one's own group) but is usually thought of as negative (actions that harm members of a group). Unlike prejudice and stereotypes, which are internal concepts that cannot be observed directly, discrimination is observable—it refers to people's overt actions toward group members. When discrimination is based on prejudice toward a racial group, it is called **racism,** and the person who performs it is called a *racist*. When discrimination is based on gender, it is called **sexism,** and the person who performs it is called a *sexist*.

Modern Racism

Almost certainly, less overt racism and negative discrimination in North America exists today than twenty-five or fifty years ago. To take some simple examples, legislated racial segregation is gone, women are getting more opportunities to advance in the business world, homosexuals are at least tolerated in the armed services (so long as they don't make their sexual orientation public), and surveys show that people express more favorable views of many minority groups than in the past. Thus, we appear to have made some real progress. But have prejudice and discrimination actually diminished, or are people just more careful about what they say and do in public? Have we reduced public discrimination while negative stereotypes and prejudice have simply gone underground?

Several researchers have suggested that, indeed, racism continues to be a problem today. These theorists argue that blatant, "old-fashioned" racism has been replaced by more subtle forms of discrimination. Common to these perspectives is the idea that white Americans know that prejudice is socially undesirable and try to control it, especially in public, but they continue to have negative stereotypes. *Norms* about acceptable racial beliefs have changed, so people's public statements of those beliefs have changed accordingly. But the beliefs themselves may not actually have changed very much.

McConahay (1986) has argued that there has been some belief change, but it has primarily been the re-

---

FIGURE 7.1   ITEMS FROM OLD-FASHIONED AND MODERN RACISM SCALES

Old-fashioned racism items

I favor laws that permit black persons to rent or purchase housing even when the person offering the property for sale or rent does not wish to rent or sell it to blacks.

Generally speaking, I favor full racial integration.

I am opposed to open or fair housing laws.

It is a bad idea for blacks and whites to marry one another.

Black people are generally not as smart as whites.

If a black family with about the same income and education as I have moved next door, I would mind it a great deal.

It was wrong for the United States Supreme Court to outlaw segregation in its 1954 decision.

Modern racism items

Over the past few years, the government and news media have shown more respect to blacks than they deserve.

It is easy to understand the anger of black people in America.

Discrimination against blacks is no longer a problem in the United States.

Over the past few years, blacks have gotten more economically than they deserve.

Blacks have more influence upon school desegregation plans than they ought to have.

Blacks are getting too demanding in their push for equal rights.

Blacks should not push themselves where they are not wanted.

Source: McConahay (1986)

placement of one type of racist belief with another. Specifically, such old-fashioned beliefs as blacks are less intelligent than whites, neighborhoods should be segregated by race, and discrimination against blacks is acceptable have been replaced by such beliefs as blacks are pushing too hard and too fast, their demands and tactics are unfair, and blacks are getting things they don't deserve as a result of their pushing. Figure 7.1 shows some items from both old-fashioned and modern racism scales.

Similarly, Kinder and Sears (1981) proposed that many white Americans have rejected old-fashioned stereotypes about African Americans but still believe that blacks threaten traditional American values like individualism, obedience, and the Protestant work ethic. This kind of prejudice has been called **symbolic racism** because it is based on perceptions that blacks threaten key American symbols (namely, traditional values). Katz and Hass (1988) suggested that white Americans are ambivalent about blacks—that is, they have both positive and negative beliefs and feelings about blacks. On the one hand, many Americans value humanitarianism and egalitarianism; these values

make whites sympathetic toward blacks and other oppressed groups. On the other hand, many Americans value the Protestant work ethic with its emphasis on being able to achieve anything you put your mind to. To the extent that African Americans are perceived to violate or not share this ethic, negative feelings result. Thus, **ambivalence**—a mix of positive and negative feelings—characterizes how many white Americans feel about black Americans.

What implications do these changes from old-fashioned to **modern racism** have? Perhaps most clearly they imply that discrimination is likely to be limited to particular situations. For example, when behavior might be interpreted as racism, people will be careful to control their negative feelings. McConahay (1986) showed that people who scored high on the modern racism scale (see figure 7.1) discriminated against blacks when evaluating mediocre white and black applicants for a job. But when the possibility that they might be seen as racist was introduced into the situation, the results were reversed: modern racists actually rated a mediocre black candidate more positively than a mediocre white candidate. Similarly, Dovidio and Gaertner (1993) have argued that discrimination is unlikely when situational norms against discrimination are clear, but when settings provide legitimization of negative treatment, minority group members will be discriminated against. For example, if an individual gets him- or herself into trouble through his or her own negligence, people have an excuse for not helping; they are more likely to take advantage of this excuse if the target needing help is black rather than white (Frey and Gaertner, 1986).

Another view of modern racism suggests that people will act on the basis of egalitarian norms in most situations, but if they are under stress, they might slip back into their old ways and act in a discriminatory manner. This form of racism—discriminatory behavior elicited under stress or arousal—is called **regressive racism.** The basic idea is that people regress—that is, go back—to their earlier modes of interaction when they feel stress or arousal. Unfortunately, what they regress or return to is an older, historical pattern of discrimination. For example, Rogers and Prentice-Dunn (1981) showed that white students who were not angered were less aggressive toward blacks than toward whites. On the other hand, when participants were angered by an experimental confederate (who insulted them), they retaliated more and expressed more hostility when that confederate was black than when he was white. In short, nonangered whites treated blacks better than whites, showing the new egalitarianism. Insulted and angry whites, however, showed regressive racism and were more hostile to blacks than to whites. The results of this experiment are presented in figure 7.2.

Motivational Factors in Prejudice

One class of factors that has been identified in theorizing about prejudice is a motivational one. From a motivational perspective, prejudice can result from tensions, emotions, fears, and underlying needs in the perceiver. In particular, prejudice and discrimination serve to reduce negative affective states and/or satisfy underlying needs. We will discuss two examples of motivational factors.

Frustration and Scapegoating

Social psychologists have found that there is a relation between frustration and many kinds of aggressive be-

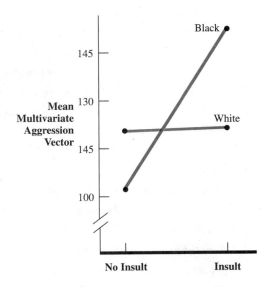

FIGURE 7.2   MEAN AGGRESSION AGAINST WHITE AND BLACK TARGETS FOLLOWING INSULT OR NO INSULT

Source: Rogers and Prentice-Dunn (1981), p. 68

havior (see chapter 10). Interference with the achievement of goals (frustration) produces emotional arousal (anger), which can result in aggression (Berkowitz, 1969). Perhaps not surprisingly, then, frustration has been posited to be a cause of prejudice and discriminatory behavior.

The **scapegoat theory of discrimination** holds that a variety of frustrations in everyday life—on the job, in the home, with friends—can lead to displaced aggression, which vents (reduces) the frustration. Thus, aggression relieves the pent-up anger produced by our daily lives and serves a useful function for the individual.

The most likely targets of emotional venting are ethnic or religious *outgroups*—groups to which the perceiver does not belong. Why are outgroups chosen as targets? Berkowitz (1962) argued that outgroups are convenient targets because they typically possess some or all of the following characteristics:

1. *Safeness*: The target group is so weak that it can be attacked without fear of strong retaliation.
2. *Visibility*: The target group has qualities that make it visible and stand out from other groups. Color, physical characteristics, or different customs can make a group visible.

3. *Strangeness*: Berkowitz argued that humans have an instinctive mistrust toward anything that is strange to them. Outgroups' unique customs may seem strange.

4. *Prior dislike for the group*: Displaced aggression will tend to be directed toward groups that are already disliked.

Thus, frustrations that occur during everyday life can be displaced onto weak, "scapegoat" targets. Prejudice and discrimination may occur as a means of relieving pent-up anger and hostility.

Desire for Superiority: Social Identity Theory

As we have already discussed in chapter 3 on the self, people want to see themselves positively. Several biases in perceptions and attributions appear to be motivated by this need to maintain a positive self-conception (such as a good person who has control over events in one's life). Could the need for a positive self-image induce a desire for superiority over other individuals and groups? One theory that answers this question affirmatively is **social identity theory** (Tajfel and Turner, 1986).

According to social identity theory, people are motivated to maintain an overall positive self-evaluation, which is determined by two components—their personal identity and their social identity. Personal identity depends on one's achievements and how they compare with those of other individuals. Like social comparison theory (discussed in chapter 3), social identity theory views comparisons with others as a key determinant of the way we both define and evaluate ourselves. If you find that you are a better writer than most of your classmates, for example, you may define yourself in part as being a writer, and you may use your view of yourself as a good writer as an important source of a positive personal identity.

Social identity theory holds that in addition to forming a personal identity based on individual characteristics and achievements, you will form a social identity based on your membership in a set of groups; that is, group memberships form your social identity. For example, you may define yourself as a woman, a soccer player, a college student, and a psychology major. Your evaluation of each of these groups (your *ingroups*) determines the overall value of your social identity. If psychology majors are held in high regard

on your campus, then being a psychology major contributes to a positive social identity.

How do we distinguish various social groups? Like many other social psychologists, Tajfel and Turner believe that we nearly always categorize people, including ourselves, into different groups on the basis of virtually any salient characteristic that allows distinctions to be drawn (Hamilton and Trollier, 1986). For example, the differences between males and females and between adults and children are very salient,

To many Americans, the visibility and strangeness of Muslim rituals make its followers in this country an outgroup and thereby a target of prejudice.

and so we categorize people into one group or the other. In Nazi Germany, differences between Jews and non-Jews were salient to many people, and so the social categories of "Aryans" and "Jews" were created.

Once we have constructed social groups, how do we evaluate them? We evaluate them *relatively*—that is, in comparison with one another. In making these comparisons, however, we are biased and nearly always assign our own groups the highest values. Thus, Aryans in Germany evaluated themselves as better than Jews, and Jews tended to evaluate themselves as better than non-Jews. Why do these biases exist? To the extent that one's ingroups are good or outgroups are bad, one's social identity will be positive. Thus, either enhancing perceptions of the ingroup or derogating outgroups improves one's social identity.

But people do more than simply perceive the outgroup as inferior. Given an opportunity, they will compete against the outgroup to actually make it inferior. One of the most consistent findings of research on social identity is that people show favoritism toward the ingroup in the allocation of rewards, a tendency to give their own group more money or resources than outgroups. Moreover, in making these allocations, people seem to be concerned primarily with seeing that their own group gets more than the outgroup even when they could get more resources for their ingroup if only they were willing to also let the outgroup have more. For example, if subjects in an experiment are confronted with the choice of giving an ingroup member 7 points and an outgroup member 1 point or an ingroup member 19 points and an outgroup member 25 points, they often select the 7–1 point combination, which is known as the **maximum differentiation strategy** (see Bourhis, 1994). There is a clear tendency to settle for less so long as the amount is more than what the outgroup gets. Social identity research has shown that people give their ingroup more than outgroups because they think it is better and therefore deserves more than outgroups. Allocating the lion's share to the ingroup confirms a positive social identity and raises self-esteem (Oakes and Turner, 1980).

Incredibly, people show ingroup favoritism even when the basis of group membership is trivial and arbitrary. For example, determining group membership by random flips of a coin still produces ingroup favoritism. These kinds of studies have been labelled the **minimal group paradigm** (Tajfel and Turner, 1986), because the groups are so trivial as to be "minimal" in any psychological sense. Yet, people seem motivated to see their ingroup on this trivial characteristic as better than the outgroup; one wonders how strong the motive for ingroup favoritism must be for meaningful and socially significant group distinctions.

What implications does social identity theory have for understanding prejudice? People have a need to achieve and maintain a high level of self-esteem. One way they can do that is by raising their social identity, and they can raise their social identity by perceiving the ingroup as better and actually treating it better than the outgroup. Thus, people will enhance perceptions of the ingroup and actively derogate and mistreat members of the outgroup. The need to maintain a high level of self-esteem can lead people to be prejudiced against and discriminate against members of outgroups. In Nazi Germany, the non-Jewish majority categorized the population into the Aryan ingroup and the Jewish outgroup. Jews were regarded as inferior to the Aryan "master race." As a consequence, they were derogated and discriminated against, eventually to the point of genocide. It seems almost unbelievable that a desire for superiority could lead to such violent and savage behavior. Certainly, there were other factors that allowed the Holocaust to go so far, but we must live with the fact that a root cause may well have been a concern for self-esteem.

Sociocultural Factors in Prejudice

When Hitler espoused his racial theories, blaming Jews for all the problems that confronted Germany, his virulent attitudes easily took root in the soil of the Third Reich. Anti-Semitism had been part of German history for centuries. Hitler learned this prejudice himself and found that his expressions of it appealed to many segments of German society. As a child and a young man, Hitler was a student of hatred toward Jews. As chancellor of the Reich, he was the teacher.

Numerous investigators have suggested that prejudice, like other attitudes (see chapter 5), is learned (Allport, 1954; Kelly, Ferson, and Holtzman, 1958). Some children may see their parents discriminate against blacks, hear their parents' disparaging remarks about blacks, and find that their parents quickly whisk them away when black children come out to play. Bird, Monachesi, and Burdick (1952) found that almost half of the white families they interviewed in the early 1950s had rules for their children against playing with black children. As children grow older, they are told by peers that blacks are bad, and they are excluded from peer groups if they are seen playing with blacks. Their parents point out media stories telling how blacks have been involved in illegal behavior. Each of these incidents teaches a child to be prejudiced against blacks. The children's parents model prejudiced attitudes, their peers reward discrimination against blacks, and both parents and peers punish associations with blacks. Thus, children are neatly taught to hate. Consistent with this perspective, researchers have found that parents' and children's levels of racial prejudice are significantly correlated (Altemeyer, 1994; Rohan and Zanna, 1996). Many children eventually internalize the norms about intergroup stereotypes and behavior that their parents and peers established.

The sociocultural learning approach can explain why there is such wide variation in the objects of prejudice. Children in different countries or in different regions of the same country can be taught to hate different ethnic groups. Indeed, the learning approach allows for the formation of prejudice in children even if they have never seen a member of the group against which they become prejudiced. Parents can instill in their children the idea that they should hate blacks (or some other group) and tell the children frightening stories about what will happen to them if they interact with blacks. The result of this schooling will be a child who hates and is afraid of blacks even though he or she may never have interacted with a black person.

Another sociocultural source of stereotypes and prejudice is the mass media. Stories in newspapers and on television often support stereotypes about groups. For example, in early television shows, blacks were often portrayed as uneducated and lazy, and more recent shows continue to present relatively low rates of interactions between blacks and whites (Rajecki, 1990; Weigel, Loomis, and Soja, 1980). In television commercials, women are more often portrayed in domestic settings than are men, whereas men are more often portrayed in positions of authority than are women (Craig, 1992; Lovdal, 1989).

To be sure, there have been attempts to "clean up" the media and eliminate the portrayal of blatant stereotypes. Further, societal values today stress equality, and discrimination, especially racial discrimination, receives almost universal disapproval. Yet, as we discussed earlier, it may be that blatant, old-fashioned racism has simply been replaced by a subtler, modern racism. From the sociocultural perspective, we might expect that when parents display public support of egalitarian norms but private rejection of equality, their children will similarly learn to distinguish between public and private settings.

Competition, Conflict, and Prejudice

Hitler may have learned and then perpetuated prejudiced attitudes in Germany, but where did those attitudes come from in the first place? Why were Jews discriminated against in Europe for so many centuries? Why have blacks been the objects of so much hatred in the United States? One answer is that, at various times in history, minority groups such as Jews and blacks have been in conflict with those in the majority and have been perceived as a threat. Usually, conflict has taken the form of competition for scarce economic or natural resources, such as jobs, housing, land, or money. The idea that competition for scarce resources is key for understanding prejudice is the central tenet of **realistic conflict theory** (Pettigrew, 1978). According to this perspective, conflict over scarce economic resources often produces intergroup discrimination. Perceived threat and competition may be part of the explanation for discrimination against women. Some men may view the women's movement for equality with alarm because they fear that women will be competing directly for jobs once reserved for men.

Conflict and competition between groups have been shown to increase the tendency to stereotype and discriminate against members of an outgroup. For example, Judd and Park (1988) found that when groups are in competition, the **outgroup homogeneity effect**—the tendency to see all members of the outgroup as similar or homogeneous—is intensified. People have a greater tendency to say "They're all alike" when referring to members of an outgroup that is in conflict with their own group. This tendency was very prominent in the early days of Nazi rule in Germany. Many people perceived Jews as competition during a time of economic hardship (the Great Depression)—Jews were a threat. The result was negative stereotypes and a range of hostile and discriminatory actions. The hostility that was unleashed did not end when the German economy improved, however, which suggests that group conflict was not the only relevant factor. Indeed, it took the total defeat of the Nazis and Hitler's death to stop the slaughter.

Personality Factors: Authoritarianism and Prejudice

Even though an entire culture may be imbued with racism and prejudice, individuals in that culture will vary in the extent to which they subscribe to racist doctrines and participate in discrimination against outgroups. Even in Nazi Germany, people varied in how much they helped or hurt Jews. In spite of the danger in protecting Jews (people could lose their lives), many Germans did so. Clearly, we must try to understand why some people accept and act on racist principles and some do not.

After World War II, the American Jewish Committee supported a large and ambitious study of anti-Semitism in the United States. It was designed to pinpoint why some people accept fascist and racist ideas and to assess the potential for fascist thinking and behavior in North America. The results of that study were published in one of the most famous books in social psychology, *The Authoritarian Personality* (Adorno, Frenkel-Brunswick, Levinson, and Sanford, 1950).

The investigators approached a large number of people who belonged to groups ranging from college fraternities to San Quentin prison inmates. The respondents, most of whom were white, middle-class Americans, were given a battery of questionnaires, and many of them were interviewed in depth about their feelings toward themselves, their families, and their childhoods. Respondents filled out an anti-Semitism scale, an ethnocentrism scale, and a political and economic conservatism scale. The anti-Semitism scale tapped respondents' attitudes toward Jews in a variety of situations and circumstances. The ethnocentrism scale measured the degree to which negative, stereotyped attitudes were held toward a variety of other groups. **Ethnocentrism** is the tendency to reject people who are culturally dissimilar to one's own ingroup while blindly accepting those who are culturally like one's ingroup (Sumner, 1906).

Adorno and his colleagues found that the correlation between the specific attitude of anti-Semitism and the general trait of ethnocentrism was extremely high: those who were anti-Semitic usually endorsed similar negative attitudes toward all ethnic, religious, and cultural outgroups (see also Altemeyer, 1994).

There was a slight tendency for ethnocentric anti-Semites to express right-wing attitudes on the political and economic conservatism scale, but the data were not conclusive in this regard.

Finally, assessments of the respondents' personalities were made in the interviews and by means of a test constructed specifically for the study: the potential-for-fascism scale, or F scale. The major findings were extremely interesting from the standpoint of viewing childhood development, adult personality, and attitudes as being inextricably interrelated. The investigators found that people with anti-Semitic and ethnocentric attitudes tended to come from homes in which discipline was severe and threatening. The parents of highly prejudiced subjects tended to have very high aspirations for their children and to measure the children in terms of their own needs rather than their children's needs. The children who were produced by this upbringing idealized their parents in questionnaires and interviews; they were more likely than children raised in less severe homes to see their father as the most influential, likable, and successful person in their lives and to see their mother as the most giving and helpful person. Prejudiced respondents saw no weakness in either themselves or their parents, whereas unprejudiced respondents were more apt to admit to some human shortcomings. The irony in the prejudiced subjects' parental adoration was that hostility was found seething beneath the surface. Although it was difficult to find prejudiced participants who would introspect and examine their feelings, the investigators reported that they could detect a lot of hostility directed at parents and authority figures in general.

The study that culminated in *The Authoritarian Personality* has drawn some criticism regarding both how the data were collected and how they were interpreted (see Brown, 1965). Nevertheless, numerous studies over the years have established clearly that there is such a thing as an **authoritarian personality** and that high authoritarians are likely to be highly racist (see Altemeyer, 1988, 1994). Thus, personality factors have been shown to predict prejudice.

Cognitive Factors in Prejudice

To this point we have discussed motivational, socio-cultural, and personality factors in prejudice, as well as the role of conflict and competition. In this section, we turn to the explanation that has received the most attention from social psychologists, especially in the last two decades: the role of *cognitive factors.* The fact that social psychologists have recently been most interested in these factors does not mean that cognitive mechanisms are the most important causes of prejudice. In fact, all of the explanations we cover in this chapter are probably important in some situations or for some people. The sad reality is that prejudice is probably "overdetermined"—that is, prejudice can be produced by many different causes, each of them sufficient for prejudice but none of them necessary. Thus, eradication of prejudice will require addressing *all* of these processes—a daunting task. We will talk more about reducing prejudice at the end of this chapter.

The fundamental cause of prejudice, according to the cognitive view, is negative stereotypes; beliefs that a group possesses negative traits often lead to dislike and to discriminatory behavior. A central aspect of the Nazis' campaign against Jews was the propaganda they spread about supposed Jewish traits. This propaganda was used to try to justify the arrest and finally the murder of Jews. In Germany and many other countries, negative stereotypes of Jews provided a foundation for such propaganda. In 1933, the year Hitler took power, American college students at Princeton described Jews as shrewd, mercenary, industrious, and grasping (Katz and Braly, 1933). Nazis assigned other traits as well: Jews were portrayed as conspiratorial, dirty, and lecherous, and not only a threat to peace and prosperity but also a danger to the health and purity of young Aryan women.

Where do such stereotypes come from? And once formed, how are they maintained? We will attempt to answer these two critical questions in this section.

Categorization: The Formation of Stereotypes

The first process that leads to stereotypes is the simple perceptual act of **categorization.** Categorizing means putting an object, person, animal, color, or other target, or stimulus, into a group—identifying what it is (what category it belongs to). Categorization is a basic and automatic cognitive process, which is extremely adaptive in our efforts to cope with a complex world. By categorizing objects, we are able to make assumptions

about what the stimulus will be like—fire will be hot, apples will be edible, and so on. As these examples show, such assumptions about objects are typically accurate and are necessary for rapid, effective behavioral decisions. But we also categorize people into groups, according to gender, race, age, occupation, and many other categories. Again, like categorization of inanimate objects, this process is automatic, and we assume that everyone in the group shares particular characteristics. Unfortunately, such oversimplification is likely to be inaccurate for most groups of humans.

Categorization of people into groups has some immediate and important cognitive consequences (see Hamilton and Sherman, 1994). One is that we magnify or accentuate the differences between people belonging to different groups. That is we see people belonging to two groups as very different from one another. Second, we minimize differences between individuals belonging to the same group. Just how much we minimize differences between individuals in the same group depends on the type of group, however. Our perceptions of groups to which we belong—ingroups—are less homogeneous (more diverse) than our perceptions of groups to which we do not belong—outgroups. This difference is primarily due to the fact that we minimize differences between members of outgroups much more than we do between members of our own group. We tend to see "them" as all alike, whereas we see "us" as considerably more variable. We are especially motivated to see "people who share our opinions" (one possible ingroup) as diverse and heterogeneous; this allows us to believe that our opinions are well considered and not just a reflection of narrow biases (Goethals, Allison, and Frost, 1979; Goethals, 1986).

Where do we get our specific stereotypes of groups? What are the sources of our beliefs about the characteristics of ingroup and outgroup members? We can refer back to processes and factors that we have already discussed to answer this question, at least in part. We learn many of our stereotypes from parents, peers, and institutions—sociocultural sources of stereotypes. We also develop stereotypes based on personal experiences with members of groups—we meet outgoing salespeople and shy librarians and generalize our experiences to all members of the groups. Of course, our personal experiences may be colored by the stereotypes we internalized from our parents; a child who has been taught to hate and fear blacks is likely to find any interactions with blacks unpleasant, which should simply confirm his or her expectancies.

Historical events provide us another kind of experience with people in different groups. During World War II, for example, Americans had experiences with Germans and Japanese that changed their perceptions of these nationalities dramatically. Before World War II, most Americans viewed Germans as scientifically minded, industrious, and intelligent. After the war and their experiences with Hitler, Americans also viewed Germans as nationalistic, aggressive, and arrogant. Nazi behavior during the Third Reich did not go unnoticed. Similarly, Japanese were seen as intelligent, industrious, and progressive before World War II, but after Pearl Harbor they were seen as sly, imitative, and treacherous (Karlin, Coffman, and Waters, 1969). Finally, we may develop stereotypes based partly on motivational factors that bias our impressions. For example, the desire for a positive social identity might motivate us to derogate outgroups— that is, to assign primarily negative traits to outgroups.

Selective Information Processing: The Maintenance of Stereotypes

We have talked about where stereotypic expectancies might originate, such as sociocultural learning and personal experiences. But how are they maintained given that they are often wrong or too extreme? It seems very likely that people with stereotypes will encounter people who do not fit their stereotypes. Surely Germans growing up in the 1930s did not find all Jews to be lecherous and dirty. How, then, did they maintain their stereotypes?

Stereotypes would be much less problematical if they changed when perceivers encountered disconfirming instances. If perceivers were unbiased information processors, who perceived disconfirming evidence accurately and revised their stereotypes on the basis of new information, then group-based expectancies would be much less worrisome.

Unfortunately, as we have said before, humans are *not* unbiased information processors. Recall our discussion in chapter 5 of the effects of attitudes on information processing; we argued that people are "selective" information processors—selective in the sense that attitude-consistent information is more likely to be processed than attitude-inconsistent information. Thus, attitudes can become more extreme even when people are exposed to mixed information. Similarly,

stereotypes bias our processing of information. Again, the bias is such that "consistent" information is more likely to be processed—in this case, consistent with stereotypes rather than with attitudes. Therefore, even when the environment contains evidence that objectively disconfirms a stereotype, individuals might perceive the evidence wrongly and conclude that their stereotype is accurate. Encountering people who disconfirm a stereotype will not necessarily change the stereotype (see Kunda and Oleson, 1997). In the following subsections, we will briefly discuss the same categories of selectivity as we did in chapter 5, but this time in the context of stereotypes rather than attitudes.

Selective Attention

Perceivers tend to see what they expect to see. They are likely to notice information that confirms their expectancies (their stereotypes) and overlook information that disconfirms their expectancies. For example, the phenomenon of illusory correlation (discussed in chapter 2) shows that we sometimes perceive covariation between two variables that are not correlated in reality. One important source of illusory correlations is our expectancies. If, for instance, someone expects that members of a group are unfriendly, he or she is more likely to notice unfriendly behaviors by members of that group (to perceive an illusory correlation between group membership and unfriendliness) than are perceivers who do not share the same expectancy (for a discussion of the relevance of illusory correlations to stereotyping, see Hamilton and Sherman, 1992).

Selective Perception

Stereotypes seem almost to have a life of their own. Real disconfirming evidence often goes unnoticed, and imagined confirming evidence sometimes serves to bolster them. But what impact do stereotypes have on our perceptions of individuals? Studies show that stereotypes do, indeed, influence our perceptions, often subtly and without our awareness. The biasing effect is such that ambiguous behaviors will often be interpreted in terms of the stereotype.

In one study (Duncan, 1976), white participants watched a videotape of either a white or a black individual interacting with another person who was white. As their conversation grew animated, the first person gave the second an "ambiguous shove." When the first person was white, the shove was interpreted as play-

TABLE 7.1   MEAN RATINGS OF BOTH WHITE AND BLACK ACTORS' BEHAVIORS BY BOTH WHITE AND BLACK SUBJECTS

		Rating Scale	
Subject Group[a]	Actor Race[b]	Mean/Threatening	Playful/Friendly
White	White	8.28	6.43
	Black	8.99	6.24
Black	White	7.38	7.19
	Black	8.40	6.74

Note: Means are based on sums of paired 7-point scales indicating how well the given adjective described the behaviors, from 1 (not at all) to 7 (exactly).

a. *n* = 40 for each group.

b. Each subject rated two white and two black actors and two white and two black targets. Means are not broken down by target race, since no statistically significant main effects or interactions were found for this variable.

Source: Adapted from Sagar and Schofield (1980)

ing around or dramatizing a point. When the first person was black, the shove was interpreted as hostile or violent. In a replication of this study, Sagar and Schofield (1980) showed pictures of white and black models engaged in aggressive behaviors to both white and black schoolchildren. As table 7.1 shows, everyone saw the black model's behavior as more threatening and mean than the same behavior exhibited by a white model—8.99 versus 8.28 for white observers and 8.40 versus 7.38 for black observers. The opposite pattern was found for ratings of playfulness, with both subject groups perceiving the white model's behavior as more playful than the black model's behavior.

Another study of social class stereotypes suggested that we can counteract the influence of our prejudices up to a point (Darley and Gross, 1983). Participants saw slides of a young girl showing where she lived and played, what her parents' backgrounds were, and so on. This information clearly told the participants that the girl had either an upper-class or lower-class background. When asked to predict how well the girl would do in school, respondents resisted their stereotypes and did not make different predictions based on social class information. When participants were shown a videotape of the girl taking some tests in school, however, those who believed she was lower class perceived her actual performance as worse than those who thought she was upper class. Thus, sometimes we can resist making gross inferences about a person from stereotypes, but it is extremely difficult to resist perceiving and interpreting people's actual behaviors from the perspective of our stereotypes.

A study by Devine (1989) showed that sometimes a stereotype that we don't even believe is true can affect our perceptions of an individual without our knowledge. In this study, white students who were either prejudiced or nonprejudiced saw words flashed on a screen so rapidly that participants had no idea what they were. Nevertheless, these rapid subliminal exposures have been shown in other research to be perceived subconsciously. In one condition, most of the words flashed were words that the white students knew were typically associated with blacks, such as *blues, rhythm, ghetto, slavery, busing,* and *welfare.* In a second condition, most of the words had no association with blacks. In this way, half of the participants were *primed* (see chapter 2) with words associated with the common stereotype of blacks and half were not. Then all the participants were asked to read about and form an impression of a person, Donald, whose behavior might or might not have been seen as hostile and aggressive (note that the specific concepts *hostile* and *aggressive* were not primed in either condition). Donald's race was not mentioned. The results, presented in table 7.2, showed that participants who had been primed with the black stereotype saw Donald's behavior as more hostile, consistent with the common stereotype of blacks, than did those who had not been primed, whereas the two conditions did not differ in ratings of traits unrelated to hostility. The results were the same for prejudiced and nonprejudiced participants. In short, a stereotype was brought to perceivers' minds without their awareness, and it affected their perceptions of Donald even when they

TABLE 7.2   **RATINGS OF DONALD'S BEHAVIOR**

Priming Condition	Rating Dimensions	
	Hostility-Related	Unrelated to Hostility
Priming of Black Stereotype	7.52	6.00
No Priming	6.87	5.89

Source: Devine (1989), p. 11

did not consciously endorse the stereotype (the non-prejudiced participants).

A recent interest in the stereotyping literature has been to identify the conditions under which perceivers are especially likely to rely on their stereotypes to form impressions. When do people use their stereotypes? Fiske and Neuberg (1990) proposed a continuum of impression formation ranging from category-based processing (based on stereotypes) to individuated processing (where impressions are based only on information about the specific target). These theorists hypothesized that perceivers initially or typically make category-based judgments about targets, but if it is important for the perceiver to form an accurate impression and if available information is inconsistent with the stereotypes, then piecemeal processing based on specific attributes of the target may occur.

Several researchers have documented that perceivers rely more on stereotypes when their processing capacities are reduced—that is, when they lack the time or ability to make the more effortful individuated judgments. For example, Pratto and Bargh (1991) manipulated the speed at which information was presented to participants. Impressions were more stereotypical when the individuating information was presented so quickly that participants did not have enough time to cope with the information. Gilbert and Hixon (1991) showed that *cognitive busyness*—giving participants a secondary task that demands attentional resources—led to more reliance on stereotypes that had been activated before the busyness manipulation was introduced. In short, reductions in processing capacity led to greater reliance on activated stereotypes. Note that cognitive busyness is probably a common state of mind in today's hectic, fast-paced world. Thus, reliance on stereotypes might be greater than it would be in a less frantic world. Box 7.1 describes a study that made a point similar to that of these exper-

iments; Bodenhausen (1990) showed that "morning people" and "night people" relied on stereotypes differently depending on the time of day.

There is also evidence that people express stereotypes (or, at least, express negative stereotypes) more when they are in a bad mood (Esses, Haddock, and Zanna, 1993, 1994). When people are feeling negative (depressed, angry, worried), it may be easier for them to retrieve negative thoughts from memory (a so-called mood congruency effect). Negative stereotypes are one type of negative thought, so bad moods might increase the accessibility and expression of negative stereotypes. Esses and her colleagues have conducted several studies in which participants were placed in good or bad moods by reading happy or sad statements or by listening to happy or sad music; in the negative mood conditions, participants expressed significantly more negative stereotypes of certain groups than in the happy (or neutral) mood conditions. When people are in a miserable mood, they seem to view outgroups in a particularly negative way.

Selective Memory

A final form of selectivity produced by stereotypes is that information consistent with stereotypes is remembered better. In one study (Cohen, 1981), participants watched a videotape of a woman having a birthday dinner with her husband. When perceivers were told that the woman was a waitress, they tended to remember that she drank beer and had a television set. When her occupation was said to be a librarian, they remembered that she wore glasses and listened to classical music.

Snyder and Uranowitz (1978) gave participants an essay to read that described the background and teenage years of a young woman. After they had finished reading the narrative, participants were told that

BOX 7.1

Circadian Variations in Stereotype Use

When do people rely on their stereotypes to make judgments about others? One factor that has been shown to be important is whether perceivers are *capable* of putting into the judgment task the extra thought that is necessary to use "individuating" (personal, idiosyncratic) information. For example, if individuating information is presented too quickly, then people will not use it (because they can't) and will rely instead on stereotypes (Pratto and Bargh, 1991).

Galen Bodenhausen (1990) of Northwestern University proposed the intriguing possibility that perceivers' natural variations in circadian arousal levels might influence the use of stereotypes. It turns out that people's mental alertness varies over the day, and these shifts in alertness are related to the capacity and efficiency of working memory (Folkard, Wever, and Wildgruber, 1983). Moreover, people differ in the time of day at which their alertness peaks: some people are "morning people" and others are "night people" (yes, these labels describe real differences). In fact, there is a questionnaire that measures this individual difference; it's called the Morningness-Eveningness Questionnaire, or MEQ (Horne and Ostberg, 1976).

Bodenhausen (1990) predicted that morning people, who are most alert in the morning, would weigh individuating information more in the morning but rely more on stereotypes later in the day. In contrast, evening people, who are more alert in the evening, were expected to rely on stereotypes more in the morning and to weigh individuating information more later in the day.

To test this reasoning, students were asked to read three cases of alleged misconduct by college students and to render a probability-of-guilt judgment. For example, participants read about a student accused of cheating on an exam and another student who allegedly sold drugs. In all cases, the evidence was circumstantial and not conclusive. Also, in each case, half of the participants learned that the accused student belonged to a particular group that was stereotypically linked with the focal behavior. The alleged cheater was sometimes identified as an athlete (pretesting showed that athletes were seen as more likely to cheat), and the alleged drug dealer was sometimes identified as an African American (pretesting also showed that African Americans were seen as more likely to sell drugs); these were the *stereotype* conditions. Other participants read about the same offenses, but the accused student was not identified as an athlete or as an African American (*no stereotype* condition). Subjects participated in the experiment at either 9 A.M., 3 P.M., or 8 P.M. (randomly determined). They also completed the MEQ and were classified as morning types or evening types based on a median split of the MEQ scores. Bodenhausen reasoned that if judgments of guilt were higher in the stereotype than in the no stereotype condition, then it could be inferred that subjects were relying on their stereotypes to make the judgments, at least in part.

The table presents the mean ratings of guilt in each condition by morning people and by evening people. The results conformed exactly to predictions. Morning people in the stereotype condition rendered higher probability of guilt ratings late in the day (3 P.M. or 8 P.M.) than in the morning (9 A.M.); that is, these people were more influenced by information about the accused student's group membership late in the day. In contrast, night people in the stereotype condition rendered higher probability-of-guilt ratings in the morning than in the afternoon or evening; they relied more on group membership information in the morning. When no stereotype was activated, the time of day did not significantly affect guilt judgments for either morning or evening people.

Continued

BOX 7.1

Continued

Thus, people were more influenced by stereotypes at whatever time of day they were least alert. Presumably, paying attention to individuating information is somewhat difficult or effortful. When people lacked the energy (at their "off" time of day), they relied more on nonindividuated, "group" information.

MEAN RATINGS OF GUILT BY MORNING PEOPLE AND BY EVENING PEOPLE AT DIFFERENT TIMES OF THE DAY WHEN A STEREOTYPE WAS OR WAS NOT ACTIVATED

	Time of Day		
	9 A.M.	3 P.M.	8 P.M.
Morning Types			
Stereotype	4.92 (13)	6.67 (18)	6.50 (16)
No Stereotype	5.39 (13)	5.61 (18)	5.79 (14)
Evening Types			
Stereotype	6.79 (19)	5.13 (16)	5.60 (15)
No Stereotype	5.05 (19)	5.67 (15)	6.45 (13)

Note: Cell sizes are indicated in parentheses.
Source: Bodenhausen (1990), p. 321

the woman was now leading either a heterosexual or a homosexual lifestyle. Without looking back at the narrative, participants' memory for the material was tested. Results showed that participants who were told that the woman was heterosexual recalled behaviors consistent with this stereotype (for example, she wore makeup in high school, she dated in high school) better than participants who were told that the woman was a homosexual. On the other hand, the latter participants recalled information consistent with the lesbian stereotype (for example, she felt closer to her father than her mother, she did not enjoy dating in high school) better than did the former participants. Thus, respondents showed heightened recall of whatever information was consistent with the stereotype that had been activated by learning the woman's sexual lifestyle. Presumably,

participants used the stereotype as a retrieval cue, searching memory in a biased manner.

Taken together, the information-processing biases described in the preceding section can serve to strengthen stereotypes even when they are wrong. By noticing confirming instances more than disconfirming instances, by interpreting ambiguous behaviors as consistent with stereotypes, and by recalling more stereotype-consistent than stereotype-inconsistent events, many perceivers will come to believe that the weight of the evidence supports their stereotypic beliefs even when the objective reality does not support their beliefs. Selective information processing is essential if we are to cope with the demands of a complex world, but it has some costs, such as putting greater faith in stereotypes and other expectancies than is warranted.

Self-Fulfilling Prophecies: Behavioral Confirmation of Stereotypes

The story does not end with selective information processing. When we have stereotypes about someone, our expectancies can cause us to behave differently toward the target than we would have behaved without the stereotypes. Sometimes these different behaviors will serve to elicit behavior from the target that confirms our expectancies. This vicious cycle, a phenomenon called a **self-fulfilling prophecy,** can produce *actual* behavioral confirmation of our expectancies (as opposed to just *perceived* confirmation that results from biased information processing).

We briefly discussed self-fulfilling prophecies in chapter 2, where we pointed out that our impressions of others can influence our behavior in such a way as to make confirmation of our impressions more likely. Stereotypes, of course, constitute one important source of impressions. Stereotypes can induce behavior in the perceiver that elicits confirmatory behavior from the target. For example, if a young man believes that Hispanics are aggressive, he might act in a defensive, aloof manner toward Hispanics. The defensive, aloof behavior might insult or anger the targets (who can tell that this man dislikes them), which might cause them to behave more aggressively than they would have behaved and thereby confirm the man's stereotype of Hispanics! Even neutral observers of this interaction (perceivers who did not possess the stereotype to begin with) might conclude that Hispanics are aggressive, thereby potentially starting yet another vicious cycle.

Several experimenters have documented self-fulfilling prophecies in the domain of stereotypes. Word, Zanna, and Cooper (1974) designed two studies that investigated the role of race in the interview process. In the first study, white participants took the role of a job interviewer. They interviewed both white and black applicants. Unknown to the participants, the applicants were carefully trained confederates who had rehearsed their answers to all the questions to be asked during the interview. When the interview took place, therefore, there were no objective differences between the verbal and nonverbal performances of the black and white applicants.

The researchers were actually observing the behavior of the interviewers. It was found that interviews with white applicants lasted longer than interviews with black applicants. Also, in the interviews with white applicants, there was a significant increase in behaviors that Mehrabian (1968) has labelled "immediacy." That is, white applicants received greater eye contact, greater forward body lean, and other responses that are usually associated with positive interactions than did black applicants.

In the second study, white participants served as applicants, and carefully trained confederates served as interviewers. The trained interviewers responded to half of the applicants with precisely the behaviors that had been directed toward black applicants in the first study; that is, the interviewers exhibited low-immediacy behaviors. The other half of the applicants received the high-immediacy behaviors that had been afforded the white applicants in the first study.

The interviews were videotaped, and naive judges subsequently rated the performances of each participant. Those applicants who were treated as the black applicants had been treated in the first study (low-immediacy behaviors) performed significantly worse than did applicants who were treated as the white applicants had been treated in the first study (high-immediacy behaviors). Also, applicants in the low-immediacy condition reported feeling significantly worse about themselves at the end of the interview.

In sum, these researchers showed in the first study that interviewers behaved differently toward black and white applicants, and in the second study that the behavior exhibited toward blacks produced worse performance. Thus, self-fulfilling prophecies can occur when interviewers evaluate black and white candidates.

In another study, Snyder, Tanke, and Berscheid (1977) told male and female participants that they would be interacting over an intercom (the participants arrived at different rooms and did not see one another). The men were given a photograph allegedly showing their partner. In fact, the photographs did not depict the actual female participant but rather showed either a physically attractive or a physically unattractive woman (the female participant did not know that her partner had been given a photograph). The man and woman then conducted a spontaneous conversation; the researchers audiotaped the conversation on separate channels for the two participants.

Part of the stereotype of physically attractive women is that they are high in sociability (friendly, outgoing, warm; see Dion, Berscheid, and Walster, 1972). Naive judges listened to the audiotapes of the female participants and scored each one for sociability. Incredibly, women interacting with a man who *believed* them to be physically attractive behaved more sociably than women interacting with a man who believed them to be unattractive. Somehow, the men's expectancies that their partner would be sociable or unsociable (based on the photographs) induced them to behave in ways that elicited the expected type of behavior. It's possible that men interacting with an allegedly attractive woman might have been more outgoing themselves, which then produced greater sociability from their partner.

Of course, prophecies will not always be fulfilled—stereotypes will not inevitably produce confirming behavioral evidence (see Olson, Roese, and Zanna, 1996). Hilton and Darley (1991) found that self-fulfilling prophecies were more likely when targets were *un*aware of the perceiver's expectancies; when targets knew how the perceiver expected them to behave, they were often careful to disconfirm erroneous expectancies. Miller and Turnbull (1986) suggested that self-fulfilling prophecies are less likely when perceivers have the explicit goal of forming accurate impressions. And Jussim (1991) has argued that perceivers' beliefs about others often predict behavior because the beliefs are accurate, not because the beliefs "create reality."

Notwithstanding these limitations, self-fulfilling prophecies are probably common in everyday life (where the explicit goal of forming accurate impressions is probably rare and where targets often do not know others' expectancies for them). Along with the biased information processing described earlier, self-fulfilling prophecies can serve to strengthen erroneous stereotypes about groups.

Sexism: Discrimination Against Women

Women constitute a disadvantaged group that is different from many other such groups (for example, blacks and Jews). For one thing, women constitute half of the total population, so all members of the advantaged group (men) have had extensive experience with women. Also, most men love several women, including their wives or girlfriends, mothers, and daughters.

Unfortunately, such relationships do not necessarily mean that men will have positive attitudes toward women as a group. Indeed, even hatred of women as a group is possible. A chilling example was provided by the murderous behavior of Marc Lepine, who broke into an engineering class at Ecole Polytechnique in Montreal in December 1989. Lepine first deliberately separated the female students from the men, then proceeded to shoot the women; thirteen died.

Such hatred is, fortunately, extremely rare. Nevertheless, discrimination is a common experience for most women. Discrimination can be both violent and nonviolent, sexual and nonsexual. The incidence of violent rape has been on the rise, and date rape continues to plague college campuses. It is estimated that 70 percent to 80 percent of all rapes are perpetrated by dates, colleagues, or other acquaintances (Chollar, 1989). Spousal abuse is another form of violence experienced by many women. Each year, approximately one and a half million American husbands use fists, knives, or guns against their wives (Strauss and Gelles, 1986).

Nonviolent discrimination is a more pervasive fact of women's lives. Although the modern workforce is 44 percent female, women are greatly underrepresented in positions of higher authority. The average salary of female workers in the United States is approximately 60 percent of that of men. In terms of promotions, women seem to be blocked by what Robertson (1989) describes as a "glass ceiling" or "invisible ceiling"—women may rise through certain levels of an organization but then suddenly hit a ceiling and proceed no further. At the same time, women shoulder the brunt of both housework and child care (Hughes and Galinsky, 1994). Although most women now work, they continue to perform about twice as much housework as their husbands—and this does not include child care (which also falls mainly to women). Husbands of working women perform a higher percentage of the housework in their homes than do husbands of nonworking women, but this higher percentage is not because the husbands of working women spend more time on housework; rather, the working wives have less time available for housework, so less housework in total gets done (Antill and Cotton, 1988; Robinson, 1988).

Gender Stereotypes

Gender stereotypes are beliefs about the typical characteristics and behaviors of men and women. In general, men are perceived as being independent, dominant, aggressive, assertive, self-confident, and intellectual, whereas women are perceived as being emotional, compassionate, home-oriented, submissive, and gentle (Bergen and Williams, 1991; Eagly and Kite, 1987). Although there is nothing wrong with being gentle or having some of the other allegedly feminine traits, these traits are clearly not the characteristics that lead to positions of authority and leadership. Thus, gender stereotypes are compatible with the differential treatment of men and women in the labor force.

"We couldn't connect. He kept spouting technobabble, and I, of course, kept coming back with psychobabble."

Are Gender Stereotypes Accurate?

As just described, gender stereotypes encompass many characteristics. Do these stereotypes reflect actual differences between the sexes? Do men and women really differ on the traits involved in gender stereotypes?

The first observation we should make is that the evidence is massive that men and women are much more similar than they are different. Men and women are about equally likely to manifest most personality traits, most physical and mental capabilities, and most hopes, fears, and wishes. Simply put, most humans share most of the features that characterize our species.

Nevertheless, a few differences between the sexes have been obtained reliably by researchers in the last two or three decades, although even these differences are typically small in an absolute sense (Ruble, 1987). For example, boys on average score higher on tests of mathematical and spatial abilities than do girls on average, whereas the opposite direction of difference (girls on average outperform boys on average) occurs on tests of verbal abilities (Hyde, Fennema, and Lamon, 1990; Maccoby and Jacklin, 1974).

One of the best-documented sex differences is that men are more aggressive than women, especially in aggression that produces pain or physical injury (Eagly and Steffen, 1986). There is some evidence that sex differences in aggression diminish with age (Hyde, 1984), although adult phenomena like spousal abuse typically involve men as the aggressors and women as the victims (Strauss and Gelles, 1986).

Eagly and Johnson (1990) reviewed the literature on leadership styles and concluded that female leaders are more likely to adopt a democratic or participative style and less likely to adopt an autocratic or directive style than are male leaders. There was also some—but not overwhelming—evidence that women are more likely than men to use an interpersonally oriented style than men, who are more likely than women to use a task-oriented style. In another literature review of leadership research, Eagly and Karau (1991) found that men were more likely than women to emerge as leaders in initially leaderless groups, especially when the groups were short-term and when they involved tasks that did not require complex social interaction (which women might be able to coordinate better than men).

Other social behaviors that have been weakly linked with sex include helping behavior, conformity, and "influenceability." Men are somewhat more likely to help in short-term interactions with strangers than are women, but sex differences in helping have not been documented in domains like close and long-term relationships (Eagly and Crowly, 1986). Women conform somewhat more than men in situations involving group pressure but not in other domains (Eagly and Carli, 1981). Women also show somewhat greater agreement with others' opinions in public group settings than do men, perhaps because women value group harmony whereas men value appearing independent (Eagly, Wood, and Fishbaugh, 1981).

So are gender stereotypes accurate? There is probably a "kernel of truth" in some expectancies about the sexes, including those noted above. For example, there is little doubt that men are more physically aggressive than women. But there is also little doubt that real differences between men and women do *not* justify the strong and multifaceted stereotypes that most people hold about the sexes. Men and women do not differ as much or as consistently as most of us believe. This point was nicely illustrated in a pair of studies at the University of British Columbia in Vancouver (Martin, 1987). Male and female participants either rated themselves on a variety of traits or estimated the prevalence of the same traits in men and women. Self-ratings by men and women revealed a few substantial differences (such as on ratings of being aggressive, egotistical, soother of hurt feelings, and whiney) and a few small differences. In contrast, stereotypes were much more extreme: Perceivers judged that men and women differ substantially on virtually every trait that was measured (in one study, for instance, thirty-four of the forty measured traits revealed significantly larger estimated sex differences than actual sex differences).

Origins of Sex Differences

Even if gender stereotypes have a kernel of truth (in the sense that some stereotypic beliefs parallel actual, though smaller, sex differences), it is important to understand where the differences between men and women originate. Are the differences between the sexes caused by biological factors, such as hormones and musculature? Or are the differences the result of the contrasting socialization experiences of boys and girls?

Theorists have taken different positions on this issue. From a biological perspective, some researchers have argued that genetic factors underlie sex differences (Benbow and Stanley, 1980), and others have proposed that evolutionary pressures have led to inborn sex differences in many characteristics, such as sex characteristics that are preferred in a mate (Buss, 1988; Feingold, 1992). Women are more likely than men to look for (and value) cues in the opposite sex that reflect material resources, such as wealth, status, and power, whereas men are more likely than women to look for (and value) cues in the opposite sex that reflect reproductive fertility, such as health, youth, and physical attractiveness. The evolutionary argument is that these differences have appeared because women invest a great deal in each child and therefore need mates who can provide physical and psychological resources to their offspring. Men, who invest relatively less than women in each child, are supposedly more

concerned with the fertility of their mate than with the mate's potential to provide resources.

A very different view of sex differences is provided by **social role theory** (Eagly, 1987; Eagly and Wood, 1991). According to this theory, sex differences arise from societal expectations about "appropriate conduct" for men and women. Eagly suggests that the central core of gender expectations is that men are expected to be more "agentic" (independent, oriented toward instrumental achievement) than women, whereas women are expected to be more "communal" (unselfish, concerned with others) than men. Further, Eagly argues that these expectations derive from the social roles that have historically been assigned to the sexes, namely working outside the home (being the bread winner) for men and child-rearing and other domestic responsibilites for women. Sex differences occur because men and women are treated very differently and because most people try to conform to society's expectations (thus, men adopt agentic behaviors and women adopt communal behaviors).

It is certainly the case that expectations differ for men and women. From the moment a newborn arrives, parents' expectations depend on whether the child is male or female. In one study of parental attitudes toward newborns within twenty-four hours after birth, parents were asked to describe their infants to a close friend. Objectively, the babies were of similar size and health, yet boys were described as better co-ordinated, stronger, more alert, and bigger than girls. Girls were described as smaller, softer, and more finely featured (Rubin, Provenzano, and Luria, 1974).

By the age of three or four, children have a reasonable understanding of their gender and are beginning to form ideas of what is appropriate for boys and for girls (Etaugh and Liss, 1992). As the child grows, the expectations of parents and others in the environment become stronger. Boys play with trucks, girls play with dolls, and research has shown that both sexes are encouraged to do so (Maccoby, 1990). Fathers tend to play more aggressively with their sons, and both parents tend to demand more independence from sons than from daughters.

By the age of seven, boys and girls have clear and stable sex identities—that is, their perception of themselves as a man or a woman will not change regardless of what they wear or are called by others. Books, institutions, and the media continue the socialization process, confirming and reinforcing society's expectations for each sex (Clark, Lennon, and Morris, 1993; Craig, 1992).

Thus, social role theory attributes sex differences to society's differential expectations for men and women—a cultural factor. Hoffman and Hurst (1990) have argued further that gender expectations and stereotypes might arise in order to rationalize or make sense of the different social roles assigned to men and women. That is, people might rationalize sex-specific social roles by attributing personality traits that "fit" the roles: because men are the breadwinners, they must be independent and competitive; because women care for the children, they must be gentle and compassionate. In support of this reasoning, Hoffman and Hurst asked participants to form impressions of two fictional groups inhabiting a distant planet, the Orinthians and the Ackmians. One group was described as consisting mostly of child raisers, whereas the other group was described as consisting mostly of city workers. When participants subsequently rated each group, they evaluated the predominantly child-

raising group as possessing many feminine traits and the predominantly city-workers group as possessing many masculine traits. More important, this effect occurred even when participants rated individuals who occupied the role that was rare for their group (for example, child raisers from the predominantly child-raising group were rated as more feminine than child raisers from the predominantly city-workers group). Participants appeared to infer personality traits from the predominant social roles of the groups.

Consequences of Gender Stereotypes

Gender stereotypes operate just like the racial and ethnic stereotypes we discussed earlier—the stereotypes constitute expectancies about men and women that can bias the perception, interpretation, and recall of gender-related information. For instance, if perceivers believe that women are emotional, they will be more likely to notice emotional behavior by women, to interpret ambiguous behavior by women as emotional,

These youngsters fixing a bicycle typify our society's expectation that boys are mechanically minded.

and to recall cases when women were emotional. An example of selective perception and interpretation related to gender is that perceivers sometimes make different causal attributions for the same behavior by men and women. Even in the face of similar performances at a task, people are more likely to attribute male success to ability than they are female success, whereas they are more likely to attribute female success to luck than they are male success (Burgner and Hewstone, 1993; Eagly, 1987).

Self-fulfilling prophesies can also occur such that expectancies change a perceiver's behavior in ways that elicit the expected behaviors from the two sexes. Stryphek and Snyder (1982) asked male participants to engage in a division-of-labor task in which they made decisions about the type of task they would do and the type of task their partner would do. When participants believed their partner was female, they tended to assign more "feminine" tasks to her than when they believed their partner was male.

In the classroom, teachers' expectancies about male and female students can influence the teachers' behavior. For example, boys receive more teacher attention—both positive and negative—than do girls, and teachers spend more time instructing and listening to boys than to girls (Sadker and Sadker, 1994).

Gender stereotypes also affect our expectancies for ourselves, of course. If a girl believes that, in general, girls are weak at math, she is more likely to expect problems in math for herself, to attribute her math success to luck, to give up quickly when encountering problems in math, and so on. When we see ourselves confirming gender stereotypes, it becomes very difficult to question their accuracy. In the next section, we will elaborate further on the psychological effects of being a target of stereotypes and prejudice.

Gender stereotypes differ from many racial stereotypes in that people often *want* to confirm them. Many men want to be "masculine" (assertive and dominant); many women want to be "feminine" (gentle and selfless). Not only do people often internalize, value, and agree with sex roles and gender stereotypes, but they also feel social pressure to conform to the stereotypes. Brown and Geis (1984) have shown that men who display "manly" traits and women who display "womanly" traits are evaluated more positively and are viewed as more psychologically healthy than those who do not.

In conclusion, gender stereotypes are constricting for both men and women, although they have interfered

with the achievements of women more than men. Biased information processing and self-fulfilling prophesies can strengthen gender stereotypes in the same way that racial and ethnic stereotypes can become stronger even when they are wrong.

Being a Target of Prejudice: The Social Psychology of Victimization

To this point in the chapter, we have focused on how stereotypes and prejudice develop in perceivers, identifying such processes as the desire for positive social identity, the sociocultural indoctrination of prejudice, competition for scarce resources, and biased information processing. Implicitly, our discussion has centered on members of majority and advantaged groups—those individuals who feel dislike for minority members or who exhibit discrimination toward disadvantaged persons. Perhaps this focus reflects, in part, ethnocentrism—mostly white, male researchers spending most of their time studying other white males to understand the topic.

What about members of minority groups? What is the reality of their lives? How do prejudice and discrimination change their lives? In this section, we discuss some of the social psychological implications of being a target of prejudice and stereotypes.

Objective Disadvantage

The first and undoubtedly most significant impact of minority group status on one's life is objective disadvantage. Minority group members are objectively worse off than they would be if stereotypes and prejudice did not exist. They suffer psychologically, economically, and physically. Knowing that you are disliked simply because of your group membership is psychologically painful—everyone wants to be liked and respected. Blacks report that experiences of discrimination are emotionally upsetting and sometimes humiliating (Schuman and Hatchett, 1974). On virtually all indices of economic and social status among North Americans, blacks and other racial minorities fall below whites, and women fall below men (see Braddock and McPartland, 1987; Jaynes and Williams,

A gathering of Mohawk Warriors and friends in their 1990 holdout against Quebec government forces at Oka, an area of special value to the Mohawks, which was designated for development. Knowing full-well the prejudice of many of the non-native people against them helped to bolster the group's self-esteem.

1989; Russo and Denmark, 1984). Minority group members have fewer jobs, less prestigious jobs, and lower paying jobs than do majority group members. As already discussed, such occupational disadvantages are true for women as well. Minority group members and women also suffer physically: their health status is worse than that of the majority group (perhaps because of their economic disadvantage), and they are more likely to be victims of violence than are members of the dominant group.

In short, the lives of many minority group members are characterized by objective disadvantage. They live in an environment where they are the targets of hatred and suspicion, where they exert little control over their outcomes, and where they have difficulty providing the basic necessities for their families. Jews in Nazi Germany constituted one of the most extreme examples of minority disadvantage in history: they paid the ultimate price for their group membership—their lives.

Attributional Implications of Minority Group Membership

One interesting line of research on minority groups has examined self-esteem. Empirical studies have indicated that members of many minority groups have self-esteem that is equal to or higher than members of majority groups. For example, several researchers have found that, in the United States, blacks report levels of self-esteem equal to that of whites (Hoelter, 1983; Rosenberg, 1979). How is that possible if they are experiencing reduced success? If blacks are excluded from occupational opportunities, denied social status, and relegated to inner-city living conditions, how can they develop a positive self-concept?

Some researchers have argued that minority group members do not suffer reduced self-esteem because they are able to attribute failure and negative outcomes to prejudice (Dion, 1986; Crocker and Major, 1989, 1994). Minority group members can protect their self-concept

TABLE 7.3   **MEAN ATTRIBUTIONS TO DISCRIMINATION AND CHANGES IN SELF-ESTEEM FROM PRETEST LEVELS FOR BLACK AND WHITE SUBJECTS GIVEN POSITIVE AND NEGATIVE FEEDBACK IN THE SEEN AND UNSEEN CONDITION**

	Race			
	Black		White	
	Visibility			
Feedback	Seen	Unseen	Seen	Unseen
Positive				
Attributions	5.62	3.40	4.70	4.40
Self-esteem	-0.50	0.40	0.38	0.04
Negative				
Attributions	9.58	7.70	5.63	4.81
Self-esteem	0.06	-0.47	0.07	-0.03

Note: Means for the attributions fall on a scale ranging from 3 (not at all due to prejudice) to 15 (very much due to prejudice). Means for self-esteem were standardized at pretest and posttest, and reported means represent differences in these standardized means.
Source: Crocker and Major (1994), p. 293

by attributing (often accurately) negative outcomes to the fact that they belong to a disliked group. As we discussed in chapter 3, taking credit for success enhances self-esteem and denying responsibility for failure protects self-esteem (see McFarland and Ross, 1982). If blacks, for example, recognize the role of prejudice and attribute negative outcomes to discrimination, then they are less likely to denigrate themselves for the failures, thus maintaining positive self-esteem even in the face of objective disadvantage.

This idea that minority group status confers attributional benefits for failure has been tested by several researchers. Dion and Earn (1975) recruited male Jewish undergraduates, who participated with three other young men in a task in which each of the participants provided positive or negative feedback on several trials to the other participants in the form of points. All participants were led to believe that they did poorly on the task, finishing with a low number of points. Half of the participants believed that the other three players were Christians and knew about their own Jewish status. The remaining participants were never given any information about the other participants' religions and believed that the others were similarly ignorant of their Jewish status. Those participants who could attribute their failure to anti-Semitism among the other players evaluated themselves more favorably on positive aspects of the Jewish identity and rated themselves more favorably on

an overall good-bad scale than did participants who could not use their religious status as an excuse because the other players were unaware of their religion.

Crocker, Voelkl, Testa, and Major (1991) led black and white students to believe that they were participating in a study of friendship development with a white partner. Half of the participants (the *seen* condition) believed that their white partner knew their racial status (black or white), and half (the *unseen* condition) believed that their partner was unaware of their race. Participants exchanged information with their partners, who then provided them with either a very positive or a very negative evaluation about the likelihood that they could be friends. Participants were asked to make attributions for this feedback and completed a measure of self-esteem. Table 7.3 presents the results for black and white participants on attributions to discrimination and changes in self-esteem from pretest levels. Black students were more likely to attribute negative feedback to discrimination than were whites, especially when they believed that their partner was aware of their racial status. Further, negative feedback did not lead to lower self-esteem among blacks when their partner allegedly knew their race. As predicted, negative feedback led to lower self-esteem only when black students could *not* use discrimination as an excuse— that is, when their partner was unaware of their race. Black students who received positive feedback from a partner who knew their race exhibited decreased self-esteem; perhaps these individuals attributed the positive feedback to false egalitarianism (reverse prejudice), which they found insulting or demeaning.

In a recent experiment, Quinn and Olson (1998) adapted the procedures of Crocker, Voelkl, Testa, and Major (1991) to examine perceived discrimination in a new way. One problem with previous studies had been that participants were not randomly assigned to "disadvantaged" or "advantaged" status—they came to the laboratory already black or white, Jewish or Christian, male or female. Quinn and Olson told white participants that the study was examining friendship development and that they would exchange self-descriptions with a partner. They were further told that the experimenter wanted to study the impact of ethnic information on friendships, and their partner would be told that they were a Native Canadian (North American Indian). Some participants were told that their partner had been chosen from among pretest subjects because he or she was prejudiced against Native Canadians, and some were told that their partner had been chosen because he or she was not prejudiced against Native Canadians. All participants subsequently received either a very favorable or very unfavorable evaluation of their friendship potential (the same feedback used by Crocker et al., 1991). Results showed that participants who believed that their partner was prejudiced against Native Canadians attributed negative feedback to discrimination more than did subjects who received negative feedback but believed their partner was unprejudiced. Moreover, the former participants exhibited higher self-esteem than the latter, suggesting that attributions to discrimination for failure served a self-protective function.

Thus, researchers have found some evidence that members of minority groups do not report lower self-esteem than members of majority groups, because minority group status provides an external attribution for failure. Of course, prejudice and discrimination result in minority group members actually failing more than majority group members, so minority group membership is certainly not an "advantage"; it simply introduces attributional ambiguity, which can protect self-esteem.

Personal-Group Discrimination Discrepancy

Another interesting finding in research on victimization has been that members of disadvantaged groups consistently report that they have personally experienced less discrimination than other members of their group. That is, disadvantaged individuals report less personal discrimination (directed at them individually) than group discrimination (directed at their group in general). Thus, most members of disadvantaged groups do not consider their own experiences to be representative of the experiences of other group members.

This discrepancy has been observed in many disadvantaged groups (for reviews, see Olson and Hafer, 1996; Taylor, Wright, and Porter, 1994). Figure 7.3, taken from Taylor, Wright, and Porter (1994), illustrates some of the diverse groups in which the discrepancy has been found: South Asian and Haitian immigrant women, inner-city black men (in both employment and housing discrimination), undergraduate and nonuniversity women, and the Inuit in Arctic Quebec.

This discrepancy might appear to be inconsistent with the preceding section, where we pointed out that attributions to discrimination can protect disadvantaged persons' self-esteem in the face of failure. In fact, though, these ideas are not necessarily incompatible. Discrimination does provide a self-protective attribution for members of disadvantaged groups, but the same individuals may also believe that other members of their group experience even more discrimination than they do personally.

Why does the **personal-group discrimination discrepancy** occur? What psychological mechanisms underlie it? Two explanations have received the most support in empirical studies, and it may be that both processes play some role. First, Crosby (1982, 1984) has argued that disadvantaged individuals may be motivated to deny or minimize personal discrimination. She suggested that denial of personal discrimination might be psychologically beneficial for several reasons. For one thing, disadvantaged individuals may be trying to maintain perceptions of control over their lives; if they believed that constant discrimination against them personally was inevitable, they might be hopeless about the future. Further, denying personal discrimination provides justification for not taking assertive action against the perpetrators of discrimination; people often do not want to attempt to rectify discrimination by powerful others because it will be costly or dangerous to do so.

A second explanation for the personal-group discrimination discrepancy focuses on bias at the group

FIGURE 7.3   EXAMPLES OF THE PERSONAL-GROUP DISCRIMINATION DISCREPANCY

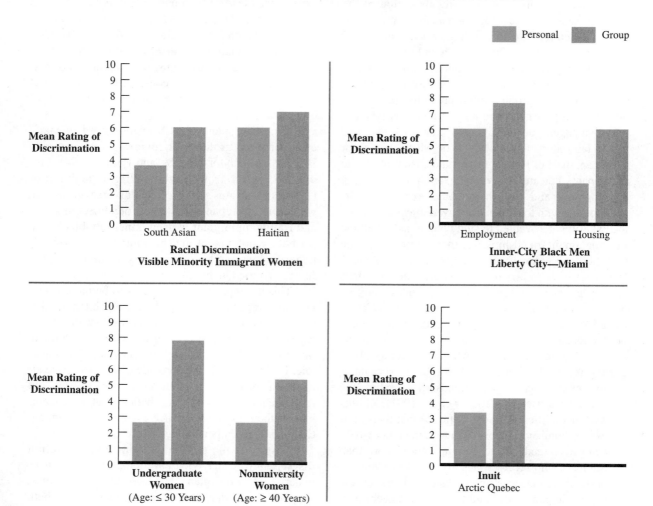

Source: Taylor, Wright, and Porter (1994), p. 235

level rather than at the personal level. Disadvantaged individuals may exaggerate group discrimination. Why might exaggeration occur? Perhaps dramatic stories in the media about discrimination lead people to overestimate the amount of discrimination that is directed against minority group members (whereas perceptions of personal discrimination may be more accurate). Disadvantaged individuals also might be motivated to exaggerate group discrimination in order to justify or stimulate corrective programs designed to improve their status (such as affirmative action programs).

Stereotype Threat and Test Performance

African Americans have a history of poorer educational and occupational achievement than white Americans (Steele, 1992). Typically, this problem has been attributed to inadequate preparation for school, resulting from historical and current socioeconomic and educational discrimination. Blacks attend poorly financed inner-city schools and are further disadvantaged by negative expectancies from teachers and peers.

These explanations may not fully explain the racial gap in achievement, however. Recently, Steele and Aronson (1995) have proposed that **stereotype threat** also undermines performance by minority group members. Stereotype threat occurs when one's behavior or performance might confirm an unfavorable stereotype about one's group. The fear of confirming the stereotype can have negative consequences. For example, the societal stereotype of African Americans includes the expectation of lower intellectual ability and performance than whites. Thus, whenever black students work on explicitly scholastic or intellectual tasks, they risk confirming the stereotype (by performing poorly). The resulting stereotype threat can interfere with performance through such mechanisms as distraction, anxiety, giving up when the task proves difficult, and so on. African Americans feel like they "represent" their group and must perform well to discredit the stereotype. White Americans do not face this kind of pressure, so their performance is not impaired.

Steele and Aronson (1995) conducted several experiments to test the idea that stereotype threat impairs the performance of African Americans on explicitly intellectual tasks. In one experiment, white and black students completed a test comprised of difficult questions from the verbal section of the Graduate Record Examination. Half of the participants were told that the study was examining "various personal factors involved in performance on problems requiring reading and verbal reasoning abilities" and that they would receive feedback on their abilities after the test; this condition was the "diagnostic" condition and was expected to arouse stereotype threat in black students. The description of the task to the remaining participants did not mention verbal ability, and they were not led to expect feedback about their own skills; this condition was the "nondiagnostic" condition and was not expected to arouse stereotype threat.

Figure 7.4 presents the average performance of white and black participants in the diagnostic and nondiagnostic conditions, corrected for the subjects' SAT scores. As the figure shows, black subjects performed worse in the diagnostic condition than in the nondiagnostic condition, whereas the performance of white subjects was not affected by the diagnosticity manipulation. Further, blacks performed worse than whites when stereotype threat was aroused but just as well as whites in the nonthreatening condition.

In another experiment, Steele and Aronson (1995) led black and white participants to expect either the diagnostic test (stereotype threat) or nondiagnostic test from the preceding experiment. Instead of measuring actual performance, however, participants answered a word completion task. In this task, participants were given fragments of a word with at least two letters missing and were asked to complete the word. Some of the words could form race-related terms (_ _ A C K for black; C O _ _ _ for color; W E L _ _ _ _ for welfare), and others could form terms reflecting self-doubt or failure (D U _ _ for dumb; S H A _ _ for shame; F L _ _ _ for flunk). Black participants who expected the diagnostic test were more likely than any other group (blacks in the nondiagnostic condition, whites in either the diagnostic or nondiagnostic condition) to complete the word fragments in race-related and failure-related ways. Thus, race and failure were highly accessible and salient to these black participants, presumably because they were feeling stereotype threat.

In a third experiment, Steele and Aronson (1995) led black and white students to expect the nondiagnostic task (no stereotype threat) from the preceding experiments. Half of the participants were asked to indicate their race on the form before completing the test, and half were not asked to indicate race. It was expected that simply identifying one's race (race prime condition) might arouse stereotype threat in black participants even though the test had not been explicitly labeled as indicative of ability, whereas the

---

FIGURE 7.4 **MEAN PERFORMANCE OF BLACK AND WHITE SUBJECTS IN THE DIAGNOSTIC AND NONDIAGNOSTIC CONDITIONS**

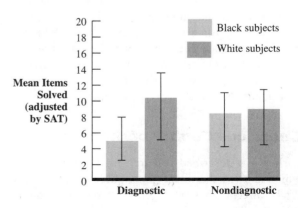

Source: Steele and Aronson (1995), p. 802

control condition (no race prime) would not arouse anxiety among black or white participants.

Figure 7.5 presents the mean performance scores for black and white subjects in the race prime and no race prime conditions, corrected for SAT scores. The results conformed exactly to predictions. In the race prime condition, black subjects performed worse than white subjects, whereas black and white subjects did not differ in the no race prime condition (indeed, the black subjects performed nonsignificantly better than the white subjects). From another perspective, blacks performed worse in the race prime than in the no race prime condition, whereas the performance of whites was not affected by the priming manipulation.

In conclusion, stereotype threat probably impairs the performance of African Americans on scholastic and intellectual tasks. As if working against objective disadvantage was not enough, blacks also carry the weight of representing their group when they complete intellectual tasks. Worried about confirming the stereotype, performance deteriorates because distraction and anxiety interfere with clear thinking. This phenomenon constitutes a vicious cycle that is reminiscent of a self-fulfilling prophesy. In a recent paper, Steele (1997) has presented data showing that stereotype threat also interferes with women's performance on mathematical tests.

Reducing Prejudice and Discrimination

Prejudice is an "overdetermined" phenomenon—it can result from several different causes. Eliminating prejudice and discrimination, therefore, may be impossible. But can we significantly improve relations between racial and ethnic groups? Have social psychologists identified any techniques that at least reduce prejudice and discrimination? The answer is yes, and we will discuss several of the techniques to conclude this chapter (some of the techniques will reappear in our chapter on intergroup relations).

Conscious Control of Stereotypes

Earlier, we described research by Devine (1989), which showed that even nonprejudiced individuals can be affected by stereotypes that are unconsciously activated. These results may seem depressing in that they imply that everyone makes stereotypical judg-

FIGURE 7.5   MEAN PERFORMANCE OF BLACK AND WHITE SUBJECTS IN THE RACE PRIME AND NO RACE PRIME CONDITIONS

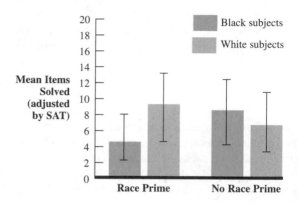

Source: Steele and Aronson (1995), p. 807

ments in certain situations. But there was another aspect of Devine's results that we did not discuss earlier and that offers a more optimistic message. Under anonymous conditions, participants were asked to list their thoughts about the racial group *blacks*. People who scored high on the modern racism scale endorsed and repeated the stereotypes of the culture. But people who scored low on the modern racism scale were reluctant to ascribe traits to the group as a whole, wrote few unfavorable thoughts about blacks, often commented on the importance of equality, and frequently expressed disagreement with the cultural stereotype.

Devine interpreted these results as showing that nonprejudiced people consciously control their thoughts about blacks; although they are aware of the negative stereotypes about members of minority groups, nonprejudiced people disbelieve and consciously override them. Devine argued that rising above or moving beyond these ingrained stereotypes is like breaking a bad habit. It takes conscious and persistent effort (or, as Devine put it, "intention, attention, and time"). It won't happen automatically. Each of us can make a difference by consciously controlling the effects of stereotypes on our own judgments about minority groups.

Legislating Against Discrimination

Many countries today have laws against discrimination on the basis of race, sex, religion, age, and other factors. These laws require that people be given equal opportunity for jobs, housing, and so on. Is such legislation a good idea? There are several reasons to think that the answer to this question should be affirmative.

For one thing, making discrimination illegal reduces the impact of prejudice on the lives of minority group members. The worst thing about prejudice and stereotypes is that they lead to negative behaviors against members of disliked groups. Such behaviors deny opportunities, inflict psychological or physical harm, and interfere with the accomplishment of goals. It is impossible to legislate against stereotypes or prejudice—we cannot make people believe or feel what we want them to. But we *can* try to ensure that members of minority groups are not *treated* differently. Legislation will never eliminate discrimination, but there is little doubt that laws against discrimination reduce the frequency and severity of such acts.

Second, laws help to establish *norms* in societies—they play a role in defining what kinds of behaviors are acceptable and unacceptable. In this sense, laws play an educative function—they teach people how to behave. To the extent that prejudiced individuals believe that discriminatory behavior is counternormative and viewed as socially unacceptable, they will be less likely to engage in such actions. Indeed, if they want to conform to social norms, they might even publicly express the desired attitudes. In Nazi Germany, laws were introduced that demanded discriminatory behavior against Jews; the German public learned that their Nazi leaders regarded anti-Semitic acts as both legal and desirable. The contrasting case of federal laws against discrimination in the United States and Canada represents the more common (and more palatable) educative function of laws.

Third, inducing conformity to nondiscriminatory behaviors might eventually produce internalization of nonprejudiced attitudes. To the extent that nondiscriminatory behavior becomes routine (a "habit"), the salience of legal sanctions as a cause of the nondiscriminatory behavior might fade. As a result, people might come to see themselves as voluntarily avoiding discrimination. Through processes of either self-perception or dissonance reduction (see chapters 3 and 6) or both, attitudes might shift to become more consistent with overt behavior. A recent example of this kind of process has been laws requiring seat belt use. When first introduced, seat belt laws have often produced howls of protest from nonusers, who feel that their freedom is being restricted. Initially, these pro-

testers used their seat belts simply to avoid fines but remained staunchly opposed to seat belts. Over time, however, seat belt use becomes habitual, and attitudes shift toward the positive pole. After a few years, the same protesters may feel unprotected without their seat belts and agree wholeheartedly with the idea that seat belts should be used regularly.

Contact

The most researched technique in social psychology for reducing prejudice is intergroup contact. Social psychologists have been in the vanguard of scientists arguing in favor of school desegregation and intergroup contact (see Stephan, 1978). The **contact hypothesis** states that contact between members of different groups leads to more positive intergroup attitudes (Pettigrew, 1986). This idea is compatible with both intuition and established social psychological principles. For example, with regard to intuition, it seems reasonable to predict that contact with members of a disliked group will teach prejudiced people that their stereotypes are wrong. From the standpoint of social psychological principles, we discussed, in chapter 5, evidence supporting the mere exposure effect, which states that familiarity with a stimulus leads to more favorable attitudes toward that stimulus; presumably, then, becoming familiar with members of a group should lead to more positive attitudes toward the group.

Some evidence supports the contact hypothesis. Researchers have found positive correlations between

The contact hypothesis states that contact between members of different groups leads to more positve intergroup attitudes.

contact with a group and attitudes toward the group. Contact with homosexuals, for example, is associated with more favorable beliefs about, and attitudes toward, this group among heterosexuals (Whitely, 1990). Altemeyer (1994) has found that highly authoritarian, ethnocentric people report having had less contact in childhood with members of outgroups. Unfortunately, these correlations are ambiguous because they may reflect that positive attitudes cause contact rather than the reverse.

Evaluations of the effects of classroom desegregation in the United States have not always found positive effects. In fact, attitudes toward minority group members among white children have sometimes been found to become more negative following desegregation (see Stephan, 1986). Why would contact be ineffective or even detrimental to reducing prejudice?

One assumption underlying the contact hypothesis is that experiences with individual members of a group will be generalized to the group as a whole. There is substantial evidence, however, that individuals who disconfirm the stereotype of their group are often dismissed as exceptions to the rule, thereby protecting the original stereotype (see Hewstone, 1994; Kunda and Oleson, 1997; Maurer, Park, and Rothbart, 1995). This process of **subtyping** presumably labels people who disconfirm the group stereotype as atypical of the group; because they are not representative, their existence does not mean that the stereotype needs to be revised.

A second assumption underlying the contact hypothesis is that experiences between members of different groups will be positive (or at least neutral) in valence rather than unpleasant or hostile. Of course, the reality is often that members of different groups act negatively toward one another, resulting in an escalating cycle of mistrust and hatred.

In order for contact to reduce prejudice, it must satisfy certain prerequisites. For one thing, it must involve cooperative behavior between the groups. A famous study in social psychology, known as the Robber's Cave experiment, demonstrated the importance of cooperation between groups in reducing prejudice. Sherif, Harvey, White, Hood, and Sherif (1961) studied boys at a summer camp in the Robber's Cave State Park in Oklahoma. The boys were divided into two groups, the Eagles and the Rattlers. Initially, activities involved intergroup competition with each of the two groups trying to defeat the other in sporting

and camping activities. Relations between the groups deteriorated as the competitive activities took place. The investigators then staged several events (such as a break in the water line to the camp) that required cooperative behavior between members of the two groups. These events produced a marked decrease in intergroup hostility; in fact, spontaneous positive interactions between members of the two groups began to occur.

In addition to being cooperative, the groups must be of equal status in order for prejudice to subside through contact (Amir, 1969). That is, members of the two groups must be approximately equal in social standing in the particular setting (such as the classroom). Often, real-life desegregation involves busing inner-city African Americans to suburban, predominantly white, schools. The black and white children are unlikely to possess equal social status in this circumstance.

Stuart Cook (1969, 1990) conducted a study in which highly prejudiced white women interacted with a black female confederate (and another white woman, also a confederate) for two hours a day for twenty days. The three women held equal status in the interactions, and the activities required cooperative behavior (the women worked on a management training simulation). The black confederate was both competent and friendly. After twenty days, approximately 40 percent of the prejudiced women showed substantial positive attitude change toward blacks. This result is both encouraging and discouraging depending on one's perspective. Compared with a control condition where only 12 percent of the women showed significant improvement in racial attitudes, the experimental condition was highly successful. On the other hand, the procedure was intensive and expensive but even so affected only a minority of the prejudiced women.

Is there hope that intergroup contact can reduce prejudice in the real world? We think so. Admittedly, the contact must satisfy the requirements of cooperation and equal status, but these characteristics can be built into programs. It is more likely that prejudiced attitudes can be reduced in children than in adults, who have held their views for a long time. Box 7.2 describes a teaching technique that has been developed by Eliot Aronson (1990) to encourage positive racial attitudes among children—the **jigsaw method.** We will return to the role of contact when we talk about intergroup relations in chapter 13.

BOX 7.2

The Jigsaw Method of Cooperative Learning

Research by Sherif, Harvey, White, Hood, and Sherif (1961), Cook (1969), and others has shown that in order for contact between racial groups to have a positive impact on interracial attitudes, it must involve cooperative behavior and must occur on an equal-status basis. Eliot Aronson and his colleagues (Aronson, 1990; Aronson, Stephan, Sikes, Blaney, and Snapp, 1978) designed a technique to be used in primary schools that rested on these findings. They called their technique the *jigsaw classroom.* This method makes cooperation requisite for successful performance by the participants and puts all of the participants on an equal level of "expertise" or knowledge.

In an initial test of this procedure, primary school students were placed in six-person, multiethnic learning groups. Each student in a group was given one-sixth of the material to be learned on a particular topic. For example, in a lesson dedicated to the life of Joseph Pulitzer, each student received one paragraph describing an aspect of Pulitzer's life (his ancestors, his early life, his middle age, and so on). No student had access to any of the paragraphs other than his or her own, so all of the group members depended on all of the other group members to learn about other aspects of Pulitzer's life.

Six weeks later, comparisons of the jigsaw classrooms with traditional classrooms showed that those in the former environment liked one another more, liked school more, had higher self-esteem, and performed better on objective tests! This positive impact of the cooperative learning strategy implemented in the jigsaw classroom has been replicated by numerous other researchers.

In a variant of the jigsaw technique, Desforges, Lord, Ramsey, Mason, Van Leeuwen, West, and Lepper (1991) had university students work in a dyad with another student (a confederate) whom they believed to be a former mental patient. The interactions lasted for one hour and involved studying the effectiveness of intravenous therapy. Each participant (the real subject and the confederate) was given one-half of the material on the topic, summarized the material for the other participant, and was not allowed to see the material given to the other participant (thus depending on that person for transmission of the information). Compared to a control condition where participants studied the material alone, the jigsaw method did not produce better learning. But when participants' attitudes toward former mental patients were assessed, the jigsaw method was shown to have produced significantly more positive evaluations, especially in those people whose initial attitudes were quite negative. Participants in the jigsaw condition appear to have generalized positive impressions from the confederate to all former mental patients.

In sum, the jigsaw method has been shown to be effective with primary school children and with university students. By structuring interactions so that cooperation is required and equal status is ensured, this procedure results in more positive intergroup attitudes. The jigsaw classroom is a clear example of applied social psychology in action.

Summary

Prejudice is an attitude, usually negative, toward members of a group. Stereotypes are beliefs that members of a group share a particular characteristic. Discrimination is behavior toward someone based on his or her group membership. When discrimination is based on prejudice toward a racial group, it is called racism, and when it is based on gender, it is called sexism. There is less overt racism and discrimination in North America now than there was twenty-five or fifty years ago, but some researchers have suggested that old-fashioned racism has simply been replaced by more subtle forms of modern racism, such as beliefs that blacks are pushing too hard. Symbolic racism is based on perceptions that blacks threaten traditional values. Many whites are ambivalent about blacks—they have both positive and negative feelings. Regressive racism occurs when discriminatory behavior is elicited under conditions of stress or arousal.

Many factors can lead to prejudice. Motivational explanations of prejudice are based on the idea that prejudice may result from tensions, emotions, fears, and underlying needs in the perceiver. For example, the scapegoat theory of discrimination holds that frustrations in everyday life lead to displaced aggression against members of weak outgroups, which vents pent-up arousal. Social identity theory proposes that people desire a positive social identity, which can be achieved by seeing one's ingroups as better than outgroups. To achieve this goal, people often give preferential treatment to ingroup members even when the basis of group membership is trivial and arbitrary—the minimal group paradigm.

Sociocultural explanations of prejudice focus on socialization processes, whereby parents, peers, the media, and institutions teach stereotypes to children, who see racial prejudice displayed and who are themselves rewarded or punished based on their actions toward members of minority groups. Realistic conflict theory proposes that intergroup prejudice and discrimination often result from actual conflict over scarce resources (such as jobs, housing). Competition increases the outgroup homogeneity effect, which is the tendency to see all members of an outgroup as similar to one another. Personality explanations of prejudice have focused on the authoritarian personality, which may result from harsh parental discipline coupled with demands of perfection and obedience. High authoritarians typically exhibit ethnocentrism, which is the tendency to reject people who are culturally dissimilar to one's ingroup while blindly accepting those who are culturally similar to one's ingroup.

Cognitive explanations of prejudice emphasize the role of negative stereotypes in the development of prejudice. The process of categorization means putting objects, people, or other stimuli into groups; categorization is a basic, automatic, and highly functional process, which allows us to cope with a complex world. Unfortunately, categorizing people into groups involves generating stereotypes (beliefs about

shared characteristics). Stereotypes can initially come from parents, peers, the media, personal experiences, and other sources. Once a stereotype is formed, it biases information processing such that the stereotype is more likely to be confirmed. To be specific, instances that are consistent with the stereotype are more likely to be noticed; ambiguous events are likely to be interpreted as consistent with the stereotype; and information consistent with the stereotype is easier to retrieve from memory. Thus, even when stereotypes are wrong, they might become stronger over time.

Self-fulfilling prophesies occur when a perceiver's expectancies about another person lead the perceiver to behave toward the target in such a way as to elicit confirmatory behavior. The vicious cycle represented by self-fulfilling prophesies can act to strengthen stereotypes over and above the impact of selective information processing.

Gender stereotypes are beliefs about the typical characteristics and behaviors of men and women. Men are typically perceived as being high in instrumental traits like assertiveness and intelligence, whereas women are typically perceived as being high in communal traits like compassion and emotionality. Although there are some real differences between men and women, both biological and psychological, gender stereotypes are more elaborate and extreme than the documented sex differences warrant. Some theorists have attributed sex differences to biological factors, such as genes or inborn differences resulting from evolutionary pressures. Other theorists have focused on social and cultural factors to understand sex differences. For example, social role theory attributes sex differences to societal expectations about "appropriate conduct" for men and women, which in turn are thought to be derived from the social roles that have historically been assigned to the sexes (work versus child care).

The reality of life for members of disadvantaged groups is deprivation—they suffer psychologically, physically, and economically compared with members of advantaged majority groups. Yet, members of disadvantaged groups typically report levels of self-esteem that are comparable to members of majority groups. One possible explanation for this finding is that minority group members can protect their self-esteem by attributing negative outcomes to discrimination. Another interesting finding in research on victimization is the personal-group discrimination discrepancy, which refers to the fact that members of disadvantaged groups typically report less personal discrimination than group discrimination. This phenomenon may reflect minimization of personal discrimination and/or exaggeration of discrimination against one's group. Stereotype threat occurs when one's behavior or performance might confirm an unfavorable stereotype about one's group. Stereotype threat can interfere with performance on intellectual tasks.

Prejudice and discrimination can be reduced by conscious control of stereotypes. Also, legislating against discrimination reduces the impact of prejudice on the lives of members of disadvantaged groups. The contact hypothesis states that contact between members of different groups leads to more positive intergroup attitudes. Unfortunately, individuals who disconfirm the stereotype of a group are often subtyped, which means that they are dismissed as being unrepresentative of their group. For contact to reduce prejudice successfully, it must involve cooperative behavior and the participants must be equal in status. The jigsaw method is a teaching technique that satisfies these prerequisites and has been shown to be effective in producing positive racial attitudes among children.

Key Terms

ambivalence
authoritarian personality
categorization
contact hypothesis
discrimination
ethnocentrism
gender stereotypes
jigsaw method
maximum differentiation
   strategy

minimal group paradigm
modern racism
outgroup homogeneity
   effect
personal-group discrimination
   discrepancy
prejudice
racism
realistic conflict theory
regressive racism

scapegoat theory of
   discrimination
self-fulfilling prophecy
sexism
social identity theory
social role theory
stereotypes
stereotype threat
subtyping
symbolic racism

Suggested Readings

Allport, G. W. (1954). *The nature of prejudice.* Reading, MA: Addison-Wesley.

Altemeyer, B. (1988). *Enemies of freedom: Understanding right-wing authoritarianism.* San Francisco: Jossey-Bass.

Basow, S. (1986). *Gender stereotypes: Traditions and alternatives.* Pacific Grove, CA: Brooks/Cole.

Dovidio, J. F., and Gaertner, S. L. (Eds.). (1986). *Prejudice, discrimination, and racism: Theory and research.* New York: Academic Press.

Eagly, A. H. (1987). *Sex differences in social behavior: A social-role interpretation.* Mahwah, NJ: Erlbaum.

Katz, P. A., and Taylor, D. A. (1988). *Eliminating racism: Profiles in controversy.* New York: Plenum.

Mackie, D. M., and Hamilton, D. L. (Eds.). (1993). *Affect, cognition, and stereotyping: Interactive processes in group perception.* New York: Academic Press.

Shaver, P., and Hendrick, C. (Eds.). (1987). *Sex and gender.* Newbury Park, CA: Sage.

Taylor, D. M., and Moghaddam, F. M. (1994). *Theories of intergroup relations: International social psychological perspectives* (2nd ed.). New York: Praeger.

Zanna, M. P., and Olson, J. M. (Eds.). (1994). *The psychology of prejudice: The Ontario symposium* (Vol. 7). Mahwah, NJ: Erlbaum.

Chapter 8

Loving, Liking, and Close Relationships

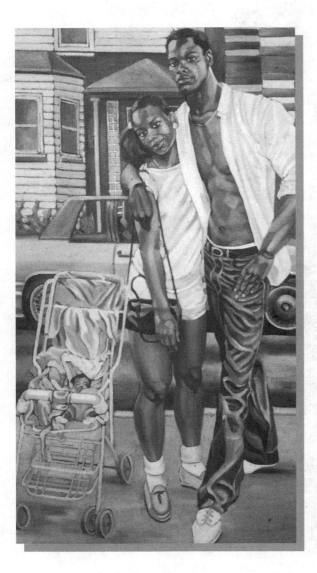

"What's in a name?" laments Juliet of the House of Capulet, "that which we call a rose by any other name would smell as sweet."

Juliet, giving expression to the irony that her greatest love bears the name of her family's greatest enemy, prepares to embark on perhaps the most compelling romantic adventure in English literature. Within two days, she and her lover, Romeo of the House of Montague, marry and consummate their love. However, they are ultimately consumed by the hostile, bitter, and violent feud between their two families. Shakespeare's romance, *Romeo and Juliet,* turns tragic as the two lovers are led by passion and fate to taking their own lives in a double suicide.

Romeo, young and impetuous, first cast eyes on Juliet when he and his friends used the occasion of a costume ball to slip into the home of the Capulets. Casting his eyes on Juliet, he is awestruck by her beauty:

Oh, she doth teach the torches to burn bright!
It seems she hangs upon the cheek of night
Like a rich jewel in an Ethiop's ear;
Beauty too rich for use, for earth too dear!!
(Act I, scene 5)

Obsessed with her beauty, Romeo returns to the Capulets' orchard later that evening and longs for the mere sight of Juliet. He is not disappointed:

But, soft! what light through yonder window breaks?
It is the east, and Juliet is the sun! . . .
It is my lady; O, it is my love! . . .
Two of the fairest stars in all the heaven,
Having some business, do entreat her eyes
To twinkle in their spheres till they return . . .
See, how she leans her cheek upon her hand!
O, that I were a glove upon that hand,
That I might touch that cheek!   (Act II, scene 2)

Juliet is equally transfixed by Romeo's figure. She muses,

> Give me my Romeo; and, when he shall die,
> Take him and cut him out in little stars,
> And he will make the face of heaven so fine,
> That all the world will be in love with night.
> (Act III, scene 2)

Swept by desire, Romeo and Juliet set out secretly to tie themselves in marriage despite the fact that Juliet's father, Lord Capulet, had promised her hand in marriage to Count Paris. Romeo beseeches Friar Laurence to marry them:

> Then plainly know my heart's dear love is set
> On the fair daughter of rich Capulet:
> As mine on hers, so hers is set on mine;
> And all combined, save what thou must combine
> By holy marriage: (Act II, scene 3)

The friar agrees to the marriage; he is struck by the strength of the passion of the two lovers and hopes that the marriage of a Capulet to a Montague may help to heal the enmity the two families have for each other.

Events will prove that, in his latter hope, he is mistaken.

While returning from their marriage vows, Romeo encounters Juliet's cousin, the fiery and angry Tybalt. Although he attempts to avoid conflict, Romeo is forced into a fight, slays Tybalt, and is banished from Verona by the Prince. Before leaving, Romeo steals into his new wife's room. There, Romeo and Juliet consummate their love. As fate will have it, they will never see each other alive again.

Angered by the murder of Tybalt, Lord Capulet announces the impending marriage of his daughter to Count Paris. With the aid of Friar Laurence, Juliet devises a plan that will permit her to join Romeo and avoid a bigamous marriage to Paris. The friar prescribes a potion that will put Juliet to sleep, simulating the symptoms of death. After she takes the potion and is believed dead, she is taken to the Capulets' mausoleum.

Though the friar's plan is to let Romeo know of the trick by which Juliet would feign death, fate intervenes. Romeo learns of Juliet's death but not of the trick that is to return her to his side. Consumed by passion, Romeo races to the mausoleum to join his love. Taking poison from an apothecary, he speaks his last words: "Thus with a kiss, I die."

When Juliet awakens from her sleep, she sees her dead lover by her side. Ignoring the friar's exhortation to leave the tomb, Juliet thrusts a knife into her breast and dies.

Positive Personal Relationships: Liking and Being Liked

Personal relationships take many forms. The relationship between Romeo and Juliet was passionate. A woman's love for her spouse of fifty years may take a more compassionate form. A boy's fondness for his Little League coach is yet a different kind of interpersonal attraction and his liking for the person who sells candy at the local store may be still different. In each case we are describing the fondness of one person for another. Some attractions are short lived; some are enduring; some are passionately hot and some are cool.

When we say that a person likes another individual, we mean that, from the perspective of that person, he or she holds a positive attitude toward the other. We will consider a **positive personal relationship** in a dyad as the positive attitude that two people hold toward each other. Love, on the other hand, adds more—and is much more difficult to define. We begin our discussion of relationships with a broad analysis of positive personal relations and then focus on the ways in which psychologists have studied the emotion of love.

What makes us like others and why do others like us? Think about the various relationships in your life. What factors have made you like certain of your friends or partners? You may find some intriguing contrasts. Some of the people you are attracted to are quite similar to you. You may have thought of going away to college and finding someone who shared your interests, came from a similar town, liked the same music, and so forth. But you can also think of people you are attracted to at least partially because they are intriguingly different. You like rock music; they like classical. You like comedies; they like serious drama. And the very fact of your differences has made them more appealing. You may also like people who like you and who always tell you how good you are. You may like others because they are brutally honest.

Leonardo DiCaprio plays Romeo to Claire Danes' Juliet in the 1996 contemporary-dress movie version of Shakespeare's play. The timeless appeal of this romantic story is the passionate relationship of the young lovers which, because they die, does not change into anything else.

Let's look at some of the broad theoretical reasons that have been proposed and tested that help to account for how we come to like and dislike others.

A Cognitive View: Better to Be Balanced

Balance theory has played an important role in many areas of social psychology. It has played an important role in the formation of attitudes and in explaining the need for consistency that is the hallmark of many theories of attitude change. It is not surprising that balance theory has also been useful to help us understand the very special attitude of liking and disliking that people hold for other people.

In this chapter we consider a form of balance theory that has been used extensively for understanding some of the issues involved in interpersonal attraction:

Theodore Newcomb's **symmetry or A-B-X model of attraction.**

Newcomb's theory takes the perspective of person A, who is in a network with person B and object X. The system considers the positive and negative bonds that exist between the actor, the other person, and the attitudinal object. In this system, the attitudinal object, X, may be a thing, such as a tree, a pineapple, or a brand of toothpaste; an issue, such as a balanced budget, abortion, or television violence; or another person.

Relationship networks may be either symmetrical (balanced) or asymmetrical (imbalanced). An example of a symmetrical system can be seen in figure 8.1(A). Romeo loves Juliet and he also likes the idea of marriage. Further, he knows that Juliet favors marriage. All of these harmonious, positive bonds are shown by the unbroken lines of figure 8.1(A). We can determine whether a system is symmetrical by using our common sense or, as it turns out, by algebraically multiplying the signs of the relationships. If the product of the three signs is positive, then the network is symmetrical. If the product is negative, the network is asymmetrical. Let's apply the mathematics to figure 8.1(A): Romeo's relation to Juliet is positive, his attitude toward marriage is positive, and he believes that Juliet's attitude toward marriage is also positive. Since the product of three pluses is plus, the network is symmetrical.

Figure 8.1(B) shows that balance can also exist when all feelings are less than positive. In this example, Romeo loves his father (Lord Montague); Lord Capulet (Juliet's father) loathes Montague. But then again, Romeo does not care much for Juliet's father. The product of the three signs is again positive, and the system is symmetrical. Figure 8.1(C) shows that Romeo loves Juliet, and Juliet loves her father. But Romeo and Capulet are enemies. The product of two pluses and a minus is negative. Therefore, the two positive relationships and the one negative relationship combine to form an asymmetrical state.

Does it matter if a network of relationships is symmetrical? According to Newcomb, it matters a great deal. People prefer symmetry in their relationships. If symmetry does not exist, people experience a "strain toward symmetry." This strain causes people to engage in cognitive and emotional activity in order to restore symmetry.

How can a person restore symmetry if it does not exist? Your best friend disapproves of your fiancée; your wife or husband disagrees with you about the desirability of having a family; one of your very best friends thoroughly dislikes another of your close friends. Such situations lack equilibrium and, according to the A–B–X model, attempts must be made to restore symmetry. Consider Romeo's predicament in figure 8.1(C). He loves Juliet; she loves him—but she also feels positive about her father and Romeo does not. Romeo (A) could:

1. try to persuade Juliet (B) to change her attitude about her father (X).
2. change his own attitude about Juliet (B).
3. change his own attitude about Lord Capulet (X).

Changing the signs in the A–B–X system in any of these ways would reduce the tension caused by the disequilibrium. There are other possibilities. The strain toward symmetry could be reduced if Romeo could:

4. reduce the *importance* of the topic about which he and Juliet disagree.
5. reduce the *common relevance* of the issue.

In the first of these alternatives, Romeo could come to feel that Juliet's father is too trivial a person to worry about. In the second, he could feel strongly about both Lord Capulet and Juliet but conclude that her opinion about a rivalry between gentlemen is irrelevant. Her opinion in this situation is not considered germane to areas that are common to him and his wife.

FIGURE 8.1   BALANCE THEORY REPRESENTATION OF RELATIONSHIPS IN SHAKESPEARE'S
ROMEO AND JULIET

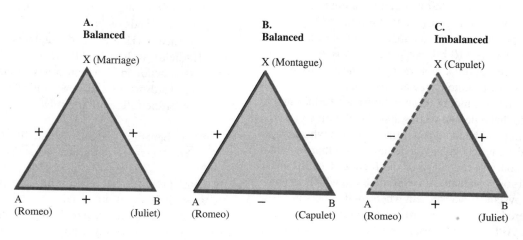

Note: Solid lines represent attraction; broken lines depict disliking.

A Reward Model of Attraction

A second model of interpersonal attraction, **reward model of attraction**, is based on the simple notion that people who are associated with rewards are liked. Such models have been put forth by Albert and Bernice Lott (1968; 1974) and by Byrne and Clore (1970). Consider a little girl sitting in a high chair who on this day, unlike every other day, picks up a spoon by herself and brings it to her mouth. Her mother responds with great delight; she smiles, kisses the baby, and gives her a cookie for her efforts. Picking up the spoon has now become a pleasurable response, since it has become associated with the pleasurable feeling generated by the mother's rewards of a kiss and a cookie. From then on, the little girl continues using the spoon to feed herself.

According to the reward model of attraction, the very same process is at the root of our interpersonal feelings: those individuals whom we associate with rewards become preferred and liked. We should also note that attraction does not occur only when rewards have been received from someone in the past or are associated with them in the present. We also tend to be attracted to those who we believe will be associated with a reward in the future (Clore and Kerber, 1981; Tedeschi, 1974). The finding that people are sensitive to rewards that others can give them in the future may help to explain why we sometimes feel an attraction to people we have known only briefly or know little about.

We are not surprised by the statement that we like people who give us rewards better than we like people who make us feel unpleasant. We can all think of occasions on which we left a situation fuming at a person who was obnoxious or unpleasant to us—the waiter who spilled soup on our sleeve, the cashier who insisted that the $10 bill we gave her was actually a $1—and we can think of as many instances of liking a person who was kind or rewarding to us.

The reward model of attraction goes further and indicates that a person who is associated with a pleasant feeling will be liked better than a person who is associated with an unpleasant feeling—whether or not that person was the cause of the feeling. Griffitt and Guay (1969) conducted an experiment in which an innocent bystander was present when another person administered either a reward or a punishment to a subject. Although that bystander had absolutely nothing to do with the reward or punishment, he was liked better when the subject experienced a reward than when the subject experienced a punishment. In a subsequent study, Griffitt (1970) directly manipulated the pleasantness of an individual's experience by varying the temperature and the humidity of an experimental room. A hypothetical stranger was liked better when the room was comfortable than when the room was hot and humid. Similarly, Veitch and Griffitt (1976) found that after a subject had heard good news on a radio report, the subject liked a stranger more than he did after bad news was broadcast. Apparently the stranger's association with the pleasantness or unpleasantness of the news report made the difference in his rated attractiveness—despite the undeniable fact that he had nothing to do with the temperature or humidity in the first case or with the nature of the news report in the last case.

Equity: Considering Both Partners' Rewards and Costs

Now let us bring both partners in a relationship into sharper focus. Thus far, we have been discussing the rewards that an individual experiences as a result of a relationship. Now consider the importance of what each partner experiences. Each individual in a two-person relationship receives a certain amount of reward. Each is benefited by pleasant feelings, each may have her or his emotional needs met, each may receive other tangible benefits. But relationships also have costs. As a partner in a relationship, you have to work to maintain that relationship. In addition, you may have to relinquish certain freedoms that you would have had if you had not been in a relationship. You may place certain demands on your partner and your partner places demands on you.

Equity theory (Hatfield and Traupmann, 1980; Walster [Hatfield], Walster, and Berscheid, 1978) proposes that satisfaction in a relationship is a function of the ratio of rewards to costs that each member experiences. Consider the following formula:

$$\frac{\text{Your benefits}}{\text{Your costs}} = \frac{\text{Partner's benefits}}{\text{Partner's costs}}$$

Equity theory proposes that relationships are most satisfying when these ratios are equal.

This is an interesting concept. If you are in a relationship with someone, equity theory suggests that your satisfaction does not depend solely upon how much you get out of the relationship—that is, it does not depend on your rewards alone. Nor does it depend on your costs alone. Instead, you will be satisfied if you feel that what you are getting from and contributing to the relationship is similar to what your partner is getting and giving. If your ratio is lower than your partner's, you may feel exploited. If your ratio is higher, you may feel guilty.

This is a provocative hypothesis. But is it true? The data are mixed (Clark and Reis, 1988). In support of equity theory, some investigators have shown that people who feel that their relationships are equitable are happier than people who feel their relationships are inequitable (Sabatelli and Cecil-Pigo, 1985). Furthermore, married people who feel their relationships are equitable are less likely to have extramarital sexual affairs (Hatfield, Traupmann, Sprecher, Utne, and Hay, 1985; Prins, Buunk, and Van Yperson, 1993). In fact, the Prins study found that women who believed that they were over-benefited from a relationship (i.e., received more from a relationship than their partner did) were the most likely to want an extramarital affair.

On the other hand, Berg and McQuinn (1986) studied couples engaged in romantic relationships at a point early in their relationship and then four months later. Couples who were still dating at the second point showed greater satisfaction, expressed greater love, and did more to maintain the relationship. However, perceptions of equity in the relationship did not predict which couples would and would not be together by the second measuring point. In a study of a different type of interpersonal relationship, Berg (1984) surveyed pairs of same-sex roommates soon after they first met each other and then again at the end of the year. Roommates' perceptions of equity in the relationship did not predict how satisfied they would be at the end of the year. Instead, the total amount of benefit the roommates felt they received was the best predictor of a good relationship.

The questions posed by equity theory are intriguing. Not all of the answers are in. Nonetheless, the work of Hatfield and her colleagues does make us think about the importance of considering others' benefits and contributions to a relationship as well as our own in estimating how satisfying the relationship is likely to be.

Long-Term Relationships

Toward Joint Outcomes

Relationships grow and change over time. Some end; some prosper. The happiness and satisfaction that peo-

ple experience in relationships change. Social psychological theories can help to identify some of the issues that become important in predicting the success of relationships over time. From the vantage point of equity theory, we saw that people's satisfaction in a relationship depends on how each person perceives his or her own versus the partner's rewards and costs. Kelley and Thibaut (1978), two theorists who have long been analyzing rewards and costs in two-person groups, suggest that lasting intimate relationships are based on a transformation of a concern with one's own outcomes ("What's in it for *me*?") or comparative outcomes ("In view of what we both contribute, am I getting as much as my partner is?") to a concern for joint outcomes ("What's in this for *us*?")

In Kelley and Thibaut's view, then, a long-lasting interpersonal relationship is characterized not by both partners' attempts to maximize their individual payoffs but rather by their attempts to maximize their joint rewards. A couple may choose to attend a football game. One may truly enjoy it; the other may yawn from the first through the fourth quarter. Although one member of the partnership is temporarily pleased, the other is not. The couple is not paying attention to the best joint reward. Ultimately, it is not a pleasing situation for either partner. More durable relationships are characterized by the kind of compromise that pleases both partners equally; for instance, going to the football game one week and to the ballet the next or skipping both and going to the theater.

An interesting feature of the transformation from a concern with individual rewards to equitable joint rewards is that the partners in the relationship are usually aware of the transformation. Fleiner and Kelley (1978) interviewed ninety-six people and had them rate their satisfaction in their personal relationships. They found that in successful partnerships, people did operate under the working rule of maximizing their joint rewards, and that each partner was aware that the other was attempting to do so.

Keeping Track of What You Give and What You Get

Do you always keep track of your rewards and costs in a relationship? Do you always feel put upon if you receive less than your partner or guilty if you receive too much? Do you always expect to receive as much as you give? Peggy Clark and her colleagues (Clark, 1984; Clark and Mills, 1979) have proposed that whether you keep track of your rewards and costs depends on the *type* of interpersonal relationship you are in. She has described two types of relationships, communal and exchange.

An **exchange relationship** is a relationship you have with an acquaintance, a stranger, or someone with whom you do business. In these relationships, there is a concern for equity, by which Clark means "comparable benefit." If you give something in the relationship, you expect something in return. Giving implies a debt assumed by the partner. Clark proposes that people keep track of the benefits they have given so that they can assess the benefits they are entitled to receive.

A **communal relationship,** on the other hand, is a long-term and deep relationship. We have communal relationships with romantic partners, friends, and family members. Clark suggests that when we desire to establish or maintain communal relationships, we stop counting. We end our recordkeeping. We do not expect our inputs to be matched by our partners. We are willing to contribute to the relationship, even if we know that our partner has no opportunity to make a similar contribution (Clark, Mills, and Powell, 1986).

How might you react if you thought you were in a potentially communal, as opposed to an exchange, relationship? Clark (1984) had students at Carnegie Mellon University enter into a relationship that they either hoped would become communal (in a romantic way) or knew would have to remain of the exchange type. This was accomplished by revealing to male participants the marital status of their partner, an attractive young woman (actually a confederate of the experimenter). Half the participants were led to believe the young woman was single, and thus participants were expected to desire a communal relationship with her. For the other participants, she was presented as being married; participants were expected to desire an exchange relationship with her, since she was unavailable as a potential romantic partner. In a game situation, the partners were given the task of locating and circling number sequences in a large matrix. As a function of the couple's performance, a reward could be won and divided between them. Clark predicted that subjects in an exchange relation would attempt to keep records—to know just how much each had contributed to the joint product so that each would know exactly how much of the reward he would eventually be entitled to. On the other hand, Clark predicted that those subjects who thought they might share a com-

munal relation would not keep records. Each would refrain from measuring his input into the relationship because the focus would be on the partnership's joint outcome.

The first person to begin the task was always the attractive woman who served as the confederate of the experimenter; she circled numbers with a colored pen. A male participant's turn followed. He could use a pen of the same color as that used by his partner or he could use a pen of a different color. Which would he use? Obviously, if he wanted to keep track of just how many correct solutions he obtained in comparison with those of his partner, he would be motivated to use a different colored pen. If he did not care about assessing the contributions made by each of them, he would not care very much which pen he used. The results showed that nearly 90 percent of all participants in the exchange relationship chose to work with a different-colored pen, while only 12.5 percent of the people in the communal condition chose the pen of a different color. Apparently Clark was correct in predicting that people are concerned with their individual equity when they are in an exchange relationship but are concerned with joint rewards when they are in a communal relationship.

Let's look at another difference in the way people react to communal and exchange relationships. Imagine that an attractive classmate asks to borrow your class notes for some lectures he or she missed. Grateful for the opportunity to get closer to this person, you readily comply. The next day, your classmate returns your notes. You notice that there is an envelope attached. You open the envelope and find a warm note of thanks—and a $5 bill! Would you rather have the note with no money in the envelope or are you pleased as can be that you have earned extra money for your kindness?

According to a study by Clark and Mills (1979), your reaction would depend on the type of relationship you anticipated with your classmate. If you thought that you might have a communal rather than an exchange relationship with your attractive classmate, then you would prefer the envelope *without* the $5. Clark and Mills designed a study whose procedure is similar to the example we have just imagined. In the course of an experimental task, male participants were given an opportunity to do a favor for an attractive female with whom they expected to work in a later phase of the study. In response to the favor, the participants received a thank-you note that the woman had

Long-term relationships depend less on the reciprocation of kind deeds than on the partners maximizing the pleasure the two of them can share.

as the partners move toward maximizing the pleasures that the two can share.

Similarity and Attraction: I'll Like You If You're Like Me

People tend to like others who have similar attitudes and characteristics. Although there are some important exceptions to this general rule, the evidence linking attitudinal similarity to attraction is considerable. Much of the empirical research that links similarity of attitudes to interpersonal attraction has been collected in a systematic series of studies by Donn Byrne and his colleagues (Byrne, 1971; Byrne, Clore, and Smeaton, 1986). The basic work was conducted exclusively in the laboratory with a consistent procedure: subjects were first asked to fill out a twelve-item attitude scale. Some time later, they entered the laboratory and were asked to form judgments about a hypothetical person "on the basis of limited information." They were given an attitude scale to read that was supposedly filled out by another person. In fact, the attitude scale was filled out by the experimenter. Depending on the particular study, the experimenter could vary the degree of similarity between the hypothetical target person and the subject. At the end of the study, the subject was given a questionnaire to complete that included two items asking the subject how much he or she liked the target person. The results of many studies reported by Byrne and his colleagues show that people like the target when they share a high proportion of similar attitudes (Byrne and Nelson, 1965). These attitudes can be political, economic, or religious.

What, then, are the variables that affect the strength of the **similarity-attraction effect?** One of them is the importance of the similarity (Clore and Baldridge, 1968). If you are similar to someone on important items, you will be more attracted to that person. Touhey (1972) conducted a study in which he found some interesting differences between men and women in the attitudes they found to be important and, consequently, the attitudes that led to greater interpersonal attraction. He had college students volunteer for computer dates. He purposely matched couples on the basis of the similarity of their religious and

written. In half of the cases, the note included a comment that the woman was also giving the participant one of the credit-hours she had earned. In effect, she was rewarding the participant with the extra credit. In order to vary the kind of relationship that the male participant might contemplate having with the woman, half of the participants were led to believe that she was married, while the other half were led to believe she was single. Participants liked the single woman more when she did not reward them with extra credit. They liked the married woman more when she did. It appears that reciprocating kind deeds in a tit-for-tat fashion may work to strengthen relationships that are formal (exchange relationships) but weaken relations that are potentially intimate and communal.

In general, research on personal relationships implicates not only rewards that a person experiences in an interaction with another person but also the equity involved in the relationship. Longer lasting, intimate relationships evolve toward a concern for the total partnership. Record keeping diminishes in importance sexual attitudes. After the couples interacted, their attraction for each other was measured. Similarity of attitudes did predict attraction. However, women assessed religious attitudes to be most important. They were more attracted to men who shared their religious attitudes and were least attracted to men with dissimilar religious attitudes. For men, sexual attitudes were most important. They were more attracted to women who had similar sexual attitudes and least attracted to women with dissimilar attitudes about sex. The results indicate that similarity of attitudes does lead to attraction, especially when the attitudes are the ones the individuals feel are important.

A recent set of studies suggests another factor that many of us might not have included on a list of occasions in which similarity of attitudes is especially related to attraction. Greenberg, Pyszczynski, and Solomon (1997) have shown that the more people think about death and mortality, the more attracted they are to people who share their attitudes and views. In their **terror management theory,** when people are faced with reminders of their mortality, they seek symbolic immortality by becoming closer to people who are like them—who hold similar views, engage in similar behaviors, belong to similar groups, and so forth. The researchers found that having people simply answer a series of questions regarding their beliefs about death caused them to increase their liking for people who shared cultural identity.

Similarity Outside the Laboratory

In the neat world of the laboratory, the similarity-attraction effect has been fairly robust. The situation is constrained, and, typically, the person to whom you are similar is only hypothetical. Does the effect hold up outside the laboratory where the people are real and the relationships are ongoing? Although there has been some controversy (Rosenbaum, 1986; Wright and Crawford, 1971), there is evidence that the relationship does occur. Susan Sprecher and Steve Duck (1994) recruited eighty-three male and eighty-three female students and randomly paired them on "get-acquainted dates." They examined whether the get-acquainted dates turned into an intention to form more long-term relationships. The most immediate predictor of the intention to move toward romantic relationships was physical attractiveness, but close behind was the perceived similarity of the dating partners.

Several decades ago, when the threat of nuclear war was salient, several studies were conducted to assess the effects of living in underground shelters designed to protect people from nuclear fallout. Griffitt and Veitch (1974) were able to study people who had been living for days in such a shelter. Before entering the shelter, the participants had filled out an attitude questionnaire. After several days, they were asked to name the two people whom they would most like to keep in the shelter with them and also to name the two whom they would most like to evict. The results indicated that the people selected to remain in the shelter were more similar to the subject in their attitudes than the people selected for eviction.

Limiting the Effect: Similarity to Whom?

It is apparently true that being in agreement with people makes us feel pleasant and causes us to come to like the people who agree with us. However, this statement may have broader implications than common sense and some data would acknowledge. Might there not be people whose agreement with us would make us feel uncomfortable rather than pleasant? Lord Montague might be chagrined to learn that his attitudes are similar to those of Lord Capulet. If he learns that he agrees with Capulet about such issues as taxes, the king, and other political events in Verona, will he come to like Capulet as a result?

Novak and Lerner (1968) conducted a study that bears on this question. They showed subjects that their attitudes and general background were similar or dissimilar to those of a mental patient. In comparison with a group that received the same information about a "normal" stranger, people who found that they were similar to the mental patient liked him less than those who found that they were dissimilar to him. Cooper and Jones (1969) showed that subjects took great pains to dissociate themselves from an obnoxious person whose attitudes were similar to their own. In a like vein, when Karuza and Brickman (1981) varied the status of a confederate, they found that subjects like similar confederates if the confederates were of high status. But subjects did not like being similar to a low-status confederate. The conclusion that can be drawn from these studies is that attitudinal similarity does not always lead to attraction. The characteristics of the target person also play an important role.

Although there are limits to the effects of similarity, the research converges on the conclusion that, in

BOX 8.1

Similarity and Sharing in the Vampire Bat and the Ground Squirrel

Similarity of characteristics has significant consequences for humans, many of which are discussed in this chapter. People with similar attitudes find each other attractive, particularly if those attitudes are ones that people find to be important. People with similar physical characteristics are often attracted to others with similar characteristics.

In the rest of the animal kingdom, similarity has far-reaching consequences, but measuring it poses a problem. Infrahuman species cannot fill out an attitude questionnaire, and human investigators have difficulty rating animals' attractiveness. Genetic similarity, however, can be assessed with some rigor and precision. The degree of genetic similarity determines some interesting social behaviors, including sharing precious resources.

Consider the vampire bat. This inhabitant of Central and South America feeds on the blood of a host animal. Armed with two razor-sharp incisors, the bat attacks mammals and birds. In the dark of night, the vampire bat locates a sleeping and unsuspecting animal. It places its bite in the blood vessels closest to the surface of the animal's skin and drinks the precious liquid. The bat is aided by an anticoagulant in its saliva that prevents the host animal's blood from clotting, thereby keeping it flowing for long periods of time. This is fortunate for the bat, because this voracious creature must consume 50 percent to 100 percent of its own body weight in blood every night.

Vampire bats have a fascinating and complex social organization. Wilkinson (1990), in his careful and systematic observations of vampire bats in Costa Rica, noted that groups of eight to twelve female vampire bats tend to cluster together, protected by a dominant male. And these clusters may live together for as long as twelve years.

The tremendous amount of blood vampire bats need must be satisfied continually; if a bat goes for two nights without the requisite amount of blood, it will die. Some nights the bat may find a large host on whom it can feed, but some nights it may find only a bird or small mammal. The bats cannot store blood from night to night, so they use their "lucky" nights to help overcome the lean evenings.

What vampires can do, however, is share their meals with other bats. Through the use of special glands, the bats are able to donate some of the blood they have drunk to a recipient bat. However, their physical need for blood is so great that sharing must be done very selectively. Sharing with the entire social group or with other social groups would surely mean death to the bat.

So, with whom does the vampire bat share? Wilkenson found that vampires share only with their close relatives. Seventy percent of sharing occurred between genetically similar vampires, and the more similar the vampires, the more likely they were to share the precious resource.

The little ground squirrel of the Sierra Nevada Mountains of California also shows favoritism for squirrels that are genetically similar. While preparing for hibernation, a squirrel may spot a predator meandering nearby and may or may not take action to warn other ground squirrels foraging in the forest. The safest plan for the squirrel is to remain perfectly still. Sherman observed that a squirrel will sound the alarm if it shares any genes with the other squirrels. And the likelihood of the warning is a direct function of the genetic similarity: the greater the similarity, the greater the likelihood of the little squirrel standing up on its hind legs, risking its own safety, to sound the warning for the other squirrels.

Continued

BOX 8.1

Continued

It is both tempting and risky to conclude that squirrels and vampire bats manifest interpersonal attraction to their fellows as a function of similarity. Nonetheless, something akin to similarity and attraction seems to occur. How much meaning we should derive from these examples is the source of considerable debate, but the potential parallels to human social psychology are intriguing.

most typical circumstances, similarity is the best predictor of interpersonal attraction and close personal relationships. By and large, similarity predicts liking inside and outside the laboratory, in dating and in marriage (Johnson and Ogasawara, 1988). There are surely some occasions in which "opposites attract," such as when complementarily of needs causes people to come together (Winch, 1958) or when people are drawn to each other because of differences in their behavior (Strong, Hills, Kilmartin, DeVries, Lanier, Nelson, Strickland, and Meyer, 1988). Given the current accumulation of research, we can conclude that similarity between two people is an excellent predictor of liking and attraction.

An Evolutionary Perspective

Why should similarity and attraction be related? Several theories in social psychology that are consistent with the similarity-attraction effect have been offered. Newcomb's symmetry theory (Newcomb, 1956; 1968) certainly predicts that if two people feel positively toward the same attitudinal object, there will be a "strain toward symmetry" that will cause them to like each other. Moreover, if two people like each other, the strain toward symmetry will motivate them to feel similarly toward a particular attitudinal object. They may also be rewarded by the statements of agreement that each expresses about the other's attitudes.

From a biosocial, or evolutionary, point of view, the effect of similarity on attraction is not at all surprising. This approach to social behavior (see Buss, Larsen, and Westen, 1996) is based on Charles Darwin's theory of the evolution of the species and holds that social behavior is predicated on the reproductive success people have had over many generations. That which is adaptive to better human functioning continues; that which

is unproductive eventually disappears. Kenrick and Trost (1987) argued that the fact that people with similar characteristics or attitudes are drawn toward each other makes sense from the evolutionary perspective. Bringing together people with similar but not identical genetic characteristics is the most adaptive mating strategy for the entire human species.

When it comes to finding a mate, men and women often present themselves in ways that are consistent with what the opposite sex favors, as discussed in chapter 7. Buss (1994) notes that men are most attracted to women who are young and beautiful. These characteristics are desired from an evolutionary perspective precisely because they are heuristic, or short-cut, signs of child-rearing capabilities and interest. Women, on the other hand, focus more on resources, wealth, and prestige—heuristic signs that their offspring will be well provided for. Thus, according to Buss (1994), in mate selection, women accommodate to men's attitudes by enhancing their physical appearance from makeup to false eyelashes to breast implants. Men accommodate to women's attitudes by enhancing their apparent resources, displaying their gold Rolex watches and fancy cars (Buss, 1994).

Obviously, the similarity-attraction effect that we have been examining is broader and pertains to more situations than heterosexual mating. And a compelling case can be made that the differences between men and women in the way they approach dating and mating is governed by the way people fulfill their socially determined roles. Nonetheless, the biosocial point of view argues that the root cause of our preferring similar individuals—and the root cause of the differences between the way males and females respond to each other's attitudes and preferences—may derive from the adaptive evolution of the human species.

The Reciprocation of Liking: I'll Like You If You Like Me

There is strong pressure to reciprocate "liking." In the absence of other information, when someone likes you, you have every reason to like that person. There is a *norm* that suggests we should like those who like us, and knowing or anticipating that people like us probably puts us in a frame of mind to like them.

This norm may well help to account for the effect of similarity on attraction. Aronson and Worchel (1966) suggested that the similarity between us and another can cause an implicit assumption that the other person likes us. If we add to this assumption the norm that we should reciprocate liking, then we should like persons who are similar to us.

Aronson and Worchel put their explanation to the test by establishing a situation in which a similar or a dissimilar confederate was said either to like or to dislike the participant. In other words, similarity information was manipulated independently of the stimulus person's evaluation of the participant. The investigators found that attraction to the confederate was affected only by the information that the stimulus person liked or disliked the participant and not by information regarding similarity. It appears that if we are given explicit information about the way another person feels about us, then that information—rather than the person's similarity to us—is what causes us to like that person.

Indeed, if we know someone likes us, it may sometimes be more gratifying to know they are dissimilar to us along important dimensions—that they like us despite our differences. For example, Jones, Bell, and Aronson (1972) had each of their subjects interact with a confederate for several minutes. During the conversation the confederate expressed attitudes and opinions either opposed to or in agreement with those expressed by the subject. Later, the subjects were allowed to overhear the confederate tell the experimenter how she felt about the subject. Half of the subjects heard a uniformly positive evaluation; that is, they heard that the confederate liked them. The other half overheard the confederate confess that she did not like the subject. When the subjects were asked how they felt about the confederate, it was clear that the confederate was liked best when she both *liked* and *disagreed with* the subject. Although we are typically attracted to people with attitudes similar to ours, knowing that others like us despite differences may make us

feel particularly good, because the implication is that they see in us qualities that are so positive that they overwhelm the differences in attitudes and opinions.

We mentioned, however, that reciprocal liking was probably only a beginning point in interpersonal attraction. It will not account for an entire relationship—not the passion of Romeo for Juliet and not even the enduring friendship of two roommates over the course of a year. A study by Backman and Secord (1959) demonstrated the declining impact of the reciprocal-liking effect on a group of subjects who met as strangers. The researchers told each subject that personality tests they had taken indicated that specific members of the group were likely to like them. In fact, this information was bogus. The subjects were to meet six times for informal discussion groups, but the members were told that there was a possibility that each group would be broken into two teams. They were asked to indicate the members with whom they would like to be paired. The data showed that after the first session the subjects chose the group members who had been designated as likely to like them. But the effect did not last; after a few sessions the pattern broke down. Feedback from group members eventually superseded the information given by the experimenters. Initially, people were attracted to those who were expected to like them, but many other factors contributed to longer-term attraction. Apparently the "I'll like you if you like me" effect is short lived.

Ingratiation: A Special Case

Although it is usually true that we enjoy being complimented and react to compliments with liking (Skolnick, 1971), this is not always the case. When we are complimented, we would like to believe that the compliments are attributable to our good nature, our fine qualities, and so on. We are less than happy if we must attribute the compliments to an ulterior motive on the part of the complimenter. A person who acts in such a way as to enhance his or her image illicitly in the eyes of another may be said to be engaging in **ingratiation.** Edward E. Jones (1964; Jones and Wortman, 1973) and his colleagues have considered the problem of ingratiation at some length. Flattery has been conceived as one tactic that an ingratiator might use to raise his or her esteem in the opinion of others. The question is; Is such a tactic successful?

The answer to this question depends on the perceived dependence of the flatterer on the object of his or her flattery. If you think that someone needs or wants something from you, you are much less likely to feel attracted to that individual as a result of compliments she or he may pay you than you are to someone who has nothing to gain by complimenting you. Evidence for this point of view can be found in a study in which women students listened to an evaluation of themselves delivered by a graduate student who had been observing them through a one-way mirror (Dickoff, 1961). The graduate student (an accomplice of the experimenter) varied her proportion of compliments depending on which experimental condition the participant was in. The subject was either (1) complimented excessively, (2) complimented within the bounds of her previously measured self-esteem, or (3) given neutral feedback.

Dickoff manipulated whether the person giving the evaluation had anything to gain by making the participant like her. In the accuracy condition, participants were led to believe that the graduate student was trying to be as accurate and honest as possible. In the ulterior-motive condition, the participant was told that the graduate student was going to ask the subject to participate in one of her studies after the current experiment was concluded.

The feedback that the subject received strongly affected her evaluation of the graduate student. As figure 8.2 shows, increasing the favorableness of the evaluation increases the liking—up to a point. When favorableness turns to flattery, the evaluation of the flatterer depends on the subject's perception of whether the flattery is in the service of ingratiation. When the possibility of an ulterior motive is present, attraction decreases as the favorableness of the compliments increases.

These results present a double-edged dilemma. An ingratiator wishing to increase his esteem must conceal any possible ulterior motivation. If he or she cannot, it is best to refrain from excessive flattery. On the other hand, a person who genuinely feels that another is worthy of considerable praise may be penalized for the expression of those feelings if the flattery can be (incorrectly) attributed to an ulterior motive.

Propinquity Breeds Attraction— Sometimes

It's probably true that throughout your life your closest acquaints will live near you, that you will marry a person who lives close to you, and that the friends you make at work will occupy positions that are physically close to you. Bossard (1932) was one of the first

FIGURE 8.2   MEAN ATTRACTION SCORES IN DICKOFF'S STUDY

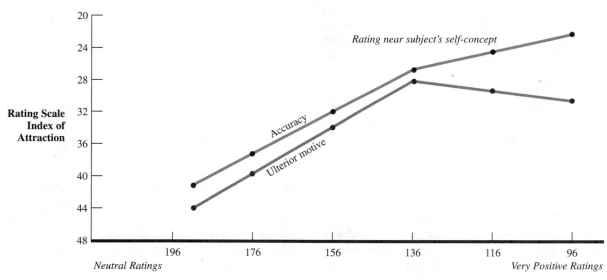

Source: Jones (1964)

FIGURE 8.3   RELATIONSHIP BETWEEN FUNCTIONAL DISTANCE AND LIKING

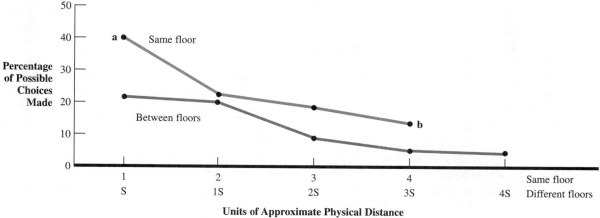

Source: Festinger, Schachter, and Back (1950)

to examine the importance of physical distance in mate selection for marriage. Examining five thousand marriage license applications in the city of Philadelphia, he found an inverse relationship between the number of such applications and the physical distance of the addresses of the two engaged partners—as the distance increased, the number of applications sharply decreased.

Perhaps the most systematic investigation of physical closeness, or propinquity, and attraction was conducted by Festinger, Schachter, and Back in 1950. Westgate West, a new housing project for married students, was constructed in the form of small two-story garden apartment complexes. Each unit contained ten apartments. New residents did not have a choice about which apartment to live in; they were assigned on a nearly random basis—that is, apartments were filled as they became vacant. Very few of the tenants knew one another before coming to Westgate West. After some time, all of the residents were asked which members of the complex they saw socially most often. The results are presented in figure 8.3. The distance between people on the same floor and on different floors was closely related to friendship patterns—the closer two individuals lived to each other, the more likely they were to be friends. Living on different floors (bottom line) reduced the likelihood of friendship because functional distance was increased. It is quite remarkable that 41 percent

of the next-door neighbors (a in figure 8.3) indicated that they got together socially whereas only 10 percent of the people at opposite ends of the hall (b in figure 8.3) mixed socially—especially since the maximum difference in distance between the closest and the farthest apartments on the same floor was only sixty-nine feet.

Nahemow and Lawton (1975) examined friendship patterns in an inner-city housing project whose residents were of various age groups and races. Consistent with the findings of Festinger and his colleagues, people of all ages and races showed an overwhelming tendency to have their best friends within the same building (an average of 93 percent). But within the same building, an interesting pattern emerged. For people whose best friends were of a similar age or the same race, the best friend was no more likely to be on the respondent's floor than on a different floor. In other words, age and racial similarity were more important in predicting friendship than the floor on which the friends lived. However, if the best friend was of a different race or age, then it was overwhelmingly likely that the person resided on the respondent's floor. Apparently, attraction in a housing project can transcend the boundaries of propinquity to some degree if similarity on an important dimension exists. In the absence of such similarity, attraction seems very much a function of physical closeness.

Explaining the Effect of Closeness on Liking

Reward. Why should propinquity lead to attraction? Why should people be more attracted to the people next to whom they live and work? One explanation is that we interact more with those who are near us and that such interactions are rewarding (Davis and Perkowitz, 1979; Werner and Latané, 1974). Newcomb has argued that "when persons interact, the reward-punishment ratio is more often . . . reinforcing" (1956, p. 576). That is, in normal everyday interaction, we are more likely to say nice things to others and to hear compliments in return than we are to say and hear negative things. So the more we interact with others, the more often we may be rewarded by them. Since it is thought that reward leads to greater liking, it would then follow that those who give us the greatest opportunity for frequent interaction would be rewarding to us and therefore would be liked by us.

Expectation. Those who are near us in our jobs, our houses, our dormitories, and so on are likely to be near us tomorrow and the next day as well. We expect to interact with them again and again. There is pressure to form a positive relationship with those with whom we constantly interact. Darley and Berscheid (1967) conducted an experiment to demonstrate that a person's expectation of interacting with another person induces a tendency in that person to like the other. College women expected to participate in a study in which they were to discuss sexual standards for female college students. Before beginning the discussion, a subject was shown information about two other women students, one of whom was designated as the subject's partner for the discussion. Although the information about each of the two was of approximately equal attractiveness, the subjects answered the question "How probable is it that you would like this girl better socially?" by picking their prospective partner 70 percent of the time.

Propinquity: A Reprise

Propinquity appears to lead to attraction in a variety of situations. This tendency may be attributable to (1) the fact that people near to us have more opportunities to reward us, (2) the expectation of future interaction with those who live and work near us, and/or (3) the phenomenon that mere exposure induces attraction. However, Berscheid and Walster [Hatfield] (1978) pointed out that attraction is not the only result of physical closeness. They cite an FBI report indicating that one-third of all murders are committed by a member of the victim's family. In addition, the FBI report indicates that "most aggravated assaults occur within family units or between neighbors." Detroit police statistics indicate that the majority of robberies are committed between family members or neighbors, and a recent New York City statistic showed that muggings are more likely to be committed by people who live in the same neighborhood as their victims than by people from different neighborhoods. One reason that social-psychological studies may demonstrate a liking-and-propinquity relationship is that the nature of the studies leads to a high reward/punishment ratio. People in housing projects, for example, do not have to interact in an intimate fashion. Nodding one's head, giving compliments, or politely agreeing with a political comment made by a neighbor while picking up the newspaper may lead to a large number of rewarding situations and an avoidance of negative situations. The possibility exists that one of the things propinquity does is to magnify the intensity of relationships regardless of direction. Consistent with this logic are data from a survey by Ebbesen, Kjos, and Konecni (1976) that showed that the majority of an individual's friends and enemies lived within the same neighborhood. Thus, physical closeness may have the effect of increasing both attractiveness and hatred depending on other factors in the situation. Determining those other factors may be the future direction of research in this area.

Mere Exposure and Liking

Have you ever thought about how fond you've become of a familiar possession, such as sweater? Have you ever thought about how much you like a familiar place or a familiar face? Robert Zajonc (1968) argued that the more familiar we are with almost any object—that is, the more we are merely exposed to an object—the more we seem to like it. This offers yet another explanation of the effect of propinquity on attraction. The closer we are to someone, the more we interact with that person, the more familiar that person becomes. And familiarity leads to attraction. We have separated "mere exposure effects" from the study of propinquity because the research on mere exposure, while relevant to propinquity, has covered a much broader spectrum of why we come to like others.

Let's look at some of the evidence. In one of the first studies on **mere exposure**, Zajonc (1968) showed participants a number of photographs of people. Some of the photos were shown often; others were shown infrequently. Later, subjects were asked how much they liked the people depicted in the photographs. People whose pictures were seen frequently were rated as more likable than people whose pictures were seen only once or twice.

Familiarity affects not only likability, as Zajonc's study demonstrated, but also perceptions of physical attractiveness. As depicted in figure 8.4, Langlois and Roggman (1990) used modern computer technology to digitize the photographs of the faces of thirty-two women. They then made a composite computer-image face that constituted the statistical "average" of the photographs. Volunteer subjects then rated all of the faces. The composite face was viewed as more attractive than any of the faces that comprised the composite. A few years later Langlois, Roggman, and Musselman (1994) extended the analysis of the original data from the Langlois and Roggman (1990) study. As we would expect from this discussion, Langlois and her colleagues concluded that the reason the original raters found the composite face more attractive was that it was perceived as more familiar.

You don't have to be aware that you are exposed to a stimulus for it to produce greater liking. This was implied in the work we just described but was made explicit in work by Kunst-Wilson and Zajonc (1980). They had subjects perform what is known as "dichotic listening task." Students were given earphones and heard a series of words in one ear. They had to match those words to words they were reading in a text that had been placed in front of them. In the other ear they heard a series of melodies, although the music was not referred to by the experimenter and seemed to have nothing to do with the task at hand. Later, subjects were asked to listen to a series of melodies and indicate whether the tunes were familiar and how much they liked each one. Subjects could not remember hearing any of the tunes, although several had been played through the earphones during the earlier portion of the experiment. Despite the fact that the students did not consciously recognize the tunes, they liked the familiar ones better. Thus, merely being exposed to the music without being aware of the previous exposure created greater liking. In a subsequent study, Bornstein and D'Agostino (1992) used a procedure much like Zajonc's original picture-viewing study except that the photographs of people's faces were viewed in a device called a "stachistiscope," which can present the pictures

FIGURE 8.4   AVERAGING FACES

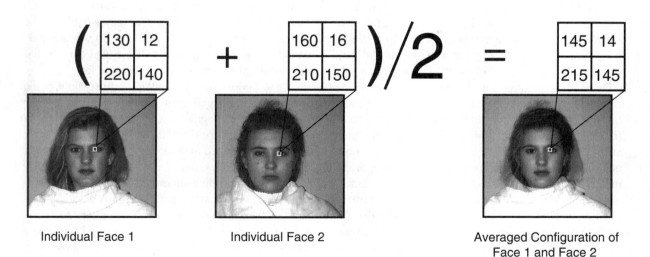

Individual Face 1   Individual Face 2   Averaged Configuration of Face 1 and Face 2

The faces are converted to digital numbers and then averaged together. The result is an averaged face that is the mathematical average of the faces that yield it. (Values are for illustrative purposes only.)

Source: Langlois and Roggman (1990)

FIGURE 8.5   RATINGS OF CONFEDERATE'S ATTRACTIVENESS AS A CONSEQUENCE OF THE NUMBER OF CLASSES SHE ATTENDED

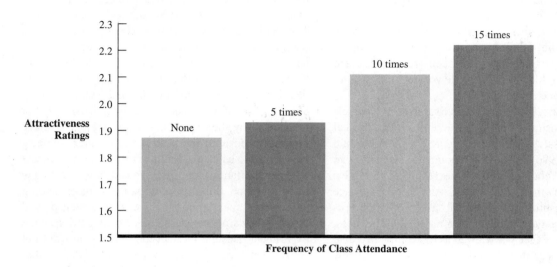

Source: Adapted from Moreland and Beach (1992), table 2

so rapidly that people cannot report seeing them. The perception is referred to as "subliminal," or below the level of awareness. Bornstein and D'Agostino found that subliminally presented photographs had an even greater effect on people's liking for the faces than did photographs that were presented more slowly such that people consciously perceived them.

Procedures like dichotic listening tasks, stachistis- copic presentation of stimuli, and the controlled pre- sentation of photographs are good experimental procedures that provide experimental control and con- vincing evidence. Nonetheless, they may seem a step removed from finding that the frequency of exposure causes interpersonal attraction in more naturalistic set- tings. Richard Moreland and Scott Beach (1992) recti- fied that in a fascinating study conducted in a classroom at the University of Pittsburgh. The study was con- ducted in a regular social psychology class of approxi- mately two hundred students. The experimenters arranged for four female confederates to attend the class at specified intervals. One woman attended the class frequently, showing up at fifteen of the lectures. She was instructed to sit in the front of the room, ask no questions or in any other way draw attention to herself, and leave promptly at the end of the lecture without making conversation with any of the other students. A second confederate came to class ten times, while a third

attended only five lectures. A fourth confederate only had her photograph taken but did not attend any lectures. Near the end of the semester, the social psychology stu- dents were asked if they would like to volunteer for a study in "social perception skills." One hundred fifty students participated. They were shown photographs of the four confederates and asked to rate them on what Moreland and Beach construed as an "attraction index." They rated: (1) the likelihood that they would like the woman and become friends with her; (2) whether they would enjoy spending time with her; and (3) whether they would like to work with her on a project.

In response to other questions, virtually none of the students could recall ever having seen any of the women in the photographs. All of the students said they did not know any of the women. Yet, when they were asked if they wanted to work with any of the women on a project, or if they would like to become friends or would enjoy spending time with the women, the stu- dents were significantly more likely to select the con- federate who had come to class more often. As figure 8.5 demonstrates, the woman who attended the lecture fifteen times was seen as most attractive, followed by the women who attended ten times. The woman who never attended class was found to be least desirable on the attraction index. These ratings were made despite the fact that none of the students could recall ever having seen the women whose faces were depicted in the photographs.

Let's examine one more intriguing effect of mere exposure: Exposure also seems to affect our attractiveness to ourselves! Think about that handsome or beautiful face that you see in the mirror several times each day. There is something a bit unusual about your perspective on your own face. It is the mirror image of what other people see. If Juliet had had a mirror, she would have seen a slightly different image than Romeo saw when he looked at her. Mita, Dermer, and Knight (1977) took note of this fact when they conducted a fascinating mere-exposure study at the University of Wisconsin. They showed college women pictures of themselves that were either their own mirror image (the perspective they had been used to seeing in the mirror) or an actual picture (the perspective that others have when looking at them). They showed the same two pictures to the students' close friends. The subjects were more attracted to their mirror image photos; the friends were more attracted to the actual photos. Apparently we are affected by mere exposure to ourselves. The view that is most familiar to us is the one we find most attractive.

Physical Attractiveness and Liking

> Beauty too rich for use. . . .
> . . . her eyes in heaven
> Would through the airy region stream so bright,
> That birds would sing, and think it were not night.
> [*Romeo and Juliet,* Act II, scene 2]

Shakespeare gives Juliet outstanding physical beauty. Surely Romeo's attraction to Juliet is partially based on her striking physical appearance. Social psychologists have studied the effect of physical attractiveness on interpersonal attraction. Their findings have shown that attractive people are liked better than homely people. Certainly, a good deal of the effect is romantic and sexually oriented, although we will soon examine some data that suggest two less obvious qualifications: (1) we sometimes prefer people who are no more attractive than we are ourselves; and (2) the observation that physical beauty is related to positive evaluations is not always sexually driven.

First, we should point out that it is well documented that physically attractive people are liked, especially as prospective dates. Recall that earlier in this chapter, in the section on similarity, we dis-

cussed the study by Sprecher and Duck (1994), who had students randomly paired for "get acquainted dates." In that study, it was found that similarity was the *second* most important reason for students wanting to pursue future dates. Physical attractiveness was the most important.

Speed and Gangested (1997) asked fraternity and sorority members at the University of New Mexico to rate the romantic popularity of their fraternity/sorority brothers and sisters and also to rate them on a series of dimensions including psychological, financial, and physical. They found that the best single predictor of romantic popularity was perceived physical attractiveness.

In an earlier study, Elaine Walster [Hatfield] and her colleagues (Walster, Aronson, Abrahams, and Rottman, 1966) arranged dates for subjects at a "Welcome Week" dance. Couples were paired randomly. Each participant was rated on physical attractiveness by a group of judges. At a break in the dance, the participants were asked how much they liked their partners. The researchers found that liking of the partner and desire for a future date were directly related to physical attractiveness—the more attractive the partner, the greater the liking.

We mentioned, however, that there are some interesting exceptions to the general rule. And, indeed, not all of the evidence indicates that people attempt to date the most attractive member of the opposite sex. The comment "She's out of your league" could be directed to an ordinary-looking man who seeks a date with the town's most beautiful woman. In fact, Walster and his colleagues did not expect the desire for a future date to be a function of attractiveness. Instead, they had predicted a "matching" hypothesis: people would choose partners who were about as attractive as they themselves were. However, these investigators realized that arranging the date at the dance did not replicate a setting in which people customarily find themselves. Usually a fear of rejection or failure might accompany an attempt to win the most attractive member of the opposite sex. In a subsequent study by Walster [Hatfield] and Walster (1969), subjects were led to believe that they would meet their prospective partners *before* the dance. They were then asked how attractive a partner they wished to have. With the fear of possible rejection reinstated, people chose potential dates who were about as attractive as they themselves were. Similar data have been collected by Berscheid and her colleagues (1971) and by Huston (1973).

Dating an attractive person, then, is something that is desired but may be tempered by fear of rejection or, as Hamilton (1981) has suggested, by experience with rejection. Research has also shown that when we are with people who are more attractive, it makes us feel less attractive (Thornton and Moore, 1993) and that in turn can cause us to feel bad about ourselves (Kenrick, Montello, Gutierres, and Trost, 1993). Gregory White (1980) has shown that there may be something beneficial about dating people whose physical attractiveness matches your own. He studied dating couples at UCLA at various points during their relationship and found that couples who were most similar in their physical appearance were the most likely to have fallen more deeply in love after a nine-month period.

It would be tempting to attribute the physical attractiveness phenomenon purely to sexual stimulation. But this is probably not the whole story. Consider some data collected by Dion, Berscheid, and Walster [Hatfield] (1972). They presented evidence that physically attractive people are perceived as being happier and more successful than less attractive people. They are also rated as having more socially desirable personality traits. And it did not matter whether a respondent was rating a member of the same or the opposite sex. Similar positive feelings have been found in young children who rated other young children (Langlois and Stephan, 1981). In neither case did sexual attraction seem to be involved.

Beauty and Performance: Altering Our Perceptions of Behavior

We have now seen that we do not always act rationally when physical attractiveness is concerned. We tend to like physically attractive people more, regardless of their sex or age. Not only do we like them more, evidence suggests we evaluate their behavior differently. We may be inclined to like the behavior of attractive people more than that of unattractive people or to expect better behavior from them. For example, Clifford

and Walster [Hatfield] (1973) showed fifth grade teachers a report card with information about a hypothetical student. Although all of the teachers saw the same information, the photograph of the student that was clipped to the card was varied so that either an attractive or an unattractive boy or girl was pictured. The teacher's assessment of the student's IQ and expected future level of attainment varied as a function of physical attractiveness. Although the test scores did not vary, an attractive child was seen as more intelligent and was expected to do better work than an unattractive child.

In another study, Landy and Sigall (1974) showed college students an essay that had been written by another student. The objective quality of the essay was varied to be either good or bad, and a photograph attached to the essay revealed that the writer was either attractive or unattractive. (Control group subjects had no photo attached to the essay.) The subjects were asked to rate the quality of the essay. It is true that objectively good essays were rated better than poor essays, but it is also true that essays written by attractive writers were seen as being of better quality than essays written by unattractive writers. And, as the results presented in table 8.1 indicate, the effect was somewhat stronger for the bad essay than for the good one. That is, an attractive writer who produced a poor essay was given an extra benefit of the doubt by the judges.

Alice Eagly and her colleagues (Eagly, Ashmore, Makhijani, and Longo, 1991) took a look at much of the evidence that had been accumulating and concluded that there is, indeed, a **beautiful-is-good stereotype.** Without being particularly conscious of making this inference, most people judge the actions of beautiful people as better, more well intentioned, and more likely to result in superior products than the behaviors of those who are not as physically attractive.

Paul Locher and his colleagues hypothesized that making the judgment that attractive people are especially worthy is automatic—that is, it occurs quickly and requires very little thought (Locher, Unger, Sociedade, and Wahl, 1993). They presented slides of male and female targets to male and female subjects. The target photographs had been rated previously by other undergraduates to be either high, medium, or low in physical attractiveness. The slides were shown for only one-tenth of a second, but subjects correctly assessed the physical attractiveness of the faces. Neither the sex of the subject nor the sex of the targets in the slides made any difference: Attractive faces were

TABLE 8.1 **SUBJECTS' RATINGS OF THE GENERAL QUALITY OF THE ESSAY IN EACH EXPERIMENTAL CONDITION**

Essay Quality	Writer's Physical Attractiveness			Total Mean
	Attractive	Control	Unattractive	
Good	6.7	6.6	5.9	6.4
Poor	5.2	4.7	2.7	4.2
Total	6.0	5.5	4.3	

Note: The higher the rating number, the better the evaluation of the essay.
Source: Adapted from Landy and Sigall (1974)

rated as more attractive than unattractive faces by everyone, regardless of gender, even though the exposure was merely for .1 second. The investigators had told all of the participants that the slides were of people applying for a managerial job. They asked the respondents which of the candidates would be better suited for the job. Subjects had no difficult rating the attractive faces as more suitable for the position. The beautiful-is-good stereotype apparently is invoked very quickly and probably automatically.

The Jury Is Out

Perhaps the most frightening situation in which physical attractiveness can affect judgments is a jury trial. A person's beauty is supposed to be extraneous to the evidence introduced in court. But if beauty affects liking and our attributions of personality and behavior, then it may also affect courtroom judgments. As legendary attorney Clarence Darrow wrote in 1933, "Jurymen seldom convict a person they like or acquit one they dislike. . . . Facts regarding the crime are relatively unimportant" (cited in Sutherland and Cressey, 1966, p. 442).

In a pioneering study, Landy and Aronson (1969) presented a case of negligent homicide to a simulated jury (student subjects pretending to serve as jurors). The defendant was accused of running over a pedestrian on Christmas Eve. The facts were identical in all cases. In half of the cases, however, the defendant was described positively (an insurance man who was going to spend Christmas Eve with his family), and in the other half he was described negatively (a janitor who was going to spend the evening with his girlfriend). Although the facts did not differ, the janitor was given significantly more years of imprisonment than the positively described defendant.

Landy and Aronson's study did not involve physical characteristics. However, Efran (1974) took this additional step. He asked subjects to decide the fate of a defendant in a college cheating case. Again the facts were held constant, but a photograph of the defendant attached to the written information was varied according to the condition of the subject in the study. Each photograph had been rated by a separate group as either attractive or unattractive. Physically attractive defendants were liked better, were judged less guilty, and received less punishment than defendants who were unattractive.

Why should attractiveness lead simulated juries to confer less guilt and punishment on a defendant? Sigall and Ostrove (1975) suggested that the reason may rest with the jurors' assumption that the attractive defendant is worthier, has greater potential, and is less likely to transgress in the future than an unattractive defendant. That people make this assumption was demonstrated in an earlier study by Dion (1972). In that study, judges attributed the transgressions of unattractive people to their stable dispositions, whereas they attributed the transgressions of attractive people to momentary circumstances.

If these are the assumptions that jurors make, Sigall and Ostrove argued, the assumptions should apply only to crimes that are not directly related to appearance. That is, if a person uses his or her good looks to put over a con game or a swindle, then the notion that an attractive person will not get involved in such activities loses its credibility. Sigall and Ostrove established a simulated jury to pass sentence on a defendant who was either attractive or unattractive. In a third condition, no information about attractiveness was provided. For half of the jurors, the crime was described as unrelated to the defendant's attractiveness. In this condition, the defendant burglarized a home of $2,200. For the other half, the defendant "ingratiated himself to a middle-aged bachelor and induced him to invest $2,200 in a nonexistent corporation." Presumably, the defendant's looks may have been a factor in this swindle.

The mean number of years of prison recommended by the jurors is depicted in table 8.2. As can be seen, the results strongly support Sigall and Ostrove's reasoning. The attractive defendant who committed a burglary was

TABLE 8.2   **MEAN SENTENCE ASSIGNED, IN YEARS (N = 20 PER CELL)**

| | Defendant Condition | | |
Offense	Attractive	Unattractive	Control
Swindle	5.45	4.35	4.35
Burglary	2.80	5.20	5.10

Source: Sigall and Ostrove (1975)

given far less punishment than the unattractive defendant or the defendant about whom no attractiveness information was provided. However, the attractive defendant who had ingratiated herself to commit the swindle was sentenced to more years in prison than the defendants in all of the other conditions.

Why Does Physical Attractiveness Lead to Liking?

Although the phenomenon has some limitations, the effect of physical attractiveness on liking seems robust. People seem to like those who are more attractive; they praise their behaviors and characteristics and find them less culpable for transgressions. What leads to this phenomenon? Why should rational human beings decide that people with more attractive physical characteristics are worthy of such praise?

First, it may be that people like attractive people for the status those people convey. We may have learned throughout our upbringing that people are impressed when we are with others who are attractive. Sigall and Landy (1973), for example, asked subjects to evaluate a man whom they saw seated with either an attractive or an unattractive woman. The man received far more positive ratings when he was seen with the attractive woman than when he was seen with the unattractive woman. Kernis and Wheeler (1981) varied both the level of association that a target had with a confederate and the attractiveness of that confederate. When the target was portrayed as being a friend of, rather than someone merely seen with, the confederate, the target was rated as being more likable and more attractive. If we are seen as attractive when we associate with attractive people, then attractive people become rewarding for us. It is reasonable to conclude then that we would come to evaluate attractive people highly.

A second principle that may govern the high regard given to attractive people comes from a study by Marks, Miller, and Maruyama (1981). These investigators asked people how similar several other people were to them on a variety of traits. Participants rated attractive people as being more similar to themselves. Could it be that there is a general tendency to view ourselves as being more similar to attractive than to unattractive people? Our positive regard for those who are attractive may be due not to their physical appeal but rather to their assumed similarity to us.

A third explanation for the positive evaluations given to physically attractive people is that there may be a kernel of truth in those evaluations. Perhaps physically attractive people do have more pleasing personalities, more varied social contacts, and more interesting friends. Perhaps they do differ from the unattractive in their ability to achieve and to perform. Reis, Nezlek, and Wheeler (1980) collected extensive notes on the social interaction patterns of attractive and unattractive people. Important differences were indeed found between the two groups with regard to the number of friends, the initiation of social contacts, and the number and quality of conversations. The lives of attractive and unattractive people do appear to differ in significant ways. Further research may tell us whether these differences support the hypothesis that there is indeed a good reason for the high ratings given to attractive people.

Finally, we should recognize the possibility that the positive characteristics of attractive people may actually be caused by our own expectations. Recall our discussion of the self-fulfilling prophecy in chapter 7 and, in particular, the experiment staged by Snyder, Tanke, and Berscheid (1977). In their study, male participants entered the laboratory and were told that they were going to be engaged in an initial "getting to know you" conversation on the telephone. Each participant was then given a photograph of their prospective phone partner. Half of the photographs were of a physically attractive woman and half were of a physically unattractive woman. Consistent with the stereotype, the investigators found that participants expected the attractive woman to possess more socially desirable traits. Then all of the participants actually engaged in the phone conversation with a female participant who did not know that the males had been given a photograph. Analyses of the phone conversations showed that men who believed that their phone partner was attractive acted in a more outgoing, animated, and charismatic way. Separate analyses of only the woman's half of the conversation found that women whose partner thought they were attractive actually reciprocated the enthusiasm and acted in a more sociable, outgoing, and friendly manner. Of course, the picture that the man had was *not* the picture of the woman to whom he was speaking. However, the man's expectation affected his behavior, which in turn affected the behavior of the woman. In the end, the attractive woman behaved as the stereotype suggested. But it was caused by the man's expectation, not the woman's characteristics.

For Whom Is Physical Attractiveness Important? The Role of Self-Monitoring

People differ in the emphasis they put on physical attractiveness, personal attributes, religious affiliation, interpersonal styles, and so forth as they choose the people with whom they interact. Are there systematic differences among people that are related to the degree to which they take physical appearance into account in choosing a potential romantic partner? Snyder, Berscheid, and Glick (1985) examined this question and suggested that the concept of **self-monitoring** may provide that systematic difference.

As you may recall, people can be classified on a scale of high to low self-monitoring. Some people pay careful attention to presenting themselves according to what they believe is demanded by the situation. They are particularly responsive to situational cues when they make decisions about appropriate behavior. And they tend to act more in accordance with what they believe is required by the situation than with what they truly believe or feel. Such people are con-

sidered high self-monitors. By contrast, low self-monitors are people who base their behaviors in social situations on their dispositions and attitudes, and not on what they think the situation demands. As we have seen, low self-monitors are more likely to demonstrate attitude-behavior consistency since they are usually more attuned to their own attitudes and less concerned with such distractions as making a good impression.

Since high self-monitors are more influenced by the appearance of a social situation, Snyder and his colleagues reasoned that they would be more inclined than low self-monitors to consider the physical attractiveness of a potential partner. Low self-monitors, on the other hand, would be more interested in discovering a potential partner's true attitudes and personal characteristics.

In an initial study, Snyder, Berscheid, and Glick (1985) gave male subjects at the University of Minnesota a choice of more than fifty files to examine. The files contained information on female students who could serve as potential partners for informal coffee dates at a nearby cafeteria. The subjects were known not to be involved with a steady romantic partner, so it was assumed that they would see the potential date as the possible start of a relationship.

Each file consisted of three pages. The first page consisted of information about the background, attitudes, and preferences of the particular woman; the second page contained some uninterpretable filler information; and the third page contained a photograph of the woman. The participants were able to spend as much time as they liked with as many of the files as they chose. Moreover, they could concentrate on any page of the file that they preferred—the physical information conveyed by the photograph on page 3 or the information about personal attributes on page 1. Observers

stationed behind a one-way mirror watched the subjects as they examined the files. One dependent measure was the degree to which participants looked at the first (personal information) page or the third (physical information) page. In addition, the subjects had to choose one of the women for a coffee date. Subjects were asked directly whether their choice was made more on the basis of the physical or the personal information.

The results were clear. High self-monitors were much more likely to pay attention to the photographs of the women than were low self-monitors. Low self-monitors were more likely to spend their time on page 1 information (personal attributes). Table 8.3 adds further support to the hypothesis by showing the subjects' stated major reason for their choice of a dating partner. Clearly, high self-monitors stated that they were influenced by physical attractiveness; low self-monitors were affected by personal characteristics.

In a second experiment, Snyder, Berscheid, and Glick (1985) constrained the male subjects' choice of a dating partner to two women. One was very attractive but had a series of unpleasant personal characteristics. The other was physically unattractive but had highly positive personal qualities. Subjects—selected so that they would be either quite high or quite low in self-monitoring—were asked to choose one of the women for an evening date at a local restaurant. Which partner did the subjects select? Of the low self-monitors, 81 percent chose to date the partner with the desirable personality and the unattractive appearance. Only 31 percent of the high self-monitors made this choice. By contrast, 69 percent of the high self-monitors chose the physically attractive woman despite her undesirable personality, while only 19 percent of the low self-monitors made this choice.

This finding also appears to apply to situations in which people are evaluating the compatibility of others. Glick, DeMorest, and Hotze (1988) had male and female subjects examine personality information and photographs of five women and five men from a nearby university. The subjects were asked to pair the men and women into couples that they thought would be "most compatible." They were led to believe that these individuals had agreed to go on a date with the person with whom they were most frequently matched. The results mirrored those of the study by Snyder, Berscheid, and Glick (1985). The pairings made by the high self-monitors reflected far more concern with physical attractiveness, whereas those made by the low self-monitors were based mainly on the personal characteristics of the target persons. Thus it appears that the differential emphasis placed on physical attractiveness between high and low self-monitors in their own relationships has a marked effect on beliefs about the foundation of compatibility in romantic relationships in general. High self-monitors think along the lines of physical attractiveness even when they make recommendations for other people.

In summary, we can say that while people may be interested in the physical attractiveness of a potential partner in a dating situation, high self-monitors are particularly concerned with this dimension. Their preoccupation with presenting an appropriate image in the dating situation leads them to focus on the physical dimension. They also assume that other people would act just as they do, and so their recommendations for dating matches are based on physical attractiveness. Low self-monitors are more concerned with personal qualities and attributes. Given a choice, they will trade physical beauty for inner qualities.

A Candle in the Wind: Some Negative Consequences of Beauty

Singer-songwriter Elton John's powerful metaphor, the "candle in the wind," captured the fragility and frailty of the human experience, even as that experience lit the way for others. John's award-winning lyrics that captured the essence of the tragic yet inspiring life of the late Princess Diana of Great Britain was originally written to lament the similarly tragic predicament of one of the world's most glamorous movie icons, Marilyn Monroe. Her mysterious suicide

---

TABLE 8.3   REASONS FOR CHOOSING A DATING PARTNER: INVESTIGATION

Stated Reason	Individuals' Self-Monitoring Category	
	Low	High
Personal attributes	15	3
Photographs	5	10

Note: Entries in this table are number of participants in each self-monitoring category who offered each type of stated reason for choosing their dating partner.
Source: Snyder, Berscheid, and Glick (1985)

at age thirty-six shocked the world and continues to intrigue observers.

> It seems to me you lived your life
> Like a candle in the wind,
> Never knowing whom to cling to
> When the rain sets in.

The lamenting lyrics of *Candle in the Wind* remind us that beauty, at least in the extreme, has its dark side.

Extremely attractive people are expected to be happier, more socially adept, and better adjusted emotionally than the rest of us (Archer and Cash, 1985). They also receive more positive feedback. But do these expectations have any negative consequences? Are these people under a great deal of pressure to conform, to be as good as such extremely attractive people are supposed to be? Furthermore, is the positive social regard that attractive people receive as believable as the same feedback received by people of more modest appearance? Recall our previous discussion of *discounting*. When people are extremely attractive *and* receive positive social feedback, they may discount that feedback. They may question whether the feedback was merely an attempt to flatter them because of their looks. Others who are told positive things have reason to believe what they are told and can use the feedback to develop a decent sense of self-esteem. It may be that, for highly attractive individuals, the ability to use social feedback, as positive as it may be, is limited. People as attractive as Marilyn Monroe may not be able to trust positive feedback. The ambiguity of the reason for positive feedback may cause anxiety and unstable self-esteem (Summers, 1986).

In one study that sheds some light on this proposition, subjects who rated themselves as extremely attractive and those who rated themselves as unattractive were asked to write creative essays (Major, Carrington, and Carnevale, 1984). The essays were supposedly rated by judges. The judges' evaluation of the subjects' work was always highly favorable. In half of the cases, however, the judges were said to be observing the subjects through a one-way mirror, while for the other half, the judge was unable to observe. The question raised by Major and her colleagues was: Who would be more likely to believe the favorable feedback? They predicted that attractive subjects whose work was evaluated by a judge who could see them would be less likely to believe the evaluation. This turned out to be true. Attractive men and attractive women were more convinced that they had done good work when their

physical attractiveness had not been seen by the judges. Attractive people whose work was praised by a judge who had seen them were less convinced that their work was really of high quality.

It seems that attractive people were less able to rely on feedback, since they believed that the feedback might have been influenced by their attractiveness. Physically attractive people may have difficulty building a clear, unambiguous image of themselves, and the result may be a sense of anxiety and uncertainty. Extreme physical attractiveness, then, seems to be a mixed blessing. Although it does lead to many social contacts and positive feedback, the very attractive person may be uncertain about the sincerity of that feedback, "never knowing whom to cling to when the rain sets in."

Another pitfall awaits us when we are compared with people more beautiful than we. As we noted earlier, others may perceive us as more physically attractive and likable if we are thought to be friends of someone who is physically attractive (Kernis and Wheeler, 1981). But what if this association is not really close? What if we just happen to be seen in either physical or temporal proximity to attractive others without the assumption that we share some kind of interpersonal relationship with them? Chances are we stand to suffer by comparison. Kenrick and Gutierres (1980) showed their subjects photographs of highly attractive people or rather unattractive people. Later these subjects were asked to rate the attractiveness of average-looking people. The results showed a "contrast effect." That is, the subjects who had been exposed to the attractive targets found the average-looking targets to be less attractive than did the subjects who had viewed the unattractive targets.

In the light of such findings, it seems reasonable to question the popular media's almost exclusive focus on exceptionally attractive and well-proportioned models whose faces and bodies monopolize the pages of such magazines as *Vogue, GQ,* and *Self.* Could such a bombardment of beauty affect the way we see and evaluate the more ordinary people who surround us? The answer appears to be yes. Doug Kenrick and his colleagues (Kenrick, Gutierres, and Goldberg, 1989; Kenrick, Neuberg, Zierk and Krones, 1993) showed both men and women slides of either beautiful nudes (from *Playboy* and *Playgirl*), average-looking nudes, or works of abstract art. Both sexes showed the expected contrast effect: average-looking nudes seen later looked uglier to subjects in the *Playboy* and *Playgirl* conditions. Moreover, men who were exposed to beautiful rather than plain-looking models reported loving their current mates *less*. This effect, it should be noted, does not implicate the viewing of erotica per se, since arousal serves mainly to intensify either attraction or revulsion. Rather, these findings seem to implicate the popular media in general, where the majority of the faces and bodies we see look like those of fashion models, body builders, and the like.

How to Win Friends and Influence People by Being Insulting and Clumsy; or, Perfection Has Its Costs

When Dale Carnegie sought to advise people on how to endear themselves to others in his book *How to Win Friends and Influence People,* he probably never dreamed of some of the less obvious and unusual facets of interpersonal attraction. Elliot Aronson and his colleagues have been active in exploring some of the more interesting situations that lead to attraction.

To Insult Is Divine

Earlier we saw that we generally like people who compliment us better than those who do not (see Skolnik, 1971; Sigall and Aronson, 1969; Tagiuri, Blake, and Bruner, 1953). However, this is not always true; after a while compliments can get boring. The doting husband who constantly compliments his wife on her clothing, makeup, and hairdo gets himself into a position where he is expected to be complimentary. His flattering statements, like the knee-jerk reflex, begin to lose their meaning.

Aronson and Linder (1965) sought to investigate the *sequence* of flattering and insulting statements that a person received. The best way to understanding their clever but complicated methodology is to imagine that you are the subject in their experiment. When you enter the laboratory, you are told that a second subject is expected. But since you arrived first, you will serve as the confederate in a study on "verbal conditioning." The experimenter tells you that the other subject will have a conversation with you and that she will then have a discussion with the experimenter, who will ask her what

she thought of you. Actually, you are told, the entire purpose of the discussion is to allow the experimenter to "reinforce" with the response "hmmmm" or "good" all plural nouns that the subject utters. You, serving as the confederate, are to count the number of plural nouns that are used by the subject (which you can hear over a sound system).

You may ask what this has to do with interpersonal perception. The experimenter has not told you the full story. In fact, the other subject is the confederate; you are not. The hoax is designed to force you to "overhear" evaluative comments made about you. The four conditions of the experiment vary in only the number and the sequence of the positive and negative evaluations you overhear; the positive and negative feedback are systematically varied over seven sessions. As depicted in figure 8.6, in the positive-positive condition, the seven sessions are devoted to flattering statements that the "other subject" makes about you. In the negative-negative condition, the other subject's statements are all derogatory and insulting ("She seems to be a rather shallow and superficial person"). In the negative-positive (gain) condition, the confederate begins by describing you as dull, ordinary, and so on, but by the fourth session she begins to change her opinion, and at the end she is describing you in very flattering terms. The positive-negative (loss) condition is the mirror image of the negative-positive condition. Here you are described in glowing terms at first; the fourth session marks the change from flattery to insult, and by the end of the study you are described with purely insulting comments.

At the end, the experimenter asks you for your "gut feeling" about the "other subject." The results of this question are shown in table 8.4. The most-liked person in the study is not the confederate in the positive-positive condition but the one in the negative-positive or gain condition. This is true even though over the course of the seven sessions the positive-positive confederate complimented you twenty-eight times without an insult, and in the gain condition she complimented you only fourteen times after delivering eight insults. The reverse is also true. Subjects liked a person who consistently insulted them better than they liked someone who began by giving them fourteen compliments and ended with eight insults. The latter effect, however, was not large enough to be statistically significant.

The Aronson and Linder study and a similar study by Mettee (1971) offer some potent advice about interpersonal attraction over time. The always perfectly complimentary husband may wonder why his wife flips for a guy who has always been insulting and belligerent and just once gave her an approving glance. Moreover, our doting husband should realize the bind that he has gotten himself into. On the one hand, he is at the mercy of the competitor with the single approving glance; but he dare not act disapprovingly himself, for if he does, he could put himself in the loss condition. That is, he would be liked less than if he had always been insulting.

Why should such an effect occur? Conceivably, the person in the gain condition may be liked because he is seen as more discriminating. In effect, he establishes credibility and proves that he is a discerning individual. To earn the praise of such a person who once insulted you indicates that you are really a good person. Another possible explanation is that the insulting person may upset you and cause some uncomfortable uncertainty about your self-esteem. But when he comes around to your side, that uncertainty is reduced. Aronson (1969) suggests that this produces a warm and pleasurable feeling—that is, it is rewarding—and therefore leads to greater attraction.

TABLE 8.4 MEAN LIKING OF THE CONFEDERATE IN EACH CONDITION

Experimental Condition	Mean
1. Negative-positive (gain)	+7.67
2. Positive-positive	+6.42
3. Negative-negative	+2.52
4. Positive-negative (loss)	+0.87

Note: Higher numbers indicate greater liking.
Source: Adapted from Aronson and Linder (1965)

Clumsiness Is Attractive: The Pratfall

In the early days of his presidency, John F. Kennedy was riding a wave of positive popular sentiment. But in 1961 came the Bay of Pigs fiasco—a U.S.-supported

FIGURE 8.6 FOUR CONDITIONS OF ARONSON AND LINDER'S STUDY OF THE SEQUENCE OF EVALUATIVE COMMENTS

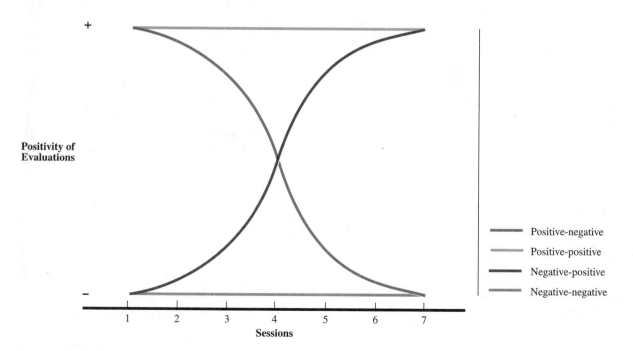

Note: Positive and negative feedback were systematically varied over seven sessions.
Source: Aronson and Linder (1965)

invasion of Cuba. At the last possible moment, Kennedy withdrew support for the incursion. He advised the American public of this and shouldered full blame and responsibility for the event, though many analysts believed that he could have legitimately transferred a major portion of the responsibility to his predecessor, President Dwight D. Eisenhower. And a good many of his advisers, with their eye on the 1964 election, wished that he had. Kennedy's political opponents had their hearts set on the forthcoming opinion polls, which they believed would show a dramatic loss of popularity for the president. The results were indeed dramatic, for they provided Kennedy with the highest ratings he was ever to receive during his presidency.

What could account for this surprising turn of events? Aronson, Willerman, and Floyd (1966) argued that a blunder, mistake, or error of judgment can be endearing in someone of extremely high competence. A man who seems to come from the land of Camelot—born to wealthy and influential parents; possessing superior intelligence, a likeable personality, and good looks; and married to a beautiful woman—may be viewed with great admiration, but such a man does not always endear himself to us. He may seem too perfect, too unapproachable. A mistake, however, is something of which we are all capable. A man who commits one has human qualities. If he is otherwise highly competent, a mistake can humanize him in our eyes and serve to increase our liking of him.

Aronson, Willerman, and Floyd (1966) designed a situation in which they could test their hypothesis. Subjects listened to a tape-recorded session in which a stimulus person was being interviewed for a spot on a college team that was to enter a quiz competition (the *College Bowl* television show). In one condition, the stimulus person was of extremely high ability. He was given a series of questions that he answered with a 92 percent score. During an interview, he said that he had been an honor student in high school, editor of the senior yearbook, and a member of the track team. The stimulus person on a second tape presented quite a different story. He answered only 30 percent of his questions correctly and said that he had received average grades in high school, that he had been a proofreader on the senior yearbook, and that he had tried out for the track team but failed to make it.

In half of the cases, both the competent and the incompetent stimulus person committed a clumsy pratfall. Near the end of the interview, a lot of shuffling

TABLE 8.5   **MEAN ATTRACTION SCORES OF THE INTERVIEWEE**

	Pratfall	No Pratfall
Superior ability	30.2	20.8
Average ability	-2.5	17.8

Note: The higher the number, the greater the attraction.
Source: Aronson, Willerman, and Floyd (1966)

was suddenly heard, and the stimulus person yelled, "Oh, my goodness, I've spilled coffee all over my new suit!" In the other half of the cases, the pratfall did not occur. At the end of the study, subjects were asked to give their impressions of the stimulus person by indicating how much they liked him. What results should be expected? In general, clumsy people are usually not liked as much as people who are not clumsy, and people who are as competent as the high-ability stimulus person tend to be liked better than incompetent people. But putting the two together presents a more complicated prediction. In the view of Aronson and his colleagues, the highly competent stimulus person was expected to be liked better, particularly if he had been the culprit in a clumsy accident. But the person of mediocre competence was not expected to benefit from his clumsiness. He had already demonstrated that he was far from perfect. Another example was hardly needed and could only work to his detriment.

The results of the study, presented in table 8.5, supported the predictions. For the person of superior ability, attractiveness increased when he acted clumsily, whereas the attractiveness of the person of average ability was markedly reduced when he was clumsy.

Social Psychology and the Study of Love

What is the experience of love? Attempts to express the meaning of love permeate literature. Shakespeare has Romeo explain:

> Love is a smoke raised with the fume of sighs;
> Being purg'd, a fire sparkling in lovers' eyes;
> Being vex'd, a sea nourish'd with lovers' tears,
> What is it else? a madness most discreet,
> (*Romeo and Juliet*, Act I, scene 1)

The "madness most discreet" drove Romeo and Juliet to their highest passion and consumed them in love's fire. We know, too, that love, like a diamond, has many intricate facets. In addition to the power of passion, of fire, and of discreet madness, love can be as deep as it is strong, as enduring as it is passionate.

You can imagine some of the difficulties studying the emotion of love. It is elusive to define if you are to encompass all of the shades of meaning contained in this powerful emotion. After defining it, you need to be able to measure it. Zick Rubin (1973) was perhaps the first social psychologist to attempt a definition and a measurement of this elusive and poetic concept. Rubin saw love as the junction of three important components: (1) caring—the feeling that another person's satisfactions are as important to you as your own; (2) attachment—the need or desire to be with the other, to make physical contact, to be approved of and cared for; and (3) intimacy—the bond or the link between two people, manifested by close and confidential communication.

Rubin then created a scale that could measure love. His scale was a self-report inventory in which people responded to items such as, "If I could never be with ____, I would be miserable." He also created a similar scale for the experience of liking. An example of a liking item is "I have great confidence in ____'s good judgment." Rubin showed that the two scales were independent of each other. A large group of respondents filled out each scale as they thought about romantic partners and friends. Romantic partners scored high on both the liking and the love scales, while friends scored high on only the liking scale.

Rubin then asked volunteer couples to come to the laboratory to participate in an experiment. The two partners were seated across a table from each other as they waited for the experiment to begin. Unknown to the partners, researchers were observing the room from behind a one-way mirror. They were keeping a close watch on the mutual glances that the partners gave to each other. Love, we have learned to expect, is associated with mutual gazing, looking into each other's eyes. And, as Rubin predicted, partners who had scored high on the love scale looked at each other more than partners who had scored below the median of the scale.

Dermer and Pyszczynski (1978) obtained evidence of the usefulness of the liking and love scales in a study of sexual arousal and romantic love. Men were shown either sexually arousing material or neutral control material. They were then asked to fill out the liking and love scales with regard to the woman they were most attracted to. Scores on the love scale were significantly higher for men who had been exposed to the erotic material than they were for men who viewed the control material. As predicted, sexual arousal did not affect scores on the liking scale.

Keith Davis (1985) conceptualized the intertwined components of love as a tapestry of elements woven together to form love's experience. Like very close friendship, love includes the partners' enjoyment of each other and their acceptance, trust, respect, mutual assistance, confiding, understanding, and spontaneity. But love has more, as you can see in the model in figure 8.7. In addition to all of the factors involved in friendship, love contains two other clusters of factors: passion and caring. Passion includes the concept of fascination: lovers tend to pay attention to each other even when they should be involved in some other activity. For example, a lover may not be able to concentrate on her or his homework because she or he is able to think only of the other. Passion also includes exclusiveness; that is, giving the romantic relationship priority over all other relationships in one's life. And passion includes sexual desire—wanting physical intimacy with the partner. The desire for physical intimacy may not be acted on if it conflicts with moral or religious values or because of practical considerations (such as fear of pregnancy), but the desire is there nonetheless.

FIGURE 8.7   LOVE AND FRIENDSHIP

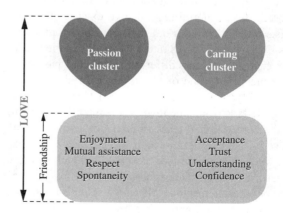

The initial model: Love is friendship plus the "passion cluster" and the "caring cluster."

Source: Davis (1985)

Love, according to Davis's analysis, also includes a caring cluster that has two components. One is "giving the utmost." Davis reminds us to consider O. Henry's famous short story "The Gift of the Magi." In that story, a man pawns his watch to get enough money to give his wife a set of combs for her beautiful long hair. Without her husband's knowledge, the wife has cut her hair and sold it to get enough money to buy her husband a gold chain for his watch. Each has given the utmost—and this is an expression of love. The caring cluster also contains the element of "being an advocate or champion" of the other, which is the notion that lovers will always take their partners' side in all disputes and see them as being able to do little wrong.

The caring cluster plays a very important role in the overall love experience (Davis and Todd, 1982). Fehr (1988) asked subjects to rate the importance of sixty-eight attributes to the experience of love. His subjects rated trust, caring, honesty, and friendship as the most important characteristics of love, while passion was seen as more peripheral. Similar findings were reported by Shaver and his colleagues (Shaver, Schwartz, Kirson, and O'Connor, 1987). As Berscheid (1988) has reminded us, we still have much work to do to discover how passion and lust interact with caring and respect to fill out a total picture of love.

The Feeling of Romantic Love

Our discussion of research on love suggests that love is multifaceted and that measurement of the experience is making significant progress. We have seen that several useful definitions of love exist as psychologists attempt to flesh out the necessary components that weave themselves into love's full experience. We have seen that across different viewpoints, passion, or romance, plays one of the key roles. Elaine Walster [Hatfield] and G. William Walster (1978) defined **passionate love** (romantic love) as the intense longing for union with another, reserving the term **companionate love** for the long-term, deeply affectionate attachment between two people (see also Hatfield and Sprecher, 1986). However, there is less consensus on just how many other elements or clusters of elements are necessary to describe and define love.

We now turn to the question, What accounts for the passionate and romantic experience? We can say that romantic love is characterized by extreme emotional intensity. It has emotional, behavioral, and chemical components (Liebowitz, 1983). It is experienced as a state of complete absorption in the other and often by the coexistence of a confusing panoply of feelings: tenderness and sexuality, elation and pain, anxiety and relief, altruism and jealousy.

Walster[Hatfield] and Walster (1978) adopted a theory we have encountered previously in this text to help explain the social-psychological factors involved in the experience of love. Recall Schachter and Singer's (1962) two-factor theory of emotions. According to that theory, emotion is essentially a union of physiological arousal and a cognitive label. That is, emotion involves both the body and the mind: general physiological arousal is combined with an interpretation of that arousal to create a particular emotional experience. So, too, with romantic love: according to Walster and Walster, it is a combination of physiological arousal and an interpretation that tells us this is love.

If romantic love is indeed based on arousal and labels, then anything that alters either the arousal or the label should affect the experience of love. At this point, the research literature is only suggestive—it can only give some clues about the degree to which passionate love is affected by the two factors. First, let's consider variations of arousal. Recall that Schachter and Singer (1962) as well as Dolf Zilmann (1978) and his colleagues had shown that if people are aroused and are not sure of the source of their arousal, then that arousal could be transferred or misattributed to other emotions to cause increased anger, humor, or aggression. White, Fishbein, and Rutstein (1981) had male subjects interact with an attractive or an unattractive female confederate. They altered the physiological arousal of the men in three unusual ways. Some men were asked to run in place, others were asked to watch portions of a Steve Martin comedy tape, and others were asked to watch portions of a grisly blood-and-gore film. In each of these conditions, physiological arousal was manipulated in ways that were quite independent of the attractiveness of the female confederate. The men were then asked to rate the attractiveness of that confederate. When the men were aroused in any of the ways that we just described, they found the attractive female more physically attractive than men who were not aroused. And what of the unattractive female confederate? She was perceived as uglier by the aroused men than by the unaroused men. Apparently the increased arousal led to increased feelings of attraction *and* revulsion. Although this study was not designed to measure love, the finding that systematic variations in arousal, regardless of the source of that arousal, could affect feelings of attraction (and its opposite) is an important link that is consistent with the two-factor theory.

Dutton and Aron (1974) conducted two fascinating experiments that lend further support to the two-factor theory. In one study conducted in the laboratory, male subjects met an attractive female confederate. Some of the males were anxious—they were anticipating being in an experiment in which they would have to undergo painful electric shocks. Other subjects anticipated no such shocks. The subjects were later asked how much they would like to date and to kiss the woman they had met. Subjects aroused through anxiety had a more intense desire to kiss the woman than those who had not experienced the arousing anxiety.

In a second study, Dutton and Aron took their research to a 450-foot suspension walkway that hangs some 230 feet above the Capilano River in British Columbia. An attractive woman approached male subjects as they traversed the 450-foot walkway. She asked them to help her fill out a questionnaire for her class. She also wrote down her name and phone number for each subject, inviting him to call. Did the physiological arousal that the subject was experiencing make the woman seem like someone he would like to be with? These subjects' responses were compared to those of other men of whom the woman made a similar request on a low, solid bridge. Men approached on the high, wobbly bridge were much more likely to call than men who were approached on the solid bridge. Men whose hearts were beating faster high above the Capilano were likely to interpret their arousal as romantic.

"From the Cradle to the Grave": Love and Styles of Attachment

The literature on passionate and companionate love has been paralleled by recent research with roots well within the traditions of developmental psychology. Psychologists are now coming to see that the way in which adults relate to each other and the patterns with which they love each other are established within the first years of life. Our ability to love and our choice of whom to love are strongly influenced by the styles of interpersonal attachment that occurred between us and our earliest caregivers—usually our parents.

John Bowlby, a British developmental psychologist, had been asked by the World Health Organization to study the mental health of the homeless children of London. The observations resulting from this project became the basis of **attachment theory** (Bowlby, 1973). Bowlby speculated that attachment patterns not only characterize the way children relate to their parents but that variations in those patterns stay with us "from the cradle to the grave" (Bowlby, 1979). Cindy Hazan and Philip Shaver (1994) adapted Bowlby's speculation and applied it to the study of love. In their approach, the styles of attachment we learn as children become one of the three central components of the way in which we, as adults, form meaningful relationships with each other.

As figure 8.8 depicts, the prototypical close relationship between two intimate adults is a function of three systems: one is the sexual system with its concomitant feelings of excitement and physical gratification; another is care giving, which is a desire to protect the other, to offer comfort and to receive the same from the partner. What differentiates Hazan and Shaver's model from other models of love is the special attention focused on the third system—the system of attachment.

Developing Attachment

Attachment is the emotional bond between two people that keeps them close both physically and emotionally. Attachment, as Bowlby conceptualized it, has an evolutionary basis. Because of the prolonged dependency of the human infant on its caregiver, there was a greater survival rate for those who maintained close proximity to the caregiver than those who did not. The absence of the caregiver activates an inborn fear in the infant, a free-floating anxiety that is quieted only by the caregiver's return. The mere physical proximity of the mother, father, or caregiver comforts the infant. Having a caregiver close by makes the infant feel secure, confident, and loved. The infant comes to learn to trust the caregiver and to tolerate short separations because the infant comes to expect that the caregiver will return. The infant can comfortably explore his or her environment because it comes to feel secure in its relationship with the caregiver.

The world of the caregiver-infant relationship is not always so rosy, however. Some caregivers are unreliable or unresponsive, some are less caring, while others are anxious and overprotective. Such caregiving styles derail the infant's quest for security and halt the trust and confidence an infant has in relationships with others.

FIGURE 8.8   THE COMPONENTS OF A PROTOTYPICAL PAIR BOND IN HAZAN AND SHAVER'S MODEL OF ATTACHMENT

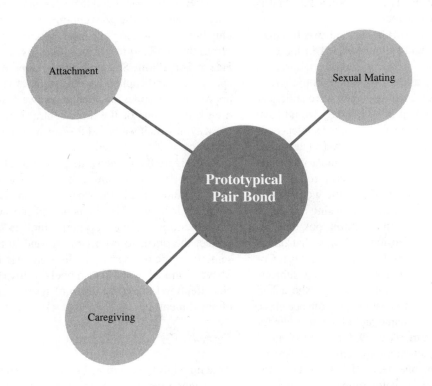

Source: Hazan and Shaver (1994)

Mary Ainsworth and her colleagues (Ainsworth, Biehar, Waters and Wall, 1978) developed a typology of attachment styles that characterize the way infants interact with their caregivers. Developed in the metaphorical "cradle," the attachment styles continue into adulthood relatively unchanged and affect adult love relationships. Dozens of children were studied as they interacted with their parents in their homes and in the laboratory. The researchers developed a technique called "Strange Situations" in which young children were observed playing in the presence of their mother. After a brief period of time, a stranger appeared, and the mother left the room but returned just a few minutes later. The researchers paid close attention to the child's reaction not only during the separation period but also during the period after the mother's return to the playroom. Three overall types of attachment styles were identified:

1. *Secure.* For secure infants, the mother's departure distressed the child momentarily, but the child was easily comforted on her return. The child was happy, exploring its environment with comfort and curiosity.

2. *Avoidant.* Avoidant infants tended to avoid contact with their mother, keeping their attention on the toys in the room. When the mother left the room, avoidant infants seemed not to be disturbed. When observed at home, these children were often ignored by their parents, who typically ignored or deflected the child's desire for close physical contact.

3. *Anxious/ambivalent.* In the homes of anxious/ambivalent children, the typical caregiver was inconsistent toward the infant. Sometimes the caregiver responded to the child's need for closeness and attention; sometimes, the child was ignored. In the laboratory, anxious/ambivalently attached infants were observed to be angry and anxious. They were so preoccupied with whether the caregiver was present that they would not allow themselves to play or explore their environment.

Taking Your Attachment Style into Adult Life

The attachment model of love, depicted in figure 8.8, holds that long-term, loving relationships depend on feelings of attachment as much, if not more, than they depend on sexual passion and the interpersonal response of "caregiving." Consider the graph in figure 8.9. It represents Hazan and Shaver's (1994) notion of the importance of the three systems over time. In the beginning, the sexual passion is strong and immediate. This is followed in time by the degree to which the two partners care for each other's needs. But as time proceeds, a couple looks toward each other as a source of comfort and security. The two bond for emotional satisfaction and safety. This is the emotional bond of attachment and becomes the most important and intense feature of a long-lasting love relationship. In a good re-

lationship, each member of the pair is secure in the responsiveness, the tenderness, and the trust of the other. Such trust leads to more open communication, more self-disclosure, and greater intimacy.

Not everyone is lucky enough to emerge from childhood with a secure attachment style. According to research by Campos and his colleagues (Campos, Barrett, Lamb, Goldsmith and Sternberg, 1983), about 60 percent of North Americans have secure attachment styles. Anxious/ambivalent attachment styles characterize approximately 25 percent of North Americans and 15 percent comprise the avoidant style. Research shows that people with secure attachment styles typically have the most stable and positive sense of self-esteem (Mikulincer, 1995) and experience the greatest happiness, friendship, and trust with their romantic partners (Hazan and Shaver, 1994). Avoidant persons are pessimistic about love, feeling

A secure child can play happily—with comfort and curiosity—with or without the close or active presence of a caregiver.

FIGURE 8.9   **THE DEVELOPMENTAL COURSE OF A PROTOTYPICAL ADULT ATTACHMENT RELATIONSHIP IN TERMS OF THREE BEHAVIORAL SYSTEMS**

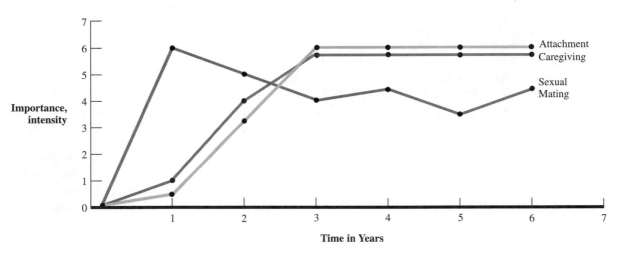

that it rarely lasts. Anxious/ambivalent adults report falling in and out of love easily. They are more likely to feel jealous and have periodic highs and lows in their relationships.

Which attachment style are you? Hazan and Shaver (1987) developed a simple, self-report inventory to determine a person's attachment style. A respondent reads a description of the three styles and chooses the one that seems closest to describing him or her. You might want to assess your own style by choosing one of the following:

1. I find it relatively easy to get close to others and am comfortable depending on them. I don't often worry about being abandoned or about someone getting too close to me.
2. I find that others are reluctant to get as close as I would like. I often worry that my partner doesn't really love me or won't want to stay with me. I want to get very close to my partner, and this sometimes scares people away.
3. I am somewhat uncomfortable being close to others; I find it difficult to trust them completely, difficult to allow myself to depend on them. I am nervous when anyone gets too close, and often love partners want me to be more intimate than I feel comfortable being.

Choosing the first of these puts you in the secure group, the second puts you in the anxious/ambivalent group and the third classifies you as avoidant.

Using this procedure, Tidwell, Reis, and Shaver (1996) asked student volunteers to fill out the attachment-style questionnaire and keep careful diaries of their social interactions for a week. Respondents with secure attachment styles indicated high levels of intimacy and enjoyment with their peers during the week. Consistent with attachment theory, avoidant subjects reported the lowest levels of intimacy and enjoyment in their relationships, especially in opposite-sex interactions. Anxious-ambivalent respondents were more volatile during the week, showing the most extreme highs and lows of all of the respondents.

Thus, finding a partner, entering a relationship, and having it last over time is a function of several factors, including styles of attachments. Attachment styles can and do change with important events that occur in the course of living (Reis and Patrick, 1996). Nonetheless, people's attachment styles show a pattern of consistency across the span of childhood (Elicker, England, and Stroufe, 1992) and adulthood (Kirkpatrick and Hazan, 1994) and even across generations within families (Benoit and Parker, 1994). These patterns, learned in the earliest years of life, endure and continue to influence our romantic long-term relationships.

When Relationships Go Sour: Losing That Loving Feeling

If the story of Romeo and Juliet had worked out differently, would they have lived happily ever after? Is it possible that the love they shared could have faded or that something could have come between them so that their marriage, like those of more than half the American population and 40 percent of the Canadian population, would have ended in a divorce?

How can we predict which relationships are likely to last and which are likely to weaken and dissolve? The factors that predict strong love relationships also predict the length and strength of satisfaction in a relationship. For relationships to last, they must meet people's needs. We know from our previous discussion that those needs include sexual passion, attachment, caring, and most likely intimacy and trust. Sexual passion may be the strongest force initiating a love relationship (recall figure 8.9). But research suggests that sexual passion decreases moderately over time (Acker and Davis, 1992; Tucker and Aron, 1993). If sexual passion decreases in importance, then there must be a strong base of attachment, caring, intimacy, and trust. In many relationships, initial physical attraction may have blinded lovers from noticing that their passion was unaccompanied by strength in other clusters such as attachment and caring. Without the emotional bonds, the security and the caring, relationships will suffer strain and be threatened with dissolution. The converse is also true. A relationship may move toward caring and attachment and provide too little passion for at least one of the partners; such a relationship is also likely to suffer strain.

Jealousy: Reacting to Threat in a Relationship

Jealousy is a potential emotional consequence whenever a relationship is formed. Losing your partner, or the possibility of losing your partner, creates a complex of emotions, thoughts, and behaviors that can be devastating. Jealousy seems to be a unique emotion that is more intense than the waning of romance over time. It is a cousin to anger, but its causes and consequences are unique. White (1981) proposed that romantic jealousy is based on two losses: first, the loss of rewards that a partner enjoys in the relationship; second the blow to self-esteem that occurs at the idea of rejection by the romantic partner.

In support of White's proposal, Mathes, Adams, and Davies (1985) described five scenarios to students at Western Illinois University. They were asked to imagine that they just lost their boyfriend or girlfriend

to a rival or to plain rejection (your partner decides he or she does not love you anymore), or to destiny (your partner moves to a faraway city), or to fate (your partner is killed in an automobile crash.) Other students were assigned to a no-loss control condition. Mathes and his colleagues reasoned that all of the loss conditions shared one common element: they all deprived the person of the rewards that he or she had enjoyed from being in the romantic partnership. But the rival and rejection conditions should be very damaging to the person's self-esteem. Losing a partner because the partner had to take a job in another city is mildly relevant to self-esteem, whereas the fate condition does not involve self-esteem at all. Mathes and his associates found that the emotion of jealousy was indeed greatest at the loss of a partner to a rival and least at the loss of a partner to a fatal accident. Jealousy does seem to depend, not only on the loss of the rewards that the relationship held for the person, but also on the magnitude of the blow to self-esteem.

Responses to Dissatisfaction

How do people usually respond to relationships that are becoming unsatisfying? Singer/songwriter Paul Simon wrote, "There must be fifty ways to leave your lover." Actually, research has identified two.

Caryl Rusboldt and her colleagues (Rusboldt and Zembrot, 1983) embarked on a systematic look at the way in which people respond to the potential dissolution of relationships. In one study, they asked twenty-five male and twenty-five female students at the University of Kentucky to describe a time when they became dissatisfied with a romantic relationship. In a second study, the same request was made of eighteen residents of Lexington, Kentucky, who ranged in age from twenty to sixty-seven. Their responses were analyzed and found to fit into four major categories: two for leaving and two for staying.

One response to a dissatisfying relationship is to *exit*. Reactions of this type were actively destructive to the relationship. "I told him I couldn't take it any more, and that it was over," and "I slapped her around a bit, I'm ashamed to say," were examples of the exit reaction.

Another way of responding to dissatisfaction was similarly destructive to the relationship's continuation. Unlike the exit response, this reaction is passive. Rusboldt and Zembrot call it *neglect*. "I guess I just kind of quit—I didn't try to salvage it—I just didn't know what to do," and, "Mostly my response was si-

BOX 8.2

Jealousy Caused by Sex and Jealousy Caused by Emotion: Can It Be Evolution?

Emergency Service (911) is flooded with calls, usually from women, about domestic violence as spouse and partner abuse occur in ever-increasing numbers. Women are threatened with physical violence, endure pain and suffering, and risk death. The leading cause of such abuse against women is male sexual jealousy (Daly and Wilson, 1989). Women also experience jealousy but are not as likely to respond violently.

Men and women not only manifest their jealousy differently, but the causes of their jealousy also differ. **Jealousy** always involves potential loss of a partner, anger at the (real or imagined) betrayal, and threats to self-esteem (Mathes, Adams, and Davies, 1985). But the kinds of threats and loss that lead to jealousy in men differ in interesting ways from what precipitates jealousy in women, sparking a debate about the reason for the differences. Might the differences be based on biosocial or genetic factors that characterize the human species through the process of evolution?

Evolutionary theory considers the following observation: Because fertilization occurs internally in women, men can never be completely confident in their parenthood. This persistent uncertainty has been codified in different colloquial phrases, such as "mama's baby, papa's maybe" (Buunk, Angleitner, Oubaid, and Buss, 1996). Therefore, the mere possibility of sexual infidelity causes great distress in men. From an evolutionary perspective, women are absolutely certain that they are the parent of their offspring but throughout history they have faced a different set of adaptive problems. The survival of children was greatly enhanced by the resources, energy, commitment, and overall parental investment of men. Women, therefore, were dependent on retaining men's interest and their resources and were thus more provoked by their *emotional* investment in other women. Buss, Larsen, Westen, and Semmelroth (1992) measured the physiological arousal and assessed the self-reports of men and women who were asked to imagine their partner's infidelity. As predicted, they found that men were more upset by imagining the *sexual infidelity* of their romantic partner, whereas women were more upset by imagining *emotional infidelity* than sexual transgression. Cross-cultural analysis suggests that such gender differences in sexual jealousy exist in a wide range of Western cultures (Buunk, et al., 1996).

Although gender differences in what provokes the most jealousy are consistent with evolutionary theory, there may well be other factors that exist within the environment that cause men and women to be more upset by sexual or emotional infidelity, respectively. One explanation for the gender difference in sexual jealousy is based on how men and women have learned to interpret the relationship between emotional and sexual infidelity. Emotional infidelity can suggest sexual infidelity, and sexual infidelity may signal emotional infidelity. Recent evidence suggests that men and women differ in their assumptions regarding the conditional probabilities, or co-occurrence, of emotional and sexual infidelity. Women believe that emotional infidelity is often accompanied by, and implies, sexual infidelity. That is, women believe that men often engage in sexual activity without being in love, but a man who is in love with a woman is almost certainly having sex with that woman. Therefore, emotional infidelity is particularly distressing for women because it implies that *both* forms of infidelity are being perpetrated. Men, on the other hand, are particularly distressed by sexual infidelity,

Continued

BOX 8.2

Continued

because they believe that women may often be in love without having sex, but if a woman is having sex, then she is likely to be in love with the man that she is having sex with. Here men are more distressed by sexual infidelity because it signals a double dose of infidelity. Consistent with these predictions, studies by both Harris and Christenfeld (1996) and DeSteno and Salovey (1996) found that female participants felt that love implied sex more than sex implied love, whereas men showed the reverse pattern. These authors suggest that men's and women's beliefs in the casual relationship between sex and love accounts for the differences found in the type of jealousy that is most easily provoked in the sexes. These theorists hold that the gender differences are products of culture and learning rather than the products of evolved characteristics.

Buss, Larsen, and Westen (1996) carry the debate further. They argue that men and women have different beliefs in the relationship between sexual and emotional infidelity because such differences are true. And they are true because biological differences have made them so. From an evolutionary viewpoint, both sexes have an investment in maintaining the species—especially producing and caring for offspring. As a result, men really do care about their number of partners and frequency of sexual intercourse. Because of their minimal parental commitment required by their biology, the evolutionary view holds that the species benefits from men's pursuit of casual sex without commitment or involvement. Because of women's heavy obligatory investment in offspring (from fertilization to gestation to lactation), they tend to be more discriminating in the selection of partners and to focus on long-term consequences and signs of commitment, such as emotional involvement. Townsend (1995) found that 76 percent of men, but only 37 percent of women, answered yes to the ques-

tion "Have you ever continued to have sex on a regular basis with someone you did not want to be emotionally involved with?" In addition, men prefer to have, on average, four times as many sexual partners in their lifetime as women do (Buss and Schmitt, 1993).

An ingenious study by Clark and Hatfield (1989) demonstrated the differential receptivity of men and women to sexual requests. The researchers had an attractive female and an attractive male approach members of the opposite sex at a local bar. After a few minutes of polite conversation, the confederate asked one of three questions: "Would you go out on a date with me tonight?"; "Would you go back to my apartment with me tonight?"; "Would you have sex with me tonight?" Fifty percent of both the women and the men agreed to go on the date. On the other two questions, the reaction of the men and women differed markedly. Whereas only 6 percent of the women agreed to go back to the man's apartment, 69 percent of the men agreed to go back to the woman's apartment. Finally, not a single woman offered a positive response towards the request for sex; 75 percent of the men, on the other hand, jumped at the chance to have sex with the woman.

The data on the differences between men and women in their experience of sexual versus emotional jealousy are substantial. So, too, are the differences between men's and women's attitudes about casual sex and emotional involvement. What the differences mean, however, is the crux of the debate. At this point in the study of sexual differences in jealousy, the data cannot be used to prove either an evolutionary or cultural learning explanation. Generating an evolutionary argument that is consistent with the data does not prove that biological differences in the evolution of the human species caused the different responses to jealousy. The evolutionary analysis is provocative and interesting; proof of its validity must await further testing.

lence to anything he might say, ignoring him," were examples of the neglect approach.

Alternatively, people who were dissatisfied with a relationship may act to salvage that relationship. Some of Rusboldt and Zembrot's respondents used the *voice* reaction. These people took active measures to try to make things better. "We talked it over and worked things out" was typical of this approach. And, finally, some people answered with a variety of *loyalty* responses. In general, these were reactions that tried to keep the relationship going but in a passive manner. "I loved her so much," said one student, "that I ignored her faults." "I prayed a lot," said another, "and left things in God's hands."

Why would people stay in a relationship that they no longer enjoy? One reason to stay is the hope that the relationship will improve. Hope, though, is rarely enough. Threatened with the dissolution of a relationship, people may go about the hard work of satisfying the unmet needs. The more commitment the couple can make to the relationship, the more likely its eventual success (Acker and Davis, 1992; Whitely, 1993). Renewing a commitment and working toward greater satisfaction would likely characterize those couples who use Rusboldt and Zumbrodt's "voice" response.

Of the 50 percent of marriages that persevere in the United States and Canada, has love persevered as well? Glenn (1991) studied a large number of couples who married in the year 1972. He found that only 25 percent were still happy in their relationships. Why do people stay in relationships that are not satisfying? Constraints such as embarrassment, children, and religious or social or financial pressures that inhibit the breakup of a relationship may be too great, causing the pair to remain together despite dissatisfaction (Stanley, 1986). An unsatisfying relationship may also endure if a better alternative is not present or expected in the near future. As alternatives become more readily available, then at least one partner may be ready to dissolve the relationship if it is not satisfactory (Drigotas and Rusbult, 1992).

Low expectations may also cause an unsatisfying relationship to continue. Individuals who have a history of relationships lacking in trust may not anticipate more from the relationship and thus will remain. Finally, people may anticipate considerable anxiety from attempting to leave a relationship. According to Hazan and Shaver (1994), anxiety can activate attachment behaviors that lead one back to the relationship. This seems to be especially true of people with anxious/ambivalent attachment styles, who never felt se-

cure with their caregivers and who, as adults, feel insecure about the stability of love.

There is an interesting converse to the anxiety people feel about leaving a relationship. If anxiety is heightened by the prospect of the ending of a relationship, is it reasonable to expect that anxiety will be lessened by the presence of a romantic partner? According to research by Brooke Feeney and Lee Kirkpatrick (1996) at the College of William and Mary, the answer seems to be yes—provided the person has a secure attachment style. Feeney and Kirkpatrick asked thirty-five women who had been dating their current male partner for at least three months to come to the laboratory with partners. The women completed a questionnaire that assessed their attachment style. Physiological recording equipment was attached to each participant to take their blood pressure and other measures of anxiety, and they were then given their experimental task. Each woman was asked to do an arithmetic problem in which she was to count backward by thirteen from a randomly selected four-digit number. The participants did the task twice: once in the presence and once in the absence of their romantic partner. The physiological measures showed that, indeed, in the presence of their romantic partners, anxiety was reduced when the romantic partner was present—but only for women who were secure in their attachment style. For women who were not secure, a heightened feeling of anxious arousal occurred regardless of whether their dating partner was present; his company did not reduce his partner's anxiety.

The Irony of the Attachment Motive

We have seen that the need for attachment provides a powerful motive for finding a relationship and that attachment may prove to be the most enduring aspect of the relationship. Ironically, the need for attachment may cause some people to enter into a relationship that is wrong for them, thus foreshadowing an unhappy, unsatisfying union. People whose attachment styles are of the anxious/ambivalent type are fearful that loving relationships are impossible to find or to rely on. As children, anxious/ambivalent types became furious when their mothers left their sight and became overly vigilant of the mother when she was present. They were unable to enjoy their play and unable to explore their environment because of their worry of losing their mother's attention. As adults, anxious/ambivalent types feel the same panic about not having closely bonded relationships or losing them if they attain them. They are too likely to seize upon a relationship that is not quite right simply because it exists. Fearful of losing whatever bond may exist with his or her partner, the anxious/ambivalent person jumps into a long-term relationship before the relationship has had a chance to mature. It's not surprising that the anxious/ambivalent type will try to hold onto a relationship beyond the point that it satisfies either partner.

Romeo and Juliet: A Reprise

> . . . never was a story of more woe
> Than this of Juliet and her Romeo (Act V, scene 3)

Shakespeare's *Romeo and Juliet* was indeed a tragedy. The two lovers' relationship was intense, yet brief, lasting only hours before the tragic double suicide. The tragedy was particularly poignant because Shakespeare convinces us that the mutual love of Romeo and Juliet was one that would have lasted and endured had it not been extinguished by the conspiracy of fateful events and the animosity of the two families.

If Romeo and Juliet had lived and had their lives been typical of people in love, the odds are that their relationship would not have been smooth sailing; there

While love relationships are not guaranteed to last and most likely will change, many endure despite conflicts, doubts, vagaries of fortune, and hard times.

would have been moments of doubt, concern about mutual and communal rewards, and questions as passion was intertwined with caring and attachment. At the very least, this Montague and Capulet would have had to work and evolve to keep the bonds of love alive. There is no one formula for a successful relationship and there is little certainty about which will last and which will dissolve. Relationships that seem so promising at the outset may turn sour. Even the marriage of the late Princess Diana to Prince Charles—a marriage that seemed to come from the pages of a fairy tale—ended in bitter dissolution. Conversely, relationships often proceed happily from romance to commitment to golden wedding anniversaries.

Relationships, like the people that form them, are diverse; no two are exactly alike. Research has provided us with the tools and the theoretical insights to begin to understand long-term relationships and to comprehend the factors that help love, and friendships, survive.

Summary

This chapter has examined some of the factors that social psychologists have found to be important in studying interpersonal attraction, long-term relationships, and love. A positive personal relationship was defined as the positive attitude two people hold toward each other. Among the factors that lead to positive personal relationships are our preference for symmetry in our relationships. Newcomb's A-B-X model posits a "strain toward symmetry" such that if persons A and B both like a certain object, X, then the strain toward symmetry will push A and B to like each other.

The reward model of attraction considers attraction to be based on associations with positive rewards. Pleasure in an interpersonal relationship depends on the rewards and costs experienced by both partners. In addition to gaining rewards, partners in long-term relationships work toward equity. Each partner hopes that the ratio of his or her rewards gained from a relationship relative to the costs expended is equal to the other partner's ratio of rewards to costs. Research has shown that people in short-term exchange relationships keep track of their contributions and rewards but that people in more meaningful and long-lasting communal relationships do not engage in such record keeping.

One of the most frequently researched aspects of liking is the relationship between similarity and attraction. In general, research has shown that similarity leads to interpersonal attraction, especially when the similarity occurs on important issues. An evolutionary, or biosocial, argument is among the explanations for the similarity-attraction effect.

We feel pressure to reciprocate attraction. We tend to like those who we believe are attracted to us. In addition, propinquity (physical closeness) is related to interpersonal attraction although it has also been linked to hostility.

People who are physically attractive have been shown to be liked. This is true in potential romantic relationships, but physical appearance has had other surprising effects as well. In simulated jury situations and in classroom situations, attractive people have been found to be judged less guilty and as having done more valuable work, respectively, than unattractive people. There is evidence that a beautiful-is-good stereotype is imposed quickly and automatically. Physical beauty can also have negative consequences. Attractive people may discount much of the positive feedback they receive from others.

Some research in interpersonal attraction has examined the more unusual features that lead to attraction. Although we tend to like people who compliment us, it has been shown that insults can lead to greater attraction if a pattern of feedback begins with insults and ends with compliments. It has also been shown that people of superior ability who have clumsy acci-

dents can be seen as more attractive after having been "humanized" by the accident.

Considerable advances have been made in the study of love. Several definitions of love exist that combine passion with other elements. Rubin specified caring and attachment as the other elements, while Davis added clusters of caring and friendship. Shaver and Hazan introduced the concept of attachment styles from developmental psychology into the study of love. Attachment styles are learned in the earliest weeks of life and can be thought of as secure, anxious/ambivalent or avoidant. Research shows that attachment styles brought into adulthood affect the type of partners people seek, the longevity of a relationship, and people's responses to a threatened dissolution of the relationship.

Two-factor theories contend that the experience of love is a function of physiological arousal and a cognitive label. If the cognitive label implies love in the presence of arousal, then emotion will be experienced as love.

The breakdown of relationships has also received the attention of psychologists. Relationships can end when people respond to dissatisfaction with neglect or exit strategies but may be maintained through loyalty and voice responses. Jealousy is a response to a relationship threat that involves the loss of reward and the threat to self-esteem. Considerable interest has developed in whether gender differences in jealousy imply an evolutionary basis to the emotion.

Key Terms

attachment theory	mere exposure
balance theory	passionate love
beautiful-is-good stereotype	positive personal relationship
communal relationship	reward model of attraction
companionate love	self-monitoring
equity theory	similarity-attraction effect
exchange relationship	symmetry or A-B-X model
ingratiation	of attraction
jealousy	terror management theory

Suggested Readings

Berscheid, E., and Reis, H.T. (1997) Attraction and close relationships. In D. T. Gilbert, S. T. Fiske and G. Lindzey (Eds.), *Handbook of social psychology. (4th ed.).* New York: Oxford University Press and McGraw-Hill.

Berscheid, E., and Walster, E. (1978). *Interpersonal attraction.* Reading, MA: Addison-Wesley.

Davis, K.E. (1985). Near and dear: Friendship and love compared. *Psychology Today,* February, pp. 22–30.

Hazan, C., and Shaver, P.R. (1994). Attachment as an organizational framework for research in close relationships. *Psychological Inquiry, 5,* 1–22.

Kelly, H.H. (1979). *Personal relationships: Their structure and processes.* Hillsdale, NJ: Erlbaum.

Jones, E.E., and Wortman, C.B. (1973). *Ingratiation: An attributional approach.* Morristown, NJ: General Learning Press.

Chapter 9

Altruism: The Psychology of Helping Others

On a hot summer night in 1995, sixteen-year-old Deletha Word was driving home from an enjoyable night at popular Belle Isle in Detroit, Michigan. On her way to the bridge that connects Belle Isle with the Detroit area, her car swerved and accidentally side-swiped another car driven by Martel Welch, Jr., causing minor damage to both cars. Before Deletha Word had the opportunity to turn her car around, she was caught in traffic on the bridge. Suddenly, her windshield and driver-side window shattered from the force of a blow—the driver of the other car, Welch, had turned back and was now attacking her! In a rage of anger, the 6-foot, 2-inch, 260-pound Welch pulled Deletha from her car, stripped off most of her clothing, and began to beat her, choke her, and slam her to the ground repeatedly. Four-foot-11-inch, 115-pound Deletha fought bravely and escaped her assailant twice, only to be caught again and subjected to more merciless brutality. Finally, as Welch went to retrieve a tire iron from his trunk, Deletha escaped and climbed over the railing on the bridge. When Welch approached Deletha swinging his weapon, Deletha, bloody, weakened from the beating, and with nowhere else to run, released her grip on the bridge railing and jumped to the cold water below. Two men who witnessed the beating immediately scaled the railing and jumped in, in an attempt to save her. But it was too late; Deletha had disappeared beneath the surface of the water. Deletha Word's body was found the next day in the water a mile from where she had jumped. Family members later revealed that Deletha had jumped from the bridge even though she had never learned how to swim.

Martel Welch pled not guilty to causing Deletha Word's death. A jury disagreed. On May 3, 1996, a jury convicted Welch of second-degree murder. He is currently serving his sentence in a Michigan penitentiary. As Deletha's mother remarked at the sentencing,

"Welch's family can still visit him in prison. I have to go to the graveyard to visit Deletha."

The story of Deletha Word is tragic. But her death becomes more tragic when we realize that Deletha was not alone when she was attacked: over forty motorists witnessed her assault on the bridge. Some accounts indicate that the passing motorists were more than just casual observers; many exited their cars and encircled the altercation. At one point, the assailant held Deletha out to the crowd of bystanders and asked if any would like to join in the assault against the young girl. But despite the fact that many of the bystanders had cellular phones, and despite the fact that a police station was located at the end of the bridge, not one witness lifted a finger to prevent the death of Deletha Word.

Why didn't any of the eyewitnesses on the bridge that night help Deletha Word? Were they afraid? Did they realize her life was in danger? The Detroit police sergeant who worked on the Word case told the *Detroit Free Press* that he could not recall any other time in which so many people had an opportunity to observe a brutal crime but failed to act. Unfortunately, what happened to Deletha Word that night on the bridge was not an isolated event. It was not unique to Detroit nor was it unique to that time period. It bears a striking similarity to an event that occurred over twenty years ago to a woman named Kitty Genovese. The place was Austin Street in the borough of Queens in New York City; the time was 3:20 A.M.

Kitty Genovese was on her way to her apartment building when a man suddenly appeared, grabbed her, and began to attack her. Kitty screamed, waking some of the neighbors. She struggled to get free and managed to reach a street corner where she could be seen and heard by more of her neighbors. She yelled, "He stabbed me! Please help me!" Lights went on in several apartments overlooking the street. From their windows above, the neighbors could see Genovese escape again, but she was bleeding. She did not get far. The attacker pursued his victim and struck again. Genovese screamed, "I'm dying! I'm dying!" This time the attack was final. This time there were no more screams and no more escapes. Kitty Genovese lay dead of stab wounds in an incident that was thought to have lasted nearly three-quarters of an hour.

What of those neighbors who were awakened that night? Reporters from the *New York Times* sought to determine what the people whose windows faced that part of Austin Street did after they heard the screams.

They discovered that at least thirty-eight people heard the screams. At least thirty-eight people had gone to their windows, but not one of them had come to the woman's aid. Not one of them had so much as lifted the telephone to call the police (Rosenthal, 1964). Had even one person done so, Kitty Genovese might have been saved.

In this chapter we will look at the reasons people refrain from helping. We will also examine the conditions under which people will help a stranger who is clearly in need. We know that the world has had its heroes who have given freely of themselves for humanity. We know that there are many who have saved people's lives despite threats to their own safety. And we know too well that there have been incidents like those that occurred to Deletha Word and Kitty Genovese in which not just one but dozens of people refused to give even the smallest degree of aid to a victim whose life might have been spared had someone helped.

Why Don't We Help? The Unresponsive Bystander

In the aftermath of the Genovese murder and *New York Times* editor A.M. Rosenthal's investigative reporting, the horror of what had occurred was on people's lips the world over. Two social psychologists, John Darley and Bibb Latané, set out to study the social-psychological factors that would cause ordinary citizens to refrain from helping someone in need. Their research on the unresponsive bystander eventually inspired work on the responsive bystander, or the reasons and causes of selfless and altruistic behavior. We begin our presentation, however, where the field began—with the scientific research on the failure of intervention in apparent emergency situations.

Bystander Intervention and the Decision Tree

Many factors can account for bystanders' failure to intervene: their personalities, the large city in which they live, the dehumanization of today's technological society, and so on. And while dispositional factors related to bystanders may be useful for understanding

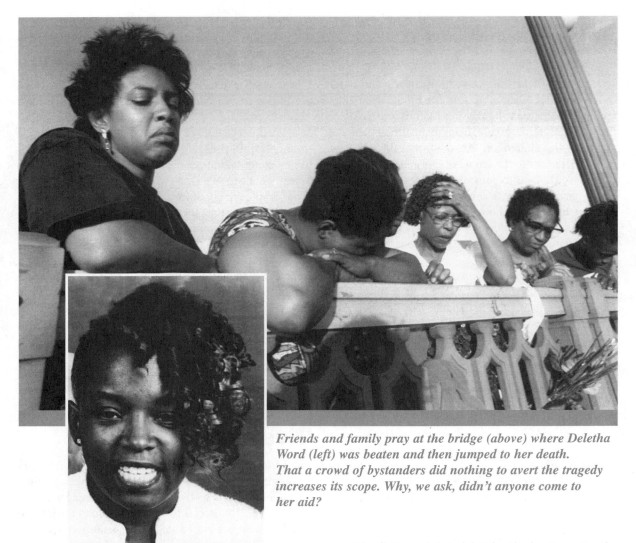

Friends and family pray at the bridge (above) where Deletha Word (left) was beaten and then jumped to her death. That a crowd of bystanders did nothing to avert the tragedy increases its scope. Why, we ask, didn't anyone come to her aid?

why they sometimes do not help, it is also useful to consider the reactions that bystanders need to have in order to help a victim in an emergency.

When a person finds himself or herself witnessing an emergency situation, Bibb Latané and John Darley (1970) pointed out that being altruistic involves not just one decision but a series of decisions. Only if a person makes an appropriate decision at each decision point will he or she intervene in the emergency. Figure 9.1 outlines these decision points in what has been called a **decision tree.** At each point, branches are available that may cause the bystander to go about his or her business without altruistic intervention.

The first crucial decision is whether to *notice* the incident at all. If a person staggers from the side of the road and waves his arms in front of your car, and your headlights shine directly on him, you have very little alternative but to notice him. A scream at a crowded snack bar at Grand Central Station, however, could go completely unnoticed, and any intervention by passersby would thus be forestalled. Somewhere between these extremes lie most of the situations that call for our intervention.

Second, we have to *interpret* an event as an emergency. Evidence will be presented shortly on just how crucial this decision is. However, we might imagine that Kitty Genovese's neighbors on Austin Street who heard screams interpreted them as something other than calls for help. "I thought I heard hammering noises," explained one of the neighbors.

We can see two factors operating here. One is at the level of *perception*. If the screams really sounded like the crash of a hammer, then it might be difficult to make the interpretation necessary for intervention. The second factor is at the level of *motivation*. People may actively want to make a nonemergency interpretation so that they will not be embarrassed by having made a mistake nor take the risk involved in intervening.

The third decision point is whether we, as bystanders, are *responsible* for helping. If we see two brothers fighting and notice that one of them is getting hurt, we may not view it as our responsibility to intervene if their father is standing there. The factors that may play a role in this decision include whether an appropriate authority who can intervene is present and the number of people who witness the emergency.

Fourth, we must decide on the *appropriate form of assistance*. We may believe that a situation requires direct or indirect intervention. People witnessing the murder of Deletha Word may have been loath to intervene directly yet may have decided that they should contact someone. But who? In the anxiety of the moment, they may not have been able to provide the answer. In short, no one may intervene because the bystanders cannot decide on the appropriate form of assistance, so they continue to tend to their own business.

Finally, people who notice an event that they in-

terpret as an emergency and decide on the appropriate form of intervention must still decide to *implement the decision*. People who observe a mugging in progress may know what to do but out of fear may decide not to implement their decisions. Such may have been the reaction of many who saw the Word attack in Detroit. And those New York City residents peering out of their windows may have felt embarrassed about describing the Genovese attack to the police or may have been fearful about the consequences of reporting the event if the assailant were not apprehended.

It is clear from the decision tree analysis that intervening in an emergency is a complex act. A series of interlocking decisions must be made, yet the final outcome may have to be achieved in a matter of seconds. Dissecting this speedy decision process is difficult, but social psychologists have uncovered a number of factors that influence the final decision regarding intervention.

Interpreting the Situation: A Need for Help or a Family Quarrel?

Before we offer help to a person in need, we have to define that person as being in need. Observers may have viewed the Deletha Word or Kitty Genovese assault as a family quarrel or as a quarrel between two lovers. Given such an interpretation, the scene takes on a different meaning and the appropriate form of

FIGURE 9.1   DECISION TREE ANALYSIS OF INTERVENTION IN AN EMERGENCY

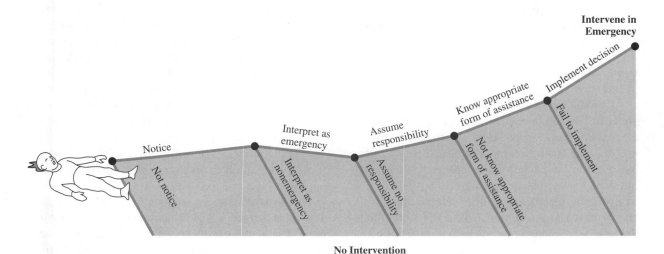

action changes. People may feel that it's appropriate to come to the aid of a woman in distress but not to become involved in an encounter between lovers. On the campus of Penn State University, Shotland and Stau (1976) staged an apparent fight in which a woman was attacked by a man. Research participants had come to the laboratory singly to fill out personality inventories. The experimenter left word that he would be late. While a participant waited for the researcher, a man and woman got off the elevator approximately fifty feet from the participant's room. They were arguing vehemently, clearly within range of the participant. Their verbal argument soon became physical. The man attacked the woman and began to throw her around the corridor. Unbeknownst to the participant, the man and woman were actors, hired to stage the fight. (The fight was apparently so realistic that, Shotland and Stau reported, some faculty members at Penn State who had been forewarned that the fight would take place but was only staged by two actors nonetheless came out of their offices to try to stop it.)

In one condition of Shotland and Stau's study, the research participant heard the woman yell, "I don't know you!" before the fight became physical. In the other condition, the woman yelled, "I don't know why I married you!" In the former condition, 65 percent of the bystanders intervened to help; but if the woman indicated that they were, or had been, married, the rate of intervention dropped to 19 percent. Neutral observers rated video tapes of the physical battle and rated the fight as equally intense and physical regardless of the experimental condition. But that is not how the subjects viewed it: the very same fight was rated as less intense and as less of an emergency when the man and woman knew each other.

The point here is a general one: the context in which an emergency takes place may affect the way we interpret the event. People may be inclined to interpret situations in a way that does not call for their intervention or help.

DeJong, Marber, and Shaver (1980) examined the effect of a victim's reaction to an emergency in another way. They carried out their study in the engineering and business library at Dartmouth College where library users saw an experimenter drop a $10 bill, which was snatched up by another person. The experimenter then acted as if he were unaware of the loss or began to search his pockets and look around. Subjects were more likely to notify the victim of the theft when he appeared to know he was missing the $10.

The investigators argued that the reaction of the victim when he knew he had lost the $10 helped witnesses *define the situation* as one that was not ambiguous but rather as one that called for help.

Why Doesn't the Bystander Intervene? Diffusing Responsibility

Even if we interpret an event as an emergency, we have to make another decision—whether it is our responsibility to help. It turns out that our perceptions of responsibility are determined largely by the number of other eyewitnesses to the situation. After reading about the Kitty Genovese incident, Darley and Latané (1968) reasoned that the *number of persons* watching the crime was primarily responsible for the inaction of the group:

> When only one bystander is present in an emergency, if help is to come, it must come from him. Although he may choose to ignore it . . . any pressure to intervene focuses uniquely on him. When there are several observers present, however, the pressures to intervene do not focus on any one of the observers; instead the responsibility for intervention is shared among all the onlookers and is not unique to anyone. As a result, no one helps. (Pp. 377–78)

To test the hypothesis that **diffusion of responsibility** discourages helping, Darley and Latané asked New York University students to participate in an honest discussion about problems they were having in adjusting to college life. Each student was to talk from a separate booth to prevent any possible embarrassment about face-to-face communication; the booths were connected by a sound system. The experimenter also explained that he would not listen to the discussion so that students could have more freedom in their comments.

Actually, only one subject participated in the experiment at a time. Each of the other voices he was to hear was a tape-recorded simulation; no other "discussants" were present. The ruse enabled the experimenters to standardize their procedure for each subject and to set the stage for the emergency.

In the "discussion," the future victim always spoke first. He talked about his difficulties in adjusting to college and then, very hesitantly, mentioned that he was prone to seizures during times of stress. The other prerecorded discussants then took their turns. The actual subject spoke last. When it was the victim's turn to talk again, the emergency took place.

The victim began by making a few calm comments and then appeared to be gripped by a seizure. Over the subject's loudspeaker came the following: "I-er-um-I think I-I need-er-if-if—could-er somebody er-er-er-er-er-er-give me a little-er give me a little-er give me a little help here because I-er-I'm . . ." (chokes, then quiet) (p. 379).

The experimenter sat outside the subject's room and recorded the amount of time it took him to seek assistance for the victim. Recall that Darley and Latané were interested in the effect of the number of witnesses to the emergency. Consequently, they systematically varied the alleged size of the discussion group. In some cases, the subject was led to believe that the group consisted of six persons: himself, the victim, and four other witnesses. In another set of cases, the subject believed that the group consisted of three persons. In the remaining cases, the subject believed that he and the victim were the only people in the discussion.

The percentage of subjects who responded to the staged emergency and the speed of their responses are shown in table 9.1. It took subjects who believed that they were the only witness to the emergency an average of 52 seconds from the beginning of the seizure to swing the door open and attempt to find help. However, as the group became larger, the average amount of time that elapsed before the subject sought help increased to 166 seconds. Moreover, only 31 percent of the subjects who thought that they were only one of a large group of witnesses ever came out to help, but an overwhelming percentage of the subjects (85 percent) eventually tried to help the victim if the responsibility for helping rested squarely on their shoulders—that is, if they believed that they were the only person to hear the attack. Thus, by systematically varying one of the factors in the emergency, Darley and Latané could conclude that the number of witnesses to an emergency is a critical determinant of whether any witnesses will take action to intervene.

It is now a well-established finding in quite a variety of situations both inside and outside of the laboratory that the more witnesses present, the less likely that any one will intervene. For example, Latané and Darley (1970) arranged to have a series of thefts occur in a New York discount store. Cases of beer were stolen in front of either one or two customers. Customers who had been lone witnesses were more likely to report the crime to the store clerk than customers who had been one of a pair of witnesses.

Schwartz and Gottlieb (1980) provided the first direct evidence that the number of bystanders had an effect on helping by affecting a witness's feeling of personal responsibility. Subjects observed an emergency situation while they were either alone or in the presence of another bystander. The presence of the bystander inhibited the subject from offering help. Subjects were then asked about their decision to help. Eighty percent of the people who were alone specifically mentioned that they felt it was their responsibility to help; only 17 percent of the people who were with another bystander felt it was their responsibility to help. Apparently, there is not much safety in numbers—the fewer the bystanders, the better our chances of obtaining immediate help.

An intriguing study by Latané and Darley (1970, pp. 81–85) shows that a person's perception of his or her responsibility not only directly affects the action he or she takes in an emergency but also affects his or her interpretation of the event. In the previous section, we saw that bystanders who define the situation as a nonemergency do not intervene. Latané and Darley wondered whether people who could not diffuse

TABLE 9.1 EFFECT OF GROUP SIZE ON THE LIKELIHOOD AND SPEED OF RESPONSE

Group Size	Number of Subjects	Percent Response by End of Seizure	Mean Time (seconds)
2 (subject and victim)	13	85%	52
3 (subject, victim, and 1 other)	26	62%	93
6 (subject, victim, and 4 others)	13	31%	166

Source: Adapted from Darley and Latané (1968)

TABLE 9.2   **THE FREQUENCY OF BELIEVING THAT THE FIGHT WAS REAL**

Condition	N	Believe	Do Not Believe
Responsibility (children are alone)	12	25%	75%
No responsibility (children are supervised)	8	88%	12%

Source: Latané and Darley (1970)

responsibility in an emergency might be motivated to alter their interpretation of the event so that they still do not have to intervene. Subjects came to the laboratory individually, ostensibly for a market research study. Each subject was placed in a room and asked to fill out some questionnaires. While alone, the subject overheard two children playing in an adjacent room. Soon the play turned into a fight, and an older bully was heard mercilessly beating a younger child. In one condition of the experiment, the subject believed that only he was aware of what was happening in the next room. Therefore, breaking up the fight was the subject's responsibility. In the no-responsibility condition, the subject believed that an adult supervisor was present at the time of the fight.

Only one subject out of eight tried to help in the no-responsibility condition, which is not surprising because an adult was with the children. But could the adult subjects possibly resist going in to break up the fight in the responsibility condition? Yes. Only one of the twelve subjects tried to help. Why was this the case, considering that there was no opportunity for responsibility diffusion? Apparently the answer lay in the subjects' *altered perception* of what was transpiring. As table 9.2 points out, three-fourths of the subjects in this condition did not believe that the fight was real. "Children don't really fight like that," said some of the subjects. Of course, they were correct; it was not a real fight. Perhaps the experimenter did a poor job of staging the fight. However, the startling finding in Latané and Darley's study was that in the no-responsibility condition, only one of the eight subjects questioned the authenticity of the fight. The vast majority of the witnesses were convinced that the children were actually fighting. The only conclusion that can be reached is that the subjects who felt that they were responsible for taking some helping action were motivated to perceive the situation as unreal.

An Analysis of the Costs

In considering people's motivation to avoid helping, we have seen that if people can avoid responsibility, they will do so, and that if they can redefine the situation, they will do so. Why shouldn't people want to help? Why don't people want to get involved? There are no entirely satisfactory answers to these questions, but a model proposed by Piliavin, Piliavin, and Rodin (1975) provides some insight. According to these researchers, witnessing an emergency situation is arousing. Generally this arousal is experienced as uncomfortable tension, and a person is motivated to reduce it. In most cases, the bystander will choose the response to an emergency that most rapidly and completely reduces the arousal.

Intervention in an emergency is not the only behavior that can reduce arousal: interpreting the situation as one that does not call for help, leaving the scene, and failing to notice the situation are other possible reactions. Which behavior will occur is a function of the analysis of the net costs of helping. In general, according to the **cost model of helping,** as the costs of helping go up, direct intervention becomes less likely. These costs are of two types. The first is the *cost of intervention to the bystander.* If Deletha Word's attacker was a truly vicious person, then attempting to help could result in a direct physical cost to the bystander. Another cost involves the potential embarrassment that might occur if the bystander overreacts; that is, if the victim is not really in trouble, the bystander would look foolish by intervening. Thus, physical or psychological costs to the bystander can prevent them from offering assistance.

The second type of cost is the *cost to the victim* if the bystander fails to help. How much trouble is the victim in? How much potential benefit can the bystander provide? A person attacked by a mob may be in genuine jeopardy, but little extra cost to the victim may be involved if the bystander fails to intervene directly because the bystander simply may not be able to accomplish very much. Table 9.3 shows the schema of the study by Piliavin and his colleagues. Direct intervention is expected to occur when the bystander does not incur high costs in trying to help and the victim will suffer great harm if the bystander fails to act. When the cost to the bystander is high, then the bystander is motivated to reduce arousal by choosing an alternative method. The right-hand column of table 9.3 suggests some of the alternatives. The most common alternative may be a redefinition of the situation so that it is viewed as a nonemergency or as a situation that does not call for a response by the bystander. The last redefinition is akin to Darley and Latané's concept of diffusion of responsibility. If the situation can be responded to by people other than a particular bystander, that bystander is especially likely to feel little responsibility when the costs of intervention are high.

Testing the Costs Model

The potential cost of intervention to a bystander can come from a variety of sources. As a bystander, you may incur costs because of the amount of effort you expend to help, because of the risk you run by helping, or because of the lack of internal reward that you derive from helping. As we pointed out earlier, helping in a situation of physical danger like that of the

Deletha Word case bears a rather salient cost. According to the model of Piliavin and his associates, this fact should reduce the degree of direct helping.

Consider the situation devised by Allen (described in Latané and Darley, 1970, pp. 21–24). In a New York City subway train, a wide-eyed, lost-looking person asks a subway rider whether a particular location is uptown or downtown. In the presence of a second subway rider, the person who has been asked gives the questioner the wrong information. The second subway rider is the real subject in this study. Both the questioner and the respondent are experimental confederates.

What this study varied were events that occurred before the asking of directions. In one condition, the person who gave the misinformation had been sitting with his feet propped up on another seat. When an innocent bystander (another confederate) tripped over the outstretched feet, the seated passenger looked up from his *Muscle* magazine and threatened the bystander with physical violence before letting the incident pass. In a second condition, he looked up and shouted some verbal abuse at the bystander. In a third condition, the bystander was neither threatened nor insulted.

The subject who witnessed these events was aware that the muscle-bound respondent had given the stranger misinformation. It would be easy to help the stranger by correcting the respondent, but what would it cost? As figure 9.2 indicates, when the costs were small because the stranger had been neither threatened nor insulted, 50 percent of the subjects

TABLE 9.3 **PREDICTED MODAL RESPONSES OF MODERATELY AROUSED OBSERVER AS A JOINT FUNCTION OF COSTS OF DIRECT HELP AND COSTS OF NO HELP TO VICTIM**

Cost of no help to victim	Cost of Direct Help	
	Low	High[a]
High	(a) Direct intervention	(c) Indirect intervention or redefinition of situation, disparagement of victim, etc.[b]
Low	(b) Variable (largely a function of perceived norms in situation)	(d) Leaving scene, ignoring, denial, etc.

a. There are some situations, generally those in which victims themselves are very likely to perish, such as severe fires, explosions, cave-ins, and ship accidents, in which the costs for helping become so high that they will be perceived as total, incalculable, or infinite. Under these limiting conditions, the actions and reactions of bystanders will deviate somewhat from those predicted here.
b. These responses lower the cost of not helping, leading to (d).
Source: Piliavin, Piliavin, and Rodin (1975)

FIGURE 9.2   **CORRECTING A STRANGER AS A FUNCTION OF THREAT**

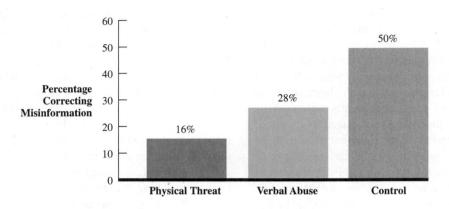

Source: Adapted from Latané and Darley (1970)

corrected the respondent. When the respondent had verbally abused a bystander, only 28 percent of the subjects corrected him; and when he had physically threatened the bystander, only 16 percent of the subjects dared to correct him.

Sterling and Gaertner (1984) tested an important assumption of the costs model. Recall that helping is based on the experience of arousal. It is arousal that motivates people to come to the aid of a victim. Sterling and Gaertner argued that if arousal is the basis of the helping response, then increasing arousal in an unambiguous emergency situation should increase the helping rate. They had male subjects perform push-ups as a part of a study that supposedly was investigating physical distraction. Some subjects performed a large number of push-ups (ten) and therefore experienced a heightened degree of physiological arousal; others performed a moderate number (five); and others performed none. The subjects then witnessed an unambiguous emergency. They believed that they heard a female student fall and become pinned under a heavy metal ladder in a room next to theirs. As in Darley and Latané's (1968) experiment, the question was the length of time it took subjects to leave their room to see if they could be of assistance to the female student. The results were clear: when the accident was unambiguous, subjects who had performed ten push-ups and therefore experienced the greatest physiological arousal helped the female confederate more than subjects in either the moderate or no-exercise conditions. Apparently, then, helping *does* seem to be based on a witness's degree of arousal.

The analysis of helping in terms of costs to the helper and the victim has provoked a considerable amount of research and has provided a guide for understanding the motivations of people who choose not to help in an emergency. But any single analysis should not be thought of as sufficient to explain the complex reasons that come together to prevent someone from helping another. For example, a study by Gruder, Romer, and Korth (1978) suggests one limitation. These investigators proposed that the social rules and norms that exist in a situation may alter the effect of the costs-to-the-victim variable in a dramatic way.

Gruder and his colleagues had a female confederate call potential helpers in their homes. Using the "wrong number" technique that had been developed in several previous studies (Gaertner, 1970; Kriss, Indenbaum, and Tesch, 1974), the confederate asked for Ralph's Garage. Of course, the confederate had not reached Ralph's Garage and the subject typically informed the caller that she had the wrong number. The caller then pleaded, "Oh, I'm sorry. Please don't hang up. I'm calling from a pay phone out here on the expressway. . . ."

For half of the phone calls, the confederate indicated her extreme reliance on the subjects' help. She continued by saying, "I don't have any more change for the phone. Do you think you could do me a favor and call Ralph's Garage for me?" For these subjects, it appeared that their not helping would have high costs for the victim. It was not clear what she could have done with no change and stranded on the highway. The other half of the subjects received their call from someone for whom the costs of not being helped were low. No mention of lack of money was made, and the subject could presume that the caller would be able to dial Ralph's Garage again.

According to the costs analysis of Piliavin and his colleagues (1975), the subjects should have been considerably more likely to help the caller when their failure to help entailed high costs to the victim. This did not always happen, however. In addition to manipulating the costs, Gruder and his associates manipulated the requester's responsibility for the emergency. For half of her phone calls, the requester added, "I was supposed to take the car into the shop last week to be repaired, but I forgot to. Now it's broken down." For the other half of her phone calls, the requester substituted, "The car was just repaired last week, and it just broke down."

Gruder and his colleagues believed that at least one principle other than the costs to the victim would bear on the decision of the potential helpers. They reasoned that it is embedded in the fabric of our social rules that people are supposed to take care of themselves, to take reasonable precautions, and to avoid negligence. They termed this concept the *norm of self-sufficiency.* Clearly, people who forget to take their car into the shop violate this norm. The investigators reasoned that the norm would be invoked to withdraw assistance from its violator if she were not greatly in need of help. Subjects who received the low-dependency call were expected to be more helpful to the caller when the emergency was not the result of the caller's negligence. On the other hand,

when the potential costs of a failure to help the caller were high, the caller's negligence was expected to be viewed as just one more illustration of the caller's incompetence and need for help. In this condition, the caller's negligence was expected to strengthen the subject's decision to help.

The results are presented in figure 9.3. When the costs of not helping the caller were high (high dependency), the subjects made more phone calls for the negligent caller than for the nonnegligent caller. However, when the dependency of the victim was low, the norm of self-sufficiency was apparently invoked and the subjects made significantly more calls to aid the nonnegligent victim than the negligent victim. Note that an analysis purely in terms of the net costs to the victim of the subjects' refusal to help would not have predicted this finding—the costs to the victim and not the victim's negligence should have determined helping. This suggests that people's motivations for not getting involved remain complex. Costs are undoubtedly a major component, but people also take into account other considerations when they decide to help.

We should also be aware that not everyone interprets the costs of a situation in exactly the same way. Some witnesses may have looked at the cost of saving Deletha Word as too high—attempting to stop the attack may have put their own physical safety in jeopardy. Others may have considered the cost of *not* intervening. They may have considered the cost of nonintervention to be low if they believed someone

---

FIGURE 9.3   PERCENTAGES OF SUBJECTS HELPING IN THE EXPERIMENTAL CONDITIONS

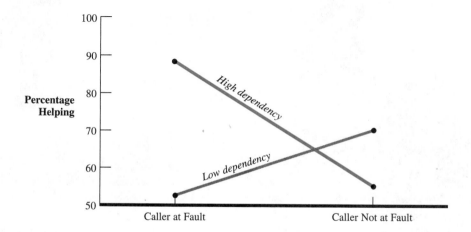

Source: Gruder, Romer, and Korth (1978)

else would offer help (for example, "I can live with my conscience because I know that the victim will be taken care of."). Kerber (1984) provided some research evidence that bears on this point. He found that students at Holy Cross who helped a person in need were much more likely to have perceived the situation's costs favorably than people who did not help. It is difficult to know from the study whether people helped because they perceived the costs of helping to be low and the costs of not helping to be high or whether they held those perceptions because they had decided to help. Nonetheless, Kerber's evidence suggests that people perceive the costs and rewards of a situation differently, and their perceptions may help to determine whether they will help a person in need.

Expanding the Costs Model

The analysis of helping in terms of its costs to the victim and to the bystander has, as we have seen, attracted a considerable amount of attention. There have also been efforts to expand the model to make it more comprehensive (Lynch and Cohen, 1978). Perhaps the most ambitious of the models was the proposal by Jane Piliavin and her colleagues (1982) that three general factors affect the likelihood that a bystander will intervene in a situation. Costs, they argue, are just one of those factors. First, the degree of *empathy* between the bystander and the victim has to be considered. How much does the potential helper identify with the victim? Variables that affect feelings of empathy include (1) situational characteristics, such as the ambiguity of the event and the number of bystanders present; (2) bystander characteristics, such as age, sex, and competence to help; (3) victim characteristics, such as sex, race, and attractiveness; and (4) family relatedness, such as the likelihood of helping our own children even in situations that entail extreme risk or cost.

The bystander's empathy for the victim determines the second factor in the helping process: psychological

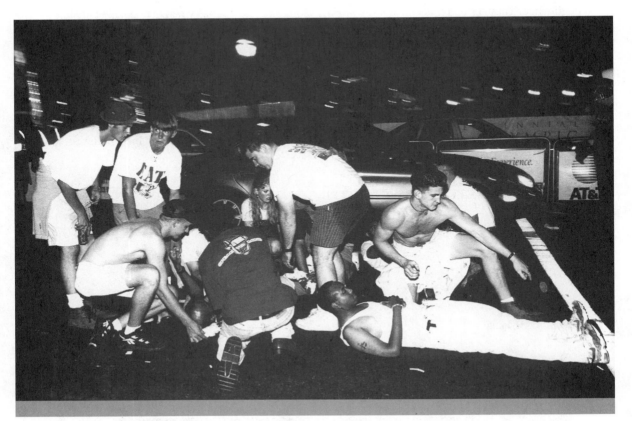

Empathy was an important factor leading to the helping of victims of the explosion in Atlanta's Olympic Centennial Park in 1996. Similarities in age and sharing an experience of peril made onlookers identify with their injured fellows.

BOX 9.1

Are Gender Differences in Helping Fact or Fiction?

Do men and women differ in their helping responses? A first glimpse at the data suggests that the answer is yes; men appear to help more than women. Reviews of the bystander intervention literature suggest that, in the United States and in other cultures, men are more likely than women to offer assistance (Eagly and Crowley, 1986; Johnson et al., 1989; Piliavin and Unger, 1985).

This first glimpse is contradicted by some other observations: For example, consider the professions that are dedicated to helping others, such as nursing and social work. In such professions women are overrepresented (Johnson et al., 1989; Schroeder, Penner, Doviodio, and Piliavin, 1995). Women are also more likely than men to do favors and provide social support to their friends (Eisenberg and Fabes, 1991; Eagly and Crowley, 1986). And although men and women do not appear to react differently to a direct request for assistance, women may be better than men at detecting the need for help when it is nonverbal or implicit (Hall, 1984; Eagly and Crowley, 1986).

Moreover, there may be gender differences in the kind of help offered by men and women. For example, men are more likely to help someone whose car has broken down (Pomazal and Clore, 1973), while women are more likely to help someone with an emotional problem (Smith, Wheller, and Diener, 1975) or a personal problem (Schwartz and Ames, 1977). Furthermore, the gender of the person in need may influence the help offered by each gender. To be specific, women provide more help to female friends and to platonic male friends than they offer to their male romantic partners (Barbee et al., 1993). It appears that gender differences cut both ways and that circumstances determine the appropriate response by men and women.

Why might men and women differ in when and how they help? One possibility concerns physical differences. On average, men tend to be taller, heavier, and physically stronger than women. Consequently, if the help requires intimidation or strength, such as might be required to stop a violent crime or to save someone who has fallen through the ice, men may be able to offer more effective help than women (Huston et al., 1981). Indeed, in their meta-analytic review, Alice Eagly and Maureen Crowley (1986) demonstrated that across a variety of helping situations, women offered less help than men when the situation was perceived as more dangerous. This suggests that in some helping situations, the costs for lending assistance may be perceived differently by men and women (Piliavin and Unger, 1985).

The source of gender differences may also be linked to gender roles. In their review of the helping literature, Eagly and Crowley (1986) argued that differences in helping may be a function of the different ways in which men and women are socialized to behave in society. The female gender role includes norms encouraging women to place the needs of others, especially those of family members, before their own. In addition, as reflected in the research discussed above, Eagly and Crowley note that women are expected to provide only certain forms of helping to certain people. Thus, the female gender role dictates that women should mainly care for others, especially in close relationships. Perhaps as a result of performing these roles, women are perceived as more stereotypically helpful, kind, compassionate, and devoted to others, and women themselves report having more empathy and sympathy toward others on self-report measures.

Continued

BOX 9.1

Continued

The male gender role, in contrast, emphasizes two different forms of helping: *heroism* and *chivalry.* Heroism emphasizes the risky self-sacrifice for the benefit of others, while the concept of chivalry emphasizes the protection of the weak and defenseless. Thus, the male gender role specifies that the helping behavior of men be nonroutine and involve risky acts of rescuing others as well as courteous and protective helping directed toward subordinates, including women.

In addition, as occupants of gender-specific social roles, men and women often acquire different skills related to helping. For example, men are more likely to occupy mechanical or technical service positions and often have the skills necessary to help someone fix a car. Alternatively, women are more likely to occupy positions that require nurtur-

ing and should therefore have the skills required to help someone who has a personal problem. Each group should then feel more confident and efficacious in gender-role-specific helping situations.

Based on their review, Eagly and Crowley concluded that "in many naturalistic settings, especially those with onlookers and multiple potential helpers and without direct appeals for help, people behave in ways that are markedly sex-typed, with men helping considerably more than women when sex-typed masculine skills are called for and when the potential dangers are more threatening to women." However, they also noted that when a man or woman was alone in a helping situation, he or she tended to ignore limitations of sex-typed skills and vulnerability to danger to help a victim in distress.

---

arousal. Not only must the arousal be experienced, it must also be interpreted as having been caused by the victim's distress. Finally, once arousal has occurred and has been interpreted as being due to the victim's plight, the third factor exerts its impact: The perceived costs will determine the actual decision to offer direct help, indirect help, or no help at all as specified in the earlier model.

When Do We Help? Situations That Promote Helping

When We Are Rewarded for Previous Helping

As implied in the discussion of costs for helping, our behavior, our values, and our goals are to a great extent molded and shaped by the pattern of rewards and punishments that we receive. General patterns of helping behavior are probably shaped in childhood by a myriad

of events involving parents, siblings, and peers (Eisenberg, 1981). In specific cases, a tendency to help may depend on the way in which similar helping was very recently rewarded. If I try to help a senior citizen cross the street and get kicked in the shins for my efforts, I probably will not try it again soon. On the other hand, if that person responds with great warmth and pleasure and even offers me a tea biscuit in return, I will probably be more inclined to help on the next such occasion.

Using a situation not unlike this one, Moss and Page (1972) set out on the streets of Dayton, Ohio, to find a relationship between rewarded helping and subsequent helping. A passerby was first approached by a stranger and asked directions to a particular part of town. Almost always the passerby willingly gave the stranger directions. The stranger, actually an experimental confederate, responded by saying something positive, such as "Thank you"; or by saying something negative, such as grumbling, "I can't understand what you're saying. Never mind, I'll ask someone else"; or by saying something neutral, such as "OK." After being reinforced positively or negatively (or not at all in the control condition), the passerby next saw a woman drop a small bag on the ground and appar-

FIGURE 9.4   **THE FREQUENCY AND TYPE OF HELPING AFTER BEING POSITIVELY OR NEGATIVELY REINFORCED**

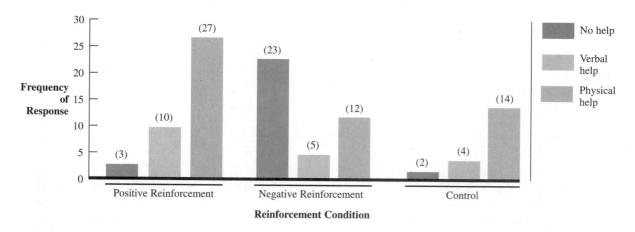

Note: Physical help = helping to pick up a dropped bag; verbal help = calling attention to dropped bag
Source: Moss and Page (1972)

ently fail to notice it. Who stopped to help the woman in this staged accident? Figure 9.4 shows that people who had been positively reinforced in their earlier encounter with a stranger were much more likely to try to help the woman retrieve her package than people who had been negatively reinforced the last time they offered help to someone.

The phenomenon known as *codependency* may be linked to the rewards gained from helping an exploitative parent. According to Deborah Lyon and Jeff Greenberg (1991), children who grow up having learned to obtain approval and self-esteem by conforming to the demands of a dysfunctional, dependent parent will seek out opportunities to help similar people in the future. Such children become codependent because their own feelings of competence and self-worth are tied to assisting a parent who, due to a dysfunction such as alcohol or substance abuse, is dependent upon them. Consequently, as adults, they should be more likely to offer help to exploitative people relative to those adults who, as children, were not raised in a codependent relationship.

To test their hypothesis, female college students were recruited to participate in a study on mood and person perception. Prior to the study, half the participants had indicated on a survey that one of their parents had a problem with alcohol. At the outset of the study, all participants met a male experimenter; for

half, he was described by a confederate as having an exploitative relationship with his girlfriend; for the other half, he was described as having a nurturing relationship with his girlfriend. Before participants completed the mood measures, the male experimenter asked them if they would be willing to donate some time for another study of his because the funding was running low. The results, presented in table 9.4, showed that females who reported having one parent with an alcohol problem volunteered significantly more time to the male experimenter when he was described as exploitative compared with when he was described as nurturing. Females who did not report having a parent with an alcohol problem donated significantly more time to the male experimenter when he was described as nurturing compared with when he was described as exploitative. The results of this study suggest that the psychological rewards gained from helping an exploitative parent may carry over into adulthood and affect future helping behavior. If their feelings of self-worth become dependent upon helping dysfunctional others, children may learn to seek out similar helping opportunities as adults.

When Our Mood Is Good

Strange things happen when we are in a good mood: we may sing on the street, offer our seat to someone

TABLE 9.4 **MEAN AMOUNT OF TIME DONATED IN MINUTES**

| | Experimenter Condition | | | |
| | Exploitive | | Nurturant | |
Group	M	SD	M	SD
Codependent	133.84	54.24	12.50	29.88
Noncodependent	0.00	0.00	60.00	70.06

Note: Time requested ranged from 0 to 180 min. Means that do not share subscripts differ at $p < .05$.
Source: Lyon and Greenberg (1991)

on the bus, maybe even offer to help people who need it. Alice Isen (1970) led teachers in a suburban school system to believe they had done either well or poorly at a task. Afterward a confederate entered the room and asked for a contribution to a fund to purchase air conditioning for the school. Teachers who had done well, and presumably felt happy and successful, contributed more money than teachers who had done poorly. Similarly, Isen and Levin (1972) varied the subjects' happiness by sneaking into a telephone booth and planting dimes in the coin return slot for subjects to find serendipitously. When such a subject came out of the phone booth, a female confederate dropped a pile of manila folders directly in the subject's path. Buoyed by their lucky feeling, the subjects who had found a coin in the phone booth were much more likely to offer help than the subjects who had not been so fortunate (cf. Isen, Clark, and Schwartz, 1976).

In a subsequent field experiment, people emerging from a local movie theater were asked to donate money to the Muscular Dystrophy Foundation. Fewer donations were made to the charity if the moviegoers had seen a sad movie than if they had seen a happy movie (Underwood et al., 1977).

Finally, we should note that, on some special occasions, a good mood does not lead to greater helping nor a bad mood to less helping. Isen and Simmonds (1978) found that people in a good mood do not wish to interrupt their happiness by taking on helping behavior that is itself unpleasant. And Rosenhan, Salovey, and Hargis (1981) showed that the happiness that does lead to helping is happiness that pertains to oneself. They found that if people were made happy because of someone else's good fortune rather than one's own good fortune, the happy mood did not lead to greater helping. On the other side of the coin, people who are in a bad mood be-

cause of something that happened to them are indeed less likely to be altruistic. But if they are in a bad mood because of something that happened to someone else (a friend, say), they seem to develop greater empathy for the victim and thus increase their helping (Thompson, Cowan, and Rosenhan, 1980).

When Someone Else Helps

The concept of modeling has wide use in psychology. Many of the things we do are learned from observing the behavior of a model such as a parent, a teacher, or a friend (Bandura and Walters, 1963). If we observe the model acting in a certain way, we are likely to try that behavior ourselves. Bryan and Test (1967) wanted to see whether male motorists would stop on a highway to assist a woman who was trying to fix a flat tire. They found that motorists were much more likely to stop if they had recently passed a scene in which a male driver had stopped to help another woman change a tire. That is, in the presence of a helping model, people were much more likely to help. Macaulay (1970) has given additional support to Bryan and Test's modeling hypothesis; she found that contributions to a Salvation Army collection box increased markedly when a model was observed making a contribution. The modeling of charitable behavior is perhaps best seen in TV telethons where we're asked to contribute both because the charitable organization needs the money and because our neighbor from Teaneck, Seattle, Columbus, or Wichita also contributed.

When Time Permits

You are probably familiar with the parable of the Good Samaritan.

A man was going down from Jerusalem to Jericho and he fell among robbers, who stripped him and beat him, and departed, leaving him half dead. Now by chance a priest was going down the road, and when he saw him he passed by on the other side. So likewise a Levite. . . . But a Samaritan, as he journeyed, came to where he was; and when he saw him, he had compassion on him and bound his wounds . . . then set him on his own beast and brought him to an inn. (Luke 10:29–37)

According to the parable, the religious outcast—the Samaritan—had more goodwill in his heart than the priest and the Levite, who were hurrying off to Jericho to conduct their business. Darley and Batson (1973) used Jesus' parable in considering some of the factors that might affect intervention to help those in need. They set up a situation to show (1) that people who are thinking ethical or moral thoughts are no more likely to help a person in need than people who are thinking other thoughts, and (2) that people who are in a hurry to attend to their business will be less likely to help someone in need than people who are not in a hurry.

Students at a theological seminary volunteered to make short speeches. Half of them were asked to speak on the ethical, moral, and social implications of the parable of the Good Samaritan. The other half were asked to make speeches on interesting employment opportunities open to seminarians. The speeches were to be tape recorded, and the room with the recording equipment was in another building. Half of the subjects were sent on their way with the knowledge that they were quite late for their appointments; the other half believed that they had ample time.

On the route between the two buildings, each of the subjects encountered a man who was sitting in a doorway, head down, eyes closed, not moving. As the subject walked by, the man coughed and groaned.

Did the subject stop to find out what was wrong or to offer assistance? Did it matter whether the subject was thinking about the parable of the Good Samaritan as he passed by the stranger in need? Did it matter whether he, like the Levite and the priest in the parable, was in a hurry to get to his destination? The victim in need of help carefully rated the reaction of each subject on a 6-point scale, ranging from failing to notice the victim at all to insisting on taking him somewhere for help.

The results supported Darley and Batson's (1973) predictions. In their words:

A person not in a hurry may stop and offer help to a person in distress. A person in a hurry *is* likely to keep going—even if he is hurrying to give a talk on the parable of the Good Samaritan, thus inadvertently confirming the point of the parable. Indeed, on several occasions a seminary student going to give his talk on the parable of the Good Samaritan literally stepped over the victim as he hurried on his way! (P. 107)

Could it be argued that another interpretation of the parable of the Good Samaritan is possible? Batson and his colleagues (1978) suggested that it is conceivable that the priest and the Levite may have made the decision to bypass the needy person because their business in Jericho was so important that it would result in greater good. In sum, the costs of not helping the needy person may have been less than the costs of failing to arrive in Jericho. Batson and his associates repeated the basic procedure of the Darley and Batson study. Half of the subjects were in a hurry; half were not. In addition, some of the subjects were made to believe that their mission was extremely important; the rest thought their mission less urgent. This time the parable of the Good Samaritan was replicated only when the subject's hurry was combined with his perception that his mission was extremely important.

A note should be added to Good Samaritan studies: Earlier, we discussed the chain of decisions that must be made if we are to decide to offer help to a victim. This chain begins with noticing that the event is occurring. Darley and Batson report that many subjects who were rushing to combat the time pressure placed on them failed to even look in the direction of the groaning victim and denied ever having heard his coughs and groans. The time pressures of our daily lives may cause us to fail to notice events that, from a more dispassionate perspective, would appear to call out for our attention.

When Making the Attribution of Altruism

People who believe that they are altruistic may be more likely to act in an altruistic manner. Earlier we noted that people use instances of behavior and the cues that situations offer to make attributions about themselves and others. Therefore, people who act altruistically may be more apt to act that way in the future if they attribute the cause of their initial behavior to an altruistic disposition.

Paulhus, Shaffer, and Downing (1977) showed that blood donors who were sensitized to the altruistic nature of donating blood (that is, the humanitarianism and selflessness) indicated a greater willingness to donate again in the future than donors who had been sensitized to the personal benefits of the donation (such as the donor's free use of blood-bank supplies). This was particularly true for first-time donors, who were probably less certain of what attribution to make for their own behavior.

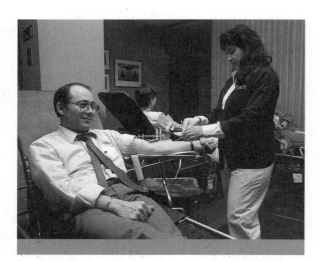

Repeat blood donors seem most motivated by the humanitarian and selfless aspects of their contribution.

In a related context, Batson and his colleagues (1978) showed that people who behaved altruistically might attribute a low degree of altruism to themselves if possible external causes existed for their behavior. Students who entered the University of Kansas administration building were met by an experimental accomplice who requested help in filling out a questionnaire. Some of the subjects received no payment for their help. Others received payment but were told about it only after they finished providing assistance. Still other subjects were promised payment before agreeing to help. This situation closely resembles the "overjustification" studies of Lepper and his colleagues (Lepper, Greene, and Nisbett, 1973), in which intrinsic motivation was undermined by the promise of an attractive reward. As in those studies, the University of Kansas students rated themselves as less al-

truistic if they helped while knowing of a reward. Even though the reward was a mere 25 cents, the subjects who behaved altruistically and knew about the reward were less able to convince themselves that they helped because of the kind of person they were. The subjects who learned of the reward only afterward and the subjects who received no reward saw themselves as altruistic. As the study by Paulhus, Shaffer, and Downing (1977) suggests, such people are likely to behave more altruistically in the future.

When Norms Direct Us to Help

We have already looked at several norms that prescribe altruistic behavior. The general idea that we should give help to people who need it can be termed a **social responsibility norm.** We saw, too, that helping was part of normative behavior to people we consider our friends. However, it is clear that we do not always behave altruistically and that we can, in fact, tolerate considerable inconsistency between the norms we say we hold and our actual behavior.

The **reciprocity norm** provides a promising approach for understanding conditions under which altruism occurs. People tend to match a partner's intimate self-disclosure with an equally intimate one of their own. Gouldner (1960) believed that the reciprocity norm is more general and incorporates the idea that we should help those who help us and not harm those who have helped us. He has argued that the only people exempt from the norm of reciprocity for helping are the old, the very young, and the weak and sick—just those people targeted for aid by the social responsibility norm.

If you ever want someone you know to do you a favor, you may be inclined to remind him of the great number of favors you have done for him: "Remember the time you asked me for a . . ." This folk wisdom is usually effective, as an experiment by Goranson and Berkowitz (1966) demonstrated. The subjects were done a favor by an experimenter who was acting either voluntarily or under compulsion. Later the subjects had a chance to help the experimenter. Even when the subjects didn't expect to see the experimenter again, they were inclined to do a favor for him if he had previously done them a favor. This effect was much more pronounced when the experimenter had performed his favor voluntarily (see also Kahn and Tice, 1973).

Whom Do We Help?

People We Like

Some people are more likely than others to get our help if they need it. It is quite obvious that a member of the family who is in trouble will receive our quick assistance. In most cases, friends will be helped more readily than strangers, although Tesser and Smith (1980) did show that if helping means the helper might be embarrassed, he or she is less likely to help a friend than a stranger.

However, as we have seen, strangers may or may not be helped even if their need seems urgent. It is not surprising then that some research efforts have shown that greater help is given to people who are liked than to those who are disliked (Goodstadt, 1971). Benson, Karabenick, and Lerner (1976) conducted a field experiment in an airline terminal to test the effect of physical attractiveness on the likelihood of receiving help. The subjects were persons who used a particular telephone booth in which a completed graduate school application, a photograph, and a stamped envelope had been placed. It was apparent that the application was to be mailed but that the applicant had left it in the booth. Would the subject offer help by placing the application in the envelope and mailing it? Observations of the subjects showed that their responses depended on the attractiveness of the applicant shown in the photograph. The subjects were much more likely to

mail the application if the photograph was of an attractive rather than an unattractive person.

Similarity: Race and Ideology

Can racial similarity influence the help received by a victim? Are people likely to help people of their own race or is the decision to help someone in need blind to skin color? Research shows that the answer to this question is not a simple one. In an important set of studies by Samuel Gaertner and John Dovidio (1986), black victims were discriminated against by white bystanders only when white bystanders could diffuse responsibility (i.e., when other bystanders were present). However, when they were the only witness to the emergency, white bystanders helped black and white victims to the same degree. The effects of racial similarity were also observed in a follow-up experiment when white bystanders could misattribute their arousal to a placebo—blacks were discriminated against when there was a plausible alternative explanation for why white participants felt distressed. The results of these studies suggest that blatant discrimination against a person of another race is unlikely when that person clearly needs help; however, if the emergency situation is ambiguous, bystanders may rely on racial similarity to determine who will get their help.

We also appear to be more disposed to helping those we perceive as being like-minded. Emswiller, Deaux, and Willits (1971) had students, dressed either as hippies or in more conservative attire, request a dime for a phone call from passersby. In the early 1970s, style of dress often signaled an entire political and social ideology (Darley and Cooper, 1972). The results indicated that people were far more likely to comply with the request when it came from a similarly dressed other. Hippies were significantly more generous to other hippies, and conservatively dressed individuals were more generous to the straight-looking requesters. It is likely that people felt more inclined to assist a person who believed as they did rather than someone whose ideology was far different.

Deserving Others

Imagine that the person in front of you at the supermarket checkout counter line turns to you and says, "Excuse me, I seem to be short on cash. Could you give me some money?" Would it make a difference to

"No, I'm sorry, I don't have a dime to spare. I did, however, see one lying in the gutter not two blocks back."

TABLE 9.5   COMPLIANCE AND INQUIRY RATES AS A FUNCTION OF TREATMENT FOR EXPERIMENT 1

| | Strange Request | | Typical Request | |
	Low 17¢	High 37¢	Low quarter	High any
Percent of compliance	42.5	30.6	30.6	15.3
Average gift	$0.32	$0.41	$0.41	$0.63
N	73	72	72	72

Source: Santos, Leve, and Pratkanis (1994)

you if you noticed that the person was buying something that was not essential? A study conducted by Bickman and Kamzan (1973) suggests that it would make a big difference. Subjects in this study were far more likely to give a female shopper a dime when she was buying a carton of milk than when she was buying a package of cookie dough. Fewer than half the subjects helped out the woman when she was buying cookie dough, but two-thirds helped her buy milk. Race was also a factor in this research. However, the researchers found that the nature of the item that the woman wished to buy (and hence the woman's perceived deservingness) had a considerably larger effect on the subjects' generosity than did the race of the requester.

How a person asks for help may also determine our perceptions of their deservingness. How would you react if a panhandler asked you for "spare change"? How about if the same panhandler asked you for 17 cents? Would your reaction be different? In a study that examined the ways in which we are asked for help, Michael Santos, Craig Leve, and Anthony Pratkanis (1994) trained college students to panhandle on the beach boardwalk in Santa Cruz, California. Some of the student panhandlers asked shoppers for "any spare change" or a "quarter"; some asked for 17 cents or 37 cents. The results, shown in table 9.5, revealed that almost twice as many shoppers helped the panhandler when the request was specific (17 or 37 cents) compared with when it was more general ("Do you have any spare change?"). Santos and his colleagues concluded that a specific dollar amount suggests to us that the person has a specific use in mind for our donation, thereby legitimating the request for help.

In chapter 2, we examined some of the theories

that describe the way in which we make attributions about persons in our environment. Not surprisingly, deciding if a request is worthy is subject to the kind of attributional scrutiny as when we make other decisions about people's characteristics. According to Bernard Weiner (1986), when the reasons for a person's needing help can be attributed to controllable causes such as lack of effort, we are more likely to respond with anger and resist helping. However, if the reasons for needing help are attributed to uncontrollable causes such as bad luck, we are more likely to respond with sympathy and offer our assistance. In one study, Schmidt and Weiner (1988) demonstrated that a student was more likely to receive lecture notes from fellow students if he claimed to have a visual disability (uncontrollable attribution) relative to when he needed notes because he went to the beach instead of class (controllable attribution). Thus, the need for help that derives from a cause that is perceived as controllable by the victim may seem less deserving relative to a request for help that derives from a cause that is beyond the victim's control.

An important finding in the study by Schmidt and Weiner (1988) was that, while the attributions made for why the student needed help determined perceptions of deservingness, the emotional reaction elicited by these attributions had a crucial effect on the decision to help. To be specific, the more sympathy participants felt when they made the uncontrollable attribution, the more likely they were to offer their assistance. As discussed in the next section, the emotional reactions we have to a victim's needs are an important determinant of whether we become motivated to give them a hand. The nature of the emotions that drive our motivation, however, is a time-honored source of controversy in the study of altruistic behavior.

What Motivates People to Help?

Altruism versus Egoism

Up to this point, we have discussed the situational antecedents of helping behavior. It is clear that the circumstances in which an emergency occurs have an important effect on our decisions to help others in need. However, you may have already wondered how situational factors, such as the number of bystanders or the rewards for helping, adequately explain the behavior of a soldier who throws himself on a live grenade to save his platoon. Or you may have questioned how situational factors explain why some people, like firefighters and lifeguards, risk their own safety on a daily basis to save the lives of others. Are these people motivated by self-serving desires for heroic status and recognition, or are they motivated out of a completely unselfish desire to benefit others?

Consider the story of Jerry Schemmel, whose behavior underscored the altruism and selflessness of the human condition. The date was July 19, 1989. It was a beautiful day in the Midwest that Wednesday. United Airlines flight 232 had taken off from Denver into a cloudless sky on what was supposed to be a routine flight to Chicago. But this day was going to be anything but routine for the 290 passengers and crew aboard the jumbo DC10 jetliner. About an hour and a half into the flight, the plane was cruising over the state of Iowa. Lunch was being served. Jerry Schemmel and the other passengers were watching an inflight video. Suddenly they heard a loud bang and the aircraft shuddered. The number two engine, mounted in the tail of the aircraft, had exploded, sending jagged debris through the control surfaces of the tail. Flight 232 was at 37,000 feet, and it was out of control.

For thirty minutes the pilot and his crew struggled to maneuver the aircraft into position to touch down on the runway at Sioux City. But five hundred feet short of the runway, the plane's right wing tip struck the ground. The plane cartwheeled and burst into flames. No one who saw the crash and the gigantic fireball that followed believed anyone could have survived.

Miraculously, the plane struck and burst in such a way that more than half of the passengers survived the impact and the initial explosion. Some climbed out through openings in the plane and walked calmly to safety. But some, such as Jerry Schemmel, had other things on their mind. Although his own route to safety was clearly visible, Schemmel chose not to use it. A baby was crying, and Schemmel was determined to find it. With smoke blanketing the airplane and flames engulfing the craft, it seemed only a matter of minutes before the remaining fuel tanks would catch fire and all remaining passengers would perish in the explosion. Still Schemmel continued his search. He came closer to the sound, searched the floor with his hands, and found one-year-old Sabrina Michaelson. He whisked

Jerry Schemmel's risking his life to retrieve and rescue a one-year-old child from a burning jetliner in 1989 was a supreme act of altruism, characterized by selfless courage.

up the infant and carried her to safety. Even better news came later. Sabrina's parents had also survived the crash, and the three were reunited by evening.

In all, 170 people survived the crash of United flight 232. Some of them survived because other passengers, strangers just moments before, risked their lives to help people in need.

There are at least two perspectives on what motivates people like Jerry Schemmel to help. These perspectives deal with fundamental questions of human nature that philosophers have wrestled with over the centuries. Do we do things for others because human beings are basically good, or must there be some ulterior, self-serving explanation for our apparent helpfulness? Let us examine this distinction. What is a self-serving motive to help others? At a very obvious level, we would not be surprised to find that a person helped an elderly gentleman across the street if that gentleman were known for bestowing lavish tips on people who helped him. If we were to witness this helping incident, we might suspect that the helping was self-serving. Clearly, as the research discussed above suggests, the reward the help-giver might obtain could explain his action. In the absence of a reward, we would probably view the behavior as selfless—done with genuine regard for the plight of another person. But here we have opened up a fascinating and subtle question: Is helping ever truly altruistic?

Think about times when you have witnessed someone being helpful. Perhaps a student knew that her roommate was ill and volunteered to attend an important class for her and take notes. You may have thought that this student behaved altruistically. She acted solely out of regard for her friend's feelings with no personal satisfactions or rewards involved. Or you may have thought that the student, in a sense, acted to please herself. For example, the student may have been distressed by her friend's illness. To leave her friend without notes for the important class might have contributed even more to the student's distress. So she volunteered to attend the class because that action reduced her own distress. That is, it was rewarding for her to act on behalf of her roommate. No one can argue that she acted in a helpful manner and her roommate benefitted from her behavior. In this example, the student is not attempting to have the favor returned later (although this consideration may sometimes be a cause of helpful behavior). Nonetheless, questions remain: Whom is the helper pleasing? Is she focused on the need of her roommate or is she reducing her own distress?

Auguste Comte, the nineteenth-century philosopher, was one of the first to comment on this distinction. He believed that some helping behavior was based on a person's own sense of self-gratification. He referred to this as **egoism.** At the same time, he believed that people also were motivated to "live for others." To describe this basically unselfish desire, Comte coined the term **altruism.** Why, then does the helper help? Why did Jerry Schemmel help? If we focus on egoism, we will look for such rewards as self-congratulations ("I'm a pretty decent person for doing what I did"), escape from guilt or shame ("I could never live with myself if I didn't help"), and relief from distress ("I felt awful when I saw the person in need; I felt better when I helped"). To argue that Schemmel risked his life to find the Michaelson baby for reasons of egoism is not to belittle in any way such helping behavior. It neither belittles nor negates helpful action if people engage in it to feel good about themselves for having come to the aid of a person in need.

Altruism, however, has as its *only* ultimate goal a benefit to another person. The focus is solely on the other without conscious attention focused on one's own self-interest. Daniel Batson and his colleagues (Batson, 1987; Batson, Duncan, Ackerman, Buckley, and Birch, 1981; Batson, Fultz, and Schoenrade, 1987; Batson, Dyck, Brandt, Batson, Powell, McMaster, and Griffith, 1988; Batson, Sager, Garst, Kang, Rubchinsky, and Dawson, 1997) have proposed that true altruism comes from **empathy**—feelings that are congruent with the feelings and perceived welfare of another person (Batson and Oleson, 1990). When a person is in need, empathy would suggest the emotions of sympathy, compassion, and tenderness. According to Batson, empathy creates a motivation for altruism, whose ultimate goal is the benefiting of the person in need.

The **empathy-altruism hypothesis** states that empathy give rise to altruism, and that this is but *one* reason that people help. The empathy-altruism link does not preclude other motivations for acting in a helpful fashion. As figure 9.5 indicates, Batson and his colleagues believe that the relief of personal distress—that is, egoism—is one motive for helping, but that the more selfless concern for others that we call altruism is yet another. According to the empathy-altruism view, if all other reasons for helping were removed, a person experiencing altruism would nonetheless offer assistance to a person in need.

In order to test the empathy-altruism hypothesis experimentally, Batson and his colleagues worked out

FIGURE 9.5   **DISTRESS AND EMPATHY**

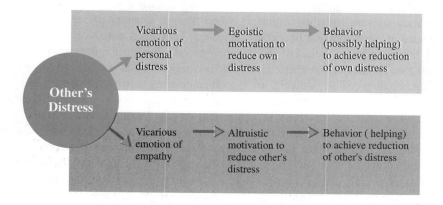

According to Batson et al. (1987), witnessing another person's distress can lead either to personal distress or to empathy. Each leads to its own motivation and behavioral goal.

Source: Batson, Fultz, and Schoenrade (1987)

a few standard scenarios in which subjects witnessed a person in distress and then decided whether or not to offer help. In one of them (Batson, Duncan, Ackerman, Buckley, and Birch, 1981) female students were introduced to a person known as Elaine. The subjects were observed in an experiment in which Elaine was considered the worker. Her job was to perform a sequence of recall tasks for two minutes. At random intervals, Elaine was to receive a series of electric shocks. Subjects watched the proceedings on videotape but believed they were watching live action on closed-circuit TV. The tape made it clear that Elaine was very disturbed by the electric shocks. The subjects were then informed that Elaine had an earlier experience with shocks that made them extremely difficult to bear. Naturally, the subjects were disturbed. The experimenters manipulated the attribution that the subjects made about their feelings. At a prior session Elaine and the participants had filled out a questionnaire to help the subjects form an impression of Elaine. Elaine's questionnaire was filled out by a confederate of the experimenter, so responses were either similar or dissimilar to those of the subjects. Half of the subjects read a similar questionnaire and thus were made to attribute their arousal to empathy, while the other half read a dissimilar questionnaire and were made to attribute their arousal to personal distress.

Subjects were then given an opportunity to help Elaine by trading places with her and receiving the

shock in her place. Which subjects would help? Batson and his colleagues predicted that both the distressed and the empathic subjects would help. Empathic subjects would help because of their true regard for Elaine. Distressed subjects would help because of the personal, egoistic relief they would experience if they traded places with Elaine. Therefore, Batson and his colleagues introduced a manipulation designed to differentiate between the two approaches. Half of the subjects were led to believe that they were free to leave the experiment whenever they wished. Elaine was given blocks of ten trials on which she was given shocks. Easy-escape subjects were told they could decide whether to switch places with Elaine, stay and watch, or leave. In this condition, then, subjects had an easy alternative way to relieve their personal distress. If it made them uncomfortable to see Elaine suffer, they could leave. The other half of the subjects were in the difficult-escape condition. They had to sit and observe Elaine throughout the ten trials. If these subjects were feeling distressed, they had only one way to relieve their discomfort: they would have to switch places with Elaine.

The results confirmed Batson and his colleagues' predictions. Whether escape was difficult or easy, empathic subjects tended to help Elaine. They seemed to be responding to her suffering, not to their own discomfort. Distressed subjects, on the other hand, helped Elaine only if that was the only way to relieve their discomfort. It if was easy to leave the situation, distressed subjects chose that route.

Batson, O'Quinn, Fultz, Vanderplas, and Isen (1983) replicated this experiment and obtained further support for the importance of the distinction between empathic and personal distress arousal. Instead of manipulating what subjects thought they were experiencing after watching Elaine, they asked subjects to describe their emotions after watching Elaine suffer. On the basis of their responses, the subjects were categorized as either personally distressed or empathic. Once again, subjects who were categorized as empathic chose to help regardless of whether escape (leaving the situation) was easy or difficult. Distressed subjects helped primarily if leaving was difficult. The data are shown in figure 9.6.

The Egoism Hypothesis Revised

Does the work we have just described lead to the conclusion that people can help others purely for altruistic reasons? Robert Cialdini and his colleagues (Cialdini, Schaller, Houlihan, Arpps, Flutz, and Beaman, 1987; Cialdini, Brown, Lewis, Luce, and Neuberg, 1997) do not think so. Cialdini and his associates (1987) suggested that Batson and his associates may have been taking the wrong view of egoism. Perhaps it is not distress in the sense of tension, agitation, and so forth but rather *sadness* that people experience when they see someone in need. They feel sad and depressed. They need to reduce that feeling and elevate their mood. Helping the person in need relieves that sadness in a way that leaving the scene does not. This is an interesting twist on the concept of egoism. It suggests that we help others in order to manage our own mood. Seeing others in a state of need causes us to feel bad, and helping is seen as a way of gratifying our own need to feel happy. Therefore, Cialdini and his colleagues are not surprised that empathic subjects help a needy person even when they have the chance to escape. Escape does not accomplish the task; it does not elevate mood, and therefore these subjects continue to help the person in need.

In one study conducted to test this notion, Cialdini and his associates (1987) reasoned that participants who interpret their emotion as empathy will help a victim under almost all conditions except when they think that helping will not serve to make themselves happy. In order to test this hypothesis, the investigators had participants witness a person in need (named Carol in this study) and then gave them an opportunity to help her. Participants were instructed either to be objective

---

FIGURE 9.6   RESULTS OF STUDY COMPARING EMPATHIC VERSUS DISTRESSED FEELINGS AND EASE OF ESCAPE ON THE PROBABILITY OF GIVING HELP

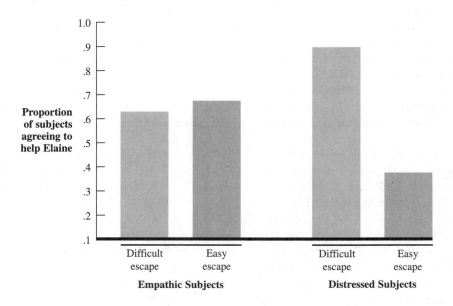

Source: Batson, O'Quinn, Fultz, Vanderplas, and Isen (1983)

FIGURE 9.7   PROPORTION OF SUBJECTS THAT HELPED CAROL AS A FUNCTION OF EMPATHY AND THE FIXEDNESS OF THEIR MOOD

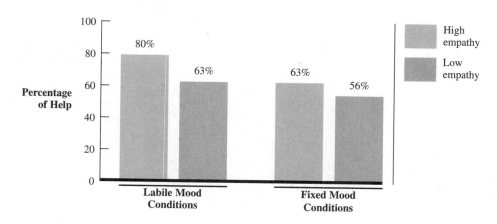

Source: Cialdini et al. (1987)

when participating in the research (low empathy) or to imagine how the other person felt (high empathy). The innovative manipulation was to have half of all subjects take a "mood-fixing" drug after observing Carol's plight. Subjects ingested a substance identified as "Mnemoxine" (actually a placebo) and were told, "This is the mood you'll be in for the next thirty minutes or so. . . . It preserves whatever mood you are in when it takes effect." If participants were saddened when they listened to Carol's difficulties, they could do nothing to elevate their mood—that was the alleged result of the Mnemoxine. To the investigators this would be the key test. Participants in the empathy-set condition could still act altruistically; they could still help Carol for her sake (altruism). However, they could not help Carol in order to make themselves feel happier (egoism). Would they nonetheless help?

In support of the revised egoism hypothesis, participants in the empathy mood-fixing condition chose not to help Carol under these conditions. Figure 9.7 demonstrates that only participants in the empathy condition who did not believe their mood had been fixed by the Mnemoxine chose to help the person in need. Cialdini and his colleagues (1987) concluded that these participants decided to help Carol to make themselves feel better, and that the decision was not motivated by altruism.

Batson and Oleson (1990) have taken issue with the Mnemoxine manipulation used by Cialdini and his colleagues on the grounds that the pill may have

distracted subjects from the plight of the victim. Using a similar procedure (this time the mood-fixing pill was called "Memorin"), a different group of investigators (Schroeder, Dovidio, Sibicky, Matthews, and Allen, 1988) found that subjects did help a person in need despite the mood-fixing pill if they were experiencing empathy.

Other investigators (Smith, Keating, and Stotland, 1989) have examined this productive debate and concluded there may be a middle position that can help to disentangle some of the conflicting evidence. They propose that people will act to help others but are in need of feedback from the victim; that is, some evidence that the victim has been helped by the intervention. Such feedback gives them a feeling of **empathic joy.** Although this feeling is egoistic in the sense that we all like to feel good, it is also empathic in the sense that we are sharing the good feeling we have imparted to the person we helped.

Batson and his colleagues were not convinced that empathic joy is an adequate substitute for true altruism. In one test of the empathic joy hypothesis, Batson, Batson, Singlsby, Harrell, Peekna, and Todd (1991, study 1) designed an experiment in which participants were asked to help a fellow student named Katie, who had recently lost her parents in a car accident. Half the participants were asked to take Katie's perspective on how the accident had affected her life (high empathy) while the other half were asked to take an objective perspective on Katie's loss (low empathy).

TABLE 9.6   **PROPORTION OF SUBJECTS AGREEING TO HELP KATIE IN EACH CELL OF EXPERIMENT 1**

Empathy Condition	No Information about Feedback	Information about Feedback	
		No Feedback	Feedback
Low			
Proportion	.42	.33	.67
M	0.67	0.33	0.92
High			
Proportion	.75	.83	.58
M	1.00	1.17	0.75

Note: n = 12 per cell. The means are those for the scaled measure of helping, ranging from *no help* (0), *3–5 hr* (1), *6–8 hr* (2), *to 9–10 hr* (3).
Source: Batson, Batson, Singlsby, Harrell, Peekna, and Todd (1991)

The amount of empathic joy participants could anticipate from their assistance was manipulated when some were told that Katie would let them know how she was doing (high empathic joy); some were told they would never hear from Katie (low empathic joy); and some were not told anything about how their help might affect Katie (no empathic joy). As seen in table 9.6 when empathy was high, more participants offered assistance regardless of how much empathic joy they expected to experience from doing so. Batson and his associates concluded that people who feel a great deal of empathy may offer help to a victim even when the potential for empathic joy is low. However, the data from the low empathy conditions suggest that the need for empathic joy can influence helping when other-directed empathy is low. Thus, empathic joy may constitute another form of egoistic motivation that can lead to helping when people are not focused on the altruistic goal of reducing another person's distress.

Fostering "Oneness": A New Frontier in the Theoretical Debate

A more recent challenge to the altruism viewpoint has emerged and has engendered yet another fascinating debate. Cialdini, Brown, Lewis, Luce, and Neuberg (1997) suggested that empathizing with another person may cause a merging of a person's sense of self with the self of the other person. Terming this merging *oneness*, Cialdini and his associates (1997) believe that, when oneness is achieved, helping the other person is tantamount to doing something positive for yourself. As Melvin Lerner had phrased it in a slightly

different context years ago, "In effect, [when we respond with empathy] we are reacting to the thought of ourselves in that situation. And, of course, we are filled with the 'milk of human kindness' for our sweet, innocent selves" (Lerner, 1980, p. 77). Thus, even if there is no sadness, empathic joy, or guilt relief, helping another person with whom you have become one is egoistic because by aiding the person in need, you aid yourself.

As a demonstration, Cialdini and his colleagues (Cialdini et al., 1997; Neuberg, Cialdini, Brown, Luce, Sagarin and Lewis, 1997) presented participants with hypothetical scenarios about people in need of help. They invented hypothetical situations involving a needy victim. They manipulated the degree of closeness that existed between the participant and the victim by asking participants to imagine that the victim was a stranger, an acquaintance, a good friend, or a close family member. They found that when instructed to perceive the victim with empathy, participants imagined that they would give more help to victims whose relationship was imagined to be close (for example, family members) rather than far (strangers). In addition, the researchers asked the participants several questions about their reasons for helping the person in need. As they predicted, the decision to help was mediated by the feeling of oneness. Only those people who felt that their own self-boundaries merged with the self-boundaries of the victims agreed to help the victim.

Batson (1997) disagreed with the interpretations of Cialdini and his associates as well as of Neuberg and his colleagues (1997). Batson, Sagen, Garst,

Kang, Rubchinsky, and Dawson (1997) conducted two new experiments to test the importance of oneness. Rather than having participants imagine whether they would provide help, the researchers had participants actively involved with another student (actually a confederate) who was in desperate need of money to support her family. Batson found that when participants empathized with the student, their decision to help her raise money for her family was dependent upon their altruistic motivation and not at all on their perception of oneness with her.

Why then do people help others? The debate between those who believe that people help others—at least sometimes—for altruistic motives and those who believe helping is always motivated by self-interest, including the feeling of oneness, has been fascinating. A definitive answer remains elusive. In sharpening the altruistic view of helping, Batson (1997) does not disagree that people can help because they want to reap rewards, absolve guilt, or help a person whose boundaries merge with their own. At issue is only whether feeling empathy with another human being establishes a motivation to be altruistic, which, at least sometimes, can be sufficient to cause us to help our fellow human beings. We can be sure that this debate will continue to be sharpened with further experimentation.

The Helping Personality: Are Some People More Likely to Help Than Others?

While the debate between egoistic and altruistic motivation continues, some psychologists have turned to examine altruism from a slightly different angle: Is there an altruistic personality? We all know people who seem to be more helpful than others, volunteering much of their time to charities or other organizations. Is there a particular set of attributes or characteristics that distinguish helpful people?

One way to investigate the influence of personality on helping is by examining the personal attributes of people who help under extraordinary conditions and comparing them to the characteristics held by people who were in the same situation but did not

help. Samuel and Pearl Oliner (1988) conducted such a study of the people who risked their lives to save Jews during the genocide that occurred under Nazi occupation in Europe during World War II. Samuel Oliner is a Holocaust survivor who grew up in Poland. During the German occupation in 1940 his family was killed by the Nazis. Oliner escaped by hiding and was finally rescued by a Christian family who owned a farm near his house. When the war was over, Samuel Oliner immigrated to the United States where he obtained his Ph.D. in sociology and became a professor at Humboldt State University. He then turned his attention to the systematic study of "rescuers"—people in Europe who had risked their own welfare to hide and care for Jews and other minorities that had been targeted for annihilation.

The Oliners located and interviewed 231 Europeans who had rescued Jews and others and compared their characteristics to a sample of 126 individuals who did not attempt to rescue anyone during the war. Of importance is that these two groups were matched on age, sex, education, and geographic region before their interview results were analyzed. The results showed that rescuers and nonrescuers could be distinguished by personality characteristics. Specifically, those who rescued victims of the Holocaust reported feeling a strong sense of responsibility for the welfare of others and an overwhelming need to act on their feelings of responsibility. In addition, they felt the pain and suffering of the victims, suggesting that feelings of emotional empathy were an important motivational force in their decision to help. But while rescuers and nonrescuers were equally likely to apply feelings of empathy and responsibility to members of their own group (other Christians), rescuers were more likely to feel empathy and responsibility for people who were perceived as dissimilar to them. Thus, rescuers could be distinguished from nonrescuers in what the Oliners called *extensivity*—the ability to feel empathy and responsibility for members of groups other than one's own.

Another factor that distinguished rescuers and nonrescuers was their socialization and upbringing. Rescuers were more likely to have been brought up by parents who did not use physical punishment to control their child's behavior. Instead, the parents of rescuers were more likely to use reason—they would explain to their children what they had done wrong, and they would then make clear what behaviors were expected of them. Thus, rescuers were punished by reason rather than by spanking. In addition, rescuers were more likely to have one parent who exemplified and modeled moral behavior. Together, these forms of child rearing may have instilled an other-oriented tendency that facilitated the decision to help when people sought shelter from the Nazi maelstrom.

Another study by Tec (1986) of rescuers and nonrescuers found other intriguing differences. First, relative to nonrescuers, rescuers tended to be marginal members of their local community—they did not report feeling integrated into the local social networks. Second, rescuers reported higher levels of independence and self-reliance relative to nonrescuers. That is, rescuers saw themselves as outsiders who would deviate from local norms to accomplish their personal goals. And, finally, rescuers reported having a history of helping others before the war, which suggests that rescuers did not become altruistic because of Nazi occupation; for them, this simply provided another opportunity to help people who were in need.

If the findings on personality differences between rescuers and nonrescuers during the Nazi occupation of Europe provide some interesting evidence for the influence of personality on helping behavior, there are important limitations to the archival methodology used to investigate these groups. For example, a large number of personality measures were administered in the questionnaires used by Oliner and Oliner (1988), yet only a handful of differences emerged (see, for example, Piliavin and Charng, 1990); and these differences might have occurred by random chance. In addition, rescuers were identified as "heroes" and "true altruists" years before they were interviewed by researchers (Schroeder, Penner, Dovidio, and Piliavin, 1995). Consequently, they may have answered the questions in the way they believed an altruist should, or they may have reconstructed their memories for events during and before the war to fit the profile of an altruist. It is difficult to know whether the personality differences found in this research are reliable, and we cannot know for sure that they are the cause and not the consequence of people having rescued someone from harm's way.

The Altruistic Volunteer: Combining Personality and Motivation

The research on rescuers in occupied Europe highlights examples of helping conducted by truly excep-

tional people under extraordinary circumstances. What evidence is there for an altruistic personality in less extreme circumstances, such as volunteerism in one's community or donating blood to a hospital or blood bank? A number of studies in social psychology have examined the relationship between various personality characteristics and volunteerism. For example, dispositional empathy has been shown to correlate with how much money students donated to the Jerry Lewis Muscular Dystrophy Telethon (Davis, 1983). Likewise, the dimension of other-oriented empathy, which is very similar to the characteristic of extensivity recognized by the Oliners among rescuers, has been shown to predict helping behavior. People who score high on other-oriented empathy report more sympathy and concern for someone who is in trouble, estimate the costs of helping as lower, and are more likely to volunteer their time in a local homeless shelter (Schroeder, Penner, Dovidio, and Piliavin, 1995). Thus, even apart from the horrors of Nazi occupation, people who experience a strong sense of empathy for others are more likely to donate their time and abilities in local communities.

Alan Omoto and Mark Snyder (Omoto and Snyder, 1990; Snyder, 1993) have added the notion of *functional volunteering*. In their view, volunteering may satisfy different motivations for different people at different times. Some people who volunteer to work at an AIDS clinic, for example, may be motivated to offer assistance because they are curious about AIDS patients; others may be motivated to feel better about themselves; still others may feel obligated to the gay community; and so forth. Volunteering, then, serves the function of satisfying a person's specific motivation. In the functionalist view, a general personality disposition to help is not so important as a person's specific motivation that can be satisfied by the volunteering behavior. Omoto and Snyder (1995) surveyed more than six hundred AIDS volunteers and found that measures of specific motivations were more predictive of how long people served in a volunteer capacity than was the personality of the volunteer.

It is likely that both motivation and personality are important factors in understanding volunteerism. Perhaps having a general disposition to be helpful is predictive of the likelihood of volunteering, but the length of time or intensity of the volunteering is predicted by the degree to which it satisfies a person's particular motivation.

Functionalists believe that a general disposition to help is less important to volunteers than a specific motivation that can be satisfied by volunteering. In this view, the helpers in this San Francisco Open Hand project for feeding PWAs may participate for a variety of reasons, including curiosity, obligation, and feeling better about oneself.

Helping Behavior Revisited: Personality or the Situation?

Which has more influence over helping behavior? The answer to this question appears to depend upon the situational influences and the type of personality variables held by those who find themselves in a helping situation. Recall that in the Good Samaritan study by Batson and Darley described earlier in this chapter, even those participants with strong religious beliefs did not stop to help the victim when they were in a hurry to get across campus. What this suggests is that even the most helpful among us can be overcome by the power of the situation and fail to assist someone in need. But what if the situation is rather mundane? Might personality differences flourish if the situation did not restrict our actions?

In one attempt to answer this question, Gustavo Carlo and his colleagues (Carlo, Eisenberg, Troyer, Switzer, and Speer, 1991) administered a series of altruism-related personality measures to college students a few weeks before they participated in an experiment on helping. When participants returned for the experiment, they found themselves observing a female (actually a confederate) who was trying to complete a difficult task. For some of the participants, the confederate appeared to become very distressed while working on the task; for the other participants, she did not become noticeably distressed. To elicit helping after struggling for a while, the confederate turned to participants and asked if they would be willing to take her place. For some of the participants, the costs for not helping were very strong—if they refused, they would have to stay and watch a highly distressed person complete the task. For the other half, the costs for not helping were relatively weak—if they refused to help, they would be able to escape the situation shortly thereafter. The results showed that when the confederate's distress was high and escape was low, 79 percent of participants took the confederate's place regardless of their level of other-directed empathy. However, when the situation was weak, scores on the personality measures significantly predicted helping—those who scored high on other-directed empathy and sympathy for the victim were significantly more likely to help the confederate relative to those who scored low on these personality dimensions. Thus, people with certain personality characteristics may be more likely to help when the situation does not demand it; however, the circumstances in which help is needed can have a powerful effect on perceptions of what the appropriate course of action should be.

BOX 9.2

Truly Heroic Helping: The Story of Oskar Schindler

In the 1993 film *Schindler's List,* Steven Spielberg told the story of Oskar Schindler, a German businessman who, from 1939 to 1945, saved more than twelve hundred Jews from the brutal savagery of Amon Goeth at his forced labor camp outside of Krakow, Poland. Schindler, at great risk to his own health and safety, first saved Jewish immigrants by employing them as workers in his factory Amelia, manufacturing pots and pans, and then later by moving his workers to a fake factory in his hometown of Zwittau, Germany. By the end of World War II, Schindler had sacrificed everything he owned to secure the safety of the Jewish families he employed.

In the first chapter of his book on which the film was based, Thomas Keneally (1982) details Schindler's background to show that "[i]t is not easy to find in [his] family's history the origins of his impulse toward rescue." (p. 31). Schindler himself was from a Catholic family but, according to Keneally, did not hold particularly strong religious beliefs, nor did his parents model the type of egalitarian beliefs common among the rescuers studied by the Oliners (1985) or Tec (1986). Schindler did not have a clear history of helping others, nor did he see himself primarily as a helpful person. He described himself as a capitalist, interested in monetary gain. His Austrian heritage, however, did place him at the fringe of his Zwittau community. Nevertheless, according to Keneally's research, there is very little evidence to suggest that Schindler's personality or upbringing played a crucial role in his decision to assist Jews during World War II.

Keneally is also careful to point out that, in the beginning, Schindler's motives for helping Jews were primarily egoistic. That is, Schindler went to Krakow after the German occupation to buy Jewish businesses that had been foreclosed by the Polish-German government. Because Jews had been stripped of their power and civil rights, Schindler viewed them as a source of inexpensive labor for his enamelware factory. Thus, Schindler's initial rescue of Jews came not from a sense of empathy for their plight but because of the wealth they could help him obtain through manufacturing kitchenware for the black market and the German armed forces.

However, Keneally's (1982) story reveals a number of events that may have played an instrumental role in shifting Schindler's motivations from egoistic to altruistic. First, Schindler was arrested twice by the German police, once for operating his black market commerce and once for expressing affection toward a Jewish girl. Although it appears he was well treated while held in jail, Schindler's captivity may have provided some perspective on how his Jewish employees lived inside the Krakow ghetto. Then, one morning shortly after his second arrest, some of Schindler's workers, including his bookkeeper, were herded off to the railway station and put into cattle cars for transport to Auschwitz. According to Keneally, as he arrived to find them, Schindler was shocked and angered by the inhumane treatment he witnessed. And, finally, Schindler himself witnessed the liquidation of the Krakow ghetto and the brutal executions of many men, women, and children. According to Keneally, after seeing the random savagery of the SS troops, Oskar Schindler no longer viewed the events in Krakow as temporary lunacies—he interpreted them as an officially sanctioned program of genocide. This realization may have provided Schindler with the perspective necessary for him to feel the sense of empathy and altruistic motivation that, according to Batson and his colleagues, is necessary for someone to put the interests of others ahead of one's own health, wealth, and personal freedom.

Reactions of the Recipients: Do They Always Love the Helper?

During the first decade of intensive research on helping behavior, almost all attention was focused on the helpers. Their costs, their rewards, their arousal, and their responsibility were the focus of research. The reaction of the recipients of aid was assumed to be positive as might be predicted by simple reinforcement theories. After all, seeking and receiving help usually results in increased material benefit for the recipient (Gross, Wallston, and Piliavin, 1975). More recently, though, attention has been paid to the psychology of receiving help. Several social-psychological theories predict negative reactions by the recipients of help under some conditions. Let's turn to the application of some of these theories (some encountered in earlier chapters and others that will be discussed more fully in later ones) to helping situations.

Equity Theory: Is It As Equal to Give As to Receive?

The heart of **equity theory** is the proposal that individuals will not only attempt to maximize their rewards in a relationship, they will also try to achieve an equitable relationship. For equity to exist, the ratio of one person's rewards to costs should be equal to his or her partner's rewards-to-costs ratio. People who find themselves in an inequitable relationship will feel distressed. A helping situation is often inequitable, with the recipient of help feeling that he or she is indebted to the helper. Several investigations have demonstrated that the recipient of help may feel negatively toward the helper when the recipient has no opportunity to reciprocate (Castro, 1974; Gross and Latané, 1974; Clark, Gotay, and Mills, 1974).

Equity theory proposes that in an inequitable relationship, both the individual who has contributed more *and* the individual who has contributed less will be distressed. However, research on helping situations has demonstrated only that the recipient of help is distressed. Helpers often feel good about their actions.

Social Exchange Theories: Helping Is Power

According to **social exchange theory,** any time individuals interact, certain *costs* must be paid and certain *rewards* result. According to Worchel (1984), an increased sense of power is one of the rewards a helper receives from the interaction. This sense flows from the fact that the helper demonstrated useful abilities and resources and was able to influence other people. The increased sense of power is independent of anything the recipient does to repay the helper, and Worchel maintains that often the increased sense of power offsets the cost of helping, which, from the helper's point of view, makes the interaction worthwhile. In contrast, an increased sense of powerlessness is a cost that the recipient experiences from the interaction, for the recipient has been forced to acknowledge dependence.

Self-Threat Theory of Recipient: Reactions to Help

Receiving help can also threaten the recipient's self-esteem. Arie Nadler and Jeffrey Fisher (1986) proposed that when help is perceived as self-supportive and signals caring and concern for the recipient, it produces such positive reactions as enhanced feelings of self-worth and appreciation directed toward the helper. However, there are conditions under which lending assistance can reduce a recipient's feelings of self-worth and elicit a negative evaluation of the helper and the help itself. First, help will be self-threatening when it conveys the message that the recipient is inferior and is dependent upon the help to avoid failure. Second, help that deviates from important socialized values such as independence, self-reliance, and fairness will pose a threat to the recipient's self-worth. Finally, help will elicit a negative reaction if it does not increase the probability of future success or if it does not reduce the need for future assistance. Aid that meets any of these three criteria will cause the recipient to suffer short-term reductions in help-seeking, more self-reliance, and an increased desire for improvement.

As we might expect from the section on the relationship between personality and helping, reactions to receiving help can be a function of individual differences. Nadler and Fisher hold that people with high self-esteem are more likely to experience negative reactions to threatening help compared with people with low self-esteem. Apparently, those who feel a strong sense of self-efficacy and competence are more likely to resent assistance that implies they may be incapable of success, are not self-reliant, and are likely to fail in the future.

Recipients' Reactions: A Postscript

This discussion should not be taken to mean that help is never appreciated. On the contrary, people who are truly in need of help respond favorably to a person who comes to their aid. But research in the area of helping has identified what might be called the helper's dilemma. The more the helping goes beyond what is absolutely required (Schwartz, 1977) or the more the favor is unsolicited or the less the opportunity for reciprocation, the more likely it is that the recipient will react negatively to the help. This may be as true of nations as it is of individuals. How often have powerful nations been surprised by the hostile reactions engendered in the people of countries to which they have given substantial assistance? So, while partners in a relationship may offer aid as a way of being helpful and getting their partner to like them, the reaction to the assistance may be the opposite of what was desired. Rather than seeming to bring benefit, the assistance may be viewed as a restriction of freedom, the creation of inequity, the usurpation of power, or the impression that the recipient is inferior and dependent upon others for success.

event, (2) interpret it as an emergency, (3) assume the responsibility to act, (4) know the appropriate form of assistance, and (5) implement their decision to help in an emergency.

Much of the research on bystander intervention has revolved about the question of responsibility. Darley and Latané showed that the number of witnesses to an emergency is related to the likelihood of acting: the more witnesses, the less action. The presence of a number of bystanders makes any single bystander feel less responsible for intervening and therefore less likely to act altruistically.

A cost model of helping has been developed to account for situations that do and do not lead to help-

This independent woman, despite her handicap, appears capable of carrying out her personal duties and would probably resent assistance from others.

ing. According to the expanded version of the model, helping increases when empathy and psychological arousal are high. If those conditions are met, the likelihood of intervention increases as the cost to the bystander decreases. Intervention also increases as the cost to the victim for the bystander's failure to help increases. Factors that affect differences in the way people perceive the various costs involved in helping must also be considered.

Research on who tends to receive help shows that we are most likely to help people we like, people who are similar to us, and people whose need

Summary

This chapter considered the factors that cause people to be apathetic when witnessing someone's need for help. The failure of bystanders to help Kitty Genovese led Latané and Darley to study bystander apathy. In their decision tree model, bystanders must (1) notice the seems to be most legitimate. Research on the situations that are likely to produce helping behavior has shown that helping increases when (1) we have been positively rewarded for previous helping, (2) we are in a good mood, (3) we observe someone else helping, (4) we are not otherwise preoccupied or hurried, (5) we attribute altruistic motivation to ourselves, and (6) norms direct us to help. Among the norms that lead to helping are reciprocity and social responsibility norms. We also tend to help those who seem deserving, which in part depends upon how they ask for help and the reasons why they need our help.

People may come to the aid of other people for altruistic or egoistic reasons. The empathy-altruism hypothesis suggests that the emotion of empathy is a motivation for altruism. Empathy is the ability to share in another person's feelings. Altruism is an unselfish desire to help another person; its ultimate goal is to benefit another's welfare. Egoism, on the other hand, is a tendency to focus on one's own gratification. Egoistic helping may be motivated by a desire to relieve one's own distress or sadness. The empathy-altruism hypothesis of Batson and his colleagues does not negate the possibility of egoistic helping but holds that pure altruism is one motivation to help. Cialdini and his colleagues' egoism hypothesis holds that all helping is essentially egoistic. Empathic joy has also been held to explain why people choose to help others, but more work in this area is needed before a conclusive answer can be provided.

There is evidence of the existence of an altruistic personality. Research on Christians and others who rescued persecuted groups from the Nazis in occupied Europe suggests that the traits of extensivity (other-directed empathy and responsibility) and independence tended to correlate with helping. In addition, socialization variables such as parenting styles and community integration tended to distinguish those who rescued from those who did not. Community volunteerism also appears to be related to measures of other-directed empathy and responsibility.

The recipient's response to helping may not always be positive. Favorable responses depend on the attribution process as the recipient determines the meaning of the helpful action. Reactions to help are also a function of how the help is provided. If perceived as demeaning, unjust, or as incompetent, help will result in negative evaluations of the helper and the help itself and will reduce the probability of success in the future. People with high self-esteem may be especially prone to the ill effects of poor help.

Key Terms

altruism	egoism	equity theory
cost model of helping	empathic joy	reciprocity norm
decision tree	empathy	social exchange theory
diffusion of responsibility	empathy-altruism hypothesis	social responsibility norm

Suggested Readings

Batson, C.D. (1987). Prosocial motivation: Is it ever truly altruistic? In L. Berkowitz (Ed.), *Advances in experimental social psychology* (Vol. 20, pp. 65–122). Orlando, FL: Academic Press.

Batson, C.D. (1997). Altruism and prosocial behavior. In D. T. Gilbert, S. T. Fiske, and G. Lindzey (Eds.) *Handbook of Social Psychology* (4th ed). New York: Oxford University Press and McGraw Hill.

Cialdini, R. B. (1991). Altruism or egoism? That is (still) the question. *Psychological Inquiry 2,* 124–126.

Keneally, T. (1982). *Schindler's list.* New York: Simon and Schuster.

Latané, B., and Darley, J.M. (1970). *The unresponsive bystander: Why doesn't he help?* Englewood Cliffs, NJ: Prentice-Hall.

Oliner, S.P., and Oliner, P.M. (1988). *The altruistic personality: Rescuers of Jews in Nazi Europe.* New York: Free Press.

Piliavin, J.A., Dovidio, J., Gaertner, S., and Clark, R.D., III. (1981). *Emergency interventions.* New York: Plenum.

Chapter 10

Aggression: Harming Others

Except for the constant drone of the television, the forced silence in the room was broken only by quiet sobbing. No one moved for almost a half hour, until one of the six fraternity men bolted from his chair and turned off the television set, apologizing in a cracked voice, "I can't watch this any more." This statement characterized the feeling of many people who watched live television coverage of the trial of the *People versus Steinberg*. Indeed, these feelings of sadness, disbelief, depression, anger, and emptiness were rekindled in us as we wrote about the incident.

Joel Steinberg seemed to have everything going for him. He grew up in a well-to-do home in Yonkers, New York. His father was a successful corporate lawyer. Joel was handsome, bright, and self-assured. He had built himself a thriving law practice in New York City and had an impressive list of wealthy clients. In 1975 he met Hedda Nussbaum at a party. Hedda was a tall, attractive woman who worked for a major New York publishing house as an editor of children's books. Although very bright and talented, Hedda lacked faith in herself and her abilities.

Joel supported and encouraged Hedda. As Hedda's self-esteem grew, her work improved and she received several promotions. The couple seemed to be on the road to living the American dream when Hedda moved in with Joel in 1976. Life took an unexpected turn, however, when Joel began to criticize Hedda. His criticism was often cruel and harsh, but he convinced her that he was doing it for her own good. Then, after they had lived together for three years, Joel struck her in the face. Both Hedda and Joel were surprised by this action. Hedda, in fact, said later that she was too surprised by the event to be angry. They both thought it wouldn't happen again.

Instead, it became a way of life. The dream quickly became a nightmare. The beatings became more frequent and sadistic. Hedda reported that the violence took many forms; Joel kicked her in the eye, strangled her, broke her nose several times, and even hung her in handcuffs from a chinning bar. One beating was so severe that Hedda had to undergo surgery for a ruptured spleen.

Just when life looked the bleakest, a turn of events promised to rescue the couple. An unmarried woman paid Steinberg to find a good home for her baby. Hedda and Joel took custody of the child. They named her Lisa. Nussbaum reported that life was a joy for about six months as she and Joel devoted themselves to Lisa. But the beatings began again and this time they were harsher and more frequent.

Hedda's injuries forced her to miss work so often that in 1982 she was fired from her job. She lost weight, going from 125 pounds to 100 pounds. She took on the appearance of a badly beaten prizefighter, and she rarely went out in public with Joel. Both Joel and Hedda began to free-base cocaine more frequently, a habit they had begun in 1978. Joel's practice suffered and he was disbarred.

In 1986 the couple was given a baby boy by a physician friend. Few people suspected that anything was wrong in their lives. The arrival of Mitchell marked a short respite in the pattern of beatings, but they soon began again. Now Hedda was not the only target; Lisa, too, became a target and was beaten because she stared too much at Joel.

By late October 1987 Joel was using cocaine almost daily. Hedda told a hushed courtroom that on the evening of November 1, Joel complained that Lisa was staring at him again. He believed she was trying to hypnotize him, and he went into her room to stop her. When Hedda next saw Lisa, she was unconscious. While Lisa lay comatose on the bed, Joel and Hedda smoked cocaine until nearly 4:00 A.M. Hedda consulted a medical dictionary to see what could be done for Lisa, but she felt that Lisa was not critically hurt. About 6:00 A.M. Joel

Joel Steinberg and Hedda Nussbaum being booked in 1987 after charges of attempted murder and assault of their adopted daughter, Lisa. Charges against Nussbaum, showing signs of her battering by Steinberg, were later dropped, because, for the violence inflicted on her, she was thought incapable of killing or saving Lisa.

discovered that Lisa had stopped breathing; an ambulance was called and Lisa was taken to a hospital. Four days later she died of a brain hemorrhage.

Initially both Hedda Nussbaum and Joel Steinberg were charged with murder. Charges against Hedda were later dropped, however, on the grounds that she had been so battered that she was incapable of killing Lisa or saving her life. Joel was brought to trial and a shocked world watched and listened as the tragic story unfolded live on television. Joel Steinberg was convicted of first-degree manslaughter and sentenced to a jail term of eight and one-half to twenty-five years.

What Is Aggression? Toward a Definition

The story of Lisa Steinberg is tragic and dramatic: the senseless violence of one man who killed an innocent child and permanently disfigured an adult who loved him. What could have caused Joel Steinberg to act with such cruelty? We are immediately tempted to leap in with the simple explanation that Joel Steinberg was "nuts." We could build a case for this explanation of Steinberg's bizarre behavior. Indeed, the more celebrated cases of extreme violence all have an element of craziness on the part of the perpetrator. Jeffrey Dahmer killed and mutilated the bodies of at least eleven victims before eating the body parts. Charles Whitman climbed the tower at the University of Texas in 1966 and slaughtered thirteen innocent victims on the campus below. But what do we make of the millions of cases of family violence committed every year? What do we make of the annual count of approximately twenty thousand murders committed in the United States each year or the one million aggravated assaults that occur annually in the United States? Can craziness account for all of these acts of aggression or the countless violent confrontations that occur on the streets each day of the year?

But we are getting a bit ahead of ourselves. Before we begin to examine the causes of aggression, let's take some time to define what we mean by aggression. As a student preparing for your upcoming exam, you probably have your pen poised to underline a concise and clear definition. Yet aggression—an act that we think we know when we see it—has some elements that are difficult to define. Don't worry, for we will offer a definition presently. But let's think a minute before opening up the dictionary. We probably all agree that Joel Steinberg's treatment of Lisa and Hedda was aggressive. But what about Hedda's actions on the night that Lisa lay comatose on her bed? Hedda did nothing to help the dying child. Her inaction may have contributed to the child's death. Was this aggression? Prosecutors initially thought that her actions opened her to the charge of murder. Later, they withdrew the charge.

And what about our agreement that Joel Steinberg's actions were aggressive? Joel argued, and he convinced Hedda, that the beatings he administered were aimed at "helping" her. He sounds much like the parent who argues that spanking the child is aimed at making the child a better person: "This hurts me more than it does you."

Thus we reach our first juncture in defining aggression. Do we focus on the act itself and say that aggression is any behavior that delivers a noxious stimulus to another person (Buss, 1961)? Or do we focus on *intention* and define aggression as any act that is intended to injure the target (Dollard, Droob, Miller, Mowrer, and Sears, 1939; Baron, 1977)? Our legal system and many researchers feel that a complete definition of aggression must include intention. If your neighbor shoots you, the action is aggressive if the neighbor intended to hurt you. It is only an unfortunate accident if the neighbor was cleaning the gun and it went off. We might find it negligent, but we would not think of it as aggressive.

Including intention in our definition makes intuitive sense, but it raises new problems for us. How do we determine intention? In an interesting study, Mummendey and Otten (1989) had subjects watch videotaped segments of an aggressive encounter between two boys. Some observers were told to take the perspective of the initiator while others were instructed to take the perspective of the recipient. The subjects who took the perspective of the recipient considered the actions to be more aggressive and were more likely to attribute harmful intentions to the aggressor. The point is that it is often difficult to determine the intention behind an act.

We present these difficulties because it is important to recognize the elusive nature of what might have seemed to be an easily recognizable concept. We also recognize that acts of aggression may be about many things other than delivering harm. People may intentionally hurt others in order to intimidate, to gain power, to express anger, or to achieve some other goal. With a better understanding of some of the difficulties of a good definition, we will proceed to offer our working definition that *aggression is an act that is intended to injure the target.*

Just as there are numerous types of aggression, so too are there many theories about its causes. No one theory may be able to explain all instances of aggression; some may best handle certain types of aggression. With this point in mind, let's examine some of those theories.

Theories of Aggression

In developing a theory to explain aggression, we can approach the topic in one of two ways. We can look inside the person (or organism) with the view that he or she is *pushed* by some internal force to aggress. The aim, then, becomes to identify that force or seat of aggression. Or we can look to external factors that may *pull* the individual to aggress. At this level of analysis, we attempt to identify environmental or social conditions that instigate aggression. Instinct and biological theories take the former approach to studying aggression, whereas frustration-aggression and social learning theories focus on the latter approach.

Instinct Theories

Among the oldest and most controversial theories of aggression are those that state aggression is an *instinct.* This concept implies that a behavior is inherited rather than learned, and that the behavior pattern is common to all members of the species. After witnessing the death and destruction of World War I, Sigmund Freud decided that humans are born with the instinct to aggress. He argued that the drive for violence arises from within people and that human aggression cannot be eliminated. It is therefore important to give people the opportunity to channel their aggression in nondestructive ways.

Another theory of instincts has been proposed by *ethologists,* scientists who study animal behavior.

Nobel prize winner Konrad Lorenz (1968) pointed out that the instinct to aggress is common to many animal species. Lorenz, however, differed from Freud in holding that aggressive behavior will not occur unless it is triggered by external cues. Unlike Freud, who saw aggression as destructive and disruptive, Lorenz viewed intraspecies aggression as adaptive and essential for the survival of animal species. An animal protects its territory, and hence its food supply, by attacking other animals that invade its territory. Aggression serves to spread out animal populations and to prevent overcrowding. In addition, as a result of the fights that animals wage over mates, the strongest animals win the mates and reproduce the species. Thus, only the fittest members of a species reproduce and the defective members are weeded out.

Instinct theories have been subjected to many attacks. One focuses on the issue of natural releasing mechanisms. Many instinct theories argue that certain animals have built-in releasing mechanisms that cause them to act aggressively in particular situations, although such mechanisms have not been identified in many animal species or in humans. Zing Yang Kuo (1930) raised some kittens with rat-killing mothers, some kittens in isolation, and a third group of kittens with rats as constant companions. After a period of time, the grown kittens were placed in the presence of rats. Of those that had been raised with the rat-killing mothers, 85 percent killed the rats, whereas only 17 percent of those that had been raised with rats attacked them.

A second criticism of instinct theories is most directly concerned with human aggression. If humans are instinctively aggressive, we would expect to find a great deal of similarity in the style and amount of aggression displayed by people. However, one of the main characteristics of human aggression is its diversity. Some people are often violent while others are seldom violent. Some people use weapons and others wound with words. Some people aggress directly and openly while others engage in passive aggression.

Cultures also vary greatly in both the amount of aggression they express and the ways in which they express it. In 1990, the U.S. homicide rate was the highest of all twenty nations surveyed. Even when you adjust for population differences, four times more people were murdered in the United States as compared with Scotland, which had the second highest homicide rate. The lowest homicide rates were found in Austria and Japan (Fingerhut and Kleinman, 1990). Firearms were also much more likely to be used in U.S. homicides. In 1987 there were 4,223 homicides involving firearms in the United States. There were 62 in Canada, 34 in Australia, 13 in Israel, and only 4 in Denmark. (For more about cultural differences in aggression, see the discussion of the South's "culture of honor" in Box 10.1). If aggression were purely human instinct unaffected by the environment, we would expect to find much more similarity in the types and numbers of homicides committed in different nations.

We do not want to ignore the role that instinct can play in aggression. Any animal breeder knows that we can develop a more aggressive animal through selective breeding and that some species of animals are more aggressive than others. But it is difficult to make the leap from here to argue that humans are instinctively aggressive. Or even that some humans are more instinctively aggressive than others. How can an instinct theory help us understand the violence of Joel Steinberg? Steinberg was not always aggressive nor did he aggress against everyone he met. Although instinct may play some role in human aggression, most research on human aggression has been directed elsewhere.

Biological Theories

Biological theories also locate the seat of aggression inside the individual. These theories, however, differ from the earlier instinct theories because they attempt to identify specific biological mechanisms that excite people to aggression.

Proponents of one biological approach have attempted to identify specific parts of the brain or nervous system that may be related to aggressive behavior. The limbic system, which influences our drives and emotions, has been identified as one such area. Some researchers feel that the amygdala, which is part of the limbic system, plays an important role in aggression (Hitchcock, 1979; Moyer, 1971). Other researchers have identified the cerebral cortex of the brain as playing an important role. The cortex is responsible for higher level thought processes, such as deciding when an action is appropriate (Weiger and Bear, 1988). It appears that when the cortex is damaged or impaired, people may commit more impulsive acts of aggression (Heinrichs, 1989; Silver and Yudofsky, 1987). Although these portions of the nervous system have been identified and linked to aggression, much research is still needed to clarify the specific role they play in the expression of aggressive behavior.

BOX 10.1

Violence and Culture in the Southern United States

More than a century ago, Redfield (1880) noted a remarkable difference between the southern and northern regions of the United States. Murder rates were ten times higher in the southern states of the nation. We may initially attribute this difference to defeated Civil War veterans or some other factor of the postwar era, but similar differences in murder rates have been found between northern and southern states ever since. Researchers in the early part of the twentieth century found smaller differences between homicide rates in the North and the South, but in 1932 Brearly still reported more than two and a half murders in the South for every murder in the rest of the United States. In the second half of the century, researchers continued to find higher homicide and assault rates in southern, as opposed to northern, states (Goldstein, 1994).

Why should individuals who live south of the Mason-Dixon line be more likely to commit homicides during a period that spans at least one hundred years? Two types of explanations have appeared. One is that there are cultural differences between the northern and southern states that lead to differences in violence. Researchers have proposed that higher levels of aggression occur in the South because of cultural norms specific to that region (Cash, 1941; Cohen, 1996; Hackney, 1969; Nisbett, 1993; for a review, see Goldstein, 1994). One such norm that has been proposed is the "culture of honor" that may characterize the southern way of life. This view holds that violence may have been seen as a legitimate and necessary way of upholding and protecting one's personal property and one's personal honor. The history of the development of the South may have encouraged the development of societal rules that legitimates violence under par-

ticular conditions. As opposed to the northeastern regions that were settled earlier, the South tended to be a more rural "frontier" area where protecting one's property, protecting the institution of slavery, and protecting one's honor as a gentleman may have served to legitimate violence until it became manifested in such statistics as murder rates.

Another class of theories disputes the interpretation that murder rates in the South are legitimized by the southern culture (for example, Bailey, 1976; Smith and Parker, 1980). These theories link crime statistics to poverty, arguing that any region, city, or neighborhood will have murder and violence rates that are inversely related to wealth. The wealthier the area, the less the violent crime; the poorer the area, the more the violent crime. As a region, the South has had less wealth than the North and thus it follows that the South would have greater rates of crime. It is also true that the South is hotter than the North and, as we note in this chapter, some social psychologists have linked warmer climates to violent behavior. In general, these theories disagree with the cultural perspective and argue that social factors, such as poverty, and environmental factors, such as heat, account for the higher crime rates.

Much of the research on this topic has been correlational, but recent work has brought the experimental method to bear on the underlying causes of the phenomenon. Cohen, Nisbett, Bowdle, and Schwarz (1996) conducted an experiment at the University of Michigan in which white male students from northern or southern states were bumped into and insulted by a white male confederate of the experimenters. After being bumped and insulted, participants who had grown up in the South showed higher cortisol and testosterone levels, and were more likely to

Continued

BOX 10.1

Continued

complete a story using a violent ending than participants who grew up in northern states. As compared with the insulted northerners, the insulted southerners also tended to view the bump and insult as more of a blow to their masculinity in the eyes of others. Cohen and his associates have interpreted these results to mean that the southerners were more physiologically and psychologically "primed" for aggression after receiving an insult. However, southerners did not report being significantly more angry than northerners after the insult, and the southerners did not actually act any more aggressively toward people whom they encountered subsequently. They were, however, less quick to get out of the way of someone who engaged them in a game of "chicken." As part of this measure, the experimenters had a second confederate walk toward the participant while the participant walked from one part of the laboratory toward the other. The confederate walked straight at the participant, so that if the participant didn't move left or right, the two would collide. The previously insulted southerner held his line of walk longer than any of the other participants.

Is there a culture of honor in the South or are murder rates due to other factors? The use of the experimental method is a promising approach to studying the problem, but the current state of the data leaves many questions unanswered. In the 1996 study by Cohen and his colleagues, southerners differed from northerners on a number of other dimensions in addition to the state where they formerly resided. As a group, southerners were farther away from their homes than northerners and they were a minority of the population at the large midwestern, but substantially northern, university (University of Michigan) where the study was conducted. Did the culture of the South dictate the participants' reactions or were other factors such as distance from home and minority status the cause? We cannot tell from this particular study, although the results are consistent with what one might expect from a culture of honor hypothesis.

What the new research on the culture of honor does point out to us is that it is at least conceivable that cultures have norms that encourage or inhibit violence and that it is possible to do experimental research across subcultures within a society. Clearly, though, much more work in this interesting field needs to be conducted. Conceptual issues need to be solved, such as defining the particular culture. What similarities and differences exist between, let's say, New York, New York, and Montpelier, Vermont, to allow us to group them as northern other than the simple notion that they are both above a particular level of latitude? Similarly, are Selma, Alabama, and Chapel Hill, North Carolina, from the same subculture because of their location south of the Mason-Dixon line? Methodological issues also need to be disentangled, as we pointed out above. It is likely that cultural norms and such factors as poverty will both be shown to have played a role in accounting for differential levels of violence. Indeed, correlational data collected by Huff-Corzine, Corzine, and Moore (1986) currently suggests that both "southernness," as measured by the proportion of a state's population that has origins in the South, and level of poverty are significant predictors of homicide rates within states.

Regardless of the answer, the difference in murder rates between the two regions seems to be decreasing and may soon disappear (Goldstein, 1994). Unfortunately, this appears to be due to increasing murder rates in the nonsouthern states (Harries, 1990). Cultures can and do change. We can only hope that our culture changes for the better.

A second line of research has focused on the relationship between aggression and gender. Recent reviews of this research make it clear that an abundance of evidence indicates that males are more aggressive than females (Bettencourt and Miller, 1996; Knight, Fabes, and Higgins, 1996). The question is, why is there a gender difference? Some investigators, such as Maccoby and Jacklin (1980), believe that the difference is hormonal and thus innate. This argument has been vigorously attacked by other investigators, such as Lightdale and Prentice (1994), who argue that gender differences in aggressiveness are due to learning and socialization rather than to differences in hormones. In addition, there is some evidence that while males are more physically aggressive than females, the gender difference narrows or disappears when we examine verbal aggression (Eagly and Steffen, 1986; Reinish and Sanders, 1986). It also narrows when males and females are directly provoked by another individual (Bettencourt and Miller, 1996).

One of the major battlegrounds for proponents and opponents of the biological predisposition theory centers on whether gender differences in aggression can be found in young children. Presumably, if these gender differences are found only at a later age, learning of role appropriate behavior, rather than biological predisposition, must play a role in aggressive behavior. Research studies show that there is a tendency for aggression to increase with the age of the child, but the type of procedures that can be used with children of different ages also differ. At the present time, there are no conclusive answers to this issue (Knight, Fabes, and Higgins, 1996).

We are left in a position similar to that of the instinct theories. Even though biological mechanisms may play a role in instigating violence, we must explain what triggers those mechanisms. To understand aggression fully, we must also look outside the person. We must investigate the ways in which these external conditions affect when and how people aggress.

Frustration-Aggression Theory

In order to understand Joel Steinberg's violence, let's reexamine his life just before he began to abuse Hedda. Steinberg had a thriving law practice in the early 1970s but things were beginning to come unraveled. He was having problems with his associates over such issues as office space and past-due rent. He moved his office at least three times in the 1970s before he began to work out of his home. His law practice started to dwindle just at the time he needed money to support his growing use of drugs. His ambitions were thwarted and he was under increasing stress. Could these conditions have contributed to his violence?

One of the earliest theories to focus on the role of external conditions was **frustration-aggression theory** (Dollard et al., 1939), which postulates that "aggression is always a consequence of frustration" and that "frustration always leads to some form of aggression" (p. 1). According to this theory, the instigation to aggress should increase as the strength of frustration increases. From these seemingly simple premises, Dollard and his associates attempted to make precise predictions about when people aggress and against whom they direct their aggression. However, the statement that frustration always results in aggression is not as uncomplicated as it appears to be.

Frustration

Dollard and his colleagues included some formal definitions of the terms used in their theory. **Frustration** was defined as an "interference with the behavior sequence" (p. 7), a statement that may be interpreted to mean that we will be frustrated if we cannot have what we want when we want it. A study by Davitz (1952) provides a good example of this kind of interference. He gave children candy bars and showed them a very interesting movie. Just before the climax of the movie, he took the candy bars away from the children and escorted them out of the film room. Needless to say, the children were frustrated.

The theory also postulates that the greater the frustration, the greater the resulting aggression. This hypothesis was supported by Harris (1974), who had confederates cut in front of either the second person or the twelfth person in line. Observations showed that the second person reacted more aggressively (with verbal abuse) to the line breaker than did the twelfth person. Supposedly the frustration was greater for the second person in line because he or she was closer to the goal than was the twelfth person.

Our feelings about ourselves also influence our reaction to frustration. Investigators found that people who had high but unstable self-esteem experienced anger and hostility rather quickly (Kernis, Gannenmann, and Barclay, 1989). These people were constantly on guard to protect their self-image, and they experienced simple frustrations as serious threats to their self-esteem.

Although the definition of frustration seems straightforward, there are still questions about what constitutes frustration. Is frustration an external state or an internal feeling? In the Davitz study, is the frustration the experimenter's action in taking the children's candy bars and removing the children from the film room, or is the frustration the feelings that those actions aroused in the children? Dollard and his colleagues (1939) viewed frustration as the entire operation.

Aggression

According to the theory of Dollard and his associates, **aggression** is a behavior whose goal is the "injury of the person toward whom it is directed." Supposedly the aggression may be either physical or verbal.

Displaced Aggression. The investigators recognized that one cannot always aggress without reprisal from either the target of the aggression or some other person. Older children are aware of this possibility; parents often mete out punishment when an older child aggresses against a younger one. Dollard and his colleagues stated that although frustration instigates aggression, the actual act of aggression may be inhibited if punishment for aggression is expected. According to frustration-aggression theory, "the strongest instigation, aroused by a frustration, is to acts of aggression directed against the agent perceived to be the source of frustration and progressively weaker instigations are aroused to progressively less direct acts of 'aggression.'" Consequently, people who are frustrated should aggress directly against the frustrating agent. However, if the frustrating agent is unavailable or if the aggressor fears punishment for aggressing against the frustrating agent, an aggressor may "displace" aggression to some other target. Using this concept, we might question whether Steinberg's frustration over his business and financial situations led him to displace aggression to Hedda and Lisa.

Identifying the targets of **displaced aggression** has led to some controversy. Miller (1948) hypothesized that the target of displaced aggression will have some similarities with the original frustrating agent. Thus, if the frustrating agent is the father, aggression may be displaced to the mother because both the mother and the father are parents. However, Miller's hypothesis does not include a clear method for determining the similarity dimension. Berkowitz and Knurek (1967) found that aggression may be displaced to a target with a name similar to that of the frustrator.

In this study, subjects who were prevented from winning money attributed more unfavorable characteristics to a bystander with the same name as that of the frustrator than to a bystander with a different name.

Frustration-aggression theory also deals with the types of aggression that can be expected to follow frustration. Dollard and his associates suggest that direct physical and verbal aggression will be the most preferred types. However, if the use of direct aggression is inhibited or blocked, an alternative type of aggression, such as spreading rumors about the frustrator or making him or her the butt of jokes, may be employed. Displacements of aggression, then, can occur in both the target and the type of aggression.

Reducing Aggression. Knowing what causes aggression is only partly satisfying. It is also important to understand how to diminish aggression. Dollard and his colleagues believed that if aggression does not follow frustration, the frustrated person retains a residue of frustration and a readiness to aggress. Each frustration that is not followed by an aggressive response adds to the residue. Finally, the residue builds up to a point at which any further addition sets off a very violent aggressive reaction. A person who is constantly frustrated at work may go home and blow up at a minor offense committed by his or her child. Normally this offense would not upset the person. The situation is analogous to blowing air into a balloon—one breath is not enough to cause the balloon to explode, but one breath can indeed cause an explosion if the balloon is already filled to capacity with air.

Frustration-aggression theory describes two ways of reducing the instigation to aggression after an individual has been frustrated. First, the frustration can be removed, thus removing the motivation to aggress. An interesting demonstration of this effect was provided by an experimenter's assistant who caused subjects to fail on a task (Ohbuchi, Kameda, and Agarie, 1989). Anger and aggression were reduced when the assistant apologized and removed the results of the test. Apology and removal of negative outcomes are also the steps necessary to restore trust after it has been breached. Second, the individual may be allowed to aggress. **Catharsis** is the term that is applied to the case in which aggression reduces future instigation to aggression. Frustration-aggression theory holds that the act of aggression should remove some of the built-up residual instigation, just as opening a balloon valve removes some of the air inside so that the balloon is less likely to explode.

According to the catharsis hypothesis, two effects should follow aggression. First, the act of aggression should reduce the individual's arousal, and second, the individual should be less likely to aggress in the near future *because* of the reduced arousal. The reduction of future aggression should occur because of the reduced arousal and not because of some other process, such as guilt or the fear of retaliation. The catharsis hypothesis is extremely important because frustration-aggression theory considers catharsis one of the main methods by which future instigations to aggression can be reduced. However, the evidence for the catharsis effect has been far less than compelling.

Some investigators have found evidence supporting the catharsis idea. Hokanson and his colleagues (Hokanson, Burgess, and Cohen, 1963; Hokanson and Shelter, 1961) demonstrated that under certain conditions, aggression reduces physiological arousal (systolic blood pressure and heart rate). However, Geen and Quanty (1977) emphasized that these effects occur only under certain conditions. In their review of the catharsis literature, they pointed out that aggression does not lead to a reduction of arousal when the target of aggression is of high power or status, when the aggressor feels that his or her aggression is foolish or inappropriately intense, and when a strong possibility of counteraggression exists. Another interesting finding centers on personal style in expressing anger. Enggebretson, Matthews, and Scheier (1989) suggest that some of us prefer to express our anger while others prefer to hold it in. Their study showed that people who were allowed to express anger in their preferred way (openly expressing it or holding it in) showed reduced arousal following frustration. Therefore, aggression may reduce arousal for some people but not for others. Thus, while a little aggression can feel good in some situations, it can result in discomfort and guilt in many others.

When we turn to the question of whether the expression of aggression reduces the instigation to future aggression, we find the picture even more clouded. Some studies have found that allowing people to participate in controlled real or fantasy aggression does reduce further aggression (Nosanchuk, 1981; Doob and Wood, 1972; Tedeschi, 1979). While these studies suggest that aggression reduces future aggression, other studies have failed to find evidence for the catharsis effect. For example, Ryan (1971) allowed some angry subjects to pound on a box with a hammer. Some of the subjects were competing with a person who had previously angered them whereas others were not. A group of control subjects were not allowed to pound on the box. All of the subjects were then given the opportunity to shock the individual who had angered them. The results showed that the subjects who had pounded on the box were as aggressive as the control subjects. This result would not have been predicted by the catharsis hypothesis.

In our discussion of social learning theory and media violence, we will examine a number of other studies that suggest that aggression leads to more aggression. Taken together, the research shows that the conditions under which a true catharsis of hostility will occur are rather limited. The minimum conditions for catharsis are that the aggressor be angry and be allowed to attack the antagonist directly. Even given these conditions, catharsis may not result; and we shall see later that aggression often leads to more aggression, not less. It is hard to argue for a catharsis effect in the Steinberg incident. Joel's violent behavior increased rather than decreased after his first attack on Hedda. Not only was he more violent to Hedda, but he also beat Lisa when she came into the family. Thus, aggression is not a good cure for aggression.

Revolution: Applying and Extending Frustration-Aggression Theory

Before leaving our discussion of frustration, let's switch our focus from individuals to large groups. Most of the world watched in awe as events in Eastern Europe and the Soviet Union unfolded during 1989 and 1990. Like dominoes, one communist government after another was overthrown as citizens who endured social and material deprivation for many years demanded more freedom and economic opportunity. In Romania, the revolution was accompanied by violence, while in other countries the governments caved in to less violent, but equally massive, demonstrations of dissatisfaction. In an effort to explain how people are moved to revolt against their leadership, psychologists, political scientists, and sociologists have drawn on the relationship between frustration and aggression.

Ted Gurr (1970) defined relative deprivation as "a perceived discrepancy between . . . value expectations and value capabilities" (p. 21). He argued that relative deprivation is loosely synonymous with frustration. Gurr described several causal models of political violence, in all of which relative deprivation plays a key

Aspirational deprivation in Romania led to revolution in 1989 and the secret execution of Romanian leader Nicolae Ceausescu and his wife, Elena, by a military tribunal.

role. According to Gurr, there are three distinct patterns of deprivation.

Decremental deprivation is the loss of what people once had thought they could have. They experience deprivation by reference to their own past condition (see figure 10.1A). A variety of situations may lead to decremental deprivation: recession or economic depression, imposition of foreign rule, a decline in the number of opportunities available to a particular group (such as unskilled labor in an increasingly technological society). Hadley Cantril (1941) did a psychological analysis of the roots of Nazism and concluded that it was able to succeed only because "old norms, old cultural standards, were no longer able to provide the framework necessary for a satisfying adjustment of the individuals who composed the culture" (p. 266). Decremental deprivation occurred for several reasons—many people had suffered reduction in status, economic distress, and personal insecurity as both social structures and normative systems disintegrated in the aftermath of World War I. Another example is seen in the rioting in Argentina when the government had to make drastic economic changes to repay its foreign debt. Decremental deprivation is credited with being the source of more collective violence historically than any other pattern of relative deprivation.

A second pattern of disequilibrium is **aspirational deprivation.** In this situation people do not feel a loss, but they feel anger at having no means of attaining new or intensified expectations. Their expectations can take one of three forms. One form is an increase in the expectation of some commodity in limited supply; the commodity could be a material good, personal freedom, political order, or justice. People may also come to expect some new value they have never had before, such as political participation or the equality of classes. And third, people may become intensely committed to something to which earlier they had given little thought (see figure 10.1B).

Aspirational deprivation may be seen in Romania's revolution. For years the population was deprived of material goods, heat, food, and a variety of personal freedoms, including freedom of expression and freedom to decide whether to have children. As nearby Eastern European countries (East Germany, Poland, Hungary) began to obtain more freedom, Romanians began to expect and demand more freedom in their own country. But this freedom was not forthcoming, and revolt followed.

FIGURE 10.1   DECREMENTAL DEPRIVATION, ASPIRATIONAL DEPRIVATION, AND PROGRESSIVE DEPRIVATION

A. Decremental Deprivation

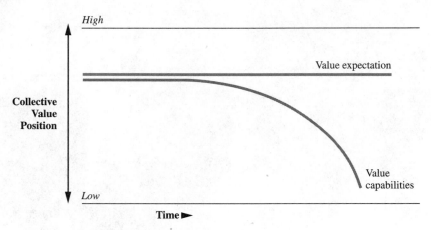

B. Aspirational Deprivation

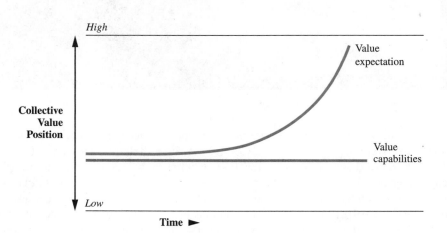

C. Progressive Deprivation

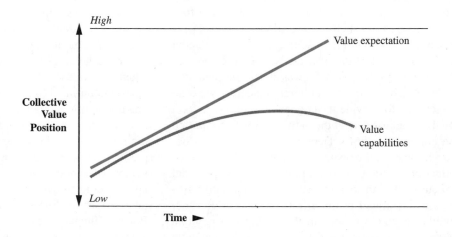

Source: Gurr (1970)

The third pattern of relative deprivation is **progressive deprivation,** or the J-curve hypothesis, which is a generalized version of a model proposed by Davies (1962). This work was fundamental in introducing a systematic empirical approach into a field whose mainstay had been the historical approach. The J-curve hypothesis predicts that a revolution is most likely to occur when a prolonged period of objective economic and social development is followed by a short period of sharp reversals. Expectations are generated after a long run of more or less steady improvement in conditions; people come to expect continued improvement. If value capabilities stabilize or decline after such a period so that improvement is discontinued and conditions stagnate or deteriorate, Davies suggests, progressive deprivation follows (see figure 10.1C). He finds this development to be most common in societies undergoing a great deal of change; the crucial factor is the vague or specific fear that ground gained over a long period of time will be quickly lost. People marveled at the speed with which radical change transformed East Germany. During the three short weeks in which Egon Krenz held office, borders were opened, the headquarters of the dreaded secret police were opened for inspection, free elections were promised, and, most dramatic, the Berlin Wall was torn down. Despite these rapid changes, the people were unhappy and demanded a new government. Actual change could not keep pace with the rising expectations, and dissatisfaction resulted.

Extensions, Revisions, and New Directions

To its credit, frustration-aggression theory was rather clear and straightforward. It stated that frustration always leads to aggression, and that catharsis should follow each aggressive act. Unfortunately, we have seen that the theory is not correct. We do not always react violently to frustration. Catharsis does not always follow aggression. Should we therefore discard the theory and look elsewhere for the cause of aggression? Probably not. It seems that repeated frustrations in many parts of Joel Steinberg's life may have contributed to his violence. If you review your own life, you will probably recall becoming very angry in the face of frustration; you may have yelled at the extremely slow driver who blocked your way to an important meeting. As we think about the theory, we begin to feel that "they might have had something

there if they had not insisted on such absolute terms as *always.*" We might be willing to buy the position that frustration sometimes causes aggression. In fact, many investigators have taken this position. However, once we start down this road, the obvious question leaps up: When (under what conditions) does frustration lead to aggression?

Aggression Cues. One investigator answered this question by suggesting that aggression follows frustration when the environment contains aggression cues that pull the person to aggress. One common aggression cue is a weapon such as a gun or knife. According to Berkowitz (1965), the presence of weapons may well elicit aggression. In fact, he has suggested that it may be the "trigger that pulls the finger." Berkowitz argued that frustration leads to a readiness to aggress, an emotional state that can be labeled *anger.* Actual aggression occurs only when there are appropriate aggression-eliciting cues in the environment. **Aggression cues,** which are defined as stimuli associated with the source of frustration and with aggressive behavior in general, may be anything from a weapon to a disliked person to a name associated with the frustrator. A cue assumes its aggression-eliciting quality when an individual associates certain instruments, situations, or persons with aggression. Further, since learning plays an important role, an object that serves as an aggression cue for one person may not be an aggression cue for another person. To predict the occurrence of aggression, one needs to know whether the individual has been frustrated and whether the immediate environment contains aggression cues.

To demonstrate the role of aggression cues in eliciting aggression, Berkowitz and his colleagues devised a number of *weapon effect* studies. They reasoned that such weapons as knives and guns would be aggression-eliciting cues and that the presence of a weapon should therefore elicit aggression from an angry individual. In one study, Berkowitz and Le Page (1967) had a confederate either anger or not anger subjects, who were then given an opportunity to administer an electric shock to the confederate. In some conditions, a 12-gauge shotgun and a .38-caliber revolver were lying on the table next to the shock apparatus (weapons condition), and in other conditions two badminton rackets were placed next to the shock apparatus. The results indicated that when the subjects were angry, they gave more shocks to the confederate (aggressed more) in the weapons condition than in the badminton condition. Berkowitz interpreted these results as supporting his hypothesis that the weapons elicited aggression from the angry subjects.

The conclusion derived from the Berkowitz and Le Page study has important implications, but the study has not escaped criticism. Some investigators (Page and Scheidt, 1971; Buss, Booker, and Buss, 1972) believed that the subjects may have been thinking about and reacting to demand characteristics in the situation. The subjects in the weapons condition may have used the presence of weapons not as a cue eliciting aggression in the sense suggested by Berkowitz but as a cue from the experimenter that it was all right to aggress or that he wanted them to aggress in this situation. A number of attempts have been made to replicate this study (some successful and others not), and there is still some controversy about exactly what role the weapons do play (aggression cue or demand characteristic).

More recently, Berkowitz (1989, 1994) broadened his theory to state that it is not just frustration or anger but rather *any* negative feelings that can lead to aggression. Aggressive cues are not necessary for aggression to occur, but they can intensify aggression once someone is angry or upset. Individuals who are angry are also more likely to notice aggression cues. In the final analysis, it seems that the presence of aggression cues will increase the likelihood of aggression following anger, but violence may well occur in the absence of these cues.

Frustration-Aggression: Some Afterthoughts

Having traveled the rather long road through frustration-aggression theory, we can now ask where we stand. It seems clear that the original theory overstated the case. Frustration can, under some circumstances, lead people to aggress. It is still unclear whether catharsis does follow aggressive actions or why it occurs. The notion of displaced aggression is intriguing, but it has not been adequately tested.

While the theory may not be correct, it has stimulated a tremendous amount of research on aggression. As we have seen, some of this research identified the conditions under which frustration leads to aggression

and the conditions under which aggression is not likely to follow frustration. Other research has attempted to reexamine the concept of aggression, arguing that it is not frustration itself that causes people to resort to aggression. One group of researchers suggested that

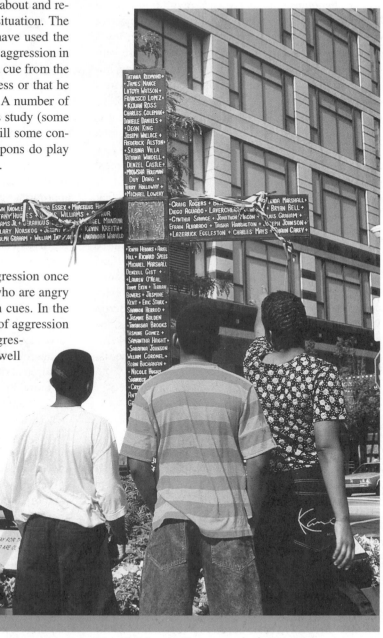

The Children's Altar was erected in Chicago as a memorial to juvenile victims of violence and as a powerful symbol which might serve to counteract aggression cues in the community.

aggression is a behavior aimed at demonstrating control over our own behavior and environment (Allen and Greenberger, 1989). They argue that such senseless acts as vandalism are a means of establishing control; we destroy things to show that we have control over them. Therefore any situation that threatens our sense of control will increase our chances of responding aggressively. In a similar vein, others have suggested that aggression is aimed at impression management (Tedeschi, Smith, and Brown, 1974; Melburg and Tedeschi, 1989). Anything that threatens our self-esteem or casts us in a poor light, be it frustration or something else, will move us to aggression. Still another position is that aggression is a response to threats to our personal freedom (Worchel, 1974). As you can see, each of these views argues for a different focus on the frustration-aggression relationship, but each holds that aggression is instigated by threat or attack on some aspect of the self.

While these approaches are concerned with the causes of aggression, they don't tell us much about the type of aggression a person may use. We can think of many forms of aggression, ranging from insults to violent attacks with knives, guns, or bombs. In fact, as we mentioned earlier, ignoring the needs of someone who is suffering or allowing someone to engage in a destructive activity may be seen as aggression from some points of view. In order to have a more complete understanding of aggressive behavior, we would like to know not only what causes it but also what factors determine how people will aggress.

Social Learning Theory

To obtain a foundation on which to base more specific predictions about the situations in which aggression will be exhibited and the forms that aggression will take, we can turn to a theory that relates aggressive behavior to learning. The major proponents of **social learning theory** (Bandura and Walters, 1963; Bandura, 1973) suggest that children learn when to aggress, how to aggress, and against whom to aggress. Although the bulk of this learning comes from observation of parents, additional learning about aggression comes from peer groups and from mass-media portrayals of aggression and violence. In extreme forms, children may actually be schooled in the techniques of aggression by parents or teachers.

Learning to Aggress: Reinforcement

People learn to be aggressive by two main mechanisms. The first is **reinforcement.** Children are often rewarded for acting aggressively; the reward may take the form of praise from a father when his son beats up a larger boy or makes a particularly vicious tackle in a football game. The child is also reinforced through the added attention that he or she receives for aggressing. Even when parents and teachers disapprove of a child's aggressive behavior, they make the child the center of attention by scolding him or her or by trying to change the behavior. The child who desires attention from adults may be very willing to suffer such negative sanctions in return for the attention that the aggression brings. Positive reinforcement is also gained directly when the aggressor reaps the fruits of the aggressive acts—when Johnny beats up Jim to get Jim's football and is rewarded by taking possession of the ball. The child can learn from instances such as these that aggression pays.

A great deal of evidence supports the position that individuals learn aggression through reinforcement. Geen and Stoner (1973) found that subjects increased the intensity of aggression when they received verbal reinforcement for violence. Cowan and Walters (1963) demonstrated that the schedule of reinforcement is important in determining future aggression. Small children were rewarded for hitting a doll. Some of the children were rewarded for every aggressive act (continuous reinforcement) whereas others were rewarded only periodically (partial reinforcement). The hitting behavior of the children increased while they were being rewarded. After a time, the experimenter stopped rewarding the aggressive behavior and studied the children's behavior. Interestingly enough, the children who had been on a partial reinforcement schedule continued to hit the doll longer than the children who had been continuously rewarded. The Cowan and Walter study is important because people are not always rewarded when they act aggressively—their aggression is successful only some of the time. The results of the study show that such partial reinforcement may be enough to sustain continued aggression even without rewards.

Learning to Aggress: Modeling

Bandura and Walters also suggest that aggression is learned through **modeling,** or imitation. People are prone to imitate the behaviors of other persons—especially persons whom they admire or like. A son who sees his father aggress or a boy who sees his favorite television hero wipe out twenty-five thugs may come to believe that violence must be a good thing because "good" people act violently. Wolfgang and Fenacuti (1967) pointed out that children are surrounded by lessons that violence is good. They are taught that the security of our nation is based on our ability to use violent weapons if we are attacked. Violence permeates our advertising—it is the hero who overcomes obstacles and brings the beer home.

In addition to learning that aggression may be "good" behavior because "good" people aggress, children can learn how to aggress from models. Arnold Schwarzenegger teaches them how to use their fists or tongues to aggress; a Power Ranger gives martial arts lessons; Beavis and Butthead show them how to set things on fire. Some children will be motivated to try out these new behaviors as they imitate their favorite characters and action heroes.

The research on imitative learning has shown that not all models are imitated to the same degree. Bandura, Ross, and Ross (1961, 1963a, 1963b) conducted a number of studies in which nursery school children first observed an adult aggressively playing with an inflated plastic clown (a "BoBo" doll). The model hit the doll, beat it with a hammer, kicked it, and sat on it. After watching the model, the children were put in a room with some toys—one of them being the BoBo doll. Their behavior was carefully observed. By varying the characteristics of the model, Bandura and his associates could study the influence of different types of models. In one study (Bandura, Ross, and Ross, 1961), they demonstrated that children are more likely to imitate same-sex models—the boys imitated the male model more than they imitated the female model, and the reverse was true for the girls. Further, imitation is more likely if the model is of high status than of low status (Turner and Berkowitz, 1972).

In another study, Bandura and his colleagues (1963a) found that children imitated a real-life adult, an adult on film, or a cartoon figure that aggressed against a BoBo doll. Thus, even cartoons can teach aggression. Myer (1972) found that adults too will imitate the behavior of a model displaying real or staged aggression. In still another example of adult imitation, Arms, Russell, and Sandilands (1979) found that spectators at sporting events involving aggression (wrestling and ice hockey) were more likely to feel hostile and to

express aggression than people who had watched a competitive but nonaggressive sporting event (swimming). This finding suggests that it is not competition that teaches aggression; it is aggressive acts themselves that teach aggression.

Other studies have focused on the act that the model performs and have shown that subjects are more likely to imitate aggression when the model is rewarded rather than punished for acting violently (Bandura, Ross, and Ross, 1963b; Bandura, 1965; Walters and Willows, 1968) and when the model's aggression is justified rather than unjustified (Geen and Stoner, 1973). Bandura (1965) allowed children to observe a model beating the BoBo doll. In one condition, the children observed no consequences to the model for the aggressive action. In a second condition, the children saw the model rewarded and praised by another adult. In a third condition, the children saw the model being punished and being called a bully for acting aggressively. The children were then allowed to play with the BoBo doll. The children who observed the punished model played less aggressively than either the children who observed the rewarded model or the children who saw no consequences to the model at all.

Committing Aggression: Behavior

Social learning theory makes an important distinction between learning to aggress and actually committing an aggressive act. People can learn to aggress by being rewarded for this activity or by observing models. However, they will generally express aggression only when there are rewards for doing so in the particular situation. In the Bandura (1965) study, for example, we saw that children did not act aggressively after watching a model being punished for aggressive behavior.

Although these results seem to suggest that watching an aggressive model will not increase aggression if the model is punished, Bandura questioned whether the effect of punishment was on the acquisition of the aggressive behavior or on its performance. That is, did the children who saw the punished model fail to learn aggressive behavior, or did they learn how to aggress but simply inhibited the behavior? To find the answer, Bandura offered all of the children a reward if they could imitate the behavior of the model they had observed previously. All of the subjects, including those who had seen the punished model, were able to reproduce the aggressive behavior with the same degree of accuracy. This result suggests that the children who observed the punished model had learned how to behave aggressively but had simply inhibited such behavior. When the circumstances were right, they too acted aggressively. This finding is significant because it shows that punishing aggressive models will not keep observers from learning aggression. To predict when people will aggress, we need to examine their past learning opportunities and conditions in the present situation.

Reducing Aggression

The social learning theory of aggression is important for a number of reasons. First, it supplies answers to questions that cannot be handled by the frustration-aggression theory. For example, frustration-aggression theory cannot explain why in the same frustrating situation one individual will lash out with fists, another will use a gun, and a third will not aggress at all. According to social learning theory, early experiences and learning determine how an individual will express aggression. We might expect, therefore, that the first individual grew up in an environment in which he or she witnessed, or was rewarded for, fist fighting. The second individual may have been reared in a family in which guns were constantly present and "shoot 'em up" movies were popular. The third individual may have grown up in an environment in which aggression was discouraged and not rewarded.

In addition to explaining why people aggress as they do, social learning theory provides a foundation on which a program to reduce aggression can be based. Bandura and Walters (1963) point out that parents' use of physical punishment for their children's misdeeds may actually lead to increased aggression. In this case the parents serve as a model for the children. The children observe the parents' use of aggression (punishment) to obtain what they want (a reduction in the children's aggression). Although the children may not aggress at home because of fear of retaliation, they are likely to use the aggressive responses learned at home in other situations. Sears and his colleagues (1953) found that children who had been severely punished for aggression at home were more likely to act aggressively outside the home than were children whose parents had punished them less severely for aggressive acts.

According to social learning theory, aggression can be decreased by the withdrawal of love or withholding of some other desired object as punishment for aggression. In this way the child receives no reinforcement or attention for aggression and does not witness an aggressive model to imitate in a later situation. Thus, social learning theory suggests that when we teach a child not to aggress, we must not use aggression as the deterrent. Brown and Elliott (1965) demonstrated this principle by having nursery school teachers reward children's cooperative and nonviolent behavior and ignore their aggressive behavior. After two weeks of this treatment, a significant reduction in the aggressive behavior displayed by the children was apparent. The children's aggressive behavior was reduced further when the teachers repeated this program of rewards three weeks later.

Egotism Threat: Combining Personality and Social Approaches to Violence

Is violence perpetrated by people who feel good about themselves or by people who feel they have low self-worth? For a long time it was considered likely that aggression was performed by people who had low self-esteem and had something to prove (Staub, 1989). However, Baumeister, Smart, and Boden (1996) propose that aggression arises primarily from those who have a high sense of self-esteem. It is people with highly positive views of themselves that, under certain circumstances, are more likely to commit acts of aggression or violence than people with more moderate (or negative) self-concepts.

Note two issues here. Baumeister and his colleagues' view may seem unusual because most of us are accustomed to thinking of high and low self-esteem as the "good guy" and "bad guy" of a grade-B movie. That is, high self-esteem is a good thing to have; low self-esteem is bad. While there are times when this is probably true, Baumeister and his associates caution us to think of self-esteem in more evaluatively neutral terms. People with high self-esteem may sometimes be competent, proud, and mentally healthy; but they may also be thought of as arrogant, conceited, and narcissistic. In this theory, high self-esteem simply refers to "a favorable, global evaluation of oneself." People with high self-esteem may be competent and confident individuals with many friends, or they may be unfriendly, conceited individuals whose views of themselves are inconsistent with reality.

The second issue to note is parallel to our earlier discussion about the instinct and biological approaches to the study of aggression. People with high self-esteem don't ordinarily go through their days committing acts of violence. The social psychologist continually asks the question, "What situations cause people to act violently?" Baumeister and his colleagues venture an answer: Violence arises when people's high sense of self-esteem, or "egotism," is threatened. In this view, people are likely to aggress when their favorable views of themselves are "impugned, mocked, challenged, or otherwise put in jeopardy." (Baumeister, Smart, and Boden, 1996, p. 8). Moreover, the aggression is most likely to be carried out against the perceived source of the threat, whether that source is an individual, an ethnic group, or a nation. Thus, these researchers provide us with a view that shows how a personality trait—high self-esteem—can interact with a social variable—encountering a threat to one's self-esteem, resulting in aggression.

Why does a threat to self-esteem cause aggression? Imagine that a friend believes she is a virtuoso at playing the piano. At least in this domain, she has a high sense of self-esteem and high regard for her ability. A second friend of yours listens to her play at a party one evening and passes a comment that disputes her appraisal of herself. The piano player's initial response to the appraisal may be to feel angry or sad. One possible response to this emotion may be to strike out against her friend by verbally abusing her, calling her names, or striking at her physically.

Figure 10.2 illustrates the threatened egotism position. At the top of the figure is the dilemma of the person who may be poised to commit violence. It depicts a person with a favorable view of himself or herself confronted with an appraisal from another person or group that contradicts the individual's view. This threat to a person's egotism sets up what Baumeister and his colleagues (1996) refer to as the "choice point." The individual may accept that appraisal, realize that she is not such a good piano player, feel a sense of sadness, and tend to withdraw from future events that might feature piano playing. On the other hand, when an individual reaches the choice point and wants to maintain that high self-appraisal, aggression might occur. Rather than sadness, these individuals typically experience anger, and it leads to aggression or violence against the source.

Joel Steinberg was a person of immense egotism. Regardless of the accuracy of his appraisal, he considered himself to be superior in most respects. He had wealth, women, and prestige. Beginning in 1975, he

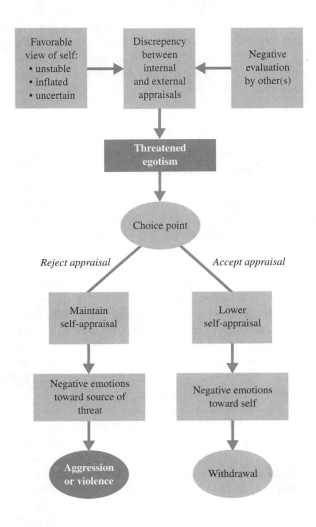

FIGURE 10.2   **SCHEMATIC REPRESENTATION OF THE RELATION OF THREATENED EGOTISM TO VIOLENT BEHAVIOR**

Source: Baumeister, Smart, and Boden (1996)

had an attractive and capable woman who was completely dependent on him for her psychological survival. As Hedda's self-esteem and confidence rose, she became less dependent on Joel's every whim. As she began to assert her own wishes and views, Steinberg's egotistical view of himself was threatened. Joel's "choice point" decision was obvious. He responded with outrageous anger, taking violent action against Hedda and, eventually, little Lisa.

Baumeister and his colleagues also note that sometimes a person's response to a threatened ego is at a level of violence well beyond what would seem rational given the magnitude of the threat. It is unpleasant to have one's view of oneself attacked and certainly unpleasant to go through the work of changing your self-concept. So aggression can also be *anticipatory*; that is, in addition to being a response to a particular threat, it also serves to anticipate future threats and discourage them from happening again. The piano-playing friend who tears into a rage when her musical skills are challenged may find it less likely to find herself challenged again.

Baumeister, Smart, and Boden (1996) examined the literature in an impressive array of areas and found support for the threatened egotism notion. Polk (1993), for example, reported that homicide is often the result of altercations between people that begin with personal insults and derogatory remarks. The person who feels he or she is losing an argument often responds violently. Similarly, Scully (1990) conducted prison interviews with men convicted of violent rape. She reported that the men often reported their satisfaction of putting the victim "in her place." It's as though the rape occurred not mainly for sexual satisfaction but rather as a demonstration of power and superiority, and for egotistical enhancement. Sometimes the woman was the direct source of threat to the man's

self-esteem, and sometimes the threat was provided by some other event. The woman, however, served as the means of the violent rapist's restoration of his egotistical sense of self-worth.

Aggression and Social Dilemmas

Aggression and violence create problems at individual, family, and societal levels. Social psychologists have explored several areas of violence in society, seeking answers that can help to shape and explain social policy. We now look at the research in some of these areas. Note that in some cases the research has made use of theoretical insights designed uniquely for a particular problem, insights that are less clearly connected to the general theories we have been discussing. In other cases the broad theories of aggression have served as meaningful guides to the research.

Family Violence

It's easy to assume that almost everyone who reads the tragic story of Lisa Steinberg will be shocked by the

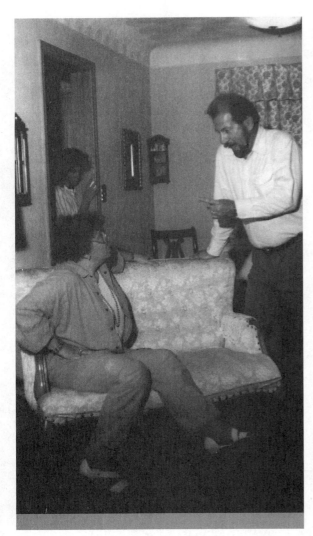

The onset of family violence: a family member feels frustrated or threatened and directs verbal aggression against another member, which in turn may lead to a physical assault.

members of their own family. Family violence is found in all racial, class, and ethnic groups. The extreme cases represent only the tip of the iceberg, so we can assume that cases of family violence range between 5 million and 25 million each year. Therefore, it is likely that some of you have been a victim of, or witness to, family violence.

How can we explain such a cruel form of human interaction? Do our theories of aggression give us some insight into the problem? To answer these questions, let's examine the typical conditions involved in family violence. First, we know what family violence is *not*. It is typically not something that can be blamed on mental illness. Robert Emery (1989) writes, "If anything conclusive can be said about child abuse research . . . it is that the psychopathological model does not apply to the great majority of abusive parents" (p. 322). The same can be said about spousal abuse. Second, and somewhat surprisingly, men and women are equally likely to perpetrate abuse (Straus, 1980), although the violence done by men against women is usually more damaging and more often reported to the police. Third, abuse is often associated with stressful events, such as the loss of a job. Fourth, violence can be transmitted through the generations (Malinosky-Rummell and Hansen, 1993; Simons et al., 1993). Fifth, many cases of abuse begin as attempts by parents to discipline their children (Parker and Collmer, 1975) or by one spouse to control another.

Do you begin to see the relevance of family violence to our theories of aggression? We can see portions of egotism threat, frustration-aggression, and social learning in the tragedy of family violence. Some aversive event sets the stage—something that causes frustration or a challenge to one's self-esteem. The resultant aggression is directed at a family member either because the family member is perceived to be the cause of the threat or frustration, or because the abuser has learned this pattern as a child. The abusive behavior is reinforced because the individual finds that it is effective in influencing the behavior of other family members and gaining power within the family (Walker, 1989).

While the pattern fits within the framework of our theories, we must add a caution. Though most family violence is perpetuated by individuals who were abused or who witnessed abuse as children, the converse is not true. Most people who come from abusive families do not become abusers (Emery, 1989). Kalmuss (1984) reports that 94 percent of people who

senseless violence of it. Testimony in the highly publicized murder trial of O. J. Simpson made spousal abuse salient to people around the globe. But to too many people, abuse within families needs no newspaper or television stories to bring home the point. It happens within their own home. It is estimated that more than seventeen hundred women die annually in the United States alone as a result of family violence (Steinmetz, 1980). More than one thousand children are killed each year as a result of family violence. And nearly 20 percent of all murder victims are killed by recalled seeing their parents hit each other were *not* physically abusive in their own marriage. Our theories help us to understand family violence, but they still do not offer a complete picture of this tragic phenomenon.

Family violence is notoriously difficult to stop. People are reluctant to report suspected cases of family violence. Often, cases are reported when the threat is imminent, then the victims recant or fail to follow through with their reports. Victims often feel that they did something to deserve the attack or assume that the violence was unusual and will not recur. Such assumptions are usually wrong, the violence tends to increase, and the attacks continue. Programs to treat family violence generally involve temporarily removing the victim from the family situation for protection, bringing the family into family therapy, and working to reduce the stress that may have led to the violence (Emery, 1989; Walker, 1989). It is also important to intervene in family violence early in the sequence. Family abuse often begins with mild forms of aggression, such as verbal abuse, and builds into major physical violence. Sugarman, Aldarondo, and Boney-McCoy (1996), who studied the continuum of abuse, suggest that therapy for family violence has a much better prognosis if it occurs when abuse is mild than when it has been allowed to evolve into destructive physical attack.

Drugs and Aggression

According to Hedda Nussbaum, both she and Joel began using cocaine in 1978; as they increased their use of the drug, the violence began. This set of events is only correlational (remember our discussion in chapter 1), but it does prompt us to question whether drug use can affect aggression. In fact, we will see that this issue actually involves a number of questions. First, does drug use itself cause people to become more aggressive? Second, do drugs increase people's aggressive behavior when they are thwarted or otherwise angered? And, finally, do all drugs have the same effect on aggression? As you might imagine, research on this topic is an ethical minefield. Many of the drugs we might like to study are illegal. Even the use of legal drugs, such as alcohol and nicotine, is restricted by state laws to adults. Given these problems and others, we are only just beginning to find answers to these questions.

Taylor and his associates (Taylor and Gammon, 1975; Taylor, Gammon, and Capasso, 1976) studied the effects of alcohol and marijuana on aggression. Subjects in the studies were given either alcohol or marijuana in large or small doses. They were then either angered or not angered by a confederate and given an opportunity to attack the confederate. The results indicated that even in rather large doses, alcohol by itself does not instigate aggression. Large doses of alcohol, however, do lead to increased aggression if the subject is angered or threatened.

Marijuana, on the other hand, has a different effect. Subjects who have consumed a large dose of marijuana and are later threatened react significantly less aggressively than either subjects who have consumed small doses of the drug or subjects who have not consumed the drug. In addition, subjects who have consumed large doses of marijuana are significantly less aggressive than subjects who have consumed large doses of alcohol.

A recent review of several studies on alcohol and aggression by Ito, Miller, and Pollock (1996) indicates that highly intoxicated individuals are also more vulnerable to the frustration-aggression effect. Compared to sober people, intoxicated individuals are more likely to act aggressively when frustrated. Another interesting effect of alcohol was uncovered when Schmutte and Taylor (1980) placed intoxicated and nonintoxicated subjects in a reaction-time task in which they could shock and be shocked by their opponent. In some conditions the subjects received little pain feedback from the opponent; in other cases, they heard the opponent express a great deal of pain and discomfort at the shock. The results showed that intoxicated subjects were more aggressive than nonintoxicated subjects, and their aggression was not influenced by the pain cues. On the other hand, the nonintoxicated subjects decreased their aggression in the pain feedback condition. Overall, the results suggest that large quantities of alcohol reduce people's awareness of, or concern about, situational conditions and the effects of their aggression. Investigators have also found that depressant drugs (diazepam) used for the treatment of anxiety affect aggression in a way similar to the effect of alcohol (Gantnot and Taylor, 1988). This finding opens up the important issue of the broad effects of drugs used for the treatment of psychological disorders. Thus, drugs can significantly affect aggressive behavior, but the direction of the effect depends on the type of drug, the size of the dose, and whether the subject is threatened.

Erotica, Violent Pornography, and Aggression

Does pornography engender aggressive acts? Does it particularly engender greater aggression by men against women? Pornographic movies rated with any number·of Xs as well as pornographic pictures and books are abundantly available. Some people can obtain pornography without even leaving home via cable television or the Internet. In one study, approximately 81 percent of all males surveyed indicated they had recently availed themselves of pornographic material and 38 percent indicated they had recently viewed violent pornographic material (Demare, Briere, and Lips, 1988). On the other hand, an analysis of crime statistics by Robert Basuerman (1996) shows no evidence that people who commit violent crimes or violent sexual crimes are any more likely than nonperpetrators to have been exposed to pornography. Can social-psychological theories inform us about the relationship of pornography and aggression?

Excitation Transfer: Predicting the Effect of Pornography

To the extent that pornography is arousing, that arousal may contribute to aggression. In chapter 3 we discussed Schachter's work on emotions (Schachter, 1964; Schachter and Singer, 1962). Schachter postulated that emotions are characterized by general, nonspecific arousal and a cognitive label. A person experiences physiological arousal and then searches the environment for the cause or an explanation. That explanation is the cognitive label that allows us to attribute our arousal to happiness, fear, anger, and so forth.

Dolf Zillmann and his associates (Zillmann, 1971, 1978, 1994; Tannenbaum and Zillmann, 1975; Zillmann and Bryant, 1988) adapted Schachter's labeling theory to the aggression paradigm. They reasoned that any angry individual who is further aroused by some other source may label the additional arousal as anger. As a consequence of this misperception, the individual will feel even more angry and therefore will be more likely to aggress. According to this **excitation transfer theory,** what is important is not the real source of arousal but rather the perceptions that people have about that arousal.

Heat: From Room Temperature to Sexually Explicit Material. As a way of demonstrating how excitation transfer may lead to aggression, let's begin with a study that involves not sexual heat but rather degrees Fahrenheit/centigrade. Researchers have discovered that more aggressive crimes are committed when the temperature is hot (Anderson, 1989; Anderson and Anderson, 1984). Murders, assaults, rapes, and family violence all increase as a function of temperature. Anderson, Deuser, and deNeve (1995) established a laboratory procedure to examine the causes of the heat effect. In the first phase of the research, participants played a video game in a room whose temperature was varied to be either comfortable (approximately 72°F) or quite hot (94°F). It was found that participants experienced more hostile and aggressive emotions and had more aggressive thoughts as a function of the temperature: the higher the temperature, the more thoughts and feelings that were aggressive.

What is quite interesting from the perspective of excitation transfer theory are the measures that Anderson, Deuser, and deNeve (1995) took of participants' real and perceived physiological arousal. As the temperature rose in the room, so did the participants' heart rates. However, subjects in the hot room thought that their arousal was quite low. Taken together, the results point to excitation transfer as being responsible for the heat effect. As temperatures rise, so does physiological arousal. However, the temperature also makes the actor less aware of that arousal. When there is a potential target who has frustrated or angered the actor, it is quite likely that the arousal that was actually caused by hot temperatures will be misattributed as angry feelings and angry thoughts directed at the target. The result of the excitation transfer is greater aggression.

Like the arousal due to heat, sexually explicit material should also fit Zillmann's excitation transfer model. And, indeed, several studies have found support for this hypothesis. For example, Zillmann (1971) investigated the effects of sexual arousal on aggression. Subjects watched either a sexually arousing film (*The Couch*), a violent boxing film (*Body and Soul*), or an interesting but nonarousing documentary (*Marco Polo's Travels*). The subjects were then either angered or not angered by a confederate. Finally, the subjects were allowed to act as teachers and administer an electric shock to the confederate. The results showed that the subjects who had watched the sexually arousing film were the most aggressive (that is, they delivered the strongest shocks), whereas the subjects who watched the nonarousing documentary were the least aggressive. This finding is consistent with the idea that the sexual arousal created by the erotic film

BOX 10.2

Road Rage: Applying Social Psychology to the Study of Aggressive Driving

By now, we have all heard of road rage, roadway anger that can result in chases, collisions, or death. "He cut me off." "She was driving too slow." "He was playing the radio too loud." These are samples of the explanations drivers gave for intentionally killing or injuring other people on the road. In fact, each of these reasons was given in at least twenty-five separate "road rage" incidents between 1990 and 1996 (Mizell, 1997).

Late in 1997, a car full of driver's education students got a lesson in road rage firsthand. As one young woman was taking her turn driving the car, she was cut off by another vehicle. The driving instructor ordered her to chase the other car. She did, and when the other car finally stopped, the instructor jumped out of the car, approached the other driver, and (allegedly) hit him in the nose. Although no charges were filed against the young woman driving the car, the instructor was later arrested.

Road rage can also lead to more serious consequences. In a much publicized case, a parkway confrontation between two men turned into an extended high-speed car chase in the Washington, D.C., area. The two cars eventually collided and shot into oncoming traffic, causing several crashes and three deaths. A study of selected newspaper, police, and insurance reports located over 10,000 reported incidents of aggressive driving within a six year period (Mizell, 1997). Yet, as David Willis of the American Automobile Association testified before a congressional committee, those incidents are but a microcosm of the full extent of the aggressive driving problem in America today.

What do psychologists know about aggression on the road? Traditionally, psychologists have studied aggression in automobiles by creating a frustrating situation and then measuring people's aggressive responses. For example, researchers have a car "stall" at a green light so that it blocks traffic. Observers then measure how long it takes other cars to honk, the number of times they honk, and how long the honks last.

This research has identified several factors that make it more likely for people to respond aggressively when trapped behind a stalled car. Temperature may often increase aggression through excitation transfer. The extra arousal caused by heat can fuel a person's anger, resulting in increased aggression. Kenrick and MacFarlane (1986) stalled a car at a green light and found that the higher the outside temperature, the more people honked their horns. Drivers who had their windows rolled down (who presumably did not have air conditioning) were even more likely to honk.

Status also appears to play a role in when people behave aggressively on the road. Researchers have noted that drivers are quicker to honk when stuck behind a low-status car than when stuck behind a more expensive, high-status car (Doob and Gross, 1968). The kind of cars people drive may also influence how quick they are to honk. A study in Germany found that people who drove high-status cars were the fastest to honk at a stalled car, while people who drove low-status cars were the slowest to honk (Diekmann, Jungbauer-Gans, Krassnig, and Lorenz, 1996).

Anonymity may also play a role in aggression on roadways. Drivers' faces are often difficult to see, and people may feel fairly anonymous while in their cars. Indeed, a study comparing people in convertibles to people in enclosed cars found that the less-anonymous convertible drivers were also less quick to honk (Ellison, Govern, Petri, and Figler, 1995).

Continued

BOX 10.2

Continued

Although much road rage is incited by events taking place on the road, some road rage may actually be displaced aggression. Imagine a woman who is angry with her boss at work. She knows she can't yell at her boss; she might lose her job. But right after work she jumps in her car and heads out on the road. Now she is free to express some of that aggression by speeding or weaving through traffic. Throw some frustration her way, such as a slow car in the fast lane, and you have a recipe for trouble.

What can be done about road rage? Structural changes, such as new or wider roadways, longer merging lanes, or more parking spaces could help reduce some fre-quent triggers of road rage. But even with improvements, driving will inevitably be frustrating on occasions, and some people will respond aggressively. Mizell (1997) offers some simple advice: try not to do things that might anger other motorists. Don't cut people off, tailgate, or drive slow in the fast lane. If you encounter an aggressive driver, back off. On the flip side, try not to drive when you are angry or under a lot of stress. Remember, people make mistakes on the road. Don't take them as personal insults. A honk, a few gestures, a high-speed chase, and you could be facing murder charges. Or you might not be alive to face any charges at all.

---

was interpreted by the subjects as anger, and the result was heightened aggression.

Is it possible to conclude that erotic or pornographic material provokes aggression? A second group of studies suggest the opposite. Baron and his colleagues (Baron, 1974; Baron and Bell, 1973; Frodi, 1977) showed that exposure to erotic stimuli can actually reduce subsequent aggression. They argued that aggression and sexuality are intrinsically incompatible. Aroused sexual feelings, they reasoned, would inhibit aggression. Zillmann and Johnson (1973) suggested that sexual arousal, by being absorbing and salient, is distracting, so people who are instigated to aggress will be distracted from their aggression by their sexual feelings.

Clearly, a more comprehensive explanation is necessary to account for the conflicting results. Zillmann, Bryant, and Carveth (1981), following earlier work by Donnerstein, Donnerstein, and Evans (1975), suggested an *excitation valence model* of the effects of pornography on aggression. In their research, they found that people who were exposed to unpleasant pornography increased their aggression toward a fellow student. Students exposed to pleasant pornography decreased their aggression. Zillmann and his associates (1981) suggested that the likelihood of aggression depends on the degree of excitation caused by the erotic material and its valence as pleasurable. For example, films of bestiality and sadomasochism produce quite negative reactions in most viewers (Zillmann, Bryant, and Carveth, 1981). Such films serve to increase aggression. More pleasing erotic films, however, may serve to reduce aggressive behavior. Thus, the same theoretical model may account for both increases and decreases in aggression.

Aggressive Pornography

Over the past several years, investigators have been increasingly concerned about aggressive erotica—films that combine sexual arousal with violence. Scenes of forcible rape, sex at gun point, and so forth are commonplace in films bearing the X rating. Malamuth and his colleagues have shown that such films have disturbing attitudinal effects on male viewers. They have demonstrated that men who see such films have more fantasies about rape (Malamuth, 1984), have a reduced sensitivity to rape (Malamuth and Check, 1981), and harbor greater feelings that they, too, could commit rape (Malamuth, Haber, and Feshbach, 1980).

Linz, Donnerstein, and Adams (1989) monitored the heart rates of undergraduates at the University of California at Santa Barbara while they were viewing film clips of violence being perpetrated by a man against a woman. Before they saw the clips, some subjects had viewed a film containing violent, explicit sex. Other subjects had watched an arousing sex scene that had no violence. Heart rate and attitude measures showed that the violence in the first film desensitized the subjects to the violence against the woman in the second film. In addition, those who had watched the violent sex in the first film attributed less injury to the victim of aggression in the second film. These subjects also saw the male perpetrator of the violence in the second film as less responsible for his aggression than subjects who had initially seen a nonviolent film. This study provides further evidence that violent pornography has both physiological and cognitive effects on viewers.

Why does violent pornography provoke aggression? Donnerstein (1980, 1983) argued that one answer may rest in Berkowitz's (1965) notion of aggressive cues. Watching a woman become the victim of sexual aggression causes arousal in men and also causes the woman to become associated with aggression. The woman, then, could become an aggressive cue that might trigger aggression by the viewer in a future incident.

Donnerstein (1980) had male subjects angered or treated in a neutral manner by a confederate and then given the opportunity to view one of three films. One

was a control film that showed neither sex nor violence; the other two films were highly erotic. One of the erotic films was entirely nonaggressive, but the other depicted the rape of a woman by a man who broke into her house and forced her into sexual activity at gun point. After the film, the subjects had an opportunity to deliver electric shocks to the confederate during what the subject thought was a learning task. The amount of electric shock that the subject wished to administer served as the dependent measure of aggression.

The results are depicted in figure 10.3. The erotic film had a mild effect in increasing the amount of electric shock, but the aggressive erotic film had a major effect. The aggressive erotic film caused a major increase in the amount of aggression shown by the subject, especially when the subject had been angered and when the confederate was a woman. Summarizing the literature, Donnerstein (1983) concluded that a direct causal link has been demonstrated between exposure to aggressive erotica and violence against women.

Recently, Mullin and Linz (1995) had students watch three films that were high in graphic violence but only mildly erotic. Participants watched three R-rated "slasher" films (such as *Friday the 13th, Part 2*) during the course of a week. Then, under the guise of a completely separate experiment on person perception,

FIGURE 10.3   MEAN SHOCK INTENSITY AS A FUNCTION OF GENDER OF VICTIM, FILM, AND ANGER

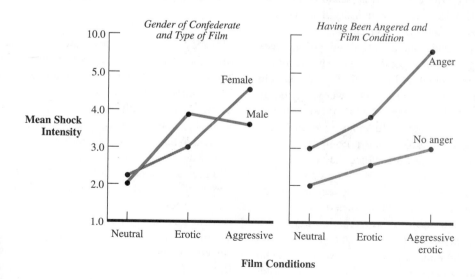

Film Conditions

Source: Donnerstein (1980)

participants viewed a twenty-minute video in which the female victim of a domestic violence attack described, in moving detail, the circumstances of her attack and detailed the extent of her injuries. Like the subjects in the Linz, Donnerstein, and Adams (1989) study, the participants who watched the three slasher films seemed desensitized to the violence and minimized the plight of the victim compared with a control group that had not seen the slasher films. At least, that is what happened when participants watched the domestic violence video three days after watching the slasher films. If the time lag between the slasher films and the domestic violence video reached five days or a week, Mullin and Linz (1995) found that the participants' reaction to the domestic violence victim and their rating of her injury had rebounded to the same level as the participants who had not seen the slasher films. Apparently, the longer delay allowed the participants to become "resensitized" to the violence and the victim. We do not know if the resensitization is a phenomenon that occurs with only mildly erotic, R-rated aggressive films or would also have occurred in the X-rated films studied by Linz, Donnerstein, and Adams (1989).

The Response of the Witness and the Target. Violent pornography tends to lead to aggression against a female target (Hui, 1986), but Leonard and Taylor (1983) showed that it makes a difference whether the female target of the aggression approves or disapproves of the pornography. They found that male subjects who viewed sexually explicit slides in the company of a female confederate who expressed approval or pleasure administered shocks of greater intensity than did subjects who received nonpermissive cues.

Now let's consider the target of aggression. Does the level of aggression depend on his or her response to a sexually violent film? In a study by Donnerstein and Berkowitz (1981), some subjects were angered by a confederate. Others were not. All of the subjects were male, but half of the confederates were male and half were female. A subject and a confederate then saw a film, and afterward the subject had an opportunity to deliver an electric shock to the confederate. The type of film a subject saw and the response of the confederate to that film were varied. The study showed that when subjects were made angry by a male confederate, shocks given to that confederate did not depend on the kind of film the subjects saw or on the confederate's response to the film. On the other hand, subjects angered by a female confederate did show different levels of aggression as a function of the

A poster for a 1943 movie contains cues of sex and violence associated with aggression.

film they saw. When they watched a violently erotic film, they tended to give more painful shocks to the confederate than when they watched a nonviolent film. Apparently the greater aggression toward women in this condition was fueled by the heightened arousal men experienced as a result of the aggressive erotica. What about the conditions in which the subjects were not previously angered by the confederate? Did they aggress against her as a function of the film they saw? A female confederate was given an intense electric shock when the film had aggressive sexual content and her response to that film was positive. When she seemed to enjoy the film, subjects perceived the film to be less aggressive, they found the film victim to be more responsible for the violence perpetrated against her, and the female confederate received more shocks.

The results of studies such as these point out the perniciousness of aggressive pornography (Donnerstein and Linz, 1986), particularly if there is any indication that the women who are being victimized—or other women viewing the victimization—experience pleasure. The message conveyed seems to reduce the perception of the seriousness of sexual aggression, justifies the aggression, and reduces inhibitions against aggressive behaviors.

Violent Television and Aggression

Turn on your television set almost any evening and odds are you will be confronted with violence. In 1992, for instance, prime-time television showed an average of 9.5 acts of violence per hour. Saturday morning cartoons were even more violent, showing an average of 32 violent encounters per hour (Goldstein, 1994). Teenagers, who watch an average of about thirty-five hours of television a week, almost inevitably are exposed to a heavy dose of violence. Researchers estimate that the average sixteen-year-old has seen 33,000 murders or attempted murders on television, and has witnessed over 200,000 acts of violence (National Coalition on Television Violence, 1990).

Because television viewing is one of the most common American pastimes and violence is one of the most common acts portrayed on television, it should not be surprising that both the public and social psychologists have been interested in the effects of violent television on aggressive behavior. Such groups as Citizens Action for Better Television have called for a decrease in media violence. They assume that such programming leads to increased aggressive behavior in viewers. As we shall see, research has generally supported this contention (Huesmann, 1982). The picture, however, may not be as clear as it is sometimes thought to be.

The two major theories about human aggression (frustration-aggression and social learning) make different predictions about the effects of television violence. On the one hand, the catharsis hypothesis of frustration-aggression theory suggests that participation in an aggressive act will lessen the instigation to future aggression. Thus, if people are allowed to play aggressively or if they vicariously experience aggression by watching violence on television, they should be less likely to aggress. From this point of view, it could be argued that violence on television (and in other media) should be allowed, if not encouraged. By witnessing violence, viewers can reduce their own needs to act aggressively because the vicarious experience of violence can lead to catharsis. On the other hand, social learning theory and Berkowitz's cue theory suggest that witnessed aggression should lead to more aggression rather than to catharsis. Portrayed aggression serves as a model for the viewer to imitate, and it can provide aggression cues that are sufficient to release the viewer's aggressiveness. Moreover, in many cases the viewer also sees the aggressor on the screen rewarded for his or her actions. This makes the aggressor an even more attractive model to follow.

Research attempting to resolve this dispute has fallen into two categories. One category has been correlational. In these studies (see Huesmann, 1982), measures are taken of aggression and of television viewing as they occur naturally. The two measures are then correlated to see if any relationship emerges. What has been consistently found is that violent television viewing and aggressive behavior are mildly but positively related. In other words, the more a person shows a preference for violent television, the more aggressive that person is. This has held true not only in the United States but in Finland, Poland, and Australia as well. This finding poses problems for a catharsis explanation of the effects of violent television; it seems more consistent with social learning theory. However, correlation does not necessarily imply causation. It could be, for instance, that people who are more aggressive to begin with prefer violent television. They may find it more exciting or a means of justifying their own aggression. If this were true, a positive correlation would be seen between the viewing of violence and aggressive behavior but *not* because television *caused* the aggressive behavior.

To answer more clearly the question of cause, researchers have turned to *experiments* as a second avenue of inquiry. Some of the earliest and most influential studies were conducted by Bandura and his colleagues (Bandura, Ross, and Ross, 1961, 1963a) that we described earlier. However, as Stein and Friedrich (1975) have observed, it is unclear how far we can generalize from these studies to violence as it is seen on commercial television. Bandura and his associates used films constructed specifically for their experiments. These films were brief and simple; the model's aggressive behavior dominated the action. But violence on commercial television may be harder to understand; the shows are longer and more complex. Therefore, the person's attention may be less focused and the violence may be less salient. Also, we do not know from Bandura's studies whether the aggression observed in subjects was lasting or more general. Typically, aggression was assessed immediately after the subjects viewed the model's behavior; the subject was given an opportunity to aggress in a similar situation using behaviors similar to the model's. Would the aggression also be observed in a different situation? And more important, would different, even more aggressive, behaviors be observed in a different context?

Further research has been somewhat contradictory. Some studies report an actual decline in aggressive behavior after witnessing violence. Feshbach (1961) demonstrated that witnessing an aggressive film can lower the viewer's subsequent aggression. He had angry and nonangry subjects watch either an aggressive film (a prizefight scene) or a nonaggressive film. Feshbach found that when given the opportunity to aggress, the angry subjects who had witnessed the aggressive film were less aggressive than the angry subjects who had seen the nonaggressive film. However, the nonangry subjects who saw the aggressive film reported feeling more hostile than the nonangry subjects who saw the nonaggressive film. This finding suggests that witnessing aggression can reduce the instigation to aggression of a viewer who is angry when he sees the film.

In a field study involving 625 boys between the ages of ten and seventeen, Feshbach and Singer (1971) found that watching violent movies reduced aggressive behavior. The subjects were upper-class boys at private boarding schools and boys in state institutions for the homeless. They were assigned to watch six weeks (one hour each night) of either aggressive programs or nonaggressive programs. Their behavior was rated for aggressiveness by staff members of the institutions. The results showed that the boys in the state institutions who watched the aggressive movies engaged in only half as many fights as, and were rated as less aggressive than, the boys who watched the nonviolent programs. The type of program was found to have no effect on the behavior of the boys in the private schools. The Feshbach and Singer study has been cited as supporting the catharsis hypothesis. However, the study has been severely criticized on methodological grounds. For example, boys at the state institution preferred aggressive programs. Thus those boys assigned to view nonaggressive programs may have felt frustrated and resentful over losing their favorite programs. This in turn may have led them to behave more aggressively.

A second body of research has suggested that violent television increases aggressive behavior. Friedrich and Stein (1973) allowed nursery school children to watch aggressive, neutral, or prosocial programs for a four-week period (see figure 10.4). The behavior of the children was observed before, during, and after the television period. Interestingly enough,

---

FIGURE 10.4   MEAN CHANGE SCORES FOR INTERPERSONAL AGGRESSION

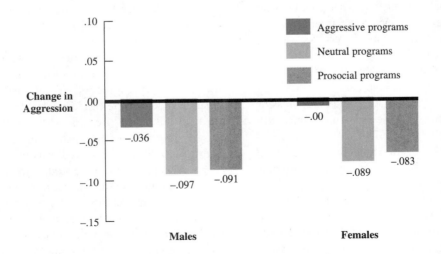

Note: The lower the score, the greater the reduction in aggression after viewing the programs. Scores are for subjects high in initial aggression.
Source: Friedrich and Stein (1973)

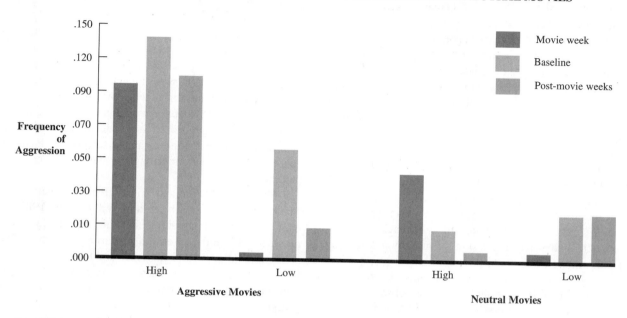

Note: "High" and "low" refer to initial tendencies to aggress.
Source: Parke et al. (1977)

the behavior of the children who had been rated as below average in aggressiveness before viewing the programs was not affected by them. For children who were initially high in aggressiveness, the results were more complex. Highly aggressive children who saw neutral and prosocial programs decreased their aggressiveness over time; those who saw aggressive programs also decreased their aggressiveness, but less. Friedrich and Stein interpreted this to mean that aggressive programs maintained what otherwise would have been a pattern of decreasing aggression and such shows thus encouraged aggression. It is important to keep in mind, however, that the aggressive programs did not increase subjects' aggressiveness. It is possible that aggressive shows had little or no impact and that the neutral or prosocial programs served to decrease aggression. Indeed, Hearold (1986) found that TV programs that show strong prosocial models have a greater influence on children's behavior than do shows that demonstrate antisocial behavior.

An experiment that did show an increase in aggression after subjects viewed violent films was reported by Parke, Berkowitz, Leyens, West, and Sebastian (1977). They conducted three extensive studies (two in the United States and one in Belgium)

with juvenile delinquents in minimum-custody institutions. The subjects' behaviors were observed for a three-week period to get a baseline measure of general aggressiveness. The subjects were then randomly divided into two groups, and for the next week half of the subjects watched aggressive movies each night and the other half watched nonaggressive movies. During the final three-week phase, the subjects were observed in their day-to-day routines and their behavior was evaluated on an aggressiveness dimension. Figure 10.5 presents results from the first study. In each case, the subjects who watched the aggressive movies behaved more aggressively than the subjects who saw the neutral movies. This is consistent with social learning theory. However, the implications of this study for understanding the impact of television violence on *typical* individuals is unclear. The films used were unedited, feature-length selections that were much more violent than actual television fare. Also, the subjects were from institutions for juvenile delinquents. Thus, at least one of the problems that Feshbach and Singer were criticized for—the use of an overly aggressive, atypical subject population—was shared by this study. Subjects from this population may have reacted differently from most other people.

An interesting experiment by Josephson (1987) provides further evidence for increased aggression following exposure to violent television. It also addresses the importance of a cue for aggression, which forms the cornerstone of Berkowitz's (1965) theory of aggression cues. Second- and third-grade boys in Winnipeg, Manitoba, watched either a violent or nonviolent action-oriented program. The nonviolent action-oriented program was an exciting motorcycle race. The violent program was an excerpt from a police action series that began with the cold-blooded killing of an off-duty police officer by a group of snipers. As the fourteen-minute episode proceeded, members of a police SWAT team systematically gunned down or knocked unconscious each member of the gang of snipers. The SWAT team members communicated with each other by walkie-talkies, and aggression was usually preceded by calls on the walkie-talkies.

After watching the violent episode, the boys played a game of floor hockey as four observers rated the boys' play. Aggression was an index composed of such things as pushing another boy down, elbowing him, insulting him, or hitting him with a hockey stick. Before beginning the game, the boys were interviewed "just the way real radio announcers interview hockey players." Half of the boys were interviewed with a microphone; the other half were interviewed with a walkie-talkie. The walkie-talkie served as the aggression cue.

Josephson found the greatest amount of aggression in boys who watched the violent episode and had the aggression cue of the walkie-talkie. These youngsters played hockey more aggressively than any other boys in the study. The boys who watched the SWAT program without the aggression cue were less aggressive and the boys who watched the motorcycle race were the least aggressive during the hockey game. These results, while offering support for the aggression cue theory of aggressive behavior, still need to be interpreted with caution. The supportive results were found only for those boys who were rated high on characteristic aggression by their classroom teachers. That is, the aggression cues tended to elicit aggressive behavior in boys already predisposed to act aggressively.

Video Games

Video games are a multi-billion-dollar industry. It is estimated that video arcades take in approximately $8 billion annually, and billions more are spent on home game systems and computer games. Even early video games such as Space Invaders and Missile Command contained a violent fantasy element; the point of the game being to blow up the characters, space ships, or planets. Later popular games, such as Mortal Kombat, included more lifelike characters that could kill or be killed by electrocution, ripping out the heart or decapitation (with a quivering spinal cord attached). The success of Mortal Kombat encouraged the production of other violent games, such as Mortal Kombat 2, Doom, and Quake. Do these games affect children and cause them to behave more aggressively? It appears that the answer is yes.

Studies by Ballard and Wiest (1996), Cooper and Mackie (1986), and Silvern and Williamson (1987) used experimental paradigms that have become familiar in the TV-and-aggression research. Silvern and Williamson (1987) studied twenty-eight children from four to six years of age. They observed pairs of children in free play to obtain baseline measures of aggression. Half of the pairs then watched a *Road Runner* cartoon, while the other half played Space Invaders. One child in the pair actually played the game, while the other merely observed. After the game or cartoon, the children were once again observed in free play. Both the violent cartoon and the video game raised the level of aggressive play above the baseline measures. The effect of the games and the TV program were far more pronounced for boys than for girls. It is interesting, too, that observers of video games were affected just as much as the players.

Cooper and Mackie's (1986) research showed similar findings: their subjects, all ten and eleven years old, behaved more aggressively after playing Missile Command. These investigators, too, found that observers of video games behaved just as aggressively as the children who actually played them. However, in contrast to Silvern and Williamson (1987), Cooper and Mackie found these effects with girls but not with boys.

The study by Mary Ballard and J. Rose Wiest (1996) measured the physiological and attitudinal effects of playing violent video games on male college students rather than children. The students played either the very violent Mortal Kombat, the ultraviolent Mortal Kombat 2, or a nonviolent video billiards game. The violent games increased students' physiological arousal (heart rate and blood pressure) and also increased students' hostile attitudes as measured by several standardized scales of hostility: the more violent the game, the more hostility it engendered in the players.

What Can We Conclude?

Policymakers want definitive answers to important questions. Whether television and video games provoke aggression in young people is one of those important questions. We have examined research that has supported the notion that viewing televised aggression causes viewers to increase their aggressive behavior. We have also seen research that supports the opposite position. Most studies find effects for males and not for females; a few studies show that females are more affected by aggressive media than males. Are there any clear and definitive answers?

A report prepared by the National Institute of Mental Health (NIMH) conceded that the television-aggression link has not been established conclusively in any single study (Pearl and Bouthilet, 1982). However, the report did conclude that the "weight of the evidence" suggested that violent television programs increased subsequent aggression by viewers. Comstock and Paik (1991) analyzed over 185 different experiments and concluded that the research shows a robust relationship between television violence and antisocial behavior. In a similar analysis, Wood, Wong, and Chachere (1991) also found a link between aggression and exposure to violent media, although the effect did not appear in many of the studies they examined.

These conclusions have not gone unchallenged. Jonathan Freedman (1984, 1986) reviewed "every available published study" and concluded that the weight of the available evidence leads to no conclusion at all—the evidence at hand is not yet sufficient to prove the hypothesis.

Freedman offered possible reasons for the less-than-conclusive findings. Suppose that televised aggression tends to lead to aggressive behavior, as has been shown in the laboratory. In the nonlaboratory world, television watching has to be placed in the context of many other behaviors and many other influences. Television viewing itself, even for a person who watches a great deal of televised violence, has to be viewed in relation to other programs in which aggression does not take place. Consequently, the real-world context provides so many other influences that the effect of television viewing may be mitigated by those other influences.

The debate engendered by Freedman's review (Freedman, 1986; Friedrich-Cofer and Huston, 1986) has raised another fascinating point. Perhaps more convincing evidence would be obtained if we paid attention to a *bidirectional hypothesis* (Gunter, 1983; Huesmann, Logerspetz, and Eron, 1984). According to this hypothesis, people who watch aggressive television may be those who are characteristically more aggressive, and the watching of the programs may provoke still greater aggression in those people. In other words, instead of seeking to prove that the causal link between TV and aggression goes only in one direction, it may be better and more fruitful to consider TV viewing and aggressive behavior as a two-way street, with each factor affecting the other.

We have placed considerable emphasis on the television-aggression question and the pornography-aggression question for several reasons: (1) they are phenomena of immense social significance; (2) they are phenomena that bring together several theories of social psychology, each of which has received considerable support in the laboratory; and (3) they are areas that demonstrate the rewards and frustrations of bringing basic research to bear on problems of societal significance. We agree with the conclusions of the NIMH and a more recent analysis by the American Psychological Association's Commission on Violence and Youth (Eron, Gentry, and Schlegel, 1994) that the weight of the evidence supports the belief that there is a causal link between watching violent television and behaving aggressively. However, the science of psychology must still refine its hypotheses in these areas and provide more definitive evidence.

Summary

Aggression is defined as an action intended to injure another person. We noted other considerations that suggest several definitions of aggression and the difficulty encountered when adopting only a single understanding of the concept. Aggressive behavior may spring from instinctual or biological origins. We have argued, however, that social-psychological theories are necessary if we are to understand when and why aggressive behavior occurs.

One of the more popular theories of aggression regards frustration as the root cause of all aggression. According to proponents of the frustration-aggression hypothesis, engaging in or witnessing acts of aggression can serve to reduce an individual's frustration via catharsis. The frustration-aggression theory also states that if aggression cannot be vented directly upon the frustrating agent, it will be displaced onto another target, the most likely targets being those that are highly similar to the source of the frustration. Critics of the theory argue that frustration does not always lead to aggression and that aggression is not always the direct result of frustration. Nevertheless, the frustration-aggression hypothesis has stimulated a tremendous amount of research that has shed light on the conditions under which frustration is likely to lead to aggressive actions.

The concept of revolution may be considered from the perspective of frustration-aggression. When a large group of people experiences frustration, or relative deprivation, through the actions of its leaders, the people may be moved to revolt. Their sense of deprivation may result from the loss of freedom or goods they once had (decremental deprivation), because they can see no hope of realizing their dreams (aspirational deprivation) or because previous improvements in economic and social conditions are suddenly cut back (progressive deprivation).

Another theoretical approach to aggression suggests that frustration merely produces the readiness to aggress; the presence or absence of aggression cues will determine whether people will actually express aggression. Still other researchers argue that aggressive behavior is a way of expressing the need to exercise control over situations or other people. Impression management and the need to maintain self-esteem are also thought to play roles in aggression.

Social learning theory suggests that aggressive behaviors are learned from others through reinforcement and, most important, from modeling. Even if an individual learns how to aggress, however, he or she will not necessarily behave aggressively unless rewarded, or at least not punished, for doing so. Research has also shown that people will imitate aggressive models. Thus, social learning theory indicates that aggressive behavior can be diminished by not providing aggressive models for children and not rewarding aggressive behavior.

A model combining personality and social-psychological approaches to aggression is the theory of egotism threat which holds that aggression is more likely to be committed by those who have high levels

Kipland Kinkel, fifteen, a student at Thurston High School in Springfield, Oregon, is led to his arraignment in May 1998 for the shooting deaths of two students and his parents. Cited at the time as the sixth occurrence of a fatal high school shooting in eight months, the incident received wide media attention. Could overreportage of school shootings contribute to their recurrence?

of self-esteem but whose self-view is threatened by others or by events in the social environment.

Theories of aggression allow us to understand a great deal about why people aggress and some ways of reducing aggression. We have seen, however, that theory is helpful to varying degrees when applied to social dilemmas that afflict society. Even though the application of theory and research is somewhat limited in the areas of family violence and drug abuse, we have a growing body of knowledge on the impact of pornography and violent television programming on aggressive behavior.

Understanding the impact of pornography on aggression has been helped by the use of excitation transfer theory. According to this theory, arousal—regardless of its true origin—will increase the likelihood of aggression if people interpret it as anger. Thus, excitation from pornography may be transferred to the experience of anger and serve to increase aggression. A more cautious approach is taken by the excitation valence model, which holds that violent and unpleasant pornography will anger men and provoke them to aggress, whereas pleasant pornography may actually reduce aggression. Other theories focus on the role of the target's response in provoking aggression-related pornography. Aggression cue theory suggests that men who watch violent sexual acts against women may come to associate the presence of a woman in a similar situation as an aggressive cue, and this may lead them to aggression.

Research on the effects of viewing television violence has generally determined that watching violent programs is associated with increased aggression, although the validity of the research has been controversial through the last several decades. The sex and age of the viewer appear to be important variables influencing the relationship between watching violent programs and engaging in violent behavior. Some research has shown that watching violent acts on television desensitizes the viewer to aggression and reduces empathy toward the victim. Similar links between exposure to violent imagery and aggressive behavior have been demonstrated with video games—both for the player and the spectator. In general, despite serious controversy surrounding both experimental and correlational studies, the weight of the evidence seems to indicate a causal link between violence in the media and aggressive behavior.

Key Terms

aggression	decremental deprivation	instinct theories
aggression cues	displaced aggression	modeling
aspirational deprivation	excitation transfer theory	progressive deprivation
biological theories	frustration	reinforcement
catharsis	frustration-aggression theory	social learning theory

Suggested Readings

Bandura, A., and Walters, R. H. (1963). *Social learning and personality development.* New York: Holt, Rhinehart and Winston.

Baumeister, R. F., Smart, L. and Boden, J. M. (1996). Relation of threatened egotism to violence and aggression: The dark side of high self-esteem. *Psychological Review, 103,* 5–33.

Dollard, J., Doob, L., Miller, N. E., Mowrer, O. H., and Sears, R. R. (1939). *Frustration and aggression.* New Haven, CT: Yale University Press.

Eron, L. D., Gentry, J. H., and Schlegel, P. (1994). *Reason to hope: A psychosocial perspective on violence and youth.* Washington, DC: American Psychological Association.

Geen, R. R. (1997). Aggression and antisocial behavior. In D. T. Gilbert, S. T. Fiske, and G. Lindzey (Eds.), *Handbook of social psychology* (4th ed.). New York: Oxford University Press and McGraw-Hill.

Gurr, T. R. (1970). *Why men rebel.* Princeton, NJ: Princeton University Press.

Lorenz, K. (1968). *On aggression.* New York: Bantam Books.

Chapter 11

Social Influence

A rather short, stocky man of thirty-four ascended a platform in the nation's capital on August 23, 1963. He looked down at a crowd of 250,000 people who were waiting for him to speak. He began slowly, but his voice gained volume and confidence as he spoke:

> I say to you today, even though we face the difficulties of today and tomorrow I still have a dream. It is a dream that is deeply rooted in the American dream. I have a dream that one day this nation will rise up, live out the true meaning of its creed: We hold these truths to be self-evident, that all men are created equal.
>
> I have a dream that one day on the red hills of Georgia the sons of former slaves and the sons of former slave owners will be able to sit down together at the table of brotherhood. I have a dream that one day even the state of Mississippi, a state sweltering with the heat of oppression, will be transformed into an oasis of freedom and justice.
>
> I have a dream that my four little children one day will live in a nation where they will not be judged by the color of their skin, but by the content of their character.
>
> I have a dream that one day every valley shall be exalted, every hill and mountain shall be made low. The rough places will be made plain and the crooked places will be made straight. This is the faith that I go back to the South with. With this faith we will be able to hew, out of the mountains of despair, the stone of hope. With this faith we will be able to work together, to pray together, to stand up for freedom together, knowing we will be free one day. (Cited in King, 1969, pp. 239–40)

When the speech ended, the audience sat in awe and then thundered its approval. The "I have a dream" speech became a rallying cry in the drive toward equal rights for blacks in the United States. The speaker, the Reverend Martin Luther King, Jr., was a strong force in the civil rights movement. He had been character-ized as the "moral leader of the nation." He was to receive the Nobel peace prize for his courageous leadership of the Black Freedom movement, and his counsel was sought by two presidents.

Martin Luther King, Jr., was born in 1929 in Atlanta, Georgia. He grew up in a middle-class black neighborhood in a relatively secure and uneventful world. His father, a Baptist minister, recalled that "we never lived in a rented house and never rode too long in a car on which payment was due" (Bennett, 1968). Young Martin was a precocious, hard-working student, deferential to his elders and considerate of his peers. He skipped the ninth and twelfth grades and entered Morehouse College at the age of fifteen. He also attended Crozer Seminary, and he received a Ph.D. in philosophy from Boston University. While at Morehouse College, King decided to become a minister, and at the age of eighteen he was ordained. In September 1954 he became head pastor at the Dexter Avenue Baptist Church in Montgomery, Alabama. It was there that his crusade for freedom began.

King was the right man in the right place at the right time. World War II had brought blacks and whites into closer contact on a more equal footing than at any other time in the history of this country (Bishop, 1971), and nonwhites were winning independence in other parts of the world—India, Africa, Southeast Asia, and the East Indies. On May 17, 1954, the U.S. Supreme Court, in the case of *Brown v. Board of Education of Topeka, Kansas,* ruled that "separate educational facilities are inherently unequal"; and on May 31, 1955, the Court ordered school desegregation "with all deliberate speed."

Then, on December 1, 1955, an incident in Montgomery precipitated King's leadership in the civil rights movement. Rosa Parks, a black seamstress, boarded a crowded bus, paid her fare, and took a seat in the "Negro section" at the back. Six whites boarded the bus at the next stop, and the bus driver then went to the back and ordered the blacks to give up their places so that the whites could be seated. Three blacks yielded to this established custom and immediately rose, but Rosa Parks remained seated. The bus driver repeated his demand, and again she refused. For this act of insubordination she was arrested. This incident provided the catalyst for the unification of the Black Freedom movement under King's leadership.

The black leaders of Montgomery felt that it was time to act—time to protest the treatment of Rosa Parks and of all blacks in the South. King urged that the protest action be nonviolent, so a one-day black boycott of the bus line was planned. King and the other leaders expected about 60 percent cooperation; to their amazement, there was almost 100 percent participation. Although no direct force was exerted to get people to support the boycott, the "silent pressure of the movement" fueled the action. Blacks who rode on the buses were subjected to hostile stares and scorn by the boycott supporters, actions that were usually enough to bring even the most stubborn person into line.

Encouraged, the black leaders met to plan further action. They elected King to head the Montgomery Freedom movement, and they decided to continue the boycott of buses until three demands were met: (1) courteous treatment of black riders by the bus operators, (2) passenger seating on a first-come, first-served basis, and (3) Negro bus drivers on predominantly Negro routes (King, 1969).

King proved a vigorous leader. He spoke to crowds of blacks about the purposes of the boycott and about the necessity for nonviolence, and he arbitrated with Montgomery's mayor, other city officials, and bus company representatives. The boycott continued. Although King's home was bombed, he continued to preach nonviolence. On February 21, 1956, the Montgomery County grand jury declared the boycott illegal, and King and other leaders were arrested. Still the boycott went on, and King's following grew. The one-day boycott evolved into a 382-day struggle that finally ended on November 14, 1956, when the Supreme Court declared illegal the Alabama law requiring segregation on buses. It was a victory for the Black Freedom movement, for its new leader, the Reverend Martin Luther King, Jr., and for King's doctrine of nonviolent protest.

The year after the Montgomery boycott, King gave 208 speeches and traveled 780,000 miles. In the following years he led drives for black freedom and equality in Georgia, Alabama, Illinois, and Mississippi, always with the goal of achieving freedom through civil disobedience and nonviolence. Despite numerous assassination attempts, he persisted in his advocacy of nonviolence in freedom marches, sit-down strikes, and civil disobedience, and thousands followed his example and his instructions. He earned the respect of blacks and whites alike, and he became a valued adviser to Presidents John F. Kennedy and Lyndon B. Johnson and to Attorney General Robert F. Kennedy. When King organized the "March on Washington" to give impetus to the Kennedy Civil Rights Bill, more than 250,000 people turned out, and King was present when the bill was eventually signed into law.

In the years following the passage of the Civil Rights Act of 1964, King became active in opposing the American war in Vietnam and in mobilizing protests against poverty in the United States. He was in Memphis, Tennessee, on April 4, 1968, organizing a march of sanitation workers demanding better working conditions when he was cut down by an assassin's bullet. He was only thirty-nine years old.

The Scope of Social Influence

The story of Martin Luther King, Jr., and the civil rights movement illustrates many types of social behavior. Among the most central is social influence. People had to be influenced to join the movement, and the nation had to be influenced to adopt the goals of the movement. In its broadest sense, social influence includes almost all of social psychology because it may be used to describe any change (physiological, attitudinal, emotional, or behavioral) that occurs in one person as the result of the real, implied, or imagined presence of others (Latané, 1981).

In its more limited usage, however, **social influence** involves the exercise of power by a person or group to influence the behavior of others. Social influence is concerned more with behavioral change than with attitudinal or emotional change. King was well aware of this distinction for he often remarked that while he would like to change people's attitudes, his main goal was to get people to act in a fair and equitable way toward others regardless of race.

The area of social influence is broad and central to social psychology. We are constantly confronted

Dr. Martin Luther King, Jr. (center), is flanked by Reverend Ralph Abernathy (right) and Bishop Julian Smith (left) in a 1968 march in Memphis, Tennessee. King's leadership in the civil rights movement is a testament to the power of social influence to peacefully alter behavior and change attitudes.

with social influence in our everyday lives; some of this influence is direct and clearly identifiable, while other influence is more indirect and less recognizable. In studying the role of social influence in the civil rights movement, we can also become aware of its role in our everyday lives.

Responses to Social Influence

It will be helpful if, at the outset, we identify three distinct types of response to the pressures of social influence (Kelman, 1961). As you will see, different kinds of individual power and group pressure result in different kinds of opinion and behavior change. The first kind of response to social influence is **compliance.** When people comply, they simply go along overtly with certain kinds of social influence; there is no genuine internal or private opinion change in the case of compliance. As a result of peer pressure, for example, a student may participate in a rally demanding that her college hire more minority faculty. The student is demonstrating compliance if she actually believes that her college should not make further efforts to hire minority faculty.

Compliance is public; that is, it does not involve private opinion change. Two kinds of responses to social influence, however, are marked by genuine opinion change. The first is called **identification.** Identification occurs when an individual adopts the standards of a person or group that he or she likes, admires, and wants to establish a relationship with. The individual privately accepts the new standards but maintains them only as long as he or she continues to admire the other person or group. A student may willingly participate in rallies for more minority faculty, for instance, as long as she likes one of the protest group leaders. When that admiration ends, however, the student may find herself surprisingly uninterested in hiring more minority faculty.

The third response to social influence involves genuine, long-lasting change of opinion based on congruence between a new opinion and the individual's overall value system. This kind of response to social influence is called **internalization.** The student who not only participates in the rally for minority faculty but also believes in that policy because it coincides with her values has internalized the aims of the protest group.

The distinction between compliance and internalization is important, as it enables us to predict how an individual will act when influence pressures have been removed. If the individual is simply complying with individual or group pressures but retains private attitudes that are inconsistent with those pressures, we would not expect his or her behavior to be the same once the social pressure has been removed. Thus, the person whose attendance at the rally only reflects public compliance will not follow through with other actions.

The distinction between compliance and internalization alerts us to the other side of the coin; that is, the fact that influence often results in private acceptance without producing public compliance. Sometimes, for example, people respond to societal minorities by accepting their ideas privately while publicly ignoring them (Nemeth, 1986).

Social Power

As we have seen, power forms the base of an individual's or group's ability to influence others. In fact, **power** is generally defined as the capacity or the potential to influence others and to resist influence by others (Michener and Suchner, 1972). The essential difference between influence and power is that influence actually changes the behavior of another person, whereas power is the ability to bring about such a change. A parent may have a great deal of power (the potential to change behavior) over a child, but some parents exercise this power (influence) more than others do.

An important clarification of the power concept was suggested by Cartwright and Zander (1968). They point out that exercising power often brings the actor rewards but may also entail costs. For example, you may have the power to get another individual to wash your automobile; and although getting that individual to wash your car may bring you some rewards (a clean

car), it will also have costs for you (money). Even though you have the money to pay someone to wash your car (power), the price may be more than you're willing to pay. Hence Cartwright and Zander employ the term *usable power* to describe the power that will bring more rewards than costs. Martin Luther King, Jr., may have had the power to persuade a group in Rio Hondo, Texas, to carry out a peaceful demonstration. This may not have been usable power, however, because it would have taken King two days of travel by plane, bus, and horse to actually meet and influence the group. Such a trip might not have been worth the benefits.

Types of Power and Their Use

People gain the potential to influence others through many routes. A policeman and a doctor may both be able to influence you to refrain from using certain drugs; however, the bases of their influence are very different. French and Raven (1959) identified five bases from which individuals gain power. They and others (Aries, 1976; Michener and Burt, 1974; Bonoma, 1976) point out that in most cases people derive power from more than one base and must decide which type of power to use in a particular situation. Further, the base of power often determines the situations in which it can be used.

Coercive Power

The potential to deliver threats and punishment to force another person to change his or her behavior is **coercive power.** A parent uses coercive power when he or she threatens to spank a child if a certain behavior is not carried out. Coercive power was used to stop King's civil rights activities: his house was bombed, he was jailed on several occasions, and there were numerous attempts on his life.

Coercive power is based on access to weapons or other resources that increase strength and the credibility of threat. Two important drawbacks deter the use of coercive power. First, the low-power individual in a coercive relationship is going to be motivated to end the relationship if the opportunity presents itself. Dictatorial governments that rely on coercive power must go to great lengths to keep citizens from leaving the country. Second, the coercive power base requires surveillance of the low-power person (Shaw and Condelli, 1986). The power of coercion is only as effective as the surveillance system. Rarely does a child rush in and announce to its mother, "I just sneaked three cookies from the cookie jar."

Because coercion requires the effort of surveillance and risks resentment, one may ask why coercion is used as a tool to wield power. One reason is that it is relatively easy to use; it takes little effort to make a threat. Another reason is that coercion may enhance the self-esteem of its user (Raven and Kruglanski, 1970; Kipnis, 1974). Being able to force another person to act in a prescribed manner leads to a feeling of mastery and superiority. Hence, Kipnis reports that supervisors who lack confidence and self-esteem often resort to coercive power. However, coercive power is the type of power that is least likely to sustain change and it is the most difficult to maintain. It is generally used as a last resort.

Reward Power

The ability to give positive reinforcement to produce change is **reward power.** The reinforcement may take the form of material commodities, such as money, or it may take a more intangible form, such as praise. Reward power is based on access to commodities that others value. Hence, an individual may have reward power over one person but not over another depending on the value that these people place on the commodities.

Reward power, unlike coercive power, motivates the low-power individual to stay in the relationship. Although surveillance is required for the effective use of reward power, the degree of such surveillance need not be as high as that required by coercive power. It is not uncommon for a child to announce, "Come look, I've just cleaned up my room." When the desired behavior is performed, the actor is likely to call the attention of the high-power individual to that performance. Canavan-Gumpert (1977) found that reward power (praise) is more effective than coercive power (criticism) in increasing performance in children. Hence, reward power should be preferred to coercive power.

Reward power may be costly to the user, however, especially when the reward is based on material assets such as money. In addition, because the reward may justify behavior, the exercise of reward power may not result in internalization, or attitude change. Remembering dissonance theory (recall chapter 6), the actor may say, "I'm doing this because of the reward and not because I believe in what I'm doing."

Thus, reward power will be effective only so long as rewards are dispensed.

Legitimate Power

The power that one derives from being in a particular role or position is **legitimate power.** Legitimate power is authority, and it is generally limited to a particular domain. For example, your boss may have the legitimate power to influence how you behave at work, but he or she doesn't have legitimate power to determine how you behave toward your spouse or what you do on your days off. Pruitt (1976) noted that legitimate power is based on the norm of "oughtness"; we are socialized to believe that we should follow the orders of persons in certain positions. For example, the child is taught to "do what your parents say because they are your parents." Martin Luther King, Jr., obtained legitimate power by virtue of the fact that he was the leader of the Black Freedom movement and the president of the Southern Christian Leadership Conference.

Possessors of legitimate power do not have to explain why they want individuals to act in a certain way. People with legitimate power are influential not because they say the right things but because they have the right to influence. Laws may be used to assign legitimate power to certain people. And it is often the case that people who have other bases of power may pass laws to ensure legitimate power for themselves. Hence, a dictator who overthrows a government by the use of coercive power may "pass laws" that give him legitimate power.

Expert Power

Often people gain power because others see them as being knowledgeable about a particular area. For example, physicians often have **expert power;** they are perceived to have special insight and knowledge about medical problems. If they advise you to have an operation, you will probably have it even if you do not necessarily understand why the operation is necessary. Expert power, like legitimate power, is usually limited to a specific area. Thus, your doctor may be able to influence you on health-related issues, but you may not necessarily follow his or her advice about what new car to buy. People often attempt to increase their expert power by the use of diplomas and citations that testify to their knowledge in a certain area. It is not uncommon to walk into a doctor's office and see a whole wall of diplomas and citations that testify to the doctor's knowledge in a certain area. Garage mechanics may also bolster their expert power by displaying diplomas and citations from courses they have taken.

Expert power has some of the advantages and disadvantages of legitimate power. It does not require surveillance; it is clearly vested in the individual; it often covers only a limited domain. It does, however, have the added advantage that internalization of attitudes may follow its use. In short, people not only follow an expert because they are awed by the credentials that the expert possesses, but they also believe that he or she has the correct information.

Referent Power

People gain the ability to influence us because we admire and like them. We want to be similar to the people we admire, and hence we often imitate them and try to act as we think they would. **Referent power** was one of the strongest bases of King's power. Because he was admired by millions for his courage, his foresight, and his charismatic personality, many people wanted to be like him and acted as he did.

Given the available evidence, it seems that referent power is the most *usable*. Its use does not require surveillance, and it tends to bring the user and the target closer together rather than forcing them apart. It is also likely to lead to an internalization of attitudes rather than simply a change in behavior. The belief in the effectiveness of referent power is one of the motivating factors behind group psychotherapy and such behavior-change groups as Weight Watchers and Alcoholics Anonymous. In these cases, peers with similar backgrounds, rather than experts, are relied upon as the agents of influence.

Informational Power

Raven and Kruglanski (1970) added a sixth basis of power to those suggested by French and Raven (1959). The five types of power that we have discussed are all dependent on the source; the basis of power lies within the particular person. That person's power may be limited to particular situations, but it is independent of the information that the person actually possesses. On the other hand, eyewitnesses to crimes have the power to influence juries solely because of the information they have and not because of their characteristics. This type of independent power

has been labeled **informational power.** As Pruitt (1976) points out, "Knowledge is power." It should be noted, however, that once the person who possesses information power dispenses the information, power is reduced. Once the eyewitness has testified, for example, he or she no longer has the power to influence the behavior of the jury.

How Does Power Influence Our Thinking?

It's possible that the mere possession of power over others influences the way we think about people—at least the people over whom we possess that power. Susan Fiske and her colleagues have proposed that possessing power reduces our ability and our desire to process information accurately about subordinates. Because they control resources, the powerful are not dependent on subordinates. Furthermore, because subordinates typically outnumber managers or supervisors, those in power may not have the time to pay attention to everyone. The net effect of decreased attention is that the powerful tend to rely on the use of stereotypes in forming impressions of subordinates (see Fiske, 1993). Using stereotypes instead of reliable, individuating information causes errors in processing that contribute to such deleterious outcomes as race or sex discrimination in the workplace (Fiske and Glick, 1995). (See Box 11.1)

Laura Stevens and Susan Fiske (in Fiske, Morling, and Stevens, 1996) manipulated power in a two-person interaction situation. They found that people who were given power were less interested in seeing diagnostic information about their partners and more likely to make stereotyped, biased attributions about their less powerful partners.

Just as you might expect, the effect of being powerless has the opposite effect on how people process information about their superiors. Because their jobs are dependent upon the behavior of managers or supervisors, the powerless are motivated to observe carefully supervisors' characteristics and behavior. The powerless pay closer attention to individuating information about those who control their fates, possibly to enhance perceptions of control and the ability to predict important outcomes.

Understanding the use of power, then, is not only a study of the relative outcomes of people in interpersonal interaction. Rather, power affects the way in which we process information about others, leading to

BOX 11.1

Sexual Harassment and the Abuse of Power in the Workplace

One especially pernicious gender difference in the use and abuse of power is sexual harassment. According to the legal definition issued by the U.S. Equal Employment Opportunity Commission (EEOC) in 1980, sexual harassment is the extortion of sexual cooperation through subtle or explicit threats of job-related consequences and pervasive sex-related verbal or physical conduct that is unwelcome or offensive. According to Louise Fitzgerald (1993), who reviewed the data gathered in surveys of federal employees, trade unions, and universities, the majority of sexual harassment is not physical, that is, it does not involve unwanted touching. Instead, Fitzgerald warned that the majority of sexual harassment is psychological in nature, experienced as "intrusive, unwanted, and coercive sexual attention from which there is frequently no viable escape" (Fitzgerald, 1993, p. 1071). Evidence shows that women are more likely to be the target of sexual harassment (cf., Gutek, 1985), and based on the results of her review, Fitzgerald predicted that one of every two women who work in an organization will experience sexual harassment sometime during their career.

The link between gender, power, and sexual harassment starts with recognition of what Eric Depret and Susan Fiske (1993) call *power asymmetries:* relative to women, men hold disproportionately more control over resources and outcomes in businesses and other organizations. Men who harass are often in a position to affect the rewards and costs of their female victims without the latter having reciprocal control. Consequently, women who file harassment complaints, or even just resist the sexual advances of a male manager or adviser, could suffer devastating economic consequences, such as lost current income (she

could get fired) or career opportunities (lost promotions or poor letters of recommendation from the harasser). Thus, men are more likely to harass in part because they are more likely to get away with it.

As implied in the chapter, the possession of power may contribute to sexual harassment when it promotes the use of stereotypes to form impressions of female subordinates. Fiske and Glick (1995) suggest that culturally shared categorizations of women as traditional, nontraditional, or "sexy" may contribute to how they are treated in the workplace. In particular, women labeled as sexy are perceived as being concerned with their own appearance for the purpose of attracting men (Six and Eckes, 1991). This female stereotype arouses sexual motives in men, and sexual harassment toward women categorized as sexy may reflect a desire for lasting intimacy or a desire for male domination. In contrast, women categorized as nontraditional are perceived to possess masculine qualities and the desire to assume male gender roles. These women may be targeted for sexual harassment to reassert both male dominance and traditional gender roles. In each case, the possession of power directly influences the impressions formed of female subordinates, which may then affect how they are treated.

Researchers are quick to point out, however, that only a minority of men in positions of power in organizations sexually harass female subordinates (Fitzgerald, 1993). Why, if men generally have more power in organizations than women, do only a minority harass? One factor suggested by recent social-psychological research is that harassment behavior has to be perceived as socially permissible or normative in a given work environment. For example, John Pryor

Continued

BOX 11.1

Continued

(1995) analyzed data on reports of sexual harassment gathered in two large national surveys. He tested the hypothesis that in organizations where management is perceived to condone or ignore sexual harassment, women are more likely to report being sexually harassed. The results in each survey showed that reports of sexual harassment by female employees were highest in organizations where male employees perceived that management condoned harassment behavior or ignored sexual harassment complaints. Although correlational in nature, these data are consistent with the notion that for men to abuse their power and harass women, they have to believe that the workplace norms support their sexual advances.

Pryor and his colleagues have further shown in experimental research that only men who associate the mental concepts of power and sex are likely to harass women when the situation is perceived as condoning the men's behavior. To identify males predisposed to harass, Pryor developed a self-report measure called the Likelihood to Sexually Harass (LSH) scale. The LSH consists of ten different scenarios in which a man is described as having a power advantage over an attractive female. In one scenario a male manager of a restaurant witnesses an attractive female waitress intentionally failing to charge her friends for a meal. Males are asked to imagine themselves in each scenario and to rate the likelihood that they would use their power advantage (e.g., the threat of firing the waitress) to gain sexual favors from the female target. Across all the scenarios, the higher the overall likelihood that a male would use power to gain sexual gratification, the stronger the association between power and sex for that person. Presumably, men with high scores on the LSH should be predis-

posed to take advantage of a woman underling if the situation were perceived as supporting harassment behavior.

A number of studies by Pryor and his colleagues support this prediction (Pryor, 1995). In one experiment by Pryor, La Vite, and Stoller (1993), high- and low-LSH men were asked to help an attractive female (a confederate) complete a computer word-processing task. Before they helped, half of the participants observed a male authority figure (a confederate) sexually harass the woman through sexually suggestive touching and verbal statements. The other half observed the "manager" treat the woman in a friendly but professional manner. When participants subsequently were asked to assist the female target, high-LSH males who observed the harassing authority figure were more likely to engage in unsolicited physical contact and make sexual comments relative to low-LSH males. After observing the professional authority figure, however, neither high- nor low-LSH males harassed the female target. These results and those of similar experiments indicate that men who make a strong connection between power and sex are more likely to take advantage of a female when they perceive the norms as supporting overt sexual behavior.

One implication of the research by Pryor is that men who are predisposed to harass are like sharks, lurking in the shallows, monitoring the surf and the waves until the opportunity presents itself for an attack on a vulnerable and unsuspecting swimmer. But do men who harass recognize and label their behavior as harassment? Do they actively search for situations in which they can abuse their power? John Bargh and Paula Raymond (1995) argue that, in fact, most males who harass are probably not aware that their behavior is upsetting to their female victims. As with the work discussed above, Bargh

Continued

BOX 11.1

Continued

and his colleagues assume that the connection between power and sex is strong, but in their research it appears to operate on behavior through nonconscious and automatic activation (e.g., Bargh, Raymond, Pryor, and Stack, 1995). Men who are high in LSH have their sexual thoughts activated whenever power becomes salient. But this activation is beneath the men's awareness and not subject to their conscious control. Thus, power makes high-LSH men aware of sexual thoughts, but they don't realize that their sexual thoughts were activated by power. High-LSH men attribute their sexual thoughts to the major focus of their awareness, namely, a female target.

They may then interpret the target's friendly, polite, and deferential behavior as a reciprocation of their sexual interest, which may help to explain why, according to Louise Fitzgerald (1993), many men accused of sexual harassment are often surprised and upset. They tend to downplay the importance and harm caused by their behavior, deny that they intentionally caused any harm, and offer a different interpretation of their behavior (i.e., it was a compliment).

The rallying cry of women during the confirmation hearings of Supreme Court Justice Clarence Thomas may accurately summarize these findings: harassers "just don't get it!"

potentially serious errors in the way those with power view their subordinates.

Gender Differences in the Use of Power

Although the type of power influences when and how power will be used, many characteristics of the target also influence the way power will be used. One factor is gender.

In an interesting study on the use of power by married couples, Raven, Centers, and Rodrigues (1975) interviewed 776 husbands and wives in the Los Angeles area. They gave examples of behaviors and asked the respondents to tell what type of power would be used by their spouses to influence those behaviors. They found that referent and expert power were used most frequently, and coercive power least frequently. Wives were most likely to attribute expert power ("knew what was best in the case") to their husbands, and husbands saw their wives as using referent power ("both part of the same family") most often. Further, expert power was used more by younger couples than by older ones, and the use of referent power increased with age. Finally, as shown in table 11.1, the use of power was also dependent on the type of behavior being influenced.

Following up on this gender difference, Falbo and Peplau (1980) had subjects write an essay describing

"how I get [my intimate partner] to do what I want." The essays were then analyzed to see what power strategy was used. The results indicated that heterosexual men tended to prefer direct and interactive strategies (bargaining, talking, reasoning, and persistence), whereas heterosexual women tended to use indirect and solitary strategies (withdrawal, negative affect). They also found that the strategies (direct-interactive) used by men were more likely to promote a satisfying relationship. Rather than indicating that men are more socially sensitive than women, Falbo and Peplau argued that because men expect compliance in their relationship, they have the "luxury" of being able to rely on these methods. Women, on the other hand, often see their position as the weaker one in the relationship. As a result, they must resort to the solitary strategies that are used when the goal is important but compliance is not expected.

Leadership

In any group, large or small, some individuals have more power and influence than others. The person with the most influence often assumes a position of prominence in the group and comes to be regarded as the leader. In fact, we can define a **leader** as the person who exerts the most influence in a group (Hollan-

TABLE 11.1 PERCENTAGE ATTRIBUTING EACH BASIS OF POWER TO THE SPOUSE AS A FUNCTION OF THE DOMAIN OF POWER

Domain of Power	N	Predominant Basis of Power Attributed to Spouse				
		Reward	Coercion	Expert	Legitimate	Referent
"Visit some friend or relative"	768	7%	8%	15%	43%	27%
"Change some personal habit"	758	6	9	35	30	20
"Repair or clean something around house"	766	5	13	28	35	19
"Change station on TV or radio"	766	14	13	8	30	35
"Go somewhere for outing or vacation"	760	10	3	10	37	40
"Go see a doctor"	768	1	2	55	22	20

Source: Raven, Centers, and Rodrigues (1975)

der, 1985; Shaw, 1981). There are many different kinds of leaders and leadership. Martin Luther King, Jr., was an exceptional leader, and he clearly fits our definition. He had an extremely high degree of influence over other people both within and outside of the Southern Christian Leadership Conference. Many times only his words kept the Black Freedom movement from turning into a violent revolt. For example, on June 30, 1956, a bomb was thrown at his home in Montgomery. A number of police officers, along with the police commissioner and the mayor, arrived on the scene shortly after the blast. A crowd of about a thousand angry blacks also gathered armed with guns, rocks, knives, and sticks and ready to do battle with the police. King walked onto the porch and asked the blacks to adhere to the doctrine of nonviolence, reminding them, "He who lives by the sword will perish by the sword." The crowd dispersed peacefully. Coretta King recalls hearing a white policeman in the crowd saying, "If it hadn't been for that nigger preacher, we'd all be dead" (King, 1969, p. 130).

Several past presidents of the United States have also been powerful leaders. Psychologists and political scientists who have discussed different kinds of presidential leadership have identified the **transformational leader** as one who senses the unexpressed wants of the populace and tries to bring those desires to expression for the purpose of changing the political system (Burns, 1984). Franklin Roosevelt fits the definition of a transformational leader as do Ronald Reagan and Bill Clinton. The last president of the former Soviet Union, Mikhail Gorbachev, perhaps exemplified the concept as well as any other recent leader. With his emphasis on *glasnost* (openness) and *perestroika* (restructuring), Gorbachev clearly signaled that he wanted the desires of the peoples of the Soviet Union and Eastern Europe to be sharply identified and used to reshape their societies. Similarly, Egypt's Anwar Sadat and Israel's Menachem Begin reflected the desires of the Egyptian and Israeli people for a lasting peace as they sought to end literally thousands of years of hostility between their two countries.

The Perception of Leaders

The concept of leadership raises many complex issues. One central question that psychologists have explored actively in recent years is how leaders are perceived (Hogg, 1996; Kinder and Fiske, 1986). Some of the research on leadership perception suggests that people have a generalized **leadership schema** (Simonton, 1986a, 1987)—an overall image of what a leader is and what a leader does. Studies of presidential leadership show that our general idea of a great leader or an "ideal president" is an individual who has three important characteristics: strength, activity, and goodness. In short, the ideal president or admired leader of any group is competent and trustworthy (Kinder, Peters, Ableson, and Fiske, 1980; Simonton, 1986a). According to this approach, when people judge leaders, salient information about their behavior activates to varying degrees this overall image of a strong, active, and good leader. Our knowledge of King's dramatic "I have a dream" speech calls to mind the overall leadership schema, and we tend to see him as strong, active, and good.

The leadership schema approach also suggests that people reveal the correspondence bias (discussed in chapter 2) in judging leaders; that is, they see their leaders' behavior as reflecting their personal traits rather than situational forces. For example, when President Clinton demonstrates strong leadership in an area of popular concern, such as taking a bold approach to protecting the environment, American citizens attribute his action to leadership qualities rather than to pressure from environmental groups or the Congress.

Leadership Behavior

The leadership schema approach shows that perceptions of leadership can be erroneous in several important ways. Therefore, it is important that we clearly identify just what it is that leaders do. Fortunately, this is something we know a good deal about. Psychologists have been doing research on leadership behavior and functions for decades, with the aim of finding out exactly what a leader does in and for a group.

One of the most widely cited studies on leadership was conducted at Ohio State University in the late 1940s. In one phase of that investigation, Halpin and Winer (1952) asked subjects to record what characteristics of a leader they felt were most important. The two most widely mentioned characteristics fell under the headings of *consideration* and *initiating structure*. The consideration category included such characteristics as (1) initiates communication, (2) explains actions, and (3) promotes trust. The initiating structure dimension included the behaviors of directing the actions of the group and group planning. Two minor factors were also found: *production emphasis* (stresses "getting the job done") and *social sensitivity* (flexibility in adjusting plans and listening to others). Lieberman, Yalom, and Miles (1973) point out that these duties of a leader are often contradictory. For example, it is difficult for an individual who is concerned with getting the job done or initiating new tasks to be involved in fraternization or in being "just one of the gang." Similarly, it is difficult to be an evaluator of a member's performance and also to be concerned about that member's feelings.

The duality of leadership and the contradictory pressures that accompany the need to be concerned about both the task and the feelings of the people working on the task would seem to ensure that one could not be an effective leader: It should be almost impossible to perform both functions at the same time. However, Bales and Slater (1955) found that one person does not generally perform both functions; usually, one person leads on task-related issues and another assumes the person-oriented functions. These investigators studied groups of three to six members working on a discussion task. They found an increas-

ing tendency over time for the best-liked individual to not be rated as the person who came up with the best ideas. The tendency was to see the individual with the best ideas as the leader because he or she provided suggestions about how the group should solve its problems. Bales and Slater named that leader the *task specialist*—mainly concerned with getting the job done. The best-liked person was called the *socio-emotional specialist* by Bales and Slater and the *maintenance specialist* by Thibaut and Kelley (1959); the chief concern of this specialist was to create a good social climate in the group. Zelditch (1955) studied families in fifty-six societies and found that in most families there was a task specialist and a maintenance specialist. Generally, the father was the task specialist, and the mother the socio-emotional leader.

Thus it is likely that there are two leaders in many groups: one leader pushes the group members to get the job done, and the other works to keep the group members happy. It is probably also true that the two types of leaders use different types of power in their role. Task leaders use legitimate, expert, and coercive power to get group members to work; socioemotional leaders should be most effective if they use referent and reward power.

A more recent study of leadership by Baumeister, Hutton, and Tice (1988) suggests that in addition to showing consideration and initiating structure, an important and quite general leadership behavior is simply assuming overall responsibility for what happens in the group. You may recall from chapter 10 that in Darley and Latané's (1968) epileptic seizure study, subjects in groups were much less likely to help than subjects who were alone. Those in groups typically diffused responsibility, assuming someone else should or would help, with the result that few of them took action and the victim was much less likely to receive needed aid. In the study by Roy Baumeister and his colleagues, however, people who were designated leaders of a group did not diffuse responsibility. In fact, 80 percent of the group leaders came out of their individual rooms to aid a group member who was having a coughing and choking fit even though this action ruined the experiment and cost them their leadership position. The 80 percent rate of helping is comparable to the helping rate of solitary subjects in other experiments, whereas the 35 percent helping rate of subordinates in this study is comparable to the rate observed among subjects in groups in those other

experiments. People who are leaders find it important to take overall responsibility in their groups even if their leadership position does not specifically require that they do so.

What Makes a Leader? Theories of Leadership

Thus far we have seen that a leader is an individual who exercises power to influence the direction of group activity. We have seen that there are many leadership behaviors and many ways to measure leadership. We can now ask: Why do some individuals arise as leaders while others do not? Why, for example, did Martin Luther King, Jr., rather than some other individual become the leader of the civil rights movement? Was it some characteristic of King, was it the particular situation, or was it some combination of the two? Hollander (1985) pointed out that the study of leadership has historically progressed by asking these three questions in turn, and that as a result attention focuses first on the trait theory, next on situational theory, and finally on the interactional theory of leadership.

Trait Theory

When we look at powerful leaders such as Martin Luther King, Jr., Mikhail Gorbachev, Franklin Roosevelt, or Golda Meir, we get the impression that these were not ordinary people. There must have been something special about them that enabled them to become such powerful leaders. The earliest studies of leadership were based on the premise that something sets leaders apart from followers—that leaders are born, not made. If this assumption is correct, it should be possible to identify certain unique traits that characterize leaders. The theory that encompasses these ideas has been labeled the great person theory of leadership, or **trait theory of leadership.** In its simplest form, the theory states that history, or the direction of a group's behavior, is shaped by the particular person in the leadership position and the course of events would be completely different if another person were in that position (Jacobs, 1971). In the case of Martin Luther King, Jr., the theory would emphasize the fact that King shaped and determined the direction of the civil rights movement in the United States and that the movement would have had a different look if someone else had been its leader.

Key assumptions of the trait theory have not been supported by empirical studies. First, the same people tend not to be the leaders in all situations and at all times. Second, leaders are not a breed apart. Sometimes they are not so different from followers; many different kinds of people can be both leaders and followers at different times and different places. Still, hundreds of studies of the characteristics of leaders have shown that leaders do tend to have distinctive traits (Stogdill, 1948). Some of the major characteristics, both physical and psychological, that have been associated with leadership include size and strength, intelligence, verbosity, motivation, the somewhat elusive quality called charisma, and sex.

Many years ago, Leo Terman (1904) pointed out that primitive tribes chose their leaders on the basis of size, strength, or age. In certain tribes the leader was the individual who could lift the largest beam and carry it longest. In one Colombian tribe, an individual was allowed to lead only after he had passed a test in which he was covered by stinging ants or whipped by other tribe members. Stogdill's data indicate that even in modern Western cultures, leaders tend to be slightly older, taller, heavier, healthier, and more energetic than the average group member. The data on physical traits makes sense if one is considering such groups as football teams, exploring expeditions, or hunting parties, where physical prowess is important. However, it is difficult to see why the strongest individual would be the leader of a debate team, where physical strength is irrelevant to the task. Because Stodgill did not differentiate his data according to the task that the group performed, generalizing from these data is somewhat risky. It is interesting to note that such powerful leaders as Gandhi, King, Napoleon, and Hitler were not stronger, taller, or heavier than most of their followers.

Among the traits most consistently associated with leadership is intelligence. The leader in most groups is somewhat more intelligent than the followers (Gibb, 1969; Mann, 1959; Stogdill, 1948). Simonton (1986b) found that intellectual brilliance is one of the few personality traits consistently linked to greatness ratings among American presidents, with Thomas Jefferson, John F. Kennedy, and Woodrow Wilson being rated the most intelligent. The correlation between intelligence and leadership, however, is not high. Mann reports the median correlation to be around .25, and some studies (for example, Loretto and Williams, 1974) found no relationship between intelligence and leadership. One possible reason for this low correlation is that a leader who is much more intelligent than the other group members will not be able to relate to them.

Another trait that paves the road for an individual's rise to leadership is verbosity, or talkativeness. A number of investigators (Riecken, 1958; Bass, 1949; McGrath and Julian, 1963) have consistently found evidence supporting the "big mouth" theory of leadership; that is, the most talkative member of the group is seen as the leader.

The relationship between talkativeness and leadership was demonstrated in a study (Bavelas, Hastorf, Gross, and Kite, 1965) in which the subjects, all males, first met in four-person discussion groups and the observers recorded the amount of time that each member spent talking. After the first discussion, the subjects rated each other on leadership. In the next session, each subject had a box in front of him with a red and green light. The subjects were told that they would receive feedback about how well they performed: a green light would signify good performance; a red light, poor performance. One subject who had been near the bottom in verbosity in the first session was chosen to receive positive feedback for talking. During the second session, he received more green lights than anyone else in the group. This positive reinforcement for talking caused him to more than double his verbal output, and the group then came to view him as the leader. A third session was run without lights. The previously reinforced subject's verbal output remained high and so did his ratings on leadership. This study strikingly demonstrated the importance of verbosity as a determinant of leadership. In support of these findings, Sorrentino and Boutillier (1975) manipulated both the quantity and quality of a confederate's remarks during a group discussion. Although quality had little effect on the confederate's leadership ratings, the more he talked the higher he was rated on leadership ability by the other group members.

Motives are also important in leadership. Recent research shows that being oriented toward achieving success and being oriented toward affiliating with others are both important in the emergence of a leader in a long-lasting group (Sorrentino and Field, 1986). Other motives may be important in a leader's success. Winter's (1987) studies of American presidents have shown that the presidents who are motivated by power, the ones who are generally energetic, autonomous, self-directed, somewhat narcissistic, and concerned with prestige and having an impact on others tend to be rated as great presidents and are credited

Charisma became an issue in the 1996 presidential campaign. Had the Republican candidate Robert Dole possessed as much special social influence as he did political influence, he might have made a better showing against President Clinton.

with great decisions. The three American presidents with the highest power motive, according to Winter's analyses of themes in their inaugural addresses, are Truman, Kennedy, and Reagan.

One other trait that is often associated with leadership has received little empirical study: **charisma,** a term used to describe the magnetic pull that certain leaders appear to have. It has been applied to such leaders as Martin Luther King, Jr., John F. Kennedy, Adolph Hitler, and Ho Chi Minh. While some leaders seem to have charisma, others do not. Max Weber (1946) used the term to mean the "gift of grace." Charisma has almost supernatural qualities that are difficult to describe and may be impossible to study. Weber felt that a leader's charisma is especially evident in times of crisis and that situational events seem to draw it out. A leader's charisma is also, in part, determined by followers' needs and emotional states. For this reason, not everyone is affected by the leader in the same way; as a result, a charismatic leader often

has a group of strongly devoted followers and a number of strong opponents. This was the case with Martin Luther King, Jr., who had both close followers and vocal antagonists among blacks.

Gender and Leadership: Does Gender Predict a Better Leader? Sex or gender has also been found to be related to leadership, though the picture is rapidly changing. Both men and women expect men to be leaders, and in early studies women were less likely to view themselves as potential leaders (Megargee, 1969). This stereotype of men as more natural leaders than women means that women leaders face an extra handicap in trying to be effective and in being perceived as such. They must "be like gold to be seen as silver" (Hollander, 1985).

An interesting group of studies, on the other hand, shows that women are more likely to become leaders in small groups now than they were three decades ago. Megargee's study, published in 1969, showed that when a man was low in dominance and his female partner was high, only 22 percent of the women became leaders. In same-sex pairs, by contrast, the high-dominance person became leader about 70 percent of the time; and in male-female pairs with high-dominance men and low-dominance women, 89 percent of the men became the leader. Two more recent studies showed change in these figures, one more than the other. Nyquist and Spence (1986) found that 35 percent of women in pairs made up of a high-dominance woman and a low-dominance man became leaders, but Fleischer and Chertkoff (1986) found that 50 percent of the women in such pairs became leaders. It is not clear how to explain the divergent findings of the two 1986 studies. The latter study was conducted in the Midwest rather than the Southwest, where Megargee and Nyquist and Spence conducted their studies. Perhaps people in the Midwest have become more accustomed to women as leaders than people in the more traditional Southwest. Regardless, both studies show that women were more likely to emerge as leaders in the mid-1980s than they were a generation ago, and it is reasonable to believe that the trend continues.

Two studies of male and female leaders at West Point, where a woman was recently graduated as overall leader of the corps of cadets, give an indication of just how fast concepts of gender and leadership are changing. A 1980 study showed that while women performed as well as men and had equally good morale in their groups, their successes were attributed to luck while men's were attributed to ability. These negative attributions were not found in a 1984 study, although female subordinates still rated female leaders quite negatively (Rice, Bender, and Vitters, 1980; Rice, Instone, and Adams, 1984).

Alice Eagly and her colleagues examined the existing literature on leadership and gender (Eagly, Karau, and Makhijani, 1995; Eagly, Makhijani, and Klonsky, 1992). They collected hundreds of studies that were conducted in the laboratory and the work place since 1980 and performed a statistical technique known as a meta-analysis to see if men or women were found to be more effective leaders. They concluded that, overall, men and women are equally effective leaders. A more detailed analysis of the studies showed, however, that men are more effective leaders in situations that put a premium on stereotypically male leadership styles—specifically, task-oriented leadership defined as "the ability to direct and control people" (Eagly, Karau, and Makhijani, 1995, p. 137). Females were more effective when the leadership style that was needed was interpersonal, or socioemotional, defined as "the ability to cooperate and get along with people" (p. 137). Eagly and her colleagues (1995) suggested, based on these findings, that men or women who are asked to perform a leadership function that diverges from gender expectations will suffer a decline in their actual or perceived effectiveness.

Zeitgeist Theory: A Situational Approach to Leadership

Psychologists found the trait approach to leadership unsatisfactory because it cannot, by itself, predict who will become a leader or explain why an individual becomes a leader. The emphasis in the study of leadership therefore shifted from traits of individuals to characteristics of particular group situations that might determine who emerges as the leader. This **situational approach** shuns the hypothesis that certain people are born to lead. Situational theorists take the position that the particular time or situation determines who will become the leader:

> At a particular time, a group of people has certain needs and requires the services of an individual to assist it in meeting its needs. Which individual comes to play the role of leader in meeting these needs is essentially determined by chance: that is, a given person happens to be at the critical place at the critical time. (Cooper and McGaugh, 1969, p. 247)

The point has been made that had Hitler espoused his doctrine in the United States rather than in Germany, he would probably have been thrown in jail or committed to a mental institution. In post–World War I Germany, however, the time and the situation were right for the people to follow the lead of such an individual.

The situation also had a great deal to do with King's rise to leadership. Blacks in the United States had made progress toward achieving a position from which they could wage their fight for freedom and dignity. World War II had been a uniting force and had also pointed up the inequities that existed: A black man could fight for his country but did not have the freedom to vote, use public restrooms, or sit next to whites on a bus. Coretta King's description of the situation that existed for blacks in 1955 also describes, to a certain extent, the situational theory of leadership:

> There is a spirit and a need and a man at the beginning of every great human advance. Each of these might be right for that particular moment of history, or nothing happens. In Montgomery, what Martin called the "Zeitgeist," or the spirit of the time, was there under the apparent passivity of the Negro people; the hour had struck, and the man was found. Yet what was done there could not have happened without a buildup of forces and an accumulation of suffering. (King, 1969, p. 108)

Several situational factors affect leadership, and some that are unsuspected can be highly influential. For example, Howells and Becker (1962) suggested that *seating arrangements* would influence leadership. They suggested that communication would naturally tend to flow across a table. They used five-man groups in which two individuals sat across the table from three. They hypothesized that if communication is important in determining the leader and if communication flows across the table, then people seated on the two-person side of the table would tend to be seen as leaders because they would be communicating to three other persons. The groups were instructed to work on a number of simple tasks, and the group members were then asked to identify the leader of their group. The results indicated that persons seated on the two-person side of the table were chosen as leaders more than twice as often as persons seated on the three-man side. It has also been found that leaders naturally chose seats at the head of rectangular tables rather than seats along the sides (Lecuyer, 1976).

Seniority is also an important factor in determining who will emerge as leader. Insko and his colleagues (1980) studied experimental groups over a period of time. During the experiment, subjects were removed, one by one, from a group and replaced with new members. The results indicated that groups at the hub of communication had the greatest influence and, within groups, members with the most seniority were accorded leadership roles. While the seniority-leadership norm emerged in all groups, it was particularly strong in powerful groups. As you can imagine, having this type of norm allows for orderly change in leadership and reduces the chances of intragroup conflict.

The *situation* facing the group will also affect leadership. Numerous investigators (Worchel, Andreoli, and Folger, 1977) have found that groups facing threat or competition are more likely to accept an authoritative leader than groups not facing such difficulties. Crisis seems to cause people to rally around their leader. In an interesting series of studies on Dutch subjects, Rabbie and Bekkers (1976) found that leaders who were threatened with losing their positions of leadership tried to engage their groups in competitive and threatening situations. Apparently they felt that they would be less likely to lose their positions if they caused the groups to perceive an external threat than if no such threat existed.

Further, the situational theorists of leadership state that the particular *needs of the group* determine who will emerge as leader. Why did King's "I have a dream" speech have such a tremendous impact on the Black Freedom movement? Situational theorists would say that the speech fitted the needs of the black people at the time; it was a message of hope, not of anger or despair. It expressed the hope for freedom and equality, and that is what the movement was fighting for. The speech also met the need of King's followers for encouragement and suggested that their goals were attainable.

According to situational theories, the needs of the group often change, and when this happens, the leader of the group will also change. Barnlund (1962) found that when the requirements of the task changed, leadership tended to shift to an individual with more appropriate qualifications. Identification of the leader at a particular time depends on the task on which the group is working. Thus, the situational theory argues that there are no general leadership traits and that the traits that make an individual a leader in one situation may not qualify him or her to lead in another situation.

Interactionist Theory

While both trait and situational theories give us some answers about the emergence of leaders, both are incomplete. Clearly, Martin Luther King, Jr., had traits that helped him rise to power, but other people also possessed many of these traits and they didn't become leaders of the movement. On the other hand, it is hard to accept an explanation that does not take into account King as a unique person; he did not become leader simply because he happened to be in the right place at the right time.

Some theorists (Katz and Kahn, 1978; Hollander, 1958) have suggested that the emergence of a leader is the result of characteristics of the leader, the followers, and the situation. Certain traits may make an individual the center of attention, but if that individual's abilities don't satisfy the needs of the members, leadership will not result. The situation influences the needs of the followers and the need of the group for a leader. Thus, the leader is influenced by the followers, and the followers are influenced by the leader (see figure 11.1). As the situation and needs of the followers change, the person who is accepted as leader will change. But the leader must possess certain abilities before he or she will be elevated to a position of leadership. As we will see, the interactionist approach has also been used to predict who will be an effective leader.

The Effective Leader

Having examined research on the emergence of a leader in a group, we can consider the kind of leader who is likely to be effective and the factors that influence that effectiveness. The question of leader effectiveness is distinct from the question of leader emergence, although the two questions are related.

Democratic versus Autocratic Styles of Leadership

One early study on leadership asked: What type of leader will be most effective? Lewin, Lippitt, and White (1939) closely observed four comparable groups of ten-year-old boys under autocratic, democratic, and laissez-faire adult leaders. The leaders were trained to respond in one of these styles and were rotated every six weeks so that each group had each type of leader. The autocratic leader determined the policy of the group, dictated all the steps and techniques for

FIGURE 11.1   THE ELEMENTS OF LEADERSHIP

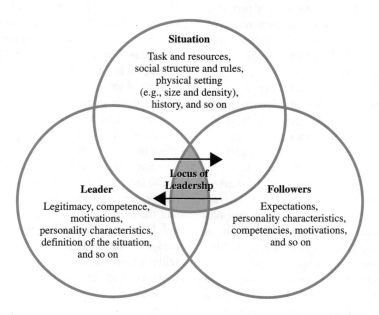

Note: The area representing the intersection of three elements of leadership—the situation, the leader, and the followers—is the locus of leadership. The arrows indicate the social exchange that occurs there between the leader and the followers.
Source: Hollander (1978)

attaining the group goals, assigned tasks and task partners, and remained aloof from the group. The democratic leader allowed the group to determine policy, offered suggestions about procedures and tasks, allowed members to choose their own tasks and task partners, was objective in his praise and criticism, and participated in the group tasks. The group engaged in such hobbies as making masks and building objects.

The results showed that under the authoritarian leader, the boys were thirty times as hostile and eight times as aggressive as they were under the democratic leader. Subjects under the authoritarian leader tended to pick out scapegoats as the targets of their aggression (two such scapegoats actually left the groups). This behavior did not occur under the democratic leader. Group unity was higher under the democratic leader than under the authoritarian leader. Although the constructiveness of work sharply decreased when the authoritarian leader temporarily left the room, it remained constant in the democratic group. Experimentally induced frustrations were very disruptive to the authoritarian-led group, but the democratic-led group tended to meet these difficulties with organized attacks.

Interesting sequential events occurred when the groups changed leaders. Figure 11.2 shows the effect of leader change in two groups. The most noticeable effect was the sharp increase in aggression when the group shifted from an autocratic leader to a laissez-faire leader, which may have been the result of repressed aggression under autocratic supervision. The boys may have become angry under the autocratic leader, but they feared the leader and were afraid to disrupt the group by expressing their anger. The laissez-faire leader gave the group a freer atmosphere, which allowed the release of pent-up aggression, a type of effect that often occurs after the overthrow of an autocratic ruler. In the history of nations, we have often seen a people, liberated after years of autocratic reign, often release pent-up hostility and frustration in a blood bath, such as the one that followed Louis XV's demise in France.

Turning from the psychological atmosphere of the group to the question of productivity, Lewin and his colleagues found that the boys worked longer and turned out more products under the autocratic leader than under the democratic leader. They did, however,

FIGURE 11.2   THE EFFECT OF DIFFERENT LEADERSHIP STYLES ON AGGRESSIVENESS IN A GROUP

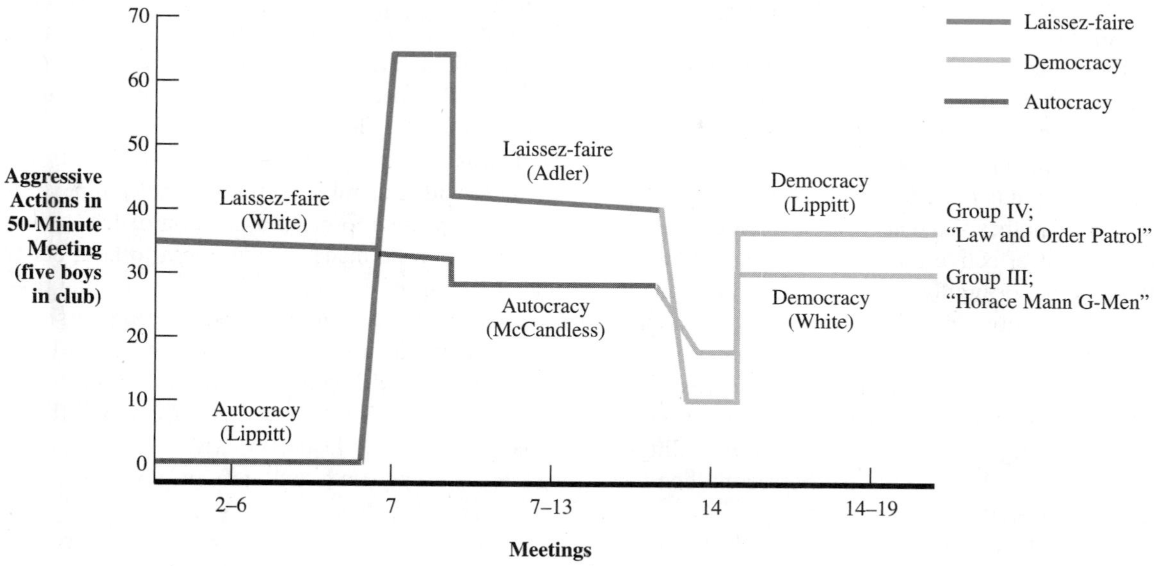

Note: Aggressiveness greatly increases in the group when an autocratic leader is replaced by a laissez-faire leader.
Source: Lewin, Lippitt, and White (1939)

tend to turn out products of somewhat better quality under the democratic leader.

Again, however, we find that the effectiveness of the leader is influenced by the situation. Research (Rosenbaum and Rosenbaum, 1971) has found that groups are more productive with an autocratic leader under stressful conditions. But when conditions are nonstressful, groups are more productive with a democratic leader. Thus, the most effective style is partly a function of the situation.

The Contingency Theory of Leadership Effectiveness

It is clear from the early work that leadership effectiveness is not simply a function of the leader's style. As the interactionist theories imply, the demands of the situation and the interaction between leaders and followers need to be considered as well. For example, to understand Martin Luther King, Jr.'s, influence in both the civil rights movement and peace movement in the 1960s, we need to consider his style, the situation facing blacks and peace activists at the time, and the relationship between King and his followers. King's effectiveness can be understood in the light of all these factors. A significant step forward in understanding leadership effectiveness was made by Fiedler (1964, 1978), who developed a theory of leadership effectiveness that considers both personal and situational factors. Fiedler's **contingency model** has been important in combining insights of the trait and situational approaches and in paving the way for other contingency models (Hollander, 1985).

Fiedler identified two different leadership styles. One is the task-oriented leader who is concerned primarily with getting the job done. The other is the relationship-oriented leader who is more concerned with feelings and relationships in the group. These two styles are similar to Bales and Slater's (1955) task and maintenance specialists. They also remind us of the two broad categories of leadership behavior, initiating structure (getting the task done) and showing consideration (thinking about relationships). The key idea in Fiedler's contingency model is that whether the task-oriented or the relationship-oriented leadership style is most effective will depend on the situation the leader faces.

Situations can be classified according to how favorable they are for the leader. Favorability of the situation depends on three factors. The first is the quality of *leader-group relations*. The situation is favorable to the leader if these relations are good, if he or she is trusted, admired, and respected. The second factor is the *task structure*. Here the situation is favorable to the leader if the task is clear and everyone knows who needs to do what. The third factor is the *leader's position power*. If the leader has a position with a great deal of power (for example, a head of state with no legislature), the situation is more favorable for that leader.

Fiedler hypothesized that the task-oriented leader would be most effective under conditions that were highly favorable or highly unfavorable for the leader. In the first condition, in which leader-group relations are good, the task is clear, the leader's position is powerful, and it is easy for the leader to be directive and task-oriented without worrying too much about feelings for everything is going well and people's feelings do not require much attention. In the second condition, in which the situation is chaotic, unpleasant, and ambiguous, a take-charge, task-oriented style will also be more effective; here the relationship-oriented leader is likely to be swamped by the chaos. On the other hand, when conditions favorable for the leader are in the middle ranges, when people need to be shown consideration, when there is some tension, and when relations between group members need to be coordinated and clarified, a relationship-oriented leader will do better than a task-oriented leader, who tends to overlook interpersonal relations.

Fiedler's theory is a complex and ambitious one. It has been tested in numerous laboratory and field studies with a wide variety of groups, such as Belgian naval officers, postmasters, basketball players, store managers, workers on open-hearth furnaces, B-29 bomber crews, and research chemists. As predicted, the general findings were that the relationship-oriented leaders were most effective in the moderately favorable situations, whereas the task-oriented leaders were most effective in either very poor or highly favorable situations (Fiedler, 1978; Chemers and Skrzypek, 1972; Hardy, 1976).

The contingency model of leadership effectiveness has generated a great deal of research and, as you might imagine with so complex a theory, a great deal of controversy (Fiedler, 1978; Schreisheim and Kerr, 1977a, 1977b). Reviews of studies of this model suggest that while it has been supported in many ways, a complete understanding of leadership effectiveness will require consideration of factors beyond leadership style and the favorableness of the situation for the leader (Rice and Kastenbaum, 1983; Peters, Hartke, and Pohlmann, 1985).

In addition to generating a large body of research and focusing attention on the interaction of personal and situational variables, the contingency theory has had practical impact in the leadership area. The usual approach to finding leaders for businesses and organizations was to rely on personality tests to identify the individual with general potential for leadership. If individuals happened to be in a position of leadership, attempts would be made to train them to be a better leader. Millions of dollars were spent on sending people to leadership conferences and training sessions. Essentially, the idea was to reshape the person to fit the situation. According to Fiedler, this approach will not succeed. He believes that it is extremely difficult to change a person's leadership style. We should instead change a person's rank, job, or power to fit his or her personality or leadership style (Fiedler, 1964); that is, we should make the environment fit the person instead of trying to make the person fit the environment. Along these lines, Fiedler, Chemers, and Mahar (1976) have developed the LEADERMATCH program, which is aimed at helping leaders to identify and create situations that are most suited to their style of leadership.

The Social Identity Theory of Leadership Effectiveness

Social psychologist Michael Hogg (1996) has recently suggested that in order to understand leadership effectiveness, we need to look at the characteristics of the group from which the leader emerges. Imagine that you are a member of a group that is particularly important to you. What kind of a leader would you like to have for your group? In whom would you place your trust and faith to lead you effectively as you compete and negotiate with other groups? The answers may depend on just how salient and important your group is to you at the moment. Like Simonton's notion of the leadership schema that we mentioned earlier, Hogg agrees that all of us carry around a mental representation or schema of what an effective leader is like. When we are not particularly involved in our group or our group is not salient to us, we are likely to think that a person who embodies these attributes would be an appropriate person to lead our group. However, if our group is salient, then it is not the person who possesses the attributes of the leadership schema whom we will want to lead us but rather the person who represents the **prototype** of our group. In an earlier chapter, we defined a prototype as the standard that incorporates the essential and most characteristic feature of a category. In the case of our own group category, we want the person who possesses the attributes that are the most fundamental, the most representative, and the most typical of our group.

Sarah Hains, Michael Hogg, and Julie Duck (in press) conducted a laboratory study in which participants were members of either a highly important and salient group or were assigned to be members of a group of considerably less salience and importance. In each group the experimenters allegedly selected a member of the group to serve as leader and described the attributes of the person they had selected. Half the time Hains and her colleagues described the leader as someone who was a prototypical group member, and half the time they described the leader as possessing stereotypical leadership characteristics. Subjects were asked how satisfied they were with the leader and how confident they were that the leader would be effective. The investigators found that when salience was high, group members were most confident that the leader would be effective if he or she fit the prototype of the group. In contrast, when salience of the group was low, members were most satisfied with the leader who fit the leadership schema.

Let's return to our original question: Whom will you want to serve as leader of your group? Social identity theory's overarching point is that to the extent the group is salient to you, then group identity is going to be important in predicting your leader's effectiveness. Hogg's theory makes the prediction that you will want as your leader the person who represents the prototype of your group's social identity.

Obedience

Martin Luther King, Jr., commanded through inspiration, rhetoric, energy, and even love. He was not an authoritarian leader who could direct interpersonal behavior by exercising coercive or reward power. By contrast, if we consider the power of an authority figure to command **obedience,** we find chilling examples of the extent to which people will do what their leaders or authorities direct. Perhaps the most vivid example of people's willingness to follow those with authority is seen in the atrocities

committed against the Jews by the Nazis during World War II; 6 million men, women, and children were tortured and executed. At the Nuremberg war trials, the Germans who served as executioners in the concentration camps maintained that they were not responsible for the deaths because they were merely following orders. This seemed a poor excuse indeed for their actions, and the executioners who were tried were themselves executed or imprisoned. The general feeling was that no human being could intentionally torture or kill another human being simply because he or she was following orders; anyone with feelings would certainly have resisted or disobeyed such orders.

Although the most common examples of blind faith in following orders occur in emergency or wartime situations, there is nowhere a more striking and, we think, more terrifying example of how blindly people follow orders than in the demonstrations of Stanley Milgram (1963, 1965). Imagine yourself in the following situation: You arrive at an experimental room, sit down, and begin talking to another subject who has signed up for the same experiment. The experimenter enters and tells you both that the experiment concerns the effects of punishment on learning. You draw straws to see which of you will be the "learner" and which the "teacher," and you draw the teacher straw. The experimenter tells you both that the teacher will ask the learner questions and that the learner will be shocked each time he answers incorrectly. The learner is led away and is supposedly hooked up to a shock apparatus in a small enclosed booth.

You are shown the "teaching machine," which supposedly generates shock. You see a lever and a row of numbers starting at 15 volts and running to 450 volts, with each 15-volt interval labeled. The lower range of numbers is marked "Slight Shock," and the upper end is labeled "Danger: Severe Shock"; 450 volts is marked "XXX." The experimenter tells you that you are to read a prepared list of questions to the learner, and that if he answers a question incorrectly, you are to shock him. You are to increase the shock by one level after each incorrect answer so that the first shock will be 15 volts, the next 30 volts, and so on.

You begin reading the questions. The learner misses one, then another, and another. After each incorrect answer you increase the voltage by 15 volts, shock the learner, and read the next question. At 90 volts, the learner cries out in pain. At 150 volts, he screams and asks to be let out of the experiment. You look to the experimenter, and he simply says: "Proceed with the next question." At 180 volts, the learner cries out that he can no longer stand the pain and bangs on the wall of the booth. You look at the experimenter and ask to stop the experiment. The experimenter calmly tells you: "You have no other choice; you must go on." At 300 volts, the learner refuses to answer any more questions and begs to be let out of the experiment. The experimenter tells you to continue; from this point on, however, there is no further response from the learner.

What would you do in this situation? Would you continue to administer shock to the 450-volt maximum? What percentage of the people in this experiment do you think would continue to the maximum shock? These were the questions that Milgram wanted to answer. He described the situation to fourteen Yale University seniors majoring in psychology and to a group of psychiatrists, and asked them to predict what percentage of subjects would continue to the 450-volt level. They predicted that less than 2 percent of the subjects would "go all the way."

Milgram conducted the actual study at Yale. His subjects were twenty to fifty years old; 40 percent of them had unskilled jobs, 40 percent had white-collar sales jobs, and 20 percent were professionals. He found that twenty-six of forty subjects, or 65 percent, continued to shock until they reached the 450-volt level! Almost two-thirds of the subjects followed orders to directly inflict intense pain on an innocent victim. In actuality, the "victim" was an experimental accomplice who had been trained to make mistakes on the questions and really did not receive any shock. However, the subjects genuinely believed that he was in pain.

The amount of obedience displayed in his studies surprised even Milgram. This was not wartime Nazi Germany; it was New Haven, Connecticut, in 1960. The subjects were not people who had been trained to injure and kill; they were everyday business people. Some critics (Baumrind, 1964; Orne, 1962; Orne and Holland, 1968) argued that the high obedience rate was obtained because the experiment was done at Yale and because the subjects believed that the experimenter would not let anything bad happen to the victim. Therefore, Milgram moved the experiment to a run-down office building in Bridgeport, Connecticut. The subjects were told nothing of

an affiliation with Yale, and the experimenter did not wear a white laboratory coat as he did in the first study. Although obedience dropped somewhat, the drop was not significant; 48 percent of the subjects administered maximum shock.

Milgram felt that he had dramatically demonstrated obedience, and he ran a series of additional experiments to determine what variables would affect obedience. In one study he varied the closeness of the authority figure. Three conditions were run: In one condition, the experimenter sat a few feet away from the subject as the subject was punishing the learner; in a second condition, the experimenter gave his instructions and left the room while the subject was shocked; and in the third condition, the subject received his instructions on a tape recorder and never saw the experimenter. Obedience dropped sharply when the authority figure was removed. The number

Three men who did not blindly follow orders were awarded the Soldier's Medal for Heroism in 1998. They intervened thirty years earlier during the My Lai massacre in Viet Nam to save civilian lives. Here, Hugh Thompson, Jr. (left) and Lawrence Colburn (right) regard a rubbing of the name of their deceased comrade Glenn Andreotta, who received the medal posthumously.

of subjects who obeyed when the experimenter was present was three times as large as the number who obeyed when he was absent. In a follow-up study, Rada and Rogers (1973) found a high degree of obedience if the experimenter gave the orders in person and then left the room.

In another study, Milgram varied the closeness of the learner. In the remote-feedback condition the learner was placed in an isolation booth and the teacher could neither see nor hear him except for an occasional pounding on the booth's walls. In a second condition (voice feedback), the teacher could hear the learner but could not see him. In the proximity condition the learner was in the same room with the teacher so that he would be seen *and* heard. Finally, Milgram introduced a touch-proximity condition in which the learner was seated right next to the teacher and the teacher had to force the learner's hand onto the shock plate when he delivered the shock. Figure 11.3 shows the results of his experiment: the closer the learner, the lower the obedience level.

Although these studies demonstrated a startling degree of obedience, Milgram reported that his subjects suffered even though they obeyed. Many of the subjects became tense; some broke into fits of nervous laughter; and some sweated profusely and begged the experimenter to stop the study.

Obedience to Other Authorities: The World Outside the Shock Paradigm

Although Milgram's experiments are the most often cited studies of obedience, researchers have also found high degrees of obedience in other situations. For example, Hofling and his colleagues (1966) investigated whether hospital nurses would obey an order to administer unusual and potentially dangerous doses of drugs to patients. The nurses were telephoned by a physician who was unknown to them. The doctor ordered the nurses to administer a drug that was not in common use in the hospital, telling them to administer it in double the amount of the maximum doses stated on the drug box. Of the twenty-two nurses, twenty-one followed the orders, even though doing so when the doctor was unknown was in violation of hospital policy and could have had harmful effects on the patient.

Another setting in which high degrees of obedience are observed involve what Meeus and Quinten Raaijmakers (1995) at the University of Utrecht in The Netherlands call "administrative." According to these researchers, the type of violence enacted by people today in response to an authority figure is indirect because it allows the obedient servant to administer the

---

FIGURE 11.3 **THE EFFECT OF THE PROXIMITY OF THE "VICTIM" ON THE AVERAGE SHOCK DELIVERED**

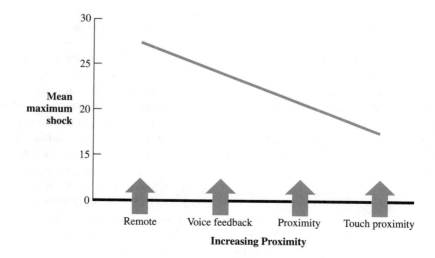

Note: The more feedback the subject received from the victim, the less shock the subject administered to him.
Source: Milgram (1965)

violence at a greater psychological distance from the victim. To illustrate this point, Meeus and Raaijmakers developed a procedure, based on Milgram's, in which an authority figure (the experimenter) and a naive participant administer a test to a job applicant (who is a confederate) during a mock job interview. The participant believes that if the applicant passes the exam, he will be hired for the job; if he does not pass, he will remain unemployed. The experimenter then instructs the participant to interrupt and disturb the applicant during the taking of the test by making a series of "stress statements"—a series of negative remarks about the applicant's test performance and derogatory statements about his personality. Further, the participant is told that the job the applicant is trying to obtain is not stressful, so the stress remarks are not relevant to the employment test. Rather, the reason for the interruption is to help the experimenter in a research project he is conducting on the effects of stress. As in the Milgram study, participants are told that they must follow the procedure and deliver fifteen negative remarks to the applicant. They are also told to continue despite the applicant's protests, which become increasingly vehement during the course of the procedure. If participants refuse at some point to make the stress-inducing remarks, the experimenter responds with four consecutive prods similar to those employed by Milgram. If a participant refuses after the fourth prod, the experiment is terminated.

In seventeen tests of this basic procedure (Meeus and Raaijmakers, 1986; 1987), the results showed remarkable similarity to the results obtained by Milgram in the shock paradigm. Meeus and Raaijmakers found that between 83 percent and 91 percent of participants delivered all fifteen of the disruptive remarks to the job applicants even though the comments cost the applicant his job and even though the stress remarks were not part of the official job-testing procedure. When asked to assign responsibility for why the applicant was not hired for the job, participants attributed most responsibility to the experimenter rather than to themselves. Also parallel to Milgram's findings was that obedience was greatest when the experimenter was physically present rather than removed from the subjects.

Obeying Commands to Harm Oneself

How likely is it that you would obey authority if the victim of the commanded behavior is yourself? There is evidence of considerable obedience even at the risk of harm or personal discomfort. High rates of obedience were found when participants were asked to eat foul-tasting crackers (Kudirka, 1965) or receive painful stimuli (Scott, 1980). In one striking example, Martin, Lobb, Chapman, and Spillane (1976) reported the results of a study that examined whether teenage participants were willing to obey a teacher and cause potential damage to their hearing. Forty-two male adolescents, ages thirteen and fourteen, volunteered to participate in research ostensibly designed to identify people who possess a rare ability to hear ultra-high-frequency sounds. Participants were told that no danger existed to people who possessed the rare trait, but that only about 5 percent of the population in fact had the trait. The participants were next introduced to the apparatus that would deliver different levels of ultra-high-frequency noise. The dial on the apparatus went from 0–10, with level 4 labeled "Danger condition 2—12% possible hearing loss," level 8 labeled "Extreme high danger level—50% hearing loss reported," and no label on level 10. Participants were instructed to turn the dial to each level and report whether they could hear the sound (in fact, no sound ever passed through the headphones). The experimenter in this case was the subjects' school teacher and the voluntary nature of participation was emphasized at several points in the study, although no prods were used to elicit obedience as in the Milgram procedure. The results showed that fully 95 percent of the participants turned the dial to up to level 6, while 54 percent turned the dial all the way to level 10! Although the participants were children responding to an adult's authority, it is striking that so many could be induced to risk such harm to their own hearing.

There are limits, however, to how much harm people are willing to cause themselves for the sake of an authority figure. For example, Orne and Evans (1965) found that not many subjects would follow an experimenter's orders to carry out such dangerous tasks as grasping a venomous snake or taking a coin from a jar containing acid. Similarly, West, Gunn, and Chernicky (1975) found that few people would follow an authority figure to engage in an illegal break-in. Finally, in one version of the administrative obedience studies by Meeus and Raaijmakers (1995), participants were warned before the task began that one recent job applicant refused to accept the way he was treated in the study and had sued the psychology department. The participants were then asked to sign a form stating they would assume legal liability for possible damages. As we might suppose, the percentage of those who made verbal assaults was significantly decreased by the legal liability manipulation. These findings indicate that there are at least some limits to obedience, at least where serious personal injury or legal troubles are concerned.

Why Obey?

The Milgram studies and similar ones raise a number of questions about obedience. One key question is: Why do people obey? Martin Orne (1962) suggested that one reason for the high degree of obedience resided in the experimental procedure itself. The subjects in Milgram's research were placed in a situation that was totally unfamiliar to them, they had little experience with electric shock, and they had no power in the study. Further, they were faced with an experimenter who seemed very familiar with the procedure and showed no signs of concern when the victim was shocked. The experimenter's behavior may have convinced the subjects that there was little need for concern. A second reason for the high degree of obedience may have been that the subjects did not feel responsible for their behavior (Milgram, 1974). The experimenter explicitly told them that the experimenter was the person responsible. A number of studies have shown that when subjects are made to feel responsible for their behavior in the Milgram paradigm, obedience drops sharply (Tilker, 1970). Indeed, that is how we might interpret the legal-liability manipulation in the Meuss and Raaijmakers (1995) study. When the subjects were asked to sign a waiver of legal liability, they not only saw a potential financial problem, they were also told that they, not the Psychology Department or their university, would be responsible. The waiver assigning responsibility to them may have been the psychological cause of the decreased obedience. Finally, we should point to a finding in Milgram's work that showed decreased obedience when the subjects saw others disobey. Seeing others disobey may have served as graphic evidence that they, the participants, were personally responsible for deciding to continue to administer the electric shocks.

Ethics and Obedience Research

Stanley Milgram ran his pioneering studies in the early 1960s and spent many years responding to criticism concerning the ethics of his research (see the section in chapter 1 on ethics). Ethical questions abound in his work. First, the studies put the unsuspecting subjects through a great deal of psychological pain—they were forced to behave in a way that made them extremely uncomfortable. Second, the subjects learned something about themselves that they may have had no desire to know—that they could be made to follow orders that might lead to the injury, and possibly even the death, of innocent individuals. This is certainly a painful thing to learn about oneself. Critics also chastised Milgram for not stopping the research when he observed the extreme discomfort that the subjects experienced. Milgram was surprised by the degree of criticism he received. He argued: "I'm convinced that much of the criticism, whether people know it or not, stems from the results of the experiment. If everyone had broken off at slight shock or moderate shock, this would be a very reassuring finding and who would protest?" (Milgram, 1977, p. 98). In a follow-up questionnaire that Milgram sent the subjects, one question asked how glad they were to have participated. Almost 84 percent of the subjects reported that they were glad they had participated.

The question of ethics is a difficult one, especially in regard to the Milgram studies. On the one hand, the results of the studies were valuable as the studies dramatically demonstrated that an individual would typically obey orders to hurt another individual. The impact of the results would have been lessened had Milgram used a more mundane task, such as asking subjects to write random numbers on paper. On the other hand, the subjects in the study clearly suffered psychological pain and were forced to learn a disturbing fact about themselves (that they would follow orders to hurt another individual). This is a difficult dilemma to resolve, but it should be pointed out that today it would be very difficult to get a departmental ethics committee to approve a study embodying Milgram's methodology.

Conformity

Although a great deal of influence is exerted by one person on another, influence is also exerted in groups and frequently results in conformity to the group's norms. Often the influence of a group is not as direct as that found in the orders of authority figures. Nonetheless, the influence is often as strong or stronger. Consider the situation that faced many blacks in the Montgomery bus boycott; many had no other means of transportation, and they had to get to their jobs. Not riding the bus meant a great deal of hardship and possible loss of jobs. While Montgomery blacks may have admired King and the other leaders of the civil rights movement, this was not the only influence on their behavior. Many stated that they joined the boycott because of their friends and neighbors; they were concerned about how their friends and other blacks would react if they rode the bus. Although they were not specifically threatened in most cases, their concern still existed. In this case the group, even a silent group, influenced their behavior.

Conformity is a change in behavior or belief in a group's standards that is a result of the group's power. In some cases, conformity results from conflict between the way an individual thinks or acts and the way the group pressures him or her to think or act (Moscovici, 1985). For example, conformity may result when a group pressures a teenage girl into having sex before she feels ready for it. In other cases, conformity results from *imagined* group pressure (Kiesler and Kiesler, 1969); the teenage girl thinking about whether to have sex may imagine that others want her to conform when that is not really true. In still other cases, conformity results when the individual is uncertain about what is correct or appropriate and adopts the group's standards, believing that they are a reliable guide. In this instance, the teenage girl may not know whether it's good for her to have sex but she goes ahead because the group's standards suggest that doing so is the correct and satisfying way to behave.

The kind of group power that produces conformity varies considerably from case to case. The group may use coercive or reward power to pressure someone into a certain action, in which case the conformity would be an instance of compliance as we defined it at the beginning of the chapter. Compliance may lead to internalization through cognitive dissonance or self-perception (see chapters 6 and 3), but it is compliance at the outset. In other instances, particularly when the person is uncertain about what is correct, the group's referent or expert power may produce internalization.

Why Conform?

Some early theories (Crutchfield, 1955) suggested that certain personality traits made individuals prone to conformity. This approach is of limited value, however, because few people conform all the time and everyone conforms sometimes. Therefore, we cannot develop a satisfying explanation simply by focusing on individual traits. For this reason, most investigators began to examine groups to determine how they influenced their members. This research identified the various kinds of influence that groups have. One kind is **informational social influence.** We often rely on groups for information about the answer to a question, what to believe, or how to behave (Asch, 1952; Deutsch and Gerard, 1955; Kelley, 1952). This is especially true if we doubt our own judgment (Campbell, Tesser, and Fairey, 1986). You might accept an answer supplied by one person, but you are more likely to accept an answer if many people supply it. In other words, a group can influence an individual by supplying information that affects his or her beliefs, attitudes, or behaviors (Festinger, 1950).

While information is power, we also know that groups influence people's behavior even when people are not looking for information. A teenager may know that smoking is bad for his health and he may hate the taste of cigarettes, yet he is quick to light up when he sees his friends smoking. Where does this type of group power come from? Anyone who has been in a group and has wanted to remain part of that group knows the anxiety that is aroused by the thought of being rejected by the group. This is not an unfounded fear; such rejection is painful. Further, anyone who has been part of a group knows that groups often reject members who act differently from the other group members, who fail to follow rules of the group, or who consistently hold and express beliefs that are different from those expressed by the group. The group may remove the nonconformist's power by denying him or her the right to vote; it may inflict physical or psychological abuse by beatings or calling out unflattering names; it may see that the nonconformist does not share in any of the rewards that the group obtains.

The individual, believing that deviance from the group may lead to rejection, feels pressure to conform to the group model. This pressure, which is referred to as normative pressure, produces **normative social influence.** We conform because of the group's capacity to reward and punish us. In particular, the group acquires its capacity to exert normative pressure from the individual's fear of the group's response to deviation from its expectations. The group may never make it explicit that deviants will receive negative sanctions, and the individual may or may not have seen the group carry out such sanctions. In reality, sanctions for deviation may not even exist. However, the group's normative power results from the fact that the individual believes that deviants will be rejected.

These two types of group pressure lead to different types of conforming behavior. The consensus among psychologists (see Allen, 1965) is that normative pressure is likely to result in public compliance without accompanying private acceptance. An individual who reacts to normative pressure is reacting out of fear or anxiety and will often conform overtly without doing so covertly. This phenomenon was seen among the prisoners of war during the Korean and Vietnamese wars who openly expressed anti-American views while in the hands of their captors but who held to their private pro-American beliefs and chose to return to the United States when the opportunity was presented to them. They were responding to normative pressures from their captors, but no private acceptance accompanied their public compliance.

On the other hand, an individual who conforms to information pressures is more likely to evidence private acceptance, compliance to the group norm that is based not on fear but on the desire to do the correct thing. Because the group decides the correct course of action or belief, public compliance is often accompanied by private acceptance. Despite these differences, investigators (Shaw, 1981) point out that in most cases groups influence individuals by using both types of pressure.

Classic Studies of Conformity

The Autokinetic Studies

One of the earliest studies of conformity was not really aimed at studying conformity at all. Rather, Sherif (1935) wanted to examine how groups develop norms. Using a phenomenon known as the **autokinetic effect,** he demonstrated that groups will establish norms that individuals in the groups will follow. He showed individual subjects a single pinpoint of light in a dark room and asked them to judge how far the light moved. In fact, the light was stationary, but to an individual focusing on a small spot of light in a dark room, the light appears to move. The amount of movement seen varies from one person to another but is relatively constant for each individual.

After the individual reported his estimation of the light movement, he was brought together with one or two other naive subjects. The subjects were then asked to continue estimating the light movement and to announce their estimates so that the other group members could hear. Without any prompting from the experimenter that they should come to a consensus, the estimates of the group members converged so that after a time each person reported that he saw about the same amount of movement as the other group members (see figure 11.4).

FIGURE 11.4 THE CONVERGENCE OF JUDGMENTS OF AUTOKINETIC MOVEMENT IN TWO GROUPS

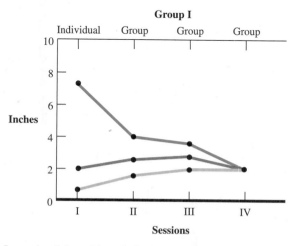 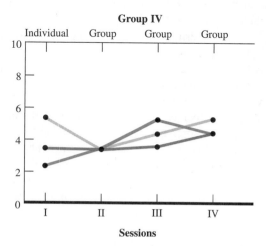

In session I the subjects judged alone. In sessions II and III they heard the judgments of other group members. In session IV they judged alone. The results show that the subjects' judgments conformed to the group norm and that this conformity continued even when the subjects were alone again in the last session.

Source: Sherif and Sherif (1969)

Sherif also found that when an individual was later asked when alone to estimate the movement of the light, these estimates were very similar to those the individual had given by the end of the group estimates. The group, then, developed a norm and the individual members of the group began to conform their judgments to that norm.

The Asch Paradigm

Although Sherif's study was not aimed at demonstrating conformity, many people interpreted the results as showing that humans are a conforming breed. Solomon Asch did not believe this. He felt that one reason why subjects conformed in Sherif's study was that the stimuli they were judging were so ambiguous, so Asch (1951) devised a unique method for studying conformity. Imagine you are a subject who has volunteered for an experiment. You enter the experimental room at the appointed time and see that six other subjects are already there. You take an empty seat at the table around which everyone is seated. The experimenter enters and tells you and the other subjects that the experiment is concerned with accuracy and visual perception. He shows your group two cards (figure 11.5). On one card is a single line, and on the other card are three lines labeled A, B, and C. The lone line is actually 10 inches long. Line A is 8¾ inches long, line B is 10 inches long, and line C is 8 inches long. The experimenter tells all of you that your task is to match the lone line with the line of equal length from the three-line card. You are to respond next to last.

The experimenter asks each subject in turn to call out the letter of the matching line. The first subject calls out B, the line that you also feel is correct. The next four subjects also call out B. When it's your turn, you call out B. The next trial goes the same as the first. The experimenter shows a 2-inch standard line, and everyone before you matches it to another 2-inch line. You do the same, and you wait for the next trial.

On the next trial, the experimenter shows a 3-inch standard line, and the three lines A, 3¾ inches; B, 4¼ inches; and C, 3 inches. You see that line C is the correct answer, and you wait for the first subject to report line C. You may also be thinking that this is really a simple-minded experiment. Suddenly, your whole world begins to collapse! The first subject reports line A. You wonder what's wrong with him; line C is obviously the correct answer. You might even laugh at the obviously incorrect response. You wait for subject two to report line C. Sub-

ject two looks the line over carefully and calls out, "Line A is correct." You sit back in disbelief, and you listen while the others who preceded you confidently report line A. It's your turn now. What do you do?

This was the question that Asch asked when he devised this procedure for studying conformity. Actually, the first five subjects were experimental confederates who had been told how to respond. On twelve of the eighteen trials, they were to respond unanimously with an incorrect answer. The second-to-last subject—you in this case—was really the only naive subject, and the experimenter was interested in finding out whether that subject would conform to the group's opinion or stick to the correct answer.

Asch set out to show that people do not conform to group opinion when they know that their own behavior is correct and that the behavior of the group is incorrect. He developed the line-judging task because he found that when people were asked to judge the lines alone without group influence, they performed almost without error. However, Asch found that his subjects conformed to the group's incorrect opinion over a third of

---

FIGURE 11.5   STIMULUS MATERIAL USED BY ASCH IN EARLY CONFORMITY RESEARCH

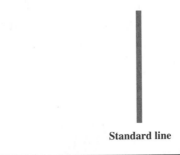

Standard line

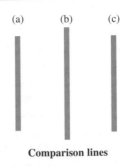

(a)   (b)   (c)

Comparison lines

Source: Adapted from Asch (1951)

BOX 11.2

Littering: A Case of Conforming to Norms

You have a piece of useless paper in your hand as you walk from one building to another. Will you throw it on the ground or hold it for the next trash bin? Holding the paper is annoying but throwing it on the ground is illegal and violates most people's idea of what is good for society. Nonetheless, littering is a growing environmental problem that has considerable aesthetic, financial, and health-related costs for all of us.

So why do people litter despite laws and social norms? Social psychologist Robert Cialdini and his colleagues (Cialdini, Reno, and Kallgren, 1990) suggest that the existence of litter itself may contribute to its increasing presence in society. Put simply, a place that is littered conveys information about what people do in that context with their refuse. When you walk across campus with that scrap of paper and you see the ground covered with paper, cans, and other discards, the litter tells you that most people use the ground as the receptacle for their litter. Thus, the presence of litter establishes a prolittering norm, and you are more likely to drop your paper on the ground.

Cialdini hypothesized that if the norms represented by a clean versus littered environment could be made salient by focusing a person's attention on the norm, the effect of a clean versus littered environment would be increased. For example, if a person enters a clearly littered environment and then observes another person walk by and drop a piece of litter, the normative conduct in this case is very clear—littering is acceptable and everyone does it.

What happens when we enter a clean environment and then observe another person drop a piece of paper onto the unpolluted ground? Cialdini makes a nonobvious prediction: littering in a clean environment would

make the antilittering norm even more powerful. In this case, we would probably not throw our paper on the ground despite the behavior of the passerby.

To investigate how the presence of litter and the salience of norms determine littering behavior, Cialdini and his students Raymond Reno and Carl Kallgren (1990) went into a parking garage located outside a local hospital. To manipulate the littering norms, they removed all the existing litter on one floor of the garage (antilittering norm). On another level, they threw brightly colored flyers all around the floor of the garage (prolittering norm). On both floors, they placed one of the flyers on the windshield of every car, positioned strategically over the driver's side so that it had to be removed to drive the car. The research participants were people returning to their cars from the hospital. To manipulate the salience of the norms, for one-half of the participants, as they returned to their cars, a confederate walked by them and got onto the elevator (low salience). For the other half of the participants, the confederate appeared to be reading one of the flyers as he approached and then threw the flyer on the floor of the garage before passing the participant (high salience). The dependent measure was the percentage of participants in each condition who deposited the flyer outside their vehicle (the researchers removed all of the trash cans before the study began).

As the data in figure 1 show, more subjects littered when the environment conveyed a norm for littering than when the environment conveyed a norm against littering. However, littering was increased when the prolittering norm was made salient by the confederate's littering behavior. In contrast, when the environment was clean and the confederate

Continued

BOX 11.2

Continued

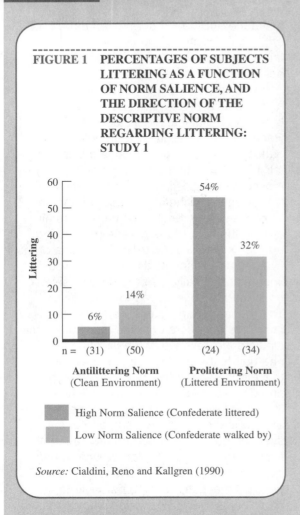

FIGURE 1   PERCENTAGES OF SUBJECTS
LITTERING AS A FUNCTION
OF NORM SALIENCE, AND
THE DIRECTION OF THE
DESCRIPTIVE NORM
REGARDING LITTERING:
STUDY 1

High Norm Salience (Confederate littered)

Low Norm Salience (Confederate walked by)

Source: Cialdini, Reno and Kallgren (1990)

it is a norm about what people *ought* to do with their litter in the garage. It is possible that both norms were operating in the parking garage. While thinking about how to separate these two norms, Cialdini and his students discovered something really unusual about the data in the parking garage study. On one day, virtually no one littered, even in the littered environment condition. In trying to figure out why this happened, they realized that it was unusually windy that day, and that it was difficult to keep the fliers strewn about the garage because the flyers were continually being blown up against a wall in a pile by the elevator. In a moment of inspired observation, the researchers realized that, in fact, the pile of flyers looked as though someone had purposely swept them up for disposal. The possibility that participants perceived the wind-swept piles of litter as man-made suggested an ingenious way to make salient the injunctive norms against littering in an area that already contains litter.

Cialdini and his team returned to the parking garage used in Study 1. This time they littered both levels of the garage, but on one parking level, they swept the litter neatly into large piles by the elevator; on the other level, the flyers were haphazardly spread around the floor. As in Study 1, they placed a flyer on the windshield of each car, and when a potential research participant emerged from the elevator, a confederate walked past them. In one condition, to make the norm salient, the confederate littered a flyer onto the floor of the garage. In the other condition, the confederate was not carrying a flyer as he passed. The dependent measure was the number of people who deposited the flyer from their windshield into the already littered environment.

littered, it appeared to focus attention on the norm against littering. In essence, the confederate was perceived as providing information about what most people did *not* do with the flyer on their car windshield.

There are at least two ways to think about what happened in the parking garage. One is *descriptive* about what people do: most people don't throw papers on the floor of this garage. The other norm is *injunctive*—that is,

Continued

BOX 11.2

Continued

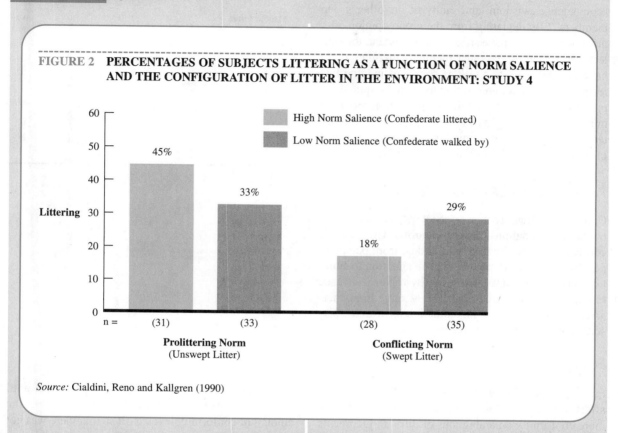

FIGURE 2   **PERCENTAGES OF SUBJECTS LITTERING AS A FUNCTION OF NORM SALIENCE
AND THE CONFIGURATION OF LITTER IN THE ENVIRONMENT: STUDY 4**

Source: Cialdini, Reno and Kallgren (1990)

The data show that when the litter had been swept, fewer participants littered than when the litter was unswept. In both cases, there were ample and equal amounts of litter in the garage. It is just that, when the litter was swept, participants recognized the normative message: The garage ought not to be littered. This effect was further enhanced by the behavior of the confederate. When the confederate littered into the swept environment, the fewest number of people followed suit, indicating that the confederate's littering behavior in the context of the swept litter made the injunctive component of the antilittering norm more salient. Hence, to decrease the amount of littering in an already littered area, some indication that other people have noticed and taken steps to eliminate the litter may go a long way toward preventing littering behavior.

the time even when they knew that the group was wrong. When faced with the group's unanimous incorrect opinion, most of the subjects conformed at least once, and only about one-fourth of the subjects were able to turn in a completely error-free performance.

Ross, Bierbrauer, and Hoffman (1976) enumerated the pressures on the subject in the Asch situation. First, the subject must wonder about his own ability to judge lines and must think, "How can everyone but me see it that way? Is there something wrong with me?"

There is, however, an additional pressure on the subject. If he reports the situation as he sees it (differently from the group response), is he not challenging the "competence, wisdom, and sanity of the other group members"? By deviating from the group opinion after the other members have stated their judgment, the subject will be telling the other members that they don't have the ability to do a task as simple as judging line lengths. This is a tough position to be in. Despite these pressures, the results obtained by Asch surprised a number of psychologists and created a great deal of interest in studying conformity. Let's examine the results of these studies in the following sections.

Factors Affecting Conformity

Conformity often involves conflict between a person's beliefs or inclinations and group norms. The way this conflict is resolved varies a great deal from person to person, from time to time, and from situation to situation. The determinants of conformity versus resistance to group pressure are complex. They range from characteristics of the conformity situation itself to the person's concerns about self-presentation.

Difficulty of the Judgments

First, consider the way the difficulty of the judgment affects conformity. Asch predicted that there would be more conformity on ambiguous or difficult judgments than on easy ones. Asch found far more conformity than he expected on relatively easy judgments, but conformity does drop when judgments become easier (Blake, Helson, and Mouton, 1956). For example, Asch (1952) found that conformity was greater when the differences between the lengths of the comparison lines were small than when they were large. In figure 11.6, it is difficult to determine the correct comparison line for judgment A but easy for judgment B. Asch found greater conformity in the hard judgment than in the easy one. From this finding we can infer that people use the group as a source of information when the task is difficult or ambiguous.

Group Size

Another important factor is the size of the group exerting pressure to conform. Asch varied the size of the group that the naive subject confronted, using one, two, three, four, eight, and fifteen confederates. He

FIGURE 11.6   EXAMPLES OF DIFFICULT (A) AND EASY (B) LINE-JUDGING TASKS

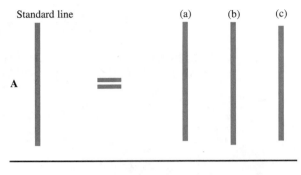

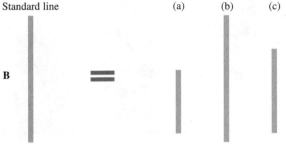

Source: Asch (1952)

found that conformity increased with group size until the group consisted of three confederates. Then the amount of conformity leveled off so that there was not more conformity to a group of fifteen members than to a group of three (see figure 11.7). More recent research shows that increasing the majority beyond three does produce more conformity, but the increases are slight (Gerard, Wilhelmy, and Conolley, 1968). Three or four people are generally enough to produce very strong conformity effects.

Other research has shown that the group size under which maximum conformity is achieved is dependent on a number of factors. The type of task may be one factor. For example, Mann (1977) studied queuing behavior (waiting in line). He had groups of two, four, six, and eight people line up at bus stops in Jerusalem and then observed how many arrivers would conform and get into line. He found that conformity increased as group size increased, with the greatest amount of conformity given to the eight-person group. Thus, the relationship between group size and conformity seems to depend on the setting and on the task (Shaw, 1981).

A second issue related to group size is the association among majority members. Wilder (1977) suggested that when people are categorized as belonging to a group, others respond to them as a group rather than as individuals. If three people from the American Red Cross ask you for a donation, you will not respond to the request as if it came from three separate individuals; rather, you will view it as a request coming from "a group from the Red Cross." Wilder argues that as a result of this categorization process, a group may lose some of its ability to influence others. He therefore suggests that instead of counting the number of people in a majority, we should examine the number of subgroups to determine the pressures toward conformity. To illustrate this point, Wilder found more conformity to a majority of four unrelated persons than to a majority of two groups of two persons each (still four people); and more conformity to a majority of six unrelated persons than to two groups of three people. Thus, both number and group categorization are important variables influencing conformity.

Group Unanimity

Asch's (1956) original research also looked at the issue of group unanimity. He studied the effect of having just one person deviate from the unanimous majority and found that deviation by the one group member reduced the amount of conformity to the group. In one set of conditions, Asch instructed one confederate to give correct judgments on all trials even when the remainder of the confederates did not. In other conditions, all of the confederates were instructed to agree on their responses. When the group gave a unanimously incorrect answer, conformity occurred about 35 percent of the time. However, when one deviant gave correct answers, conformity dropped to about 9 percent. In addition, it did not seem to matter whether the group size was three or fifteen—one deviant drastically reduced the amount of conformity. Conformity by naive subjects even decreased when the deviant gave an *incorrect* answer!

Why does a single deviant have such a drastic impact on conformity? Allen and Wilder (1980) suggest that a unanimous majority may force the individual to reinterpret the situation; the presence of a deviant, even one, shows the individual that there may be many ways to view the situation and that a reinterpretation is not necessary. Although this explanation may apply when there is some doubt about the meaning of events, a broader interpretation focuses on the deviant's effect on normative social influence. If an individual feared group rejection for not conforming, observing a deviant who was not rejected could alleviate this fear and significantly reduce the amount of normative pressure. The effects of the deviation would quite likely have been very different had the remainder of the group laughed at or threatened the deviant. Then the group's

FIGURE 11.7   ERRORS MADE BY SUBJECTS TO CONFORM WITH UNANIMOUS MAJORITIES OF VARIOUS SIZES

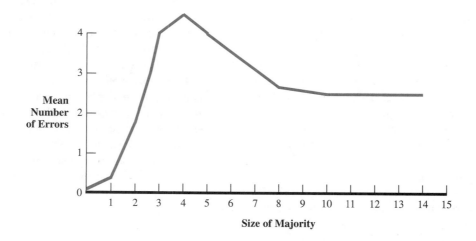

Source: Asch (1951)

response to the deviant might have actually increased conformity. The group must ensure that the deviant does not "get away with it" lest additional group members decide to act against the desires of the group. One function of brutal public executions is to demonstrate how badly a deviant will be treated by the group. Such penalties cause others to think twice before they try to break away from the group's norm.

Time Factors

Time has some interesting effects on conformity. One important consideration is at what point pressure is applied in the development of group conformity. There is reason to think that it is easier to produce conformity in the early stages of interaction than in later stages. In the early stages the group is attempting to establish norms and individuals are responsive to each other—the so-called **forming stage** (Tuckman, 1965). During later periods of group interaction, people are trying to negotiate their position in the group and are less likely to conform—the **storming stage** of group development. Consistent with the idea of forming versus storming stages of group development is the finding that conformity can be produced by *either* self-doubt *or* high group pressure in the early stages of interaction.

Another time factor is the length of time an individual has to think about other people's positions. It may seem surprising, but if people know that the others with whom they are going to interact have opinions that differ from their own on an issue, they tend to conform more to those opinions if they are asked to write down their thoughts about the issue before they state their own opinions. When people think about the issue before they say what they think, they tend to empathize with the group's opinions, and they open themselves up to those views. If they are simply asked to state their opinions before they are given the chance to think, they simply express their own views and conform less (Tetlock, Skitka, and Boettger, 1989). When you interact with people who don't agree with you, you will be more influenced by their views if you think about their position before you simply proclaim your own.

Personal Factors

A variety of personal factors affect conformity. One is the individual's concern about his or her position or status in the group, especially when the individual is attracted to the group. Overall, research indicates that

people who feel insecure about their position are most likely to conform. Hancock and Sorrentino (1980) found a high degree of conformity in subjects who had received no support from the group in previous meetings but who expected future interaction with it. The lack of prior support reduced the subjects' self-confidence, and the expectation of future interaction made acceptance as group members an important issue. Related research has found that conformity is greater when people are attracted to the group (Back, 1951; Brehm and Festinger, 1957) and when the individual has somewhat lower status than other group members (Raven and French, 1958; Stang, 1972). In these cases, it seems that individuals are responding to normative group pressures and trying to "buy" themselves a secure position in the group by conforming. Hollander (1958), in fact, suggested that people earn *idiosyncrasy credits* when they conform to group expectations. These credits give individuals status in the group and allow them the opportunity to deviate without being rejected by the group. Each time members deviate, they must pay by giving up some of their credits. Therefore, conformity may well help an individual buy a more secure place in the group.

Even though some research has focused on personal characteristics in isolation, most has studied how personal and situational variables interact to influence conformity. Two lines of research show the value of this approach: the first is sex differences in conformity. A number of early studies (Gerard, Wilhelmy, and Conolley, 1968; Julian, Regula, and Hollander, 1968) found that women were more likely to conform than men. These results were often explained by reference to sex roles: men were expected to be independent while women were expected to be "reasonable" and sensitive to others. This explanation fits many of the earlier results, but it does not explain subsequent findings. For example, Sistrunk and McDavid (1971) found that women conformed more than men when the task was one in which men should have been expert. However, when the task involved female-related items, men conformed more than women. Eagly, Wood, and Fishbaugh (1981) found that women conformed more than men when their behavior was being observed, but that there was no sex difference when there was no surveillance. Although surveillance did not affect the amount of conformity shown by women, men conformed less under surveillance than under no-surveillance conditions. The investigators suggested that surveillance increased concerns with

Social impact theory helps to explain the mass suicide in 1978 of the followers of Jim Jones. The combined influence of the fanatical leader's command and the cumulative peer pressure to obey was enough to induce everyone to take a dose of liquid cyanide.

self-presentation: men conformed less than women under these conditions because they were more interested than women in presenting themselves as being independent. Thus, sex and sex roles do not necessarily breed conformity; rather, they breed concern with presenting a certain image to others. While there is still some debate about why sex differences in conformity occur (Eagly and Carli, 1981), these studies show that sex alone does not determine conformity: sex interacts with the situation to determine conformity.

Santee and Maslach (1982) also adopted a self-presentation approach to explain conformity, arguing that people vary in the degree to which they want to be seen as distinct and separate from others (this desire can be measured by a number of scales). However, the situation determines when this personality variable will influence conformity. For example, individuals can more

readily present themselves as distinct by deviating from a unanimous group as opposed to a nonunanimous group. If other people are already dissenting, an individual who also dissents will not look particularly unusual. Santee and Maslach found, in fact, that the desire for distinctiveness had a greater influence on conformity when the group was unanimous than when it was not. Once again, the role of individual characteristics can best be understood in relation to situational variables.

Social Impact Theory

Obedience and conformity are two important consequences of social influence pressures that can lead to behaviors few people would have predicted had they not actually been demonstrated in laboratory research. The

Drinking on Campus: A Case of Misperceiving the Norm

Alcohol use on college campuses in the United States has reached alarming proportions. Students at M.I.T., Louisiana State, and elsewhere have died from alcohol abuse. University health services and local hospitals routinely treat students whose binge drinking has made them critically ill. Alcohol, especially as implicated in driving fatalities, has been cited as the number one cause of death among young people. Surveys reveal that between one-fifth and one-fourth of all college students exhibit symptoms of problem drinking (Engs, Diebold, and Hanson, 1996).

What accounts for the heavy abuse of alcohol by students? Deborah Prentice and Dale Miller have argued that a social psychological process known as *pluralistic ignorance* accounts for a remarkable portion of the problem (Prentice and Miller, 1996). As Prentice and Miller define it, pluralistic ignorance "describes the case in which virtually every member of a group of society privately rejects a belief, opinion or practice, yet believes that virtually every other member privately accepts it" (1996, p. 161). In their view, students come to college believing that drinking to excess is a behavior that is supported by most of their peers. Indeed, much of the talk during the first few days on campus is of drinking, parties, fraternities, and so forth. To "fit in," students speak bravely and boldly about their drinking exploits and desires. Privately, they may feel uncomfortable about drinking, but they are convinced that the sentiments that they are hearing from others are true and honest descriptions of their peers' affinity toward alcohol.

Imagine Richard at a hypothetical party during the first week of school. Everyone drinks and seems comfortable. However, at the very moment that he is drinking and par-

tying, Richard may feel that his behavior is not a genuine reflection of his private attitude. He feels uncomfortable, but he assumes that everyone else's drinking is indicative of their comfort with heavy drinking. Prentice and Miller believe that many people are like Richard. Each person looks at his or her peers and believes that their public expressions are true representations of their love of alcohol. And in this latter view, Richard and others are simply incorrect.

Prentice and Miller (1993) asked Princeton University students to rate their own comfort with the alcohol drinking habits of their fellow students and to estimate the comfort of the average Princeton undergraduate toward drinking. The figure shows that, for men and women, comfort about drinking is significantly lower than the comfort they believe is experienced by the average student. Of course, they have to be wrong about their assessment of the "average student," because the true comfort level of the average student is the mean of the "self" ratings of all of the students in the survey. Nonetheless, the students have created a view of the "average student" that makes them believe that there is an *injunctive norm* on campus (a norm that dictates how one *should* act regarding alcohol).

Perkins and Berkowitz (1986) conducted surveys on four other college campuses and found results that fit the portrait that Prentice and Miller propose. They asked students to select from five statements the one that best represented their own feeling about drinking. They also asked the students to select the statement that best represented "the general campus attitude toward drinking alcoholic beverages" (p. 964). Overwhelmingly, the students endorsed a moderate position to represent their own attitudes. However, more

Continued

BOX 11.3

Continued

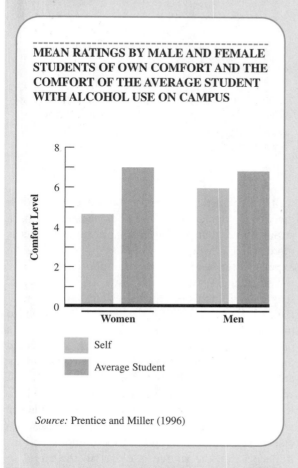

MEAN RATINGS BY MALE AND FEMALE STUDENTS OF OWN COMFORT AND THE COMFORT OF THE AVERAGE STUDENT WITH ALCOHOL USE ON CAMPUS

Comfort Level

Women   Men

- Self
- Average Student

Source: Prentice and Miller (1996)

than 60 percent of the respondents felt that the general campus attitude was reflected by a more permissive statement that endorsed frequently getting drunk even if it interfered with responsibilities and grades. As in Prentice and Miller's (1993) study, people privately felt less comfortable with excessive drinking and misperceived the group's norm, believing it was considerably more permissive toward alcohol than it really was.

Prentice and Miller (1996) reported an experiment in which women students came to a discussion group during the first week of college to talk about "the role of alcohol in campus life." Prior to the conversation, each student privately recorded her comfort with alcohol and then engaged in a ten minute discussion on the topic. Prentice and Miller found that students believed that (1) the others in the group were considerably more comfortable about drinking than they were; (2) they had given the impression to the others in their group that they were comfortable about alcohol but that the impression was not true; and (3) the impression that others in the group gave about being comfortable about alcohol was a true reflection of the group's attitudes. Thus, when conversing with other Princeton students, the participants believed that the conversation was reliable evidence that the others were more comfortable about alcohol. The students recognized that their own conversation also conveyed a pro-alcohol attitude, but they knew that their own behavior was not a true reflection of their attitudes. Each person continued to believe that there was a norm supporting or even requiring permissive drinking on campus.

If people are not comfortable engaging in the destructive pattern of drinking on campus, how can drinking be brought closer to the moderate level that most students privately endorse? Although it is simplistic to believe there is any single answer to the problem, the work by Prentice and Miller suggests one component to a solution. Part of the problem on campus is that students are simply wrong about what the collegiate norm is regarding drinking. They believe they know how their classmates feel, but they are incorrect. One straightforward solution is to correct their knowledge of the student norm. Schroeder and Prentice (1998) had entering students at Princeton participate in one of two types of discussions about alcohol use during their first week on campus. In the *peer-oriented* condition, students were shown data that revealed the systematic mis-

Continued

BOX 11.3

Continued

perception of other students' comfort with campus drinking and were encouraged to talk about this phenomenon during the discussion. In the *individual-oriented* condition, students engaged in a discussion of how to make responsible personal decisions in a drinking situation. Approximately four to six months following the discussions, students were contacted and asked to fill out a self-

report measure of their alcohol consumption. The students who had participated in the peer-oriented discussion reported having an average of 3.1 drinks per week, whereas students in the individual-oriented discussion reported drinking 5.05 drinks per week. Revealing their pluralistic ignorance to students in the very beginning of school led to a significant reduction in college drinking behavior.

---

research on these phenomena helps us to understand a variety of dramatic instances of social influence, including the deaths of 6 million Jews and 14 million others under the direction of Adolf Hitler, the mass suicide that took place in Jonestown, Guyana, in 1978, under the direction of the fanatical preacher Jim Jones, and the "Heaven's Gate" suicide of thirty-nine people at the Rancho Santa Fe mansion in Spring 1997 under the leadership of Marshall Applewhite (also known as Do).

Social psychologist Bibb Latané proposed a general theory of social influence that helps us to understand and relate some of the factors that affect obedience, conformity, and other kinds of social influence. **Social impact theory** (Latané 1981; see also Jackson, 1987; Nowak, Szamrej, and Latané, 1994) states that the social impact or force felt by a person, or target, is a function of the strength, immediacy, and number of sources of social influence that are present. That is, a person will be more affected when there are stronger sources of influence, when the sources are physically closer or more immediate, and when there are more of them. Social impact works just like physical impact—for example, the amount of light falling on a table is a function of the strength of the lights overhead, their distance from the table, and their number. In figure 11.8, Latané presents a pictorial view of the combination of the strength, immediacy, and number components of social influence, which forms the tongue-in-cheek equation that impact is a function of SIN.

Let's consider how these basic principles of strength, immediacy, and number might apply to some of the issues already discussed in this chapter. Social impact theory predicts more impact and thus more influence when the source of influence is strong, a fact

well documented in Milgram's obedience work. When the person demanding the obedience represents a strong force, that passion has more impact. This is represented in Milgram's procedure by presenting the experimenter as someone of authority, someone whose authority was conveyed by a major institution. It is unlikely that the subjects would have administered shock if a person of low authority had demanded obedience. We can envision a scenario in which a passerby or a custodian entered the room and ordered the participant to shock the victim; here we would not anticipate much influence. We can also recall that when the investigator's authority was conveyed by a less prestigious organization in Bridgeport, obedience was reduced (although by no means eliminated). Social impact theory also predicts more impact and influence when the source is closer to the target of influence, a prediction directly tested in the obedience experiments where Milgram found more obedience when the experimenter—one source of social impact—was closer to the subject but less obedience when the learner—another source of social impact—was closer to the subject (Milgram, 1974).

Now let's consider number. Social impact tells us that there is more influence as the number of sources of influence increases; however, the relationship is not a simple one. If one classmate tries to convince you of something, you may or you may not believe it. A second person will add to the impact. By the time a third friend tells you the same thing, the impact influences are probably growing. Does the twentieth person add as much to nineteen earlier influence attempts as the fourth did to the third? Probably not. By the time you hear many, many attempts to influence you, you may

FIGURE 11.8   MULTIPLICATION OF IMPACT:
$I = f(\text{SIN})$

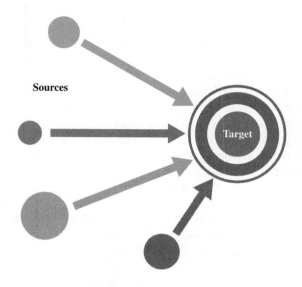

Sources

Target

Source: Latané (1981)

ciples to his advantage. He brought his fight to the heart of segregation (the South) and to Washington, D.C., where laws are enacted (immediacy). He worked hard to gather as many people as possible to attend his rallies and marches (number). And unlike some other black leaders, he invited powerful white political leaders, such as President Kennedy, to join the movement (strength).

Another principle of social impact theory states that the impact of any source of social influence is *diffused* as the strength, immediacy, and number of targets of social influence increase. For example, there should be less impact on a strong target than on a weak one. We just saw that people with less status in a group conform more. As their strength (measured by status) increases, the group's impact is diffused and they conform less. This finding is exactly what social impact theory predicts. The number of targets was explored in one of the variations of Milgram's (1977) research. When two confederates were posing as subjects, the experimenter's orders to the actual subject had less impact. These confederates also displayed defiance of the experimenter's orders, so it is unclear if the number of targets alone reduces social impact; the targets' behavior also has an effect, but it is plausible to conclude that the number of targets alone reduces the experimenter's impact (Brown, 1986).

Imagine that you were one of the multitude who stood in the shadows of the Washington Monument in 1963 listening to Martin Luther King, Jr's., speech. Latané's theory makes a nonobvious prediction: Although you likely would have been moved, as the entire nation was moved, the number of people sharing that event with you actually diminished the speech's impact on you. Cumulatively, the speech had enormous impact. But social impact theory's prediction about the impact on *you* as an individual would be that you were less influenced than if you had been one of a small group invited to be present while Dr. King delivered the speech in your college auditorium.

Social impact theory is about conformity, obedience, and influence but in a slightly, yet importantly, different way than most theories. Note that it does not specify any mechanism or process that causes people to conform or obey or be influenced. Rather, it holds that any theory that deals with the various topics of social influence must take into account the impact of strength, immediacy, and number on the magnitude of the influence.

be pretty well convinced. Adding one more does not add that much to what you now feel. Social impact theory sees the increase in number of influence attempts to be a curved line (known as a *power function*) rather than a straight line. Each new source of influence adds to the previous sources, but as the numbers increase the influence of adding yet one more source of influence to the previous ones adds less to the total impact than earlier ones.

Number clearly played an important role in conformity research. After two people put pressure on the real subject, the next source of influence made an enormous difference. After that, increasing the numbers did not increase the magnitude of conformity in any significant way. We should point out that Asch's data do not quite fit social impact theory's predictions because increasing the numbers past three should have had *some* impact even though it was not as much as adding that third conforming confederate. The data from subsequent conformity studies, such as Gerard, Wilhelmy, and Conolley's (1968), fit the social impact prediction better. Although still showing the tremendous importance of having three conforming confederates, their data did show small tendencies to increase conforming behavior as the number of confederates increased.

It is interesting to think about some of the ways in which Martin Luther King, Jr., used social impact prin-

An interesting study by Jackson and Latané (1981) shows the relevance of social impact variables on quite a different area of people's behavior: stage-fright. Jackson and Latané showed that people singing in front of an audience experience more impact in the form of anxiety as the number of pairs of eyes staring at them from the audience increases. The increase was a power function: the more people in the audience, the more anxiety. However, as the size of the audience increased, each new pair of eyes did not add as much anxiety as did the previous pair of eyes. This study also showed that the number of singers who join someone on stage—that is, the number of cotargets—has the effect of decreasing the amount of anxiety. In that case, the audience's impact is diffused. Research on bystander intervention by Latané and Darley (1970), discussed in chapter 9, also shows that the impact of a source—for example, a person in distress—is diffused if there are a large number of bystanders.

Social Impact in Dynamic Systems

Latané and his colleagues have focused more recently on the way in which social influence occurs in dynamic, or changing, systems. Imagine that you live in a dormitory of, let's say, one hundred other people. An issue arises in your university that causes you and the others in your dorm to form an opinion. When you do,

you notice that not everyone shares your opinion. You may be in the majority, but there is also a sizable minority opinion. You all talk about the issue. We can predict that you will talk to people who are physically close to you and that you will try to convince nonbelievers to believe as you do. On the basis of social impact and other theories of influence, we can predict that your influence will be most effective as a function of strength (perhaps your expertise on the issue), the number of people to whom you are talking, and the immediacy of your communication.

But, as you and others communicate, the situation changes in interesting ways. You may have been in the majority, and perhaps the persons on your left and right were in the minority. However, if those persons focus their communication on you, the SIN variables may cause you to change. But you also have friends in the majority who will exert influence forces on you, and you will exert influence forces on them. That is what Andrzej Nowak and Jacek Szamrej of the University of Warsaw and Bibb Latané (1990) refer to as a *dynamic system*. The pieces of the influence puzzle all interact with each other; as the pieces change, so does the whole puzzle.

How do we conduct research on large systems when they are undergoing subjection to social influence and observe their changes? Nowak, Szamrej, and Latané (1990) suggested that computer simulations of

It has been demonstrated by people singing in front of an audience that as the audience increases so does anxiety among the singers, but that anxiety decreases with an increase in number of singers.

FIGURE 11.9   THE INITIAL, RANDOM DISTRIBUTION OF ATTITUDES IN TWO GROUPS OF 400 PEOPLE, EACH WITH A 30 PERCENT MINORITY

A. 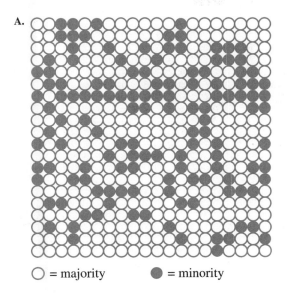   B.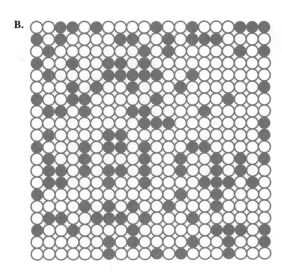

○ = majority   ● = minority

Source: Latané, Nowak, and Liu (1994)

social systems would add insights into the likely outcome of real people interacting. They reasoned that if the SIN variables of social impact theory (strength, immediacy, and number) were correctly built into the simulation, then the outcome of the computer program would reveal the way social influence occurs and how the system reacts to that change.

One such simulation was conducted by Latané, Nowak, and Liu (1994). Figure 11.9 shows a random grouping of four hundred people who are either for (represented by open circles) or opposed (represented by solid circles) to a particular issue. Approximately 30 percent held the minority view, randomly scattered through the four hundred people in the system. Latané and his associates (1994) assumed that communication would occur and that influence would result as a function of the SIN variables. When the computer finished a large number of iterations, it produced two possible outcomes, shown in figure 11.10. In each, the proportion of people holding the minority position decreased from its original 30 percent. And the minority viewpoint showed marked clusters. People who believed in the same position, clustered spatially either in one large group or in several small groups. We know from work with real participants, such as those studied by Festinger, Schachter, and Back (1950) in

the Westgate housing project (see chapter 8), that such clustering of similar attitudes is a likely occurrence.

Properties of large, interacting groups often emerge from social influence. Computer simulations may provide a way to see what those properties are. In the Latané, Nowak, and Liu (1994) computer simulation, spatial clustering is one of those emergent properties. We must remember, though, that the outcome is only the result of a computer program, and the participants were not real human beings but just computer codes. Nonetheless, using the variables of social impact theory, this new methodology allows investigators to begin to examine the consequences of social influence in large, continually changing, dynamic groups.

Deviation and Resistance to Social Influence

The discussion thus far has shown many of the factors that lead people to respond to social influence. Many pressures act on us as targets of social influence, pressures that can be very difficult to resist. Indeed, a person who deviates and refuses to go along with the crowd runs many risks. In one demonstration of such risks, Schachter (1951) set up groups of naive subjects and planted three experimental confederates to act as

FIGURE 11.10   **EQUILIBRIUM DISTRIBUTIONS OF ATTITUDES AFTER SEVERAL ROUNDS OF DISCUSSION**

A.

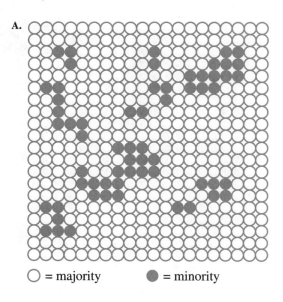

B.

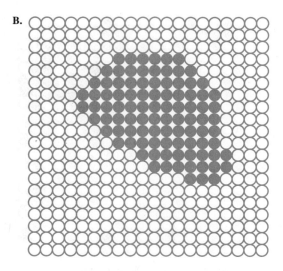

○ = majority   ● = minority

Source: Latané, Novak, and Liu (1994)

subjects in each of the groups. The task of the groups was to discuss how to handle a juvenile delinquent named Johnny Rocco. One of the confederates (the deviant) consistently disagreed with the group's opinion about how to handle Johnny. A second confederate (the slider) began by disagreeing with the majority opinion but soon switched positions to conform to that of the majority. The final confederate (the mode) agreed with the majority opinion throughout the discussion. Schachter manipulated cohesiveness by making half of the groups believe that they would be working on very attractive tasks (high cohesive) and by making the other half believe that they would be working on relatively unattractive tasks (low cohesive). After the groups had discussed the Johnny Rocco case, the subjects were asked to rate how much they liked the other members of the group and to nominate group members to serve in various functional positions in the group.

At first the group directed a great deal of its communication and attention to the deviant, apparently in an attempt to persuade him to conform to group opinion. Finally, the group members seemed to give up; they stopped talking to him. In essence, they rejected him. When the jobs in the group were divided up, the

deviant was consistently given the worst job. Thus, he was not only rejected, but also punished for not conforming to group opinion. Interestingly enough, the rejection of the deviant was greatest in the highly cohesive groups. Schachter also found that the slider, who began by deviating but later switched to a conforming posture, was liked as much as the mode, who consistently agreed with the group. The slider was often assigned popular and attractive jobs, and he received a great deal of the group's attention. Apparently the slider's switch to conformity was interpreted by the group as recognition that he had been wrong and was "mature enough" to admit it. Thus, consistent deviation from a group is met with rejection whereas conformity is rewarded. Recent research suggests that the tendency to reject deviants is strongest when the group feels that evaluating an issue is a group goal rather than an individual goal and when the issue being discussed is a matter of facts rather than values (Earle, 1986). The group that is most likely to reject deviant opinions is one that needs to define reality, not values, for the group as a whole. For example, a labor or management negotiating team trying to predict what the other side will accept in a strike settlement is likely to reject deviant opinion. Even though this is just the kind of group that may need to hear divergent views, it may be the least likely to tolerate them.

Despite all the pressures to comply, noncompliance is often as common as, if not more common than, compliance. Every study of conformity found nonconformity by subjects—in fact, nonconformity was more common than conformity in the Asch studies. Many of the great men of history have been nonconformists. Galileo was tortured because he argued that the earth revolved around the sun when the prevailing view was that the earth was the focal point of the universe. Columbus was ridiculed because he believed that the world was round at a time when most people believed that it was flat. Freud was not allowed to publish many of his writings because his theories offended his contemporaries. Why do such men deviate from the majority and risk ridicule and punishment?

Most of the social-psychological work on conformity has studied the conformist, not the deviant or the nonconformist. However, some theories do apply to the question of why a person does not conform. One of these is **reactance theory** (Brehm, 1966; West and Wicklund, 1980). Brehm hypothesized that an individual whose freedom to perform certain behaviors is threatened or eliminated will experience a motivational arousal that is aimed at regaining the freedom. This motivational arousal is labeled *reactance*. When individuals feel pressure from the group to conform, whether that pressure is normative or informational, they should experience reactance because the pressure threatens their freedom not to conform. Nonconformity should then become a more attractive behavioral option, and individuals should attempt to demonstrate that they are free not to conform. In the reactance view of nonconformity, therefore, the pressure a group applies on a person to conform causes that person to experience reactance and results in his or her nonconformity.

The desire to be unique is another reason why people resist influence (Maslach, 1974; Snyder and Fromkin, 1980). Most of us believe that we have certain traits or abilities that are different from those possessed by others. Further, in most societies value is placed on being different and standing apart from the crowd. One way of demonstrating uniqueness is by not conforming to the group. Santee and Maslach (1982) found that people who place a high value on uniqueness resist conformity, especially when the rest of the group adopts a unanimous position. Further, being different attracts the attention of others. As we saw in the Schachter (1951) study, early in the group's

Contract negotiators from the United Auto Workers (left) and General Motors begin 1996 contract negotiations. While labor and management groups would benefit from hearing divergent views, they are probably not likely to tolerate them.

life the majority of communications were aimed at those people who held deviant attitudes. People may thus adopt anticonformity as a way of showing their uniqueness and attracting attention.

Summary

Social influence is the exercise of power by a person or group to influence the behavior of others. Power is viewed as the potential to influence others. There are many kinds of power, including coercive, legitimate, expert, referent, and informational power.

A leader is the individual who exerts the most influence in a group. Leaders tend to be either task oriented or relationship oriented. Often groups have two leaders, each characterized by a different orientation. One of the earliest theories about leadership suggested that leaders have certain traits that make them leaders. This position, however, has received only limited support. The *zeitgeist* theories argue that the situation determines who will become the group's leader. Although some situational factors, such as seniority and physical position, do influence leadership, the situational approach has also proved too limited in scope. The most accepted view is that the situation and the personal characteristics of the individual and the followers interact to determine who will be leader. Research on leadership style shows that while autocratic leaders may have productive groups, members are happiest with a democratic leader. The contingency model of leadership suggests that the situation determines what will be the most effective style of leadership.

Obedience is conformity to the direct orders of a person in a position of authority. Milgram's research found that people are surprisingly obedient. One reason is that they feel the leader will assume responsibility for their behavior.

Conformity is a yielding to the real or imagined pressures of the group. Groups use informational and normative social influence to get members to conform. Conformity is affected by both situational and personal factors.

Social impact theory states that the impact of a source or sources of influence on a target increases with the strength, immediacy, and number of the sources of influence. Social impact is diffused as the strength, immediacy, and number of the targets of influence increase. Deviation from group opinion can lead to rejection from the group. Nonconformity may be caused by reactance or by a desire to appear unique or to attract attention.

Key Terms

autokinetic effect
charisma
coercive power
compliance
conformity
contingency model
expert power
forming stage
identification
informational power
informational social
   influence
internalization
leader
leadership schema

legitimate power
normative social influence
obedience
power
prototype
reactance theory
referent power
reward power
situational approach
social impact theory
social influence
storming stage
trait theory of leadership
transformational leader

Suggested Readings

Asch, S. (1956). Studies of independence and conformity: I. A minority of one against a unanimous majority. *Psychological Monographs, 70*(9).

Cialdini, R. B., and Trost, M. R. (1997). Influence, social norms, conformity and compliance. In D. T. Gilbert, S. T. Fiske, and G. Lindzey (Eds.), *Handbook of social psychology* (4th ed.). New York: Oxford University Press and McGraw-Hill.

Fiedler, F. E., and Chemers, M. M. (1974). *Leadership and effective management.* Glenview, IL: Scott, Foresman.

Latané, B. (1981). The psychology of social impact. *American Psychologist, 36,* 343–356.

Milgram, S. (1975). *Obedience to authority.* New York: Harper and Row.

Moscovici, S. (1985). Social influence and conformity. In G. Lindzey and E. Aronson (Eds.), *The handbook of social psychology* (Vol. 2, pp. 347–412). New York: Random House.

Chapter 12

Intergroup Conflict

If you drive westward from Charleston, the capital of West Virginia, there is winding road that takes you through mountain passes and over some rugged but beautiful country. When you think you've left civilization behind, you strike the Tug Fork of the Big Sandy River and the Kentucky-West Virginia border. The beauty of the place is enhanced by its remoteness, but if you are a history buff, a shiver of excitement may run up your spine, for this is the location of one of the most famous family feuds in American history.

It's hard to determine all the reasons that led the Hatfields and McCoys to take up arms against each other, but it is easy to identify the incident that set the guns blazing. The Big Sandy not only separated two states, it also divided the Hatfield and the McCoy families, the Hatfields residing in West Virginia and the McCoys in Kentucky. In the Autumn of 1873, Floyd Hatfield went into the hills and rounded up his hogs, driving them into his pigsty near Stringtown, Kentucky. A few days later, Randolph McCoy stopped by to chat with Floyd and noticed the hogs. The common bond between the two men because of their marriage to sisters was suddenly shattered when Randolph proclaimed: "Floyd, that thar ain't yo' hog . . . hit's mine" (Jones, 1948, p. 18). The men squabbled over the ownership of the porker, and Randolph stomped away to swear out a warrant accusing Floyd of stealing his pigs.

A trial was held in Preacher Anse Hatfield's makeshift court. Spectators packed the court to hear witnesses for both sides. Recognizing that he was in a no-win situation because bad blood had existed between the two families since the Civil War, Preacher Anse appointed a jury of twelve men, six Hatfields and six McCoys, to hear the case. As expected, Hatfield witnesses supported Floyd's claim, and McCoy witnesses supported Randolph. One by one, the jury was polled, and it began to divide along family lines until Selkirk McCoy, to everyone's surprise, stated

that there was not enough evidence to take the pigs away from Floyd Hatfield. "There have been bigger trials, bigger courts, bigger crimes, but rarely a verdict so ponderous. In this outcome, the die was cast. Years would pass before the hatred thus engendered would fade; generations would follow in which the family names of Hatfield and McCoy could never be mentioned without the thought of feuds and dangerous mountaineers" (Jones, 1948, p. 21).

The seething hatred boiled to the surface, and the McCoys vowed to take revenge on those who had taken away their pigs. In the next few days, heated words were exchanged and tension escalated. It wasn't long before words gave way to bullets, and Bill Stanton, who had testified for Floyd Hatfield, was killed by Sam McCoy when the men happened upon each other while hunting. Sam stood trial for the murder but was acquitted on a ruling of self-defense. The verdict infuriated the Hatfields, who vowed their own revenge.

Each side armed itself, seeking an opportunity to kill members of the opposing family. The feud was in full swing. In many ways the hatred between the two families is difficult to understand because they were similar in so many ways. Both families traced their origins to Scotland. Both were engaged in farming, logging, and moonshining. "In their physical attributes and their attitudes, the Hatfields and the McCoys showed striking similarities" (Rice, 1978). Intermarriage between the two families was not uncommon, but once the battle lines were drawn, these romances served as a source of added tension.

The fighting raged for over fifty years. As news of the feud spread, the governors of West Virginia and Kentucky were drawn into the conflict, each supporting its native clan. Distrust was rampant, and those cases that went to trial only increased the distrust between the families. One of the bloodiest incidents occurred on January 1, 1888, when a group of Hatfields attacked Randolph McCoy's home, killing Calvin, his son, and Alifair, his daughter, and burning his home. It is estimated that nearly one hundred people were killed as a result of the feud, which did not end until 1928 when Tennis Hatfield offered his hand to Uncle Jim McCoy and "Jim grasped it."

In this chapter, we discuss the social psychology of intergroup conflict. We explore factors that influence the relations between groups—some that contribute to intergroup conflict and some that help to resolve it.

The Nature of Intergroup Relations

It seems rather strange that the relationship between the Hatfields and McCoys could deteriorate so quickly. The clans had lived next to each other for generations, intermarriage between clan members was common, and although there had been periods of conflict, there were also many incidents of cooperation between the two families. Unfortunately, the pattern of relations between these two groups is not unusual. History is filled with examples of neighbor killing neighbor because of group membership, even after long periods of peace and harmony. One of the saddest examples of this situation has occurred in Bosnia and other countries formerly part of Yugoslavia, where Croats, Muslims, and Serbs once lived together peacefully but now often hate and distrust one another. Before the war, Dancia Sandor, a Croat, lived next to Jovanka Ciric, a Serb, in the small town of Vukovar. Their children played together, they cooked meals for each other, and their husbands worked together (*Wall Street Journal,* September 23, 1994). Now, after the conflict, both their houses lie in ruins, and the two families are bitter enemies. How can we explain these and similar patterns of behavior between members of different groups?

Preacher Anse Hatfield and his clan. The half-century feud between the Hatfields and the McCoys is an egregious, and legendary, example of intergroup conflict in this country.

As a first step, we should consider findings by Insko and Schopler (1987) (see also Schopler, Insko, Drigotas, and Graetz, 1993; Drigotas, Insko, and Schopler, 1998) that document what they label the **discontinuity effect.** In a variety of laboratory studies involving small groups, these investigators consistently found that individuals are more competitive and less cooperative when they are interacting in a context where group membership is salient than when they are more focused on the interpersonal nature of their interactions. Intergroup interactions, in short, tend to bring out the competitiveness in people. The investigators suggested a couple of possible reasons for this effect. One is that greed or self-interest is more salient in intergroup relations than in the interpersonal context. Individuals may have received support from their groups in the past for "taking all they can" from other groups, but no such support is available for purely interpersonal interactions. A second possibility is that people may harbor "fear" of outgroups, believing them to be competitive, dishonest, and aggressive. They may, therefore, react competitively when they view the situation as involving intergroup relations rather than interpersonal relations.

Another explanation for the competitiveness of groups is based on **social identity theory** (Tajfel, 1970; Tajfel and Turner, 1986; see chapter 7). Recall that social identity theory argues that part of our identity (our social identity) is based on the groups to which we belong. Because most people wish to create the most positive identity possible, they are motivated to join attractive groups. In addition to joining the best groups, individuals will do all they can to enhance the position of their own groups relative to that of outgroups (groups of which they are not members). Enhancing one's group may occur through biased perceptions (focusing on the good points of one's own group and the bad points of outgroups) and discriminating against outgroups (giving more points, money, or opportunities to the ingroup and withholding these from the outgroups). Therefore, simply categorizing the social landscape into an ingroup and outgroups sets up the motivation to compete against outgroups (Turner, 1987). Greater competition arises in the intergroup setting (the discontinuity effect) because it is clear that the opponent is not a member of one's ingroup. In the interpersonal situation, on the other hand, competition may be muted because the involved parties may categorize each other as being members of the same group (both students, both farmers and mountain people, or both residents of Vukovar).

Regardless of the underlying cause, it is clear that in many situations, relationships between people deteriorate when they view themselves as belonging to different groups. Both perceptions and behaviors are affected in these cases, which might be of little consequence except for the fact that our relationships so often become tinged with an intergroup perspective even when they do not involve actual groups of people. When Randolph McCoy saw "his" pigs in Floyd Hatfield's pen, his response was not solely that Floyd was a thief; rather, he shouted that this was an example of the Hatfields "up to their no good, again." And Floyd's reaction was based on the fact that he saw the McCoys trying to bully the Hatfields. The interpersonal quickly became the intergroup. Similarly, in our own interactions it takes very little to entice us to categorize the other person into a group (woman, psychology major, student, Democrat) and to emphasize the "group" tone of our interaction. As these examples illustrate, intergroup relations may involve interactions between large numbers of people from different groups, or they may involve relations between two people who are viewed as representing different groups. Because of the wide scope involved in intergroup relations, it is important to understand the processes involved and the steps that can be taken to improve the relationship. Let's begin our study of intergroup relations with an examination of how the formation of groups affects the perceptions of the ingroup and outgroups.

Setting the Battlefield: The Role of Cognition in Creating Groups

We can present the famous "pig incident" in many ways. The simplest is to suggest that two men disagreed about which owned the pigs in Floyd Hatfield's pigsty. This seems to be quite a reasonable approach from our perspective as outsiders. If we were to act as a judge or jury in this situation, we'd probably limit our concern to which of the two men could prove ownership of the porkers. But this was not the perspective of either Floyd Hatfield or Randolph McCoy. Although they were related by marriage, each saw the dispute as concerning two groups, the Hatfields and the McCoys. Indeed, there is a tendency for humans to view interpersonal relationships as involving intergroup relations (Moya, 1998; Deschamps and Devos, 1998). More recently, this tendency was exhibited in the murder trial of O. J. Simpson, who was accused of killing his ex-wife Nicole Brown Simpson and her friend Ron Goldman. Much of the discussion of the incident focused on racial issues, Simpson being black and the victims white.

Our social landscape is exceedingly complex. Because we may come into contact with hundreds of people in the course of a day, it's extremely difficult to treat each one as a separate, unique entity. So, according to Turner (1987), we simplify our world by placing people, including ourselves, into categories that become the basis for dividing our world into groups. Groups, therefore, are developed and exist in our minds rather than being only a product of our environment. Indeed, we perceive our social world at three levels: the superordinate level that includes all people as human beings, the intermediate level of ingroup-outgroup based on similarities and differences between human beings, and the subordinate level that identifies us as unique individuals.

To argue that our groups are actually products of our minds is a subtle, but critical, point. Most important, it implies that perceived "groups" can change dramatically in a short period of time without physical changes in the environment. Oakes, Haslam, and Turner (1994) argue that groups are formed on the basis of elements that happen to be *salient* at the time, and that people are assigned to these groups on the rule of *fit*. Those who share common characteristics considered central to the group are placed (cognitively) within that category or group. For example, Randolph McCoy initially visited Floyd Hatfield to discuss plans for the spring planting of corn. At that time, the category of "farmer" was the salient one, and Randolph felt that he and Floyd belonged to this common category. However, upon seeing the pigs, Randolph recalled times when the members of the Hatfield clan had cheated members of the McCoy clan. Suddenly, the Hatfield-McCoy grouping became salient, and Randolph and Floyd were members of different groups.

All this might seem like innocent mind games. What harm can come from creating these cognitive groups? The answer is that the categorization of people into groups can have far-reaching consequences because we respond to people based on the groups to which they belong. Hamilton and Trollier (1986) state that the "basis for all stereotyping is the differential perception of groups. Without such differentiation between groups, stereotyping cannot occur" (p. 134). As we pointed out in chapter 7, categorization sets the stage for stereotyping because we assign characteristics to the groups that we form. For the most part, we anoint the groups to which we belong (ingroups) with positive characteristics and dump negative characteristics on outgroups (Hinkle and Schopler, 1986). And Sumner (1906) pointed out that "one's own group (becomes) the center of everything, and all others are rated and scaled with reference to it." In other words, we organize our social landscape into groups, giving our own groups the most positive descriptions and making them the center of the universe by which all other groups are judged. And we maintain our stereotypes through a combination of selective information processing efforts: selective attention, selective perception, and selective memory (see chapter 7).

Each of these processes tends to preserve the positive image of our own group. But there are other effects associated with creating ingroups and outgroups. These effects don't necessarily intrude on how positively we view the ingroup and outgroup, but they do have important implications for interactions between members of different groups. Let's consider just a few of these effects to illustrate our point.

They're All Alike

"Floyd, he's like all them other Hatfields. They're all the same, no damned good." With this pronouncement, Randolph wrapped all the Hatfields into one neat package. But this tendency is not unique to Randolph McCoy. Numerous investigators (Linville and Jones, 1980; Quattrone and Jones, 1980; Park and Rothbart, 1982) have found that we tend to notice variability within our own group and to perceive similarities within outgroups. For example, Jones, Wood, and Quattrone (1981) asked members of various eating clubs at Princeton University how members of their own eating club and other clubs could be described on a number of trait dimensions. The respondents perceived significantly greater variability between the members of their own club than between members of other clubs. In another example of this **outgroup homogeneity effect,** Park and Rothbart (1982) found that people were more likely to recall information that differentiated members of their own groups (that is, information that made members of their own group seem different from one another) than information that differentiated members of outgroups.

If people do view outgroup members as being similar, we might expect that they would generalize from an experience with one outgroup member to the whole outgroup: "know one, know them all." Indeed, Quattrone and Jones (1980) found this to be true when they had students observe the behavior of a target person. The participants were told that the target was either from their college or from a neighboring college (outgroup). Participants were more likely to state that the "average person" from the target's college would act as he did when the target person was from a neighboring college than when he supposedly came from the participant's college.

How can we explain these differences in perceptions? The most widely accepted explanation suggests that we have more experience with members of our own group than with members of outgroups (Quattrone, 1986; Rothbart and Lewis, 1994). With regard to our ingroup, we generally have frequent contact with a variety of members across a variety of situations. Our experience with the outgroup, however, is usually limited to a few members in a few situations. Therefore, we know that our group is composed of people with different views, characteristics, and preferences. However, because of our limited knowledge and experience, we are willing to believe that the outgroups are populated by people who are similar to each other.

Although there is a tendency to perceive more variability in our ingroups than in outgroups, there are some exceptions. Brown and Smith (1989) found that members of minority groups viewed their groups as being more homogeneous than did members of majority groups. And Worchel, Coutant-Sassic, and Grossman (1992) found that members of newly formed groups perceived their groups as homogeneous *and* described themselves as "typical" of the members of the group. In these cases, acceptance by the group may have been especially important to the individuals. Viewing themselves as typical members of a homogeneous group may have increased their feeling of belonging to the group.

The tendency to view outgroups as homogeneous has important consequences for interaction between members of different groups. Recalling our discussion of person perception in chapter 2, we reported that people often attribute the behavior of others to internal dispositions (traits). If we combine this tendency

with the belief that all members of the outgroup are similar, we find that observers are likely to develop stereotypes of outgroups based on very little information. In order to illustrate this chain of events, imagine a prospective student paying his first visit to your university. As he steps off the bus, he is bumped by a student who is rushing to class. Our prospective student concludes that the offending individual is clumsy and rude (attributes behavior to internal dispositions). Further, he concludes that all students at the university are clumsy and rude, a logical conclusion if he believes that all students at your university are similar. Armed with this view, the student spends the remainder of his visit focusing on examples of clumsiness and rudeness (selective information processing).

One further consequence of deciding that all members of the outgroup are similar is that we are likely to restrict our interaction with members of the outgroup. If you believe that all the Hatfields are similar, you only have to meet one or two members of the clan to "know" what they are all like. This perspective not only limits your desire to interact with many different members of the group but also reduces the opportunities you will have to change your impression of the group. Therefore, the tendency to view outgroups as homogeneous combined with the motivation to perceive ingroups more positively than outgroups has wide-ranging implications for intergroup behavior and can increase the chances of intergroup conflict.

Extremity of Evaluations

One effect of being a member of a group is that it influences the extremity of our evaluations of other ingroup members and members of the outgroup. The direction of this extremity effect has been the source of some controversy, however. In an early study, Linville and Jones (1980) asked white college students to rate a black or white law school applicant. In some cases, the description of the applicant showed him to be either a strong or weak candidate. The findings indicated that the black (outgroup) applicant was rated more extremely than the white (ingroup) applicant. In other words, when the description was positive, the black applicant was rated more favorably than the white applicant. When the description indicated that the applicant had weak credentials, however, the black applicant was rated more negatively than the white applicant. Linville (1982) argued that our evaluations of outgroup members are more extreme because we generally have less complex information about outgroups than about ingroups. Therefore, information we receive about an outgroup member can strongly influence our evaluations of him or her.

Although this position seems logical, Marques, Yzerbyt, and Leyens (1988) seemed to throw a monkey wrench into the situation. They had Belgian students rate the likability of either an ingroup (Belgian student) or outgroup (North African student) member who was described in either favorable or unfavorable terms. Their results indicated that more extreme ratings were given to the ingroup member. The ingroup target was rated most positively when the information was favorable and least positively when the information was negative. The investigators dubbed this latter pattern of responses the **black sheep effect,** suggesting that we generally are favorably disposed toward ingroup members except when those members are negative. In this case, the member threatens the favorable impression of the ingroup, and we react strongly by rejecting the offensive ingroup member.

How can we reconcile these seemingly opposing findings? One team of investigators has suggested that the degree to which the ingroup is important to the rater may influence the pattern of responses (Branscombe, Wann, Noel, and Coleman, 1993). They argued that people who strongly identify with the ingroup will be motivated to reject an unfavorable ingroup member, thereby showing the black sheep effect. However, individuals who have a low identification with the ingroup will be more influenced by the complexity of information they possess about the groups, and the result will be more extreme ratings of outgroup members. In their study, they asked students to evaluate the author of a newspaper article on a basketball game. In some cases, the author was a member of the student's university (ingroup member), and in other cases, the author was from the rival university (outgroup member). In the article, the author either strongly supported his university's team (loyal) or did not support the team (disloyal). As can be seen in figure 12.1, those raters who indicated that they strongly identified with their school's basketball team rated the ingroup author more extremely than the outgroup author. In contrast, those raters who had little identification with their school's basketball team showed the opposite pattern of ratings, with the most extreme ratings going to the outgroup author.

Our evaluations of others may be influenced not only by the group to which they belong but also by our identification with our ingroup and the favorability of the target's behavior. Jones (1948) reported similar patterns of responses from members of the Hatfield clan. Hatfields who were strongly involved in the feud were

FIGURE 12.1   EVALUATIONS OF INGROUP AND OUTGROUP TARGETS

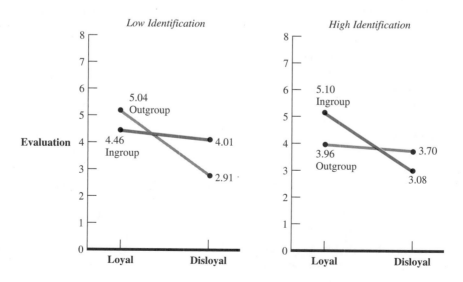

Note: Higher numbers indicate more positive evaluations.
Source: Branscombe, Wann, Noel, and Coleman (1993)

very judgmental of their own clan members. Those who expressed extreme contempt for the McCoys were viewed very positively, but those who were unwilling to give blanket condemnation of the McCoys were quickly rejected. The Hatfield clan members who were less involved in the feud, however, were rather accepting of their own clan members regardless of their opinions. Also, these less involved Hatfields condemned McCoys who attacked the Hatfields but spoke kindly of McCoys who refrained from attacks.

Belief in a Just World

One of the most provocative theories in social psychology is Lerner's **just-world theory** (1980; Lerner and Miller, 1978). Lerner proposed that people *want* to believe, and generally *do* believe, that the world is a fair and just place. There is evidence that this belief in a just world can contribute to intergroup conflict. By a "just" world, Lerner meant a place where people usually get what they deserve: hard work and virtue are rewarded, laziness and vice punished. Lerner argued that the belief in a just world is adaptive (in fact, essential) and develops during childhood. Infants enter the world wanting to satisfy all of their impulses immediately and to avoid all pain (the **pleasure principle**). Eventually they learn that if they delay gratification or incur short-term costs, they can sometimes obtain even more rewards (the **reality principle**). For example, parents might promise their daughter a reward if she cleans her room. But willingness to incur the "costs" of cleaning her room will depend on the assumption that the world is an orderly place where promises are kept and agreements are honored. Therefore, Lerner proposed that children must develop a belief that the world is generally fair to be willing to delay gratification or incur costs.

Many sources of information in society support the sanctity of individuals' belief in a just world. In fairy tales, the prince and princess always find happiness in the end. In the mass media, stories of criminals being captured and punished are prominent. Ideologies emphasize the relation between personal actions and ultimate success (for example, the Protestant work ethic). And, of course, our world often *is* fair—hardworking students do tend to get higher grades, thoughtful people do have many friends, careful investments often do produce profits, and so on.

Unfortunately, if believing that the world is a just place means that people get what they deserve, it also

This twenty-year-old mother of two children, after losing her job and running out of money, was forced to move into a family shelter. Pending approval of the welfare agency, she hopes to move into an apartment. She finds it hard both to look for work and take care of an infant and a two-year-old. Some people derogate unemployed welfare recipients as a group for being "unreliable" or "lazy."

implies that people *deserve what they get*. That is, successful people must have "earned" their success, and unsuccessful people must have somehow brought on their failures. After all, if the world is just, then winners must be better or more deserving people than losers. Thus, this belief can result in people derogating victims, a phenomenon that has been documented in many studies (see Furnham and Proctor, 1989; Lerner, 1980; Montada and Lerner, 1998).

If this tendency to derogate those who are unsuccessful is applied to groups, then people might believe that minority groups, who are typically disadvantaged, must be responsible for their own plight. Similarly, victims of various negative events must be

---

FIGURE 12.2 MOST COMMON MEANS OF DELEGITIMIZATION

1. *Dehumanization:* labeling a group as inhuman by characterizing members as different from the human race—using either categories of subhuman creatures, such as "inferior races" and animals, or categories of negatively valued superhuman creatures, such as demons, monsters, and satans.

2. *Trait characterization:* describing a group as possessing extremely negative traits that are unacceptable in a given society, such as aggressors, idiots, or parasites.

3. *Outcasting:* categorizing members of a group as transgressors of such pivotal social norms that they should be excluded from society and/or institutionalized—for example, murderers, thieves, psychopaths, or maniacs.

4. *Use of political labels:* describing a group as a political entity that threatens the basic values of the given society, is a danger to its system, and is therefore totally unacceptable—for example, Nazis, fascists, communists, or imperialists.

5. *Group comparison:* labeling with the name of a group that is negatively perceived, such as "Vandals" or "Huns." Each society has a cultural repertoire of groups that serve as symbols of malice, evil, or wickedness.

Source: Bar-Tal (1990), pp. 65–66

---

blameworthy. Unemployed persons are "unreliable workers," welfare recipients "don't want to work," rape victims "behaved riskily," and AIDS victims are "suffering the consequences of a sexually promiscuous life-style." These kinds of **victim blaming** are very common and also imply that assistance or help may not be warranted because the victims caused their own misfortune. Thus, in intergroup relations, the belief in a just world can contribute to outgroup derogation and opposition to programs of assistance.

Delegitimization: An Extreme Form of Categorization

As we have seen, there is a tendency to divide our social world into us and them, ingroups and outgroups. And we generally look on our own group more favorably than the outgroups. At times, however, this process can be carried to extremes. Bar-Tal (1990) coined the term **delegitimization** to describe "categorization of a group or groups into extremely negative social categories that are excluded from the realm of acceptable norms and/or values" (p. 65). In other words, delegitimization involves excluding the target group from the perceived "world" of humanity. Figure 12.2 describes the most common means used to delegitimize a group. As you can see, the process involves denying the relevance of traditional values and morals to the target group, and it implies that the target group does not deserve humane treatment. The belief in a just world can support this connection between negative categorization and negative treatment.

According to Bar-Tal, delegitimization is most likely to occur when people perceive great threat to their ingroup or when they strongly identify with their group. In both of these cases, individuals desire a clear structure to their social world and experience a sense of urgency to act toward the outgroup. They want a fast, simple, and unequivocal foundation on which to base their actions. Delegitimization provides this foundation. It characterizes the outgroup as dangerous and justifies responding to the group with violence and harm. Such labels as "terrorist" or "fascist" encourage extreme forms of discrimination and aggression against the target and define the outgroup as a threat to the ingroup's existence.

Viewed in these terms, delegitimization plays two sinister roles in intergroup relations. On one hand, it provokes harm against the outgroup. Labeling the outgroup as inhuman or evil instigates discrimination and aggression. "They are evil and threatening and therefore we must harm them." On the other hand, delegitimization may follow incidents of harm. In this situation, the negative labels justify the mistreatment aimed at the outgroup. "We harmed them because they are evil and a threat to our group."

Bar-Tal (1990) presents several examples of delegitimization in extreme conflicts. At the height of the Cold War, many United States politicians accused the Soviet Union of seeking world dominance; it was the "Evil Empire" that had no respect for human rights or human life (Bronfenbrenner, 1961; White, 1984). Early settlers justified their brutal treatment of Indians by delegitimizing them: "Without religion or

government, having nothing more than diverse super-
stitions and a type of democracy similar to that of ants"
(Forbes, 1964, pp. 16–17). And slavery was justified in
the description of blacks as being barbarians (Stampp,
1956). Delegitimization has also frequently characterized the interactions between Israeli Jews and the Palestinians, prolonging the conflict and keeping the two
sides separate and distrusting of each other.

Fanning the Flames: Emotions and Intergroup Conflict

In the preceding section, we focused on the role of
cognition in the perception of groups. The tendency to
categorize people into groups was shown to have consequences like ingroup favoritism and perceived outgroup homogeneity. But intergroup conflict does not
arise solely from cognitive factors. Emotions can fan
the flames: anger, fear, and other kinds of feelings can
intensify hostility and aggression.

Relative Deprivation

Relative deprivation is the feeling of resentment that
occurs when individuals believe that their own or their
group's outcomes are unfair. It refers to the emotional
experience of injustice—people feel unjustly deprived
of a reward or outcome. What factors cause people to
feel unjustly treated? And what are the behavioral
consequences of such feelings? These are the questions that theorists of relative deprivation have attempted to answer.

Causes of Relative Deprivation

Probably the most influential recent theorist of relative deprivation has been Faye Crosby (1976, 1982).
Crosby proposed a model of the causes of relative deprivation, in which she suggested that perceivers will
feel resentful about their outcomes only when they see
other people, who are similar to themselves, possessing something desirable that they feel they deserve
too. When perceivers see other people possessing an
object or outcome that they want and to which they
feel entitled, they will experience anger or resentment.
For example, someone will feel resentful about his or
her salary to the extent that he or she (1) wants or

needs a higher salary and (2) feels that he or she deserves a higher salary (other people doing the same
work are earning more money). These critical factors
of "wanting" and "deserving" (or entitlement) are presumed to cause resentment because they imply that
there are no good reasons why the perceivers do not
possess the desired object themselves.

Many researchers have tested Crosby's model of
relative deprivation. Olson, Roese, Meen, and Robertson (1995) surveyed sixty-two working women who
varied considerably in their own objective conditions—
the sample included low-wage secretaries, nurses, managers, and university professors. Participants completed
a questionnaire that assessed their resentment about
their own job situation and their resentment about the
status of women as a group in the workforce; that is,
respondents reported the extent to which they felt
angry about their own job situation (*personal* relative
deprivation) and the extent to which they felt angry
about the job situations of women as a group (*group*
relative deprivation). In addition, participants were
asked a variety of items that tapped possible preconditions (causes) of these feelings of resentment. Results showed that perceptions of wanting and
deserving were critical predictors of resentment. For
example, the extent to which respondents wanted a
better job for themselves and felt that they personally
deserved a better job predicted their dissatisfaction
with their own job situation (but not their dissatisfaction with the job situations of women as a group). In
contrast, the extent to which respondents thought that
women in general wanted and deserved better jobs
predicted their dissatisfaction with the job situations
of women as a group (but not their dissatisfaction with
their own job). Thus, personal and group relative deprivation were distinct constructs: women who were
most angry about the job situations of women as a
group were not necessarily unhappy with their own
job situations. In addition, the determinants of personal and group relative deprivation were distinguish-
able, with the former emotion dependent upon how
much perceivers wanted and felt entitled to a better
job for themselves and the latter emotion dependent
upon how much perceivers thought that women as a
group wanted and deserved better outcomes.

Consequences of Relative Deprivation

The importance of relative deprivation for understanding intergroup conflict rests on the assumption

that resentment has important behavioral consequences. In short, theorists have assumed that people who feel angry about their group's status will act in constructive or destructive ways to change the status quo. Has evidence supported this assumption?

The answer to this question is affirmative—relative deprivation does predict behavior. The intensity of the emotion is particularly important. As we have already explained, relative deprivation is the feeling of resentment that results from the cognitive perception that oneself or one's group is poorly treated. The

Francophones in Quebec protest a 1992 constitutional reform package for keeping Canada unified. Support for the independence movement is based more on anger about how Francophones are treated than on the simple perception of the nature of their treatment.

feeling of resentment seems more important for behavior than the simple perception of poor treatment. For example, Guimond and Dubé-Simard (1983) surveyed Francophones in Quebec to rate how well or badly they were treated and to report their anger about this treatment. Support for the independence movement in Quebec (the movement to have the province of Quebec withdraw from Canada to form a separate country) was predicted by respondents' anger about the status of Francophones but not by their simple ratings of how well or badly Francophones were treated. Thus, for example, if someone believed that Francophones were treated poorly but was not angry about this treatment, he or she tended not to support the independence movement, whereas if someone believed that Francophones were treated neutrally but was angry about this treatment, he or she tended to support the independence movement strongly. In a similar demonstration, Tougas and Veilleux (1988) found that the intensity of working women's anger about the treatment of women predicted their support for affirmative action programs better than did beliefs about the objective status of working women. Again, the emotion of relative deprivation was associated with support for actions designed to address the deprivation, whereas the simple perception of deprivation did not predict support as well.

Another important hypothesis concerning the behavioral effects of relative deprivation is that personal relative deprivation has different consequences than group relative deprivation. To be specific, if individuals are dissatisfied with their condition, they may engage in behaviors designed to improve it, such as looking for a new job or obtaining additional qualifications. In contrast, if individuals are dissatisfied with the condition of their group, they may engage in behaviors designed to improve the group's condition, such as protest marches or collective action. Thus, to understand intergroup behaviors (which, obviously, are at the group level), we need to know people's resentment about the treatment of their group, not their satisfaction or dissatisfaction with their own treatment. This hypothesis is consistent with the historical observation that revolutions and protests have often been led, not by people who are among the most downtrodden, but rather by people who may be reasonably well-off themselves but who feel keenly that their group has been treated unfairly (see Gurr, 1970).

In a test of this reasoning, Dubé and Guimond (1986) surveyed 146 students at the University of

Montreal less than three months after an intense period of protest had occurred on the campus in support of Quebec nationalism. Students were asked to report their discontent with their own personal situation at the university (personal relative deprivation) and their discontent with the collective situation of students in Quebec (group relative deprivation). They also reported the extent of their involvement in ten protest actions that had occurred, ranging from mild actions like meeting the administration to more militant actions like occupying buildings and boycotting classes. Each participant was classified as either high or low on personal discontent and high or low on group discontent, and each received an "activism" score that reflected his or her involvement in the collective actions. Table 12.1 presents the mean activism scores for the various groups of students. Group discontent was strongly predictive of activism, with high-group-discontent individuals engaging in much more activism than low-group-discontent individuals. Personal discontent was not significantly related to activism.

Dubé and Guimond's study showed that group relative deprivation, not personal relative deprivation, predicted collective, group-directed actions. But what about individual, self-directed actions? Presumably, personal discontent should predict such actions better than group discontent. In the study of working women described earlier, Olson and his associates (1995) asked respondents how willing they would be to engage in various behaviors. Some actions were self-directed, self-improvement behaviors (such as increase productivity to get a better job, obtain training to increase qualifications), other actions were group-directed and

normative (such as join a women's action group, sign a petition), and a final set of actions were group-directed and counternormative (such as sabotage the job performance of someone who is unsympathetic to the plight of women, join a work slowdown). The self-improvement behaviors were best predicted by measures of personal relative deprivation, whereas the group-directed behaviors (both normative and counternormative) were best predicted by measures of group relative deprivation. Thus, each type of relative deprivation was associated with behavioral consequences, but the particular actions differed for personal resentment versus group resentment.

Box 12.1 describes a study that drew connections between relative deprivation and the belief in a just world. The researchers tested the hypothesis that people who believe strongly that the world is a fair place will tend not to report much relative deprivation.

The Threat of Similarity

Perceived similarity wears two masks, one in interpersonal relationships and a different one in intergroup relationships. As discussed in chapter 8, we are attracted to people who are similar to us (Byrne, 1971). Likewise, similarity between people encourages placing them into the same category. Similarity can take many forms, including physical appearance, attitudes, and beliefs. Horwitz and Rabbie (1989) suggested that sharing a common fate or similar experience is one of the most important characteristics for creating an ingroup. But once distinct groups have been formed, similarities between groups can fan the flames of intergroup conflict. Indeed, the similarities between the Hatfields and McCoys were so striking that historians often dwelled on them (Rice, 1978). As we pointed out earlier, we tend to compare ourselves with similar others, but similarity between groups can obscure the unique identity of our own group. Similarity can also be threatening if another group is doing better than our own.

In an effort to demonstrate the role of similarity in intergroup relations, Rothgerber and Worchel (1997) examined the relationship between groups of varying status. The investigators suggested that minority groups often compare themselves with each other, and to find that one disadvantaged group is prospering can be particularly threatening to the others. In their study, participants were divided into three groups. The experimenter told them that one group would work

TABLE 12.1   **ACTIVISM AS A FUNCTION OF PERSONAL DISCONTENT AND GROUP DISCONTENT**

| | | Personal Discontent | |
		Low	High
Group Discontent	Low	21.0 ($n = 51$)	27.6 ($n = 7$)
	High	41.9 ($n = 30$)	43.0 ($n = 35$)

Note: Entries are means on the activism scale ranging from 10 (not at all active) to 90 (frequently active in various protest actions). *Source:* Dubé and Guimond (1986), p. 209

BOX 12.1
Beliefs in a Just World and Relative Deprivation

Lerner (1980) hypothesized that people need to believe that the world is a fair and just place where they generally get what they deserve. We have already discussed how this belief can lead people to blame or derogate victims and members of minority groups. One interesting direction that researchers have taken is toward identifying people who differ in the *strength* of their belief in a just world. Rubin and Peplau (1975) developed a scale to measure individual differences in the belief in a just world, and subsequent researchers have shown that strong and weak believers differ in their reactions to others' misfortunes, with strong believers exhibiting more derogation of victims than weak believers (see Furnham and Proctor, 1989).

But what about instances of our own misfortune, deprivation, or suffering? Isn't the occurrence of bad things to ourselves or to our ingroup inconsistent with a belief in a just world given that we presumably regard ourselves and our ingroup as good? If so—and if we want to maintain our belief—then perhaps we might downplay the extent of our deprivation or even blame ourselves or our ingroup for misfortunes. Further, this tendency should be stronger among people who believe firmly in a just world than among weak believers.

To test this idea, Hafer and Olson (1993) recruited seventy working women who represented a broad range of occupation types and salary levels (ranging from secretaries to medical doctors). These women first completed a questionnaire that assessed their resentment about their own job situation (personal relative deprivation), their resentment about the job situation of women generally (group relative deprivation), and the strength of their belief in a just world.

One month later, the women completed another questionnaire, which measured a wide variety of behaviors potentially related to discontent. Twenty items assessed self-directed actions designed to improve the respondent's own job situation, such as "Looked for another job," "Obtained information about courses I can take to improve my professional qualifications," and "Increased the quality of my work so I can get ahead." Another twenty items assessed group-directed actions designed to improve the status of working women as a group, such as "Argued in favor of giving women special opportunities for jobs," "Signed a petition which expresses concern about an issue involving working women," and "Supported a walkout or strike (either by actively participating or by offering moral support) meant to protest the status of working women." Participants were instructed to place a check mark beside all behaviors that they had performed in the past month.

The strength of participants' belief in a just world was significantly correlated with their reports of group relative deprivation. Specifically, consistent with the expected impact of just-world beliefs, strong believers in a just world reported less resentment about the status of working women than did weak believers. Perhaps strong believers were inclined to assume that disparities between men and women in the workplace either were minor or were justified. Beliefs in a just world did not predict personal relative deprivation (participants' dissatisfaction with their own jobs).

Even more interesting were the findings that beliefs in a just world predicted participants' reports of behaviors potentially related to discontent. Beliefs in a just world predicted both self-directed and group-directed actions, with strong believers engaging in significantly fewer of both kinds of behaviors than weak believers. Thus, strong believers in a just world were less likely than weak believers to report having worked to improve either their own job situation or the job situations of women as a group. Strong believers seemed

Continued

BOX 12.1

Continued

to be more satisfied with the status quo than weak believers, which makes sense given that they perceived the status quo (the current world) to be generally fair.

Consistent with our discussion earlier in the chapter, the behavior measures were also predicted by the "appropriate" measures of resentment. That is, the self-directed behaviors were predicted by respondents' per-

sonal relative deprivation (but not by their group relative deprivation), whereas the group-directed behaviors were predicted by respondents' group relative deprivation (but not by their personal relative deprivation). Thus, individual differences in both beliefs in a just world and relative deprivation were shown to predict assertive actions designed to change the status quo.

under ideal environmental conditions (advantaged group), whereas the other two groups would have to work under impoverished conditions (disadvantaged groups). The groups would work on a series of tasks and receive feedback about their performance and that of the other groups after each task. All participants were led to believe that they were in a disadvantaged group. They were also led to believe that their group was performing relatively poorly on each task and that the advantaged group always did well. The feedback they received about the performance of the other disadvantaged group, however, was varied. Some participants were led to believe that the other disadvantaged group was performing better than their own group, whereas other participants believed that the other disadvantaged group was performing either similarly to, or worse than, their own group. Later in the procedure, participants were given the opportunity to help or injure one of the outgroups.

Participants were more likely to injure the other disadvantaged group when it did better than or equal to their own group; they behaved kindly to the other disadvantaged group only when it was performing poorly. Figure 12.3 presents the results of the study. Participants' verbal reports indicated they were likely to compare their group with the other disadvantaged group. When the other disadvantaged group was doing better than or equal to their own group, the comparison was not favorable and participants did not like the group. But when the disadvantaged outgroup was doing poorly, a favorable comparison resulted and the outgroup was liked. Participants reported that they were less likely to compare themselves with the advantaged outgroup because it labored under different conditions.

Hence, perceived similarity between the groups invited comparisons, and when the comparisons introduced threat because they were unfavorable to the ingroup, the outgroup was disliked. Emotions fanned the flames ignited by group categorization.

The Escalating Path of Conflict

It seems almost incredible that a disagreement about the ownership of some pigs could have grown into a feud that lasted over fifty years, resulted in the death of one hundred people, and drew two states (West Virginia and Kentucky) to a point of confrontation. Indeed, after a number of years, few on either side remembered the details of the situation that started their feud, but neither side was prepared to call it quits. Although the intensity of this conflict is unusual, the path of escalation is not. Rather than burning itself out after a time, conflict left untended often grows in intensity and the number of people involved. Deutsch (1973) referred to this course as the **conflict spiral.** As we will see, conflict often leads two sides to distrust each other and cease communication. Individuals become entrapped in the conflict, feeling that they have few alternatives besides conflict and disagreement (Brockner and Rubin, 1985). Each side attempts to threaten and cajole the other, and winning becomes more important than resolving the discord.

We have already described cognitive factors that produce perceptions of groups and emotional factors like anger and threat that can intensify con-

FIGURE 12.3 HARM AS A FUNCTION OF DISADVANTAGED OUTGROUP PERFORMANCE

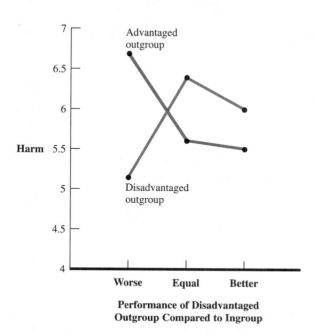

Source: Rothgerber and Worchel (1997)

flict. There are also a host of factors that conspire to maintain or even escalate conflict. Let's examine some of these forces to see why conflict, once initiated, tends to grow.

Use of Threats and Counterthreats

When Preacher Anse Hatfield rendered his decision that Floyd Hatfield should retain possession of the pigs, Randolph McCoy vowed revenge. Two nights after the trial, bullets smashed into Floyd's house. Not long afterward, Sam McCoy killed Bill Stanton. Each family armed itself to the teeth, attempting to demonstrate to the other side that it was the stronger. But all the saber rattling and threats did not force a resolution. Rather, each threat increased the intensity of the conflict.

Threats are "messages of the intention by [one person or group] to behave in ways that are detrimental to the interests of [another person or group], depending on what the latter does or does not do" (Rubin, Pruitt, and Kim, 1994, p. 58). According to Rubin and his colleagues (1994), threats are one of the most common responses to conflict. They cost the ini-

tiator nothing and can gain concessions, especially when the target is weak. However, threats may not be as effective as we think in most situations.

In an interesting experiment, Rothbart and Hallmark (1988) asked participants to play the role of a defense minister of a nation involved in a conflict in which both parties were developing threatening weapons. When asked to indicate the tactic that would be most likely to lead to a settlement, participants reported that their nation would respond most positively if the other nation made some conciliatory response, such as reducing the level of its threatening weapons. However, they believed that the other nation would be most likely to agree to settle the conflict in response to an increased threat. Thus, we see ourselves as being most influenced by a reduction in threat, but we see others as being most influenced by increased threat! In fact, research suggests that our beliefs about how others will respond to increased threat are inaccurate; threat typically leads to spiraling conflict.

In one of the earliest experiments on the effects of threat (Deutsch and Krauss, 1960), participants played a "trucking game" in which they imagined that they were heads of opposing trucking companies (Acme and Bolt). The players' task was to move their truck from the start to the finish as quickly as possible; the quicker the trip, the more money the player earned. The participants were then shown a road map (see figure 12.4) that indicated that each player could take two routes to the finish. The longest route was filled with curves, so a player taking this route was sure to lose money on the trip. The second route was the most direct but had a stretch of one-lane road. If the players' trucks met on this road, neither could proceed unless one of the trucks backed up. Here was the point of conflict: which player would back up and let the other pass?

To make matters more interesting, Deutsch and Krauss also built in a manipulation of "threat." At each end of the one-lane section, there was a gate that was under the control of the player whose starting point was closest to that end. By closing the gate, one player could prevent the other player's truck from reaching its destination by way of the one-lane section. Each player's gate was a threat because the player could close it (thus preventing the other from passing) and then take the alternate route. Deutsch and Krauss ran three conditions by varying the availability of the gates: no threat (no gates), unilateral threat (only one player has a gate), and bilateral threat (both players have gates). After each trial, the experimenter

FIGURE 12.4   ROAD MAP IN DEUTSCH AND KRAUSS TRUCKING GAME

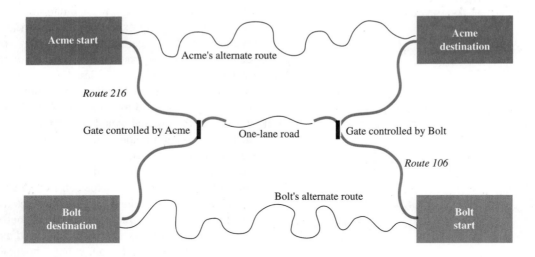

Source: Deutsch and Krauss (1960)

announced how much each player had won or lost. The game was played over twenty trials.

The results indicated quite dramatically that the best payoffs occurred when neither player had access to a threat, and the worst payoffs occurred when both players could threaten. The results are presented in table 12.2. Profit was realized only in the no-threat condition. The presence of either a unilateral or bilateral threat resulted in *both* players losing money. Moreover, a unilateral threat was better for both players (even the low-power player) than bilateral threat. These results indicate that the greater the threat potential in a conflict situation, the harder it is to work out a cooperative solution. In fact, it has been suggested that the use of threats might itself be a sign that negotiations are breaking down and the parties are far from achieving a resolution (Barner-Barry and Rosenwein, 1985).

Terrorism: The Threat of the Weak

In recent times, new and more dramatic terrorist acts seem to occur every year. In some cases the act involves the bombing of a building or airplane; in other cases terrorism comes in the form of a kidnapping or a hostage taking. Recent examples include an occupation of the Japanese embassy in Lima, Peru, which ended with the death of one hostage and all of the hostage-takers, a drive-by shooting that killed two Jews in Israel, and terrorist bombings that injured or killed bystanders in

France, Russia, Ireland, and Spain. Each of us is left to wonder, "Will I be the next victim?"

Terrorism is actual or threatened violence against noncombatants for avowed political ends (McCauley and Segal, 1987). The aim of terrorism, unlike many situations we have discussed, is not an immediate resolution to conflict or even to short-term goals. The major aim of terrorism is to achieve worldwide attention and to instill widespread fear (Friedland, 1988). Terrorists capture attention by enlisting the media. A terrible fire that claims the life of several people may receive little more than a note in a local newspaper. But a hostage-taking by terrorists is likely to make headlines in newspapers around the world until the situation is resolved.

Beyond the goal of arousing fear, terrorists aim to create conflict within the governments involved. Governments are placed in a no-win situation. If they take a hard-line stand and refuse to negotiate, they jeopardize the safety of innocent people and risk being branded as cold and uncaring. If they negotiate and make concessions to the terrorists, the governments will be seen as weak and may invite future acts of terrorism. Thus, terrorists create conflict within a conflict. In an effort to enhance the level of chaos and conflict, terrorists often target the most innocent as their victims: children, women, the elderly. And they make rather modest demands, such as the release of a few prisoners or the opportunity to get their message to the world. In this way, terrorists enlist the aid of the public

TABLE 12.2   PAYOFFS IN THE DEUTSCH AND KRAUSS TRUCKING GAME

	Means		
Variable	No Threat	Unilateral Threat (Acme has threat)	Bilateral Threat
Summed payoffs (Acme and Bolt)	203.31	−405.88	−875.12
Acme's payoff	122.44	−118.56	−406.56
Bolt's payoff	80.88	−287.31	−468.56

Source: Deutsch and Krauss (1960)

to put pressure on governments to negotiate (Merari and Friedland, 1988).

Terrorists also often count on the fact that their threats and violence will be met with counterthreats and counterviolence by their target, thereby escalating the scope of the conflict (Worchel, in press). For example, a terrorist act such as a bombing in Israel conducted by Hamas generally ignites a swift retaliation by the Israelis. The retaliation may include closing the border to Palestinian workers or the bombing of a village in Lebanon that is suspected of housing the terrorists. The response is not only of greater intensity than the initial terrorist act, but it often affects a large number of people, many of whom were not involved with the terrorists. Because they are impacted by the retaliatory acts, many of these people will view the Israelis as aggressors and be more willing to support the terrorist faction in the future.

Terrorism is generally a response to conflict by a weak group with few resources. By itself, a single act of terrorism is generally not effective in achieving political goals or in overthrowing governments. But the acts can have broad implications and exact great costs from the target. For example, in 1983, terrorist acts worldwide resulted in the deaths of 720 people and injuries to 963 people (Cordes, Hoffman, Jenkins, Kellen, Moran, and Slater, 1984). During that same year, there were close to 45,000 deaths in traffic accidents in the United States alone. Yet the terrorism prompted the U.S. government to institute broad security measures in airports and greatly increase the number of law enforcement officials assigned to deal with terrorism. The cost ran to multimillions of dollars (Merari and Friedland, 1985). In addition, countless numbers of people changed or canceled travel plans, and others feared for their lives and safety. The point is that when terrorism is stirred into the stew of intergroup conflict, the impact can be quite dramatic and wide-ranging, generally escalating the degree and scope of the conflict.

The Importance of Saving Face

It seems to be an increasingly common practice in many countries to resolve conflicts in the courts. Whether the conflicts involve two individuals in a divorce or countries in dispute over boundaries or trade practice, the courts are an increasingly popular forum in which to air disputes. Indeed, when Floyd and Randolph disagreed over ownership of the pigs, they took their problem into the court of Preacher Anse Hatfield. Although we do not wish to debate the merits and demerits of the court system, one of the consequences of submitting conflicts to courts is that the dispute and its resolution become public. In Randolph's case, Anse Hatfield's decision not only resulted in his loss of the pigs, he also lost face in front of the whole community. The trial was the center of attention in their small corner of the world, and people packed the courtroom. Some people snickered after the verdict that the McCoys couldn't even "keep their pigs at home."

If we examine conflicts closely, we find that participants have two motives. One is to gain as much as possible from the eventual resolution of the conflict. The second goal, often more important than the first, is to appear strong and tough (recall our discussion of self-presentation motives in chapter 4). Group appearances in conflict are important for a number of reasons. If opposing groups perceive the group as weak or reluctant to take a strong stand, they may act to take advantage of this weakness by making more extreme demands. Second, as we pointed out, groups survive by their ability to retain existing members and to attract new members.

Hence, it is important that groups have a positive public image. As a result, when the conflict gets played out in a public forum, groups often take a more extreme position and attempt to portray their strength by being unyielding (Moscovici and Doise, 1994).

The concern with appearances in conflict situations is referred to as **face-saving.** A number of investigators (Brockner and Rubin, 1985; Streufert and Streufert, 1986) have suggested that the desire to save face often motivates people to resort to threats. People may feel that yielding is an admission of weakness. Such an admission not only is a blow to one's self-esteem but also can lead to embarrassment and distress if other people witness this weakness. Brown (1968) had participants play against a confederate in another trucking game experiment. The participants

were told that they were being observed by other participants through a one-way mirror. During the first half of the experiment, the confederate had the greatest power and exploited the participants. At one point in the experiment, the participants were given notes that had supposedly been written by the observers. Half of the participants received insulting notes saying that they looked like suckers, and the other half received more flattering notes. After receiving the notes, the participants were given control of the gates and could charge the confederate a high toll to allow him to pass through. The one catch was that using the gates and charging a high toll would also reduce the participant's ability to win. The results showed that participants who felt that they had lost face during the first part of the study (that is, who received insulting notes

In 1997, after a four-month crisis, Peruvian soldiers stormed the Japanese ambassdor's mansion in Lima where terrorists were holding dozens of hostages. In this instance, the terrorists, who were probably counting on counterviolence by soldiers so that public opinion would turn against them, lost out: the soldiers guided all but one of the captives to safety and killed all the terrorists.

from the observers) were more likely to use the costly threat than participants who had not lost face.

Conditions other than public observation can also cause people to attempt to save face in conflicts. For example, the more a person has invested in a conflict, the more he or she will attempt to save face and resist yielding to demands (Teger, 1980). This investment can take the form of time, effort, personal commitment, or material. This need to rationalize investments (costs) is similar to the phenomenon of "effort justification," which we discussed in chapter 6 in the section on dissonance theory.

Trust and Distrust

Even before the "pig incident," an air of distrust hung over the relationship between the Hatfields and McCoys. Historians suggest that this dated back to the Civil War, when members of the families fought on different sides (Rice, 1978). Whatever its beginning, the lack of trust constantly worked against even the most well-intentioned efforts to reduce the conflict. The Hatfields resisted efforts to have their kin and friends tried in Kentucky courts because they believed they would not receive fair treatment. The McCoys felt the same way about their relatives going to courts in West Virginia. Even when the Hatfield clan leader, Devil Anse Hatfield, wrote a letter on December 26, 1886, expressing his sorrow for the feud and his desire to end it, the McCoys dismissed his efforts as a trick and vowed revenge for the killing of Jeff McCoy. Once distrust infected the conflict, it seemed that no force could reduce it. "The perception of the other group as untrustworthy is probably a major source of tensions leading to conflict. The history of labor/management strife, interracial violence, war, and revolution demonstrates the significance of distrust" (Webb and Worchel, 1986, p. 213).

Researchers (for example, Schlenker, Helm, and Tedeschi, 1973; Swinth, 1976) have suggested that for trust to develop, one person has to let down his or her guard and become vulnerable to see whether the other person abuses that vulnerability. Many such tests are necessary before a trusting relationship can be established.

Whereas trust is difficult to develop and a series of positive encounters are often required to develop a trusting relationship, Webb and Worchel (1986) pointed out that, often, only one betrayal is necessary to establish distrust, which is then very resistant to change. Distrust is difficult to change because it leads to the conflict spiral: the other person is perceived as a threat, which leads to conflict, which leads to even greater distrust, and so on. Once a person has committed one betrayal, it is difficult for him or her to "make up" with the other person, because the wronged individual may believe that the betrayal will recur in the future.

We have presented distrust as a rather terminal state; that is, once it develops, it continues. This is certainly true in many cases, but the tide of distrust can be reversed if the wrongdoer confesses the betrayal and convinces the wronged person that he or she is remorseful. Further, if the wrongdoer has gained from the betrayal, the wrongdoer must attempt to make restitution. Some of the most popular U.S. presidents (George Washington, Abraham Lincoln, Harry Truman) made public apologies for events in which they were involved and accepted personal blame. Truman, in fact, is famous for a plaque on his desk that read: "The buck stops here."

Communication

Implied in the concept of trust is communication; trust is built on the communication of intentions and promises, and it develops as people exchange information. Communication is also an important key to the resolution of conflict. Yet, the initial tendency of parties in a conflict is often to withdraw and cease communication. This response has been called **autistic hostility** (Newcomb, 1947), because it is a form of hostility that ignores the reality that communication is essential for the resolution of problems.

The parties soon realize, however, that communication will be necessary if the conflict is to be resolved. And here arises an interesting dilemma (McClintock, Stech, and Keil, 1983). On the one hand, neither side wants to give the other information about its strengths, weaknesses, and desires that may be used against it. On the other hand, communication is vital if the parties are to ascertain the issues and develop solutions to the problem.

The results of many studies show that, overall, communication increases the chances for a positive resolution of conflict (Grzelek, 1988). But people in conflict often must be *forced* to engage in communication, as the study described in Box 12.2 shows. The timing of communication can also be important; for example, communication later in a conflict is more likely to have a positive effect than communication early in the conflict (Stech and McClintock, 1981).

BOX 12.2

The Importance of Communication in Resolving Conflict

The experiment by Deutsch and Krauss (1960) described earlier in this chapter is one of the most famous in all of social psychology. These researchers used a trucking game to investigate the impact of threats on resolving conflict. Their study showed that the presence of any kind of threat—unilateral or bilateral—greatly reduced the payoffs for the players. It seemed that when threat was part of the equation, participants had difficulty working out a cooperative solution.

The same researchers conducted another well-known study, again utilizing the trucking game procedure, a couple of years after the first one (Deutsch and Krauss, 1962). As in the earlier study, players could either cooperate with one another and use an efficient, one-lane road that yielded profit or fail to cooperate and be forced to use a winding, inefficient road that guaranteed losses (see figure 12.4). Also as in the earlier study, threat potential was manipulated. In the bilateral threat condition, both players had a gate that they could use to close the direct, single-lane road; in the unilateral threat condition, only one player had a gate that could close the road; and in the no-threat condition, neither player had a gate.

The important addition to this study was a manipulation of the potential for *communication.* In the compulsory communication condition, players were told that they must communicate with each other; thus, these participants were forced to exchange information with their adversary. In the permissive communication condition, players were told that they could communicate with each other if they wanted to; thus, these participants could choose to communicate or not, depending on their wishes. Finally, in the no-communication condition, there was no possibility of communication or exchange of information.

The table presents the average-per-trial joint payoffs (that is, combining both players' payoffs) in the various conditions. Notice first that, as in the earlier study, the only condition in which profits (positive values) occurred was the no-threat condition. Also, the communication manipulation had little impact in this condition; the absence of threat seemed to promote cooperation with or without communication. The outcomes were quite different in the other conditions, however. When either one or both players had a gate, both players experienced losses (negative values); in addition, the extent of loss was dramatically influenced by the manipulation of communication in the unilateral threat condition. When only one player controlled a gate, compulsory communication greatly reduced the amount of loss compared with either permissive or no communication. Thus, when players were forced to communicate with their adversary, they were able to overcome the obstacles imposed by unilateral threat. On the other hand, simply having the opportunity to exchange information was not enough to avoid losses. Perhaps participants thought that voluntary communication with their adversary would be taken as a sign of weakness or willingness to compromise and, therefore, did not take advantage of the opportunity to communicate. Whatever the reason, only compulsory communication produced better outcomes than no communication in the unilateral threat condition. Not even compulsory communication, however, could overcome the negative impact of bilateral threat on payoffs: all three communication conditions experienced substantial losses when both players controlled gates. It appears that when deadlock could be imposed by either player, there was simply so much tension or distrust that a cooperative relationship could not be established no matter what communication occurred.

Continued

Continued

These findings provide reason for both optimism and pessimism about resolving real-life intergroup conflict. On the positive side, communication was shown to be capable of encouraging cooperation and improving participants' outcomes. Thus, keeping channels of communication open appeared capable of ameliorating conflict. On the negative side, participants had to be *forced* to communicate, which may be rare in real-life intergroup conflicts. Also, the presence of bilateral threat—the situation that is probably most common in real-life conflicts—produced negative outcomes in all communication conditions. Although the results in the forced communication/unilateral threat condition offer support for the benefits of communication, Deutsch and Krauss's (1962) findings are at least as discouraging as they are encouraging.

JOINT PAYOFFS (ACME PLUS BOLT) PER TRIAL IN MODIFIED TRUCKING GAME

	No Threat	Unilateral Threat	Bilateral Threat
Compulsory communication	6.09	−5.14	−41.73
Permissive communication	8.54	−34.58	−41.32
No communication	10.41	−22.13	−47.44

Source: Deutsch and Krauss (1962)

Late communication may focus attention on cooperative aspects of the relationship and ways to reduce conflict, whereas early communication often focuses on the conflict and on threats.

Reducing Conflict and Improving Intergroup Relations

As we have seen, the relationship between groups can quickly turn contentious. A disagreement between two people can become a struggle between two groups. We have examined some of the causes of conflict and identified factors that contribute to maintaining the conflict once ignited. Now we must ask the question of how intergroup conflict can be reduced or managed. If we had happened to visit Stringtown, Kentucky, in 1880 after the Hatfield-McCoy feud had erupted, what steps could we have recommended to contain the situation?

Our approach to resolving the conflict would most likely be based on our views of the *causes* of intergroup conflict. For example, at the foundation of Buddhism is the belief in the importance of individual action. The *Samyutta Nikaya* relates the story of King Kosla, who attempted to get Queen Millika, his wife, to profess her love for him. He decided on a roundabout approach, asking Millika, "Is there anyone who is more dear to you than yourself?" He was shocked when Millika answered that there was no one dearer to her than herself. The troubled king sought counsel from the great Buddha. After listening to his story, the Buddha responded, "Nowhere will you find anything more dear to you than yourself. In the same way, the self is extremely dear to others. Therefore, one who loves himself should cause no harm to another" (Kraft, 1992, p. 75). From this perspective, the resolution to conflict between even the largest groups must begin with individual action, because it is within the individual where the seeds of intergroup conflict can be found. Hence, if we take this advice, our efforts would be focused on educating individuals and helping each person secure his or her own identity.

If we believe that intergroup conflict arises from a combination of individual and group processes, however, we will broaden our search to include group

factors. And in doing this, we confront two basic approaches that have guided national programs to create harmony between ethnic and cultural groups living within a nation (Worchel, in press). These two perspectives can help us understand the goal of specific steps that we will soon examine.

Recall the discussion of social identity theory and categorization earlier in this chapter. These concepts argue that the division of people into groups lays the foundation for conflict and discrimination between the groups. Whether the categorization is accompanied by a common fate or is based on shared characteristics, members will be motivated to enhance the position of their group relative to that of outgroups. If intergroup tension is created by categorizing people into different groups, then it follows that intergroup conflict can be reduced by eliminating group boundaries and encouraging people to view themselves as members of the same group. This **recategorization** approach (Gaertner, Mann, Dovidio, Murrell, and Pomare, 1990) suggests that we could dampen the intensity of the Hatfield–McCoy feud by reducing the salience of clan identity and by inducing the members of both families to view themselves as belonging to the same, albeit larger, group, Appalachian mountain people. This is the reasoning behind the "melting pot" approach adopted by the United States and proponents of a global society (Featherstone, 1990). Proponents argue that the conflict between ethnic groups is reduced when the salience of ethnic group boundaries is reduced. Rather than emphasizing ethnic identity, individuals are encouraged to place themselves and others within a larger common category. For example, identity as an "American" or a "citizen of planet Earth" could be stressed to create a common group.

The other approach, often labeled **multiculturalism** when applied at a national level, takes the position that intergroup conflict arises when groups experience threats to their collective identity (Worchel, Coutant-Sassic, and Wong, 1993). Groups, these theorists argue, have a desire to establish secure identities that give them a unique position in the social universe. Threats to the group's identity lead members into conflict and confrontation with members of other groups in an effort to reestablish the ingroup identity (Brewer, 1991). Groups that are secure have little motivation to engage in conflict with other groups. Based on this viewpoint, intergroup conflict will be reduced to the extent that each group feels that its identity is respected by others and is positive. If we adopted this approach, we would attempt to reduce the conflict between the Hatfields and McCoys by enhancing group identity and emphasizing the positive aspects of each clan. We might, for example, have members of each clan learn more about the history of their clan and exchange this information with members of the other clan. Developing two strong and well-organized clans would allow members to negotiate more effectively with each other. Multicultural approaches are found in New Zealand, Canada, and Switzerland. In these cases, the identities of the various ethnic groups that populate the country are emphasized. Individuals are encouraged to maintain and share their native language and customs. The country itself will adopt multiple languages, celebrate the holidays of all major ethnic groups, and introduce school children to classes on the different groups. The aim of this approach is to build harmony and understanding between separate and unique groups.

As we review some of the specific actions designed to reduce conflict between groups, keep these two perspectives in mind. In many cases, the two perspectives would prescribe the same action but with different emphases. For example, we will see that contact between members of different groups can reduce conflict under some circumstances. From the recategorization perspective, the contact is valuable because it encourages individuals to recategorize themselves as belonging to the same group. However, from the multicultural perspective, the contact is useful to the extent that it maintains separate group identities but allows each group to learn about and develop an understanding of the other group. Hence, although focused on different processes, the two approaches recommend similar activities to reduce intergroup conflict.

Our discussion will make clear that reducing conflict between groups is no small task, a fact that may explain why we are surrounded by intergroup conflicts. We may take hope, however, from the knowledge that intergroup conflict *can* be resolved, and we *can* identify some of the steps that are most likely to lead to resolution.

Contact

When the feud ignited, the Hatfields tended to keep to the West Virginia side of the Big Sandy, and the McCoys stayed on the Kentucky side much of the time. They had little opportunity to discuss their differences or identify common attributes. Indeed, this lack of contact may have served to prolong the conflict. Although this is a tempting position to adopt, the story of the feud shows that some of the most violent confrontations occurred when the families were forced into contact at the election polls. In the spring election of 1880, Johnse Hatfield and Rose Anna McCoy began a romance at the Blackberry Creek precinct poll that ignited a round of violence between the clans. And at the same polling place in 1882, a fight broke out between members of the two clans that resulted in the death of Ellison Hatfield and, eventually, of three McCoys. These exam-

ples prompt us to question the role that contact plays in the resolution of conflict.

We discussed the role of contact in reducing prejudice in chapter 7. Recall that contact must satisfy certain prerequisites in order to reduce intergroup hostility. First, it must involve *cooperation;* we will elaborate on this point in the next section. Second, members of the group must be of *equal status* in order for contact to have positive consequences (Amir, 1969); that is, the situation under which the group members have contact must ensure that they have equal status or power. In many attempts to integrate schools, for example, whites who had had superior schooling were placed in schools with blacks who had had inferior schooling. When students were then given tasks that the whites were better prepared to handle

Canada is a country that attempts to support the identities of its various ethnic groups in such multicultural events as Vancouver's Pacific National Exhibition.

because of their past schooling history, this contact emphasized the differences between blacks and whites and often increased the conflict.

A third factor that increases the positive consequences of contact (which we did not mention in chapter 7) is preceding the contact with positive information about the outgroup. In a study that looked at the attitudes of Israeli tourists in Egypt (Ben-Ari and Amir, 1988), the results showed that those Israelis who had received information about Egyptians before their visit to Egypt had the most positive attitudes. Neither positive information alone (without visiting Egypt) nor contact alone (without positive information) had much effect on attitudes. Thus, the contact situation can serve to promote perceptions of outgroup members as individuals when perceivers possess positive information about the group.

Cooperation and Interdependence

One of the most productive means for reducing intergroup conflict is cooperation. For cooperation to occur, members of different groups must work together toward a **superordinate goal,** which is one that is attractive to the members of two groups but cannot be achieved without cooperation between the groups.

In Aronson's **jigsaw method** of cooperative learning discussed in chapter 7 (see Box 7.2), each member of a group of students is given a part of the lesson that he or she must present to the other group members. Under these circumstances, all the group members become motivated to help each other learn their parts of the lesson. Aronson found that when the groups were composed of people of different racial or ethnic groups, the jigsaw method reduced ethnic stereotyping and increased attraction between members of the various ethnic groups.

Cooperation is a good means to reduce hostility for a number of reasons. First, it focuses the group members' attention away from their conflict and onto trying to solve the problem that confronts them. Second, cooperation reduces the salience of the ingroup/outgroup distinction (Miller and Davidson-Podgorny, 1987; Worchel, 1986). Groups that work together become more concerned with the task at hand and are less likely to categorize themselves as ingroup and outgroup. In a sense, all the members are now one group and have increased motivation to see others in a positive light because each person is dependent on all the others.

With this point in mind, it is interesting to note that conflict is not reduced when one party offers to help the other (Worchel, Wong, and Skeltema, 1989). Similarly, foreign aid programs often engender bad feelings in the recipients (Taormina and Messick, 1983). It seems that helping, unlike cooperation, draws a distinct boundary between the helper and the recipient and places the helper in a more powerful position. As a result, the group boundary remains salient, and the conflict continues. Also, although cooperation

is effective in reducing conflict when the group succeeds in its efforts, failure in the cooperative effort can result in scapegoating (blaming the other group) and increased intergroup hostility (Worchel, Andreoli, and Folger, 1977).

Reducing Conflict by Reducing Threat

Earlier in this chapter, we discussed the destructive effects of threat on conflict resolution. Not only does threat escalate conflict, but conflict often motivates the use of threat. Osgood (1962) recognized this and pointed out that negotiations between the United States and the Soviet Union were proceeding on a path directly contrary to conflict resolution. Each side was amassing threat potential, and the huge increase in weapons was making the possibility of accidental war more likely. Osgood suggested a way out of this spiraling increase in conflict. He called his plan the **graduated reciprocation in tension reduction (GRIT)** policy. In the first phase, which is aimed at enlisting public support, one party publicly announces that it intends to reduce tension and clearly states the unilateral initiatives that it plans to take to do so. That party should also invite the other party to reciprocate with its own initiatives. The second phase is aimed at establishing the initiator's credibility and authenticity. During this phase, the initiator must carry out the announced tension-reducing moves in a way that is unambiguous and open to verification. These steps must be taken even in the absence of reciprocation. The final points of the GRIT strategy relate to the need to have the initiator retain enough power to avoid being exploited by the other party. These steps specify that the initiatives should be risky and create a vulnerability in the initiator; yet they should not be so drastic that the initiator loses the ability to protect itself or to retaliate if the opponent responds aggressively. The idea behind GRIT is that moves by one nation or person to reduce threat capabilities will likely be met with similar reductions by others (Lindskold, 1986).

Overall, research suggests that GRIT does work; that is, unilateral reductions of threat are often responded to with cooperative efforts on the part of an opponent. Research has found this effect even when the competition is very keen and has lasted for some time (Walters and Lindskold, 1982). Other research has found that GRIT is most likely to be successful when the opponent has equal or less power than the initiator (Lindskold and Aronoff, 1980); thus, high power people can use GRIT particularly effectively.

We also know today that the end to the Cold War between the United States and the former USSR was almost certainly hastened by a series of moves in the late 1980s and early 1990s, when each country made unilateral moves to reduce conventional forces and nuclear arsenals. A real-life approximation of GRIT worked to reduce tension and conflict.

Depersonalizing Conflict: The Use of Norms

Randolph McCoy became the center of the feud for a number of reasons. His pride had been damaged by the incident over the pig. He was loath to show any weakness. The situation quickly became the McCoys against the Hatfields. This is often the course of conflict, but it puts all parties in a position where "backing down" or "fighting on" appear to be the only alternatives. This perspective clearly places one party against the other. Such a highly personal view of the confrontation often works against a resolution because reputations are on the line and face must be saved.

Our analysis suggests that conflict may be more readily resolved if the personal nature of it is reduced. Thibaut (1968) suggested that invoking general rules or norms to identify solutions often depersonalizes the conflict and unfreezes the positions of the parties. This procedure eliminates the "us" versus "them" mentality and challenges the parties to find a general rule they can apply to the situation.

Norms are rules that determine how behavior should legitimately progress (see chapter 11). They are impersonal in that they are concerned with the situation rather than with the personalities of the people in conflict. Efforts at conflict resolution that rely on norms are directed toward identifying a just and fair solution rather than which side is stronger or more capable.

Some norms focus on the distribution of resources. One such norm deals with the *needs* of the two parties. Simply put, this norm states that the more need a person has, the more he or she should receive. A second norm is based on *equality*. According to this norm, resources should be divided equally among the people involved in a social relationship. A third norm (the one studied most by social psychologists) is **equity**. According to this norm, the amount people receive from a relationship should be determined by how much they put into it. For example, suppose that

you work eight hours painting a fence, and your friend works two hours. Together, you receive $100 for the job. The relationship will be equitable if you receive $80 (80 percent of the pay for 80 percent of the work) and your friend receives $20 (20 percent of the pay for 20 percent of the work).

Certain norms tend to be used or preferred in certain situations. For example, need and equality norms are most likely to be used in cohesive groups that enjoy a positive emotional climate (friendships, families), whereas equity norms are common in noncohesive groups. Deutsch (1975) argued that equity norms will be used in groups whose greatest concern is productivity, whereas equality norms will be used when the main concern is developing positive social relations (recall the distinction in chapter 8 between exchange relationships, where equity guides resource distribution, and communal relationships, where equal distribution is preferred).

Although norms can depersonalize conflict, they do not always ensure smooth resolutions. There may be disagreement over which norm is the most appropriate one to use in the situation (Austin, 1986). Also, in fundamental disagreements over such things as ownership of resources—like the Hatfield-McCoy pig dispute—norms do not provide an obvious framework for satisfying both parties; after all, the disputed pigs can belong to only one owner!

Third-Party Intervention: Arbitration and Mediation

Outside parties can sometimes be recruited to help resolve conflict. Consider the following story attributed to anthropologist William Ury by Rubin, Pruitt, and Kim (1994). An elderly man instructed his three sons that at his death his property should be divided by giving the eldest son half, the middle son a third, and the youngest son one-ninth. When the man died, the sons struggled to determine how to divide his seventeen camels according to his instructions. In the middle of a heated argument, the village elder rode up on a camel, and after hearing the problem, offered to add her camel to their father's estate if it would help. Indeed, it did help. The older brother took nine camels (one-half), the middle brother got six camels (one-third), and the youngest received two camels (one-ninth). The total number of camels taken by the brothers was seventeen, and the elder rode away on her camel.

This story illustrates that third parties can often intervene and present a new perspective that helps to resolve disputes. "A third party is an individual or collective that is external to a dispute between two or more people and that tries to help them reach agreement" (Rubin, Pruitt, and Kim, 1994, p. 197). Third parties can take many roles. The most common is a **mediator,** who generally serves as an advisor, helping the parties clarify issues and agree on a solution (Duffy, 1991). Another common third party is the **arbitrator,** who is invested with the power to impose the final solution after hearing the arguments of both sides. Most recently, a hybrid has been introduced: the **mediator/ arbitrator (Med/Arb),** who will impose a settlement if mediation is not successful (Pruitt, Fry, Castrianno, Zubek, Welton, McGillicuddy, and Ippolito, 1989).

The mere presence of the third party changes the nature of the interaction between the disputing parties, often diverting the attention of the parties away from their immediate disagreement and onto influencing that third party. This can have a positive effect on the conflict, except in cases where the parties are themselves making progress toward a settlement (Hiltrop, 1985).

Mediators can help to resolve conflicts in a number of ways. They can encourage communication between the parties and instruct them on methods of effective communication (recall our discussion of the importance of communication). They may help to focus attention on important issues rather than on more peripheral ones. They can help to identify new alternatives and suggest different perspectives on problems. They can help to balance power in the situation so that one party is not overwhelmed by the other (Carnevale and Pruitt, 1992). And they can help to resist premature conclusion to resolution efforts.

Pruitt and his colleagues (1989) reported that parties who felt that they had had a fair opportunity to voice their concerns seemed most happy with mediation. In other words, the perception that the procedure was open and fair may be one of the most important ingredients for successful and satisfying negotiation (Lind and Tyler, 1988).

Mediation is becoming increasingly popular as a means of handling civil conflicts, such as property settlements in divorce, landlord-tenant disputes, and consumer complaints (Duffy, Grosch, and Olczak, 1991). These efforts keep the disputes from clogging the court system and give participants an opportunity to develop resolutions they are comfortable with.

Many states have training and licensing procedures for mediators. We can speculate whether or not a mediator might have been effective in the "pig dispute," thereby changing the course of history at the Tug Fork.

The Other Side of the Coin: The Positive Value of Conflict

No one could deny the tragedy of the Hatfield–McCoy dispute. Lives were lost, families destroyed, and bitter feelings gripped a region for fifty years. Most conflicts do not lead to this degree of destructiveness and misery, but even this feud can be said to have had some positive outcomes. The feud focused national attention on this remote corner of the world. The governors of West Virginia and Kentucky sent some of the best state judges and law officers into the area, and a strong court system developed. Both families produced a number of teachers, businesspeople, political figures, physicians, and, ironically, lawyers. In fact, Henry Drury Hatfield, nephew of Devil Anse Hatfield, became a respected surgeon who was elected president of the West Virginia Senate in 1911. In 1913 he became governor of West Virginia. Conflict, then, can have positive, as well as negative, results.

From the group perspective, Worchel, Coutant-Sassic, and Wong (1993) argued that intergroup conflict helps to establish group boundaries and identity. In fact, when groups experience threats to their identity, they may seek conflict with other groups. The investigators found that newly formed groups preferred a competitive relation over a cooperative one with outgroups, presumably as a way of developing a clear group identity. The conflict forces people to take sides, creating a clearer distinction between "we" and "they." Intergroup conflict often strengthens the bonds between members within each group.

Sociologist George Simmel (1995) suggested another positive role of conflict: it gives rise to social change. Open conflict between blacks and whites in the United States has led to numerous social changes that have afforded opportunities to increase equality in our society. The black power movement, which resulted in new solidarity among blacks, was a direct result of racial conflict.

Intergroup conflict can have positive effects. The militant Black Panther Party, which promoted conflict between blacks and whites and among blacks themselves, helped eventually to bring blacks together in their struggle for power.

Deutsch (1973) summed up the positive roles of conflict:

> It [conflict] prevents stagnation; it stimulates interest and curiosity; it is the medium through which problems can be aired and solutions arrived at; it is the root of personal and social change. Conflict is often part of the process of testing and assessing oneself and, as such, may be highly enjoyable as one experiences the pleasure of the full and active use of one's capacities. In addition, conflict demarcates groups from one another and thus helps establish group and personal identities; external conflict often fosters internal cohesiveness. (P. 9)

We might conclude by suggesting that relationships between groups will often be tinged with conflict and competition. This situation by itself is not necessarily negative. The important issue concerns how the groups *manage* their conflict. One approach may cre- ate tragedy and destruction, whereas another approach may give rise to the positive outcomes we have identified in this section. The challenge to intergroup relations is to develop a constructive response to conflicts.

Summary

People tend to be more competitive and less cooperative when interacting in a context where group membership is salient than when interacting as individuals, a phenomenon that has been labeled the discontinuity effect. Therefore, interactions between groups often involve conflict. This effect may be due to increased greed in intergroup settings or to the desire of people to enhance their social identity by increasing the position of their ingroup relative to other groups.

People impose structure on their social world by placing themselves and others into categories, which become the basis on which individuals create their social identities and place others into groups. Categories are developed around salient features, and people are assigned to them on the basis of *fit*. Groups, then, have their origins in our cognitive processing rather than simply being a product of the physical environment.

We generally perceive more similarity between members of outgroups than between members of our ingroup, an effect that has been called the outgroup homogeneity effect. Because of this tendency, we often generalize from the experience with one member of an outgroup to all members of that outgroup. The belief in outgroup homogeneity also tends to limit our interactions with outgroup members.

There are conflicting findings concerning the extremity of ratings of ingroup and outgroup members. Some studies show more extreme ratings of ingroup members (the black sheep effect), whereas other studies show greater extremity in ratings of outgroup members. One group of investigators suggested that people who strongly identify with their group will exhibit the black sheep effect, whereas people who have a low identification with their group will evaluate outgroup members more extremely than ingroup members.

Just-world theory proposes that people want and need to believe that the world is basically a fair place where people get what they deserve. This belief allows children to move from satisfying all impulses immediately (the pleasure principle) to delaying gratification and incurring costs in order to obtain greater future rewards (the reality principle). An unfortunate consequence of this belief that people get what they deserve can be victim blaming, whereby victims of negative events and members of disadvantaged minority groups are assumed to be responsible for their own plight.

Delegitimization involves placing people or groups into very negative social categories that are outside the realm of acceptable norms or values. Delegitimization is most likely to occur when perceivers feel highly threatened.

Relative deprivation is the feeling of resentment that occurs when individuals believe that their own or their group's outcomes are unfair. This feeling of injustice is hypothesized to depend on perceptions of wanting and deserving—that is, people feel relatively deprived when they want a desired object and feel entitled to that object. Personal relative deprivation refers to resentment about one's own outcomes and tends to cause behaviors designed to improve one's own outcomes (self-improvement behaviors). Group

relative deprivation refers to resentment about the outcomes of one's ingroup and tends to cause behaviors designed to improve the group's outcomes (collective action).

Minority groups often compare themselves with each other. Therefore, if one group is doing better than the other, the worse-off group may feel threatened. A consequence of this threat can be that members of the worse-off group will dislike members of the prospering group.

Once initiated, conflict often increases in intensity and scope, a pattern that has been called the conflict spiral. The use of threat is often met with counterthreat, resulting in greater conflict. Giving in to a threat, especially in public, often involves losing face, which individuals and groups strive to avoid. Terrorism is actual or threatened violence against noncombatants for avowed political ends. The aims of terrorism are to achieve worldwide attention and to instill widespread fear.

Distrust also maintains or contributes to the escalation of conflict. Trust is difficult to develop but is easily destroyed. Communication is key to the resolution of conflict, but the initial tendency of parties in a conflict is often to withdraw and cease communication—a reaction called autistic hostility. Although communication increases the chances for a positive resolution of conflict, the participants must often be forced to engage in communication before they positively resolve their conflict.

There are two general approaches to reducing intergroup conflict. One approach, called recategorization, encourages the opposing groups to reduce existing identities and adopt a common identity. The other approach, called multiculturalism at a national level, involves strengthening and securing group identities while encouraging cooperation and learning between the distinct groups. Contact, especially equal-status contact, can help to reduce conflict between groups. The positive effects of contact are enhanced if it involves cooperation between the groups to obtain a superordinate goal.

Just as the use of threat increases conflict, a reduction in threat helps to reduce conflict. The policy called graduated reciprocation in tension reduction (GRIT) is based on the idea that unilateral moves to reduce threat by one side in a conflict will likely be met with similar reductions by the opponent. The use of norms, such as equity, helps to depersonalize conflict by applying general "rules" to the solution of the disagreement. A mediator serves as an advisor to the parties in a conflict, helping the parties clarify issues and agree on a solution. An arbitrator has the power to impose the final settlement after hearing the arguments of both sides. A mediator/arbitrator (Med/Arb) combines both roles by being able to impose a settlement if mediation is unsuccessful.

Although conflict often has negative, even tragic, consequences, it can also have positive results. Conflict helps groups establish their identities, can lead to social change, and can encourage creative thinking. Therefore, conflict is not necessarily a state to be avoided. Constructive approaches to conflict management are important, however, for reaching positive goals.

Key Terms

arbitrator
autistic hostility
black sheep effect
conflict spiral
delegitimization
discontinuity effect
equity
face-saving
graduated reciprocation in
   tension reduction (GRIT)

jigsaw method
just-world theory
mediator
mediator/arbitrator
   (Med/Arb)
multiculturalism
norms
outgroup homogeneity
   effect
pleasure principle

reality principle
recategorization
relative deprivation
social identity
   theory
superordinate goal
terrorism
victim blaming

Suggested Readings

Abrams, D., and Hogg, M. A. (Eds.). (1990) *Social identity theory: Constructive and critical advances.* London, England: Harvester Wheatsheaf.

Bar-Tal, D. (1990). *Group beliefs: A conception for analyzing group structure, process, and behavior.* New York: Springer-Verlag.

Brown, R. J. (1988). *Group processes: Dynamics within and between groups.* Oxford, England: Blackwell.

Hewstone, M., and Brown, R. J. (Eds.). (1986). *Contact and conflict in intergroup encounters.* London, England: Blackwell.

Hogg, M. A., and Abrams, D. (1988). *Social identifications: A social psychology of intergroup relations and group processes.* London, England: Routledge.

Messick, D. M., and Mackie, D. M. (1989). Intergroup relations. *Annual Review of Psychology, 40,* 45–81.

Stroebe, W., Kruglanski, A. W., Bar-Tal, D., and Hewstone, M. (Eds.). (1988). *The social psychology of intergroup conflict: Theory, research, and applications.* Berlin: Springer-Verlag.

Taylor, D. M., and Moghaddam, F. M. (1994). *Theories of intergroup relations: International social psychological perspectives* (2nd ed.). New York: Praeger.

Turner, J. C. (1987). *Rediscovering the social group: A self-categorization theory.* Oxford, England: Blackwell.

Worchel, S., and Austin, W. G. (Eds.). (1986). *The psychology of intergroup relations.* Chicago: Nelson-Hall.

Chapter 13

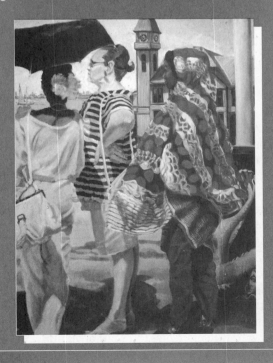

Group Dynamics

The museum director smiled at the young man. "That's an interesting theory, but it has one major flaw. It would have been impossible for anyone to sail a balsa raft from Peru to the Polynesian islands. Do you realize that the journey is over 4,300 miles?"

Thor Heyerdahl pressed his point. "Look at the similarity between these artifacts found in Peru and on the Polynesian islands. And how do you explain the fact that both the ancient Incas of Peru and the Polynesians have a god named Kon Tiki? The Polynesian islands must have first been settled by peoples from Peru."

"You will never be able to make a strong case by showing similarities in artifacts and gods," responded the director. "These coincidences mean nothing if it is impossible to get from Peru to Polynesia by raft. You have to show that this feat could be done before your theory will be taken seriously:"

Thor left this meeting more determined than ever to prove his theory. He would show that it was possible to sail a raft from Peru to Polynesia. He spent weeks in the library studying the type of raft that was used by the Incas during the period between A.D. 500 and 1100. Thor found that they built large rafts out of balsa trees by lashing the logs together with hemp rope. They erected cloth sails and used long rudders to steer the rafts. Could such a raft make a 4,300-mile trip over some of the roughest ocean in the world?

Clearly, Thor could not make the trip by himself. Someone had to man the helm at all times and there were many chores to do on board. With little effort, Thor talked five other men into accompanying him on the trip. Herman would keep the instruments and measure the currents and winds. Erik was an expert at patching sails, splicing ropes, and navigating. Knut and Torstein had had experience with wireless radios during World War II, and they would be responsible for communication. Bengt would take scientific notes

and act as quartermaster. And Thor would captain the expedition and keep the logbook.

With the crew assembled and financial backing secured, the group set off for Peru to build their raft. They had to go deep into the jungle to find large balsa trees, and with great effort they moved nine gigantic logs to Callao harbor. There they worked on lashing the logs together, building a small cabin on the deck, and making their sails. They followed drawings of the ancient Inca rafts, and they accepted no help from the curious audience that gathered each day to watch them build their raft. The native Peruvians watched the strange raft take shape, and each day the size of the crowd grew.

Finally the raft was ready. The logs ranged from thirty- to forty-five-feet long. On the large sail they painted a picture of the Tiki and they christened their raft the *Kon Tiki*. Each man had worked with the knowledge that the raft would be only as good as the worst piece of work. Finally, on April 27, 1947, food and water were brought on board and the *Kon Tiki* was ready.

Early the next morning, the raft was towed slowly out to sea. As they waved farewell to the tugboat, the men knew that they would see no other people but each other for at least three months—if all went well.

Three days into their voyage, the men held a meeting to discuss rules. Although each man had been assigned certain duties, all the routine jobs such as steering, watch, and cooking were divided equally. Every man had two hours each day and two hours each night at the steering oar. All meals were to be eaten outside the cabin, and "the 'right place' was only at the farthest end of the logs astern" (Heyerdahl, 1950). Each position also had its rules. For example, the night watch had to be secured by a rope around his waist at all times.

Days wore into weeks, weeks into months. The sturdy raft was battered by high waves and fierce

On the ninety-third day of their trans-Pacific voyage, the crew of the **Kon Tiki** *sight land, the Polynesian island Angatau. To bring the venture to a successful conclusion required six individuals of widely different backgrounds to form a tightly knit group capable of working together and making complex decisions.*

storms, but it always emerged the victor. Each morning the men anxiously checked the ropes to make sure that their raft was holding together.

Coordination of effort was essential if the voyage was to succeed. Each man had to do his part, and they all had to work together during crises such as storms. Life in such close quarters offered little room for bickering, so when trouble arose, the group held a powwow.

Finally, ninety-three days into the journey, the watch shouted, "Land ahead!" All the men scrambled to the deck and saw the island of Puka Puka in the distance. However, the winds were not in their favor, and they sailed past this island. During the next several days, they passed a number of islands; often the inhabitants rowed out toward the raft.

On the one hundred first day, a strong wind blew them onto a reef off a small Polynesian island. They had made it! They had shown that ancient inhabitants of Peru could indeed have been the first settlers of Polynesia. These six men had overcome storms, navigational problems, and interpersonal squabbles. Using only the most primitive means, they had duplicated a trip that may have been made over one thousand years earlier. They were hailed as heroes throughout the world, and President Truman received members of the expedition.

The voyage of the *Kon Tiki* is notable in many respects. One is how six individuals of very different backgrounds could be formed into a closely knit group capable of carrying out such a venture. These men were able to work together and make the complex decisions that ensured success. Their experience tells us a great deal about the dynamics of groups.

What Is a Group?

Let's assume that we wanted to do a closer study of the crew of the *Kon Tiki* to understand how its members made this incredible voyage. In beginning our study, we might ask whether we should focus only on each crew member as an individual or whether we should study the unit—the group. This may seem like a rather simple question, but social scientists have been asking it for almost one hundred years without agreeing on an answer. When we examine the issue more closely, we can see that it is rather complex and, in fact, guides the study of group dynamics. We are asking whether the group is greater than the sum of its parts, or members.

Emile Durkheim, the eminent sociologist, had a direct answer to the question: "The group thinks, feels, and acts quite differently from the way in which its members would were they isolated. If we begin with the individual, we shall be able to understand nothing of what takes place in the group" (Durkheim, 1898, p. 104).

Floyd Allport (1924) had an equally clear answer about the nature of groups. But he took the opposite position. He stated that groups don't think, feel, or act—people do. He capped his argument for studying individuals with the profound observation that nobody ever stumbled over a group, so how could they be real?

The debate refused to die, and in 1952 Solomon Asch offered an interesting analogy. He pointed out that water (H_2O) is composed of hydrogen and oxygen. Even though it's important to know the characteristics of these two elements, we would not have a good understanding of the nature of water with only this knowledge. He suggested that a group is like water: it helps to understand the individual members, but a clear grasp of group behavior requires an examination of the unit. And to a large degree, recent research has taken Asch's suggestion by studying the behavior of both individual members and the group. With this position in mind, we can now ask: What is a group?

Today social psychologists view the group as a dynamic whole that is different from the sum of its parts: it is neither greater nor less than these parts, but it is clearly different from the collection of individual members. Although investigators have offered various definitions of the group, most would be comfortable with the idea that a **group** consists of "two or more persons who are interacting with one another in such a manner that each person influences and is influenced by each other person" (Shaw, 1981, p. 8). Group members generally feel that they belong together; they see themselves as forming a single unit. This feeling of group unity usually results because the group members share common beliefs and attitudes and accept certain norms of the group. Group members also share at least one common goal.

The crew of the *Kon Tiki* fits the definition of a group. They were involved in constant face-to-face interaction during their voyage. They saw themselves as forming a group and felt that they belonged together. In talking with others, they often referred to themselves as "the *Kon Tiki* crew." In other words, the awareness of being a group became part of their own identity. Finally, they shared the common goal of completing the journey from Peru to Polynesia. We can contrast this group with the collection of people who gathered to watch them build their raft. These people did not interact with each other and had no feeling of belonging together. They simply happened to be in the same place at the same time and thus engaged in a similar activity. The term **collective** has been used to describe a gathering of individuals who do not have face-to-face interactions but are engaged in a common activity (Milgram and Toch, 1968).

The Development of Groups and Their Members

If we examine the *Kon Tiki* crew, one point becomes apparent immediately: crew members and their relationships with each other changed over time. The members thought, acted, and felt differently as they worked together, and the crew functioned differently. In other words, the group was a *dynamic* unit, constantly changing. A great deal of attention has been paid recently to **group development**—the process by which groups form, flourish, and decline along with the changes that take place in the group and in its members over time.

Looking first at the individual, we find that potential group members are faced with an immediate problem: whether to join the group (Mackie and Goethals, 1987; Montgomery, 1989). Being a group member clearly has its advantages. We can accomplish tasks that would be impossible to do alone; a single person could not sail the *Kon Tiki*. Being with other people allows us to evaluate ourselves on several dimensions, as we shall see. You cannot determine how good a tennis player you are by banging a tennis ball against a wall. The protection and sense of security that result from membership in a group tend to make accepted group members healthier and happier than loners (Moreland, 1987). But these and other advantages are balanced by costs. Being a member of a group requires you to give up some of your independence. You may have to change your attitudes and behaviors to become accepted into the group. You must consider the desires of others in addition to your own. Hence the first step toward becoming a group member is to decide whether you're prepared to accept the costs of membership in order to reap the benefits.

But the conflict does not end there. Upon entry into the group, the individual steps into the category of new member. The group attempts to change the individual so that the individual can make the maximum contribution to the group (Moreland and Levine, 1982, 1988). At the same time, the new member attempts to change the group so that it will meet his or her needs. We can see this negotiation in the *Kon Tiki* crew when it was formed. As each new member was recruited, the crew stated what was expected of him. And each new member attempted to exact promises and commitments from the crew.

Once a person becomes a full member of a group, the focus of negotiations changes somewhat. The group identifies roles or positions it wants the member to occupy—such as navigator or helmsman in our example. And the full member defines the jobs associated with those roles that he or she desires. During the time you belong to a group, you find that the group is not meeting all of your needs. You begin to question the value of membership in this group, search for other groups, and become a marginal member (see figure 13.1). If the group does not move to recapture you, you leave the group. The other group members often discuss former members, evaluating their former colleagues' contributions. The ex-member also looks back on the group, remembering the benefits and costs of being a member of the group.

If you examine your own experience in groups, several points may come to mind. First, you may see

how you passed through these stages. You may also see that at any one time you are a member of numerous groups, and you may be in a different stage of membership in each of these groups. Finally, in examining any one group to which you belong, you will find that it has members at each of these stages. In this sense, a group is like a highway, with members scattered at various points along the road. The group therefore must deal with members at these various stages at any one time.

While the image of a highway may allow us to visualize members passing through a group, it may be misleading if it causes us to picture groups as stable, unchanging units. Groups, like individual members, are in a constant state of flux. Groups change and develop just as members do. One analysis suggested that new groups begin at a *forming* stage (Tuckman, 1965). During this stage, group members identify a leader and discuss the nature of their task. Groups next enter a *storming* stage, in which members try to change the group to meet their personal needs. Conflict erupts as each member attempts to gain control. In the *norming* stage the group focuses on reducing conflict and works to develop rules to guide members' behavior. At the fourth stage, *performing*, members work together to achieve mutual goals.

Tuckman's analysis focused mostly on small work groups. In an effort to expand this focus, Worchel,

---

FIGURE 13.1 A MODEL OF GROUP SOCIALIZATION

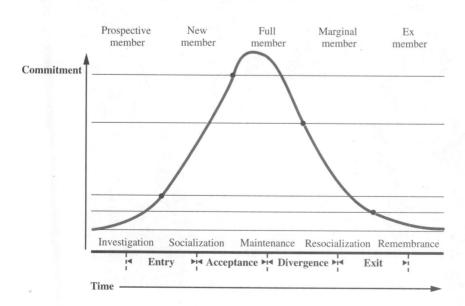

Source: Moreland and Levine (1982)

Coutant-Sasic, and Grossman (1991) studied larger groups and social movements, such as political parties and the Solidarity Union in Poland. They found that new groups often begin to form when some significant event, such as an assassination of a prominent person or a repressive action by a controlling group, brings people together in a common cause. The new group then enters an *identification* stage much like the forming stage proposed by Tuckman. During this stage the group is concerned with establishing its identity. It demands conformity from its members and punishes deviants. The group may establish a uniform dress code to define its members and often invites conflict with other groups because such conflict establishes group boundaries. During this stage, group members will work for the good of the group, often placing the group's needs ahead of their own. In the next stage, *production*, the group's focus turns from identity to productivity. The group becomes concerned with achieving task goals and meeting the needs of its members. The cooperation of other groups to achieve these goals may be invited. Groups then enter the *individualization* stage, in which the focus is on the individual members. Members begin to examine what they are receiving from the group. They want to be recognized for their individual accomplishments. They may dress to set themselves apart from other members. And they may explore the advantages of membership in other groups. In the final stage, *decay*, members whose needs are not being met by the group begin to complain and demand changes in leadership and structure. Group cohesion decreases and the stage is set for the forming of new groups.

Several points emerge from this discussion of group and member development. The major point is that any group, such as the *Kon Tiki* crew, is con-

The members of this Bible study group share many of the same attitudes, beliefs, and behaviors.

stantly undergoing change and development. A snapshot of the group taken at one time may give a very different picture from a snapshot taken at another time. It is important to discuss groups within the framework of time (McGrath, 1988). Further, the development process of groups and their members does seem to follow a predictable pattern. This is not to say that all groups or all members undergo precisely the same process in a stepwise fashion; but in most cases there is an order to development. Finally the changes experienced by group members affect the group and the changes in the group affect the members. In order to understand this point, you may want to review your own family. Events such as your going to college probably changed the nature of your family, just as the family's move from one neighborhood to another had effects on you. With this dynamic picture of groups in mind, let's look more closely at two key facets of group dynamics: (1) how groups affect individuals and (2) how group processes affect decision making.

The Group's Impact on the Individual

Being in a group has a number of significant effects on individual performance and individual behavior. Let's consider first how being in a group influences your *individual* performance. From your own perspective, you may want to ask whether it would be better for you to work (study, take a test, jog) in a group or alone.

Social Facilitation

Social scientists became interested in questions of performance in groups about one hundred years ago. In 1897, as we saw in chapter 1, Norman Triplett devised one of the first social psychology experiments when he asked children to wind string on a fishing reel as fast as they could, either alone or in competition with another child. Triplett found that the children worked faster in competition than they did alone.

Much of the research that followed Triplett's studies also found that people performed better in groups or in front of audiences than alone (Travis, 1925; Allport, 1924). This effect of others has been found with animals and insects. For example, Chen (1937) counted the balls of dirt that ants excavated as

they built their tunnels. In some cases he had an ant work alone, and in other cases the ant worked with one or two other ants. Chen found that the individual ant worked harder (removed more balls of dirt) when it worked with other ants than when it worked alone. These results suggest that the presence of others facilitates performance. However, since the test subjects performed in front of a passive audience in a number of the studies—an audience composed of people taking no action—it seems that the effects of **social facilitation** were due to the mere presence of others rather than to direct competition between individuals.

Given these results, we might conclude that groups are good for people (and other animals). Unfortunately, the picture is not quite so clear. At about the same time that the social facilitation results were reported, a number of investigators reported **social inhibition** effects. For example, Pessin and Husband (1933) found that the presence of an audience slowed the learning of a maze task and a nonsense-syllable task. Of interest is that after the subjects had learned the maze and nonsense-syllable tasks, they performed better in front of spectators. These contradictory results caution us against indiscriminately using groups to upgrade an individual's performance.

It was not until Zajonc (1965) proposed his theory of social facilitation that some theoretical sense was made of the contradictory results. Zajonc drew a distinction between the learning or acquisition phase of task performance and the performance or emission phase. Zajonc (1965, 1972) proposed that the mere presence of others increases an individual's arousal and drive. He argued that the presence of others in the environment increases alertness. The alertness (or arousal) results because the presence of others may require that the individual act quickly or in novel or unique ways. The arousal is important because it has been shown that an increase in drive increases the likelihood that an individual will perform what psychologists call the "dominant response." The dominant response is defined as the one that the individual is most likely to make in a particular situation. Hence Zajonc proposed that the mere presence of others facilitates the performance of the dominant response because it increases drive and arousal. He further pointed out that when an individual is learning a new behavior, the correct behavior has not yet become the dominant response. Thus, according to Zajonc, the mere presence of others should inhibit the learning of new or complicated responses but facilitate the

performance of well-learned behaviors that have become dominant responses.

Overall, psychologists have agreed about the effect groups have on individual performance, but there has been considerable disagreement about why these effects occur (Berger, Carli, Garcier, and James, 1982; Guerin and Innes, 1982). One alternative position is that audience effects are due to the performer's concern about being evaluated (Cottrell, Wack, Sekerak, and Rittle, 1968). According to this position, people learn that others are potential sources of evaluation, and the presence of these others creates an anticipation of positive or negative outcomes. Therefore, social facilitation should occur only when the audience is in a position to evaluate the individual's performance. In support of this position, Henchy and Glass (1968) found greater social facilitation when the audience was perceived as being experts on the task than when the audience knew little about the task. Supposedly the experts were in a better position to evaluate performance than the nonexperts. In an interesting variation on this theme, some psychologists suggest that the effect of an audience on one's performance depends on whether one fears negative evaluation for poor performance or expects positive evaluation for good performance (Paulus, 1983; Wilke and Van Knippenberg, 1988). This hypothesis suggests that a focus on a positive outcome will improve performance on both simple and complex tasks. Concern about a negative outcome, on the other hand, will facilitate performance on simple tasks but inhibit performance on complex tasks. This idea still awaits careful testing.

Other research, however, has suggested that concern about evaluation is not necessary to achieve social facilitation. For example, one study (Haas and Roberts, 1975) found that a blindfolded audience that could not evaluate performance did improve the worker's performance but not as much as an audience that was not blindfolded. More recently, research by Baumeister, Hamilton, and Tice (1985) has found that too much concern about evaluation may lower performance. Results from this study showed that people performed less well in front of an audience that expected success than in front of an audience that did not hold such high expectations.

Another alternative explanation (Sanders, 1981) suggests that the audience serves as a distraction for the performer. In such a situation, the performer is placed in the conflictual position of having to decide whether to pay attention to the audience or to the task. This conflict leads to increased drive and facilitates the performance of simple tasks. In support of this position, a number of studies (Sanders and Baron, 1975) found that low levels of distraction enhanced the performance of simple tasks.

Finally, it has been proposed that the presence of others creates arousal which leads to attention overload and the lack of attention to environmental cues. If the task is simple, then the cues ignored are likely to be irrelevant to the task, and performance will be enhanced. On the other hand, if the task is complex, the narrowing of attention will lead to the overlooking of task-relevant information and a decline in performance (Geen and Bushman, 1987).

It seems that many factors, including arousal, concern for evaluation, distraction, and attention overload only enhance social facilitation effects. In fact, all of these processes may occur simultaneously in some situations.

Social Loafing

The findings on social facilitation *seem* quite straightforward and clear. However, as is often the case, human behavior manages to create some interesting wrinkles and challenges for social psychologists. The first hint of such a wrinkle appeared in a rope-pulling study by Ringelmann (1913). Male subjects pulled either alone or in groups of two, three, or eight persons. Ringelmann found that two-man groups pulled 1.9 times as hard as a single individual, that three-man groups pulled 2.5 times as hard, and that eight man groups pulled 4 times as hard. Hence, the larger the group, the greater the force that was exerted on the rope. As the size of the group increased, however, the output from each individual decreased. In other words, people worked less hard or "loafed" when they worked in the group.

Appropriately, this effect has been called **social loafing,** and research has replicated it many times. For example, it has been found that people clap less loudly in a group than alone. And a result that will interest waiters and waitresses is that individuals leave smaller tips when they are part of a group than when they are tipping alone (Jackson, 1987; Latané, 1981).

Before we scrap everything that we learned about social facilitation, let us examine some of the explanations for the loafing effect. As you may remember, in the studies on social facilitation, subjects performed alone or in front of others: in each case, the person knew that his or her performance could be observed and identified by others. In the social loafing research, on the other hand, the person performs with others and believes that only the group product can be measured (Harkins and Szymanski, 1989). Further, the group product has little personal implication for the individual. In this case, the individual believes that his or her output cannot be specifically identified. In an effort to demonstrate the importance of identifiability, Williams, Harkins, and Latané (1981) had subjects shout either alone or in groups. In some conditions, however, subjects believed that their individual performance was always being monitored (always identifiable); in others they believed it was identifiable only when they were alone; and in still other conditions, they believed their output was never identifiable. As can be seen in figure 13.2, performance was lower when subjects felt that their efforts were not being identified. Further support for this position comes from research showing that social loafing does not occur if the result of the group performance has clear personal relevance for the individual members (Brickner, Harkins, and Ostrom, 1986). Hence, one explanation for loafing suggests that the effect results when the individual cannot be identified with a specific output and the output has little implication for the individual.

A second explanation has been termed the **free-rider effect** (Kerr and Brunn, 1983). To understand

---

FIGURE 13.2   SOUND PRESSURE AS A FUNCTION OF GROUP SIZE AND IDENTIFIABILITY

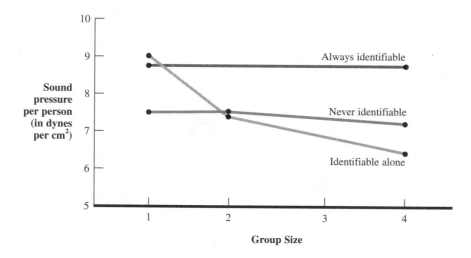

Source: After Williams, Harkins, and Latané, 1981

BOX 13.1

Using Unshared Information

In many decision-making groups, there is a combination of shared and unshared information. Some information everyone knows when entering the discussion, but other things only one person or a minority of group members knows. Numerous studies have shown that the information known to everyone gets more attention and has more influence than the unshared information (Larson, Christensen, Abbott, and Franz, 1996; Larson, Foster-Fishman, and Keys, 1994; Stewart and Stasser, 1993). There seem to be three major reasons for this imbalance. First, shared information may be easier to recall, because every group member has it from the outset. Unshared information, in contrast, becomes available for most people only in the course of discussion itself. Second, information that comes to a group's attention late is often less influential in the group's decisions than information that was available early. Plans have already taken shape around the early information. Third, unshared information may seem less reliable than shared information. Groups members can verify the accuracy of shared information but they cannot do the same for unshared information; yet it may be unshared information that gives the truer picture of the problem at hand—that is, a "hidden profile" of key facts may be contained in a group but not widely shared (Stasser, 1988; Larson, Foster-Fishman, and Keys, 1994). How can the disadvantages of unshared information be overcome so that groups can make decisions based on all the information?

Larson and his colleagues have suggested two ways that these problems can be overcome: group decisions training and effective leadership. In one study, groups went through several training procedures, including devising plans of action, reviewing barriers to effective decision making, and watching videos outlining sound decision-making practices, such as considering all alternatives carefully, not changing positions without a good reason, and considering all important information. The results of training were promising, although they could not completely eliminate the stubborn advantage of shared information. Decision training significantly increased the amount of unshared information that was discussed (Larson et al., 1994).

The role of leadership was investigated in a study of medical diagnoses made by groups of physicians. In these groups the older, more experienced hospital residents assumed the leadership positions in groups including interns and medical students. They took control of the discussions about the proper diagnosis and played a key role in seeing that unshared information was repeated and not forgotten during the group's deliberations. In this way they muted the usual tendency to overlook unshared information (Larson et al., 1996).

The tendency of groups to overlook and underweigh unshared information is often a serious problem in group discussions and group decisions. Research on minority influence and on groupthink shows how widespread the problem can be. Fortunately, there are ways to ease the problem of unshared information. More work needs to be done to train groups in making the problem go away completely, but we already know that group decision training and effective leadership are a good start.

---

this effect, assume that you are a crew member on the *Kon Tiki*. The job is to pull up the sail. Everyone is pitching in, and you see the sail going up nicely. Because all is going well, you may feel that great effort is not needed from you in this situation; you therefore reduce your efforts and become a "free rider." Loafing in this case results because the group members believe that their contributions are dispensable and the group will succeed without them. From the group's point of view, this is a dangerous situation because if all the members become free riders, the task performance will suffer.

Another explanation for social loafing has been called the **sucker effect** (Kerr, 1983). Again, assume that you are working to pull up the sails on the *Kon Tiki*; but this time you are working your hardest and turn to see another crew member doing very little. You realize that it is the crew as a whole and not you as an individual that will get credit for getting the job done. This lazy member is therefore playing you for a sucker; you are doing all the work, and he will receive as much credit as you. As a result, you may reduce your efforts and not work as hard as you did when you were working alone. In a study demonstrating this effect, subjects worked on a task with another group member who did poorly (Kerr, 1983). The subjects believed that the other member either had or did not have the ability to do better. They reduced their efforts (loafed) to the greatest extent when they felt the other person could do better but simply was not trying. It seems that we especially want to avoid being a sucker for others who can do well but are intentionally acting lazy.

A final point may have occurred to you as you read about the social loafing experiments. Although the subjects worked on their tasks in sight of each other, they had little feeling of being a group. A number of investigators have suggested that loafing is most likely to occur when the workers have little feeling of "groupness" (Petrovsky, 1985). For example, one study found no loafing when group members were given a standard and led to believe their group would be evaluated against this standard (Harkins and Szymanski, 1989). In another study, subjects actually worked harder in the group when their interdependence was emphasized by the possibility of a group reward for good performance. In fact, they worked harder for a group reward than for individual rewards (Worchel, Hart, and Buttermeyer, 1989). Therefore, loafing may occur in collectives rather than in groups of people who feel bound together by a common fate.

These studies and a number of others conducted in recent years suggest overall that being in a group enhances individual performance when a person's output is clearly identifiable and can be evaluated, the task is easy, a sense of groupness is emphasized, and people feel that the task is important and their efforts are important (Karau and Williams, 1993). However, when the output cannot be matched to the individual and people feel little sense of belonging to the group, social loafing may occur.

Deindividuation: Getting Lost in the Group

We turn now to one of the most dramatic effects of groups on individuals—**deindividuation**. Herman Watzinger, one of the crew members on the *Kon Tiki*, anticipated our discussion when he stated that as the voyage wore on, he lost his concern about himself and focused on "the crew." He felt that his own identity became that of the group. For Watzinger, the effect was enjoyable and enhanced his performance on the voyage. In other cases the effect has not been positive. In the now infamous "snowball" game between the Denver and San Francisco professional football teams during the 1985 season, a snowball was hurled from the crowd as San Francisco was preparing to kick a short field goal. The snowball distracted the players and San Francisco missed the goal; Denver won the game by two points. The young man who threw the snowball said he was ashamed of his actions; he had become carried away by the excitement of the crowd and had acted without thinking of the consequences.

As far back as 1895, the French sociologist Gustave Le Bon observed that individuals often become "lost" in crowds and do things they would not do if they were alone. He observed:

> Whoever be the individuals that compose it, however like or unlike be their mode of life, their occupations, their character, or their intelligence, the fact that they have been transformed into a crowd puts them in possession of a sort of collective mind. (1895, p. 20)

In addition to having a collective mind, a crowd is irrational, and its intellectual level is always below that of the isolated individual. Le Bon also described crowds as emotional and said that when in them, the individual begins to feel and express the emotions of a "primitive being." According to Le Bon, three mechanisms are responsible for creating the monster known as a crowd. First, because individuals are anonymous, they lose the sense of individual responsibility and thus participate in acts they would not normally engage in. Second, contagion causes individuals in the crowd to act as they like in ways they would not act under other circumstances. Contagion reduces individuals' inhibitions and allows them to behave as the model behaves. Third, people become more suggestible in crowds; the crowd hypnotizes the individual, who then follows the suggestions of other members or the crowd's leader.

Other investigators have expanded the view of the deindividuation process, and three models have been proposed. One suggests that conditions such as large groups, anonymity, and a heightened state of arousal are the precursors of deindividuation. These conditions lead individuals to become submerged in the group, losing their own sense of identity (Zimbardo, 1970; Taylor, O'Neal, Langley, and Butcher, 1991). When this identity loss occurs, people no longer feel responsible for their behavior; their attention is drawn to the group and behavior becomes regulated by fleeting cues in the immediate situation.

When people lose a sense of personal responsibility for their actions, they are no longer governed by the norms and inhibitions that are present in most situations. Their behavior becomes impulsive, emotional, and difficult to terminate.

At the extreme, this view suggests that deindividuation releases the "beast" inside each of us. When Watson (1973) studied the warfare patterns of more than two hundred cultures, for example, he found that warriors who were deindividuated by masks and paint had a greater tendency to torture captives than warriors in cultures that did not use such devises. Taking a somewhat different approach, Worchel and Andreoli (1978) found that aggressors deindividuated their victims before harming them. This deindividuation of the victim occurred when the aggressor selectively recalled information, thereby removing the victim's identity and uniqueness. It was easier to attack a dein-

Crowd violence seems endemic among soccer fans. Riots erupting from fights between fans of the English and Tunisian teams in the 1998 World Cup competition resulted in numerous arrests and injuries.

dividuated victim than a more individuated one. Finally, Diener, Fraser, Beaman, and Kelem (1976) found that Halloween trick-or-treaters were more likely to steal when they wore masks and remained anonymous than when they were clearly identifiable.

A second position also suggests that people lose their personal identity in a crowd. Rather than becoming unrestrained and unrestricted, this position argues, people take on a new identity, one defined by their role in the group (Brown, 1988; Reicher, 1984; Reicher and Levine, 1994; Diener, 1979). This new identity then guides their behavior. Consider the following experiment (Johnson and Downing, 1979). Subjects in the study were deindividuated by a uniform. In some cases, however, the experimenter commented that the uniform was similar to that worn by the Ku Klux Klan, a group known for violence. In other cases the experimenter mentioned the similarity of the uniform to that worn by nurses, a nonviolent group. Subjects were then given the opportunity to shock another person in a learning situation. Aggression increased slightly when the uniform was compared with that of the Ku Klux Klan. The intensity of shocks administered *decreased* significantly when the connection with nurses was salient. When the salience of the individual identity was reduced, the subjects performed more like the group they felt they represented.

In order to understand the third position, consider your own feelings in large groups. Many of us may find losing our identity to the group disturbing or uncomfortable. At many large universities, students complain of being lost in the crowd; they are treated like numbers and no one knows or cares about them. Feeling lost in the crowd may motivate people to do something that makes them stand out from the group, to gain identity, and to be recognized. Hence animated, exaggerated, and sometimes antisocial behavior may represent people's attempts to gain recognition (Maslach, Stapp, and Santee, 1985). We might therefore explain the act of the snowball hurler at the football game by focusing on loss of responsibility; being in the group freed him from inhibitions against throwing the snowball. On the other hand, we might argue that being submerged in the crowd motivated him to do something to gain recognition; throwing the snowball separated him from the rest of the crowd.

Clearly, deindividuation is a complex process that may be partially explained by all three hypotheses. But there's another side of deindividuation. We have shown that deindividuation can lead to negative anti-social behaviors, but deindividuation can also have positive consequences. Deindividuation often leads to a reduction in conformity to group norms. In some cases, freeing the individual from the shackles of group norms can give rise to creativity that would otherwise be inhibited. For example, some authors adopt pseudonyms because they feel fewer restraints when they write anonymously. Finally, we find deindividuation in some professions in which individuals must violate social norms to carry out their jobs. For example, surgeons must handle and cut into their patients' bodies. For many years it was believed that surgeons should not become well acquainted with their patients; and when the operation took place, the surgeon was covered from head to foot and the patient was draped with a cloth so that only the affected area was visible. We might speculate that deindividuation here freed the surgeon from concerns and fears that might have interfered with his or her job. However, many patients and doctors complained that they felt uncomfortable with this impersonal transaction; today many doctors spend time getting to know their patients before operations. All the same, though deindividuation has its darker side, it can also have positive effects.

Groups and Decisions

Groups affect decisions in a number of ways. First, group involvement can affect the decisions that individuals make. Second, minorities and majorities within groups can use different processes to affect the decisions that groups as a whole make. Third, group dynamics can lead groups to make some extreme decisions. Finally, group dynamics can lead groups to make some disastrous decisions. In this section we will consider all of these aspects of groups and decisions.

The Influence of Groups on Individual Decisions

One of the critical activities engaged in by the *Kon Tiki* crew was decision making. From the beginning they were faced with a number of tough issues: how to build the raft; the kinds and quantities of provisions to take with them; and who performed which tasks. And they had to make numerous rules to govern their behavior during the voyage. The decisions they made determined the success or failure of the voyage; and some of these decisions would affect their very lives.

Often the group would discuss the issues, but the final decisions and actions rested with the individual crew members. This situation leads to some interesting questions concerning how being a member of a group affects our individual decisions and actions.

One of the earliest questions to be researched in this area was how making a decision in a group affects the individual's behavior (Lewin, 1943). Kurt Lewin's interest arose out of a practical problem that existed in this country during World War II. The price of food, especially meat, increased rapidly and supplies ran short. There was no shortage of beef kidneys, brains, and sweetbreads, but American homemakers were not accustomed to serving such things to their families. The government, interested in getting homemakers to serve these items, launched an extensive media campaign to persuade them to do so. Lewin reasoned that this method would not be effective. He believed that because groups to which the homemakers might belong were responsible for the norm of not serving these products, propaganda attempts should be aimed at the groups, not at the individual.

Lewis felt that it was important to change group norms regarding these products, and he set up an experiment to demonstrate how this could be done. He brought women who were Red Cross volunteers together in groups of thirteen to seventeen. Half of the groups heard a lecture on the positive values of using these nourishing but unpopular parts of animals and how their use would help the war effort (lecture condition). The lecturer told how the products could be cooked and even passed out recipes. The other half of the groups were in the group-decision condition; a trained group leader summarized the problem briefly and then let the women discuss their feelings about using these products. The discussion leader succeeded in getting a 100 percent vote in favor of the proposal that these meats be served at least once a week. One week later, the women from all of the groups were interviewed to see who had actually served them. Ten percent of the women in the lecture condition compared with 52 percent of the women in the group-decision condition had done so.

The Lewin study clearly demonstrates that group discussion and decision can be used to change the norms and the behavior of group members. It is sometimes difficult, however, to have every member of a group involved in the discussion and decision-making process. Hence it would be nice to find that the same change can be achieved by the use of group represen-

tatives instead of the whole group. Coch and French (1948) had a chance to investigate this question when they were asked to look at productivity at the Harwood Manufacturing Corporation, a pajama factory. The plant often had to make minor adjustments in the work procedure. Although management expected temporary decreases in productivity after such changes, it found that the declines in productivity were often drastic and long-lasting. Supervisors explained the reasons for the work adjustments to the employees, but these explanations failed to increase productivity. Coch and French designed a study in which some groups of workers (no involvement) were simply told the reasons for the changes and exhorted to work harder. Other groups (total involvement) were given the opportunity to discuss with management the reasons for the changes and how they could improve work conditions. In a third condition, group representatives were brought together to discuss the changes with management. The results indicated that workers in the total-involvement condition adjusted more quickly to the changes than no-involvement workers, and that the productivity of the total-involvement workers rose to a much higher level than that of the no-involvement workers. The performance of the workers in the representative condition was higher than that of the no-involvement groups but did not reach the level of the total-involvement groups. Hence, direct involvement in discussions by all group members is the most effective way to bring about group change.

Who Influences Group Decisions: Majority and Minority Influence

Now that we know something about how groups influence individual decisions, let's look at the way groups themselves make decisions. When an issue is first introduced, opinions are often split, with a majority favoring one position and a minority favoring another. Examining the *Kon Tiki* group, we can find numerous instances when the crew initially split four to two or five to one. Such splits occurred when the crew was deciding how to move the large balsa logs from the jungle to the coast and when they were charting their original sailing plans. In most such instances the group eventually adopted the majority position.

Indeed, this seems to be the case in much of the research: the majority usually wins. Much of the research on this question has examined the decisions made by mock juries. Subjects are given "evidence" about a case and told to arrive at a verdict. A series of studies (Davis, Kerr, Atkin, Holt, and Meek, 1975; Davis, Bray, and Holt, 1977) found that the majority generally wins; that is, the view held by the majority before discussion begins usually determines the verdict. Thus, if we find that ten out of twelve jurors believe the defendant is guilty, it is likely that a guilty verdict will be returned if the jury is forced to deliberate to unanimity. On the other hand, there are some important process differences to consider. For example, Foss (1981) formed twelve-member mock juries and had them listen to a trial proceeding. Some of the juries were told that they had to reach a unanimous decision before a verdict could be accepted, while others were told that a verdict supported by a majority of members (a quorum) could be accepted. The results indicated that the verdicts reached by the two types of juries were roughly the same. However, the quorum juries reached a decision twice as fast and were less likely to be "hung" than the unanimous juries. Further, members of the quorum juries were more cooperative and willing to compromise than the members of the unanimous juries. The individual has much less power in a quorum jury than in a unanimous jury, which can be hung by one member. These findings are important because they may mean that juries required to reach a unanimous verdict are more likely to consider all the evidence carefully than are juries under majority rule. (If you were on trial, it would not be very comforting to know that the members of your jury were willing to compromise so that they could reach a quick verdict!)

Some interesting processes help ensure the power of the majority. First the majority may simply reject the minority members and expel them from the group. However, this is not the case with juries or with the *Kon Tiki* crew. Second, a majority can put pressure on group members by making clear their expectation that they align themselves with the majority opinion. This pressure can lead group members to think about issues in ways that support the majority position (Wood, Pool, Leck, and Purvis, 1996). Third, a group with a fixed membership often fails to consider information held by the minority, focusing instead on information known by the majority of the group (Stasser and Titus, 1985).

In one study, subjects in groups of three or six members were given information about candidates for student body president (Stasser, Taylor, and Hanna, 1989). Some of the information was given to all sub-

jects (shared) and some of the information was known by only one subject in each group (unshared). When the subjects met as a group to discuss each candidate, it was found that they more often discussed shared information than unshared information. Further, discussion of shared information was greater in six-person groups than in three-person groups. A study of physicians making medical diagnoses involving fainting spells and blood in the urine revealed a similar finding. Shared information was much more often discussed than unshared information (Larson, Christensen, Abbott, and Franz, 1996). We might argue that it would be better for groups to seek out unshared information than to focus on shared information. Regardless of our views on this matter, we can see that the focus on shared information favors adoption of the majority opinion. The minority has an uphill battle if the group refuses to consider and discuss unshared information about a topic.

The majority, then, often determines the position taken by the group. But before accepting this tendency as a general rule, consider the groups in which you have been a member. How often is the group ready to adopt a majority position when someone says, "No, I don't think we should do that. I think we should take this other course of action"? The other group members probably let out an audible groan, but after trying to change the dissenter's mind, the group may well have slowly shifted to the dissenter's direction. In fact, this **minority influence** was the theme of a classic movie, *Twelve Angry Men*, in which Henry Fonda portrayed one of twelve jurors at a murder trial. After hearing the evidence, the jury retired to the jury room to reach a verdict. Many of the jurors wanted to decide quickly because they had other things planned after the trial. On their first ballot, eleven jurors found the defendant guilty. The one not-guilty vote was cast by Henry Fonda, who believed strongly that there was not enough evidence to prove beyond a reasonable doubt that the defendant was guilty. The remainder of the movie shows how the other jurors tried to get Fonda to change his vote. When he held to his convictions, one by one the other jurors began to agree with him; at the end, the jury voted unanimously for acquittal.

How could Henry Fonda or any other individual or minority within a group change the opinion of the majority? According to investigators (Moscovici and Mugny, 1983), minorities become influential to the extent that they can become visible to other group members and create conflict and tension within the group. This can best be done when decision-making procedures are devised that allow minorities within larger groups to coordinate their views prior to a discussion with the full group and stick to them (Kameda and Sugimori, 1995). Often the group attempts to silence the minority, but the tension may lead others to consider the minority position.

In an interesting display of regionalism in social psychology, a number of European psychologists took the lead in examining the influence of the minority while American psychologists focused on the power of the majority. The European investigators argued that the minority can influence the group if it takes a clear

In this early scene from the movie Twelve Angry Men (1957), *the juror played by Henry Fonda keeps his right hand under the table as the others raise theirs to signify a vote of guilty for the defendant.*

and consistent stand (Moscovici, 1976; Moscovici and Nemeth, 1974; Maass and Clark, 1984). The minority must hold to its position in the face of pressure from the majority, but the minority must show that it is willing to compromise if a better alternative is found (Papastamos and Mugny, 1989). This display of openness is necessary to avoid the appearance of rigidity and dogmatism.

With this discussion in mind, you may rush off to a group meeting and adopt a minority position only to

find that you not only fail to sway the group but lose some of your popularity among the members. Were we wrong about minority influence? The answer is found in the type of influence the minority has on the group. Investigators have found that the influence of the majority is generally direct, immediate, and public. That is, when the majority of group members suggest an alternative, the group may quickly and openly adopt this position. Minority influence is more subtle. The minority is more likely to influence members' private beliefs (Mucchi-Faina, 1989). The influence may be delayed (Nemeth and Staw, 1989); that is, members will not immediately jump to the alternative suggested by the minority, but they may change their position after thinking about the minority alternative. And minority influence may show up in indirect ways. One study found that a minority message in support of the right to abortion resulted in little change on the abortion issue, but group members did change their formerly negative attitudes toward birth control (Perez and Mugny, 1987). Other studies have shown that hearing a minority position in the group leads members to develop more creative solutions to problems that can be either related or unrelated to the issue addressed by the minority (Maass and Volpato, 1989; Nemeth and Chiles, 1988).

The suggestion that minorities have a different kind of influence than majorities is fascinating. Investigators argue that upon hearing the majority position, people become concerned about how they will be treated if they deviate from it. They feel that the majority must be correct and focus their attention on the immediate alternatives suggested by the majority and minority. In other words, their thinking *converges* on a few alternatives (Nemeth, 1989). Hearing the minority position sets up a very different process: the minority position gets attention because it is distinctive (Martin, 1989). As we witness the minority hold to its position in the face of pressure from the majority, we view the minority as courageous and as believing in their position; why else would they suffer for it (Moscovici, 1976)? We then try to figure out why the minority would adopt its position, and this leads us to consider the issue from a variety of perspectives. Thus, our thoughts *diverge* from the stated alternatives and we may create new alternatives and solutions (Nemeth, 1989). In general, the minority can encourage understanding issues from multiple perspectives and in flexible, integrative modes of thinking (Peterson and Nemeth, 1996). Taking this line of reasoning, we can see that investigators are suggesting that the majority motivates us to quickly adopt a position that favors either the majority or the minority. The minority, on the other hand, does not force us into taking an either-or stand but instead frees up our thinking so that we can consider a variety of positions.

Therefore, both the majority and the minority influence the group's decisions. We are more likely to see the group quickly and publicly adopt the position of the majority. But the minority will have a more subtle and longer lasting effect, especially on the private positions accepted by individual group members.

Group Polarization

When Thor Heyerdahl began thinking about his voyage, he proposed his idea to a number of people in the scientific community. He met with disbelief and discouragement that began to shake his commitment to the trip. In somewhat dampened spirits, he had a chance meeting with other sailors and explorers at the New York Explorers' Club. After a long discussion of the pros and cons of the trip, Thor emerged completely committed to making the risky voyage. What could have transformed Thor's growing caution into absolute certainty?

If we were to look at the early literature on group decision making, we would be surprised at this turn of events; we would have expected Thor to have emerged from the group in a more cautious frame of mind. William Whyte, in his insightful analysis of business bureaucracies, *The Organization Man* (1956), speculated that the group lowers the creativity and risk-taking behavior of its members to the least-common denominator. Because they fear they will be ridiculed by the more conservative power structure, people rarely risk being creative and innovative.

The view of group effects on individuals was challenged in a classic study. Stoner (1961) found that people chose riskier courses of action in groups than when they were alone. Following up on this finding, a group of investigators (Wallach, Kogan, and Bem, 1962) asked a large group of college students to fill out a questionnaire consisting of twelve potential dilemmas that a person might face in life, each choice presenting a risky and a conservative alternative. The risky alternative had a very high payoff if successful, but if unsuccessful it had dire consequences. Here are four of the dilemmas (Wallach, Kogan, and Bem, 1962, p. 77):

1. A captain of a college football team, in the final seconds of a game with the college's traditional rival, may choose a play that is almost certain to produce a tie score *or* a more risky play that would lead to sure victory if successful, sure defeat if not.
2. The president of an American corporation that is about to expand may build a new plant in the United States, where returns on the investment would be moderate, *or* build in a foreign country with an unstable political history where, however, returns on the investment would be very high.
3. A college senior planning graduate work in chemistry may enter a university where, because of rigorous standards, only a fraction of the graduate students manage to receive the Ph.D., *or* a university that has a poorer reputation but where almost every graduate student receives the Ph.D.
4. A low-ranked participant in a national chess tournament, playing an early match with the top-ranked opponent, has the choice of attempting *or* not trying a deceptive but risky maneuver that might lead to quick victory if successful or almost certain defeat if it fails.

The students were asked what probability of success they would require before they recommended the risky alternative. When the subjects had completed the questionnaire, they were asked to get together in groups of five to discuss the various dilemmas and arrive at a group consensus—a recommendation that could be agreed to by all members of the group. On ten of the twelve items, the groups arrived at decisions that were riskier (required less probability of success) than the average risk that had

BOX 13.2

Gender Differences in Group Performance

The *Kon Tiki* crew was an all-male group. Would the results of the voyage have been different if Heyerdahl had chosen an all-female crew or a mixed-sex crew? Researchers have been interested in comparing groups of men and women for more than fifty years. The issue is particularly important in today's social and economic climate, where equality is the watchword and women are playing increasingly important roles at all levels of the workforce.

In addressing the issues of gender differences, we might first ask whether all-male groups perform differently than all-female groups. In a review of fifty-two studies on this question, Wendy Wood concluded that the evidence suggests that all-male groups are more productive than all-female groups in some types of tasks. The research further suggests that males in general are more task oriented, whereas women are oriented more toward social factors and feelings (Carli, 1982; Amancio, 1989; Wood, 1987). Such a broad statement, however, tells only part of the story. Many of the tasks used in the research were "male-oriented" problem-solving tasks involving math or mechanical abilities. Men often perform better than women on these tasks when they work alone, so we might well expect a group effect to favor men. Differences between male and female groups decline when their tasks are less sex typed. Another issue is that men expect women to be socially oriented rather than task oriented and do not respond well to task-oriented women. Men prefer women who are likable, and who like them in return, and men grant women influence only when women behave in a social manner (Carli, LaFleur, and Loeber, 1995).

The research raises another interesting issue. For most groups to function well, attention must be focused on task behavior and social interactions within the group. Cohesive groups generally perform better than groups whose members are experiencing conflict and dissatisfaction. If men tend to be predominantly task oriented and women are concerned with group feelings, we should expect mixed-sex groups to function better than same-sex groups. In fact, the few studies that have been conducted on the topic indicate that mixed-sex groups do perform better than same-sex groups (either all-male or all-female groups). Although mixed-sex groups have a broader range of styles and abilities, the problem

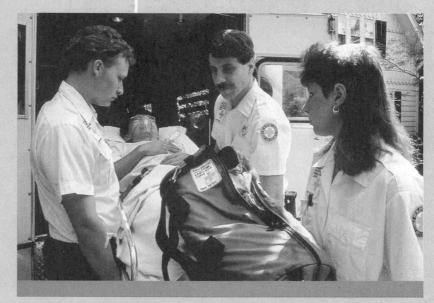

Paramedics assisting an injured person. Studies indicate that mixed-sex groups perform better than same-sex groups by offering a broader range of styles and abilities. Their challenge is to make best use of this variety.

Continued

BOX 13.2

Continued

confronting such groups is to make the best use of this variety. An interesting twist to this problem is seen in the effect of gender on a partner's behavior. Carli (1989) found that both male and female subjects showed more positive socially oriented behavior when they were paired with a female work partner and more task-oriented behavior when their partner was male.

Now that we have considered these issues, what do we think about the composition of Thor Heyerdahl's crew? Assuming that the nature of the tasks and the work setting do not favor men or women, a mixed-sex group might have been considered for maximum functioning of the group.

---

been acceptable only moments earlier to the individuals who made up the groups.

In the final step in this study, the subjects were retested individually. The group shift to a risky position may have been one that the individual group members publicly agreed to but did not actually accept; perhaps they had acceded to the will of a few strong individuals. The results showed that the group discussion and decision had caused a change of attitude. The subjects' opinions in the second individual testing remained at the risky position that they had adopted in the group discussion. Some subjects who were tested as much as six weeks after the group session continued to show the shift toward risk.

This and a number of other studies with similar results (Muhleman, Bruker, and Ingram, 1976; Cartwright, 1973) led investigators to conclude that being in groups led individuals to adopt riskier positions; the term *risky shift* was coined to refer to this effect. But the picture became cloudy when some other studies discovered that people in groups adopted more conservative positions than they had had on entering the group. For example, Fraser, Gouge, and Billig (1971) were able to identify several items on which the subjects shifted toward caution. McCauley, Stitt, Woods, and Lipton (1973) and Knox and Safford (1976) examined bets on horses at the racetrack. In their field studies, the subjects bet either alone or after group discussion. In both of these cases, groups were more cautious than individuals, as groups bet on the favorite more often than did individuals.

The general picture that emerged was that groups do not necessarily produce a risky shift. Rather, they

seem to produce a polarization effect in the direction that was initially preferred. The average postgroup response was more extreme in the same direction as the average pregroup response. If the initial tendency was toward risk, the group response was toward more risk; if the initial tendency was toward conservatism, the group response was even more conservative. It has subsequently been found that group discussions produce more extreme or polarized opinions and actions in line with any of a group's important values (Kerr, 1992). For example, groups of French high school students discussing France's World War II hero Charles DeGaulle, became more positive in their evaluations of DeGaulle (Moscovici and Zavalloni, 1969). This area of study became known as **group polarization.** Given that groups do lead to polarization in decisions, the next question was why this effect occurred. A variety of hypotheses were suggested.

An explanation that focuses on social comparison (see chapter 3) suggests that people do not want to be seen as taking wishy-washy or neutral positions; they want to appear at least as certain and extreme as others (Goethals and Zanna, 1979; Myers, 1982). According to this explanation, people use group discussion to compare their position with that of others. As a result of this comparison, they shift their own position until it is at least as extreme as that of other group members. Along these lines, one study found that people become more confident of their opinion when they perceive consensus in the group and must soon act on their opinion (Orive, 1988). Most group polarization studies find little difference in subjects' initial opinions. Therefore, when you hear other group members agree with your opinion, your confidence in that opinion may increase and this increased confidence may cause your opinion to become more extreme.

Social comparison may be responsible for some of the polarization effects but not all. Studies of the impact of simply exchanging information about preferred positions without group discussion typically show some degree of polarization but not as much as is found with full discussion. If people simply want to compare their position with that of others, an information exchange should produce complete polarization effects. This finding suggests that social comparison by itself is one factor affecting polarization, but that other factors are important as well.

A second hypothesis (Burnstein and Vinokur, 1977; Burnstein, 1982) suggests that it is not the positions of the other people but the arguments they use to support their positions that create group polarization. According to this hypothesis, members listen to the arguments presented by people during a group discussion, and they shift their opinions in the direction of the position that has the most persuasive arguments. Laughlin and Earley (1982) found that the direction of polarization was related to the number of persuasive arguments supporting a position: risky shift occurred when the risky extreme had the most arguments, and conservative shift occurred when the conservative side had the most arguments.

Although the persuasive arguments theory does have support, Sanders and Baron (1977) argue that the theory does not explain why the most compelling arguments favor a particular and relatively extreme position. That is, would it not be just as likely that strong arguments might favor a more neutral and middle-of-the-road stand?

In an effort to reconcile the various positions, several social psychologists (Isenberg, 1986; Brown, 1986) suggested that social comparison and persuasive arguments work together to produce group polarization. According to these investigators, group members first compare their position with that of other group members. This comparison motivates them to present arguments supporting their position. These arguments influence not only the presenter but other members as well. Another intriguing idea is that both social comparison and persuasive arguments affect the extremity of our opinions, but the two forces work in different situations (Kaplan, 1987). According to this position, when the issue involves facts, we will be concerned with the information presented in the arguments. Our

position becomes more extreme as we garner information from the discussion. However, on tasks requiring values (for example, the right to abortion), we compare our position with the position (not the reasons for the position) of others. In this case, social comparison plays a strong role in pushing our opinions toward extremity.

Looking back over our discussion of group decision making, we can see that groups may increase the extremity and confidence of our opinions. What does this imply about the wisdom of making decisions in groups? We have seen that groups offer a wealth of information and perspectives that can improve decisions. But it is important to be aware of the influence groups can have on the decision-making process and guard against the negative dynamics. Using this advice, investigators have found that groups that have received information about group dynamics can perform better than even the best individual member (Hall and Williams, 1970; Michaelson, Watson, and Black, 1989).

Groupthink

We have many reasons for believing that groups should make better decisions than individuals. Groups have members with different experiences, expertise, and points of view. We might further expect that highly cohesive groups—groups in which members like each other and want to stay in the group—would be best able to use the diverse talents of the members and arrive at the best decisions. Indeed, there is evidence that groups often make better decisions than isolated individuals (Shaw, 1981). However, there are so many examples to the contrary that we cannot conclude that groups are always superior decision makers.

One of the clearest examples of a situation in which a group made a poor decision occurred on April 17, 1961, when fourteen hundred Cuban exiles landed at the Bay of Pigs in Cuba. Their mission was to establish a beachhead and to join with Cuban rebels in the Escambray Mountains. Together, these forces were expected to unite the Cuban people in a rebellion to overthrow Premier Fidel Castro. The exiles were armed by the United States. Their mission had been planned by one of the best intelligence organizations in the world, the Central Intelligence Agency (CIA), and approved by one of the most popular leaders of the time, President John F. Kennedy. Despite all of these advantages, the whole plan fell flat on its face. Castro's army was well prepared for the invasion;

there was little discontent among the Cuban people; and eighty miles of dense swamp separated the Bay of Pigs from the Escambray Mountains. Within two days of the invasion, the exiles had been surrounded by Castro's army and the entire force either killed or captured. The United States suffered a severe political setback, and it was besieged by cries of outrage and indignation from countries around the world.

It's easy to see why the invasion failed. It's not so easy, however, to see how such a misconceived plan could have been devised and set in motion. Janis (1972, 1982) carefully analyzed the decision-making process that produced the Bay of Pigs fiasco and similar blunders, such as lack of preparedness for the Pearl Harbor attack and increasing U.S. involvement in Vietnam. From these analyses, he concluded that a situation of groupthink may develop in cohesive decision-making groups. According to Janis, **groupthink** is "a mode of thinking that people engage in when they are deeply involved in a cohesive group, when members' striving for unanimity overrides their motivation to realistically appraise alternative courses of action" (1972, p. 9). In other words, groupthink is excessive concurrence seeking in groups (t'Hart, 1988).

Janis and his colleagues (Janis and Mann, 1977) developed a model that shows the groupthink process. As figure 13.3 indicates, groupthink has three causes. One is a highly cohesive group. A second is structural faults in the organization. Groups that are relatively isolated from the scrutiny of others and have members with similar attitudes and backgrounds are most likely to exhibit groupthink. The presence of a strong and respected leader who does not remain impartial is another structural problem that helps set the stage for groupthink. In fact, recent work suggests that the leader's behavior may be more responsible for groupthink than the cohesiveness of the group (t'Hart and Kroon, 1989; Vinokur, Burnstein, Sechrest, and Wortman, 1985). The third cause of groupthink, "provocative situational context," simply means that the group is under a great deal of stress, and the members may have had their self-esteem lowered by past failures or the difficulty of their task. One recent study shows that time pressure can increase the extent to which people advance arguments without systematic processing of relevant information, information that is needed to make good decisions, making groupthink more likely (Kelly, Jackson, and Huston-Comeaux, 1997).

These factors leading to groupthink have a variety of observable consequences, as shown in figure 13.3.

1. The group develops the illusion of *invulnerability*. As Arthur Schlesinger (1965) reported, the Kennedy group felt that they had the Midas touch; they had done everything right and won the election against all odds. They were euphoric, and the possibility of failure hardly crossed their minds.

FIGURE 13.3 **ANALYSIS OF GROUPTHINK, BASED ON COMPARISONS OF HIGH- AND LOW-QUALITY DECISIONS BY POLICY-MAKING GROUPS**

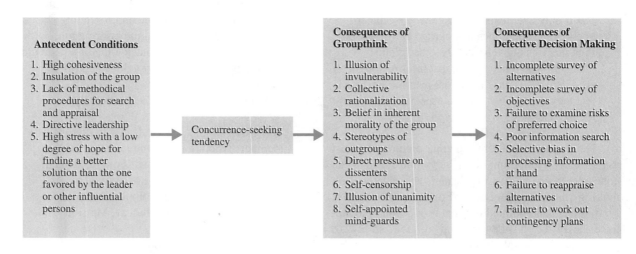

Antecedent Conditions		Consequences of Groupthink	Consequences of Defective Decision Making
1. High cohesiveness 2. Insulation of the group 3. Lack of methodical procedures for search and appraisal 4. Directive leadership 5. High stress with a low degree of hope for finding a better solution than the one favored by the leader or other influential persons	Concurrence-seeking tendency	1. Illusion of invulnerability 2. Collective rationalization 3. Belief in inherent morality of the group 4. Stereotypes of outgroups 5. Direct pressure on dissenters 6. Self-censorship 7. Illusion of unanimity 8. Self-appointed mind-guards	1. Incomplete survey of alternatives 2. Incomplete survey of objectives 3. Failure to examine risks of preferred choice 4. Poor information search 5. Selective bias in processing information at hand 6. Failure to reappraise alternatives 7. Failure to work out contingency plans

Source: Based on Janis (1972)

2. The group members view themselves as having a high degree of *morality*. Kennedy's advisers saw themselves as fighting the evil forces of communism.

3. The group members share *common stereotypes*. In the Bay of Pigs case, Kennedy's cabinet members reinforced one another's view that the Cubans were a bunch of unorganized bandits who could not fight.

4. One of the most disastrous consequences is that the group develops an *illusion of agreement and unanimity*. Each person simply assumes that the other group members hold the same opinions and there is no need to encourage discussion on issues on which everyone agrees.

5. As a result of this illusion, there are strong group *pressures toward conformity* and the group members become reluctant to *express disagreement*. A member or members of the group assume the role of "mind guard" and work to protect the agreement and cohesive feeling of the group.

6. Another possible consequence is the *discussion pattern* that develops in the group and discourages examination of all alternatives. In a careful analysis of group communication, investigators (Stasser and Titus, 1985; Stewart and Stasser, 1993) found that information is more likely to enter group discussion if it is shared by all or most group members. Groups tend to avoid considering unique information that is not already known by most group members. Further, group discussion is generally biased in favor of preferences that already exist in the group. This tendency suggests that if only one member of Kennedy's cabinet knew of the conditions that existed at the Bay of Pigs site, it is unlikely that the other group members would have given that information much consideration even if the initial member proposed that they do so. This effect is especially likely if the member has low status in the group.

Having painted a rather dismal picture, we must ask whether groupthink is an inevitable result when cohesive groups with strong leaders are charged with making important decisions. Fortunately, it is not. First, it has been pointed out that groupthink may not necessarily be a phenomenon related solely to groups; an individual who rationalized decisions and failed to carefully examine the risks involved would also make poor decisions (Abelson and Levi, 1985). Group pressures may increase the likelihood of this process, but they are not solely responsible for it. Second, cohesive groups do not always fall prey to groupthink; in fact, such groups can make excellent decisions if they take steps to avoid groupthink. To demonstrate this point, Janis cited another decision made by Kennedy's cabinet. Just over a year after the Bay of Pigs invasion, Kennedy learned that the Soviets were deploying missiles with nuclear warheads in Cuba. Kennedy called a series of meetings of his advisers, many of whom were the same men who had planned the Bay of Pigs invasion. This time, however, Kennedy pushed to ensure that numerous proposals for action were discussed and carefully weighed; recommendations were considered and reconsidered. Persons outside the group of advisers were called on to supply information and opinions. Kennedy intentionally excluded himself from many of the meetings so that the discussants would not be unduly influenced by him. In this case, groupthink was avoided and a successful plan was adopted by the group. A shipping blockade was imposed to prevent the Soviets from delivering additional men and supplies to Cuba; and ensuing events led to the eventual removal of the missiles already in Cuba.

As the nuclear missile crisis illustrates, groupthink is most likely to be avoided if the following steps are taken:

1. The leader should avoid stating a preference and should encourage group members to consider all alternatives (Flowers, 1977).

2. Group members should be encouraged to play the role of devil's advocate and force the discussion to focus on unique information.

3. When possible, persons outside the group should be brought in to express opinions and offer suggestions.

4. New information should be continually reassessed.

5. The group should consist of highly dominant members who are not prone to anxiety about disagreement. Research has shown that such groups are less likely to show symptoms of groupthink than groups composed of low-dominance members (Callaway, Marriott, and Esser, 1985).

6. Individual members should be told that they will be held personally accountable for the group

decision and will have to justify it (t'Hart and Kroon, 1989).

Groupthink is an important concept; it's unfortunate that more research has not addressed it. Much of the support for the theory comes from case studies. Although the verdict on the theory is not in, the concept of groupthink cautions us to pay attention to the characteristics of the members, structure, and process of decision-making groups.

Summary

A group may be defined as two or more people who are interacting with one another in such a manner that each person influences, and is influenced by, each other person. People in groups consider themselves as belonging together and sharing common goals. From the individual's perspective, joining a group has both positive and negative consequences. Groups allow people to accomplish a variety of tasks that could not be achieved alone, and social comparison is possible in groups. On the other hand, people must give up some freedom and personal identity when they join a group.

Group members go through a variety of stages: new member, full member, marginal member, ex-member. Groups, like members, go through a series of stages as they develop and change. These stages affect the dynamics of the group and the behavior of individual group members.

Groups may influence the performance and behavior of individual members. Research on social facilitation shows that people perform simple and well-learned tasks better in groups than alone, but that learning of new material will be inhibited by the presence of others. The last effect seems to occur because others arouse the individual and increase the drive to exhibit the dominant response. Many explanations have been offered for the social facilitation effect, including evaluation apprehension, distraction, narrowing of attention, and social comparison. Social loafing is the tendency of individuals to work less hard in groups than alone, an effect that may be the result of reduced feelings of responsibility for the final product and the lack of identifiability of individual performance in a group. Social loafing has also been attributed to the free-rider effect and the sucker effect. Social loafing is reduced when people feel a sense of groupness and a concern that the group product can be evaluated.

Deindividuation occurs when people lose their personal identity and adopt that of the group. It generally occurs in large groups in which people feel anonymous and arousal is heightened. People in deindividuated conditions focus on immediate cues. Doing so often lowers inhibitions against performing socially disapproved actions. A second explanation for the deindividuation effect is that people lose their personal identity in a crowd and take on an identity defined by their role in the group. A third explanation for the behaviors of deindividuated people is that they are attempting to gain personal recognition and distinctiveness.

Decisions made in groups following group discussion are most likely to influence an individual's behavior.

Although the majority usually determines the group's decision, the minority can be effective if it adopts a consistent and unyielding stand. Minorities are effective because they create conflict and challenge the group norm of conformity. Majority influence is generally direct, immediate, and public; minority influence is usually indirect, delayed, and private. The minority often motivates divergent thinking that results in creativity.

Membership in a group often leads individuals to adopt more extreme positions than they held before they became part of the group. Group polarization has been explained by social comparison and persuasive argument processes.

Groupthink occurs when group members make a quick and ill-conceived decision in an effort to maintain group harmony. Groupthink is most likely to occur in highly cohesive groups that have a strong and respected leader. The chances that groupthink will occur can be reduced by a careful consideration of proposals, by the leader's avoidance of stating a clear preference, and by solicitation of opinions by people who are not members of the group.

Key Terms

collective	group development	social facilitation
deindividuation	group polarization	social inhibition
free-rider effect	groupthink	social loafing
group	minority influence	sucker effect

Suggested Readings

Brown, R. (1988). *Group processes: Dynamics within and between groups.* Oxford, England: Blackwell.

Forsyth, D. (1990). *An introduction to group dynamics* (2nd ed.). Pacific Grove, CA: Brooks/Cole.

Hendrick, C. (Ed.). (1987). *Group processes.* Newbury Park, CA: Sage.

Janis, I. (1982). *Groupthink.* Boston: Houghton Mifflin.

Levine, J. M., and Moreland, R. L. (1998). Small groups. In D. T. Gilbert, S. T. Fiske, and G. Lindzey (Eds.), *The handbook of social psychology* (Vol. 2, pp. 415–469). New York: McGraw-Hill.

McGrath, J. (1984). *Groups: Interaction and performance.* Englewood Cliffs, NJ: Prentice-Hall.

McGrath, J. E. (Ed.). (1988). *The social psychology of time.* Newbury Park, CA: Sage.

Moscovici, S., Mugny, G., and van Avermaet, E. (1985). *Perspectives on minority influence.* Cambridge, England: Cambridge University Press.

Mullen, B., and Goethals, G. R. (1987). *Theories of group behavior.* New York: Springer-Verlag.

Petrovsky, A. V. (1985). *The individual and the collective.* Moscow: Progress.

Pfeffer, J. (1998). Understanding organizations: Concepts and controversies. In D. T. Gilbert, S. T. Fiske, and G. Lindzey (Eds.), *The handbook of social psychology* (Vol. 2, pp. 733–777). New York: McGraw-Hill.

Turner, J. C. (1987). *Rediscovering the social group: A self-categorization theory.* Oxford, England: Blackwell.

Chapter 14

Culture and Behavior

If you examine a world map, New Zealand looks like two ships drifting alone in the South Pacific. As tiny as the country seems, its landscape is a mosaic of contrasts that seem not to fit together in such a small country. Lush rain forests are bordered by stark, dry desert land punctuated with volcanic mountains, and the rather gentle north island seems to look with dismay at its southern partner, an island of towering jagged mountains and deep fjords. In some ways, however, this geography is appropriate because it mimics New Zealand's social landscape. The country is inhabited by the Maori people, the early settlers who now compose about 12 percent of the population. The Maori are striking in their physical appearance, their bodies sometimes adorned with intricate tattoos. The majority of the country's population (over 80 percent) are of European extract, mostly Dutch and English. These people are called *Pakeha*; their ancestors were settlers who fought bitter wars with the Maori to establish their hold on the island nation. When both sides were exhausted by these armed conflicts, they called a truce, deciding that living as neighbors was preferable to war. But each neighbor retained its own culture and identity.

Maori author Witi Ihimaera (1973) tells the story of Tama Mahana, a young man who tried to live in both cultures, "half in light and half in darkness." Tama grew up in the small Maori village of Waituhi. He was the eldest son in a family of eight. The people of Waituhi viewed themselves as one large family, related by the fact that they all traced their lineage to one of the original seven canoes that carried the first Maori to discover New Zealand. In fact, it was customary for a person who wished to speak in the meetinghouse to recite his or her lineage before addressing the group. Decisions in the village were often made in the meetinghouse only after everyone who wished to state a position had an opportunity. People were

A reunion between a Maori grandmother and granddaughter. The young woman returned from city life to rejoin her family and community in their homeland, where the Maori are the majority population.

woven into the fabric of their extended family. As Tama recalled, "If somebody got married, you didn't wait for an invitation, you just went to the wedding, because you were a member of the family. And if there was a *tangi,* you stopped whatever you were doing, no matter whether you were working in some flash factory or at some flash job, and you went home to help out. One of the family had died and the *tangi,* it was the homecalling" (p. 120).

Greetings involved pressing noses together and schedules were guidelines rather than strict masters. This view of time often led to conflict with the *Pakeha* neighbors who viewed schedules as solemn commitments. In fact, one Maori son complained to his father, "I can't work to Maori time like you do. There's a *Pakeha* world which is my world, Dad. Gosh, if the whole world was full of Maoris, it would be chaotic! People would make appointments for one hour and arrive the next. Trains, boats, planes, nothing would run to schedule!" (p. 121). One's role in the group took precedence over one's personal wishes in guiding behavior. Tama's father never tired of telling him, "You are the eldest, Son. The eldest always looks after the younger ones of the family. I was taught that when I was a child. I teach you the same thing now. Never forget" (p. 192).

When Tama was eighteen years old, he decided to spread his wings and strike out on his own. He would go to the city of Wellington, live among the Pakeha, and try a new life. His decision created terrible conflict in his family. The Maori way was for families, including even distant relatives, to live together. But Tama was determined and off he went to Wellington. He was fortunate to land a job in the post office. His life was now run by a strict schedule. He lived in his own apartment and was now responsible for himself. There was no one with whom he must share his possessions, but no one to share with him. Few people cared about Tama's Maori lineage or his position in his family. These and many other items were private matters.

A certain excitement and freedom came from embracing the *Pakeha* world. But at times Tama felt a nagging discomfort, a sense of isolation, a feeling that his march to the *Pakeha* drumbeat was just slightly out of step. At these times, he would quiet himself and remember, "Dad and my *whanau,* my big Maori family, and my world would right itself" (p. 79). Tama managed to straddle both worlds for four years. Then he received the fateful telephone call from his sister, "Come home, Tama. Dad . . . he's dead."

Tama's world came crashing down. His grief for his father was made worse by his guilt for having left his village. As he took the sad journey to Waituhi, he vowed that he would remain there, assuming the position of leadership bestowed on the eldest child. He would not only reenter the Maori world but he would teach his younger siblings "of Maori *aroha,* the love we hold for one another" and of the Maori customs and traditions. Trying to live in two cultures had been surprisingly difficult. Although the distance between Waituhi and Wellington was relatively short when measured in miles, the distance between the Maori and Pakeha cultures seemed quite large many times.

Culture: Software of the Mind

Tama spent his first eighteen years in the Maori culture followed by four years in the culture of the Pakeha. We might begin our discussion by comparing the two cultures, or by asking how each culture affected his life. But before attempting to deal with these questions, let's ask a more basic question: What is **culture?** This seems like a fairly straightforward question, one that should have a straightforward answer. But the issue is not so simple. Indeed, many recent books devote whole chapters or several chapters to defining culture (Triandis, 1994; Matsumoto, 1997), and the definitions that are given are not completely in agreement. For example, Matsumoto (1996) defines culture as: "The set of attitudes, values, beliefs, and behaviors shared by a group of people, but different for each individual, communicated from one generation to the next" (p. 32).

Although this definition may seem quite comprehensive, Triandis (1994) renders a more expanded one: "Culture is a set of human-made objective and subjective elements that in the past have increased the probability of survival and resulted in satisfactions for the participants in an ecological niche, and thus become shared among those who could communicate with each other because they had a common language and they lived in the same time and place" (p. 22). Although this seems like a mouthful, both of these definitions make certain common points about culture. First, culture is shared by a group of people and is transmitted across generations. For example, one characteristic of the Maori culture was the role of the eldest son; his father had taught Tama that the eldest son's role was to take care of the family. This role was shared by most Maori people, but it was not entrenched in the *Pakeha* culture.

Second, culture involves attitudes, values, beliefs, and behaviors (subjective elements). Triandis (1994) argues that culture also includes objective elements such as the tools, methods of transportation, style of houses, and furniture that characterize a people. This definition is a useful addition because we find that people often pass on these objective elements from generation to generation. In some cases the objective elements include traditional dress and sacred objects, whereas in other cases these elements are more mundane. Consider the use of chopsticks by many Asian cultures versus such eating utensils as forks and spoons in many European and American cultures. Differences in these basic utensils are associated with different ways in which food is cooked and served.

Culture is the result of a group's adaptation to its world. A culture that is faced with periodic floods may build houses that rest on high poles; a nomadic culture, on the other hand, may use dwellings such as tents that can be easily dismantled and carried. Being adaptive, culture is also constantly changing to deal with such events as wars or environmental and technological change. For example, the traditional Anglo culture of the United States identified the role of the woman as a homemaker, wife, and mother. The Second World War, however, changed the culture. Casualties reduced the number of men, and during the war women had to take over many jobs that were traditionally reserved for men. As a result, the role of the modern woman in the culture is one that is more equal to that of the man and allows (encourages) women to hold positions outside the home.

Culture plays a cunning role in our lives. As Triandis (1994) points out, we are often not aware of our culture until we come into contact with other ones. At this point we realize the broad influence culture has on us.

Taking into account the pervasive influence of culture on our behavior, several investigators have developed shorthand definitions of culture. Hofstede, for example, suggested that "culture is like a computer program that controls behavior" (1980), and "culture is the software of the mind" (1991). To this view we might add that culture is the stage on which the drama of human behavior unfolds. Regardless of the definition, culture affects all aspects of human behavior, and therefore, it is vital to consider its influence within the

domain of social psychology. Social psychology, however, is largely a science developed in the United States and most of the studies in the field include subjects from this country. Because of this situation, we are only just beginning to recognize the role of culture, but the results from **cross-cultural studies,** which compare behaviors across cultures, have opened up new vistas for understanding and predicting human behavior.

Classifying Cultures

Our world is a mosaic of cultures that differ on nearly any dimension you can name. Trying to compare and contrast all these cultures seems like a daunting task. Where would we start? Several attempts to classify cultures into manageable categories have been made. Probably the most influential is attributed to Hofstede (1980, 1991), who was initially interested in measuring work-related values in cultures. He surveyed more than 117,000 IBM employees in sixty-six countries and identified four dimensions on which cultural values could be arranged. Hofstede believed that these dimensions represented the core values that influenced social arrangements, institutions, customs, and practices in the society. One dimension was **uncertainty avoidance,** which referred to the extent that individuals in the culture were disturbed by and avoided ambiguity and uncertainty.

A second dimension was **power distance,** which was the degree of inequality that existed between a less powerful and a more powerful person. Individuals in high power-distance cultures tended to behave submissively in the presence of high-power persons, and they tended to prefer autocratic supervisors. **Masculinity** was the third dimension. Cultures low on the masculinity continuum tended to have sex roles that were fluid and flexible; power was not necessarily associated with sex roles or sex, and ideals were unisex or androgynous (Hofstede, 1996). On the other hand, societies high on the masculinity dimension believe that "men should be dominant in all settings," sex roles are clearly differentiated, and *machismo* is valued.

Although these dimensions have received some attention and support (Hofstede and Bond, 1984; Bochner and Hesketh, 1994; Kim, Triandis, Kagitcibasi, Choi, and Yoon, 1994), most attention has been focused on Hofstede's (1980) **individualism** and **collectivism** categories. Societies high in individualism, often referred to as individualistic soci-

BOX 14.1

Culture: Adapting to a Changing World

Triandis (1994) points out that culture is the result of a group's effort to adapt to its environment. As a result, a group's culture is in constant flux, changing as its environment changes. The following article provides an interesting example of this point. Consider it from the standpoint that groups must develop means to ensure that those in the society (the young and the very old) who cannot care for themselves receive the care they need. Within Asian cultures, as with many collective groups, the responsibility for family members rests squarely with the family. But as times change, the society must adapt and find ways to ensure that its values are heeded.

In Singapore, Mother of All Lawsuits Is Often Filed by Mom

* * *

Act to Protect Aging Parents From Neglect Spurs Rash Of Interfamily Litigation

By PETER WALDMAN
Staff Reporter of THE WALL STREET JOURNAL

SINGAPORE — It was supposed to be a safety net, a last resort, a legal reckoning for the handful of Singaporean parents whose reprobate children abandon them in old age.

But since the Maintenance of Parents law took effect here June 1, requiring citizens of this tiny republic to financially support their aged parents in need, already more than 100 mothers and fathers have filed suits against their children.

"It seems that our daughter prefers paying for the living expenses of her dogs than for ours," complained C.K. Wong, 71-years-old, who sought redress from the Tribunal for the Maintenance of Parents on the court's first day in business.

Mother of Invention

Leave it to Singapore to find a legal remedy for the burgeoning moral and economic problems of elderly care, problems that plague aging populations everywhere. This high-tech city state, mostly jungle and beach just 30 years ago, today has one of the globe's highest per-capita incomes. Its strict laws — meting out death to drug traffickers, caning to graffiti artists and big fines to chewing-gum sellers and litter bugs — have kept the island clean, green and tranquil.

And now, it is hoped, filial. Neglect of parents wasn't considered a big problem in Singapore, whose three main cultures, Chinese, Malay and Indian, have strong traditions of family loyalty. But backers of the parent-support law were looking to the future, when, by the year 2020, the proportion of Singaporeans over 60 is projected to quadruple to 26% of the population. As the overall population ages, advocates for the elderly fret that younger generations are becoming more self-centered, raising the specter of more and more elderly becoming wards of the state.

"We're in a balancing act," says Anamah Tan, a prominent family lawyer. "In Singapore we tell young people to go, go, go, to strive for economic success. But we don't want them to forget their other responsibilities. This law provides needed ballast."

Suits of Surprise

The fact that scores of aggrieved parents rushed to sue their kids after the law took effect surprised even the act's sponsors, who assumed the parents' tribunal would remain largely symbolic. The court, to protect privacy, won't disclose details of the cases, nor will tribunal members be interviewed.

But accounts from Singaporean lawyers,

Continued

BOX 14.1

Continued

doctors and social workers, as well as interviews with some petitioners to the new court, show how the bonds of filial piety are straining, even here. "When it comes to money from your pocket, you see how fast those traditional 'Asian values' can dissipate," Ms. Tan says.

Mr. Wong and his wife, W.H. Soh, filed their claim just hours after the parents' court opened its doors. The couple, parents of seven, have told advocates they scrape by on less than $350 a month because a wealthy daughter cut them off several years ago. Fighting back tears, Mrs. Soh, 67, said the couple could barely make ends meet, yet her daughter's family lived comfortably in a large house with a maid and three dogs. Under the parents' law, parents over 60 can sue their kids.

The tribunal first tries to settle cases through mediation, with no lawyers allowed. Failing that, it can order progeny to pay parents as much financial support as the court deems fair and feasible. Only offspring who prove they have been "abandoned, abused or neglected" by their parents can get off the hook. Proving something as emotional as parental misconduct, however, isn't easy; in most cases, right and wrong are buried beneath years of family trauma.

Sue Thy Brother

Many of the cases involve sibling rivalries. Recently, a woman who calls herself Madam Yee squared off at the tribunal against her two brothers, whom she is suing on their 85-year-old mother's behalf. As a court mediator watched, the invective flew, says Madam Yee, 52.

The brothers, one older than Madam Yee and one younger, accused her of squandering money on herself, and insisted the mother, who lives with Madam Yee, be placed in a nursing home. Madam Yee, who is unmarried, says the older brother

absconded with their mother's savings. Her brothers, she says, seldom visit their mother and pay nothing for her support.

"Mom can pretty much take care of herself; she just needs companionship and moral support," says Madam Yee, who works in a hospital as a nurse. "A nursing home wouldn't provide that."

The brothers — one a vice principal at a private school and the other a bank manager — have offered to pay $350 a month, between them, in maternal support. Madam Yee wants $550 a month — from each. The mediator scheduled another meeting for October, when he plans to review the costs of maintaining the mom. He instructed Madam Yee to bring her along next time.

"I've been telling her what's going on, but she doesn't show any response," Madam Yee says. "I'm not sure she understands."

Tangled Circumstances

In another case, a man's children from his second marriage are suing the kids from his first, seeking help to pay the father's medical bills after a recent stroke. The man left his first family years ago. Now the tribunal finds itself in the knotty position of apportioning a significant financial burden on the basis of a dad's uneven treatment of his children.

Foreseeing troubles like that, the parents' bill caused a passionate, and rare, debate when it was first proposed by an independent member of Singapore's parliament two years ago. Singapore's long-ruling People's Action Party was neutral on the idea, clearing the way for what Walter Woon, the bill's author, calls "the only real debate we've ever had in parliament."

Opponents accused the bill's sponsors of debasing the core "Asian values" by reducing them to a "Western" legal obligation. Love for parents can't be legislated, they said;

Continued

BOX 14.1

Continued

attempting to do so will only sour relations between the generations. What happens to a people's sense of shame under such a law, opponents asked. One lawmaker said some of his constituents were already saving evidence — check stubs, receipts — to prove their "loyalty," should the need ever arise.

In the end, the government supported the bill and it became law. Mr. Woon, a law professor and an appointed member of parliament, had anticipated a "couple of dozen" parents would take recourse to the new law. The 100-plus suits filed so far "took me by surprise," he says. Noting that the rate of filings has steadily declined since the law's enactment, Mr. Woon says he's "not worried yet. We're talking about 25 years of pent-up demand."

In the field, Singaporeans who work with seniors welcome the legislation. At giant Alexandra Hospital, the staff has grown ac-

customed to seeing relatives of elderly patients arrive for visits in late-model luxury cars, only to find that, "as soon as you mention discharge, they just disappear," says Chan Kin Ming, the hospital's head of geriatrics. The new law provides a useful "last resort" against those who would completely abandon their parents, he says.

For now, most elderly Singaporeans still shudder at the thought of suing their own children, says Lim Chan Yong, a physician and president of Singapore Action Group for the Elderly, an advocacy group. Those days, however, may soon end, he says. Among the Chinese who make up the largest segment of Singapore's population, "filial piety is one of the pillars of Confucianism," he says. "But I'm sure the next generation will be more conscious of their rights. Parents won't have a problem suing their kids."

eties, emphasize personal autonomy and independence. Everyone is expected to look after himself or herself and the immediate family. These societies stress individual initiative, personal privacy, self-containment, and self-reliance. Many of the individualistic cultures tend to be rooted in the Judeo-Christian tradition that emphasizes the existence of the individual soul along with the concept of free will (Morris and Peng, 1994).

On the other hand, societies that are low in individualism—collective cultures—emphasize collective or group identity. These societies view individuals in relation to their position in the group. Dependence or interdependence between people is the foundation of collective cultures. A high premium is placed on duties and obligations to one's groups; group decisions rather than individual decisions are important. Many of these cultures reflect the Confucian doctrine of the importance of role-appropriate behavior and the notion that social relationships are of paramount importance (King and Bond, 1985). If we consider the two cultures faced by Tama, it is clear that the Maori society is strongly

collective, while the *Pakeha* culture is individualistic. Table 14.1 lists the placement on Hofstede's individualism scale of a number of cultures.

In reviewing this list, several points can be made. First, the United States and Canada along with most western European countries are high on individualism, whereas Asian and Hispanic cultures are more collective. Second, individualistic cultures tend to be found in the more highly industrialized areas, and the collective cultures are less industrialized. However, before adopting this list, we must offer two cautions. The first is clearly seen in the story of Tama. Although New Zealand is rated as highly individualistic, the Maori culture within New Zealand is very collective. Hofstede's ratings are for whole countries, but within any country there may be cultures that differ from the country's norm. The second caution is that even within a culture, individuals may differ in their degree of individualism (Triandis, 1994; Ayerstaran, 1996). For example, if we examine the Maori culture (even within Waituhi) there are likely to be individuals who are highly

TABLE 14.1   INDIVIDUALISM/COLLECTIVISM SCORES ACROSS COUNTRIES IN HOFSTEDE'S STUDY

Country	Actual IDV	Country	Actual IDV
U.S.A.	91	Argentina	46
Australia	90	Iran	41
Great Britain	89	Brazil	38
Canada	80	Turkey	37
Netherlands	80	Greece	35
New Zealand	79	Philippines	32
Italy	76	Mexico	30
Belgium	75	Portugal	27
Denmark	74	Hong Kong	25
Sweden	71	Chile	23
France	71	Singapore	20
Ireland	70	Thailand	20
Norway	69	Taiwan	17
Switzerland	68	Peru	16
Germany (F.R.)	67	Pakistan	14
South Africa	65	Colombia	13
Finland	63	Venezuela	12
Austria	55		
Israel	54	Mean of 39 countries	
Spain	51	(HERMES)	51
India	48	Yugoslavia (same industry)	27
Japan	46		

Note: Work goal scores were computed for a stratified sample of seven occupations at two points in time. Actual values and values predicted on the basis of multiple regression on wealth, latitude, and organization size.
Source: Hofstede (1980)

collective in their values and others more individualistic. The ratings, therefore, should be viewed as only a crude estimation of the general tendency within a culture.

The characterization of cultures along these dimensions gives us a starting point on which to compare them. As we will see, culture has an influence on nearly every type of behavior we have discussed throughout this text. It would take another book to describe the range of behaviors touched by culture, so we examine only a sample. Most attention has been placed on the individualism/collective dimension identified by Hofstede (1980), and most of our discussion will deal with this dimension. The important point about culture is that we generally take it for granted, rarely thinking about its influence on us until we are faced with someone from another culture who acts, feels, or thinks differently from us. Let's begin our examination of culture by focusing on the self.

Culture and the Self-Concept

When Tama recalled his interactions with his father, he remembered his father stressing two points: Tama was a Maori, and he was the eldest son in the family. In general, collective cultures view individuals as they relate to the group. However, when we recall our interactions with our parents, we may remember that they emphasized that we were beautiful or handsome, intelligent, or funny. These traits are unique to the individual, often labeled **ideocentric.** One characteristic of individualistic cultures is the emphasis on the person as an independent, unique being separate from the group. Given these differences, we might expect that people from collective cultures would develop a self-concept that emphasizes their role in, and relationship to, groups. On the other hand, individuals from highly individualis-

Commune workers in the People's Republic of China picking tea leaves. Asian cultures tend to be more collective than individualistic.

tic cultures should tend to see themselves in terms of unique personal traits.

Bochner (1994) found support for this prediction when he asked individuals from Malaysia (collective culture), Australia (individualistic culture), and Great Britain (individualistic culture) to describe themselves by completing ten sentences that began with "I am . . ." Coders categorized the responses into three types: group, ideocentric, and allocentric. Group statements referred to group membership, demographic characteristics, and groups with which people experience a common fate; examples might include referring to oneself as a son, a teacher, or a Roman Catholic. The second category was ideocentric, which included statements about personal qualities, attitudes, beliefs, behaviors, and traits; for example, "I am happy," "I am intelligent," and "I am attractive." The final category, "allocentric," included statements about interdependence, friendship, and responsiveness to others; "I am a person who wants to help others" or "I am able to tell when someone is angry with me."

As can be seen in table 14.2, individuals from the collective culture of Malaysia described themselves by using more group and fewer ideocentric characteristics than people from the more individualistic cultures of Australia and Great Britain. There were no differences between the cultures in the number of allocentric statements made by the participants.

Viewing the self as independent from others has another interesting implication for the self-concept—

the self is not only an independent entity but also a unique one. We can see this viewpoint in the advice to "stand up and be counted" or in advertisements that entice us to "break away from the crowd." On the other hand, if your view of yourself is highly embedded in your group, your concern about being unique should not be strong. In fact, you would want to blend into the group, to be similar to others in your group. This desire to "blend in" is reflected in the popular warning in some collective cultures, "The tall poppy gets cut first." In other words, it is ill advised to stand out from others in your group (Feather, 1996).

Taking these cultural differences into account, Yamaguchi (1990) had a sample of Japanese students complete several questionnaires. One was designed to

TABLE 14.2 WEIGHTED GROUP, IDIOCENTRIC, AND ALLOCENTRIC MEAN SCORES IN THREE CULTURES

	Nationality of Subjects		
Self-References	Malaysian	Australian	British
Group	11.38	5.53	5.10
Idiocentric	13.42	18.97	17.10
Allocentric	3.15	3.56	5.80

Note: The higher the score, the greater the salience.
Source: Bochner (1994)

FIGURE 14.1   **MEAN PERCEIVED SIMILARITY OF SELF TO OTHER AND OTHER TO SELF BY SUBJECTS WITH EASTERN AND WESTERN CULTURAL BACKGROUNDS**

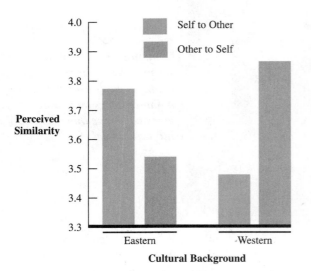

Source: Kitayama et al. (1995)

measure their degree of collectivism, another their need for uniqueness, and a third the degree to which they monitored (or paid attention) to their own behavior. When the various scales were correlated, they showed that the higher people scored on collectivism, the less was their desire for uniqueness and the greater their tendency to monitor their own behavior. Yamaguchi argued that these results demonstrated that as people adopt collective values, they not only have less desire to appear as unique individuals but they also monitor their own behaviors to ensure that they will not be viewed as different or unique.

Taking a somewhat different approach, Kitayama, Markus, Tummala, Kurokawa, and Kato (1990) suggested that in individualistic cultures the self is viewed as the standard by which others are judged. However, in collective societies, people see others as standing in the center, and the self is compared with these others. These investigators found that students from India (a more collective culture) were more likely to view their selves as being similar to the selves of others than to perceive others' selves as being similar to their selves (figure 14.1). However, the pattern was reversed when students from the

United States placed their selves in relation to those of others. U.S. students saw others' selves as being more similar to their selves than they saw their selves being similar to others'. Likewise, Ma and Schoeneman (1997) found that U.S. students were less likely to use social comparison statements (how they compared to others) than were Kenyans (a collective culture). This difference was greatest in the responses of Kenyans from more rural and traditional societies than those in large urban areas. This may seem like a fine distinction, but it shows how culture influences the role of the self in making judgments. The self is central and unique in individualistic cultures, whereas it is more related to others in collective cultures.

The overall picture, then, is that people in collective cultures adopt an interdependent self-image. They view themselves as being woven into the fabric of their groups and as representing the qualities of their group (Markus and Kitayama, 1991). On the other hand, individuals from more individualistic societies have an independent picture of themselves. They stand apart from their groups and their self-image is unique (figure 14.2).

We can see these different views of the self reflected in the organizational settings of cultures. For example, employee selection in individualistic cultures such as the United States and Canada is likely to be based solely on interviews and tests (ability, personality). In collective cultures, employees are often selected on the basis of their social relationship (friend, cousin, sibling) with current employees (Redding and Wong, 1986). Further, rewards in individualistic cultures are often given for short-term personal performance, whereas collective cultures often reward long-term group productivity (Hofstede, 1991). Also organizations in collective cultures are often more concerned with how well an employee "fits into" the work group than in individual productivity.

Protecting the Self

As you will recall from our discussions of attribution, information processing, and the self (chapters 2 and 3), we not only process information to develop mental images of ourselves but often engage in self-deception to create the best possible personal image. In other words, we distort reality in ways to enhance our self-image. We "protect" ourselves by making downward social comparisons (Wills, 1981), which involves making social comparisons with people who are

A.

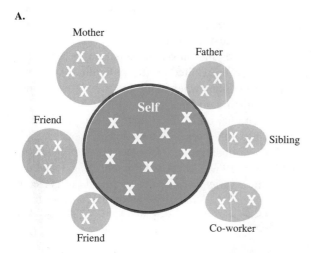

B.

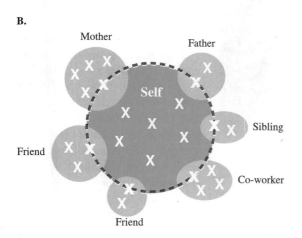

Source: Markus and Kitayama (1991)

slightly inferior to us. We also emphasize our uniqueness (uniqueness bias, Goethals et al. 1990) by perceiving our abilities and strengths as being unusual, and we overestimate our control over events (beneffectance). If we consider all these tendencies in light of our discussion of culture, we should expect them to be most strongly exhibited in cultures that stress the concept of the independent (and responsible) self—in other words, individualistic cultures.

If we consider the situation in collective cultures, we should expect a very different set of attributions in service of the self. Rather than standing apart from others, the positive image of the self in collective cultures should involve attributions that help embed the individual within the group (see also next section). Indeed, studies in Asian cultures have found individuals less likely to place confidence in positive information about the self (Takata, 1992) or to internalize success and externalize failure (Kashima and Triandis, 1986) than people in Western cultures. Likewise, Heine and Lehman (1995) found that Canadians were more likely to hold unrealistic optimism (belief that they are more likely to experience positive future events and less likely to experience negative events than similar others) than Japanese respondents. In addition, the Canadian subjects stated that they would have more control over both positive and negative future events than did the Japanese.

From Image to Feeling

According to a number of investigators, culture not only affects how we view ourselves but also guides what we will experience or feel about events in our lives. It shapes our emotions and influences how we will express those emotions. To capture these points, let's recall the situation faced by Tama. He spent four years building his life in Wellington. He had a good job, a close circle of friends, and an exciting lifestyle. The death of his father signaled an end to all this, because, as the eldest son, he was expected to return to his small village, assume responsibility for his mother and five siblings, and cultivate the small family farming plot. How would you feel if you faced this prospect? Most of us would answer that we would feel some disappointment and sadness at having to give up all that we had worked for. We might even feel anger and resentment. If you examine these feelings, you will find that they are based on a very self-focused approach. Your focus would be on what "you" had achieved, what "you" were sacrificing, and the responsibilities that "you" must accept. According to Markus and Kitayama (1994), these feelings are based on a very individualistic or independent view of the self. Emotions, in this case, are based on what happens to the independent self, what one gains or loses.

A collective or interdependent foundation for the self gives rise to a very different perspective and set of emotions. In fact, we find that Tama expressed joy and pride in his decision to return home. He promised his dead father, "I will be your son, e pa. I will make you proud" (Ihimaera, 1973, p. 192). Mixed with his grief over his father's passing, Tama felt proud about taking his role as family head. "Most of all, I will teach Hone and Marama (his young siblings) of Maori *aroha,* the love we hold for one another, so that they will never be alone" (p. 79). As his sister broke into sobs at the funeral, Tama told himself, "Hug her tightly. Forget your own tears. . . . Her wounds will be deep; you must salve them. . . . Take her hand now. Look how your shadows join on the ground. Your hands reach out to each other, and slowly become one shadow" (p. 150). In this case, Tama's emotions were based on his interpretation of the situation as validating his role in his group (the family). The

Octoberfest celebrations typify the German propensity for good cheer and emotional engagement.

definition of the self as it relates to the group in collective societies leads to emotions based on how events affect the relationship of the self to the group. Tama's return to Waituhi was an occasion that reinforced his position in his family. There was joy and pride in meeting the needs of the family and taking the responsibilities of his role in the family.

Markus and Kitayama (1994) suggest that emotions in collective cultures arise from interpretations of the self in relation to the group, while in individualistic cultures emotions are based on an independent self. But there is more to this story. In an interesting study, Levenson, Ekman, Heider, and Friesen (1992) had people in the United States and West Sumatra (the Minangkabau) assume facial expressions that mimicked positive and negative emotional states. In both

groups the posed expressions led to systematic arousal of the autonomic nervous system. However, only the U.S. participants reported feeling the emotions they were expressing. The Minangkabau had difficulty describing how they were feeling presumably because they were alone. The Minangkabau, a collective society, were accustomed to experiencing emotions in groups and relying on others to define the nature of emotions. In the United States, individuals often experience emotions when alone and they "look inside" to define their emotional state.

Culture not only affects how we experience emotions, it also influences our expression of emotions. Early studies by Ekman and his associates (Ekman, Sorenson, and Friesen, 1969; Ekman and Friesen, 1971) found that people in a variety of cultures were able to correctly identify emotional expressions when shown pictures of faces. And other investigators (Aronoff, Barclay, and Stevenson, 1988) found striking similarities in the expressions of masks picturing threatening faces in many cultures. These findings suggested that there may be universal patterns of expressing and experiencing emotions across cultures, but are some limitations to this conclusion. First, a large body of research suggests that people in collective cultures tend to experience emotions for a shorter duration of time than people in individualistic cultures (Matsumoto, Kudoh, Scherer, and Wallbott, 1988). Second, research suggests that people in collective cultures tend to experience emotions that relate to others (shame, feelings of respect, feelings of indebtedness) while not experiencing or inhibiting ego-focused emotions (frustration, anger, feeling superior).

As you can see, ego-focused emotions are those that foster an independent self and are based on personal inner feelings (Markus and Kitayama, 1991). Related to this point, investigators report that people in collective cultures (Costa Rica) express more discomfort with expressing negative emotions than do people in individualistic societies (United States) (Stephan, Stephan, and de Vargas, 1996). Finally, the expression of emotions in collective societies is often more muted and less intrusive than expression in more individualistic cultures (Triandis, 1994). For example, investigators report that both Japanese and Australian students view Australians as more expressive of emotions than Japanese (Pittman, Gallois, Iwawaki, and Kroonenberg, 1995). You can quickly see this difference by watching people from the two types of cultures in a restaurant. At a table of Germans, you will likely hear raised voices and loud laughing, and see a great deal of arm-waving; at a table of Chinese patrons, in contrast, you'll notice relative quiet and frequent use of the hands to cover the face when emotions are expressed.

Emotions are often personal expressions of feelings, and these expressions have less importance in collective societies than in individualistic cultures. Further, the expression of emotions, especially negative ones such as anger, call attention to the self and they disrupt the decorum of the group and therefore have less of a place in collective cultures.

From Acts to Dispositions . . . in Individualistic Cultures

In chapters 2 and 3 we examined how people attribute the cause of behaviors. One finding was so common that it was labeled the *fundamental attribution error*; that is, observers attribute the cause of others' behaviors to the others' internal dispositions to a much greater extent than the situation would warrant (Ross, 1977). In other words, observers give less weight to situational causes and more to dispositional causes. If we consider our discussion of collective societies, we find that people are less likely to see others as independent actors. Rather, people's behavior is determined or guided by the situation and their role. Therefore, we would expect people in these societies to be more likely to refer to situational causes when explaining the behavior of others. In other words, we should find less tendency to make the fundamental attribution error in collective societies than in individualistic cultures. Indeed, this was exactly the pattern uncovered by Miller (1984) when he asked American and Hindu Indians to explain why someone they knew well did something good or bad to another person. American respondents typically referred to traits and made such comments as "she was irresponsible." The Hindu subjects tended to refer to situational causes such as the actor's duties and roles.

In another interesting study, Morris and Peng (1994) examined newspaper accounts of two mass murders in the United States, one committed by a Chinese person and one committed by an Irish American.

As we might expect from our previous discussion, when American reporters speculated about the reasons for the murders, they were more likely to focus on personal dispositions, such as attitudes (belief that guns were an important means for settling grievances), personality traits (bad temper, violent person), and psychological problems of the murderer. Chinese reporters, on the other hand, were more likely to suggest situational causes, such as relationships (rivalry with others) and situational factors (pressures and stress on the individual, job problems). Even more intriguing was the finding that the attributions made by American reporters were affected by the culture of the murderer. Situational factors were stressed when he was an American (ingroup member), but there was no difference in reference to situational and personal factors when the murderer was Chinese (outgroup). The ethnicity of the murderer made no difference in the attributions made by the Chinese reporters (see figure 14.3). The investigators suggested that personal characteristics (ingroup or outgroup member) are less important to the attributions of Chinese because their attributions focus on situational variables. However, because Americans tend to employ dispositional variables (traits of the actor), they attend to the characteristics of the actor. This is an intriguing suggestion, but it seems to contradict the view that collective cultures make more definite distinctions between ingroups and outgroups. We will have to await further research to reconcile these viewpoints.

Turning to explanations of our own behavior, we discussed the likelihood of a *self-serving bias*; that is, we make attributions to protect a positive self-image. Recall the study that found that people tended to attribute their success to their own ability but attributed failure to external causes such as task difficulty (De-Jong, Koomen, and Mellenbergh, 1988). Most of us can easily relate to this tendency. But consider the situation from the perspective of someone in a collective culture. Attributing success to one's own ability and failure to the situation elevates our position relative to others. If you are concerned about not standing out and with maintaining harmony, modesty should characterize your explanations.

We would expect individuals in collective cultures to avoid self-serving attributions. In fact, this pattern of responses has been found in several studies. For example, Shikanai (1978) led Japanese students to believe that they had either done very well or poorly on a task. The students were then asked to indicate which of five

FIGURE 14.3 **PROPORTIONS OF TOTAL ITEMS CODED AS PERSONAL AND AS SITUATIONAL ATTRIBUTIONS IN AMERICAN NEWSPAPERS (*NEW YORK TIMES*) AND CHINESE NEWSPAPERS (*WORLD JOURNAL*)**

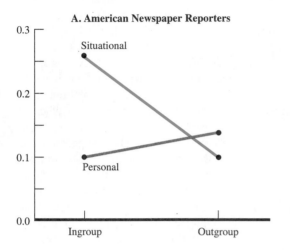

A. American Newspaper Reporters

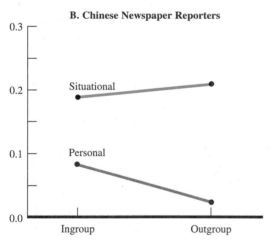

B. Chinese Newspaper Reporters

Note: Broken down by whether the murderer was ingroup or outgroup (relative to the reporter).
Source: Morris and Peng (1994)

causes (ability, effort, task difficulty, luck, or mental-physical "shape" of the day) was most responsible for their performance. The students generally avoided using their ability as an explanation for their behavior. They further showed a "modesty" bias by attributing success to the ease of the task, luck, and shape while avoiding ability and effort as factors. However, failure was more likely to be attributed to their ability (lack of)

and their effort. Of interest is that work on achievement motivation (Yu and Yang, 1994) implies that individuals may resort to self-serving bias when they refer to their group: "my group" succeeded because of its ability and effort or failed because of external causes.

One other example of the role of culture in attributions draws a more complete picture. When it comes to positive traits, we often show a *uniqueness bias,* seeing our own strengths and abilities as being unusual (Campbell, 1986; Goethals, Messick, and Allison, 1990). In addition, we also tend to overestimate the number of people who agree with our opinions or behave as we do—in other words, a *false consensus effect* (Ross, 1977). As with much of the research in social psychology, these two effects are found among people in individualistic cultures. When we turn to collective cultures, we find one of these effects more pronounced and the other less frequent. Can you guess what pattern is found?

Markus and Kitayama (1991) asked students at American and Japanese universities, "What proportion of students at this university has a higher intellectual ability than yourself?" They found that on average, American students answered that 30 percent of other students were more intelligent than they were, while Japanese students gave an estimate of 50 percent. In other words, the false uniqueness effect was alive and well in the individualistic culture but clearly ailing in the collective Japanese society. Japanese students did not believe themselves to be better than the majority of their groups.

On the other hand, Yamaguchi (1990) had Japanese students complete a scale that measured their degree of collectivism. Students were then given a series of decision problems to solve and asked to estimate the percentage of students who would have chosen the same answer. The results indicated that the more collective the individual was, the more likely it was that he or she would assume that other students would make the same choices. In other words, the higher the collectivism, the more likely there would be a false consensus effect.

Overall, then, in collective cultures attributions about others and the self do not stress internal causation of behavior; rather, they stress the relationship and similarity between members of a group. We are not suggesting that people in other cultures do not make attributions about the causes of behaviors. Cultures do, however, affect the way information is processed and interpreted. The processing of information follows the values of the culture. In cultures high on individualism, processing stresses the independent and unique self; in more collective cultures, attributions affirm the interrelatedness of individuals.

The (Nonverbal) Language of Culture

Imagine meeting a close friend in the middle of your university campus. The friend smiles at you, shakes your hand, and then presses his nose to yours. How would you react? This, in fact, is the traditional Maori greeting between close friends and relatives.

Edward Hall (1959, 1966) observed that people interact at predictable distances. He suggested that individuals feel a sense of ownership of the space that surrounds them, it is their **personal space.** In Western societies, people typically have four levels of personal space, each with a close and a far distance. The size of this space is determined, in part, by the nature of the relationship between the interacting people (see table 14.3). When the proper spacing is violated, individuals become uncomfortable and try to position themselves to create the "proper" spacing.

The size of the personal space bubble we keep around ourselves is influenced by a number of factors. For example, male-male interactions are typically undertaken with larger interpersonal distances than female-female or mixed-sex interactions (Brady and Walker, 1978). Interpersonal distance also increases from childhood to adolescence (Aiello and Aiello, 1974; see figure 14.4). But of most interest here are Hall's observations that spacing is influenced by culture. Latin Americans, the French, and Arabs generally interact at closer distances than people from the United States, Sweden, Japan, and England. People in these latter cultures are also less prone to touch each other when interacting. And as figure 14.5 shows, culture also influences what parts of the body can be touched when interacting (Barnlund, 1975).

This is an interesting finding but it also has some serious implications. When people from different cultures interact, each will attempt to establish the spacing that he or she is comfortable with. When the proper space is violated, the individual will become uncomfortable and possibly irritated with the conversational partner. This is not a problem when the "proper" space is the same for both people; but if "proper" space is close for one person but far for the other, the conversation is likely to become the stage

---

TABLE 14.3 HALL'S INTERPERSONAL DISTANCES IN WESTERN SOCIETIES

	Close Phase	Far Phase
Intimate Distance	0 to 5 inches; two parties touch each other; make love, wrestle, comfort, give protection	6 to 18 inches; used when touching is not permitted; conversation in low tones, as when telling secrets
Personal Distance	18 to 30 inches; used by close friends or by a married couple when they converse	30 to 48 inches; ordinary social interaction between friends and acquaintances
Social Distance	4 to 7 feet; personal business and conversations at casual social gatherings	7 to 12 feet; formal business and social discourse
Public Distance	12 to 25 feet; formal interactions	25 or more feet distance set around important public figures

Source: Hall (1966)

FIGURE 14.4   **MEAN INTERACTION DISTANCES OF MALE AND FEMALE DYADS AT SIX GRADE LEVELS**

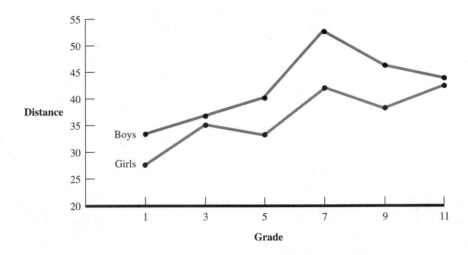

Source: Aiello and Aiello (1974)

on which each tries to establish a comfortable space and views the other as impolite or rude. Because our spacing is so automatic and we rarely think about the influence of our culture, cultural differences in spacing may lead to unpleasant interactions.

It is not only spacing that is influenced by culture. Cultures often have their own unique gestures. Maoris greet by touching noses, Americans shake hands, and Mexicans embrace. Matsumoto (1997) gives the following example about how cultural differences in gestures can result in more than an uncomfortable situation:

Japanese often signify that someone is angry by raising the index fingers of both hands, in a pointing fashion, toward the sides of their heads, pointing up. In Brazil and other South American countries, however, this signifies that one wants sex (is horny). Imagine what would happen if a Japanese person were trying to tell someone from Brazil that someone else is angry and the Brazilian interpreted the signal to mean the Japanese person is horny! (P. 44)

Other cultural differences in signs and signals are identified by Axtell (1991). For example, in the United States, forming a circle by touching the thumb and index finger means "OK." In many Latin American countries, this sign is considered an obscene gesture similar to that of raising the middle finger from a closed fist. And in southern France, the same sign is taken to mean "worthless" or "zero." So you may want to think twice before you give another a nonverbal signal that they are OK. Many of us are accustomed to beckoning someone to come to us by curling our index finger in and out. But in Malaysia and Yugoslavia, this signal is used only for calling animals, and in Indonesia and Australia it is reserved for beckoning prostitutes. So, watch your (nonverbal) language.

In general, greetings in collective cultures are often longer and more elaborate than in individualistic cultures. Triandis (1994) points out that greetings in collective cultures are used to determine information about the status and group positions of the participants. This is an important function because status and group position determine how the parties will interact. Some languages (for example, Japanese) have different forms that are used when communicating to someone of lower status than to someone of higher status. By determining status, the greeting also determines which form of the language will be used in later discussions.

The structure of a culture influences the language of people in that culture (Gudykunst, 1991). For example, in individualistic cultures such as the United States, the family is a rather small circle including mother, father, children, uncles, aunts, grandparents, cousins, nephews, and nieces. However, in many col-

FIGURE 14.5   TABOOS RELATED TO TOUCHING

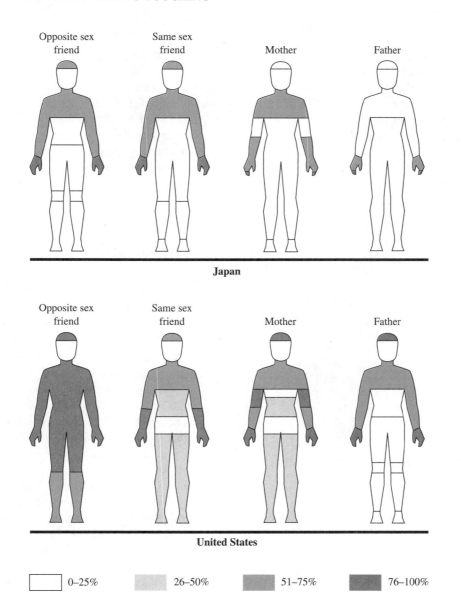

One can touch certain parts of the body in one culture that are taboo in other cultures. Barnlund (1975) obtained the frequencies of touching different parts of the body. In the United States one can touch all parts of the body on an opposite-sex friend, but the region around the genitals is taboo in the case of all others. In Japan larger areas of the body, even the areas below the waist of opposite-sex friends, are taboo. You can count the number of body parts that are taboo to obtain index of the "tightness" of the culture.

Source: Barnlund (1975)

lective cultures, the family is much larger. In the Maori culture, one's family might include an aunt's aunt. In such cultures there are terms that identify these people; we do not find such terms in our culture because these people are not considered relations. Similarly, collective cultures typically have terms to describe complex other-focused emotions that can only be approximated by a string of words in less-collective cultures. For example, *sonkei* is the Japanese term for feeling respect for someone, whereas *fureai* means feeling connection with someone (Markus and Kitayama, 1991). And because the relationship with others is so important in Japanese culture, there are

served her tea and bananas, but because tea is not commonly served with bananas, "this communicated that the two (the boy and girl) could not mix" (Triandis, 1994). By giving this sign, the girl's mother avoided creating an unpleasant interaction by having to directly refuse the request for marriage. In individualistic cultures, communication is generally more direct because the culture does not stress harmony.

The hand of culture, therefore, is clearly evident in the communication between people. Culture affects the structure of language, the nature of spoken communication, and nonverbal behavior.

Culture and Social Behavior

When Tama was waiting in the Wellington airport to take his flight home, he ran into his cousin. He told his cousin of his father's death, and the cousin promised to be at the *tangi*. As they were departing, the cousin put his hands in his pocket and pulled out all the money he had. He thrust the money into Tama's pockets and walked away.

"Forgive me, but my people often find yours cold and distant!"

three terms that describe feelings of interdependence: *fureai* (feeling of connection), *shitashimi* (feeling of familiarity), and *sonkei* (feeling of respect).

Finally, culture can have a strong impact on the nature of communication between people. Triandis (1994) states that because collective cultures place such a strong emphasis on harmony, "one says what the other wants to hear, and does not contradict the other" (p. 185). As a result, one must pay careful attention to signs and gestures to interpret meaning. An instructive example is found in the case of an Indonesian boy who wanted to marry a girl of a higher class. The boy's mother went to discuss the possibility of this marriage with the girl's mother. The girl's mother

In general, collective cultures make definite distinctions between the ingroup and outgroups, and their social behavior reflects these distinctions more clearly than that found in individualistic cultures. Once these distinctions are drawn, individuals in collective cultures act to create smooth relations within the ingroup and more negative relations with the outgroups. Within collective societies, people typically belong to relatively few groups, but these groups are often life-long associations and form a central part of social identity (Tajfel and Turner, 1986). Although Tama left his village, he remained a member and easily returned to assume his place. Individuals in individualistic cultures, on the other hand, typically join more groups but for a shorter period of time. They are less likely to make such clear distinctions between the ingroup and outgroups. There is less difference between the treatment of ingroup and outgroup members in individualistic cultures than in collective cultures. And within the ingroup, individuals are likely to emphasize personal needs and goals in individualistic cultures (Matsumoto, 1996). The impact of this difference in the cultural view of groups is seen in nearly every type of social interaction. Let's take a moment to examine a few examples.

Attraction and Love in Social and Family Relationships

Looking first at similarities between cultures, Buss (1989) found that males generally preferred younger mates while females preferred older ones. Males across cultures rated physical attractiveness more important in a mate than did females. Overall, males tended to be attracted to a mate for her reproductive capacity, whereas females often looked to mates to provide resources and protection.

Despite these similarities, there are some notable differences, especially evident in marriage and long-term romantic relationships. In collective cultures, marriage is viewed as a union that unites families rather than simply two individuals. Therefore, the "right" union is one that creates a comfortable bond between families. For this reason, marriages in collective cultures are often arranged, and while the individual's feelings may be considered, the needs of the two families are paramount. Marriage in individualistic cultures is based on the love and the desire of the two individuals who will exchange vows. As a result, romance is more highly valued in individualistic cultures than in collective ones (Simmons, vom-Kolke, and Shimizu, 1986), but there is considerable variation within culture type. For example, investigators asked students in eleven countries how important love was for marriage (Levine, Sato, Hashimoto, and Verma, 1995). As can be seen in table 14.4, students in the more individualistic societies (United States, England, Australia, and European Brazil) placed high importance on love. On the other hand, several collective cultures (India, Pakistan, Thailand, and the Philippines) placed less importance on love, but other col-

A study of Indian marriages revealed that couples who married for love were more in love during the first five years but less in love after the fifth year than couples in arranged marriages. In later years these differences increased.

TABLE 14.4   **RESPONSES TO QUESTION 1**

"If a man (woman) had all the other qualities you desired, would you marry this person if you were not in love with him (her)?"

Response	India	Pakistan	Thailand	United States	England	Japan	Philippines	Mexico	Brazil	Hong Kong	Australia
Yes	49.0	50.4	18.8	3.5	7.3	2.3	11.4	10.2	4.3	5.8	4.8
No	24.0	39.1	33.8	85.9	83.6	62.0	63.6	80.5	85.7	77.6	80.0
Undecided	26.9	10.4	47.5	10.6	9.1	35.7	25.0	9.3	10.0	16.7	15.2

Note: Figures given are in percentages.
Source: Levine, Sato, Hashimoto, and Verma (1995)

lective cultures reported it as being important (Mexico, Hong Kong).

But this does not mean that love is absent from arranged marriages. Gupta and Singh (1982) examined couples in India, some who married for love and others who had arranged marriages. Responses to a scale designed to measure intensity of love indicated that couples who married for love were more in love during the first five years of marriage. However, they were less in love than couples in arranged marriage after the fifth year, and the difference increased in this direction in later years.

Collectivity is not the only cultural dimension that affects love and attraction. Hofstede (1996) delineated several Asian cultures along the masculinity dimension and examined the characteristics single working women between the ages of twenty and thirty considered important in boyfriends and husbands. Overall, the women indicated that health, wealth, and social status were more important for husbands than boyfriends, while a sense of humor and personality were less important in husbands than boyfriends. However, the results also indicated that women in the more masculine cultures were more likely to distinguish important traits between husbands and boyfriends than were women in the more feminine cultures. Hofstede suggested that these results might indicate that love (boyfriend) and family (husband)

are more often separated in masculine cultures than in feminine societies.

We may find the practices of other cultures unusual, but such practices are deeply ingrained within the culture. Problems arise, however, when marriage and relationship patterns accepted in one culture are practiced in another. As can be seen in the newspaper story in figure 14.6, the patterns of one culture may violate the laws of another culture or society. The result may present a difficult moral dilemma, and it raises the question of how accommodating a society may be to the practices of different cultures.

A final issue of interest on this topic concerns family structure. Triandis (1994) suggests that the nuclear family is the standard unit in individualistic cultures, whereas the more extended family is emphasized in collective cultures. In collective cultures, for example, individuals are more likely to live close to extended family members (grandparents, cousins, aunts, and uncles). Children are often cared for by extended family members (especially grandparents) in collective cultures. Supporting this position, a team of researchers (Georgas, Christakopoulou, Poortinga, Angleitner, Goodwin, and Charalambous, 1997) questioned university students in five European countries about their relationship with their families. There were no differences between the collective cultures (Greece, Cyprus) and individualistic

---

FIGURE 14.6   IRAQI MAN CHARGED WITH FORCING HIS TEENAGE DAUGHTERS TO MARRY

By J.L. Schmidt, Associated Press

LINCOLN, Neb. — An Iraqi refugee accused of forcing his 13- and 14-year-old daughters to marry men twice their age in an Islamic ceremony was jailed on child abuse charges, and the alleged husbands were charged with rape.

A university professor from Iraq and a lawyer for the so-called husbands said the three were following Islamic tradition and did not intend to violate state law.

"It is a clash between cultural mores and U.S. law," said Terry Cannon, a lawyer for the alleged husbands, Latif Al-Hussani, 34, and Majed Al-Tamimy, 28. The two recent immigrants were jailed on $50,000 bail each and could get up to 50 years in prison.

The father, a school janitor on disability who was identified only by the first name Salaam, was jailed on $10,000 bail. He faces up to six months and a $1,000 fine.

Police said Hussani and the 13-year-old were married Nov. 9 against the girl's will in a ceremony at her father's home. The 14-year-old daughter claimed she was forced to marry Tamimy at the same ceremony, but the father allegedly told authorities the girl and Tamimy simply became engaged.

Court papers said the two men took the girls to their homes and had sex with them to consummate the marriages. The 14-year-old ran away from the apartment, and the father reported her to police as a runaway.

Police found the girl, heard her story, arrested the men and put the girls in protective custody.

"They're not aware of the kind of civil rules here," Mohamed Nassir of the Lincoln Islamic Foundation told the Lincoln Journal Star. Nassir, a University of Nebraska-Lincoln professor, did not attend the ceremony but said it was conducted according to Islamic tradition, which includes both sides publicly saying they want the marriage.

Source: Bryan–College Station (TX) *Eagle,* Nov. 20, 1996

Easter Sunday is a time of reunion for the Loukas Sklavounos family in the village of Vasilika. Whether a priest, grandfather, or chic young Athenian, Greeks remain united by family ties.

cultures (Netherlands, Germany, Great Britain) in emotional closeness, frequency of meetings, or telephone contact with members of the nuclear family (parents, siblings). But students from the collective cultures reported more frequent contact, more geographic closeness, and more emotional closeness with extended family members than did students from the individualistic societies. These and other findings suggest that culture affects how we define our family and how much contact and emotional closeness we will have with various family members.

Cultural differences in family structure are also reflected in the treatment of the elderly. Many collective cultures, especially Asian societies, have strong filial piety ethics that requires "absolute obedience to and obligation for support of parents on the parts of sons and daughters-in-law" (Cogwill, 1986, p. 114). In fact, in many Asian cultures these obligations were part of the law, and although many of the laws have been repealed, the custom remains (Treas, 1977). For example, 60 percent of the elderly in Japan live with their children, while 15 percent in the United States do so (Organization for Economic Cooperation and Development, 1994). This pattern results in many children in collective families having more frequent contact with grandparents and cousins than children in individualistic families (Matsumoto, 1996). Indeed, we can see this difference in the opening incident. Tama felt a strong sense of guilt for moving away from his family even though he went less than

one hundred miles. The majority of the family lived in the same small village, and at the *tangi*, each family member, including more distant relatives, had an explicit role.

Helping Behavior

The actions of Tama's cousin in the airport may seem quite unusual to many of us. Without being asked, he gave Tama all his money, and Tama, with little protest, accepted the funds. We might explain this behavior by suggesting that the cousin felt sorry for Tama and wanted to show him how badly he felt about his father's death. But this was probably not the case. In chapter 9 we discussed research on altruism and helping behavior. You might have been surprised to find the degree of reluctance to help in many of the studies. Some investigators (Ho and Chiu, 1994) have suggested that collective cultures generally value altruism more highly than individualistic cultures.

This finding does not necessarily mean that individuals in collective cultures will always help each other more often than individualistic people. Rather, it seems that collective people draw a clear distinction between ingroup, or potential ingroup, members and outgroup members. They are more likely to help ingroup members but less likely to help outgroup members (Triandis, 1994). Triandis made the point that Greeks are often more willing to help a stranger than

BOX 14.2

The Shocking Side of Culture

In addition to examining the influence of culture on a variety of social behaviors, social psychologists have been interested in how people are affected when they move from one culture to another. Much has been said about how technology has "shrunk" our world, but one clear consequence of the technology revolution is that many more people than ever before will visit or work in a foreign country with a different culture. Although the prospect of crossing cultures is exciting, the leap can prove difficult for some people. *Culture shock* often results when people are submerged, even for a short time, in another culture (Oberg, 1954). A host of physical and psychological symptoms have been associated with culture shock. These symptoms may include fatigue, homesickness, helplessness, depression, fits of anger, and excessive fear of being robbed, cheated, or hurt (Triandis, 1994). Furnham and Bochner (1986) found that German, Polish, and American women living in Great Britain were twice as likely to commit suicide as were British women. Supposedly, this was the result of the stress of living in a foreign culture.

Most studies find that less than 10 percent of travelers experience "severe" culture shock (Weaver, 1994), and the severity of culture shock is related to the difference between one's home culture and the new one (Gao and Gudykunst, 1990). If you imagine yourself in a strange culture, you can anticipate why people experience culture shock. A major factor involves *loss of control* and the accompanying uncertainty (see chapter 3). Even the simplest tasks such as ordering food in a restaurant, cashing a check, or buying groceries can be confusing in another culture. The difficulties one encounters in these endeavors may lead to a feeling of *learned helplessness* (Abramson, Seligman, and Teasdale, 1978) and damage one's sense of *self-efficacy* (Bandura, 1982). To

make matters worse, when one experiences these conditions there is often no one there to discuss one's concerns; the familiar *social support* network (Rook, 1987) is absent and a sense of isolation sets in. As we have seen in earlier chapters, each of these conditions is associated with depression and damage to one's self-image.

Although culture shock is a problem for tourists and others who spend a short time in another culture, adjustment to a foreign culture takes on greater importance for those who must spend longer periods of time abroad, such as business people, students, and missionaries. Triandis (1994) identified five phases of adjustment that characterize many of these long-term sojourners. In the first phase, there is a sense of optimism and excitement; the new situation is perceived as a challenge. The second phase begins when difficulties with language, schools, and daily activities are experienced. The loss of control often leads to anger at the culture and to depression. Individuals may seek out "co-nationals with whom they compare notes about 'how awful the natives are' " (Triandis, 1994, p. 265). The third phase is rock bottom, often characterized by severe depression and psychosomatic illness. During this phase, people may flee the culture or be sent home by their company. However, if they remain in the culture, a U-shaped curve begins to develop. In the fourth phase, people learn new coping skills, and a sense of optimism returns. The fifth phase occurs when people feel "at home" in the new culture. They develop long-term goals and close friends from the host culture.

The adaptation to a new culture not only takes its toll on the individual, it also has important implications for organizations that have sent people to foreign cultures to work or study. It is estimated that between $2 billion to $2.5 billion are lost to corporations because

Continued

BOX 14.2

Continued

of adjustment difficulties of workers in foreign cultures (Lublin, 1990). As a result, nearly half of the businesses who send workers to foreign locales have instituted culture-training programs to facilitate adjustment. These programs have diverse agendas, but the table illustrates the range of topics covered (Paige and Martin, 1996). The format of these programs is also widely varied but many include such multiple approaches as lectures, discussion groups, films, role-playing, group problem-solving exercises, and simulations.

As you can see, an understanding of social psychology theories and research gives insight into the difficulties people experience when crossing cultures and an appreciation of the steps that can be taken to help the adjustment process. The task of preparing people to comfortably move across cultural boundaries is one that will grow in importance and urgency as cross-cultural contact expands in the coming years.

CONTENT FOUNDATIONS OF INTERCULTURAL TRAINING

Intercultural Communication Phenomena
    Culture and Communication
    Language and Communication
    Nonverbal Behavior and Communication
    Role of Values, Beliefs, and Norms in Communication
    Cognitive Differentiation: Categories, Classification Systems
    Learning Styles
    Communication Styles
    Culture Learning, Adjustment, "Shock"
Characteristics of the Intercultural
Communication and Interaction Process
    Alternative Responses to Cultural Differences
    Stages of Development Toward Intercultural Communication
        Competence/Sensitivity
    Describing, Interpreting, and Evaluating Intercultural Events and
        Persons

Intercultural Relations and Cultural Differences
    Intercultural Relations Continuum: From Similarity to Difference
    Cultural Differences That Make a Difference: Values, Attitudes,
        Beliefs, Behaviors
    Cultural Differences Associated With Race, Ethnicity, Gender,
        Nationality, Socioeconomic Status, Religion, Sexual
        Orientation, Etc.

Factors That Inhibit and Promote Intercultural Communication
    Personal Characteristics: Degree of Flexibility, Openness,
        Emotional Resilience, Etc.
    Situational Variables: Degree of Status Equality, Shared Goals,
        Cooperation, Supportive Environment, Role and Work
        Assignment Clarity, Etc.
    Cultural Variables: Language Differences and Language Ability
        of Interactants, Cultural Differences and Target Culture Skills
        of the Interactants

Area Studies/Target Culture Knowledge
    History
    Political and Economic Systems
    Religions
    Ethnic Diversity
    Etc.

Source: Paige and Martin (1996)

another Greek who is clearly not a member of their ingroup. At first glance, this might seem to contradict our earlier point. However, it seems that Greeks see the stranger as a potential ingroup member, so they are willing to extend help until it is determined that the stranger is not going to be included in the ingroup. In Tama's case, he was clearly an ingroup member to his cousin, and therefore it was only natural for the cousin to extend aid. Culture, then, not only influences our willingness to extend aid but also helps determine whom we will help.

One note of caution here. Yousif and Korte (1995) examined willingness to help in urban and nonurban areas in England and Sudan (a collective culture). In both countries, helping was more frequent in the nonurban areas than in the urban areas. Therefore, it is possible that differences between collective and individualistic cultures may be caused by differences in urban development rather than by cultural norms.

Conformity and Group Behavior

Culture also plays an interesting role in regard to conformity (see chapter 11). Although we might expect the Japanese, a collective people, to be more likely to conform than Germans, an individualistic people, studies using the Asch line method found conformity in both Japan and Germany to be relatively low (Mann, 1980). At first this result seems surprising until we examine the situation more closely. Typically, the naive subject in the Asch experiment is faced with a dissenting majority composed of strangers, who are clearly not ingroup members. Therefore, we would not expect individuals from a collective society to show high levels of conformity in this situation. However, in a study that involved cohesive groups (composed of ingroup members), Matsuda (1985) found a high degree of conformity in Japan even when responses were given in private.

In 1965, Vietnamese leader Ho Chi Minh (right) and Chinese official Deng Xiaoping (left) bade each other farewell. From the Asian perspective, today's ally may have been yesterday's enemy and vice-versa, and one should not expect peace in one's lifetime. A people can learn to endure and help provide for better times in future generations.

Expanding on the issue of groups, Brislin (1993) points out that people in individualistic cultures have considerable choice about joining a group, whereas individuals in collective cultures are *expected* to be a member of certain groups. In individualistic cultures, groups often last only as long as is needed to complete a task. In collective cultures, groups are often more enduring and individuals are responsible to and for the group. Brislin mentions an incident in Japan in which good students complained about the behavior of several rowdy students. The teacher told the good students that they were responsible for their classmates and that they should solve the problem. Hence, children in collective cultures learn from an early age to be responsible for members of their group. This sense of mutual obligation and responsibility for other group members is also evident in Hispanic cultures (Hines, Garcia-Preto, McGoldrick, Almeida, and Weltman, 1992) and is shown in high group loyalty and the avoidance of complaining about or identifying members that break organizational rules.

Conflict and Conflict Resolution

An underlying assumption in many individualistic cultures is that conflict arises because of the dispositions of the involved parties (Rubin, Pruitt, and Kim, 1994). It is likely that you will view your opponent as aggressive, unyielding, and obstinate. Galtung (1997) notes that individualistic cultures also have a very defined view of time, suggesting that a clear beginning and end point to interactions can be identified. We can add to these characteristics the fact that individualistic cultures value the open expression of emotions and a direct approach to interpersonal relations. This recipe of ingredients results in personalized conflicts in these cultures involving direct confrontations between the parties. The conflicts typically involve one party attempting to directly force the other party to yield. There is also little patience so that if a conflict is not quickly resolved, the parties will turn to a third party (mediator, arbitrator, judge) to find a solution.

The approach to conflict and conflict resolution is generally very different in collective cultures. The underlying cause of conflict is seen as the situation (Fry and Fry, 1997) rather than the dispositions of the parities. The resolution, therefore, rests in changing the situation rather than the attitudes or characteristics of the parties. Instead of openly confronting the conflict, people in collective cultures often resort to avoidance (Triandis, 1994). They are reluctant to bring in impartial third parties, waiting instead for alterations in the situation to reduce the level of conflict. For people in Western cultures, this approach would be maddeningly slow, prolonging the conflict for an extended time. But Galtung's (1997) analysis of Buddhism shows that for Buddhists "time is infinite. For all practical purposes, there is no beginning and no end. . . . Conflict would be seen as interminable, with no beginning and no end" (p. 42).

The important point here is that culture helps define our schema of conflict and conflict resolution. Perceptions about the causes of conflict are rooted in culture, as are the approaches toward the management of conflict. This creates difficulties when conflict arises between people of different cultures.

The Importance of Culture: A Concluding Comment

We are not suggesting that culture completely changes the nature of human behavior. Indeed, regardless of the culture, individuals perceive, process, and interpret social information, they develop views of themselves, they love and hate, they deal with conflict, and they are influenced by others. Schwartz and his colleagues (Schwartz, 1992; Schwartz and Sagiv, 1995), for example, argue that there are basic values that are recognized and dealt with in all cultures. These investigators identify ten motivationally distinct types of values that they believe are recognized in the value systems of all cultures (see figure 14.7). Based on data collected from over forty countries, Schwartz argues that two basic dimensions (openness to change versus conservatism and self-transcendence versus self-enhancement) are universal in all cultures, and these dimensions affect the relationship between the ten basic values. Therefore, injecting culture into the study of social psychology does not negate theories and research on social behavior.

Culture, however, does have a pervasive, albeit often subtle, influence on our attitudes, values, perceptions, and behaviors. Culture shapes the way we view ourselves and interpret the actions of others. Culture influences the features of situations that we attend to and use to make sense of our social world. Our culture affects how we relate to others and to groups.

FIGURE 14.7   **DEFINITIONS OF MOTIVATIONAL
TYPES OF VALUES IN TERMS OF
THEIR GOALS AND THE SINGLE
VALUES THAT REPRESENT THEM**

Power: Social status and prestige, control or dominance over people and resources. (Social Power, Authority, Wealth) [Preserving My Public Image, Social Recognition]

Achievement: Personal success through demonstrating competence according to social standards. (Successful, Capable, Ambitious, Influential) [Intelligent, Self-Respect]

Hedonism: Pleasure and sensuous gratification for oneself. (Pleasure, Enjoying Life)

Stimulation: Excitement, novelty, and challenge in life. (Daring, A Varied Life, An Exciting Life)

Self-direction: Independent thought and action-choosing, creating, exploring. (Creativity, Freedom, Independent, Curious, Choosing Own Goals) [Self-Respect]

Universalism: Understanding, appreciation, tolerance and protection for the welfare of all people and for nature. (Broadminded, Wisdom, Social Justice, Equality, A World at Peace, A World of Beauty, Unity With Nature, Protecting the Environment)

Benevolence: Preservation and enhancement of the welfare of people with whom one is in frequent personal contact. (Helpful, Honest, Forgiving, Loyal, Responsible) [True Friendship, Mature Love]

Tradition: Respect, commitment and acceptance of the customs and ideas that traditional culture or religion provide the self. (Humble, Accepting My Portion in Life, Devout, Respect for Tradition, Moderate)

Conformity: Restraint of actions, inclinations, and impulses likely to upset or harm others and violate social expectations or norms. (Politeness, Obedient, Self-Discipline, Honoring Parents and Elders)

Security: Safety, harmony, and stability of society, of relationships, and of self. (Family Security, National Security, Social Order, Clean, Reciprocation of Favors) [Sense of Belonging, Healthy]

Note: Values in brackets are not used in computing indexes for value types. Additional values included to measure a possible spirituality value type that was not found were: A Spiritual Life, Meaning in Life, Inner Harmony, Detachment.
Source: Schwartz and Sagiv (1995)

Finally, attempts to categorize cultures involve descriptions of central tendencies. Therefore, within cultures there is considerable variation in people's attitudes, behaviors, and outlook on life. Culture is a framework for helping us understand the foundation of social behavior rather than a straightjacket for segregating people into tightly defined groups.

The study of culture's influence on social behavior is a growing and developing field. It not only allows social psychologists to determine how broadly their findings generalize across populations but it has identified new areas for research. The approach represents one of the new directions in the field of social psychology.

Summary

Culture is defined as a "set of human-made objective and subjective elements that in the past have increased the probability of survival and resulted in satisfactions for the participants in an ecological niche, and thus become shared among those who could communicate because they had a common language and they lived in the same time and place" (Triandis 1994, p. 22). Culture, in short, is viewed as the software of the mind. It is transmitted across generations, and it influences nearly every aspect of life and social interaction.

Hofstede classified cultures along four dimensions: uncertainty avoidance, masculinity, power distance, and individualism/collectivism. Most cross-cultural research focuses on the individualism-collectivism continuum. Individualistic cultures emphasize the independent individual; personal privacy and individual initiative are stressed. Collective cultures, on the other hand, emphasize the group and the interdependent individual; individuals are defined by the groups to which they belong and the roles they play in these groups. Individualistic cultures tend to be found in highly industrialized societies.

People from individualistic cultures tend to use personal traits to describe themselves, while those from collective cultures use group membership as their personal identities. People in individualistic cultures stress their personal uniqueness, while those in collective cultures avoid "standing out" from the group.

Emotions in individualistic cultures are often based on internal experiences and expression is open and public. Emotional expression in collective societies is generally controlled and nonobtrusive. Feelings arise from relations with others and one's group. Cultures have emotional expressions that are common across cultures, but they also have unique gestures and expressions.

The fundamental attribution error, self-serving bias, and uniqueness bias are more likely to be found in individualistic cultures than in collective cultures. In collective cultures, individuals make attributions to enhance their groups but downplay their unique role in success. Behavior is viewed as being under the control of the situation rather than the individual.

Personal space differs between cultures, with some having large spaces while others use smaller interaction distances. The culture is often reflected in the language. For example, cultures that place strong emphasis on status often have different forms of language for interactions between people at different status levels. In general, people in collective cultures avoid conflict and disdain direct confrontation.

In many collective cultures, marriages are arranged based on group considerations. Love is less important in marriage decisions than in individualistic cultures.

People in collective cultures make clearer distinctions between ingroups and outgroups than do people in individualistic societies. As a result, "collective" people show greater differences in their social behavior when they are interacting with ingroup and outgroup members than do people in individualistic cultures. For example, people in collective societies are likely to help ingroup members but not outgroup members. They are likely to conform to their ingroup but not to outgroups. These differences are more pronounced than those found in individualistic cultures.

Culture affects both perceptions of the cause of conflict and approaches to resolving conflict. Individualistic cultures often view conflict as resulting from the dispositions of the involved parties, whereas collective cultures see conflict as arising from situations. Although people from individualistic cultures attempt to deal with conflict directly, people in collective cultures prefer avoidance.

Schwartz has suggested that there are ten basic values that are dealt with by all cultures. In general, the study of cultures helps us determine how general the findings in social psychology are across populations. Understanding the influence of culture on behavior helps us understand how these behaviors develop and are influenced by learning and situation.

Key Terms

collectivism	ideocentric	personal space
cross-cultural studies	individualism	power distance
culture	masculinity dimension	uncertainty avoidance

Suggested Readings

Brislin, R. (1993). *Understanding culture's influence on behavior.* Fort Worth, TX: Harcourt Brace.

Hall, E. T. (1966). *The hidden dimension.* New York: Doubleday.

Hofstede, G. (1991). *Cultures and organizations: Software of the mind.* London, England: McGraw-Hill.

Kim, U., Triandis, H., Kagitcibasi, C., Choi, S., & Yoon, G. (1994). *Individualism and collectivism: Theory, method, and applications.* Thousand Oaks, CA: Sage.

Kitayama, S., and Markus, H. (1994). *Emotion and culture: Empirical studies of mutual influence.* Washington, D C: American Psychological Association.

Matsumoto, D. (1997). *Culture and modern life.* Pacific Grove, CA: Brooks/Cole.

Triandis, H.T. (1994). *Culture and social behavior.* New York: McGraw-Hill.

Glossary

A-B-X model   The theory that the relationship between two persons and an attitude object will strain to become symmetrical.

accessibility   The extent to which an attitude comes to mind quickly and automatically when the attitude object is encountered; the strength of the association in memory between the attitude object and the evaluation of the object.

actor-observer bias   The tendency of actors to attribute their behavior to situational factors and of observers to attribute it to stable dispositions.

aggression   A behavior whose goal is the injury of the person toward whom it is directed.

aggression cues   Stimuli associated with the source of frustration and with aggressive behavior in general; when paired with frustration, aggression cues may elicit aggression.

alcohol myopia   Alcohol intoxication reduces cognitive capacity, which leads to a focus on only the most salient cues in the environment.

allocentric   Traits or descriptions that concern interdependence and relationships between people.

altruism   An unselfish desire to help others; an unselfishly helpful act.

ambivalence   A mix of positive and negative feelings.

analysis of variance test   A statistical procedure that takes into account both the mean and the variability of experimental data to determine the statistical significance of the results.

arbitrator   In dispute settlement, a third party who is invested with the power to impose the final solution after hearing the arguments of both sides.

archival research   A method of study by which the investigator examines historical accounts of events that have one or more features in common and identifies common responses to those events.

aspirational deprivation   Loss of hope of attaining something in limited supply, something one has come recently to value, or something to which one has recently become committed.

attitude   A general and enduring positive or negative feeling about some person, object, or issue; an evaluative judgment of a target.

attitude polarization via mere thought   Merely thinking about an issue often makes attitudes more extreme (polarized).

attributions   Inferences about the cause of a person's action.

audience pleasing   Self-presentational behavior designed to make an audience happy.

authoritarian personality   A complex of characteristics that includes ethnocentrism, hostility toward outgroups, and emphasis on obedience, discipline, and respect for authority.

autistic conspiracy   The tendency for an ingratiator and a target person to pretend or believe that ingratiation is not occurring, because neither one wants to acknowledge it.

autistic hostility   Withdrawal from a conflict situation and avoidance of interaction.

availability bias   The tendency of a stimulus that comes easily or quickly to mind to be seen as the cause of an event.

balance theory   Theory concerning the way attitudes toward persons, objects, and issues are formed, based on the supposition that people prefer orderly, consistent, and harmonious relationships among their cognitions.

base-rate information   Data or information about the frequency of specific events or behaviors in particular groups.

beautiful-is-good stereotype   The belief that actions of beautiful people are better, more well intentioned, and more likely to result in superior products than the behavior of those who are not as physically attractive.

beliefs   The characteristics that perceivers associate with an object.

beneffectance   The tendency to take credit for success and deny responsibility for failure; from *beneficent + effectance*.

black sheep effect   People generally are favorably disposed toward ingroup members except when those members are negative.

case history   A method of inquiry that examines the responses of a few individuals and analyzes their reactions in depth.

categorization   The tendency to conceptualize objects and people as members of groups; a basic human cognitive process.

catharsis   The reduction in the instigation to aggress following some instances of aggression.

central route to persuasion   Persuasion caused by thinking about the arguments contained in the message.

charisma   A personal attribute of certain leaders that tends to draw others' support and admiration.

check on the manipulation   A procedure that ensures that the variable that investigators intended to manipulate was accurately perceived by participants in the experiment.

circumplex   Leary's classification scheme for interpersonal behavior, which arrays behaviors in a circle created by crossing a dominant-submissive dimension and a friendly-hostile dimension.

classical conditioning   Modification of behavior by the pairing of a neutral stimulus with another stimulus that produces an unconditioned response.

coercive power   The capacity to deliver threats and punishments to force compliance.

cognition   An element of knowledge; any thought that an individual has about him- or herself or the environment.

cognitive consonance   A relationship among cognitions such that each fits with or psychologically follows from the others.

cognitive dissonance   A relationship among cognitions such that one cognition follows from the opposite of another.

cognitive dissonance theory   A theory proposed by Leon Festinger that unpleasant psychological tension arises when cognitions are not in harmony.

cognitive response approach   The effectiveness of a message depends on the cognitive responses generated by the recipients as they anticipate, receive, or reflect on the persuasive communication.

collective   A gathering of people who have no structure or face-to-face interaction but are engaged in a common activity.

collectivism   Tendency of a culture to emphasize interdependence and the relationship of the individual to the group.

communal relationship   A long-term relationship in which benefits given are not balanced against benefits received.

companionate love   A long-term, deep, affectionate attachment between two people.

compatibility of attitude and behavior measures   Because general attitudes predict only general behaviors, and specific attitudes predict only specific behaviors, measures of attitudes and behaviors must be both general or both specific.

compliance   Overt behavioral conformity while maintaining one's own attitude.

conflict spiral   Conflict that grows in intensity and number of people involved as two sides distrust each other and cease communication, and winning becomes more important than resolving the problem.

conformity   Change in behavior or belief in a group's standards that is a result of the group's power.

consonant cognitions   Cognitions that are compatible or that support each other.

contact hypothesis   Contact between members of different groups leads to more positive intergroup attitudes.

contingency model   The theory that the effectiveness of the task-oriented and relationship-oriented leadership styles depends on the situation the leader faces.

correlation   The degree of association between two events; a statistical measure.

correspondence bias (also known as **fundamental attribution error**)   The tendency of perceivers to infer

that behavior reflects internal dispositions and to ignore external factors that might explain it.

cost model of helping   A model of altruistic behavior that considers the observer's cost of helping and the cost to the victim of not receiving help.

credibility   Attribute of a communicator, based on expertise and trustworthiness, that enhances persuasion.

cross-cultural studies   Studies that examine and/or compare the attitudes, beliefs, values, and behavior of people in different cultures.

culture   Set of attitudes, values, beliefs, and behaviors shared by a group of people and communicated from one generation to the next. Culture is the result of a group's adaptation to its environment.

deception (in an experiment)   The practice of giving subjects false information about the reasons for the study or the manipulations.

decision tree   A model of intervention in emergencies that considers decisions about noticing, interpreting, assessing responsibility, knowing an appropriate form of assistance, and implementing the decision.

decremental deprivation   The loss of what one once had or thought one could have.

deindividuation   The loss of individuality that occurs when the individual becomes submerged in the group and feels relatively anonymous.

delegitimization   According to Bar-Tal, the categorization of a group or groups into extremely negative social categories that are excluded from the realm of acceptable norms and/or values.

demand characteristics   Cues in the experimental setting that communicate to subjects the behavior that is expected of them.

dependent variable   The subject's response in an experiment.

depressive realism   The tendency of depressed people to see themselves and the world realistically, without the self-deceiving biases that protect nondepressed people.

destructive cult   According to MacHovec (1989), a rigidly structured absolutist group, usually under an authoritarian, charismatic leader, which isolates itself from established societal traditions, values, and norms, recruits members deceptively without informed consent, and retains them by continually reinforced direct and indirect manipulative techniques, which cause personality and behavior change, deny freedom of choice, and interrupt and obstruct optimal personality development.

differential decay   Source information often decays faster than message information.

diffusion of responsibility   The sharing of responsibility among several individuals; when no one person can be held accountable, no one may intervene in an emergency.

dilution effect   The tendency of an inference to be weakened by irrelevant information.

direct experience   An attitude derived from personal contact with the object of the attitude, rather than from hearing or reading about the experience of others.

discontinuity effect   Individuals are more competitive and less cooperative when interacting in a context where group membership is important than when they are involved in interpersonal interactions.

discounting In attribution, reducing the perceived importance of one possible cause of behavior when another possible cause is also present; in persuasion, suppressing attitude change when the message comes from a low-credibility source.

discrimination Usually negative, often aggressive behavior aimed at someone because of his or her group membership.

displaced aggression Aggression that varies either in type or in target from that most preferred by the attacker.

dispositions Qualities or traits that distinguish one person or group from another.

dissociation In memory, over time, a message becomes separated from information about the source.

dissonant cognitions Cognitions that contradict one another psychologically.

effort justification paradigm Defense of what one has voluntarily suffered for as a means to reduce cognitive dissonance.

egocentricity A bias toward perceiving oneself as the central actor and causal agent in events.

ego defensive functions Attitudes may protect people from admitting to themselves an uncomplimentary truth.

egoism A tendency to focus on one's own gratification; behavior directed at self-gratification.

elaboration likelihood model (ELM) A model of attitude change that focuses on the distinction between scrutinizing the content of a message (central route) and the other factors (peripheral route) that affect persuasion.

empathy The ability to share in another's feelings.

empathy-altruism hypothesis The hypothesis that helping behavior is based, at least in part, on feelings of empathy with another person.

equity The amount people receive from a relationship should be determined by how much they put into it.

equity theory The theory that an individual compares inputs and outcomes with those of the other party to determine the fairness of a relationship.

ethnocentrism A tendency to reject people who are culturally dissimilar to one's own ethnic group and to accept without question those who are culturally like one's ethnic group; a characteristic of the authoritarian personality.

exchange relationship A relationship in which benefits given are balanced against benefits received.

excitation transfer The transfer of arousal produced by one source to the energization of an unrelated response.

excitation transfer theory A theory, usually applied to aggression, that holds that arousal from one source can be misperceived and therefore transferred to another source.

exemplification Behavior designed to get others to believe that one is moral and self-sacrificing.

expectancy effects (self-fulfilling prophecy) The tendency of a perceiver's expectations about a target person's behavior or performance to be confirmed because the expectations change how the perceiver acts toward the target.

experiment A method of study aimed at determining the cause-and-effect relationship between events; the experimenter exercises control over the independent variable.

experimental realism The degree to which experimental manipulations have impact and involve the subjects in the experimental situation.

experimenter bias Influence on subjects' behavior as a function of the investigators' expectations.

expert power Power derived from a reputation for special insight or knowledge about a particular area.

external attribution An inference that a person's behavior is caused by an environmental or situational factor.

external locus of control A perception that one's outcomes are due to factors outside of one's control, such as luck, chance, or fate.

external validity The degree to which research findings may be generalized to situations outside the laboratory.

extraneous variables Factors that may influence the dependent variable, though they have nothing to do with the independent variable.

face The positive social value we claim for ourselves in social interactions.

face saving Behaviors designed to maintain a positive public image.

face work In Goffman's theory of self-presentation, behavior designed to maintain other people's faces.

false consensus The tendency to overestimate the number of people who think and act as we do.

field experiment An experiment that is run in a natural setting, and subjects often do not know that they are in an experiment; the realism should allow greater opportunity for generalization and more mundane realism.

foot-in-the-door technique A compliance technique whereby the communicator leads the target to commit him- or herself to the desired action in small incremental steps.

forbidden toy paradigm A version of the induced compliance paradigm that produces counterattitudinal behavior.

free-choice paradigm A strategy for research in cognitive dissonance in which an individual is asked to choose one of two or more items. Dissonance is aroused by the choice, owing to rejection of desirable aspects of the rejected item and acceptance of undesirable aspects of the chosen alternative.

free-rider effect Social loafing as a consequence of a belief that one's contributions to the group are dispensable and that the group will succeed without one's efforts.

frustration Interference with or thwarting of an ongoing behavior.

frustration-aggression theory The theory that aggression is always a consequence of frustration and that frustration always leads to some form of aggression.

fundamental attribution error. *See* **correspondence bias.**

gender stereotypes Beliefs about the typical characteristics and behaviors of women and men.

generalization The process of deriving from a sample of situations information that predicts and explains behavior in other situations of a similar sort.

graduated reciprocation in tension reduction (GRIT) A policy developed by Osgood to reduce international tension through the unilateral reduction of threat capability.

group Two or more persons who are interacting with one another in such a manner that each person influences and is influenced by each other person.

group development The process by which groups form, flourish, and decline, and the changes that take place in groups and in their members over time.

group polarization The tendency of group discussion to cause an individual to make a more extreme decision than he or she would make alone.

groupthink A form of thinking in a decision-making situation in which the group suspends objectivity and careful analysis in an effort to preserve group cohesiveness.

heritability coefficient An estimate of the amount of variance in a particular characteristic within a sample that is attributable to genetic factors.

heuristic processing. *See* **peripheral route to persuasion**.

heuristics Assumptions or rules that allow people to make rapid judgments; peripheral cues.

hypocrisy The realization that one has publicly advocated behavior that one does not practice personally.

hypothesis A statement that expresses the nature of the relationship between events; it expresses *what* relationship exists between the events, not *why* they are related.

idealized performance Behavior suggesting we live up to ideal standards of social behavior more than we actually do.

identification Adoption of the standards of a person or group that one likes, admires, and wants to establish a relationship with.

ideocentric Traits unique to the individual.

illusory correlation A correlation erroneously perceived between a person or group and a characteristic on the basis of a few specific coincidences.

IBM model of AIDS-preventive behavior Information, motivation, and behavioral skills are joint determinants of safer sex behavior.

impression management theory Behavior is designed to control what others think, especially so as to maintain power in relation to them.

independent variable A variable manipulated by the experimenter to study its effect on the dependent variable.

individualism Tendency of culture to emphasize and value independence and the primacy of the individual over the group.

induced compliance paradigm A paradigm of research in cognitive dissonance in which individuals are persuaded to behave in ways that are discrepant with their private attitudes.

informational power Power derived from the possession of a specific piece of information.

informational social influence Influence based on a group's capacity to supply information.

informed consent Consent given to participate in an experiment after the procedures to be used have been explained and the subject has been given an opportunity to withdraw from the experiment.

ingratiation Use of a variety of strategies to enhance one's image illicitly in the eyes of others.

ingratiator's dilemma A problem posed by the fact that a low-power position makes a person want to ingratiate but alerts the target person to the possibility of ingratiation and thus makes it more difficult; also, the problem of wanting to ingratiate but not wanting to see oneself as an ingratiator.

institutional review boards (IRBs) Committees in which a cross section of professionals considers the risks and benefits of research to participants and ensures that proposed research methods protect subjects' safety and rights.

internal attribution An inference that a person's behavior is caused by a personal disposition.

internalization The process by which one genuinely accepts an opinion as a result of its good fit with one's other values and opinions.

internal locus of control A perception that one's outcomes are due to one's own efforts and actions.

internal validity Freedom of an experimental design from contamination by an extraneous variable; allows the investigator to state that manipulations of the independent variable are responsible for changes in the dependent variable.

intimidation Behavior designed to get others to believe that one is dangerous.

jigsaw method A technique for reducing conflict in a racially mixed group of students by which the group is given a problem to solve such that each member holds a part of the solution; if the group is to succeed, each member must master his or her part.

just-world theory People want to believe that the world is a fair and just place.

knowledge function Attitudes help perceivers to understand their environments by providing summary evaluations of objects and groups of objects.

leader The person who exerts the most influence in a group.

leadership schema An overall image of what a leader is and does.

learned helplessness A state resulting when the individual perceives no control over his or her environment.

legitimate power Power derived from a particular role or position.

Likert scale A scale that measures the direction and intensity of attitudes.

love bombing In cult recruitment meetings, expressions of unconditional love and caring from cult members.

masculinity dimension dimension used to differentiate and describe cultures by referring to the degree to which sex roles within the culture are fluid and flexible.

matching to standards Attempting to meet ideal standards of behavior in a situation; caused or increased by self-awareness.

maximum differentiation strategy The tendency to settle for less so long as the amount is more than what the outgroup gets.

mean Average, computed by dividing the sum of the terms by the number of terms.

mediator A third party who helps the principal parties to a conflict develop their own resolution.

mediator/arbitrator (Med/Arb) In a dispute, a third party who will impose a settlement if mediation is not successful.

mere exposure effect Exposure to a person or objects in the absence of any factor other than familiarity, leads to feelings of attraction.

mere thought Thought alone, in the absence of the object contemplated or new information about it, causes preexisting attitudes toward it to become more extreme.

minimal group paradigm Membership in a group based on nothing more than random assignment to it. Research shows that ingroup bias results from even this situation.

minority influence The ability of a minority opinion to affect the thinking of individual group members.

modeling Imitation of another person's behavior.

modern racism Compared to old-fashioned racism, prejudice and discrimination today may be expressed in more subtle ways and appear in limited situations.

multiculturalism The idea that the distinct cultural identities of ethnic groups in a society should be maintained and harmony between the groups encouraged.

multiple-act behavioral criterion A measure that includes a wide variety of behaviors related to an attitude.

mundane realism The degree to which the experimental setting approximates a real-life setting.

need for cognition An individual's preference for and tendency to engage in effortful thought.

negative memory bias The tendency of depressed people to remember more negative than positive experiences.

norms Rules that govern specific behavior and apply to everyone in the group.

normative beliefs One's beliefs about what other people want one to do.

normative social influence Influence based on a group's capacity to reward and punish, including the capacity to accept or reject the individual.

norming stage A stage of group development marked by a high degree of conformity, in which members attempt to establish norms.

obedience Conformity to direct orders from a person of high status and authority.

outgroup homogeneity effect The tendency to see all members of the outgroup as similar or homogeneous.

outgroup polarization effect The tendency to have extreme reactions to information about outgroup members, overvaluing both positive and negative information.

overjustification effects The tendency of inappropriately large rewards to be counterproductive.

perceived behavioral control People take into account whether they are capable of performing a behavior when they formulate their intentions.

perceived self-efficacy One's confidence in one's ability to produce a positive outcome.

peripheral cues. *See* **heuristics.**

peripheral route to persuasion Persuasion effected by factors other than the content of the persuasive message.

personal-group discrimination discrepancy Members of disadvantaged groups report that they personally experience less discrimination than other members of their group.

personal space Area that surrounds the individual over which he or she feels ownership or control.

person attribution An inference that a person's behavior is caused by an internal disposition.

pleasure principle Individuals want to satisfy all of their impulses immediately and to avoid all pain.

positive personal relationship The positive attitude that two people hold toward each other.

postdecisional dissonance Dissonance experienced when one makes a choice between two or more alternatives; associated with the free-choice paradigm.

power The capacity to influence others and to resist influence by others.

power distance Dimension used to differentiate and describe cultures by referring to the degree of inequality that exists between people in different power positions.

prejudice An unjustified negative attitude toward an individual based solely on that individual's membership in a group.

priming The process of bringing certain things, typically behaviors or personal characteristics, to mind, activating them.

progressive deprivation Loss of momentum or deterioration of conditions after a prolonged period of steady improvement.

protection motivation theory Threatening messages produce attitude change by motivating the listener to protect him- or herself from dangers described in the message.

prototype A standard that incorporates the essential and most characteristic features of a category.

racism Discrimination or prejudice based on race.

random assignment Assignment of subjects to experimental conditions in such a way that all subjects have equal opportunities to be in each experimental condition.

reactance theory The theory that a threat to behavioral freedom arouses a motivation to regain that freedom.

realistic conflict theory The theory that discrimination can be traced to competition for scarce resources.

reality principle Individuals learn to delay gratification to obtain greater rewards.

recategorization In an intergroup conflict situation, eliminating group boundaries and encouraging people to view themselves as members of the same group.

reciprocity A mutual exchange of confidences, self-disclosures, or resources.

reciprocity norm A rule specifying that people should reciprocate another's self-disclosure and helpful acts to the same degree.

reference group A group toward which one orients oneself; it forms the basis of comparison for attitudes, values, and behaviors.

referent power Power derived from being admired and liked.

reflected appraisal A view of the self based on other people's appraisals.

regressive racism Discriminatory behavior elicited under stress or arousal.

reinforcement Rewards offered for approved behavior, which tend to increase the probability that the approved behavior will be repeated.

related attributes hypothesis In social comparison theory, the hypothesis that we evaluate our opinions and abilities by comparing them with those of people whose opinions and performance should be similar to ours, given their standing on characteristics related to opinion and performance.

relative deprivation Feeling of resentment that occurs when individuals believe that their own or their group's outcomes are unfair.

representativeness bias The tendency to assume that a person who shares some characteristics of a group probably belongs to that group.

revised learned helplessness (RLH) model The theory that people learn to become helpless, and eventually become depressed, as a result of attributing their negative outcomes to internal, stable, and global causes.

reward model of attraction The theory that we like people whom we associate with rewards.

reward power The capacity to give positive reinforcements to achieve compliance.

role A set of norms that defines how a particular person in a given position must act.

role ambiguity Uncertainty as to what is expected of one in a specific situation or position.

role conflict The inner struggle that results when incompatible behaviors are demanded either by the various requirements of a role or by the various roles that one occupies.

romantic love A passionately intense attachment to another person.

saliency bias The tendency to attribute behavior to any stimulus that is most vivid or salient in the situation.

scapegoat theory of discrimination The theory that outgroups are convenient targets for hostility stemming from the frustrations of everyday life.

schema A body of general knowledge and expectations about a person, object, or event.

science A set of rules guiding the inquiry and study of events.

selective exposure hypothesis Perceivers actively control their exposure to information so that consistent information is approached and inconsistent information is avoided.

selective memory Information consistent with one's attitudes will be overrepresented in memory relative to inconsistent information.

selective perception Perceivers tend to interpret information as being more supportive of their attitudes than it really is.

self-affirmation theory People can reduce dissonance by affirming their worth in any way that shows they are good people.

self-complexity The condition of perceiving oneself to have many aspects, which differ greatly from one another.

self-concept theory Any threat to the self-concept induces dissonance.

self-construction Self-presentational behavior designed to confirm a desired view of the self.

self-disclosure The act of revealing personal information to others.

self-discrepancy theory The theory that one's psychological well-being is affected by the match or mismatch between one's self-concept and one's self-guides: one's ideal self and the self one thinks one ought to be.

self-efficacy Confidence in one's ability to produce positive outcomes.

self-fulfilling prophecy *See* **expectancy effect.**

self-handicapping Putting obstacles in the way of one's own success, for the purpose of providing an excuse for poor performance.

self-monitoring A personality variable that reflects the extent to which individuals behave according either to their internal states or to external cues in the environment.

self-perception theory A theory that people infer their own attitudes and feelings from their behaviors and the situations in which they take place.

self-promotion Behavior designed to get others to believe that one is competent and talented.

self-regulation The process by which self-awareness leads to matching to standards if outcome expectancy is positive.

sexism Discrimination or prejudice based on sex.

similarity-attraction effect People like someone with whom they share similar attitudes and characteristics.

similarity hypothesis We evaluate ourselves by comparing our opinions and abilities with those of other people who are similar to us.

situated identity The conception one has of oneself in a specific situation.

sleeper effect The increase in the strength of a communication's effect on attitudes over time.

social cognition The processing, organizing, and retrieval of information about other people.

social comparison The process whereby individuals reduce uncertainty about their opinions, abilities, and emotions by observing those of similar others.

social exchange theory Theory that views human interaction as a cost-reward transaction.

social facilitation An increase in the quality of performance in the presence of an audience or co-actors, whether or not in competition.

social identity theory The theory that people evaluate themselves by their membership in groups, and therefore are motivated to evaluate the ingroup more positively than the outgroup.

Social impact theory The theory that social influence is a function of the strength, immediacy, and number of sources of influence.

social influence The exercise of power by a person or group to change the opinions or behavior of others.

social inhibition A restraint on performance effected by the presence of an audience or co-actors.

social learning theory The theory that individuals learn behavior by imitating others and receiving rewards.

social loafing The tendency of individuals to work less hard in a group than alone, perhaps because of lack of individual identifiability or reduced feelings of personal responsibility.

social psychology A discipline that employs scientific methods to understand and explain how the thoughts, feelings, and behavior of individuals are influenced by the actual, imagined, or implied presence of others.

social responsibility norm A general rule specifying that we should give help to people who need it.

social role theory Sex differences arise from societal expectations about "appropriate conduct" for men and women.

spontaneous trait inferences The concept that when people observe behavior, they automatically make trait inferences.

statistically significant Reliable; a finding is considered statistically significant if a statistical test indicates that the event could have occurred by chance fewer than 5 times out of 100 (p <.05).

stereotype Sets of beliefs about the characteristics of the people in a group, generalized to nearly all group members.

stereotype threat When one's behavior or performance might confirm an unfavorable stereotype about one's group.

storming stage A stage of group development marked by a low degree of conformity, in which members negotiate their positions in the group.

subjective norms Behavior-guiding rules based on what we think other people want us to do.

subtractive rule In attribution theory, the principle that perceivers should subtract the contribution of situational inducements from the personal disposition implied by the behavior.

subtyping Individuals that disconfirm the stereotype of their group may be considered exceptions to the group stereotype.

sucker effect Social loafing as a consequence of a belief that other group members are not contributing their maximum effort.

superordinate goal A goal that is attractive to members of two groups but cannot be achieved without cooperation between the two groups.

supplication Behavior designed to make others feel sorry for you and want to help.

survey A method of research by which the investigator asks questions of a large sample of subjects.

symbolic racism Hostility toward racial minorities based on the belief that they threaten the values of the majority culture.

symmetrical relationships In the perception of individuals, a set of relationships that are harmonious and consistent.

systematic processing. *See* **central route to persuasion.**

systemic-heuristic model Chaiken's theory that attitude change can occur in two ways: systematic processing and heuristic processing.

terrorism Actual or threatened violence against noncombatants for avowed political ends.

terror management theory When people are faced with reminders of their mortality, they seek symbolic immortality by becoming closer to people who are like them.

theory A systematic statement that seeks to explain *why* two or more events are related.

theory of planned behavior The theory that planned behavior is linked to an attitude toward specific behavior, subjective norms, and degree of perceived control.

theory of reasoned action People are assumed to be rational, deliberate thinkers, who act on the basis of what they know; attitudes and subjective norms determine intentions.

totalitarian ego The biased organization of information about the self that functions to preserve a favorable self-impression.

transformational leader A leader who can sense and articulate the unexpressed desires of a populace and who expresses those desires to change the political system.

two-factor theory of emotions Schachter's theory that emotional experience is based on a combination of physiological arousal and cognitive labeling or interpretation of the causes of arousal.

uncertainty avoidance Dimension that describes cultures by referring to the extent individuals are disturbed by and avoid uncertainty and ambiguity.

uncertainty orientation Tendency to seek out new information and to approach uncertain situations.

unobtrusive measures Experimental methods that permit subjects' behavior to be measured without their awareness.

utilitarian function Attitudes serve to maximize rewards and minimize punishments.

value-expressive function Attitudes may communicate individual's values and identities to other people.

variability The extent to which scores vary about the mean. The closer the scores cluster about the mean, the lower the variability.

victim blaming Tendency to derogate those who are unsuccessful, physically or economically disadvantaged, or victims of disease or crime and consider them blameworthy.

visual dominance behavior Staring or other assertive, dominating nonverbal behavior.

References

Abelson, R. (1995). *Statistics as principled argument.* Mahwah, NJ: Erlbaum.

Abelson, R. P. (1981). The psychological status of the script concept. *American Psychologist, 36,* 715–729.

Abelson, R. P., & Levi, A. (1985). Decision making and decision theory. In G. Lindzey & E. Aronson (Eds.), *The handbook of social psychology* (3rd ed.). New York: Random House.

Abramson, L. Y., Alloy, L. B., & Metalsky, G. I. (1986). The cognitive diathesis-stress theories of depression: Toward an adequate evaluation of the theories validity. In L. B. Alloy (Ed.), *Cognitive processes in depression.* New York: Guilford.

Abramson, L. Y., Seligman, M. E. P., & Teasdale, J. D. (1978). Learned helplessness in humans: Critique and reformulation. *Journal of Abnormal Psychology, 87,* 49–74.

Acker, M., & Davis, M. H. (1992). Intimacy, passion and commitment in adult romantic relationships: A test of the triangular theory of love. *Journal of Social and Personal Relationships, 9,* 21–50.

Adorno, T. W., Frenkel-Brunswick, E., Levinson, D. J., & Sanford, R. N. (1950). *The authoritarian personality.* New York: Harper.

Aiello, J. R., & Aiello, T. (1974). The development of personal space: Proxemic behavior of children 6 through 16. *Human Ecology, 2*(3), 177–189.

Ainsworth, M. D. S., Biehar, M. C., Waters, E., & Wall, S. (1978). *Patterns of attachment: A psychological study of the strange situation.* Hillsdale, NJ: Erlbaum.

Ajzen, I. (1985). From actions to intentions: A theory of planned behavior. In J. Kuhl & J. Beckman (Eds.), *Action control: From cognition to behavior.* New York: Springer-Verlag.

Ajzen, I. (1991). The theory of planned behavior. *Organizational behavior and human decision processes, 50,* 179–211.

Ajzen, I., & Fishbein, M. (1980). *Understanding attitudes and predicting social behavior.* Englewood Cliffs, NJ: Prentice-Hall.

Ajzen, I., & Madden T. J. (1986). Prediction of goal-directed behavior: Attitudes, intentions, and perceived behavioral control. *Journal of Experimental Social Psychology, 22,* 453–474.

Alden, L. (1987). Attributional responses of anxious individuals to different patterns of social feedback: Nothing succeeds like improvement. *Journal of Personality and Social Psychology, 52,* 100–106.

Alee, W. et al. (1935). *A handbook of social psychology.* Edited by Humphrey Milford. London: Oxford University Press.

Alexander, C. N., Jr., & Rudd, J. (1981). Situated identities and response variables. In J. T. Tedeschi (Ed.), *Impression management theory and social psychological research.* New York: Academic Press.

Alicke, M. D., Klotz, M. L., Breitenbecher, D. L., Yurak, T. J., & Vredenburg, D. S. (1995). Personal contact, individuation, and the better-than-average effect. *Journal of Personality and Social Psychology, 68,* 804–825.

Allen, V., & Greenberger. (1989). Destruction and perceived control. In A. Baum & J. Singer (Eds.), *Advances: Environmental Psychology, Vol. 2.* Hillsdale, NJ: Erlbaum.

Allen, V. L. (1965). Situational factors in conformity. In L. Berkowitz (Ed.), *Advances in experimental social psychology* (Vol. 2). New York: Academic Press.

Allen V. L., & Wilder, D. A. (1980). Impact of group consensus and social support on stimulus meaning: Mediation of conformity by cognitive restructuring. *Journal of Personality and Social Psychology, 39,* 1116–1125.

Allison, S. T., & Kerr, N. L. (1994). Group correspondence biases and the provision of public goods. *Journal of Personality and Social Psychology, 66,* 688–698.

Allison, S. T., Mackie, D. M., & Messick, D. M. (1996). Outcome biases in social perception: Implications for dispositional inference, attitude change, stereotyping, and social behavior. In M. P. Zanna (Ed.), *Advances in experimental social psychology* (Vol. 28). Boston: Academic Press.

Alloy, L. B., & Ahrens, A. H. (1987). Depression and pessimism for the future: Biased use of statistically relevant information in predictions for self versus others. *Journal of Personality and Social Psychology, 52,* 366–378.

Allport, F. H. (1924). *Social psychology.* Cambridge, MA: Riverside Press.

Allport, G. W. (1935). Attitudes. In C. Murchison (Ed.), *Handbook of social psychology* (pp. 798–844). Worcester, MA: Clark University Press.

Allport, G. W. (1954). *The nature of prejudice.* Reading, MA: Addison-Wesley.

Allport, G. W. (1985). The historical background of social psychology. In G. Lindzey & E. Aronson (Eds.), *Handbook of social psychology* (3rd ed., Vol 1. pp. 1–46). New York: Random House.

Altemeyer, B. (1988). *Enemies of freedom: Understanding right-wing authoritarianism.* San Francisco, CA: Jossey-Bass.

Altemeyer, B. (1994). Reducing prejudice in right-wing authoritarians. In M. P. Zanna & J. M. Olson (Eds.), *The psychology of prejudice: The Ontario symposium* (Vol. 7, pp. 131–148). Mahwah, NJ: Erlbaum.

Amancio, L. (1989). Social differentiation between "dominant" and "dominated" groups: Toward an integration of social stereotypes and social identity. *European Journal of Social Psychology, 19,* 1–10.

American Psychological Association. (1982). *Ethical principles in the conduct of research with human participants.* Washington, DC: Author.

Amir, Y. (1969). Contact hypothesis in ethnic relations. *Psychological Bulletin, 71,* 319–341.

Anderson, C. (1989). Temperature and aggression: Ubiquitous effects of heat on the occurrence of human violence. *Psychological Bulletin, 106,* 74–96.

Anderson, C., & Anderson, D. (1984). Ambient temperature and violent crime: Tests of the linear and curvilinear hypotheses. *Journal of Personality and Social Psychology, 46,* 91–97.

Anderson, C. A., Anderson, K. B., & Deuser, W. E. (1996). Examining an affective aggression framework: Weapons and temperature effects on aggressive thoughts, affect, and attitudes. *Personality and Social Psychology Bulletin, 22*(4), 366–376.

Anderson, C. A., Deuser, S. B., & DeNeve, K. M. (1995). Hot temperatures, hostile affect, hostile cognition and arousal: Tests of a general model of affective aggression. *Personality and Social Psychology Bulletin, 21,* 434–448.

Anderson, D., & Rosenthal, R. (1968). Some effects of interpersonal expectancy on institutionalized retarded children. *Proceedings of the 76th Annual Convention of the American Psychological Association* (pp. 479–480). Washington, DC: American Psychological Association.

Anderson, N. H. (1981). *Foundations of information integration theory.* New York: Academic Press.

Antill, J. K., & Cotton, S. (1988). Factors affecting the division of labor in households. *Sex Roles, 18,* 531–553.

Archer, D., & Akert, R. M. (1977). Words and everything else: Verbal and nonverbal cues to social interpretation. *Journal of Personality and Social Psychology, 35,* 443–449.

Archer, R. L. (1980). Self-disclosure. In D. M. Wegner & R. R. Vallacher (Eds.), *The self in social psychology.* New York: Oxford University Press.

Archer, R. L., & Burleson, J. A. (1980). The effect of timing of self-disclosure on attraction and reciprocity. *Journal of Personality and Social Psychology, 38,* 120–130.

Archer, R. P., & Cash, T. F. (1985). Physical attractiveness and maladjustment among psychiatric in-patients. *Journal of Social and Clinical Psychology, 3,* 170–180.

Aries, D. (1976). Interaction patterns and themes of male, female, and mixed groups. *Small Group Behavior, 7,* 7–18.

Arkin, R. M. (1980). Self-presentation. In D. M. Wegner & R. R. Vallacher (Eds.), *The self in social psychology.* New York: Oxford University Press.

Arms, R. L., Russell, G. W., & Sandilands, M. L. (1979). Effects on the hostility of spectators of viewing aggressive sports. *Social Psychology Quarterly, 42,* 275–279.

Aron, A., Paris, M., & Aron, E. N. (1995). Falling in love: Prospective studies of self-concept change. *Journal of Personality and Social Psychology, 69,* 1102–1112.

Aronoff, J., Barclay, A., & Stevenson, L. (1988). The recognition of threatening facial stimuli. *Journal of Personality and Social Psychology, 54,* 647–655.

Aronson, E. (1968). Dissonance theory: Progress and problems. In E. Aronson, R. Abelson, W. McGuire, T. Newcomb, M. Rosenberg, & P. Tannenbaum (Eds.), *Theories of cognitive consistency: A sourcebook* (pp. 5–27). Chicago: Rand-McNally.

Aronson, E. (1969). Some antecedents of interpersonal attraction. In W. J. Arnold & D. Levine (Eds.), *Nebraska symposium on motivation* (Vol. 17). Lincoln: University of Nebraska Press.

Aronson, E. (1989). Analysis, synthesis, and the treasuring of the old. *Personality and Social Psychology Bulletin, 15,* 493–507.

Aronson, E. (1990). Applying social psychology to desegregation and energy conservation. *Personality and Social Psychology Bulletin, 16,* 118–132.

Aronson, E. (1992). The return of the repressed: Dissonance theory makes a comeback. *Psychological Inquiry, 3*(4), 303–311.

Aronson, E., Brewer, M. & Carlsmith, J. M. (1985). Experimentation in social psychology. In G. Lindzey & E. Aronson (Eds.), *Handbook of social psychology* (3rd ed., Vol. I. pp. 1–46). New York: Random House.

Aronson, E., & Carlsmith, J. M. (1963). Effect of the severity of threat on the devaluation of forbidden behavior. *Journal of Abnormal and Social Psychology, 66,* 584–588.

Aronson, E., Fried, C. B., & Stone, J. (1991). Overcoming denial and increasing the intention to use condoms through the induction of hypocrisy. *American Journal of Public Health, 81,* 1636–1638.

Aronson, E., & Linder, D. E. (1965). Gain and loss of esteem as determinants of interpersonal attractiveness. *Journal of Experimental Social Psychology, 1,* 156–171.

Aronson, E., & Mills, J. (1959). The effect of severity of initiation on liking for a group. *Journal of Abnormal and Social Psychology, 59,* 177–181.

Aronson, E., Stephan, C., Sikes, J., Blaney, N., & Snapp, M. *The jigsaw classroom.* Beverly Hills, CA: Sage.

Aronson, E., Willerman, B., & Floyd, J. (1966). The effect of a pratfall on increasing interpersonal attractiveness. *Psychonomic Science, 4,* 227–228.

Aronson, E., & Worchel, P. (1966). Similarity versus liking as determinants of interpersonal attractiveness. *Psychonomic Science, 5,* 157–158.

Asch, S. (1946). Forming impressions on personality. *Journal of Abnormal and Social Psychology, 41,* 258–290.

Asch, S. (1951). Effects of group pressure upon the modification and distortion of judgment. In H. Geutzkow (Ed.), *Groups, leadership, and men.* Pittsburgh, PA: Carnegie Press.

Asch, S. (1952). *Social psychology.* New York: Prentice-Hall.

Asch, S. (1956). Studies of independence and conformity: I. A minority of one against a unanimous majority. *Psychological Monographs, 70*(9).

Austin, W. G. (1986). Justice in intergroup conflict. In S. Worchel & W. G. Austin (Eds.), *The psychology of intergroup relations,* (pp. 153–176). Chicago: Nelson-Hall.

Axsom, D., Yates, S. M., & Chaiken, S. (1987). Audience response as a heuristic cue in persuasion. *Journal of Personality and Social Psychology, 53,* 30–40.

Axtell, R. (1991). *Gestures: The do's and taboos of body language around the world.* New York: Wiley.

Ayerastaran, S. (1996, July). Paper presented at the European Association of Experimental Social Psychology, Gmunden, Austria.

Ayllon, T., & Azrin, N. (1968). *The token economy: A motivational system for therapy and rehabilitation.* New York: Appleton-Century-Crofts.

Babad, E., Bernieri, F., & Rosenthal, R. (1989). Nonverbal communication and leakage in the behavior of biased and unbiased teachers. *Journal of Personality and Social Psychology, 56,* 89–94.

Back, K. W. (1951). Influence through social communication. *Journal of Abnormal and Social Psychology, 46,* 9–23.

Backman, C. W., & Secord, P. F. (1959). The effect of perceived liking on interpersonal attraction. *Human Relations, 12,* 379–384.

Bailey, W. C. (1976). Some further evidence on homicide and a regional culture of violence. *Omega, 2,* 145–170.

Baldwin, M. W., & Holmes, J. G. (1987). Salient private audiences and awareness of the self. *Journal of Personality and Social Psychology, 52,* 1087–1098.

Bales, R. F. (1958). Task roles and social roles in problem-solving groups. In E. E. Maccoby, T. M. Newcomb, & E. L. Hartly (Eds.), *Readings in social psychology* (3rd ed.) New York: Holt, Rinehart and Winston.

Bales, R. F., & Slater, P. (1955). Role differentiation in small decision-making groups. In T. Parsons & R. F. Bales (Eds.), *Family, socialization and interaction processes.* Glencoe, IL: Free Press.

Ballard, M. E., & Wiest, J. R. (1996). Mortal Kombat: The effects of violent videogame play on males' hostility and cardiovascular responding. *Journal of Applied Social Psychology, 26,* 717–730.

Bandura, A. (1965). Influences of models' reinforcement contingencies on the acquisition of initiative responses. *Journal of Personality and Social Psychology, 1,* 589–593.

Bandura, A. (1973). *Aggression: A social learning analysis.* New York: Holt, Rinehart and Winston.

Bandura, A. (1977). Self-efficacy: Toward a unifying theory of behavior change. *Psychological Review, 84,* 191–215.

Bandura, A. (1982). Self-efficacy mechanisms in human agency. *American Psychologist, 37,* 122–147.

Bandura, A., Ross, D., & Ross, S. A. (1961). Transmission of aggression through imitation of aggressive models. *Journal of Abnormal and Social Psychology, 63,* 575–582.

Bandura, A., Ross, D., & Ross, S. A. (1963a). Imitation of film-mediated aggressive models. *Journal of Abnormal and Social Psychology, 66,* 3–11.

Bandura, A., Ross, D., & Ross, S. A. (1963b). A comparative test of the status envy, social power, and secondary reinforcement theories of identificatory learning. *Journal of Abnormal and Social Psychology, 67,* 527–534.

Bandura, A., & Walters, R. H. (1963). *Social learning and personality development.* New York: Holt, Rinehart and Winston.

Barbee, A. P. (1993). Effects of gender role expectations on the social support process. *Journal of Social Issues, 49,* 175–190.

Bardach, L., & Park, B. (1996). The effect of in-group/out-group status on memory for consistent and inconsistent behavior of an individual. *Journal of Personality and Social Psychology, 70,* 169–178.

Bargh, J. A., Bond, R. N., Lombardi, W. J., & Tota, M. E. (1986). The additive nature of chronic and temporary sources of construct accessibility. *Journal of Personality and Social Psychology, 50,* 869–878.

Bargh, J. A., & Raymond, P. (1995). The misuse of power: Nonconscious sources of sexual harassment, *Journal of Social Issues, 51,* 85–96.

Bargh, J. A., Raymond, P., Pryor, J. B., & Stack, F. (1995). The attractiveness of the underling: An automatic power—sex association and its consequence for sexual harassment and aggression. *Journal of Personality and Social Psychology, 68,* 768–781.

Bargh, J. A., & Tota, A. E. (1988). Content-dependent automatic processing in depression: Accessibility of negative constructs with regard to self but not others. *Journal of Personality and Social Psychology, 54,* 925–939.

Barner-Barry, C., & Rosenwein, R. (1985). *Psychological perspectives on politics.* Englewood Cliffs, NJ: Prentice-Hall.

Barnlund, D. (1975). *Public and private self in Japan and the United States.* Tokyo: Simul Press.

Barnlund, D. C. (1962). Consistency of emergent leadership in groups with changing tasks and members. *Speech Monographs, 29,* 45–52.

Baron, R. A. (1974). The aggression-inhibiting influence of heightened sexual arousal. *Journal of Personality and Social Psychology, 30,* 318–322.

Baron, R. A. (1977). *Human aggression.* New York: Plenum.

Baron, R. A. (1979). Effects of victim's pain cues, victim's race, and level of prior instigation upon physical aggression. *Journal of Applied Psychology, 9,* 103–114.

Baron, R. A., Albright, L., & Malloy, T. E. (1995). Effects of behavioral and social class information on social judgment. *Personality and Social Psychology Bulletin, 21,* 308–315.

Baron, R. A., & Bell, P. A. (1973). Effects of heightened sexual arousal on physical aggression. *Proceedings of the 81st Annual Convention of the American Psychological Association, 8,* 171–172.

Barr, C. L., & Kleck, R. E. (1995). Self-other perception of the intensity of facial expressions of emotion: Do we know what we show? *Journal of Personality and Social Psychology, 68,* 608–618.

Bar-Tal, D. (1990). Causes and consequences of delegitimization: Models of conflict and ethnocentrism. *Journal of Social Issues, 46*(1), 65–81.

Bass, B. M. (1949). An analysis of the leadership group discussion. *Journal of Applied Psychology, 33,* 527–533.

Bassili, J. N. (1996). Meta-judgmental versus operative indexes of psychological attributes: The case of measures of attitude strength. *Journal of Personality and Social Psychology, 71,* 637–653.

Batson, C. C., Duncan, B. D., Ackerman, P., Buckley, T., & Birch, K. (1981). Is empathic emotion a source of altruistic motivation? *Journal of Personality and Social Psychology, 40,* 290–302.

Batson, C. D. (1987). Prosocial motivation: Is it ever truly altruistic? In L. Berkowitz (Ed.), *Advances in experimental social psychology* (Vol. 20, pp. 65–122). Orlando, FL: Academic Press.

Batson, C. D. (1997). Self-other merging and the empathy-altruism hypothesis. *Journal of Personality and Social Psychology, 73,* 517–522.

Batson, C. D., Batson, J. G., Singlsby, J. K., Harrell, K. L., Peekna, H. M., & Todd, R. M. (1991). Empathy joy and the empathy-altruism hypothesis. *Journal of Personality and Social Psychology, 61,* 413–426.

Batson, C. D., Coke, J. S., Jasnoski, M. L., & Hanson, M. (1978). Buying kindness: Effect of an extrinsic incentive for helping on perceived altruism. *Personality and Social Psychology Bulletin, 4*(1), 86–91.

Batson, C. D., Dyck, J. L., Brandt, J. R., Batson, J. G., Powell, A. L., McMaster, M. R., & Griffitt, C. (1988). Five studies testing two new egoistic alternatives to the empathy-altruism hypothesis. *Journal of Personality and Social Psychology, 55,* 52–77.

Batson, C. D., Fultz, J., & Schoenrade, P. A. (1987). Distress and empathy: Two qualitatively distinct vicarious emotions with different motivational consequences. *Journal of Personality, 55,* 19–39.

Batson, C. D., & Oleson, K. (1990). Current status of the empathy-altruism hypothesis. *Review of Personality and Social Psychology, 12.*

Batson, C. D., O'Quinn, K., Fultz, J., Vanderplas, N., & Isen, A. M. (1983). Influence of self-reported distress and empathy on egoistic versus altruistic motivation to help. *Journal of Personality and Social Psychology, 43,* 706–718.

Batson, C. D., Sager, K., Garst, E., Kang, M., Rubchinsky, K., & Dawson, K. (1997). Is empathy-induced helping due to self-other merging? *Journal of Personality and Social Psychology, 73,* 495–509.

Baumeister, R. F. (1982). A self-presentational view of social phenomena. *Psychological Bulletin, 91,* 3–26.

Baumeister, R. F. (1985, April). The championship choke. *Psychology Today,* pp. 48–52.

Baumeister, R. F. (1986). *Public self and private self.* New York: Springer-Verlag.

Baumeister, R. F. (1989). *Masochism and the self.* Hillsdale, NJ: Erlbaum.

Baumeister, R. F. (1990). Suicide as escape from self. *Psychological Review, 97,* 90–113.

Baumeister, R. F. (1996). The self. In D. T. Gilbert, S. T. Fiske, & G. Lindzey (Eds.), *Handbook of social psychology* (4th ed.). New York: McGraw-Hill.

Baumeister, R. F., Hamilton, J., & Tice, D. (1985). Public versus private expectancy of success: Confidence booster or performance pressure? *Journal of Personality and Social Psychology, 48,* 1447–1457.

Baumeister, R. F., & Hutton, D. G. (1987). A self-presentational perspective on group processes. In B. Mullen & G. R. Goethals (Eds.), *Theories of group behavior.* New York: Springer-Verlag.

Baumeister, R. F., Hutton, D. G., & Tice, D. M. (1989). Cognitive processes during deliberate self-presentation: How self-presenters alter and misinterpret the behavior of their interaction partners. *Journal of Experimental Social Psychology, 25,* 59–78.

Baumeister, R. F., & Jones, E. E. (1978). When self-presentation is constrained by the target's knowledge: Consistency and compensation. *Journal of Personality and Social Psychology, 36,* 608–618.

Baumeister, R. F., Smart, L., & Boden, J. M. (1996). Relation of threatened egotism to violence and aggression: The darker side of high self-esteem. *Psychological Review, 103,* 5–33.

Baumeister, R. F., & Steinhilber, A. (1984). Paradoxical effects of supportive audiences on performance under pressure: The home field disadvantage in sports championships. *Journal of Personality and Social Psychology, 47,* 85–93.

Baumeister, R. F., & Tice, D. M. (1984). Role of self-presentation and choice in cognitive dissonance under forced compliance: Necessary or sufficient causes. *Journal of Personality and Social Psychology, 46,* 5–13.

Baumeister, R. F., & Tice, D. M. (1985). Toward a theory of situational structure. *Environment and Behavior, 17,* 147–172.

Baumgardner, A. H., Heppner, P. P., & Arkin, R. M. (1986). Role of causal attribution in personal problem solving. *Journal of Personality and Social Psychology, 50,* 636–643.

Baumrind, D. (1964). Some thoughts on ethics of research: After reading Milgram's "Behavioral Study of Obedience." *American Psychologist, 19,* 421–423.

Bauserman, R. (1996). Sexual aggression and pornography: A review of correlational research. *Basic and Applied Social Psychology, 18,* 405–427.

Bavelas, A., Hastorf, A. H., Gross, A. E., & Kite, W. R. (1965). Experiments on the alteration of group structure. *Journal of Experimental Social Psychology, 1,* 55–71.

Baxter, T. L., & Goldberg, L. R. (1987). Perceived behavioral consistency underlying trait attributions to oneself and another: An extension of the actor-observer effect. *Personality and Social Psychology Bulletin, 13,* 437–447.

Beaman, A. L., Klentz, B., Diener, E., & Svanum, S. (1979). Objective self-awareness and transgression in children: A field study. *Journal of Personality and Social Psychology, 37,* 1835–1846.

Beckett, N. E., & Park, B. (1995). Use of category versus individuating information: Making base rates salient. *Personality and Social Psychology Bulletin, 21,* 21–31.

Beckman, L. (1970). Effects of students' performance on teachers' and observers' attributions of causality. *Journal of Education Psychology, 61,* 76–82.

Belmore, S. M., & Hubbard, M. L. (1987). The role of advance expectancies in person memory. *Journal of Personality and Social Psychology, 53,* 61–70.

Bem, D. J. (1967). Self-perception: An alternative interpretation of cognitive dissonance phenomena. *Psychological Review, 74,* 183–200.

Bem, D. J. (1970). *Beliefs, attitudes, and human affairs.* Belmont, CA: Brooks/Cole.

Bem, D. J. (1972). Self-perception theory. In L. Berkowitz (Ed.), *Advances in experimental social psychology* (Vol. 6). New York: Academic Press.

Ben-Ari, R., & Amir, Y. (1988). Intergroup contact, cultural information, and change in ethnic attitudes. In W. Stroebe et al. (Eds.), *The social psychology of intergroup conflict* (pp. 151–166). Berlin: Springer-Verlag.

Benbow, C. P., & Stanley, J. C. (1980). Sex differences in mathematical ability: Fact or artifact? *Science, 210,* 1262–1264.

Bennett, L. (1968). *What manner of man? A biography of Martin Luther King, Jr.* Chicago: Johnson.

Benoit, D., & Parker, K. (1994). Stability and transmission of attachment across three generations. *Child Development, 65,* 1444–1456.

Benson, P. L., Karabenick, S. A., & Lerner, R. M. (1976). Pretty pleases: The effect of physical attraction, race and sex on receiving help. *Journal of Experimental Social Psychology, 12,* 409–415.

Bentwich, N. (1981). Kristallnacht: Pogrom in Emden. In A. Eisenberg (Ed.), *Witness to the holocaust.* New York: Pilgrim Press.

Berg, J. H. (1984). Development of friendship between roommates. *Journal of Personality and Social Psychology, 46,* 346–356.

Berg, J. H., & McQuinn, R. D. (1986). Attraction and exchange in continuing and non-continuing dating relationships. *Journal of Personality and Social Psychology, 50,* 942–952.

Bergen, D. J., & Williams, J. E. (1991). Sex stereotypes in the United States revisited: 1972–1988. *Sex Roles, 24,* 413–423.

Berger, S. M., Carli, L. C., Garcier, R., & James, J. B. (1982). Audience effects in anticipatory learning: A comparison of drive and practice inhibition analysis. *Journal of Personality and Social Psychology, 42,* 478–486.

Berkowitz, L. (1962). *Aggression: A social psychological analysis.* New York: McGraw-Hill.

Berkowitz, L. (1965). The concept of aggressive drive: Some additional considerations. In L. Berkowitz (Ed.), *Advances in experimental social psychology* (Vol. 2). New York: Academic Press.

Berkowitz, L. (Ed.). (1969). *Roots of aggression: A reexamination of the frustration-aggression hypothesis.* New York: Atherton.

Berkowitz, L. (1989). Frustration-aggression hypothesis:

Examination and reformulation. *Psychological Bulletin, 106,* 59–73.

Berkowitz, L. (1994). Is something missing? Some observations prompted by the cognitive-neoassociationist view of anger and emotional aggression. In L. R. Heusmann (Ed.), *Aggressive behavior: Current perspectives* (pp. 35–57). New York: Plenum.

Berkowitz, L., & Knurek, D. (1967). Label-mediated hostility generalization. *Journal of Personality and Social Psychology, 5,* 364–368.

Berkowitz, L., & Le Page, A. (1967). Weapons as aggression-eliciting stimuli. *Journal of Personality and Social Psychology, 7,* 202–207.

Berman, P. (1994, February 28). The other and almost the same. *New Yorker,* p. 71.

Berry, J. (1979). *Human ecology and cognitive style.* Beverly Hills, CA: Sage.

Berscheid, E. (1988). Some comments on love's anatomy; or, whatever happened to old-fashioned lust? In R. J. Sternberg & M. L. Barnes (Eds.), *The anatomy of love.* New Haven, CT: Yale University Press.

Berscheid, E., Dion, K., Walster, E., & Walster, G. W. (1971). Physical attractiveness and dating choice: A test of the matching hypothesis. *Journal of Experimental Social Psychology, 7,* 173–189.

Berscheid, E., Graziano, W., Monson, T., & Dermer, M. (1976). Outcome dependency: Attention, attribution, and attraction. *Journal of Personality and Social Psychology, 34,* 978–989.

Berscheid, E., & Walster, E. (1978). *Interpersonal attraction.* Reading, MA: Addison-Wesley.

Bettencourt, B. A., & Miller, N. (1996). Gender differences in aggression as a function of provocation: A meta-analysis. *Psychological Bulletin, 119,* 422–447.

Bickman, L., & Kamzan, M. (1973). The effect of race and need on helping behavior. *Journal of Social Psychology, 89,* 73–77.

Bird, C., Monachesi, E. D., & Burdick, M. (1952). Studies of group tensions: III. The effect of parental discouragement of play activities upon the attitudes of white children toward Negroes. *Child Development, 23,* 295–306.

Bishop, J. (1971). *The days of Martin Luther King, Jr.* New York: Putnam.

Blake, R. R., Helson, H., & Mouton, J. S. (1956). The generality of conformity behavior as a function of factual anchorage, difficulty of task and amount of social pressure. *Journal of Personality, 25,* 294–305.

Blanck, P. D., & Rosenthal, R. (1982). Developing strategies for decoding "leaky" messages: On learning how and when to decode discrepant and consistent social communications. In R. S. Feldman (Ed.), *Development of nonverbal behavior in children* (pp. 203–229). New York: Springer-Verlag.

Blaney, P. H. (1986). Affect and memory: A review. *Psychological Bulletin, 99,* 229–246.

Bochner, S. (1994). Cross-cultural differences in self-concept: A test of Hofstede's individualism/collectivism distinction. *Journal of Cross-Cultural Psychology, 25,* 273–283.

Bochner, S. & Hesketh, B. (1994). Power distance, individualism/collectivism and job-related attitudes in culturally diverse work groups. *Journal of Cross Cultural Psychology, 25,* 233–257.

Bodenhausen, G. V. (1990). Stereotypes as judgmental heuristics: Evidence of circadian variations in discrimination. *Psychological Science, 1,* 319–322.

Bogart, K., Loeb, A., & Rittman, J. D. (1969). *Behavioral consequences of cognitive dissonance.* Paper presented at the Eastern Psychological Association meeting.

Bond, M., & Yang, K. (1982). Ethnic affirmation versus cross-cultural accommodation: The variable impact of questionnaire language on Chinese bilinguals in Hong Kong. *Journal of Cross-Cultural Psychology, 13,* 169–185.

Boninger, D. S., Gleicher, F., & Strathman, A. (1994). Counterfactual thinking: From what might have been to what may be. *Journal of Personality and Social Psychology, 67,* 297–307.

Bonoma, T. V. (1976). Social psychology and social evaluation. *Representative Research in Social Psychology, 7,* 147–156.

Bornstein, R. F. (1989). Exposure and affect: Overview and meta-analysis of research, 1968–1987. *Psychological Bulletin, 106,* 265–289.

Bornstein, R. F., & D'Agostino, P. R. (1992). Stimulus recognition and the mere exposure effect. *Journal of Personality and Social Psychology, 63,* 545–552.

Bossard, J. (1932). Residential propinquity as a factor in marriage selection. *American Journal of Sociology, 38,* 219–224.

Bostrom, R. N., & White, N. D. (1979). Does drinking weaken resistance? *Journal of Communication, 29,* 73–80.

Bourhis, R. Y. (1994). Power, gender, and intergroup discrimination: Some minimal group experiments. In M. P. Zanna & J. M. Olson (Eds.), *The psychology of prejudice: The Ontario symposium* (Vol. 7, pp. 171–208). Hillsdale, NJ: Erlbaum.

Bowlby, J. (1973). *Attachment and love:* Vol. 2. *Separation: Anxiety and anger.* New York: Basic Books.

Bowlby, J. (1979). *The making and breaking of affectional bonds.* London, England: Tavistock.

Bradbury, T. N., & Fincham, F. D. (1992). Attributions and behavior in marital interaction. *Journal of Personality and Social Psychology, 63,* 613–628.

Braddock, J. H., II, & McPartland, J. M. (1987). How minorities continue to be excluded from equal employment opportunities: Research on labor market and institutional barriers. *Journal of Social Issues, 43,* 5–10.

Bradley, G. W. (1978). Self-serving biases in the attribution process: A re-examination of the fact or fiction question. *Journal of Personality and Social Psychology, 35,* 56–71.

Brady, A., & Walker, M. (1978). Interpersonal distance as a function of situationally induced anxiety. *British Journal of Social and Clinical Psychology, 17,* 127–133.

Branscombe, N. R., Wann, D. L., Noel, J. G., & Coleman, J. (1993). In-group or out-group extremity: Importance of the threatened social identity. *Personality and Social Psychology Bulletin, 19,* 381–388.

Brearly, M. C. (1932). *Homicide in the United States.* Montclair, NJ: Patterson-Smith.

Brehm, J. W. (1956). Postdecision changes in the desirability of alternatives. *Journal of Abnormal and Social Psychology, 52,* 384–389.

Brehm, J. W. (1966). *A theory of psychological reactance.* New York: Academic Press.

Brehm, J. W., & Festinger, L. (1957). Pressures toward uniformity of performance in groups. *Human Relations, 10,* 85–89.

Brewer, M. B. (1988). A dual process model of impression formation. In T. K. Srull & R. S. Wyer, Jr. (Ed.s), *A dual process model of impression formation. Advances in social cognition* (Vol. 1). Hillsdale, NJ: Erlbaum.

Brewer, M. B. (1991). The social self: On being the same and different at the same time. *Personality and Social Psychology Bulletin, 17*(5), 475–482.

Brickman, P., & Bulman, R. J. (1977). Pleasure and pain in social comparison. In J. M. Suls & R. L. Miller (Eds.), *Social comparison processes: Theoretical and empirical perspectives.* New York: Wiley.

Brickner, M., Harkins, S., & Ostrom, T. (1986). Effects of personal involvement: Thought-provoking implications for social loafing. *Journal of Personality and Social Psychology, 51,* 763–769.

Briggs, S. R., & Cheek, J. M. (1988). On the nature of self-monitoring: Problems with assessment, problems with validity. *Journal of Personality and Social Psychology, 54,* 663–678.

Briggs, S. R., Cheek, J. M., & Buss, A. H. (1980). An analysis of the self-monitoring scale. *Journal of Personality and Social Psychology, 38,* 679–686.

Brislin, R. (1980). Translation and content analysis of oral and written materials. In H. Triandis & J. Berry (Eds.), *Handbook of cross-cultural psychology* (Vol. 2), Boston, MA: Allyn and Bacon.

Brislin, R. (1993). *Understanding culture's influence on behavior.* Ft. Worth, TX: Harcourt Brace Jovanovich.

Brock, T. C. (1965). Communicator-recipient similarity and decision change. *Journal of Personality and Social Psychology, 1,* 650–654.

Brockner, J., & Rubin, J. Z. (1985). *Entrapment in escalating conflicts.* New York: Springer-Verlag.

Bronfenbrenner, U. (1961). The mirror image in Soviet-American relations: A social psychologist's report. *Journal of Social Issues, 27*(3), 45–56.

Brophy, J. E. (1982). *Research on the self-fulfilling prophecy and teacher expectations.* Paper delivered at annual meeting of the American Educational Research Association, New York.

Brown, B. R. (1968). The effects of need to maintain face on interpersonal bargaining. *Journal of Experimental Social Psychology, 4,* 107–122.

Brown, J. D., & Dutton, K. A. (1995a). Truth and consequences: The costs and benefits of accurate self-knowledge. *Personality and Social Psychology, 21,* 1288–1296.

Brown, J. D., & Dutton, K. A. (1995b). The thrill of victory, the complexity of defeat: Self-esteem and people's emotional reactions to success and failure. *Journal of Personality and Social Psychology, 68,* 712–722.

Brown, J. D., & Siegel, J. M. (1988). Attributions for negative life events and depression: The role of perceived control. *Journal of Personality and Social Psychology, 52,* 316–322.

Brown, P., & Elliott, R. (1965). Control of aggression in a nursery school class. *Journal of Experimental Child Psychology, 2,* 103–107.

Brown, R. (1965). *Social psychology.* New York: Free Press.

Brown, R. (1986). *Social psychology—The second edition.* New York: Free Press.

Brown, R. (1988). *Group process: Dynamics within and between groups.* Oxford, England: Basil Blackwell.

Brown, R., & Smith, A. (1989). Perceptions of and by minority groups: The case of women in academia. *European Journal of Social Psychology, 19,* 61–76.

Brown, V., & Geis, F. L. (1984). Turning lead into gold: Evaluations of men and women leaders and the alchemy of social consensus. *Journal of Personality and Social Psychology, 46,* 811–824.

Bryan, J., & Test, M. (1967). Models and helping: Naturalistic studies in aiding behavior. *Journal of Personality and Social Psychology, 6,* 400–407.

Bureau of HIV/AIDS & STD Laboratory, Centre for Disease Control, Health Canada (1995). *1994 annual report on AIDS.* Ottawa, ON: Health Protection Branch, Health Canada.

Burger, J. M., & Burns, L. (1988). The illusion of unique invulnerability and the use of contraception. *Personality and Social Psychology Bulletin, 14,* 264–270.

Burgner, D., & Hewstone, M. (1993). Young children's causal attributions for success and failure: 'Self-enhancing' boys and 'self-derogating' girls. *British Journal of Developmental Psychology, 11,* 125–129.

Burns, J. M. (1984). *The power to lead: The crisis of the American presidency.* New York: Simon and Schuster.

Burnstein, E. (1982). Persuasion as argument processing. In M. Brandstatter, J. M. Davis, & G. Stocker-Kreichgauer (Eds.), *Group decision processes.* London, England: Academic Press.

Burnstein, E., & Vinokur, A. (1977). Persuasive argumentation and social comparison as determinants of attitude polarization. *Journal of Experimental Social Psychology, 9,* 123–137.

Buss, A. H. (1961). *The psychology of aggression.* New York: Wiley.

Buss, A. H. (1980). *Self-consciousness and social anxiety.* San Francisco: Freeman.

Buss, A. H., Booker, A., & Buss, E. (1972). Firing a weapon and aggression. *Journal of Personality and Social Psychology, 27,* 296–302.

Buss, D. M. (1988). The evolution of human intrasexual competition: Tactics of mate attraction. *Journal of Personality and Social Psychology, 54,* 616–628.

Buss, D. M. (1989). Sex differences in human mate preferences: Evolutionary hypotheses tested in 37 cultures. *Behavioral and Brain Sciences, 12,* 1–49.

Buss, D. M. (1994). *The evolution of desire: Strategies of human mating.* New York: Basic Books.

Buss, D. M., Larsen, R. J., & Westen, D. (1996). Sex differences in jealousy: Not gone, not forgotten and not explained by alternative hypotheses. *Psychological Science, 7,* 373–375.

Buss, D. M., Larsen, R. J., Westen, D., & Semmelroth, J. (1992). Sex differences in jealousy: Evolution, physiology and psychology. *Psychological Science, 3,* 251–255.

Buss, D. M., & Schmitt, D. P. (1993). Sexual strategies theory: An evolutionary perspective on human mating. *Psychological Review, 100,* 204–232.

Buunk, B. P., Angleitner, A., Oubaid, V., & Buss, D. M. (1996). Sex differences in jealousy in evolutionary and cultural perspective: Tests from the Netherlands, Germany and the U.S. *Psychological Science, 7,* 359–363.

Byrne, D. (1971). *The attraction paradigm.* New York: Academic Press.

Byrne, D., & Clore, G. L. (1970). A reinforcement model of evaluative responses. *Personality: An International Journal, 1,* 103–128.

Byrne, D., Clore, G. L., & Smeaton, G. (1986). The attraction hypothesis: Do similar attitudes affect anything? *Journal of Personality and Social Psychology, 51,* 1167–1170.

Byrne, D., & Nelson, D. (1965). Attraction as a linear function of proportion of positive reinforcements. *Journal of Personality and Social Psychology, 1,* 659–663.

Cacioppo, J., Ctites, S., & Gardner, W. (1996). Attitudes to the right: Evaluative processing is associated with lateralized late positive event-related brain potentials. *Personality and Social Psychology Bulletin, 22,* 1205–1219.

Cacioppo, J. T., Marshall-Goodell, B. S., Tassinary, L. G., & Petty, R. E. (1992). Rudimentary determinants of attitudes: Classical conditioning is more effective when prior knowledge about the attitude stimulus is low rather than high. *Journal of Experimental Social Psychology, 28,* 207–233.

Cacioppo, J. T., & Petty, R. E. (1985). Central and peripheral routes to persuasion: The role of message repetition. In L. F. Alwitt & A. A. Mitchell (Eds.), *Psychological processes and advertising effects* (pp. 91–111) Hillsdale, NJ: Erlbaum.

Cacioppo, J. T., Petty, R. E., & Kao, C. (1984). The efficient assessment of need for cognition. *Journal of Personality Assessment, 48,* 306–307.

Cacioppo, J. T., Petty, R. E., & Morris, K. (1983). Effects of need for cognition on message evaluation, recall, and persuasion. *Journal of Personality and Social Psychology, 45,* 805–818.

Cacioppo, J., Priester, J., & Berntson, G. (1993). Rudimentary determinants of attitudes: II Arm flexion and extension have different effects on attitudes. *Journal of Personality and Social Psychology, 65,* 5–17.

Caldwell, D. F., & O'Reilly, C. A. (1982). Boundary spanning and individual performance: The impact of self-monitoring. *Journal of Applied Psychology, 67,* 124–127.

Callaway, M., Marriott, R., & Esser, J. (1985). Effects of dominance on group decision making: Toward a stress-reduction explanation of group think. *Journal of Personality and Social Psychology, 49,* 949–952.

Campbell, D. T., & Stanley, J. C. (1963). *Experimental and quasi-experimental designs for research.* Chicago: Rand-McNally.

Campbell, J. D. (1986). Similarity and uniqueness: The effects of attribute type, relevance, and individual differences in self-esteem and depression. *Journal of Personality and Social Psychology, 50,* 281–293.

Campbell, J. D., Tesser, A., & Fairey, P. J. (1986). Conformity and attention to the stimulus: Some temporal and contextual dynamics. *Journal of Personality and Social Psychology, 51,* 315–324.

Campos, J. J., Barrett, K., Lamb, M. E., Goldsmith, H. H., & Stenberg, C. (1983). Socioemotional development. In P. H. Mussen (Ed.), *Handbook of child psychology:* Vol 2. *Infancy and developmental psychobiology* (pp. 783–915). New York: Wiley.

Canavan-Gumpert, D. (1977). Generating reward and cost orientations through praise and criticism. *Journal of Personality and Social Psychology, 35,* 501–514.

Cantril, H. (1940). *The invasion from Mars: A study in the psychology of panic.* Princeton, NJ: Princeton University Press.

Cantril, H. (1941). *The psychology of social movements.* New York: Wiley.

Carli, L. (1982). *Are women more social and men more task oriented? A meta-analytic review of sex differences in group interaction, coalition formation, and cooperation in prisoner's dilemma games.* Unpublished manuscript, University of Massachusetts.

Carli, L. (1989). Gender differences in interaction style and influence. *Journal of Personality and Social Psychology, 56,* 565–576.

Carli, L. L., LaFleur, S. J., & Loeber, C. C. (1995). Nonverbal behavior, gender, and influence. *Journal of Personality and Social Psychology, 68,* 1030–1041.

Carlo, G., Eisenberg, N., Troyer, D., Switzer, G., & Speer, A. L. (1991). The altruistic personality: In what contexts does it appear? *Journal of Personality and Social Psychology, 61,* 450–458.

Carlsmith, J. M., Ellsworth, P. C., & Aronson, E. (1976). *Methods of research in social psychology.* Reading, MA: Addison-Wesley.

Carlston, D. E., & Skowronski, J. J. (1994). Savings in the relearning of trait information as evidence for spontaneous inference generation. *Journal of Personality and Social Psychology, 66,* 840–856.

Carlston, D. E., Skowronski, J. J., & Sparks, C. (1995). Savings in relearning: II. On the formation of behavior-based trait associations and inferences. *Journal of Personality and Social Psychology, 69,* 420–436.

Carnegie, D. (1936). *How to win friends and influence people.* New York: Simon and Schuster.

Carnevale, P., & Pruitt, D. (1992). Negotiation and mediation. *Annual Review of Psychology, 43,* 531–582.

Carroll, J. M., & Russell, J. A. (1996). Do facial expressions signal specific emotions? Judging emotion from the face in context. *Journal of Personality and Social Psychology, 70,* 205–218.

Carson, R. C. (1969). *Interaction concepts of personality.* Chicago: Aldine.

Cartwright, D. (1973). Determinants of scientific progress: The case of research on the risky shift. *American Psychologist, 28,* 222–231.

Cartwright, D. (1979). Contemporary social psychology in historical perspective. *Social Psychology Quarterly, 42,* 82–93.

Cartwright, D., & Zander A. (Eds.). (1968). *Group dynamics: Research and theory* (3rd ed.). New York: Harper and Row.

Carver, C. S., & Scheier, M. F. (1981). *Attention and self-regulation: A control-theory approach to human behavior.* New York: Springer-Verlag.

Carver, C. S., & Scheier, M. F. (1990). Self-regulation and the self. In J. Strauss & G. R. Goethals (Eds.), *The self: Interdisciplinary perspectives.* New York: Springer-Verlag.

Cash, W. (1941). *The mind of the South.* New York: Knopf.

Castro, M. A. C. (1974). Reactions to receiving aid as a function of cost to donor and opportunity to aid. *Journal of Applied Social Psychology, 4,* 194–209.

Catania, J. A., Coates, T. J., Stall, R., Turner, H., Peterson, J., Hearst, N., Dolcini, M. M., Hudes, E., Gagnon, J., Wiley, J., & Groves, R. (1992). Prevalence of AIDS-related risk factors and condom use in the United States. *Science, 258,* 1101–1106.

Ceci, S. J., Peters, D., & Plotkin, J. (1985). Human subjects review, personal values, and the regulation of social science research. *American Psychologist, 40,* 994–1002.

Centers for Disease Control. (1994, June). *HIV/AIDS surveillance report.* Atlanta, GA: Center for Infectious Diseases, Centers for Disease Control and Prevention.

Chaiken, S. (1980). Heuristic versus systematic information processing and the use of source versus message cues in persuasion. *Journal of Personality and Social Psychology, 39,* 752–766.

Chaiken, S. (1987). The heuristic model of persuasion. In M. P. Zanna, J. M. Olson, & C. P. Herman (Eds.), *Social influence: The Ontario symposium* (Vol. 5, pp. 3–39). Hillsdale, NJ: Erlbaum.

Chaiken, S., & Baldwin, M. W. (1981). Affective-cognitive consistency and the effect of salient behavioral information on the self-perception of attitudes. *Journal of Personality and Social Psychology, 41,* 1–12.

Chapman, L. J. (1967). Illusory correlation in observational report. *Journal of Verbal Learning and Verbal Behavior, 6,* 151–155.

Chemers, M. M., & Skrzypek, G. J. (1972). Experimental test of the contingency model of leadership effectiveness. *Journal of Personality and Social Psychology, 24,* 172–177.

Chen, S. C. (1937). Social modification of the activity of ants in nest-building. *Physiological Zoology, 10,* 420–436.

Chollar, S. (1989). An epidemic of acquaintance rape. *Psychology Today, 23,* 73.

Chu, G. C. (1966). Fear arousal, efficacy and imminency. *Journal of Personality and Social Psychology, 4,* 517–524.

Cialdini, R. B. (1993). *Influence: Science and practice* (3rd ed.). New York: HarperCollins.

Cialdini, R. B., Borden, R. J., Thorne, A., Walker, M. R., Freman, S., & Sloan, L. R. (1976). Basking in reflected glory: Three (football) field studies. *Journal of Personality and Social Psychology, 34,* 366–375.

Cialdini, R. B., Brown, S. L., Lewis, B. P., Luce, C., & Neuberg, S. L. (1997). Reinterpreting the empathy-altruism relationship: When one into one equals oneness. *Journal of Personality and Social Psychology, 73,* 481–494.

Cialdini, R. B., & De Nicholas, M. E. (1989). Self-presentation by association. *Journal of Personality and Social Psychology, 57,* 626–631.

Cialdini, R. B., Reno, R. R., & Kalgren, C. A. (1990). A focus theory of normative conduct: Recycling the concept of norms to reduce littering in public places. *Journal of Personality and Social Psychology, 58,* 1015–1026.

Cialdini, R. B., Schaller, M., Houlihan, D., Arps, K., Fultz, J., & Beaman, A. L. (1987). Empathy-based helping: Is it selflessly or selfishly motivated? *Journal of Personality and Social Psychology, 52,* 749–758.

Clark, M. S. (1984). Record keeping in two types of relationships. *Journal of Personality and Social Psychology, 47,* 549–557.

Clark, M. S., Gotay, C. C., & Mills, J. (1974). Acceptance of help as a function of the potential helper and opportunity to repay. *Journal of Applied Social Psychology, 4,* 224–229.

Clark, M. S., & Mills, J. (1979). Interpersonal attraction in exchange and communal relationships. *Journal of Personality and Social Psychology, 37,* 12–24.

Clark, M. S., Mills, J., & Powell, M. C. (1986). Keeping track of needs in communal and exchange relationships. *Journal of Personality and Social Psychology, 51,* 333–338.

Clark, M. S., & Reis, H. T. (1988). Interpersonal processes in close relationships. *Annual Review of Psychology, 39,* 609–672.

Clark, R. D., & Hatfield, E. (1989). Gender differences in receptivity to sexual offers. *Journal of Psychology and Human Sexuality, 2,* 39–55.

Clark, R., Lennon, R., & Morris, L. (1993). Of Caldecotts and kings: Gendered images in recent American children's books by black and non-black illustrators. *Gender and Society, 7,* 227–245.

Clay, C. (1987). *No freedom for the mind: A study of the cult phenomenon from a Canadian perspective.* Burlington, ON: Trinity Press.

Clifford, M., & Walster, E. (1973). The effect of physical attractiveness on teacher expectation. *Sociology of Education, 46,* 248.

Clore, G. L., & Baldridge, B. (1968). Interpersonal attraction: The role of agreement and topic interest. *Journal of Personality and Social Psychology, 9,* 340–346.

Clore, G. L., & Kerber, K. W. (1981). *Toward an affective theory of attraction and trait attribution.* Unpublished manuscript.

Coch, L., & French, J. R. P. (1948). Overcoming resistance to change. *Human Relations, 1,* 512–532.

Cogwill, D. (1986). *Aging around the world.* Belmont, CA: Wadsworth.

Cohen, A. R. (1962). An experiment on small rewards for discrepant compliance and attitude change. In J. W. Brehm & A. R. Cohen (Eds.), *Explorations in cognitive dissonance.* New York: Wiley.

Cohen, C. E. (1981). Person categories and social perception: Testing some boundaries of the processing effects of prior knowledge. *Journal of Personality and Social Psychology, 40,* 441–452.

Cohen, D. (1996). Law, social policy and violence: The impact of regional cultures. *Journal of Personality and Social Psychology, 70,* 961–978.

Cohen, D., Nisbett, R. E., Bowdle, B. F., & Schwartz, N. (1996). Insult, aggression and the southern culture of honor: An "experimental ethnography." *Journal of Personality and Social Psychology, 70,* 945–960.

Cohn, N. B., & Strassberg, D. S. (1983). Self-disclosure reciprocity among preadolescents. *Personality and Social Psychology Bulletin, 9,* 97–102.

Comstock, G. A., & Paik, H. (1991). The effects of television violence on aggressive behavior: A meta-analysis. In *A preliminary report of the National Research Council on the understanding and control of violent behavior.* Washington, DC: National Research Council.

Conn, L. K., Edwards, C. N., Rosenthal, R., & Crowne, D. (1968). Perception of emotion and response to teachers' expectancy by elementary school children. *Psychological Reports, 22,* 27–34.

Cook, S. W. (1969). Motives in a conceptual analysis of attitude-related behavior. In W. J. Arnold & D. Levine (Eds.), *Nebraska symposium on motivation* (Vol. 17). Lincoln: University of Nebraska Press.

Cook, S. W. (1990). Toward a psychology of improving justice: Research on extending the equality principle to victims of social injustice. *Journal of Social Issues, 46*(1), 147–161.

Cooley, C. H. (1902). *Human order and the social order.* New York: Scribner's.

Cooper, H., & Hazelrigg, P. (1988). Personality moderators of interpersonal expectancy effects: An integrative research review. *Journal of Personality and Social Psychology, 55,* 937–949.

Cooper, J., & Axsom, D. (1982). Effort justification in psychotherapy. In G. Weary & H. Mirels (Eds.), *Integrations of clinical and social psychology* (pp. 214–230). New York: Oxford University Press.

Cooper, J., Bennett, E. A., & Sukel, H. L. (1996). Complex scientific testimony: How do jurors make decisions? *Law and Human Behavior, 20,* 379–394.

Cooper, J., & Fazio, R. H. (1984). A new look at dissonance theory. In L. Berkowitz (Ed.), *Advances in experimental social psychology* (Vol. 17, pp. 229–262). New York: Academic Press.

Cooper, J., & Jones, E. E. (1969). Opinion divergence as a strategy to avoid being miscast. *Journal of Personality and Social Psychology, 13,* 23–30.

Cooper, J., & Mackie, D. (1986). Video games and aggression in children. *Journal of Applied Social Psychology, 16*(8), 726–744.

Cooper, J., & Worchel, S. (1970). Role of undesired consequences in arousing cognitive dissonance. *Journal of Personality and Social Psychology, 16,* 199–206.

Cooper, J. E., & McGaugh, J. L. (1969). Leadership: Integrating principles of social psychology. In C. A. Gibb (Ed.), *Leadership*. Baltimore, MD: Penguin.

Cordes, B., Hoffman, B., Jenkins, B., Kellen, K., Moran, S., & Slater, W. (1984). *Trends: International terrorism, 1982 and 1983* (Report No. R-3183-52). Santa Monica, CA: Rand Corporation.

Cotton, J. L. (1981). A review of research on Schachter's theory of emotion and the misattribution of arousal. *European Journal of Social Psychology, 11,* 365–397.

Cottrell, N., Wack, D., Sekerak, G., & Rittle, R. (1968). Social facilitation of dominant responses by the presence of an audience and the mere presence of others. *Journal of Personality and Social Psychology, 6,* 245–250.

Cowan, P. A., & Walters, R. H. (1963). Studies of reinforcement of aggression: I. Effects of scheduling. *Child Development, 34,* 543–551.

Cox, F. D. (1996). *The AIDS booklet* (4th ed.). Dubuque, IA: Brown.

Cozby, P. C. (1972). Self-disclosure, reciprocity, and liking. *Sociometry, 35,* 151–60.

Craig, R. S. (1992). The effect of television day part on gender portrayals in television commercials: A content analysis. *Sex Roles, 26,* 197–211.

Crider, A. B., Goethals, G. R., Kavanaugh, R. D., & Solomon, P. R. (1993). *Psychology* (4th ed.). Glenview, IL: Scott, Foresman.

Crocker, J., Hannah, D. B., & Weber, R. (1983). Person memory and causal attributions. *Journal of Personality and Social Psychology, 44,* 55–66.

Crocker, J., & Major, B. (1989). Social stigma and self-esteem: The self-protective properties of stigma. *Psychological Review, 96,* 608–630.

Crocker, J., & Major, B. (1994). Reaction to stigma: The moderating role of justifications. In M. P. Zanna & J. M. Olson (Eds.), *The psychology of prejudice: The Ontario symposium* (Vol. 7, pp. 289–314). Mahwah, NJ: Erlbaum.

Crocker, J., Voelkl, K., Testa, M., & Major, B. (1991). Social stigma: The affective consequences of attributional ambiguity. *Journal of Personality and Social Psychology, 60,* 218–228.

Crosby, F. (1976). A model of egoistical relative deprivation. *Psychological Review, 83,* 85–113.

Crosby, F. (1982). *Relative deprivation and working women.* New York: Oxford University Press.

Crosby, F. (1984). The denial of personal discrimination. *American Behavioral Scientist, 27,* 371–386.

Crowne, D. P., & Marlowe, D. (1964). *The approval motive: Studies in evaluative dependence.* New York: Wiley.

Crutchfield, R. A. (1955). Conformity and character. *American Psychologist, 10,* 191–198.

Cunningham, J. D. (1981). Self-disclosure intimacy: Sex, sex-of-target, cross-national, and "generational" differences. *Personality and Social Psychology Bulletin, 7,* 314–319.

Curtis, R. C., & Miller, K. (1986). Believing another likes or dislikes you: Behaviors making the beliefs come true. *Journal of Personality and Social Psychology, 51,* 284–290.

Daly, M., & Wilson, M. (1989). Killing the competition: Female/female and male/male homicide. *Human Nature, 1,* 81–107.

Damrad-Frye, R., & Laird, J. D. (1989). The experience of boredom: The role of self-perception of attention. *Journal of Personality and Social Psychology, 57,* 315–320.

Danheiser, P. R., & Graziano, W. G. (1982). Self-monitoring and cooperation as a self-presentational strategy. *Journal of Personality and Social Psychology, 42,* 497–505.

Dardenne, B., & Leyens, J. P. (1995). Confirmation bias as a social skill. *Personality and Social Psychology Bulletin, 21,* 1229–1239.

Darley, J. M., & Aronson, E. (1966). Self-evaluation vs. direct anxiety reduction as determinants of the fear-affiliation relationship. *Journal of Experimental Social Psychology, 2,* 66–79.

Darley, J. M., & Batson, C. D. (1973). "From Jerusalem to Jericho": A study of situational and dispositional variables in helping behavior. *Journal of Personality and Social Psychology, 27,* 100–108.

Darley, J. M., & Berscheid, E. (1967). Increased liking caused by the anticipation of personal contact. *Human Relations, 10,* 29–40.

Darley, J. M., & Cooper, J. (1972). The "Clean for Gene" phenomenon: Deciding to vote for or against a candidate on the basis of the physical appearance of his supporters. *Journal of Applied Social Psychology, 2,* 24–33.

Darley, J. M., & Fazio, R. H. (1980). Expectancy and confirmation processes arising in the social interaction sequence. *American Psychologist, 5,* 867–881.

Darley, J. M., Fleming, J. H., Hilton, J. L., & Swann, W. B. (1988). Dispelling negative expectancies: The impact of interaction goals and target characteristics on the expectancy confirmation process. *Journal of Personality and Social Psychology, 54,* 19–36.

Darley, J. M., & Gross, P. H. (1983). A hypothesis-confirming bias in labeling effects. *Journal of Personality and Social Psychology, 44,* 20–33.

Darley, J. M., & Latané, B. (1968). Bystander intervention in emergencies: Diffusion of responsibility. *Journal of Personality and Social Psychology, 8,* 377–383.

Darrow, C. (1993). Quoted in E. H. Sutherland & D. R. Cressy, *Principles of criminology* (p. 44). Philadelphia, PA: Lippincott, 1996.

Darwin, C. (1873). *The expression of the emotions in man and animals.* New York: Appleton.

Davidson, A. R., & Duberman, L. (1982). Friendship: Communication and interactional patterns in same sex dyads. *Sex Roles, 8,* 809–822.

Davidson, A. R., & Jaccard, J. J. (1979). Variables that moderate the attitude-behavior relation: Results of a longitudinal survey. *Journal of Personality and Social Psychology, 37,* 1364–1376.

Davies, J. C. (1962). Toward a theory of revolution. *American Sociological Review, 27,* 5–19.

Davis, C. G., Lehman, D. R., Silver, R. C., Wortman, C. B., & Ellard, J. H. (1996). Self-blame following a traumatic event: The role of perceived avoidability. *Personality and Social Psychology, 22,* 557–567.

Davis, C. G., Lehman, D. R., Silver, R. C., Wortman, C. B., & Thompson, S. C. (1995). The undoing of traumatic life events. *Personality and Social Psychology Bulletin, 21,* 109–124.

Davis, D. N., & Perkowitz, W. T. (1979). Consequences of responsiveness in dyadic interaction: Effect of probability of response and proportion of content-related responses in interpersonal attraction. *Journal of Personality and Social Psychology, 37,* 534–550.

Davis, J., Bray, R., & Holt, R. (1977). The empirical study of decision processes in juries. In J. Tapp & F. Levine (Eds.), *Law, justice, and the individual in society: Psychological and legal issues.* New York: Holt, Rinehart and Winston.

Davis, J., Kerr, N. L., Atkin, R. S., Holt, R., & Meek, D. (1975). The decision processes of 6- and 12-person mock juries assigned unanimous and two-thirds majority rules. *Journal of Personality and Social Psychology, 32,* 1–14.

Davis, K. E. (1985, February). Near and dear: Friendship and love. *Psychology Today,* pp. 22–30.

Davis, K. E., & Florquist, C. C. (1965). Perceived threat and dependence as determinants of the tactical usage of opinion conformity. *Journal of Experimental Social Psychology, 1,* 219–236.

Davis, K. E., & Todd, M. (1982). Friendship and love relationships. In K. E. Davis and T. O. Mitchell (Eds.), *Advances in descriptive psychology.* Greenwich, CT: JAI Press.

Davis, M. H. (1983). Empathic concern and the muscular dystrophy telethon: Empathy as a multidimensional construct. *Personality and Social Psychology Bulletin, 9,* 223–229.

Davis, M. H., & Franzoni, S. L. (1986). Adolescent loneliness, self-disclosure, and private self-consciousness: A longitudinal investigation. *Journal of Personality and Social Psychology, 51,* 595–608.

Davitz, J. R. (1952). The effects of previous training on post-frustrative behavior. *Journal of Abnormal and Social Psychology, 47,* 309–315.

Deford, F. (1996a). Year of the women: Why female athletes are our best hope for Olympic gold. *Newsweek,* 62–82.

Deford, F. (1996b, June 10). Jackie! Oh! *Newsweek,* 72–77.

DeJong, P. F., Koomen, W., & Mellenbergh, C. J. (1988). Structure of causes for success and failure: A multidimensional scaling analysis of preference judgements. *Journal of Personality and Social Psychology, 55,* 718–725.

DeJong, W., Marber, S., & Shaver, R. (1980). Crime intervention: The role of a victim's behavior in reducing situational ambiguity. *Personality and Social Psychology Bulletin, 6,* 113–118.

Demare, D., Brier, J., & Lips, H. M. (1988). Violent pornography and self-reported likelihood of sexual aggression. *Journal of Research in Personality, 22,* 140–153.

DePaulo, B. M., Kashy, D. A., Kirkendol, S. E., Wyer, M. M., & Epstein, J. A. (1996). Lying in everyday life. *Journal of Personality and Social Psychology, 70,* 996–1011.

Deppe, R. K., & Harackiewicz, J. M. (1996). Self-handi-capping and intrinsic motivation: Buffering intrinsic motivation from the threat of failure. *Journal of Personality and Social Psychology, 70,* 868–876.

Depret, E. F., & Fiske, S. T. (1993). Social cognition and power: Some cognitive consequences of social structure as a source of deprivation. In G. Weary, F. Gleischer, & K. L. Marsh (Eds.), *Control motivation and social cognition* (pp. 176–202). New York: Springer-Verlag.

Dermer, M., & Pyszczynski, T. A. (1978). Effects of erotica upon men's loving and liking responses for women they love. *Journal of Personality and Social Psychology, 36,* 1302–1309.

Deschamps, J., & Devos, T. (1998). Regarding the relationship between social identity and personal identity. In S. Worchel, F. Morales, D. Paez, & J. Deschamps (Eds.), *Social identity: International perspectives.* London, England: Sage.

Desforges, D. M., Lord, C. G., Ramsey, S. L., Mason, J. A., Van Leeuwen, M. D., West, S. C., & Lepper, M. R. (1991). Effects of structured cooperative contact on changing negative attitudes toward stigmatized social groups. *Journal of Personality and Social Psychology, 60,* 531–544.

DeSteno, D. A., & Salovey, P. (1996). Evolutionary origins of sex differences in jealousy? Questioning the "fitness" of the model. *Psychological Science, 7,* 367–372.

Deutsch, M. (1973). *The resolution of conflict.* New Haven, CT: Yale University Press.

Deutsch, M. (1975). Introduction. In M. Deutsch & H. A. Hornstein (Eds.), *Applying social psychology: Implications for research, practice, training* (pp. 1–12). Hillsdale, NJ: Erlbaum.

Deutsch, M., & Gerard, H. (1955). A study of normative and informational social influences upon individual judgment. *Journal of Abnormal and Social Psychology, 51,* 629–636.

Deutsch, M., & Krauss, R. M. (1960). The effect of threat upon interpersonal bargaining. *Journal of Abnormal and Social Psychology, 61,* 181–189.

Deutsch, M., & Krauss, R. M. (1962). Studies of interpersonal bargaining. *Journal of Conflict Resolution, 6,* 52–76.

Devine, P. G. (1989). Stereotypes and prejudice: Their automatic and controlled components. *Journal of Personality and Social Psychology, 56,* 5–18.

Dickoff, H. (1961). *Reactions to evaluations by another person as a function of self-evaluation and the interaction context.* Unpublished doctoral dissertation. Duke University, Durham, NC.

Diekman, A., Jungbauer-Gans, M., Krassnig, H., & Lorenz, S. (1996). Social status and aggression: A field study analyzed by survival analysis. *Journal of Social Psychology, 136,* 761–768.

Diener, E. (1979). Deindividuation, self-awareness, and disinhibition. *Journal of Personality and Social Psychology, 37,* 1160–1171.

Diener, E., Fraser, S., Beaman, A., & Kelem, Z. (1976). Effects of deindividuation variables on stealing among Halloween trick-or-treaters. *Journal of Personality and Social Psychology, 33,* 178–183.

Diener, E., & Larson, R. J. (1993). The subjective experience of emotional well-being. In M. Lewis & J. M. Haviland (Eds.), *Handbook of emotions* (pp. 405–415). New York: Guilford.

Diener, E., Wolsic, B., & Fujita, F. (1995). Physical attractiveness and subjective well-being. *Journal of Personality and Social Psychology, 69,* 120–129.

Dion, K. K. (1972). Physical attractiveness and evaluation on children's transgressions. *Journal of Personality and Social Psychology, 24,* 207–213.

Dion, K. K., Berscheid, E., & Walster, E. (1972). What is beautiful is good. *Journal of Personality and Social Psychology, 24,* 285–290.

Dion, K. L. (1986). Responses to perceived discrimination and relative deprivation. In J. M. Olson, C. P. Herman, & M. P. Zanna (Eds.), *Relative deprivation and social comparison: The Ontario symposium* (Vol. 4, pp. 159–179). Mahwah, NJ: Erlbaum.

Dion, K. L., & Earn, B. M. (1975). The phenomenology of being a target of prejudice. *Journal of Personality and Social Psychology, 32,* 944–950.

Dodson, J. A., Tybout, A. M., & Sternthal, B. (1978). Impact of deals and deal retraction on brand switching. *Journal of Marketing Research, 15*(1), 72–81.

Dollard, J., Doob, L., Miller, N., Mowrer, O., & Sears, R. (1939). *Frustration and aggression.* New Haven, CT: Yale University Press.

Donnerstein, E. (1980). Aggressive erotica and violence against women. *Journal of Personality and Social Psychology, 39,* 269–277.

Donnerstein, E. (1983). Erotica and human aggression. In R. G. Geen & E. Donnerstein (Eds.), *Aggression: Theoretical and empirical reviews* (Vol. 1). New York: Academic Press.

Donnerstein, E., & Berkowitz, L. (1981). Victim reactions in aggressive erotic films as a factor in violence against women. *Journal of Personality and Social Psychology, 41,* 710–724.

Donnerstein, E., Donnerstein, M., & Evans, R. (1975). Erotic stimuli and aggression: Facilitation or inhibition. *Journal of Personality and Social Psychology, 32,* 237–244.

Donnerstein, E., & Linz, D. G. (1986, December). The question of pornography. It is not sex, but violence, that is an obscenity in our society. *Psychology Today,* pp. 56–59.

Doob, A. N., & Gross, A. E. (1968). Status of frustrator as an inhibitor of horn-honking responses. *Journal of Social Psychology, 76,* 213–218.

Doob, A. N., & Wood, L. E. (1972). Catharsis and aggression: Effects of annoyance and retaliation on aggressive behavior. *Journal of Personality and Social Psychology, 22,* 156–162.

Dovidio, J. F., & Gaertner, S. L. (1993). Stereotypes and evaluative intergroup bias. In D. M. Mackie & D. L. Hamilton (Eds.), *Affect, cognition, and stereotyping: Interactive processes in group perception.* New York: Academic Press.

Drigotas, S. M., Insko, C. A., & Schopler, J. (1998). Mere categorization and competition: A closer look at social identity theory and the discontinuity effect. In S. Worchel, F. Morales, D. Paez, & J. Deschamps (Eds.), *Social identity: International perspectives.* London, England: Sage.

Drigotas, S. M., & Rusbult, C. E. (1992). Should I stay or should I go? A dependence model of break-ups. *Journal of Personality and Social Psychology, 62,* 62–87.

Dubé, L., & Guimond, S. (1986). Relative deprivation and social protest: The personal-group issue. In J. M. Olson, C. P. Herman, & M. P. Zanna (Eds.), *Relative deprivation and social comparison: The Ontario symposium* (Vol. 4, pp. 201–216). Hillsdale, NJ: Erlbaum.

Duclos, S. E., Laird, J. D., Schneider, E., Sexter, M., Stern, L., & Van Lighten, O. (1989). Emotion-specific effects of facial expressions and postures on emotional experience. *Journal of Personality and Social Psychology, 57,* 100–108.

Duffy, K. (1991). Introduction to community mediation programs: Past, present, and future. In K. Duffy, J. Grosch, & P. Olzak (Eds.), *Issues in community mediation: A handbook for practitioners and researchers.* New York: Guilford.

Duffy, K., Grosch, J., & Olzak, P. (Eds.). (1991). *Issues in community mediation: A handbook for practitioners and researchers.* New York: Guilford.

Duncan, D. L. (1976). Differential social perception and attribution of intergroup violence: Testing the lower limits of stereotyping of blacks. *Journal of Personality and Social Psychology, 34,* 590–598.

Durkheim, E. (1898). *The rules of sociological method.* New York: Free Press.

Dutton, D. G., & Aron, A. P. (1974). Some evidence for heightened sexual attraction under conditions of high anxiety. *Journal of Personality and Social Psychology, 30,* 510–517.

Duval, S., Duval, V. H., & Neely, R. (1979). Self-focus, felt responsibility, and helping behavior. *Journal of Personality and Social Psychology, 37,* 1769–1778.

Duval, S., & Wicklund, R. A. (1972). *A theory of objective self-awareness.* New York: Academic Press.

Eagly, A. H. (1987). *Sex differences in social behavior: A social role interpretation.* Mahwah, NJ: Erlbaum.

Eagly, A. H., Ashmore, R. D., Makhijani, M. G., & Longo, L. C. (1991). What is beautiful is good, but. . . . A meta-analytic review of research on the physical attractiveness stereotype. *Psychological Bulletin, 110,* 109–128.

Eagly, A. H., & Carli, L. L. (1981). Sex of researchers and sex-typed communications as determinants of sex differences in influenceability: A meta-analysis of social influence studies. *Psychological Bulletin, 90,* 1–20.

Eagly, A. H., & Chaiken, S. (1984). Cognitive theories of persuasion. In L. Berkowitz (Ed.), *Advances in experimental social psychology* (Vol. 17, pp. 267–359). New York: Academic Press.

Eagly, A. H., & Chaiken, S. (1993). *The psychology of attitudes.* Fort Worth, TX: Harcourt Brace Jovanovich.

Eagly, A. H., & Crowley, M. (1986). Gender and helping behavior: A meta-analytic review of the social psychological literature. *Psychological Bulletin, 100,* 283–308.

Eagly, A. H., & Johnson, B. T. (1990). Gender and leadership style: A meta-analysis. *Psychological Bulletin, 108,* 233–256.

Eagly, A. H., & Karau, S. J. (1991). Gender and the emergence of leaders: A meta-analysis. *Journal of Personality and Social Psychology, 60,* 685–710.

Eagly, A. H., Karau, S. J., & Makhijani, M. G. (1995). Gender and effectiveness of leaders: A meta-analysis. *Psychological Bulletin, 117,* 125–145.

Eagly, A. H., & Kite, M. E. (1987). Are stereotypes of nationalities applied to both women and men? *Journal of Personality and Social Psychology, 53,* 457–462.

Eagly, A. H., Makhijani, M. G., & Klonsky, B. G. (1992). Gender and the evaluation of leaders: A meta-analysis. *Psychological Bulletin, 111,* 3–22.

Eagly, A. H., & Steffen, V. J. (1986). Gender and aggressive behavior: A meta-analytic review of the social psychological literature. *Psychological Bulletin, 100,* 309–330.

Eagly, A. H., & Wood, W. (1991). Explaining sex differences in social behavior: A meta-analytic perspective. *Personality and Social Psychology Bulletin, 17,* 306–315.

Eagly, A. H., Wood, W., & Chaiken, S. (1978). Causal inferences about communicators and their effect on opinion change. *Journal of Personality and Social Psychology, 36,* 424–435.

Eagly, A. H., Wood, W., & Fishbaugh, L. (1981). Sex differences in conformity: Surveillance by the group as a determinant of male nonconformity. *Journal of Personality and Social Psychology, 40,* 384–394.

Earle, W. B. (1986). The social context of social comparison: Reality versus reassurance? *Personality and Social Psychology Bulletin, 12,* 159–168.

Eaves, L. J., Eysenck, H. J., & Martin, N. G. (1989). *Genes, culture, and personality: An empirical approach.* London, England: Academic Press.

Ebbesen, E. B., Kjos, G. E., & Konecni, J. J. (1976). Spatial ecology: Its effect on the choice of friends and enemies. *Journal of Experimental Social Psychology, 12,* 505–518.

Efran, M. G. (1974). The effect of physical appearance on the judgment of guilt, interpersonal attraction, and severity of recommended punishment in a simulated jury task. *Journal of Experimental Research and Personality, 8,* 45–54.

Eisenberg, A. (Ed.). 1981. *Witness to the holocaust.* New York: Ballantine Books.

Eisenberg, N., & Fabes, R. A. (1991). Prosocial behavior and empathy: A multimethod and developmental perspective. In M. S. Clark (Ed.), *Review of personality and social psychology* (Vol. 12, pp. 34–61). Newbury Park, CA: Sage.

Eisenstadt, D., & Lieppe, M. R. (1994). The self-comparison process and self-discrepant feedback: Consequences of learning you are what you thought you were not. *Journal of Personality and Social Psychology, 67,* 611–626.

Ekman, P., & Friesen, W. V. (1969). Nonverbal leakage and clues to deception. *Psychiatry, 32,* 88–106.

Ekman, P., & Friesen, W. V. (1971). Constants across cultures in face and emotion. *Journal of Personality and Social Psychology, 117,* 124–129.

Ekman, P., Friesen, W. V., & Ellsworth, P. C. (1982). What are the similarities and differences in facial behavior across cultures? In P. Ekman (Ed.), *Emotion in the human race* (Vol. 2, pp. 56–97). Cambridge, England: Cambridge University Press.

Ekman, P., Friesen, W. V., & O'Sullivan, M. (1988). Smiles when lying. *Journal of Personality and Social Psychology, 54,* 414–420.

Ekman, P., Sorenson, E., & Friesen, W. V. (1969). Pan-cultural elements of facial displays of emotion. *Science, 164,* 86–88.

Elicker, J., Englund, M., & Sroufe, L. A. (1992). Predicting peer competence and peer relationships in childhood from early parent-child relationships. In R. D. Parke and G. W. Ladd (Eds.), *Family-peer relations: Modes of linkage.* Hillsdale, NJ: Erlbaum.

Ellison, P. A., Govern, J. M., Petri, H. L., & Figler, M. H. (1995). Anonymity and aggressive driving behavior: A field study. *Journal of Social Behavior and Personality, 10,* 265–272.

Ellsworth, P. C., & Carlsmith, J. M. (1968). Effect of eye contact and verbal consent on affective response to a dyadic interaction. *Journal of Personality and Social Psychology, 10,* 15–20.

Elms, A. C. (1975). The crisis of confidence in social psychology. *American Psychologist, 30,* 967–976.

Emery, R. E. (1989). Family violence: Children and their development: Knowledge base, research agenda, and social policy application. (Special issue). *American Psychologist, 44*(2), 321–328.

Emswiller, R., Deaux, K., & Willits, J. (1971). Similarity, sex, and requests for small favors. *Journal of Applied Social Psychology, 1,* 284–291.

Enggebretson, T. O., Matthews, K. A., & Scheier, M. F. (1989). Relations between anger expression and cardiovascular reactivity: Reconciling inconsistent findings through a matching hypothesis. *Journal of Personality and Social Psychology, 59,* 513–521.

Engs, R. C., Diebold, B. A., & Hanson, D. J. (1996). The drinking patterns and problems of a national sample of college students, 1994. *Journal of Alcohol and Drug Education, 41,* 13–33.

Epstein, R., & Komorita, S. S. (1966). Childhood prejudice as a function of parental ethnocentrism, punitiveness, and outgroup characteristics. *Journal of Personality and Social Psychology, 3,* 259–264.

Erdley, C. A., & D'Agostino, P. R. (1988). Cognitive and affective components of automatic priming effects. *Journal of Personality and Social Psychology, 54,* 741–747.

Eron, L. D., Gentry, J. H., & Schlegel, P. (1994). *Reason to hope: A psychosocial perspective on violence and youth.* Washington, DC: American Psychological Association.

Esses, V. M., Haddock, G., & Zanna, M. P. (1993). Values, stereotypes, and emotions as determinants of intergroup attitudes. In D. M. Mackie & D. L. Hamilton (Eds.), *Affect, cognition, and stereotyping: Interactive processes in group perception* (pp. 137–166). New York: Academic Press.

Esses, V. M., Haddock, G., & Zanna, M. P. (1994). The role of mood in the expression of intergroup stereotypes. In M. P. Zanna & J. M. Olson (Eds.), *The psychology of prejudice: The Ontario symposium* (Vol. 7, pp. 77–101). Mahwah, NJ: Erlbaum.

Etaugh, C., & Liss, M. B. (1992). Home, school, and playroom: Training grounds for adult gender roles. *Sex Roles, 26,* 129–147.

Ethier, K., & Deaux, K. (1994). Negotiating social identity when contexts change: Maintaining identification and responding to threat. *Personality and Social Psychology Bulletin, 67,* 243–251.

Exline, R. V., Ellyson, S. L., & Long, B. (1974). Visual behavior as an aspect of power role relationships. In P. Pliner, L. Krames, & T. Galloway (Eds.), *Nonverbal communication of aggression* (Vol. 2). New York: Plenum.

Fabrigar, L. R., & Krosnick, J. A. (1995). Attitude importance and the false consensus effect. *Personality and Social Psychology Bulletin, 21,* 468–479.

Falbo, T., & Peplan, L. S. (1980). Power strategies in intimate relationships. *Journal of Personality and Social Psychology, 38,* 618–628.

Fazio, R. H. (1981). On the self-perception explanation of the overjustification effect: The role of the salience of initial attitude. *Journal of Experimental Social Psychology, 38,* 618–628.

Fazio, R. H. (1990). Multiple processes by which attitudes guide behavior: The MODE model as an integrative framework. In M. P. Zanna (Ed.), *Advances in experimental social psychology* (Vol. 23, pp. 75–109). San Diego, CA: Academic Press.

Fazio, R. H., & Williams, C. J. (1986). Attitude accessibility as a moderator of the attitude-perception and attitude-behavior relations: An investigation of the 1984 presidential election. *Journal of Personality and Social Psychology, 51,* 505–514.

Fazio, R. H., & Zanna, M. P. (1978). Attitudinal qualities relating to the strength of the attitude-behavior relationship. *Journal of Experimental Social Psychology, 14,* 398–408.

Fazio, R. H., & Zanna, M. P. (1981). Direct experience and attitude-behavior consistency. In L. Berkowitz (Ed.), *Advances in experimental social psychology* (Vol. 14, pp. 161–202). San Diego, CA: Academic Press.

Feather, N. (1996). Values, deservingness, and attitudes toward high achievers: Research on tall poppies. In C. Seligman, J. Olson, & M. Zanna (Eds.), *The psychology of values: The Ontario symposium* (Vol. 8). Mahwah, NJ: Erlbaum.

Featherstone, M. (1990). *Global culture: Nationalization, globalization, and modernity.* London, England: Sage.

Feeney, B. C., and Kirkpatrick, L. A. (1996). Effects of adult attachment style and presence of romantic partners on physiological responses to stress. *Journal of Personality and Social Psychology, 70,* 255–270.

Fehr, B. (1988). Prototype analysis of the concepts of love and commitment. *Journal of Personality and Social Psychology, 55,* 557–579.

Feingold, A. (1992). Gender differences in mate selection preferences: A test of the parental investment model. *Psychological Bulletin, 112,* 125–139.

Felson, R. B. (1989). Parents and the reflected appraisal process. A longitudinal analysis. *Journal of Personality and Social Psychology, 57,* 965–971.

Feshbach, S. (1961). The stimulating versus cathartic effects of a vicarious aggressive activity. *Journal of Abnormal and Social Psychology, 63,* 381–385.

Feshbach, S., & Singer, R. D. (1971). *Television and aggression: An experimental field study.* San Francisco: Jossey-Bass.

Festinger, L. (1950). Informal social communication. *Psychological Review, 57,* 271–282.

Festinger, L. (1954). A theory of social comparison processes. *Human Relations, 7,* 117–140.

Festinger, L. (1957). *A theory of cognitive dissonance.* Palo Alto, CA: Stanford University Press.

Festinger, L. (1964). *Conflict, decision, and dissonance.* Palo Alto, CA: Stanford University Press.

Festinger, L. (1980). *Retrospections on social psychology.* New York: Oxford University Press.

Festinger, L., & Carlsmith, J. M. (1959). Cognitive consequences of forced compliance. *Journal of Abnormal and Social Psychology, 58,* 203–210.

Festinger, L., Schachter, S., & Back, K. (1950). *Social pressures in informal groups: A study of a housing community.* Palo Alto, CA: Stanford University Press.

Fiedler, F. E. (1964). A contingency model of leadership effectiveness. In L. Berkowitz (Ed.), *Advances in experimental social psychology* (Vol. 1). New York: Academic Press.

Fiedler, F. E. (1978). Recent developments in research on the contingency model. In L. Berkowitz (Ed.), *Group process* (pp. 209–225). New York: Academic Press.

Fiedler, F. E., Chemers, M. M., & Mahar, L. (1976). *Improving leadership effectiveness: The leader match concept.* New York: Wiley.

Fiedler, K., Semin, G. R., Finkenauer, C., & Berkel, I. (1995). Actor-observer bias in close relationships: The role of self-knowledge and self-related language. *Personality and Social Psychology Bulletin, 21,* 525–538.

Fincham, F. D. (1985). Attribution processes in distressed and non-distressed couples: 2. Responsibility for marital problems. *Journal of Abnormal Psychology, 94,* 183–190.

Fingerhut, L. A., & Kleinman, J. C. (1990). International and interstate comparisons of homicide among young males. *Journal of the American Medical Association, 263,* 3292–3295.

Finison, L. J. (1986). The psychological insurgency, 1936–1945. *Journal of Social Issues, 42,* 21–34.

Fischer, K., Schoeneman, T. J., & Rubanowitz, D. E. (1987). Attributions in the advice columns. II. The dimensionality of actors' and observers' explanations for interpersonal problems. *Personality and Social Psychology Bulletin, 13,* 458–466.

Fishbein, M., & Ajzen, I. (1975). *Belief, attitude, intention, and behavior: An introduction to theory and research.* Reading, MA: Addison-Wesley.

Fisher, J. D., & Fisher, W. A. (1992a). *People like us.*

Videotape. Department of Psychology, University of Connecticut, Storrs, CT.

Fisher, J. D., & Fisher, W. A. (1992b). Changing AIDS risk behavior. *Psychological Bulletin, 111,* 455–474.

Fisher, J. D., Fisher, W. A., Misovich, S. J., Kimble, D. L., & Malloy, T. E. (1996). Changing AIDS risk behavior: Effects of an intervention emphasizing AIDS risk reduction information, motivation, and behavioral skills in a college student population. *Healthy Psychology, 15,* 114–123.

Fisher, J. D., Fisher, W. A., Williams, S. S., & Malloy, T. E. (1994). Empirical tests of an information-motivation-behavioral skills model of AIDS preventive behavior. *Health Psychology, 94,* 238–250.

Fisher, W. A., Fisher, J. D., & Rye, B. J. (1995). Understanding and promoting AIDS-preventive behavior: Insights from the theory of reasoned action. *Health Psychology, 14,* 255–264.

Fiske, S. T. (1993). Controlling other people: The impact of power on stereotyping. *American Psychologist, 48,* 621–628.

Fiske, S. T., & Glick, P. (1995). Ambivalence and stereotypes cause sexual harassment. *Journal of Social Issues, 51,* 97–115.

Fiske, S. T., Morling, B., & Stevens, L. F. (1996). Controlling self and others: A theory of anxiety, mental control and social control. *Personality and Social Psychology Bulletin, 22,* 115–123.

Fiske, S. T., & Neuberg, S. L. (1990). A continuum of impression formation, from category-based to individuating processes: Influences of information and motivation on attention and interpretation. In M. P. Zanna (Ed.), *Advances in experimental social psychology* (Vol. 23, pp. 1–74). Boston, MA: Academic Press.

Fiske, S. T., & Taylor, S. E. (1984). *Social cognition.* New York: McGraw-Hill.

Fiske, S. T., & Taylor, S. E. (1991). *Social cognition* (2nd ed.). New York: McGraw-Hill.

Fitzgerald, L. (1993). Sexual harassment: Violence against women in the workplace. *American Psychologist, 48,* 1070–1076.

Fleiner, S., & Kelley, H. H. (1978). Study cited (but not referenced) in H. H. Kelley, *Personal relationships: Their structures and processes.* Hillsdale, NJ: Erlbaum.

Fleischer, R. A., & Chertkoff, J. M. (1986). Effects of dominance and sex on leader selection in dyadic work groups. *Journal of Personality and Social Psychology, 50,* 94–99.

Fleming, J. H., & Darley, J. M. (1989). Perceiving choice and constraint: The effects of contextual and behavioural cues on attitude attribution. *Journal of Personality and Social Psychology, 56,* 27–40.

Flowers, M. L. (1977). A laboratory test of some implications of Janis' groupthink hypothesis. *Journal of Personality and Social Psychology, 35,* 888–896.

Folkard, S., Wever, R. A., & Wildgruber, C. M. (1983). Multi-oscillatory control of circadian rhythms in human performance. *Nature, 305,* 223–226.

Follette, V. M., & Jacobson, N. S. (1987). Importance of attribution as a predictor of how people cope with failure. *Journal of Personality and Social Psychology, 52,* 1205–1211.

Forbes, J. D. (1964). *The Indian in America's past.* Englewood Cliffs, NJ: Prentice-Hall.

Ford, T. E., & Kruglanski, A. W. (1995). Effects of epistemic motivations on the use of accessible constructs in social judgment. *Personality and Social Psychology Bulletin, 21,* 950–962.

Foss, R. D. (1981). Structural effects in simulated jury decision making. *Journal of Personality and Social Psychology, 40,* 1053–1062.

Frank, M. G., & Gilovich, T. (1988). The dark side of self- and social perception: Black uniforms and aggression in professional sports. *Journal of Personality and Social Psychology, 54,* 74–85.

Fraser, S., Gouge, C., & Billig, M. (1971). Risky shifts, cautious shifts, and group polarization. *European Journal of Social Psychology, 1,* 7–29.

Freedman, J. L. (1984). Effect of television violence on aggressiveness. *Psychological Bulletin, 96*(2), 227–246.

Freedman, J. L. (1986). Television violence and aggression: A rejoinder. *Psychological Bulletin, 100*(3), 372–378.

Freedman, J. L., & Fraser, S. C. (1966). Compliance without pressure: The foot-in-the-door technique. *Journal of Personality and Social Psychology, 4,* 195–202.

Freedman, J. L., & Sears, D. O. (1965). Selective exposure. In L. Berkowitz (Ed.), *Advances in experimental social psychology* (Vol. 2, pp. 57–97). San Diego, CA: Academic Press.

French, J. R. P., Jr., & Raven B. H. (1959). The bases of social power. In D. Cartwright (Ed.), *Studies in social power* (pp. 150–167). Ann Arbor: University of Michigan Press.

Frey, C. L., & Gaertner, S. L. (1986). Helping and the avoidance of inappropriate interracial behavior: A strategy that perpetuates a nonprejudiced self-image. *Journal of Personality and Social Psychology, 50,* 1083–1090.

Frey, D. (1986). Recent research on selective exposure to information. In L. Berkowitz (Ed.), *Advances in experimental social psychology* (Vol. 19, pp. 41–80). San Diego, CA: Academic Press.

Fridlund, A. J. (1991). Sociality of solitary smiling: Potentiation by an implicit audience. *Journal of Personality and Social Psychology, 60,* 229–240.

Friedland, N. (1988). Political terrorism: A social psychological perspective. In W. Stroebe et al. (Eds.), *The social psychology of intergroup conflict* (pp. 103–116). Berlin: Springer-Verlag.

Friedman, H. S., & Riggio, R. (1981). Effect of individual differences in nonverbal expressiveness on transmission of emotion. *Journal of Nonverbal Behavior, 6,* 96–104.

Friedman, H. S., Riggio, R., & Casella, D. F. (1988). Nonverbal skill, personal charisma, and initial attraction. *Personality and Social Psychology Bulletin, 14,* 203–211.

Friedrich, L. K., & Stein, A. H. (1973). Aggressive and prosocial television programs and the natural behavior of preschool children. *Monographs of the Society for Research in Child Development, 38*(4), Whole No. 151.

Friedrich-Cofer, L., & Huston, A. C. (1986). Television violence and aggression: The debate continues. *Psychological Bulletin, 100,* 364–371.

Frieze, I., & Weiner, B. (1971). Cue utilization and attributional judgments for success and failure. *Journal of Personality, 39,* 591–606.

Frodi, A. (1977). Sexual arousal, situational restrictiveness, and aggressive behavior. *Journal of Research in Personality, 11,* 48–58.

Fry, D. & Fry, V. (1997). Culture and conflict resolution models: Exploring alternatives to violence. In D. Fry et al. (Eds.), *Cultural variation in conflict resolution: Alternatives to violence.* Mahwah, NJ: Lawrence Erlbaum Associates.

Fuhrman, R. W., & Funder, D. C. (1995). Convergence between self and peer in the response-time processing of trait-relevant information. *Journal of Personality and Social Psychology, 69,* 950–960.

Furnham, A., & Bochner, S. (1986). *Culture shock: Psychological reactions to unfamiliar environments.* London, England: Methuen.

Furnham, A., & Proctor, E. (1989). Belief in a just world: Review and critique of the individual difference literature. *British Journal of Social Psychology, 28,* 365–384.

Gabrenya, W. K., & Arkin, R. M. (1980). Self-monitoring scale: Factor structure and correlates. *Personality and Social Psychology Bulletin, 6,* 12–22.

Gaertner, S. L. (1970). A "call" for help: Helping behavior extended to black and white victims by New York City Liberal and Conservative party members. *Proceedings of the 78th Annual Convention of the American Psychological Association* (Vol. 5), pp. 441–442.

Gaertner, S. L., & Dovidio, J. F. (1986). The aversive form of racism. In J. F. Dovidio & S. L. Gaertner (Eds.), *Prejudice, discrimination, and racism* (pp. 61–90). New York: Academic Press.

Gaertner, S. L., Mann, J., Dovidio, J., Murrell, A., & Pomare, M. (1990). How does cooperation reduce intergroup bias? *Journal of Personality and Social Psychology, 59,* 692–704.

Galanter, H. (1989). *Cults: Faith, healing, and coercion.* New York: Oxford University Press.

Gantnot, A. B., & Taylor, S. P. (1988). Human physical aggression as a function of diazepam. *Personality of Social Psychology Bulletin, 14,* 479–484.

Gao, G., & Gudykunst, W. (1990). Uncertainty, anxiety, and adaptation. *International Journal of Intercultural Relations, 14,* 301–317.

Geen, R. G., & Bushman, B. J. (1987). Drive theory: Effects of socially engendered arousal. In B. Mullen & G. R. Goethals (Eds.), *Theories of group behavior.* New York: Springer-Verlag.

Geen, R. G., & Quanty, M. (1977). The catharsis of aggression: An evaluation of a hypothesis. In L. Berkowitz (Ed.), *Advances in experimental social psychology* (Vol. 10). New York: Academic Press.

Geen, R. G., & Stoner, D. (1973). Context effects in observed violence. *Journal of Personality and Social Psychology, 25,* 145–150.

Georgas, J., Christakopoulou, S., Poortinga, Y., Angleitner, A., Goodwin, R., & Charalambous, N. (1997). The relationship of family bonds to family structure across cultures. *Journal of Cross Cultural Psychology, 28,* 284–302.

Gerard, H. B. (1963). Emotional uncertainty and social comparison. *Journal of Abnormal and Social Psychology, 66,* 568–573.

Gerard, H. B., Wilhelmy, R. A., & Conolley, E. S. (1968). Conformity and group size. *Journal of Personality and Social Psychology, 8,* 79–82.

Gergen, K. J. (1971). *The concept of self.* New York: Holt.

Gergen, K. J., & Taylor, M. G. (1969). Social expectancy and self-presentation in a status hierarchy. *Journal of Experimental Social Psychology, 5,* 79–92.

Gergen, M. (1989). Induction and construction: Teetering between two worlds. *European Journal of Social Psychology, 19,* 431–438.

Gibb, C. A. (1969). Leadership. In G. Lindzey & E. Aronson (Eds.), *The handbook of social psychology* (2nd ed., Vol. 4). Reading, MA: Addison-Wesley.

Gibbons, F. X. (1978). Sexual standards and reaction to pornography: Enhancing behavioral consistency through self-focused attention. *Journal of Personality and Social Psychology, 36,* 976–987.

Gibbons, F. X. (1986). Social comparison and depression: Company's effect on misery. *Journal of Personality and Social Psychology, 51,* 140–148.

Gibbons, F. X. (1990). Self-attention and behavior: A review and theoretical update. In L. Berkowitz (Ed.), *Advances in experimental social psychology* (Vol. 23, pp. 249–303). New York: Academic Press.

Gibbons, F. X., Benbow, C. P., & Gerrard, M. (1994). From top dog to bottom half: Social comparison strategies in response to poor performance. *Journal of Personality and Social Psychology, 67,* 638–652.

Gifford, R., & O'Connor, B. (1987). The interpersonal circumplex as a behavior map. *Journal of Personality and Social Psychology, 52,* 1019–1026.

Gilbert, D. T., Giesler, R. B., & Morris, K. A. (1995). When comparisons arise. *Journal of Personality and Social Psychology, 69,* 227–236.

Gilbert, D. T., & Hixon, J. G. (1991). The trouble of thinking: Activation and application of stereotypic beliefs. *Journal of Personality and Social Psychology, 60,* 509–517.

Gilbert, D. T., & Jones, E. E. (1986). Perceiver-induced constraint: Interpretations of self-generated reality. *Journal of Personality and Social Psychology, 50,* 269–280.

Gilbert, D. T., Krull, D. S., & Pelham, B. W. (1988). Of thoughts unspoken: Social inference and the self-regulation of behavior. *Journal of Personality and Social Psychology, 55,* 685–694.

Gilbert, D. T., & Malone, P. S. (1995). The correspondence bias. *Psychological Bulletin, 117,* 21–38.

Gilbert, D. T., Pelham, B. W., & Krull, D. S. (1988). On cognitive busyness: When person perceivers meet persons perceived. *Journal of Personality and Social Psychology, 54,* 733–740.

Gilligan, C. (1982). *In a different voice: Psychological the-*

ory and women's development. Cambridge, MA: Harvard University Press.

Ginosar, Z., & Trope, Y. (1980). The effects of base rates and individuating information on judgments about another person. *Journal of Experimental Social Psychology, 16,* 228–242.

Glenn, N. D. (1991). The recent trend in marital success in the United States. *Journal of Marriage and the Family, 53,* 261–270.

Glick, P., DeMorest, J. A., & Hotze, C. A. (1988). Self-monitoring and beliefs about partner compatibility in romantic relationships. *Personality and Social Psychology Bulletin, 14,* 485–494.

Goethals, G. R. (1972). Consensus and modality in the attribution process: The role of similarity and information. *Journal of Personality and Social Psychology, 21,* 84–92.

Goethals, G. R. (1986). Fabricating and ignoring social reality: Self-serving estimates of consensus. In J. M. Olson, C. P. Herman, & M. P. Zanna (Eds.), *Relative deprivation and social comparison: The Ontario symposium* (Vol. 4, pp. 135–157). Hillsdale, NJ: Erlbaum.

Goethals, G. R., Allison, S. J., & Frost, M. (1979). Perceptions of the magnitude and diversity of social support. *Journal of Experimental Social Psychology, 15,* 570–581.

Goethals, G. R., & Darley, J. M. (1977). Social comparison theory: An attributional approach. In J. M. Suls & R. L. Miller (Eds.), *Social comparison processes: Theoretical and empirical perspectives.* Washington, DC: Hemisphere/Halsted.

Goethals, G. R., & Darley, J. M. (1987). Social comparison theory: Self-evaluation and group life. In B. Mullen & G. R. Goethals (Eds.), *Theories of group behavior.* New York: Springer-Verlag.

Goethals, G. R., Messick, D. M., & Allison, S. T. (1990). The uniqueness bias: Studies of constructive social comparison. In J. M. Suls & T. A. Wills (Eds.), *Social comparison: Contemporary theory and research.* Hillsdale, NJ: Erlbaum.

Goethals, G. R., & Zanna, M. P. (1979). The role of social comparison in choice shifts. *Journal of Personality and Social Psychology, 37,* 1469–1476.

Goffman, E. (1955). On face work: An analysis of ritual elements in social interaction. *Psychiatry, 18,* 213–231.

Goffman, E. (1959). *The presentation of self in everyday life.* Garden City, NY: Doubleday/Anchor.

Goffman, E. (1967). *Interaction ritual.* New York: Doubleday/Anchor.

Goldstein, A. P. (1994). *The ecology of aggression.* New York: Plenum.

Goodstadt, M. (1971). Helping and refusal to help: A test of balance and reactance theories. *Journal of Experimental Social Psychology, 7,* 610–622.

Goranson, R. E., & Berkowitz, L. (1966). Reciprocity and responsibility reactions to prior help. *Journal of Personality and Social Psychology, 3,* 227–232.

Gorassini, D. R., & Olson, J. M. (1995). Does self-perception change explain the foot-in-the-door effect? *Journal of Personality and Social Psychology, 69,* 91–105.

Gordon, C. M., & Carey, M. P. (1996). Alcohol's effects on requisites for sexual risk reduction in men: An initial experimental investigation. *Health Psychology, 15,* 56–60.

Gordon, R. (1996). Impact of ingratiation on judgments and evaluations: A meta-analytic investigation. *Journal of Personality and Social Psychology, 71,* 54–70.

Gorenflo, D. W., & Crano, W. D. (1989). Judgmental subjectivity/objectivity and locua of choice in social comparison. *Journal of Personality and Social Psychology, 57,* 605–614.

Gouldner, A. (1960). The norm of reciprocity: A preliminary statement. *American Sociological Review, 25,* 161–178.

Graumann, C. F. (1988). Introduction to a history of social psychology. In M. Hewstone, W. Stroebe, J. Codol & G. M. Stephenson (Eds.), *Introduction to social psychology.* Oxford, England: Basil Blackwell.

Greenberg, J., & Musham, C. (1981). Avoiding and seeking self-focused attention. *Journal of Research in Personality, 15,* 191–200.

Greenberg, J., Pyszczynski, T., & Solomon, S. (1982). The self-serving attributional bias: Beyond self-presentation. *Journal of Experimental Social Psychology, 18,* 56–67.

Greenberg, J., Solomon, S., & Pyszczynski, T. (1997). Terror management theory of self-esteem and cultural world view: Empirical assessment and conceptual refinement. In M. P. Zanna (Ed.), *Advances in Experimental Social Psychology* (pp. 61–141). New York: Academic Press.

Greenwald, A. G. (1968). Cognitive learning, cognitive response to persuasion, and attitude change. In A. G. Greenwald, T. C. Brock, & T. M. Ostrom (Eds.), *Psychological foundations of attitudes* (pp. 147–170). New York: Academic Press.

Greenwald, A. G. (1980). The totalitarian ego: Fabrication and revision of personal history. *American Psychologist, 35,* 603–613.

Gregory, S. W., & Webster, S. (1996). A nonverbal signal in voices of interview partners effectively predicts communication accommodation and social status perceptions. *Journal of Personality and Social Psychology, 70,* 1231–1240.

Griffitt, W. (1970). Environmental effects on interpersonal affective behavior: Ambient effective temperature and attraction. *Journal of Personality and Social Psychology, 15,* 240–244.

Griffitt, W., & Guay, P. (1969). "Object" evaluation and conditioned affect. *Journal of Experimental Research in Personality, 4,* 1–8.

Griffitt, W., & Veitch, R. (1971). Hot and crowded: Influence of population density and temperature on interpersonal affective behavior. *Journal of Personality and Social Psychology, 17,* 92–98.

Griffitt, W., & Veitch, R. (1974). Preacquaintance attitude similarity and attraction revisited: Ten days in a fallout shelter. *Sociometry, 37,* 163–173.

Gross, A. E., Wallston, B. S., & Piliavin, I. M. (1975). Beneficiary attractiveness and costs as determinants of responses to routine requests for help. *Sociometry, 38,* 131–140.

Gross, E., & Latané, J. G. (1974). Receiving help, reciprocation, and interpersonal attraction. *Journal of Applied Social Psychology, 4,* 210–223.

Gruder, C. L. (1977). Choice of comparison persons in evaluating oneself. In J. M. Suls & R. L. Miller (Eds.), *Social comparison processes: Theoretical and empirical perspectives.* Washington, DC: Hemisphere/Halsted.

Gruder, C. L., Cook, T. D., Hennigan, K. M., Flay, B. R., Alessis, C., & Halamaj, J. (1978). Empirical tests of the absolute sleeper effect predicted from the discounting cue hypothesis. *Journal of Personality and Social Psychology, 36,* 1061–1074.

Gruder, C. L., Romer, D., & Korth, B. (1978). Dependency and fault as determinants of helping. *Journal of Experimental Social Psychology, 14,* 227–235.

Grzelak, J. (1988). Conflict and cooperation. In M. Hewstone, W. Stroebe, J. Codol, & G. M. Stephenson (Eds.), *Introduction to social psychology* (pp. 288–313). Oxford, England: Blackwell.

Gudykunst, W. (1991). *Bridging differences.* Newbury Park, CA: Sage.

Guerin, B., & Innes, J. (1982). Social facilitation and social monitoring: A new look at Zajonc's mere presence hypothesis. *British Journal of Social Psychology, 21,* 7–18.

Guimond, S., & Dubé-Simard, L. (1983). Relative deprivation theory and the Quebec nationalist movement: The cognition-emotion distinction and the personal-group deprivation issue. *Journal of Personality and Social Psychology, 44,* 526–535.

Gump, B. B., & Kulik, J. A. (1995). The effect of a model's HIV status on self-perceptions: A self-protective similarity bias. *Personality and Social Psychology Bulletin, 21,* 827–833.

Gunter, B. (1983). Do aggressive people prefer violent television? *Bulletin of the British Psychological Society, 36,* 166–168.

Gupta, U., & Singh, P. (1982). Exploratory studies in love and liking and types of marriage. *Indian Journal of Applied Psychology, 19,* 92–97.

Gurr, T. R. (1970). *Why men rebel.* Princeton, NJ: Princeton University Press.

Gutek, T. R. (1985). *Sex and the workplace: Impact of sexual behavior on harassment on women, men and organizations.* San Francisco, CA: Josey-Bass.

Haas, J., & Roberts, G. C. (1975). Effect of evaluative others upon learning and performance of a complex motor task. *Journal of Motor Behavior, 7,* 81–90.

Hackney, S. (1969). Southern violence. *American Historical Review, 74,* 906–925.

Hafer, C. L., & Olson, J. M. (1993). Beliefs in a just world, discontent, and assertive actions by working women. *Personality and Social Psychology Bulletin, 19,* 30–38.

Hafer, C. L., Reynolds, K. L., & Obertynski, M. A. (1996). Message comprehensibility and persuasion: Effects of complex language in counterattitudinal appeals to laypeople. *Social Cognition, 14,* 317–337.

Hains, S. L., Hogg, M. A., & Duck, J. M. (1997). Self-categorization and leadership: Effects of group prototypicality and leader stereotypicality. *Personality and Social Psychology Bulletin, 23,* 1087–1099.

Hall, E. T. (1959). *The silent language.* New York: Fawcett.

Hall, E. T. (1966). *The hidden dimension.* New York: Doubleday.

Hall, J., & Williams, M. S. (1970). Group dynamics training and improved decision making. *Journal of Applied Behavioral Science, 6,* 27–32.

Hall, J. A. (1984). *Nonverbal sex differences: Communication accuracy and expressive style.* Baltimore, MD: Johns Hopkins University Press.

Hall, J. A., & Taylor, S. E. (1976). When love is blind: Maintaining idealized images of one's spouse. *Human Relations, 29,* 751–761.

Halpin, A., & Winer, B. (1952). *The leadership behavior of the airplane commander.* Columbus: Ohio State University Research Foundation.

Hamilton, D. L. (1981). Cognitive representations of persons. In E. T. Higgins, C. P. Herman, & M. P. Zanna (Eds.), *Social cognition: The Ontario symposium* (Vol. 1). Hillsdale, NJ: Erlbaum.

Hamilton, D. L., & Gifford, R. K. (1976). Illusory correlation in interpersonal perception: A cognitive basis of stereotypic judgements. *Journal of Experimental Social Psychology, 12,* 392–407.

Hamilton, D. L., & Sherman, J. W. (1994). Stereotypes. In R. S. Wyer, Jr., & T. S. Srull (Eds.), *Handbook of social cognition* (2nd ed.) (Vol. 2: Applications, pp. 1–68). Hillsdale, NJ: Erlbaum.

Hamilton, D. L., & Sherman, S. J. (1992). Illusory correlations: Implications for stereotype theory and research. In D. Bar-Tal, C. F. Graumann, A. W. Kruglanski, & W. Stroebe (Eds.), *Stereotypes and prejudice: Changing conceptions* (pp. 59–82). New York: Springer-Verlag.

Hamilton, D. L., & Sherman, S. J. (1996). Perceiving persons and groups. *Psychological Review, 103,* 336–355.

Hamilton, D. L., & Trollier, T. (1986). Stereotypes and stereotyping: An overview of the cognitive approach. In J. Dovidio & S. L. Gaertner (Eds.), *Prejudice, discrimination, and racism.* New York: Academic Press.

Hancock, R. D., & Sorrentino, R. M. (1980). The effects of expected future interaction and prior group support on the conformity process. *Journal of Experimental Social Psychology, 16,* 261–270.

Haney, C., & Manzolati, J. (1984). Television criminology: Network illusions of criminal justice realities. In E. Aronson (Ed.), *Readings about the social animal* (4th ed.). New York: Freeman.

Hansen, C. H., & Hansen, R. D. (1988). Finding the face in the crowd: An anger superiority effect. *Journal of Personality and Social Psychology, 54,* 917–924.

Hansen, C. H., Hansen, R. D., & Crano, W. D. (1989). Sympathetic arousal and self-attention. The accessibility of interceptive and exteroceptive arousal cues. *Journal of Experimental Social Psychology, 25,* 437–449.

Hardy, R. C. (1976). A test of the poor leader: Member relations cells of the contingency model on elementary school children. *Child Development, 46,* 958–964.

Harkins, S. G., & Szymanski, K. (1989). Social loafing and group evolution. *Journal of Personality and Social Psychology, 56,* 934–941.

Harmon-Jones, E., Brehm, J. W., Greenberg, J., Simon, L., & Nelson, D. E. (1996). Evidence that the production of aversive consequences is not necessary to create cognitive dissonance. *Journal of Personality and Social Psychology, 70,* 5–16.

Harries, K. D. (1990). *Serious violence patterns of homicide and assault in America.* Springfield, IL: Charles C. Thomas.

Harris, B. (1986). Reviewing 50 years of the psychology of social issues. *Journal of Social Issues, 42,* 1–20.

Harris, C. R., & Christenfeld, N. (1996). Gender, jealousy and reason. *Psychological Science, 7,* 364–366.

Harris, M. B. (1974). Mediators between frustration and aggression in a field experiment. *Journal of Experimental Social Psychology, 10,* 561–571.

Harris, M. J., & Rosenthal, R. (1985). Mediation of interpersonal expectancy effects: 31 meta-analyses. *Psychological Bulletin, 97,* 363–386.

Hassan, S. (1988). *Combatting cult mind control.* Rochester, VT: Park Street Press.

Hastie, R. (1980). Memory for behavioral information that confirms or contradicts a personality impression. In R. Hastie, T. M. Ostrem, E. B. Ebbesen, R. S. Nyer, D. L. Hamilton, & D. E. Carlston (Eds.), *Person memory: The cognition basis of social perception.* (pp. 141–172). Hillsdale, NJ: Erlbaum.

Hatfield, E., Greenberger, J., Traupmann, S., & Labert, P. (1980). Equity and sexual satisfaction in recently married couples. *Journal of Sex Research, 18,* 18–32.

Hatfield, E., & Sprecher, S. (1986a). Measuring passionate love in intimate relationships. *Journal of Adolescence, 9,* 383–410.

Hatfield, E., & Sprecher, S. (1986b). *Mirror, mirror . . . : The importance of looks in everyday life.* Albany: SUNY Press.

Hatfield, E., & Traupmann, J. (1980). Intimate relationships: A perspective from equity theory. In S. Duck & R. Gilmour (Eds.), *Studying Personal Relationships.* London, England: Academic Press.

Hatfield, E., Traupmann, J., Sprecher, S., Utne, M., & Hay, J. (1985). Equity and intimate relations: Recent research. In W. Ickes (Eds.), *Compatible and incompatible relationships.* New York: Springer-Verlag.

Hazan, C., & Shaver, P. R. (1987). Romantic love conceptualized as an attachment process. *Journal of Personality and Social Psychology, 52,* 511–524.

Hazan, C., & Shaver, P. R. (1994). Attachment as an organizational framework for research in close relationships. *Psychological Inquiry, 5,* 1–22.

Hazlewood, J. D., & Olson, J. M. (1986). Covariation information, causal questioning, and interpersonal behavior. *Journal of Experimental Social Psychology, 22,* 276–291.

Hearold, S. (1986). A synthesis of 1043 effects of television on social behavior. In G. Comstock (Ed.), *Public communication and behavior* (Vol. 1, pp. 65–133.) Orlando, FL: Academic Press.

Heatherton, T. F., & Baumeister, R. F. (1991). Binge eating as escape from self-awareness. *Psychological Bulletin, 110,* 86–108.

Heider, F. (1944). Social perception and phenomenal causality. *Psychological Review, 51,* 358–374.

Heider, F. (1958). *The psychology of interpersonal relations.* New York: Wiley.

Heine, S., & Lehman, D. (1995). Cultural variation in unrealistic optimism: Does the West feel more invulnerable than the East? *Journal of Personality and Social Psychology, 68,* 595–607.

Heinrichs, R. W. (1989). Frontal cerebral lesions and violent incidents in chronic neuropsychiatric patients. *Biological Psychiatry, 25,* 174–178.

Helgeson, V. S., & Mickelson, K. D. (1995). Motives for social comparison. *Personality and Social Psychology Bulletin, 21,* 1200–1209.

Henchy, T., & Glass, D. C. (1968). Evaluation apprehension and the social facilitation of dominant and subordinate responses. *Journal of Personality and Social Psychology, 10,* 446–454.

Hendrick, S. S. (1981). Self-disclosure and marital satisfaction. *Journal of Personality and Social Psychology, 40,* 1150–1159.

Henley, N. M. (1977). *Body politics: Power, sex, and nonverbal communication.* Englewood Cliffs, NJ: Prentice-Hall.

Herek, G. M. (1986). The instrumentality of attitudes: Toward a neofunctional theory. *Journal of Social Issues, 42*(2), 99–114.

Herr, P. M. (1986). Consequences of priming: Judgment and behavior. *Journal of Personality and Social Psychology, 51,* 1106–1115.

Hess, U., Banse, R., & Kappas, A. (1995). The intensity of facial expression is determined by underlying affective state and social situation. *Journal of Personality and Social Psychology, 69,* 280–288.

Hewstone, M. (1994). Revision and change of stereotypic beliefs: In search of the elusive subtyping model. In W. Stroebe & M. Hewstone (Eds.), *European review of social psychology* (Vol. 5, pp. 69–109). New York: Wiley.

Heyerdahl, T. (1950). *Kon-Tiki.* Chicago: Rand-McNally.

Higgins, E. T. (1989). Self-discrepancy theory: What patterns of self-beliefs cause people to suffer? In L. Berkowitz (Ed.), *Advances in experimental social psychology* (Vol. 22, pp. 181–227). San Diego, CA: Academic Press.

Higgins, E. T., Bond, R. N., Klein, R., & Strauman, T. (1986). Self-discrepancies and emotional vulnerability: How magnitude, accessibility, and type of discrepancy influence affect. *Journal of Personality and Social Psychology, 51,* 5–15.

Higgins, E. T., & McCann, C. D. (1984). Social encoding and subsequent attitudes, impressions, and memory: Context-driven and motivational aspects of processing. *Journal of Personality and Social Psychology, 47,* 26–39.

Higgins, E. T., & Rholes, W. S. (1978). "Saying is believing": Effects of message modification on memory and liking for the person described. *Journal of Experimental Social Psychology, 14,* 363–378.

Higgins, E. T., Rholes, W. S., & Jones, C. R. (1977). Category accessibility and impression formation. *Journal of Experimental Social Psychology, 13,* 141–154.

Higgins, E. T., Roney, C. J. R., Crowe, E., & Hymes, C. (1994). Ideal versus ought predilections for approach and avoidance: Distinct self-regulatory systems. *Journal of Personality and Social Psychology, 66,* 276–286.

Hilton, D. J. (1990). Conversational processes and causal explanation. *Psychological Bulletin, 107,* 65–81.

Hilton, D. J., & Sugolski, B. R. (1986). Knowledge-based causal attribution: The abnormal conditions focus model. *Psychological Review, 93,* 75–88.

Hilton, J. L., & Darley, J. M. (1991). The effects of interaction goals on person perception. In M. P. Zanna (Ed.), *Advances in experimental social psychology* (Vol. 24, pp. 235–267). New York: Academic Press.

Hilton, J. L., & Fein, S. (1989). The role of typical diagnosticity in stereotype-based judgments. *Journal of Personality and Social Psychology, 57,* 201–211.

Hiltrop, J. M. (1985). Mediator behavior and the settlement of collective bargaining disputes in Britain. *Journal of Social Issues, 41*(2), 83–99.

Hines, P., Garcia-Preto, N., McGoldrick, M., Almeida, R., & Weltman, S. (1992). Intergenerational relationships across cultures. *Families in Society: The Journal of Contemporary Human Services, 73,* 323–337.

Hinkle, S., & Schopler, J. (1986). Bias in the evaluation of in-group and out-group performance. In S. Worchel and W. G. Austin (Eds.), *Psychology of intergroup relations.* Chicago: Nelson-Hall.

Hiroto, D. S., & Seligman, M. E. P. (1975). Generality of learned helplessness in man. *Journal of Personality and Social Psychology, 31,* 311–327.

Hitchcock, E. (1979). Amygdalotomy for aggression. In M. Sandler (Ed.), *Psychopharmacology of aggression* (pp. 205–215). New York: Raven Press.

Ho, D., & Chiu, C. (1994). Component ideas of individualism, collectivism, and social organization: An application in the study of Chinese culture. In Kim et al. (Eds.), *Individualism and collectivism: theory, method, and applications.* Thousand Oaks, CA: Sage.

Hoelter, J. W. (1983). Factorial invariance and self-esteem: Reassessing race and sex differences. *Social Forces, 61,* 834–846.

Hoffman, C., & Hurst, N. (1990). Gender stereotypes: Perception or rationalization? *Journal of Personality and Social Psychology, 58,* 197–208.

Hofling, C. K., Brotzman, E., Dalrymple, S., Graves, N., & Pierce, C. M. (1966). An experimental study in nurse-physician relationships. *Journal of Nurses and Mental Diseases, 143*(2), 171–180.

Hofstede, G. (1980). *Culture's consequences: International differences in work-related values.* Beverly Hills, CA: Sage.

Hofstede, G. (1991). *Cultures and organizations: Software of the mind.* London, England: McGraw-Hill.

Hofstede, G. (1996). Gender stereotypes and partner preferences of Asian women in masculine and feminine cultures. *Journal of Cross Cultural Psychology, 27,* 533–546.

Hofstede, G., & Bond, M. (1984). Hofstede's cultural dimensions: An independent validation using Rokeach's value survey. *Journal of Cross-Cultural Psychology, 15,* 417–433.

Hogg, M. A. (1996). Social identity, self-categorization and the small group. In E. H. Witte and H. H. Davis (Eds.), *Small group processes and interpersonal relationships: Understanding group behavior* (Vol. 2, pp. 227–253). Mahwah, NJ: Erlbaum.

Hokanson, J. E., Burgess, M., & Cohen, M. F. (1963). Effect of displaced aggression on systolic blood pressure. *Journal of Abnormal and Social Psychology, 67,* 214–218.

Hokanson, J. E., & Shelter, S. (1961). The effect of overt aggression on physiological arousal level. *Journal of Abnormal and Social Psychology, 63,* 446–448.

Holden, S. (1996, June 16). Ella Fitzgerald, the voice of jazz, dies at 79. *New York Times.*

Hollander, E. P. (1958). Conformity, status, and idiosyncrasy credit. *Psychological Review, 65,* 117–127.

Hollander, E. P. (1978). *Leadership dynamics: A practical guide to effective relationships.* Glencoe, IL: Free Press.

Hollander, E. P. (1985). Leadership and power. In G. Lindzey & E. Aronson (Eds.), *Handbook of social psychology* (3rd ed., Vol. 2, pp. 485–537). New York: Random House.

Holtgraves, T., Srull, T. K., & Socall, D. (1989). Conversation memory: The effects of speaker status on memory for the assertiveness of conversation remarks. *Journal of Personality and Social Psychology, 56,* 149–160.

Horne, J. A., & Ostberg, O. (1976). A self-assessment questionnaire to determine morningness-eveningness in human circadian rhythms. *International Journal of Chronobiology, 4,* 97–110.

Horneffer, K. J., & Fincham, F. D. (1996). Attributional models of depression and marital distress. *Personality and Social Psychology Bulletin, 22,* 678–689.

Horwitz, M., & Rabbie, J. (1989). Stereotypes of groups, group members, and individuals in categories: A differential analysis. In D. Bar-tal, C. Graumann, A. Kruglanski, & W. Stroebe (Eds.), *Stereotyping and prejudice: Changing conceptions.* New York: Springer-Verlag.

Hosch, H. M., & Platz, S. J. (1984). Self-monitoring and eyewitness accuracy. *Personality and Social Psychology Bulletin, 10,* 289–292.

Houston, D. A., & Fazio, R. H. (1989). Biased processing as a function of attitude accessibility: Making objective judgments subjectively. *Social Cognition, 7,* 51–66.

Hovland, C. I., Janis, I. L., & Kelley, H. H. (1953). *Communication and persuasion.* New Haven, CT: Yale University Press.

Hovland, C. I., & Weiss, W. (1951). The influence of source credibility on communication effectiveness. *Public Opinion Quarterly, 15,* 635–650.

Howells, L. T., & Becker, S. W. (1962). Seating arrangement and leadership emergence. *Journal of Abnormal and Social Psychology, 64,* 148–150.

Hoyt, W. T. (1994). Development and awareness of reputations in newly formed groups: A social relations analysis. *Personality and Social Psychology Bulletin, 20,* 464–472.

Huesmann, L. F., Logerspetz, K., & Eron, L. D. (1984). Intervening variables in the TV violence-aggression relation: Evidence from two countries. *Developmental Psychology, 20*(5), 746–775.

Huesmann, L. R. (1982). Television violence and aggressive behavior. In D. Pearl & L. Bouthilet (Eds.). *Television and behavior: Ten years of scientific progress and implications for the 80s.* Washington, DC: U. S. Government Printing Office.

Huff-Corzine, L., Corzine, J., & Morre, D. C. (1986). Southern exposure: Deciphering the South's influence on homicide rates. *Social Forces, 64,* 906–924.

Hughes, D. L., & Galinsky, E. (1994). Gender, job and family conditions, and psychological symptoms. *Psychology of Women Quarterly, 18,* 251–270.

Hui, C. H. (1986). Fifteen years of pornography research: Does exposure to pornography have any effects? *Bulletin of the Hong Kong Psychological Society, 16–17,* 41–62.

Hull, J. G., Van Treuren, R. R., & Propsom, P. M. (1988). Attributional style and the components of hardiness. *Personality and Social Psychology Bulletin, 14,* 505–513.

Hull, J. G., Young R. D., & Jouriles, E. (1986). Applications of the self-awareness model of alcohol consumption: Predicting patterns of use and abuse. *Journal of Personality and Social Psychology, 51,* 790–796.

Huston, T. L. (1973). Ambiguity of acceptance, social desirability, and dating choice. *Journal of Experimental Social Psychology, 9,* 32–42.

Huston, T. L., Ruggiero, M., Connor, R., & Geis, G. (1981). Bystander intervention into crime: A study based on naturally occurring episodes. *Social Psychology Quarterly, 44,* 13–23.

Hyde, J. S. (1984). How large are gender differences in aggression? A developmental meta-analysis. *Developmental Psychology, 20,* 722–736.

Hyde, J. S., Fennema, E., & Lamon, S. J. (1990). Gender differences in mathematics performance: A meta-analysis. *Psychological Bulletin, 107,* 139–155.

Ickovics, J. R., & Rodin, J. (1992). Women and AIDS in the United States: Epidemiology, natural history, and mediating mechanisms. *Health Psychology, 11,* 1–16.

Ihimaera, W. (1973). *Tangi.* New Zealand: Secker and Warburg.

Imada, A. S., & Hakel, M. D. (1977). Influence of nonverbal communication and rater proximity on impressions and decisions in simulated employment interview. *Journal of Applied Psychology, 62,* 295–300.

Ingram, R. E., Cruet, D., Johnson, B. R., & Wisnicki, K. S. (1988). Self-focused attention, gender, gender role, and vulnerability to negative affect. *Journal of Personality and Social Psychology, 55,* 967–978.

Insko, C. A., & Schopler, J. (1987). Categorization, competition, and collectivity. In C. Hendrick (Ed.), *Group processes: Review of personality and social psychology* (Vol. 8), Newbury Park, CA: Sage.

Insko, C. A., Thibaut J., Moehle, D., Wilson, M., Dia-

mond, W. D., Gilmore, R., Soloman, M. K., & Lipsitz, A. (1980). Social evolution and the emergence of leadership. *Journal of Personality and Social Psychology, 39,* 431–449.

Isen, A. M. (1970). Success, failure, attention, and reactions to others: The warm glow of success. *Journal of Personality and Social Psychology, 15,* 294–301.

Isen, A. M., Clark, M., & Schwartz, M. F. (1976). Duration of the effect of good mood on helping: "Footprints on the sands of time." *Journal of Personality and Social Psychology, 34,* 385–393.

Isen, A. M., & Levin, P. F. (1972). The effect of feeling good on helping: Cookies and kindness. *Journal of Personality and Social Psychology, 21,* 284–288.

Isen, A. M., & Simmonds, S. F. (1978). The effect of feeling good on a helping task that is incompatible with good mood. *Social Psychology, 41,* 346–349.

Isenberg, D. J. (1986). Group polarization: A critical review and meta-analysis. *Journal of Personality and Social Psychology, 50,* 1141–1151.

Ito, T. A., Miller, N., & Pollock, V. E. (1996). Alcohol and aggression: A meta-analysis on the moderating effects of inhibitory cues, triggering events and self-focused attention. *Psychological Bulletin, 120,* 60–82.

Jackson, J. M. (1987). Social impact theory. In B. Mullen & G. R. Goethals (Eds.), *Theories of group behavior.* New York: Springer-Verlag.

Jackson, J. M., & Latané, B. (1981). All alone in front of all those people: Stage fright as a function of number and type of co-performance and audience. *Journal of Personality and Social Psychology, 40,* 73–85.

Jacobs, T. O. (1971). *Leadership and exchange in formal organizations.* Alexandria, VA: Human Resources Research Organization.

James, B. (1988). *The Bill James historical baseball abstract.* New York: Villard.

James, K. (1986). Priming and social categorizational factors: Impact on awareness of emergency situations. *Personality and Social Psychology Bulletin, 12,* 462–467.

James, W. (1890). *Psychology.* New York: Holt.

Janis, I. L. (1972). *Victims of groupthink: A psychological study of foreign policy decisions and fiascoes.* Boston, MA: Houghton Mifflin.

Janis, I. L. (1982). *Groupthink* (2nd ed.), Boston, MA: Houghton-Mifflin.

Janis, I. L., & Feshbach, S. (1953). Effects of fear-arousing communications. *Journal of Abnormal and Social Psychology, 48,* 78–92.

Janis, I. L., Kaye, D., & Kirschner, P. (1965). Facilitating effects of "eating while reading" on responsiveness to persuasive communications. *Journal of Personality and Social Psychology, 1,* 181–186.

Janis, I. L., & Mann, L. (1977). *Decision making: A psychological analysis of conflict, choice, and commitment.* New York: Free Press.

Jaynes, G. D., & Williams, R. M., Jr. (Eds.). (1989). *A common destiny: Blacks and American Society.* Washington, DC: National Academy Press.

Jemmott, J. B., Jemmott, L. S., & Fong, G. T. (1992). Reductions in HIV risk-associated sexual behaviors among Black male adolescents: Effects of an AIDS prevention intervention. *American Journal of Public Health, 82,* 372–377.

Jemmott, J. B., Jemmott, L. S., Spears, H., Hewitt, N., & Cruz-Collins, M. (1992). Self-efficacy, hedonistic expectancies, and condom-use intentions among inner-city Black adolescent women: A social cognitive approach to AIDS risk behavior. *Journal of Adolescent Health, 13,* 512–519.

Jessop, D. J. (1982). Topic variation in levels of agreement between parents and adolescents. *Public Opinion Quarterly, 46,* 538–559.

John, M., Eckardt, G., & Hiebsch, H. (1989). Kurt Lewin's early intentions (Dedicated to his 100th birthday), *European Journal of Social Psychology, 19,* 163–169.

John, O. P., & Robins, R. W. (1994). Accuracy and bias in self-perception: Individual differences in self-enhancement and the role of narcissism. *Journal of Personality and Social Psychology, 66,* 206–219.

Johnson, C., & Mullen, B. C. (1994). Evidence for the accessibility of paired distinctiveness in distinctiveness-based illusory correlation in stereotyping. *Personality and Social Psychology Bulletin, 20,* 65–70.

Johnson, J. T., & Boyd, K. R. (1995). Dispositional traits versus the content of experience: Actor/observer differences in judgments of the "authentic self." *Personality and Social Psychology Bulletin, 21,* 375–383.

Johnson, J. T., Boyd, K. R., & Magnani, P. S. (1994). Causal reasoning in the attribution of rare and common events. *Journal of Personality and Social Psychology, 66,* 229–242.

Johnson, R. C., Danko, G. P., Darvill, T. J., & Bochner, S. (1989). Cross-cultural assessment of altruism and its correlates. *Personality and Individual Differences, 15,* 855–868.

Johnson, R. C., & Ogasawara, G. M. (1988). Within and across-group dating in Hawaii. *Social Biology, 35,* 103–109.

Johnson, R. D., & Downing, L. L. (1979). Deindividuation and violence of cues: Effects of prosocial and antisocial behavior. *Journal of Personality and Social Psychology, 37,* 1532–1538.

Johnson, R. J., Feigenbaum, R., & Weiby, M. (1964). Some determinants and consequences of teachers' perceptions of causation. *Journal of Educational Psychology, 55,* 237–246.

Jones, E. E. (1964). *Ingratiation.* New York: Irvington.

Jones, E. E. (1985). Major developments in social psychology during the past five decades. In G. Lindzey & E. Aronson (Eds.), *Handbook of social psychology* (3rd ed., Vol. 1, pp. 1–46). New York: Random House.

Jones, E. E., & Archer, R. L. (1976). Are there special effects of personalistic self-disclosure? *Journal of Experimental Social Psychology, 12,* 180–193.

Jones, E. E., Bell, L., & Aronson, E. (1972). The reciprocation of attraction from similar and dissimilar others: A study in person perception and evaluation. In C. C. McClintock (Ed.), *Experimental social psychology.* New York: Holt, Rinehart and Winston.

Jones, E. E., & Berglas, S. (1978). Control of attributions about the self through self-handicapping strategies: The appeal of alcohol and the role of underachievement. *Personality and Social Psychology Bulletin, 4*(2), 200–206.

Jones, E. E., & Davis, K. E. (1965). From acts to dispositions: The attribution process in person perception. In L. Berkowitz (Ed.), *Advances in experimental social psychology* (Vol. 2). New York: Academic Press.

Jones, E. E., Farina, A., Hastorf, A. H., Markus, H., Miller, D. T., & Scott, R. A. (1984). *Social stigma: The psychology of marked relationships.* New York: Freeman.

Jones, E. E., Gergen, K. J., & Jones, R. G. (1964). Tactics of ingratiation among leaders and subordinates in a status hierarchy. *Psychological Monographs, 77*(3) (Whole no. 566).

Jones, E. E., & Gordon, E. M. (1972). Timing of self-disclosure and its effects on personal attraction. *Journal of Personality and Social Psychology, 24,* 358–365.

Jones, E. E., & Jones, R. G. (1964). Optimum conformity as an ingratiation tactic. *Journal of Personality, 32,* 436–458.

Jones, E. E., & Nisbett, R. E. (1971). *The actor and the observer: Divergent perceptions of the causes of behavior.* Morristown, NJ: General Learning Press.

Jones, E. E., & Pittman, T. S. (1982). Toward a general theory of strategic self presentation. In J. M. Suls (Ed.), *Psychological perspectives on the self.* Hillsdale, NJ: Erlbaum.

Jones, E. E., Rhodewalt, F., Berglas, S., & Skelton, J. A. (1981). Effects of strategic self-presentation on subsequent self-esteem. *Journal of Personality and Social Psychology, 41,* 407–421.

Jones, E. E., Wood, G. C., & Quattrone, G. A. (1981). Perceived variability of personal characteristics of in-groups and out-groups: The role of knowledge and evaluation. *Personality and Social Psychology Bulletin, 7,* 523–528.

Jones, E. E., & Wortman, C. (1973). *Ingratiation: An attributional approach.* Morristown, NJ: General Learning Press.

Jones, R. A., & Brehm, J. W. (1970). Persuasiveness of one- and two-sided communications as a function of awareness there are two sides. *Journal of Experimental Social Psychology, 6,* 47–56.

Jones, V. (1948). *The Hatfields and the McCoys.* Chapel Hill: University of North Carolina Press.

Josephson, W. (1987). Television violence and children's aggression: Testing the priming, social script, and disinhibition predictions. *Journal of Personality and Social Psychology, 53,* 882–890.

Jourard, S. M. (1971). *The transparent self* (2nd ed.). New York: Van Nostrand Reinhold.

Judd, C. M., & Park, B. (1988). Out-group homogeneity: Judgments of variability at the individual and group levels. *Journal of Personality and Social Psychology, 54,* 778–788.

Julian, J. W., Regula, C. R., & Hollander, E. P. (1968). Effects of prior agreement from others on task confidence and conformity. *Journal of Personality and Social Psychology, 9,* 171–178.

Jussim, L. (1991). Social perception and social reality: A reflection-construction model. *Psychological Review, 98,* 54–73.

Jussim, L., Eccles, J., & Madon, S. (1996). Social perception, social stereotypes, and teacher expectations: Accuracy and the quest for the powerful self-fulfilling prophecy. In M. P. Zanna (Ed.), *Advances in experimental social psychology* (Vol. 28). Boston, MA: Academic Press.

Kahn, A., & Tice, T. (1973). Returning a favor and retaliating harm: The effects of stated intentions and actual behavior. *Journal of Experimental Social Psychology, 9,* 43–56.

Kahneman, D., & Tversky, A. (1973). On the psychology of prediction. *Psychological Review, 80,* 237–251.

Kahneman, D., & Tversky, A. (1982). The simulation heuristic. In D. Kahneman, P. Slovic, & A. Tversky (Eds.), *Judgment under uncertainty: Heuristics and biases* (pp. 201–208). New York: Cambridge University Press.

Kalmuss, D. (1984). The intergenerational transmission of marital aggression. *Journal of Marriage and Family, 47,* 11–19.

Kameda, T., & Sugimori, S. (1995). Procedural influence in two-step group decision making: Power of local majorities in consensus formation. *Journal of Personality and Social Psychology, 69,* 865–876.

Kaplan, M. F. (1987). The influencing process in group decision making. In C. Hendrick (Ed.), *Group processes* (pp. 189–212). Newbury Park, CA: Sage.

Karasawa, K. (1995). An attributional analysis of reactions to negative emotions. *Personality and Social Psychology Bulletin, 21,* 456–467.

Karau, S. J., & Williams, K. D. (1993). Social loafing: A meta-analytic review and theoretical integration. *Journal of Personality and Social Psychology, 65,* 681–706.

Kardes, F. R., Sanbonmatsu, D. M., Voss, R. T., & Fazio, R. H. (1986). Self-monitoring and attitude accessibility. *Personality and Social Psychology Bulletin, 12,* 468–474.

Karlin, M., Coffman, J., & Walters, G. (1969). On the fading of social stereotypes: Studies in three generations of college students. *Journal of Personality and Social Psychology, 13,* 1–16.

Karney, J. R., Bradbury, T. N., Fincham, F. D., & Sullivan, K. T. (1994). The role of negative affectivity in the association between attributions and marital satisfaction. *Journal of Personality and Social Psychology, 66,* 413–424.

Karuzza, J., Jr., & Brickman, P. (1981). Preference for similarity in higher and lower status others. *Personality and Social Psychology Bulletin, 7,* 504–508.

Kashima, Y., & Triandis, H. (1986). The self-serving bias in attribution as a coping strategy: A cross-cultural study. *Journal of Cross-Cultural Psychology, 17,* 83–97.

Katz, D. (1960). The functional approach to the study of attitudes. *Public Opinion Quarterly, 24,* 163–204.

Katz, D., & Braly, K. W. (1933). Racial stereotypes of 100 college students. *Journal of Abnormal and Social Psychology, 28,* 280–290.

Katz, D., & Kahn, R. L. (1978). *The social psychology of organizations* (2nd ed.). New York: Wiley.

Katz, I., & Hass, R. G. (1988). Racial ambivalence and American value conflict: Correlational and priming studies of dual cognitive structures. *Journal of Personality and Social Psychology, 55,* 893–905.

Keating, C. F., & Heltman, K. R. (1994). Dominance and deception in children and adults: Are leaders the best misleaders? *Personality and Social Psychology Bulletin, 20,* 312–321.

Kelley, H. H. (1950). The warm-cold variable in first impressions. *Journal of Personality, 18,* 431–439.

Kelley, H. H. (1952). Two functions of reference groups. In G. E. Swanson, T. M. Newcomb, & E. L. Hartley (Eds.), *Readings in social psychology* (2nd ed.). New York: Holt, Rinehart and Winston.

Kelley, H. H. (1967). Attribution theory in social psychology. In D. Levine (Ed.), *Nebraska symposium on motivation, 15,* 192–238.

Kelley, H. H. (1972). Attribution in social interaction. In E. E. Jones, D. E. Kanouse, H. H. Kelley, R. E. Nisbett, S. Valins, & B. Weiner (Eds.), *Attribution: Perceiving the causes of behavior.* Morristown, NJ: General Learning Press.

Kelley, H. H. (1997). The "stimulus field" for interpersonal phenomena: The source of language and thought about interpersonal events. *Personality and Social Psychology Review, 1,* 140–169.

Kelley, H. H., & Thibaut, J. W. (1978). *Interpersonal relations: A theory of interdependence.* New York: Wiley Interscience.

Kelly, J. A., St. Lawrence, J. S., & Brasfield, T. L. (1991). Predictors of vulnerability to AIDS risk behavior relapse. *Journal of Consulting and Clinical Psychology, 59,* 163–166.

Kelly, J. G., Ferson, J. E., & Holtzman, W. H. (1958). The measurement of attitudes toward the Negro in the South. *Journal of Social Psychology, 48,* 305–312.

Kelly, J. R., Jackson, J. W., & Huston-Comeaux, S. L. (1997). The effects of time pressure and task differences on influence modes and accuracy in decision-making groups. *Personality and Social Psychology Bulletin, 23,* 10–22.

Kelman, H. C. (1961). Processes of opinion change. *Public Opinion Quarterly, 25,* 57–78.

Keltner, D. (1995). Signs of appeasement: Evidence for the distinct displays of embarrassment, amusement, and shame. *Journal of Personality and Social Psychology, 68,* 441–454.

Keneally, T. (1982). *Schindler's list.* New York: Simon and Schuster.

Kenny, D. A. (1985). Quantitative methods for social psychology. In G. Lindzey & E. Aronson (Eds.), *Handbook of social psychology* (3rd ed., Vol. 1, pp. 1–46). New York: Random House.

Kenrick, D. T., & Gutierres, S. E. (1980). Contrast effects and judgments of physical attractiveness: When beauty becomes a social problem. *Journal of Personality and Social Psychology, 38,* 131–140.

Kenrick, D. T., Gutierres, S. E., and Goldberg, L. L.

(1989). Influence of popular erotica on judgments of strangers and mates. *Journal of Experimental Social Psychology, 25,* 159–167.

Kenrick, D. T., & MacFarlane, S. W. (1986). Ambient temperature and horn honking: A field study of the heat/aggression relationship. *Environment and Behavior, 18,* 179–191.

Kenrick, D. T., Montelo, D. R., Gutierres, S. E., & Trost, M. R. (1993). Effects of physical attractiveness on affect and perceptual judgments: When social comparison overrides social reinforcement. *Personality and Social Psychology Bulletin, 19,* 195–199.

Kenrick, D. T., Neuberg, S. L., Zierk, K. L., & Krones, J. M. (1994). Evolution and social cognition: Contrast effects as a function of sex, dominance and physical attractiveness. *Personality and Social Psychology Bulletin, 20,* 210–217.

Kenrick, D. T., & Trost, M. R. (1987). A biosocial model of heterosexual relationships. In K. Kelley (Ed.), *Males, females, and sexuality: Theory and research.* Albany: SUNY Press.

Kerber, K. W. (1984). The perception of nonemergency helping situations: Costs, rewards, and the altruistic personality. *Journal of Personality, 52,* 177–187.

Kernis, M. H., Gannenmann, B. D., & Barclay, L. C. (1989). Stability and level of self-esteem as predictors of anger arousal and hostility. *Journal of Personality and Social Psychology, 56,* 1013–1022.

Kernis, M. H., & Wheeler, L. (1981). Beautiful friends and ugly strangers: Radiation and contrast effects in perception of same-sex pairs. *Personality and Social Psychology Bulletin, 7,* 224–231.

Kerr, N. L. (1983). Motivation loss in small groups: A social dilemma analysis. *Journal of Personality and Social Psychology, 45,* 819–828.

Kerr, N. L. (1992). Issue importance and group decision making. In S. Worchel, W. Wood, & J. A. Simpson (Eds.), *Group processes and productivity* (pp. 68–88). Newbury Park, CA: Sage.

Kerr, N. L., & Brunn, S. (1983). Dependability of member effort and group motivation loss: Free-rider effects. *Journal of Personality and Social Psychology, 44,* 78–94.

Kiesler, C. A., & Kiesler, S. B. (1969). *Conformity.* Reading, MA: Addison-Wesley.

Kim, U., Triandis, H., Kagitcibasi, C., Choi, S., & Yoon, G. (1994). Introduction. In Kim et al. (Eds.), *Individualism and collectivism: Theory, method, and applications.* Thousand Oaks, CA: Sage.

Kinder, D. R., & Fiske, S. T. (1986). Presidents in the public mind, In M. G. Hermann (Ed.), *Political psychology.* San Francisco, CA: Jossey-Bass.

Kinder, D. R., Peters, M. D., Ableson, R. R., & Fiske, S. T. (1980). Presidential prototypes. *Political Behavior, 2,* 315–338.

Kinder, D. R., & Sears, D. O. (1981). Prejudice and politics: Symbolic racism versus racial threats to the good life. *Journal of Personality and Social Psychology, 40,* 414–431.

King, A., & Bond, M. (1985). The Confucian paradigm of man: A sociological view. In W. Tseng, D. Wu (Eds.).

Chinese culture and mental health (pp. 29–46). New York: Academic Press.

King, C. (1969). *My life with Martin Luther King, Jr.* New York: Holt, Rinehart and Winston.

Kipnis, D. M. (1974). Inner direction, other direction and achievement motivation. *Human Development, 17,* 321–343.

Kirkpatrick, L. A., & Hazan, C. (1994). Attachment styles and close relationships: A four-year prospective study. *Personal Relationships, 1,* 165–184.

Kitayama, S., & Markus, H. (1990, August). *Culture and emotion: The role of other-focused emotions.* Paper presented at 98th Convention of American Psychological Association, Boston, MA.

Kitayama, S., & Markus, H. (1994). *Emotion and culture.* Washington, DC: American Psychological Association.

Kleinke, C. L., & Kahn, M. L. (1980). Perceptions of self-disclosers: Effects of sex and physical attractiveness. *Journal of Personality, 48,* 190–205.

Knight, G. P., Fabes, R. A., & Higgins, D. A. (1996). Concerns about drawing causal inferences from meta-analyses: An example in the study of gender differences in aggression. *Psychological Bulletin, 119,* 410–421.

Knox, R. E., & Safford, R. K. (1976). Group caution at the racetrack. *Journal of Experimental Social Psychology, 12,* 317–324.

Kobasa, S. C. (1979). Stressful life events, personality, and health: An inquiry into hardiness. *Journal of Personality and Social Psychology, 37,* 1–11.

Koch, H. (1940). *The panic broadcast: Portrait of an event.* Princeton, NJ: Princeton University Press.

Koestner, R., Zuckerman, M., & Koestner, J. (1989). Attributional focus of praise and children's intrinsic motivation: The moderating role of gender. *Personality and Social Psychology Bulletin, 15,* 61–72.

Kolditz, T. A., & Arkin, R. M. (1982). An impression management interpretation of the self-handicapping strategy. *Journal of Personality and Social Psychology, 43,* 492–502.

Kraft, M. (1992). *Inner peace, world peace: Essays on Buddhism and nonviolence.* Albany: SUNY Press.

Kring, A. M., Smith, D. A., & Neale, J. M. (1994). Individual differences in dispositional expressiveness: Development and validation of the emotional expressivity scale. *Journal of Personality and Social Psychology, 66,* 934–949.

Kriss, M., Indenbaum, E., & Tesch, F. (1974). Message type and status of interactants as determinants of telephone helping behavior. *Journal of Personality and Social Psychology, 30,* 856–859.

Krueger, J., & Clement, R. W. (1994). The truly false consensus effect: An ineradicable and egocentric bias in social perception. *Journal of Personality and Social Psychology, 67,* 596–610.

Kudirka, N. (1965). Defiance of authority under peer influence. (Doctoral dissertation, Yale University). *Dissertation Abstracts, 26,* 4103.

Kulik, J. A., & Mahler, H. I. M. (1989). Stress and affiliation in a hospital setting: Preoperative roommate preferences. *Personality and Social Psychology Bulletin, 15,* 183–193.

Kunda, Z., & Oleson, K. C. (1997). When exceptions prove the rule: How extremity of deviance determines the impact of deviant examples on stereotypes. *Journal of Personality and Social Psychology, 72,* 965–979.

Kunst-Wilson, W. R., & Zajonc, R. B. (1980). Affective discrimination of stimuli that cannot be recognized. *Science, 207,* 557–558.

Kuo, Zing Yang. (1930). The genesis of the cat's response to the rat. *Journal of Comparative Psychology, 11,* 1–35.

La France, M., & Hecht, M. A. (1995). Why smiles generate leniency. *Personality and Social Psychology Bulletin, 21,* 207–214.

Landy, D., & Aronson, E. (1969). The influence of the character of the criminal and his victim on the decisions of simulated jurors. *Journal of Experimental Social Psychology, 5,* 141–152.

Landy, D., & Sigall, H. (1974). Beauty is talent: Task evaluation as a function of the performer's physical attractiveness. *Journal of Personality and Social Psychology, 29,* 299–304.

Langer, E. J. (1981). Old age: An artifact? In J. McGaush & S. Kiesler (Eds.), *Aging: Biology and behavior.* New York: Academic Press.

Langer, E. J. (1989). Minding matters: The consequences of mindlessness-mindfulness. In L. Berkowitz (Ed.), *Advances in experimental social psychology* (Vol. 22, pp. 137–173). New York: Academic Press.

Langlois, J. H., & Stephan, C. W. (1981). Beauty and the beast: The role of physical attractiveness in the development of peer relations and social behavior. In S. S. Brehm, S. M. Kassin, & F. X. Gibbons (Eds.), *Development social psychology.* New York: Oxford University Press.

Langlois, J. H., & Roggman, C. A. (1990). Attractive faces are only average. *Psychological Science, 1,* 115–121.

Langlois, J. H., Roggman, L. A., & Musselman, L. (1994). What is average and what is not average about attractive faces? *Psychological Science, 5,* 214–220.

LaPiere, R. T. (1934). Attitudes vs. actions. *Social Forces, 13,* 230–237.

Larson, J. R., Jr., Christensen, C., Abbott, A. S., & Franz, T. M. (1996). Diagnosing groups: Charting the flow of information in medical decision-making teams. *Journal of Personality and Social Psychology, 71,* 315–329.

Larson, J. R., Jr., Foster-Fishman, P. G., & Keys, C. B. (1994). Discussion of shared and unshared information in decision-making groups. *Journal of Personality and Social Psychology, 67,* 446–461.

Lassiter, G. D., Stone, J. I., & Weigold, M. F. (1987). Effect of leading questions on the self-monitoring-memory correlation. *Personality and Social Psychology Bulletin, 13,* 537–545.

Latané, B. (1981). The psychology of social impact. *American Psychologist, 36,* 343–356.

Latané, B. & Darley, J. M. (1970). *The unresponsive bystander: Why doesn't he help?* Englewood Cliffs, NJ: Prentice-Hall.

Latané, B., Nowak, A., & Liu, J. H. (1994). Measuring emergent social phenomena: Dynamism, polarization and clustering as order parameters of social systems. *Behavioral Science, 39,* 1–24.

Laughlin, P. R., & Earley, C. (1982). Social combination models, persuasive arguments theory, social comparison theory, and choice shift. *Journal of Personality and Social Psychology, 42,* 273–281.

Leary, T. (1957). *Interpersonal diagnosis of personality.* New York: Ronald Press.

LeBon, G. (1895, 1969). *The crowd: A study of the popular mind.* New York: Ballantine.

Lécuyer, R. (1976). Man's accommodation to space, man's accommodation of space. *Travail Humain, 39,* 195–206.

Lefcourt, H. M. (1982). *Locus of control: Current trends in theory and research* (2nd ed.). Hillsdale, NJ: Erlbaum.

Leonard, K. E., & Taylor, S. P. (1983). Exposure to pornography, permissive and nonpermissive cues, and male aggression toward females. *Motivation and Emotion, 7,* 291–299.

Lepper, M. R., Greene, D., & Nisbett, R. E. (1973). Undermining children's intrinsic interest with extrinsic reward: A test of the overjustification hypothesis. *Journal of Personality and Social Psychology, 28,* 129–137.

Lerner, M. J. (1980). *The belief in a just world: A fundamental delusion.* New York: Plenum.

Lerner, M. J., & Miller, D. T. (1978). Just world research and the attribution process: Looking back and ahead. *Psychological Bulletin, 85,* 1030–1051.

Levenson, R., Ekman, P., Heider, K., & Friesen, W. (1992). Emotion and autonomic nervous system activity in the Minangkabau of West Sumatra. *Journal of Personality and Social Psychology, 62,* 972–988.

Levine, R., Sato, S., Hashomoto, T., & Verman, J. (1995). Love and marriage in eleven cultures. *Journal of Cross-cultural Psychology, 26,* 554–571.

Levine, S. V. (1984). *Radical departures: Desperate detours to growing up.* San Diego, CA: Harcourt Brace Jovanovich.

Lewin, K. (1935). *A dynamic theory of personality.* New York: McGraw-Hill.

Lewin, K. (1943). Forces behind food habits and methods of change. *Bulletin of the National Research Council, 108,* 35–65.

Lewin, K. (1948). *Resolving social conflicts: Selected papers on group dynamics.* New York: Harper.

Lewin, K., Lippitt, R., & White, R. (1939). Patterns of aggressive behavior in experimentally created social climates. *Journal of Social Psychology, 10,* 271–299.

Lieberman, M. A., Yalom, I. D., & Miles, M. B. (1973). *Encounter groups: First facts.* New York: Basic Books.

Liebowitz, M. R. (1983). Patient's dramatic mood swings present challenge for therapist. *Hospital and Community Psychiatry, 34,* 305–308.

Lightdale, J. R., & Prentice, D. A. (1994). Rethinking sex differences in aggression: Aggressive behavior in the absence of social roles. *Personality and Social Psychology Bulletin, 20,* 34–44.

Likert, R. (1932). A technique for the measurement of attitudes. *Archives of Psychology, 140,* 5–53.

Lind, E., & Tyler, T. (1988). *The social psychology of procedural justice.* New York: Plenum Press.

Lindskold, S. (1986). GRIT: Reducing distrust through carefully introduced conciliation. In S. Worchel & W. G. Austin (Eds.), *The psychology of intergroup relations.* Chicago: Nelson-Hall.

Lindskold, S., & Aronoff, J. R. (1980). Conciliatory strategies and relative power. *Journal of Experimental Social Psychology, 16,* 187–198.

Linville, P. W. (1982). The complexity-extremity effect and age-based stereotyping. *Journal of Personality and Social Psychology, 42,* 193–211.

Linville, P. W. (1987). Self-complexity as a cognitive buffer against stress-related illness and depression. *Journal of Personality and Social Psychology, 52,* 663–676.

Linville, P. W., & Jones, E. E. (1980). Polarized appraisals of outgroup members. *Journal of Personality and Social Psychology, 38,* 689–703.

Linz, D., Donnerstein, E., & Adams, S. M. (1989). Physiological desensitization and judgments about female victims. *Human Communication Research, 15,* 509–522.

Litt, M. D. (1988). Self-efficacy and perceived control: Cognitive mediators of pain tolerance. *Journal of Personality and Social Psychology, 54,* 149–160.

Locher, P., Unger, R., Sociedade, P., & Wahl, J. (1993). At first glance: Accessibility of the physical attractiveness stereotype. *Sex Roles, 28,* 729–742.

Lofland, J., & Stark, R. (1965). Becoming a world saver: A theory of conversion to a deviant perspective. *American Sociological Review, 30,* 862–874.

Loftus, G. (1996). Psychology will be a much better science when we change the way we analyze data. *Current Directions in Psychological Science, 5,* 161–171.

Lonner, W. (1980). The search for psychological universals. In H. Triandis & W. Lambert (Eds.), *Handbook of cross-cultural psychology* (Vol. 1). Boston: Allyn & Bacon.

Lord, C. G., Ross, L., & Lepper, M. R. (1979). Biased assimilation and attitude polarization: The effects of prior theories on subsequently considered evidence. *Journal of Personality and Social Psychology, 37,* 2098–2109.

Lorenz, K. (1968). *On aggression.* New York: Harcourt, Brace & World.

Loretto, R., & Williams, D. (1974). Personality, behavioral and output variables in a small group task situation: An examination of consensual leader and nonleader differences. *Canadian Journal of Behavioral Science, 6,* 59–74.

Lott, A. J., & Lott, B. E. (1968). A learning theory approach to interpersonal attitudes. In A. G. Greenwald, T. C. Brock, & T. M. Ostrom (Eds.), *Psychological foundations of attitudes.* New York: Academic Press.

Lott, A. J., & Lott, B. E. (1974). The role of reward in the formation of positive interpersonal attitudes. In T. Huston (Ed.), *Foundations of interpersonal attraction.* New York: Academic Press.

Lott, B. E., & Lott, A. J. (1985). Learning theory in contemporary social psychology. In G. Lindzey & E. Aronson (Eds.), *Handbook of social psychology* (3rd ed., Vol. 1, pp. 1–46). New York: Random House.

Lovdal, L. T. (1989). Sex role messages in television commercials: An update. *Sex Roles, 21,* 715–724.

Lublin, J. (1990). Companies use cross-cultural training to help their employees abroad. *Wall Street Journal.*

Lynch, J. G., Jr., & Cohen, J. (1978). The use of subjective expected utility theory as an aid to understanding variables that influence helping behavior. *Journal of Personality and Social Psychology, 36,* 1138–1151.

Lyon, D., & Greenberg, J. (1991). Evidence of co-dependency in women with an alcoholic parent: Helping out Mr. Wrong. *Journal of Personality and Social Psychology, 61,* 435–439.

Ma, V., & Schoeneman, T. (1997). Individualism versus collectivism: A comparison of Kenyan and American self-concepts. *Basic and Applied Social Psychology, 19,* 261–273.

Maass, A., & Clark, R. D. (1984). Hidden input of minorities: Fifteen years of minority influence research. *Psychological Bulletin, 95,* 428–450.

Maass, A., & Volpato, C. (1989, June). *Theoretical perspectives on minority influence: Conversion vs. divergence.* Paper presented at the Third Workshop on Minority Influence, Perugia, Italy.

Macauley, J. (1970). A skill for charity. In J. Macauley & L. Berkowitz (Eds.), *Altruism and helping behavior: Social psychological studies of some antecedents and consequences.* New York: Academic Press.

Maccoby, E. E. (1990). Gender and relationships: A developmental account. *American Psychologist, 45,* 513–520.

Maccoby, E. E., & Jacklin, C. N. (1974). *The psychology of sex differences.* Palo Alto, CA: Stanford University Press.

MacDonald, T. K., Zanna, M. P., & Fong, G. T. (1995). Decision making in altered states: Effects of alcohol on attitudes toward drinking and driving. *Journal of Personality and Social Psychology, 68,* 973–985.

MacDonald, T. K., Zanna, M. P., & Fong, G. T. (1996). Why common sense goes out the window: Effects of alcohol on intentions to use condoms. *Personality and Social Psychology Bulletin, 22,* 763–775.

MacHovec, F. J. (1989). *Cults and personality.* Springfield, IL: Charles C. Thomas.

Mackie, D. M., & Goethals, G. R. (1987). Individual and group goals. In C. Hendrick (Ed.), *Review of personality and social psychology* (Vol. 8). Newbury Park, CA: Sage.

Mackie, D. M., & Worth, L. T. (1991). Feeling good, but not thinking straight: The impact of positive mood on persuasion. In J. Forgas (Ed.), *Emotion and social judgments* (pp. 201–219). Oxford, England: Pergamon Press.

Maddux, J. E., & Rogers, R. W. (1983). Protection motivation and self-efficacy: A revised theory of fear appeals and attitude change. *Journal of Experimental Social Psychology, 19,* 469–479.

Mahoney, M. J. (1977). Publication prejudices: An experimental study of confirmatory bias in the peer review system. *Cognitive Therapy and Research, 1,* 161–175.

Maier, S. F., Seligman, M. E. P., & Solomon, R. L. (1969). Pavlovian fear conditioning and learned helplessness. In B. A. Campbell & R. M. Church (Eds.), *Punishment.* New York: Appleton-Century-Crofts.

Maio, G. R., & Olson, J. M. (1995). Relations between values, attitudes, and behavioral intentions: The moderating role of attitude function. *Journal of Experimental Social Psychology, 31,* 266–285.

Major, B. (1981). Gender patterns in touching behavior. In C. Mayo & N. Henley (Eds.), *Gender, androgyny, and nonverbal behavior.* New York: Springer-Verlag.

Major, B., Carrington, P. I, & Carnevale, P. J. D. (1984). Physical attractiveness and self-esteem. Attributions for praise from an other-sex evaluator. *Personality and Social Psychology Bulletin, 10,* 43–50.

Major, B., Cozzarelli, C., Testa, M., & McFarlin, D. B. (1988). Self-verification versus expectancy confirmation in social interaction: The impact of self-focus. *Personality and Social Psychology Bulletin, 14,* 346–359.

Malamuth, N. M. (1984). Aggression against women: Cultural and individual causes. In N. M. Malamuth & E. Donnerstein (Eds.), *Pornography and sexual aggression.* Orlando, FL: Academic Press.

Malamuth, N. M., & Check, J. V. P. (1981). The effects of mass media exposure on acceptance of violence against women: A field experiment. *Journal of Research in Personality, 15,* 436–446.

Malamuth, N., Haber, S., & Feshbach, S. (1980). Testing hypotheses regarding rape: Exposure to sexual violence, sex differences, and the "normality" of rapists. *Journal of Research in Personality, 14,* 121–127.

Malinosky-Rummell, R., & Hansen, D. J. (1993). Long-term consequences of childhood physical abuse. *Psychological Bulletin, 68–79.*

Mann, L. (1980). Cross-cultural studies of small groups. In H. Triandis & R. Brislin (Eds.), *Handbook of cross-cultural psychology* (Vol. 5). Boston: Allyn and Bacon.

Mann, R. (1959). A review of the relationship between personality and performance in small groups. *Psychological Bulletin, 56,* 241–270.

Mann, S. H. (1977). The use of social indicators in environmental planning. In I. Altman & J. R. Wohlwill (Eds.), *Human behavior and environment* (Vol. 2). New York: Plenum Press.

Markman, K. D., Gavanski, I., Sherman, S. J., & McMullen, M. N. (1995). The impact of perceived control on the imagination of better and worse possible worlds. *Personality and Social Psychology Bulletin, 21,* 588–595.

Marks, G., & Miller, N. (1987). Ten years of research on the false-consensus effect: An empirical and theoretical review. *Psychological Bulletin, 102,* 72–90.

Marks, G., Miller, N., & Maruyama, G. (1981). Effect of targets' physical attractiveness on assumptions of similarity. *Journal of Personality and Social Psychology, 41*(1), 198–206.

Markus, H., & Kitayama, S. (1991). Culture and the self: Implications for cognition, emotion, and motivation. *Psychological Review, 98,* 224–253.

Markus, H., & Kitayama, S. (1994). The cultural construction of self and emotion: Implications for social behavior. In H. Markus & S. Kitayama (Eds.), *Emotion and culture.* Washington, DC: American Psychological Association.

Markus, H., & Zajonc, R. (1985). The cognitive perspective in social psychology. In G. Lindzey & E. Aronson (Eds.), *The handbook of social psychology* (3rd ed., Vol. 1, pp. 137–230). New York: Random House.

Marques, J., Yzerbyt, V., & Leyens, J. P. (1988). The "black sheep effect": Extremity of judgment toward ingroup members as a function of identification. *European Journal of Social Psychology, 18,* 1–16.

Martin, C. L. (1987). A ratio measure of sex stereotyping. *Journal of Personality and Social Psychology, 52,* 489–499.

Martin, J., Lobb, B., Chapman, G. C., & Spillane, R. (1976). Obedience under conditions demanding self-immolation. *Human Relations, 29,* 345–356.

Martin, N. G., Eaves, L. J., Jardine, R., Heath, A. C., Feingold, L. F., & Eysenck, H. J. (1986). Transmission of social attitudes. *Proceedings of the National Academy of Sciences of the U.S.A., 83,* 4364–4368.

Martin, R. (1989, June). *Minority influence, majority influence and social identification: Some thought and contradictions.* Paper presented at the third Workshop on Minority Influence, Perugia, Italy.

Maslach, C. (1979). Negative emotional biasing of unexplained arousal. *Journal of Personality and Social Psychology, 37,* 953–969.

Maslach, C., Stapp, J., & Santee, R. (1985). Individuation: Conceptual analysis and assessment. *Journal of Personality and Social Psychology, 49,* 729–738.

Mathes, E. W., Adams, H. E., & Davies, R. M. (1985). Jealousy: Loss of relationship rewards, loss of self-esteem, depression, anxiety, and anger. *Journal of Personality and Social Psychology, 48,* 1552–1561.

Matsuda, N. (1985). Strong, quasi- and weak conformity among Japanese in a modified Asch procedure. *Journal of Cross-Cultural Psychology, 16,* 83–97.

Matsumoto, D. (1996). *Culture and psychology.* Pacific Grove, CA: Brooks/Cole.

Matsumoto, D. (1997). *Culture and modern life.* Pacific Grove, CA: Brooks/Cole.

Matsumoto, D., Kudoh, T., Scherer, K., & Wallbott, H. (1988). Antecedents and reactions to emotions in the United States and Japan. *Journal of Cross-Cultural Psychology, 19,* 267–286.

Maurer, K. L., Park, B., & Rothbart, M. (1995). Subtyping versus subgrouping processes in stereotype representation. *Journal of Personality and Social Psychology, 69,* 812–824.

Mayo, C., & Henley, N. M. (Eds.). (1981). *Gender and nonverbal behavior.* New York: Springer-Verlag.

McArthur, L. Z. (1972). The how and what of why: Some determinants and consequences of causal attribution. *Journal of Personality and Social Psychology, 22,* 171–193.

McArthur, L. Z., & Post, D. (1977). Figural emphasis and person perception. *Journal of Experimental Social Psychology, 13,* 520–535.

McCauley, C., Stitt, C. F., Woods, K., & Lipton, D. (1973). Group shift to caution at the race track. *Journal of Experimental Social Psychology, 9,* 80–86.

McClintock, C., Stech, F., & Keil, L. (1983). The influence of communication on bargaining. In P. Paulus (Ed.),

Basic group processes (pp. 205–234). New York: Springer-Verlag.

McConahay, J. B. (1986). Modern racism, ambivalence, and the Modern Racism Scale. In J. F. Dovidio & S. L. Gaertner (Eds.), *Prejudice, discrimination, and racism* (pp. 91–126). New York: Academic Press.

McCrae, R. R., & Costa, P. (1997). Personality trait structure as a human universal. *American Psychologist, 52,* 509–516.

McCrae, R. R., & Costa, P. T. (1989). The structure of interpersonal traits: Wiggins's circumplex and five-factor model. *Journal of Personality and Social Psychology, 56,* 586–595.

McCrae, R. R., Zonderman, A. B., Costa, P. T., Jr., Bond, M. H., & Paunonen, S. V. (1996). Evaluating replicability of factors in the revised NEO personality inventory: Confirmatory factor analysis versus procrustes rotation. *Journal of Personality and Social Psychology, 70,* 552–566.

McCusker, J., Stoddard, A. M., McDonald, M. Zapka, J. G., & Mayer, K. H. (1992). Maintenance of behavioral change in a cohort of homosexually active men. *AIDS, 6,* 861–868.

McDougall, W. (1908). *An introduction to social psychology.* London: Methuen.

McFarland, C., & Ross, M. (1982). Impact of causal attributions on affective reactions to success and failure. *Journal of Personality and Social Psychology, 43,* 937–946.

McGrath, J. E. (Ed.). (1988). *The social psychology of time.* Newbury Park, CA: Sage.

McGrath, J. E., & Julian, J. W. (1963). Interaction process and task outcome in experimentally created negotiation groups. *Journal of Psychological Studies, 14,* 117–138.

McGuire, W. J. (1968a). Personality and attitude change: An information processing theory. In A. G. Greenwald, T. C. Brock, & T. M. Ostrom (Eds.), *Psychological foundations of attitudes* (pp. 171–196). New York: Academic Press.

McGuire, W. J. (1968b). Personality and susceptibility to social influence. In E. F. Borgatta & W. W. Lambert (Eds.), *Handbook of personality theory and research* (pp. 1130–1187). Chicago: Rand-McNally.

McGuire, W. J. (1969). The nature of attitudes and attitude change. In G. Lindzey & E. Aronson (Eds.), *Handbook of social psychology* (2nd ed., Vol. 3, pp. 136–314). Reading, MA: Addison-Wesley.

McGuire, W. J. (1972). Attitude change: The information-processing paradigm. In C. G. McClintock (Ed.), *Experimental social psychology* (pp. 108–141). New York: Holt, Rinehart, and Winston.

McGuire, W. J. (1985). Attitudes and attitude change. In G. Lindzey & E. Aronson (Eds.), *Handbook of social psychology* (3rd ed., Vol. 2). New York: Random House.

McGuire, W. J., & McGuire, C. V. (1981). The spontaneous self-concept as affected by seasonal distinctiveness. In M. D. Lynch, A. Norem-Hebeisen, & K. J. Gergen (Eds.), *Self-concept: Advances in theory and research.* Cambridge, MA: Ballinger.

McGuire, W. J., McGuire, C. V., Child, P., & Fujioka, T.

(1978). Salience of ethnicity in the spontaneous self-concept as a function of one's ethnic distinctiveness in the social environment. *Journal of Personality and Social Psychology, 36,* 511–520.

McGuire, W. J., & Padawar-Singer, A. (1976). Trait salience in the spontaneous self-concept. *Journal of Personality and Social Psychology, 33,* 743–754.

McNulty, S. E., & Swann, W. B., Jr. (1994). Identity negotiation in roommate relationships: The self as architect and consequence of social reality. *Journal of Personality and Social Psychology, 67,* 1012–1023.

Mead, G. H. (1934). *Mind, self and society.* Chicago: University of Chicago Press.

Medvec, V. H., Madey, S. F., & Gilovich, T. (1995). When less is more: Counterfactual thinking and satisfaction among Olympic medalists. *Journal of Personality and Social Psychology, 69,* 603–610.

Mehrabian, A. (1972). *Nonverbal communication.* Chicago: Aldine-Atherton.

Meeus, W. H., & Raaijmakers, Q. A. W. (1986). Administrative obedience: Carrying out orders to use psychological-administrative violence. *European Journal of Social Psychology, 16,* 311–324.

Meeus, W. H., & Raaijmakers, Q. A. W. (1987). Administrative obedience as a social phenomenon. In W. Doise & S. Moscovici (Eds.), *Current issues in European social psychology* (pp. 183–230). Cambridge, England: Cambridge University Press.

Meeus, W. H., & Raaijmakers, Q. A. W. (1995). Obedience in modern society: The Utrecht studies. *Journal of Social Issues, 51,* 155–176.

Megargee, E. I. (1969). Influence of sex roles on the manifestation of leadership. *Journal of Applied Psychology, 53,* 377–382.

Mehrabian, A. (1968). Relationship of attitudes to seated posture, orientation, and distance. *Journal of Personality and Social Psychology, 10,* 26–30.

Mellema, A., & Bassili, J. N. (1995). On the relationship between attitudes and values: Exploring the moderating effects of self-monitoring and self-monitoring schematicity. *Personality and Social Psychology Bulletin, 21,* 885–892.

Melburg, V., & Tedeschi, J. T. (1989). Displaced aggression: Frustration or impression management? *Environmental Journal of Social Psychology, 19,* 139–146.

Merari, A., & Friedland, N. (1985). Social psychological aspects of political terrorism. *Applied Social Psychology Annual, 6,* 185–206.

Merari, A., & Friedland, N. (1988). Negotiating with terrorists. In W. Stroebe et al. (Eds.), *The social psychology of intergroup conflict* (pp. 135–150). Berlin: Springer-Verlag.

Metalsky, G. I., Halberstadt, L. J., & Abramson, L. Y. (1987). Vulnerability to depressive mood reactions: Toward a more powerful test of the diathesis-stress and causal mediation component reformulated theory of depression. *Journal of Personality and Social Psychology, 52,* 386–393.

Mettee, D. R. (1971). Rejection of unexpected success as a function of the negative consequences of accepting success. *Journal of Personality and Social Psychology,* *17,* 332–341.

Mettee, D. R., & Aronson, E. (1974). Affective reactions to appraisal from others. In T. L. Huston (Ed.), *Foundations of interpersonal attraction.* New York: Academic Press.

Michaelson, L. K., Watson, W. E., & Black, R. H. (1989). A realistic test of individual versus group consensus decision making. *Journal of Applied Psychology, 74,* 834–839.

Michenbaum, D. H., Bowers, K. S., & Ross, R. R. (1969). A behavioral analysis of teacher expectancy effects. *Journal of Personality and Social Psychology, 13,* 306–316.

Michener, H. A., & Burt, M. R. (1974). Legitimacy as a base of social influence. In J. Tedeschi (Ed.), *Perspectives on social power.* Chicago: Aldine.

Michener, H. A., & Suchner, R. (1972). The tactical use of social power. In J. Tedeschi (Ed.), *The social influence process.* Chicago: Aldine.

Mikulincer, M. (1986). Attributional processes in the learned helplessness paradigm: Behavioral effects of global attributions. *Journal of Personality and Social Psychology, 51,* 1248–1256.

Mikulincer, M. (1995). Attachment style and the mental representation of the self. *Journal of Personality and Social Psychology, 69,* 1203–1215.

Mikulincer, M., & Nizan, B. (1988). Causal attribution, cognitive interference, and the generalization of learned helplessness. *Journal of Personality and Social Psychology, 55,* 470–478.

Milgram, S. (1963). Behavioral study of obedience. *Journal of Abnormal and Social Psychology, 67,* 376.

Milgram, S. (1965). Some conditions of obedience and disobedience to authority. *Human Relations, 18,* 57–76.

Milgram, S. (1974). *Obedience to authority.* New York: Harper and Row.

Milgram, S. (1977). *The individual in a social world.* Reading, MA: Addison-Wesley.

Milgram, S., Liberty, H. J., Toledo, R., & Wackenhut, T. (1986). Response to intrusion into waiting lines. *Journal of Personality and Social Psychology, 51,* 683–689.

Milgram, S., & Toch, H. (1968). Reply to the critics. *International Journal of Psychiatry, 6,* 294–295.

Miller, C. T. (1982). The role of performance-related similarity in social comparison of abilities: A test of the related attributes hypothesis. *Journal of Experimental Social Psychology, 18,* 513–523.

Miller, C. T. (1984). Self-schemas, gender, and social comparison: A clarification of the related attributes hypothesis. *Journal of Personality and Social Psychology, 46,* 1222–1229.

Miller, D. T., & Turnbull, W. (1986). Expectancies and interpersonal processes. *Annual Review of Psychology, 37,* 233–256.

Miller, D. T., Turnbull, W., & McFarland, C. (1988). Particularistic and universalistic evaluation in the social comparison process. *Journal of Personality and Social Psychology, 55,* 908–917.

Miller, D. T., Turnbull, W., & McFarland, C. (1990). Counterfactual thinking and social perception: Thinking about what might have been. In M. P. Zanna (Ed.),

Advances in experimental social psychology (Vol. 23, pp. 305–331). New York: Academic Press.

Miller, J. (1984). Culture and the development of everyday social explanation. *Journal of Personality and Social Psychology, 46,* 961–978.

Miller, L. C., & Kenny, D. A. (1986). Reciprocity of self-disclosure at the individual and dyadic levels: A social relations analysis. *Journal of Personality and Social Psychology, 50,* 713–719.

Miller, M. L., & Thayer, J. F. (1989). On the existence of discrete classes in personality: Is self-monitoring the correct joint to carve? *Journal of Personality and Social Psychology, 57,* 143–155.

Miller, N., & Davidson-Podogrny, G. (1987). Theoretical models of intergroup relations and the use of cooperative terms as an intervention for desegregated settings. In C. Hendrick (Ed.), *Group process and intergroup relations* (pp. 41–67). Newbury Park, CA: Sage.

Miller, N. E. (1948). Theory and experiments relating psychoanalytic displacement to stimulus-response generation. *Journal of Abnormal and Social Psychology, 43,* 155–178.

Minton, H. L. (1984). J. F. Brown's social psychology of the 1930's: A historical antecedent to the contemporary crisis in social psychology. *Personality and Social Psychology Bulletin, 10,* 7–30.

Mita, T. H., Dermer, M., & Knight, J. (1977). Reversed facial images and the mere-exposure hypothesis. *Journal of Personality and Social Psychology, 35,* 597–601.

Mizell, L. (1997). Aggressive driving. In *Aggressive driving: Three studies.* Washington, DC: AAA Foundation for Traffic Safety.

Montada, L., & Lerner, M., Jr. (Eds.). (1998). *Responses to victimizations and belief in a just world.* New York: Plenum.

Montgomery, R. L. (1989). *Social influence and conformity: A transorientational model.* Unpublished manuscript, University of Missouri—Rolla.

Moreland, R. L. (1987). The formation of small groups. In C. Hendrick (Ed.), *Group processes* (pp. 80–110). Newbury Park, CA: Sage.

Moreland, R. L., & Beach, S. R. (1992). Exposure effects in the classroom: The development of affinity among students. *Journal of Experimental Social Psychology, 28,* 255–276.

Moreland, R. L., & Levine, J. M. (1982). Socialization in small groups: Temporal changes in individual group relations. In L. Berkowitz (Ed.), *Advances in experimental social psychology* (Vol. 15). New York: Academic Press.

Moreland, R. L., & Levine, J. M. (1988). Group dynamics over time: Development and socialization in small groups. In J. E. McGrath (Ed.), *The social psychology of time* (pp. 151–181). Newbury Park, CA: Sage.

Moretti, M. M., & Higgins, E. T. (1990). Relating self-discrepancy to self-esteem: The contribution of discrepancy beyond actual-self ratings. *Journal of Experimental Social Psychology, 26,* 108–123.

Morris, M., & Peng, K. (1994). Culture and cause: American and Chinese attributions for social and physical events. *Journal of Personality and Social Psychology, 67,* 949–971.

Morris, W., Worchel, S., Bois, J., Pearson, J., Roundtree, C., Samaha, G., Wachtler, J., & Wright, S. (1976). Collective coping with stress: Group reactions to fear, anxiety, and ambiguity. *Journal of Personality and Social Psychology, 13,* 131–140.

Morse, S. J., & Gergen, K. J. (1970). Social comparison, self-consistency, and the concept of self. *Journal of Personality and Social Psychology, 16,* 149–156.

Moscovici, S. (1976). *Social influence and social changes.* London, England: Academic Press.

Moscovici, S. (1985). Social influence and conformity. In G. Lindzey & E. Aronson (Eds.), *The handbook of social psychology* (3rd ed., Vol. 2., pp. 347–412). New York: Random House.

Moscovici, S., & Doise, W. (1994). *Conflict and consensus.* London, England: Sage.

Moscovici, S., & Mugny, G. (1983). Minority influence. In P. Paulus (Ed.), *Basic group process.* New York: Springer-Verlag.

Moscovici, S., & Nemeth, C. J. (1974). Minority influence. In C. J. Nemeth (Ed.), *Social psychology: Classic and contemporary integrations.* Chicago: Rand-McNally.

Moscovici, S., & Zavalloni, M. (1969). The group as a polarizer of attitudes. *Journal of Personality and Social Psychology, 12,* 125–135.

Moskowitz, D. S. (1988). Cross-situational generality in the laboratory: Dominance and friendliness. *Journal of Personality and Social Psychology, 54,* 829–839.

Moskowitz, D. S. (1994). Cross-situational generality and the interpersonal circumplex. *Journal of Personality and Social Psychology, 66,* 921–933.

Moss, M. K., & Page, R. A. (1972). Reinforcement and helping behavior. *Journal of Applied Social Psychology, 2,* 360–371.

Moya, M. (1998). Social identity and interpersonal relationships. In S. Worchel, F. Morales, D. Paez, & J. Deschamps (Eds.), *Social identity: International perspectives.* London, England: Sage.

Moyer, K. E. (1971). *The physiology of hostility.* Chicago: Markham.

Mucchi-Faina, A. (1989, June). *Minority influence processes: Assimilation, reactive differentiation, active differentiation.* Paper presented at the third Workshop on Minority Influence, Perugia, Italy.

Muhleman, J. T., Bruker, C., & Ingram, C. M. (1976). The generosity shift. *Journal of Personality and Social Psychology, 34,* 344–351.

Mullen, B. (1983). Operationalizing the effect of the group on the individual: A self-attention perspective. *Journal of Experimental Social Psychology, 19,* 295–322.

Mullen, B. (1986). Atrocity as a function of lynch mob composition: A self-attention perspective. *Personality and Social Psychology Bulletin, 12,* 187–197.

Mullen, B. (1987). Self-attention theory. In B. Mullen & G. R. Goethals (Eds.), *Theories of group behavior.* New York: Springer-Verlag.

Mullen, B., Atkins, J. L., Champion, D. S., Edwards, C., Hardy, D., Story, J. E., & Vanderklok, M. (1985). The false consensus effect: A meta-analysis of 115 hypothesis tests. *Journal of Experimental Social Psychology, 21,* 262–283.

Mullen, B., & Goethals, G. R. (1990). Short note: Social projection, actual consensus, and valence. *British Journal of Social Psychology.*

Mullin, C. R., & Linz, D. (1995). Desensitization and resensitization to violence against women: Effects of exposure to sexually violent films on judgments of domestic violence victims. *Journal of Personality and Social Psychology, 69,* 449–459.

Mummendey, A., & Otten, S. (1989). Perspective-specific differences in the segmentation and evaluation of aggressive interaction sequences. *European Journal of Social Psychology, 19,* 23–40.

Myer, T. (1972). The effect of sexually arousing and violent films on aggressive behavior. *Journal of Sex Research, 8,* 324–333.

Myers, D. G. (1982). Polarizing effects of social interaction. In H. Brandstatter, J. H. Davis, & G. Stocker-Kreichgauer (Eds.), *Group decision processes.* London, England: Academic Press.

Myers, D. G. (1983). *Social Psychology.* New York: McGraw-Hill.

Nadler, A., & Fisher, J. D. (1986). The role of threat to self-esteem and perceived control in recipient reactions to help: Their development and empirical validation. In L. Berkowitz (Ed.), *Advances in experimental social psychology* (Vol. 19). Orlando, FL: Academic Press.

Nahemow, L., & Lawton, M. P. (1975). Similarity and propinquity in friendship formation. *Journal of Personality and Social Psychology, 32,* 205–213.

Napolitan, D. A., & Goethals, G. R. (1979). The attribution of friendliness. *Journal of Experimental Social Psychology, 15,* 105–113.

National Coalition on Television Violence. (1990 July–September). *NCTV News* (Vol. 2). Champaign, IL: Author.

Nemeth, C. (1986). Differential contributions of majority and minority influence. *Psychological Review, 93,* 1–10, 23–32.

Nemeth, C. (1989, June). *The stimulating properties of dissent: The case for recall.* Paper presented at the third Workshop on Minority Influence, Perugia, Italy.

Nemeth, C., & Chiles, C. (1988). Modeling courage: The role of dissent in fostering independence. *European Journal of Social Psychology, 18,* 275–280.

Nemeth, C., & Staw, B. M. (1989). The tradeoffs of social control and innovation in groups and organizations. In L. Berkowitz (Ed.), *Advances in experimental social psychology* (Vol. 23, pp. 175–210). Orlando, FL: Academic Press.

Neuberg, S. L. (1989). The goal of forming accurate impressions during social interactions: Attenuating the impact of negative expectancies. *Journal of Personality and Social Psychology, 56,* 374–386.

Neuberg, S. L. (1994). Expectancy-confirmation processes in stereotype-tinged social encounters: The moderating role of social goals. In M. P. Zanna & J. M. Olson

(Eds.), *The psychology of prejudice: The Ontario symposium on personality and social psychology* (Vol. 7, pp. 103–130). Hillsdale, NJ: Erlbaum.

Neuberg, S. L., Cialdini, R. B., Brown, S. L., Sagarin, B. J., & Lewis, B. P. (1997). Does empathy lead to anything more than superficial helping? Comment on Batson et al. (1997). *Journal of Personality and Social Psychology, 73,* 510–516.

Newcomb, T. A. (1947). Autistic hostility and social reality. *Human Relations, 1,* 69–86.

Newcomb, T. M. (1943). *Personality and social change.* New York: Dryden.

Newcomb, T. M. (1956). The prediction of interpersonal attraction. *American Psychologist, 11,* 575–586.

Newcomb, T. M. (1963). Persistence and regression of changed attitudes: Long-range studies. *Journal of Social Issues, 19,* 3–14.

Newman, L. S. (1996). Trait impressions as heuristics for predicting future behavior. *Personality and Social Psychology Bulletin, 22,* 395–411.

Newman, L. S., & Baumeister, R. F. (1996). Toward an elaboration of the U.F.O. abduction phenomenon: Hypnotic elaboration, extraterrestrial sadomasochism, and spurious memories. *Psychological Inquiry, 7,* 99–126.

Nisbett, R. E. (1993). Violence and the U.S. regional culture. *American Psychologist, 48,* 441–449.

Nisbett, R. E., & Ross, L. (1980). *Human inference: Strategies and shortcomings of social judgment.* Englewood Cliffs, NJ: Prentice-Hall.

Nisbett, R. E., Zukier, H., & Lemley, R. E. (1981). The dilution effect: Nondiagnostic information weakens the implications of diagnostic information. *Cognitive Psychology, 13,* 248–277.

Nolen-Hoeksema, S., Seligman, M. E. P., & Girgus, J. S. (1986). Learned helplessness in children: A longitudinal study of depression, achievement, and explanatory style. *Journal of Personality and Social Psychology, 51,* 435–442.

Noller, P. (1980). Misunderstandings in marital communication: A study of couples' nonverbal communication. *Journal of Personality and Social Psychology, 39,* 1135–1148.

Norman, R. (1976). When what is said is important: A comparison of expert and attractive sources. *Journal of Experimental Social Psychology, 12,* 294–300.

Nosanchuk, T. A. (1981). The ways of the warrior: The effects of traditional martial arts training on aggressiveness. *Human Relations, 34,* 435–444.

Novak, D., & Lerner, M. (1968). Rejection as a consequence of perceived similarity. *Journal of Personality and Social Psychology, 9,* 147–152.

Nowak, A., Szamrej, J., & Latané, B. (1990). From private attitude to public opinion: A dynamic theory of social impact. *Psychological Review, 97,* 362–376.

Nyquist, L. V., & Spence, J. T. (1986). Effects of dispositional dominance and sex role expectations on leadership behaviors. *Journal of Personality and Social Psychology, 50,* 87–93.

Oakes, P. J., Haslam, S., & Turner, J. (1994). *Stereotyping and social reality.* London, England: Blackwell.

Oakes, P. J., & Turner, J. C. (1980). Social categorization and intergroup behavior: Does minimal intergroup discrimination make social identity more positive? *European Journal of Social Psychology, 10,* 295–301.

Oberg, K. (1954). *Culture shock.* (The Bobbs-Merrill Reprint Series, No. A-329). Boston: Bobbs-Merrill.

Ohbuchi, K., Kameda M., & Agarie, N. (1989). Apology as aggression control: Its role in mediating appraisal of and response to harm. *Journal of Personality and Social Psychology, 56,* 219–227.

Oliner, S. P., & Oliner, P. M. (1988). *The altruistic personality: Rescuers of Jews in Nazi Europe.* New York: Free Press.

Olson, J. M., & Hafer, C. L. (1996). Affect, motivation, and cognition in relative deprivation research. In R. M. Sorrentino & E. T. Higgins (Eds.), *Handbook of motivation and cognition: The interpersonal context* (Vol. 3, pp. 85–117). New York: Guilford.

Olson, J. M., & Roese, N. J. (1995). The perceived funniness of humorous stimuli. *Personality and Social Psychology Bulletin, 21,* 908–913.

Olson, J. M., Roese, N. J., Meen, J., & Robertson, D. J. (1995). The preconditions and consequences of relative deprivation: Two field studies. *Journal of Applied Social Psychology, 25,* 944–964.

Olson, J. M., Roese, N. J., & Zanna, M. P. (1996). Expectancies. In E. T. Higgins & A. W. Kruglanski (Eds.), *Social psychology: Handbook of basic principles* (pp. 211–238). New York: Guilford.

Olson, J. M., Vernon, P. A., Harris, J., & Jang, K. (in press). The heritability of attitudes: A study of twins. *Journal of Personality and Social Psychology.*

Olson, J. M., & Zanna, M. P. (1993). Attitudes and attitude change. *Annual Review of Psychology, 44,* 117–154.

Omoto, A., & Snyder, M. L. (1990). Basic research in action: Volunteerism and society's response to AIDS. *Personality and Social Psychology Bulletin, 16,* 152–166.

Omoto, A., & Snyder, M. L. (1995). Sustained helping without obligation: Motivation, longevity of experience and perceived attitude change among AIDS volunteers. *Journal of Personality and Social Psychology, 68,* 671–686.

Organization for Economic Cooperation and Development. (1994). *Caring for frail elderly people: New directions in care.* (Social Policy Studies, No. 14). Paris: OECD Publications.

Orive, R. (1988). Social projection and social comparison of opinions. *Journal of Personality and Social Psychology, 54,* 953–964.

Orne, M. T. (1962). On the social psychology of the psychological experiment: With particular reference to demand characteristics and their implications. *American Psychologist, 17,* 776–783.

Orne, M. T., & Evans, F. J. (1965). Social control in the psychological experiment: Antisocial behavior and hypnosis. *Journal of Personality and Social Psychology, 1,* 189–200.

Orne, M. T., & Holland, C. C. (1968). On the ecological validity of laboratory deceptions. *International Journal of Psychiatry, 6,* 282–293.

Osgood, C. E. (1962). *An alternative to war or surrender.* Urbana: University of Illinois Press.

Osgood, C. E., Suci, G. J., & Tannenbaum, P. H. (1957). *The measurement of meaning.* Urbana: University of Illinois Press.

Oskamp, S. (1991). *Attitudes and opinions* (2nd ed.). Englewood Cliffs, NJ: Prentice-Hall.

Overmier, J. B., & Seligman, M. E. P. (1967). Effects of inescapable shock upon subsequent escape and avoidance learning. *Journal of Comparative and Physiological Psychology, 63,* 28–33.

Page, M., & Scheidt, R. J. (1971). The elusive weapons effect: Demand awareness, valuation apprehension, and slightly sophisticated subjects. *Journal of Personality and Social Psychology, 20,* 304–318.

Paige, R. M., & Martin, J. (1996). Ethics in intercultural training. In D. Landis & R. Bhagat (Eds.), *Handbook of intercultural training* (2nd ed.). Thousand Oaks, CA: Sage.

Pallak, S. R. (1983). Salience of a communicator's physical attractiveness and persuasion: A heuristic versus systematic processing interpretation. *Social Cognition, 2,* 158–170.

Papastamos, S., & Mugny, G. (1989, June). *Synchronic consistency and psychologization in minority influence.* Paper presented at the third Workshop on Minority Influence, Perugia, Italy.

Park, B., & Rothbart, M. (1982). Perception of out-group homogeneity and levels of social categorization: Memory for the subordinate attributes of in-group and out-group members. *Journal of Personality and Social Psychology, 42,* 1051–1068.

Parke, R., Berkowitz, L., Leyens, J. P., West, S. G., & Sebastian, R. J. (1977). Some effects of violent and nonviolent movies on the behavior of juvenile delinquents. In L. Berkowitz (Ed.), *Advances in experimental social psychology* (Vol. 10, pp. 139–169). New York: Academic Press.

Parker, R. D., Collmer, C. W. (1975). Child abuse: An interdisciplinary analysis. In M. E. Hetherington (Ed.), *Review of Child Development Research, Vol. 5.* Chicago: University of Chicago Press.

Patrick, C. J., Craig, K. D., & Prkachin, K. M. (1986). Observer judgements of acute pain: Facial action determinants. *Journal of Personality and Social Psychology, 50,* 1291–1298.

Paulhus, D. L., Shaffer, D. R., & Downing, L. L. (1977). Effects of making blood donor motives salient upon donor retention. *Personality and Social Psychology Bulletin, 3,* 99–102.

Paulus, P. (1983). Group influence on task performance and informational processing. In P. Paulus (Ed.), *Basic group processes.* New York: Springer.

Pearl, D., & Bouthliet, L. (Eds.). (1982). *Television and behavior: Ten years of scientific progress and implications for the 80's.* Washington, DC: U.S. Government Printing Office.

Pelham, B. W. (1995). Self-investment and self-esteem: Evidence for a Jamesian model of self-worth. *Journal of Personality and Social Psychology, 69,* 1141–1150.

Pendry, L. F., & Macrae, C. N. (1996). What the disinterested perceiver overlooks: Goal-directed social categorization. *Personality and Social Psychology, 22,* 249–256.

Pepitone, A. (1981). Lessons from the history of social psychology. *American Psychologist, 36,* 972–985.

Perez, J. A., & Mugny, G. (1987). Paradoxical effects of categorization in minority influence: When being an out-group is an advantage. *European Journal of Social Psychology, 17,* 157–169.

Perkins, H. W., & Berkowitz, A. D. (1986). Perceiving the community norms of alcohol use among students: Some research implications for campus alcohol education programming. *International Journal of the Addictions, 21,* 961–976.

Perlman, D., & Oskamp, S. (1971). The effects of picture content and exposure frequency on evaluations of Negroes and whites. *Journal of Experimental Social Psychology, 7,* 503–514.

Perloff, R. M. (1993). *The dynamics of persuasion.* Hillsdale, NJ: Erlbaum.

Pessin, J., & Husband, R. (1933). Effects of social stimulation on human maze learning. *Journal of Abnormal and Social Psychology, 28,* 148–154.

Peters, L. H., Hartke, D., Pohlmann, J. T. (1985). Fiedler's contingency theory of leadership: An application of the meta-analysis procedures of Schmidt and Hunter. *Psychological Bulletin, 97,* 274–285.

Peterson, C., & Barrett, L. C. (1987). Explanatory style and academic performance among college freshmen. *Journal of Personality and Social Psychology, 53,* 603–607.

Peterson, R. S., & Nemeth, C. J. (1996). Focus versus flexibility: Majority and minority influence can both improve performance. *Personality and Social Psychology Bulletin, 22,* 14–23.

Petrovsky, A. V. (1985). *Studies in psychology: The collective and the individual.* Moscow: Progress.

Pettigrew, T. F. (1978). Three issues in ethnicity: Boundaries, deprivations, and perceptions. In J. M. Yinger & S. J. Cutler (Eds.), *Major social issues: A multidisciplinary view.* New York: Free Press.

Pettigrew, T. F. (1986). The intergroup contact hypothesis reconsidered. In M. Hewstone & R. Brown (Eds.), *Contact and conflict in intergroup encounters.* Oxford, England: Basil Blackwell.

Petty, R. E., & Cacioppo, J. T. (1981). *Attitudes and persuasion: Classic and contemporary approaches.* Dubuque, IA: Brown.

Petty, R. E., & Cacioppo, J. T. (1984). The effects of involvement on responses to argument quantity and quality: Central and peripheral routes to persuasion. *Journal of Personality and Social Psychology, 46,* 69–81.

Petty, R. E., & Cacioppo, J. T. (1986). The elaboration likelihood model of persuasion. In L. Berkowitz (Ed.), *Advances in experimental social psychology* (Vol. 19, pp, 123–205). New York: Academic Press.

Petty, R. E., Cacioppo, J. T., & Goldman, R. (1981). Personal involvement as a determinant of argument-based persuasion. *Journal of Personality and Social Psychology, 41,* 847–855.

Petty, R. E., Cacioppo, J. T., & Schumann, D. (1983). Central and peripheral routes to advertising effectiveness: The moderating role of involvement. *Journal of Consumer Research, 10,* 134–148.

Petty, R. E., Wegener, D. T., & Fabrigar, L. R. (1997). Attitudes and attitude change. *Annual Review of Psychology, 48,* 609–642.

Petty, R. E., Wells, G. L., & Brock, T. C. (1976). Distraction can enhance or reduce yielding to propaganda: Thought disruption versus effort justification. *Journal of Personality and Social Psychology, 34,* 874–888.

Phares, E. J. (1984). *Introduction to personality.* Columbus, OH: Merrill.

Piliavin, I. M., Piliavin, J. A., & Rodin, J. (1975). Cost, diffusion, and the stigmatized victim. *Journal of Personality and Social Psychology, 32,* 429–438.

Piliavin, J. A., & Charng, H. W. (1990). Altruism: A review of present theory and research. *Annual Review of Sociology, 16,* 27–65.

Piliavin, J. A., Dovodio, J. F., Gaertner, S. L., & Clark, R. D., III. (1982). Responsive bystanders: The process of intervention. In V. J. Derlega & J. Grzelak (Eds.), *Cooperation and helping behavior: Theories and research.* New York: Academic Press.

Piliavin, J. A., & Unger, R. K. (1985). The helpful but helpless female: Myth or reality? In V. O'Leary, R. K. Unger, & B. S. Wallston (Eds.), *Women, gender, and social psychology* (pp. 149–190). Hillsdale, NJ: Erlbaum.

Pittman, J., Gallois, C., Iwawaki, S., & Kroonenberg, P. (1995). Australian and Japanese concepts of expressive behavior. *Journal of Cross-Cultural Psychology, 26,* 451–473.

Polk, K. (1993). Observations on stranger homicide. *Journal of Criminal Justice, 21,* 573–582.

Pomazal, R. J., & Clore, G. L. (1973). Helping on the highway: The effects of dependency and sex. *Journal of Applied Social Psychology, 3,* 150–164.

Pratkanis, A. R., & Aronson, E. (1992). *Age of propaganda: The everyday use and abuse of persuasion.* New York: Freeman.

Pratkanis, A. R., & Greenwald, A. G. (1989). A sociocognitive model of attitude structure and function. In L. Berkowitz (Ed.), *Advances in experimental social psychology* (Vol. 22, pp. 245–285). San Diego, CA: Academic Press.

Pratkanis, A. R., Greenwald, A. G., Leippe, M. R., & Baumgardner, M. H. (1988). In search of reliable persuasion effects: III. The sleeper effect is dead. Long live the sleeper effect. *Journal of Personality and Social Psychology, 54,* 203–218.

Pratto, F., & Bargh, J. A. (1991). Stereotyping based on apparently individuating information: Trait and global components of sex stereotypes under attention overload. *Journal of Experimental Social Psychology, 27,* 26–47.

Prentice, D. A., & Miller, D. T. (1993). Pluralistic ignorance and alcohol use on campus: Some consequences of misperceiving the social norm. *Journal of Personality and Social Psychology, 64,* 243–256.

Prentice, D. A., & Miller, D. T. (1996). Pluralistic ignorance and the perpetuation of social norms by unwitting actors. In M. P. Zanna (Ed.), *Advances in experimental social psychology* (Vol. 28, pp. 161–209). New York: Academic Press.

Prins, K. S., Buunk, B. P., & VanYperson, N. W. (1993). Equity, normative disapproval and extramarital relationships. *Journal of Social and Personal Relationships, 10,* 39–53.

Pruitt, D., Fry, W., Castrianno, L., Zubek, J., Welton, G., McGillicuddy, N., & Ippolito, C. (1989). The process of mediation: Caucusing, control, and problem solving. In M. Rahim (Ed.), *Managing conflict: An interdisciplinary approach.* New York: Praeger.

Pruitt, D. G. (1976). Power and bargaining. In B. Seidenberg & A. Snadowsky (Eds.), *Social psychology: An introduction.* New York: Free Press.

Pryor, J. B. (1995). The psychosocial impact of sexual harassment on women in the U.S. military. *Basic and Applied Social Psychology, 17,* 581–603.

Pryor, J. B., Lavite, C., & Stoller, L. (1993). A social psychological analysis of sexual harassment. The person/situation interaction. *Journal of Vocational Behavior, 42,* 68–83.

Pyszczynski, T., Hamilton, J. C., Herring, F. H., & Greenberg, J. (1989). Depression, self-focused attention, and the negative memory bias. *Journal of Personality and Social Psychology, 57,* 351–357.

Quattrone, G. A. (1986). On the perception of a group's variability. In S. Worchel & W. G. Austin (Eds.), *The psychology of intergroup relations* (pp. 25–48). Chicago: Nelson–Hall.

Quattrone, G. A., & Jones, E. E. (1978). Selective self-disclosure with and without correspondent performance. *Journal of Experimental Social Psychology, 14,* 511–526.

Quattrone, G. A., & Jones, E. E. (1980). The perception of variability with in-groups and out-groups: Implications for the law of small numbers. *Journal of Personality and Social Psychology, 38,* 141–152.

Quinn, K. L., & Olson, J. M. (1998). Attributional ambiguity and stigmas: Self-protective effects of minority status. Manuscript submitted for publication.

Rabbie, J. M., & Bekkers, F. (1976). Threatened leadership and intergroup competition. *Nederlands Tijdschrift voor de Psychologie en haar Grensaebieden, 31,* 269–283.

Rada, J. B., & Rogers, R. W. (1973, October). *Obedience to authority: Presence of authority and command strength.* Paper presented at the meeting of the Southwestern Psychological Association, New Orleans.

Rajecki, D. W. (1990). *Attitudes* (2nd ed.). Sunderland, MA: Sinauer.

Raven, B. H., Centers, R., & Rodrigues, A. (1975). The bases of conjugal power. In Cromwell, R. E., & Olson, D. H. (Eds.), *Power in families* (pp. 217–234). Newbury Park, CA: Sage.

Raven, B. H., & French, J. R. (1958). Legitimate power, coercive power and observability in social influence. *Sociometry, 21,* 83–97.

Raven, B. H., & Kruglanski, A. (1970). Conflict and

power. In P. Swingle (Ed.), *The structure of conflict.* New York: Academic Press.

Redding, G., & Wong, G. (1986). The psychology of Chinese organizational behavior. In M. Bond (Ed.), *The psychology of the Chinese people.* New York: Oxford University Press.

Redfield, H. V. (1880). *Homicide, north and south.* Philadelphia, PA: Lippincott.

Regan, P. C., Snyder, M., & Kassin, S. M. (1995). Unrealistic optimism: Self-enhancement or person positivity? *Personality and Social Psychology Bulletin, 21,* 1073–1082.

Reicher, S. D. (1984). The St. Paul riot: An explanation of the limits of crowd action in terms of social identity model. *European Journal of Social Psychology, 14,* 1–21.

Reicher, S. D., & Levine, M. (1994). On the consequences of deindividuation manipulations for the strategic communication of self: Identifiability and the presentation of social identity. *European Journal of Social Psychology, 24,* 511–524.

Reinisch, J. M., & Sanders, S. A. (1986). A test of sex differences in aggressive response to hypothetical conflict situations. *Journal of Personality and Social Psychology, 50,* 1045–1049.

Reis, H. T., Nezlek, J., & Wheeler, L. (1980). Physical attractiveness in social interaction. *Journal of Personality and Social Psychology, 38,* 604–617.

Reis, H. T., & Patrick, B. (1996). Attachment and intimacy: Component process. In A. Kruglanski & E. T. Higgins (Eds.), *Social psychology: Handbook of basic principles* (pp. 523–563). New York: Guilford.

Rhodewalt, F., & Hill, S. C. (1995). Self-handicapping in the classroom: The effects of claimed self-handicaps on responses to academic failure. *Basics of Applied Social Psychology, 16,* 397–416.

Rhodewalt, F., Sanbonmatsu, D. M., Tschanz, B., Feick, D. L., & Waller, A. (1995). Self-handicapping and interpersonal trade-offs: The effects of claimed self-handicaps on observers' performance evaluations and feedback. *Personality and Social Psychology, 21,* 1042–1050.

Rice, O. (1978). *The Hatfields and the McCoys.* Lexington: University of Kentucky Press.

Rice, R. W., Bender, L. R., & Vitters, A. G. (1980). Leader sex, follower attitudes toward women, and leadership effectiveness: A laboratory study. *Organizational Behavior and Human Performance, 25,* 46–78.

Rice, R. W., Instone, D., & Adams, J. (1984). Leader sex, leader success, and leadership process: Two field studies. *Journal of Applied Psychology, 69,* 12–31.

Rice, R. W., & Kastenbaum, D. R. (1983). The contingency model of leadership: Some current issues. *Basic and Applied Social Psychology, 4,* 373–392.

Rickels, K., & Downing, R. (1967). Drug- and placebo-treated neurotic outpatients. *Archives of General Psychiatry, 16,* 369–372.

Riecken, H. W. (1958). The effect of talkativeness on ability to influence group solutions of problems. *Sociometry, 21,* 309–321.

Riess, M., Rosenfeld, R., Melburg, V., & Tedeschi, J. T.

(1981). Self-preserving attributions: Biased private perceptions and distorted public descriptions. *Journal of Personality and Social Psychology, 41,* 224–231.

Riggio, R. E., Tucker J., & Throckmorton, B. (1987). Social skills and deception ability. *Personality and Social Psychology Bulletin, 13,* 568–577.

Ringelmann, M. (1913). Recherches sur les moteurs animes: Travail de l'homme. *Annale de l'Instint National Agronomigre, 2nd Series, 12,* 1–40.

Roberts, D. F., & Maccoby, N. (1985). Effects of mass communication. In G. Lindzey & E. Aronson (Eds.), *Handbook of social psychology* (3rd ed., pp. 539–598). New York: Random House.

Roberts, J. V. (1984). Selective recall for personally relevant communications. *Canadian Journal of Behavioral Science, 16,* 208–215.

Robertson, I. (1989). *Society: A brief introduction.* New York: Worth.

Robinson, J. P. (1988). Who's doing the housework? *American Demographics, 10*(12), 24–28, 63.

Roese, N. (1994). The functional basis of counterfactual thinking. *Journal of Personality and Social Psychology, 66,* 805–818.

Rogers, R. W. (1983). Cognitive and physiological processes in fear appeals and attitude change: A revised theory of protection motivation. In J. T. Cacioppo & R. E. Petty (Eds.), *Social psychophysiology: A sourcebook* (pp. 153–176). New York: Guilford.

Rogers, R. W., & Mewborn, C. R. (1976). Fear appeals and attitude change: Effects of a threat's noxiousness, probability of occurrence, and the efficacy of coping responses. *Journal of Personality and Social Psychology, 34,* 54–61.

Rogers, R. W., & Prentice-Dunn, S. (1981). Deindividuation and anger-mediated interracial aggression: Unmasking regressive racism. *Journal of Personality and Social Psychology, 41,* 63–73.

Rohan, M. J., & Zanna, M. P. (1996). Value transmission in families. In C. Seligman, J. M. Olson, & M. P. Zanna (Eds.), *The psychology of values: The Ontario symposium* (Vol. 8, pp. 233–276). Mahwah, NJ: Erlbaum.

Rook, K. (1987). Social support versus companionship: Effects of life stress, loneliness, and evaluation by others. *Journal of Personality and Social Psychology, 52,* 1132–1147.

Rosenbaum, L. L., & Rosenbaum, W. B. (1971). Morale and productivity consequences of group leadership style, stress, and type of task. *Journal of Applied Psychology, 55,* 343–348.

Rosenbaum, M. E. (1986). The repulsion hypothesis: On the nondevelopment of relationships. *Journal of Personality and Social Psychology, 51,* 1156–1166.

Rosenberg, M. (1979). *Conceiving the self.* New York: Basic Books.

Rosenhan, D. L., Salovey, P., & Hargis, K. (1981). The joys of helping: Focus of attention mediates the impact of positive effect on altruism. *Journal of Personality and Social Psychology, 40,* 899–905.

Rosenthal, A. M. (1964). *Thirty-eight witnesses.* New York: McGraw-Hill.

Rosenthal, R. (1973). The Pygmalion effect lives. *Psychology Today, 7*(4), 56–63.

Rosenthal, R., & Benowitz, L. I. (1985). Sensitivity to nonverbal communication in normal, psychiatric, and brain-damaged samples. In P. D. Blanck, R. W. Buck, & R. Rosenthal (Eds.), *Nonverbal communication in the clinical context.* University Park: Pennsylvania State University Press.

Rosenthal, R., & Evans, J. (1968). Unpublished data. Harvard University.

Rosenthal, R., & Fode, K. L. (1963). Psychology of the scientist: V. Three experiments in experimenter bias. *Psychological Reports, 12,* 491–511.

Rosenthal, R., & Jacobson, L. (1968). *Pygmalion in the classroom: Teacher expectation and pupils' intellectual development.* New York: Holt, Rinehart and Winston.

Rosenthal, R., & Rubin, D. B. (1978). Interpersonal expectancy effects: The first 345 studies. *The Behavioral and Brain Sciences, 3,* 377–386.

Ross, E. A. (1908). *Social psychology: An outline and a source book.* New York: Macmillan.

Ross, L. (1977). The intuitive psychologist and his shortcomings: Distortions in the attribution process. In L. Berkowitz (Ed.), *Advances in experimental social psychology* (Vol. 10). New York: Academic Press.

Ross, L., Bierbrauer, G., & Hoffman, S. (1976). The role of attribution processes in conformity and dissent: Revisiting the Asch situation. *American Psychologist, 31,* 148–157.

Ross, L., Greene, D., & House, P. (1977). The "false consensus effect": An egocentric bias in social perception and attribution processes. *Journal of Experimental Social Psychology, 13,* 279–301.

Ross, M. (1981). Self-centered biases in attribution of responsibility: Antecedents and consequences. In E. T. Higgins, C. P. Herman, & M. P. Zanna (Eds.), *Social cognition: The Ontario symposium* (Vol. 1). Hillsdale, NJ: Erlbaum.

Ross, M. (1989). Relation of implicit theories to the construction of personal histories. *Psychological Review, 96,* 341–357.

Ross, M., & Fletcher, G. J. O. (1985). Attribution and social perception. In G. Lindzey & E. Aronson (Eds.), *The handbook of social psychology* (3rd ed., Vol. 2). New York: Random House.

Ross, M., McFarland, C., & Fletcher, G. J. O. (1981). The effect of attitude on the recall of personal histories. *Journal of Personality and Social Psychology, 40,* 627–634.

Ross, M., & Sicoly, F. (1979). Egocentric biases in availability and attribution. *Journal of Personality and Social Psychology, 37,* 322–336.

Roth, S., & Kubal, L. (1975). Effects of noncontingent reinforcement on tasks of differing importance: Facilitation and learned helplessness. *Journal of Personality and Social Psychology, 32,* 680–691.

Rothbart, M., & Hallmark, W. (1988). In-group—out-group differences in the perceived efficacy of coercion and conciliation in resolving conflict. *Journal of Personality and Social Psychology, 55,* 248–257.

Rothbart, M., & Lewis, S. H. (1994). *Cognitive processes and intergroup relations: A historical perspective.* San Diego, CA: Academic Press.

Rothgerber, H., & Worchel, S. (1997). The view from below: Intergroup relations from the perspective of the disadvantaged group. *Journal of Personality and Social Psychology, 73,* 1191–1205.

Rotter, J. B. (1966). Generalized expectancies for internal vs. external reinforcement. *Psychological Monographs, 80*(1), Whole no. 609.

Rotter, J. B. (1971, June). External and internal control. *Psychology Today,* pp. 37–42, 58–59.

Rubin, J., Pruitt, D., & Kim, S. (1994). *Social conflict: Escalation, stalemate, and settlement.* New York: McGraw-Hill.

Rubin, J. Z., Provenzano, F. J., & Luria, Z. (1974). The eye of the beholder: Parents' views on sex of newborns. *American Journal of Orthopsychiatry, 44,* 512–519.

Rubin, Z. (1970). Measurement of romantic love. *Journal of Personality and Social Psychology, 16,* 265–273.

Rubin, Z. (1973). *Liking and loving.* New York: Holt, Rinehart and Winston.

Rubin, Z., & Peplau, L. A. (1975). Who believes in a just world? *Journal of Social Issues, 31,* 65–89.

Rubin, Z., & Schlenker, S. (1978). Friendship, proximity, and self-disclosure. *Journal of Personality, 46,* 1–22.

Ruble, D. N. (1987). The acquisition of self-knowledge: A self-socialization perspective. In N. Eisenberg (Ed.), *Contemporary topics in developmental psychology.* New York: Wiley.

Rudin, J., & Rudin, M. (1980). *Prison or paradise?: The new religious cults.* Philadelphia, PA: Fortress Press.

Rusboldt, C. E., & Zembrot, I. M. (1983). Responses to dissatisfaction in romantic involvement. *Journal of Experimental Social Psychology, 19,* 274–293.

Russo, N. E., & Denmark, F. L. (1984). Women, psychology, and public policy: Selected issues. *American Psychologist, 39,* 1161–1165.

Ryan, W. (1971). *Blaming the victim.* New York: Vintage Books.

Sabatelli, R. M., Buck, R., & Dreyer, A. (1982). Nonverbal communication accuracy in married couples: Relationship with marital complaints. *Journal of Personality and Social Psychology, 43,* 1088–1097.

Sabatelli, R. M., & Cecil-Pigo, E. F. (1985). Relational interdependence and commitment in marriage. *Journal of Marriage and Family, 47,* 931–937.

Sadker, M. P., & Sadker, D. M. (1994). *Failing at fairness: How America's schools cheat girls.* New York: Scribner's.

Sadler, O., & Tesser, A. (1973). Some effects of salience and time upon interpersonal hostility and attraction during social isolation. *Sociometry, 36,* 99–112.

Sagar, H. A., & Schofield, J. W. (1980). Racial behavioral cues in black and white children's perceptions of ambiguously aggressive acts. *Journal of Personality and Social Psychology, 39,* 590–598.

Sanbonmatsu, D. M., Shavitt, S., Sherman, S. J., & Roskos-Ewoldsen, D. R. (1987). Illusory correlation in the perception of performance by self or a salient other. *Journal of Experimental Social Psychology, 23,* 518–543.

Sande, G. N., Goethals, G. R., & Radloff, C. E. (1988). Perceiving one's own traits and others': The multifaceted self. *Journal of Personality and Social Psychology, 54,* 13–20.

Sanders, G. S. (1981). Driven by distraction: An integrative review of social facilitation theory and research. *Journal of Experimental Social Psychology, 17,* 227–251.

Sanders, G. S., & Baron, R. S. (1975). The motivating effects of distraction on task performance. *Journal of Personality and Social Psychology, 32,* 956–963.

Sanders, G. S., & Baron, R. S. (1977). Is social comparison irrelevant for producing choice shifts? *Journal of Experimental Social Psychology, 13,* 303–313.

Sansone, C. (1986). A question of competence: The effect of competence and task feedback on intrinsic interest. *Journal of Personality and Social Psychology, 51,* 918–931.

Sansone, C. (1989). Competence feedback, task feedback, and intrinsic interest: An examination of process and context. *Journal of Experimental and Social Psychology, 25,* 343–361.

Santayana, G. (1920). *Character and opinion in the United States.* New York: Scribner's.

Santee, R. T., & Maslach, C. (1982). To agree or not to agree: Personal dissent amid social pressure to conform. *Journal of Personality and Social Psychology, 42,* 690–701.

Santos, M. D., Leve, C., & Pratkanis, A. R. (1994). Hey buddy, can you spare seventeen cents? Mindful persuasion and the pique technique. *Journal of Applied Social Psychology, 24,* 755–764.

Schachter, S. (1951). Deviation, rejection, and communication. *Journal of Abnormal and Social Psychology, 46,* 190–207.

Schachter, S. (1959). *The psychology of affiliation.* Palo Alto, CA: Stanford University Press.

Schachter, S. (1964). The interaction of cognitive and physiological determinants of emotional state. In L. Berkowitz (Ed.), *Advances in experimental social psychology* (Vol. 1). New York: Academic Press.

Schachter, S. (1971). *Emotion, obesity, and crime.* New York: Academic Press.

Schachter, S., & Singer, J. (1962). Cognitive, social and physiological determinants of emotional state. *Psychological Review, 69,* 379–399.

Schank, R. C., & Abelson, R. P. (1977). *Scripts, plans, goals and understanding: An inquiry into human knowledge structures.* Hillsdale, NJ: Erlbaum.

Schlenker, B. R. (1980). *Impression management: The self-concept, social identity, and interpersonal relations.* Pacific Grove, CA: Brooks/Cole.

Schlenker, B. R., & Britt, T. W. (1996). Depression and the explanation of events that happen to self, close others, and strangers. *Journal of Personality and Social Psychology, 71,* 180–191.

Schlenker, B. R., Dlugolecki, D. W., & Doherty, K. (1994). The impact of self-presentations on self-appraisals and behavior: The power of public commitment. *Personality and Social Psychology, 20,* 20–33.

Schlenker, B. R., Helm, B., & Tedeschi, J. T. (1973). The effects of personality and situational variables on behavioral trust. *Journal of Personality and Social Psychology, 25,* 419–427.

Schlesinger, A. M., Jr. (1965). *The thousand days.* Boston: Houghton–Mifflin.

Schmidt, G., & Weiner, B. (1988). An attribution-affect-action theory of behavior: Replications of judgments of help-giving. *Personality and Social Psychology Bulletin, 14,* 610–621.

Schmidt, J. L. (1996, November 20). Iraqi man charged with forcing his teenage daughters to marry. *Bryan-College Station (TX) Eagle.*

Schmutte, G. T., & Taylor, S. P. (1980). Physical aggression as a function of alcohol and pain feedback. *Journal of Social Psychology, 110,* 235–245.

Schopler, J., Insko, C. A., Drigotas, S., & Graetz, K. A. (1993). Individual-group discontinuity: Further evidence for mediation by fear and greed. *Personality and Social Psychology Bulletin, 19*(4), 419–431.

Schreisheim, C. A., & Kerr, S. (1977a). R.I.P. LPC: A response to Fiedler. In J. F. Hunt & L. L. Larson (Eds.), *Leadership: The cutting edge* (pp. 51–56). Carbondale: Southern Illinois University Press.

Schreisheim, C. A., & Kerr, S. (1977b). Theories and measures of leadership: A critical appraisal of current and future directions. In J. G. Hunt & L.L. Larson (Eds.), *Leadership: The cutting edge* (pp. 9–45). Carbondale: Southern Illinois University.

Schroeder, C. M., & Prentice, D. A. (In press). Exposing pluralistic ignorance to reduce alcohol use among college students. *Journal of Applied Social Psychology.*

Schroeder, D. A., Dovidio, J. F., Sibicky, M. E., Matthews, L. L., & Allen, J. L. (1988). Empathy concern and helping behavior: Egoism or altruism. *Journal of Experimental Social Psychology, 24,* 333–353.

Schroeder, D. A., Penner, L. A., Dovidio, J. F., & Piliavin, J. A. (1995). *The psychology of helping and altruism.* New York: McGraw-Hill.

Schuman, H., & Hatchett, S. (1974). *Black racial attitudes: Trends and complexities.* Ann Arbor: University of Michigan Press.

Schwartz, S. (1992). Universals in the content and structure of values: Theoretical advances and empirical tests in 20 countries. In M. Zanna (Ed.), *Advances in experimental social psychology* (Vol. 25). Orlando, FL: Academic Press.

Schwartz, S., & Sagiv, L. (1995). Identifying culture-specifics in the content and structure of values. *Journal of Cross-Cultural Psychology, 26,* 92–116.

Schwartz, S. H. (1977). Normative influences on altruism. In L. Berkowitz (Ed.), *Advances in experimental social psychology* (Vol. 10). New York: Academic Press.

Schwartz, S. H., & Ames, R. E. (1977). Positive and negative referent others as sources of influences: A case of helping. *Sociometry, 40,* 12–21.

Schwartz, S. H., & Gottlieb, A. (1980). Bystander anonymity and reactions to emergencies. *Journal of Personality and Social Psychology, 39,* 418–430.

Scott, D. S. (1980) Pain endurance induced by a subtle variable (demand) and the "reverse Milgram effect." *British Journal of Social and Clinical Psychology, 19,* 137–139.

Scully, D. (1990). *Understanding sexual violence: A study of convicted rapists.* New York: HarperCollins.

Sears, R. R., Whiting, J. W. M., Nowlis, J., & Sears, P. S. (1953). Child rearing antecedents of aggression and dependency in young children. *Genetic Psychology Monographs, 47,* 135–234.

Sedikides, C. (1995). Central and peripheral self-conceptions are differentially influenced by mood: Tests of the differential sensitivity hypothesis. *Journal of Personality and Social Psychology, 69,* 759–776.

Seeman, M., & Evans, J. W. (1962). Alienation and learning in a hospital setting. *American Sociological Review, 27,* 772–782.

Seligman, C., Olson, J. M., & Zanna, M. P. (1996). *The psychology of values: The Ontario symposium* (Vol. 8). Mahwah, NJ: Erlbaum.

Shaffer, D. R., Pegalis, L. J., & Bazzini, D. G. (1996). When boy meets girl (revisited): Gender, gender-role orientation, and prospect of future interaction as determinants of self-disclosure among same- and opposite-sex acquaintants. *Personality and Social Psychology Bulletin, 22,* 495–506.

Sharp, M. J., & Getz, J. G. (1996). Substance use as impression management. *Personality and Social Psychology, 22,* 60–67.

Shaver, P., Schwartz, J., Kirson, D., & O'Connor, C. (1987). Emotion knowledge: Further exploration of a prototype approach. *Journal of Personality and Social Psychology, 52,* 1061–1086.

Shavitt, S. (1990). The role of attitude objects in attitude functions. *Journal of Experimental Social Psychology, 26,* 124–148.

Shaw, J. I., & Condelli, L. (1986). Effects of outcome and basis of power on the powerholder-target relationship. *Personality and Social Psychology Bulletin, 12,* 236–246.

Shaw, M. E. (1981). *Group dynamics: The psychology of small group behavior.* New York: McGraw-Hill.

Sheppard, J. A., & Arkin, R. M. (1989). Self-handicapping: The moderating roles of public self-consciousness and task importance. *Personality and Social Psychology Bulletin, 15,* 252–265.

Sherif, M. (1935). A study of some social factors in perception. *Archives of Psychology, 27*(187), 1–60.

Sherif, M., Harvey, O., White, B., Hood, W., & Sherif, C. (1961). *Intergroup conflict and cooperation: The Rober's Cove experiment.* Norman: Institute of Group Relations, University of Oklahoma.

Sherif, M., & Sherif, C. W. (1969). *Social Psychology.* New York: Harper.

Shikanai, K. (1978). Effects of self-esteem on attributions of success-failure. *Japanese Journal of Experimental Social Psychology, 18,* 47–55.

Shotland, R. L., & Stau, M. K. (1976). Bystander response to an assault: When a man attacks a woman. *Journal of Personality and Social Psychology, 34,* 990–999.

Showers, C. J., & Kling, K. C. (1996a). Organization of

self-knowledge: Implications for recovery from sad mood. *Journal of Personality and Social Psychology, 70,* 578–590.

Showers, C. J., & Kling, K. C. (1996b). The organization of self-knowledge: Implications for mood recovery. In L. L. Martin & A. Tesser (Eds.), *Striving and feeling: Interactions among goals, affect, and self-regulation* (pp. 151–173). Hillsdale, NJ: Erlbaum.

Showers, C. J., & Ryff, C. D. (1996). Self-differentiation and well-being in a life transition. *Personality and Social Psychology Bulletin, 22,* 448–460.

Sidanius, J. (1993). The psychology of group conflict and dynamics of oppression: A social dominance perspective. In S. Iyengar & W. McGuire (Eds.), *Explorations in political psychology.* Durham, NC: Duke University Press.

Sigall, H., & Aronson, R. (1969). Liking for an evaluator as a function of her physical attractiveness and nature of the evaluations. *Journal of Experimental Social Psychology, 5,* 93–100.

Sigall, H., & Landy, D. (1973). Radiating beauty: Effects of attractive partner on person perception. *Journal of Social Psychology, 28,* 218–224.

Sigall, H., & Ostrove, N. (1975). Beautiful but dangerous: Effects of offender attractiveness and nature of the crime on juridic judgments. *Journal of Personality and Social Psychology, 31,* 410–414.

Silver, J. M., & Yudofsky, S. C. (1987). Aggressive behavior in patients with neuropsychiatric disorders. *Psychiatric Annals, 17,* 367–370.

Silvern, S. B., & Williamson, P. A. (1987). The effects of video game play on young children's aggression, fantasy, and prosocial behavior. *Journal of Applied Developmental Psychology, 8*(4), 453–462.

Simmel, G. (1955). *Conflict.* New York: Free Press.

Simmons, C., vonKolke, A., & Shimizu, H. (1986). Attitudes toward romantic love among Americans, Germans, and Japanese students. *Journal of Social Psychology, 126,* 327–336.

Simons, R. L., Johnson, C., Beaman, J., & Conger, R. D. (1993). Explaining women's double jeopardy: Factors that mediate the association between harsh treatment as a child and violence by a husband. *Journal of Marriage and the Family, 55,* 713–723.

Simonton, D. K. (1986a). Dispositional attributions of (presidential) leadership: An experimental simulation of historiometric results. *Journal of Experimental Social Psychology, 22,* 389–418.

Simonton, D. K. (1986b). Presidential personality: Biographical use of the Gough Adjective Check List. *Journal of Personality and Social Psychology, 51,* 149–160.

Simonton, D. K. (1987). Presidential inflexibility and veto behavior: Two individual-situational interactions. *Journal of Personality, 55,* 1–18.

Sistrunk, F., & McDavid, J. W. (1971). Sex variables in conforming behavior. *Journal of Personality and Social Psychology, 17,* 200–207.

Six, B., & Eckes, T. (1991). A closer look at the complex structure of gender stereotypes. *Sex Roles, 24,* 57–71.

Skolnick, P. (1971). Reactions to personal evaluations: A failure to replicate. *Journal of Personality and Social Psychology, 18,* 62–67.

Smith, K. D., Keating, J. P., & Stotland, E. (1989). Altruism reconsidered: The effect of denying feedback on a victim's status to empathetic witnesses. *Journal of Personality and Social Psychology, 57,* 641–650.

Smith, M. D., & Parker, R. N. (1980). Type of homicide and variation in regional rates. *Social Forces, 59,* 136–147.

Smith, R. E., Wheeler, G., & Diener, E. (1975). Faith without works: Jesus people, resistance to temptation, and altruism. *Journal of Applied Psychology, 5,* 320–330.

Smith, R. H., & Insko, C. A. (1987). Social comparison choice during ability evaluation: The effects of comparison publicity, performance feedback, and self-esteem. *Personality and Social Psychology Bulletin, 13,* 111–122.

Smith, T. W., Snyder, C. R., & Handlesman, M. M. (1982). On the self-serving function of an academic wooden leg: Test anxiety as a self-handicapping strategy. *Journal of Personality and Social Psychology, 42,* 314–321.

Smith, T. W., Snyder, C. R., & Perkins, S. C. (1983). The self-serving function of hypochondrical complaints: Physical symptoms as self-handicapping strategies. *Journal of Personality and Social Psychology, 44,* 787–797.

Snell, W. E. (1989). Willingness to self-disclose to female and male friends as a function of social anxiety and gender. *Personality and Social Psychology Bulletin, 15,* 113–125.

Snyder, C. R., & Fromkin, H. L. (1980). *Uniqueness: The human pursuit of difference.* New York: Plenum.

Snyder, M. (1974). Self-monitoring of expressive behavior. *Journal of Personality and Social Psychology, 30,* 683–689.

Snyder, M. (1979). Self-monitoring processes. In L. Berkowitz (Ed.), *Advances in experimental social psychology* (Vol. 12, pp. 85–128). New York: Academic Press.

Snyder, M. (1987). *Public appearances, Private realities.* New York: Freeman.

Snyder, M., Berscheid, E., & Glick, P. (1985). Focusing on the exterior and the interior: Two investigations of the initiation of personal relationships. *Journal of Personality and Social Psychology, 48,* 1427–1439.

Snyder, M., & Gangestad, S. (1982). Choosing social situations: Two investigations of self-monitoring processes. *Journal of Personality and Social Psychology, 43,* 123–135.

Snyder, M., & Gangestad, S. (1986). On the nature of self-monitoring: Matters of assessment, matters of validity. *Journal of Personality and Social Psychology, 51,* 125–139.

Snyder, M., & Haugen, J. A. (1995). Why does behavioral confirmation occur? A functional perspective on the role of the target. *Personality and Social Psychology Bulletin, 21,* 963–974.

Snyder, M., & Kendzierski, D. (1982). Acting on one's attitudes: Procedures for linking attitude and behavior. *Journal of Experimental Social Psychology, 18,* 165–183.

Snyder, M., & Swann, W. B., Jr. (1976). When actions reflect attitudes: The politics of impression management. *Journal of Personality and Social Psychology, 34,* 1034–1042.

Snyder, M., Tanke, E. D., & Berscheid, E. (1977). Social perception and interpersonal behavior: On the self-fulfilling nature of social stereotypes. *Journal of Personality and Social Psychology, 35,* 656–666.

Snyder, M., & Uranowitz, S. W. (1978). Reconstructing the past: Some cognitive consequences of person perception. *Journal of Personality and Social Psychology, 36,* 941–950.

Snyder, M. L. (1993). Basic research and practical problems: The promise of a "functional" personality and social psychology. *Personality and Social Psychology Bulletin, 19,* 251–264.

Sorrentino, R. M., Bobocel, D. R., Gitta, M. Z., Olson, J. M., & Hewitt, E. C. (1988). Uncertainty orientation and persuasion: Individual differences in the effects of personal relevance on social judgments. *Journal of Personality and Social Psychology, 55,* 357–371.

Sorrentino, R. M., & Boutillier, R. G. (1975). The effect of quantity and quality of verbal interaction on ratings of leadership ability. *Journal of Experimental Social Psychology, 11,* 403–411.

Sorrentino, R. M., & Field, N. (1986). Emergent leadership over time: The functional value of positive motivation. *Journal of Personality and Social Psychology, 50,* 1091–1099.

Sorrentino, R. M., & Higgins, E. T. (1986). Motivation and cognition: Warming up to synergism. In R. M. Sorrentino & E. T. Higgins (Eds.), *Handbook of motivation and cognition: Foundations of social behavior* (Vol. 1, pp. 3–19). New York: Guilford.

Sorrentino, R. M., Short, J. C., & Raynor, J. O. (1984). Uncertainty orientation: Implications for affective and cognitive views of achievement behavior. *Journal of Personality and Social Psychology, 46,* 189–206.

Speed, A., & Gangestad, S. W. (1997). Romantic popularity and mate preferences: A peer-nomination study. *Personality and Social Psychology Bulletin, 23,* 928–936.

Sprecher, S., & Duck, S. (1994). Sweet talk: The importance of perceived communication for romantic and friendship attraction experienced during a get-acquainted date. *Personality and Social Psychology Bulletin, 20,* 391–400.

Stagner, R. (1986). Reminiscences about the founding of SPSSI. *Journal of Social Issues, 42,* 35–42.

Stampp, K. M. (1956). *The peculiar institution: Slavery in the ante-bellum South.* New York: Vintage.

Stang, D. J. (1972). Conformity, ability, and self-esteem. *Representative Research in Social Psychology, 3,* 97–103.

Stanley, S. M. (1986). *Commitment and the maintenance and enhancement of relationships.* Unpublished doctoral dissertation. University of Denver, Denver, CO.

Stasser, G. (1988). Computer simulation as a research tool: The DIS-CUSS model of group decision making. *Journal of Experimental Social Psychology, 24,* 393–422.

Stasser, G., Taylor, L. A., & Hanna, C. (1989). Information sampling in structured and unstructured discussions in three- and six-person groups. *Journal of Personality and Social Psychology, 57,* 67–78.

Stasser, G., & Titus, W. (1985). Pooling of unshared information in group decision making: Biased information sampling during discussion. *Journal of Personality and Social Psychology, 48,* 1467–1478.

Staub, E. (1989). *The roots of evil: The origins of genocide and other group violence.* New York: Cambridge University Press.

Stech, F. J., & McClintock, C. G. (1981). Effects of communicating timing on duopoly bargaining outcomes. *Journal of Personality and Social Psychology, 40,* 664–674.

Steele, C. M. (1988). The psychology of self-affirmation: Sustaining the integrity of the self. In L. Berkowitz (Ed.), *Advances in experimental social psychology* (Vol. 21, pp. 261–302). New York: Academic Press.

Steele, C. M. (1992, April). Race and the schooling of black Americans. *Atlantic Monthly.*

Steele, C. M. (1997). A threat in the air: How stereotypes shape intellectual identity and performance. *American Psychologist, 52,* 613–629.

Steele, C. M., & Aronson, J. (1995). Stereotype threat and the intellectual test performance of African Americans. *Journal of Personality and Social Psychology, 69,* 797–811.

Steele, C. M., Critchlow, B., & Liu, T. J. (1985). Alcohol and social behavior: II. The helpful drunkard. *Journal of Personality and Social Psychology, 97,* 196–205.

Steele, C. M., & Josephs, R. A. (1990). Alcohol myopia: Its prized and dangerous effects. *American Psychologist, 45,* 921–933.

Steele, C. M., & Liu, T. J. (1981). Making the dissonance act unreflective of self: Dissonance avoidance and the expectancy of a value-affirming response. *Personality and Social Psychology Bulletin, 7,* 393–397.

Steele, C. M., Southwick, L. L., & Critchlow, B. (1981). Dissonance and alcohol: Drinking your troubles away. *Journal of Personality and Social Psychology, 41,* 831–846.

Stein, A. H., & Freidrich, L. K. (1975). The impact of television on children and youth. In E. M. Hetherington (Ed.), *Review of Child Development Research.* Chicago: University of Chicago Press.

Steinmetz, S. K. (1980). Women and violence: Victims and perpetrators. *American Journal of Psychotherapy, 34,* 334–350.

Stephan, W. G. (1978). School desegregation: An evaluation of predictions made in *Brown v. Board of Education. Psychological Bulletin, 85,* 217–238.

Stephan, W. G. (1986). Effects of school desegregation: An evaluation 30 years after *Brown.* In L. Saxe & M. Saks (Eds.), *Advances in applied social psychology* (Vol. 4, pp. 181–206).

Stephan, W. G., Stephan, C., & de Vargas, M. (1996). Emotional expression in Costa Rica and the United States. *Journal of Cross Cultural Psychology, 27,* 147–160.

Sterling, B., & Gaertner, S. L. (1984). The attribution of

arousal and emergency helping: A bi-directional process. *Journal of Experimental Social Psychology, 6,* 586–596.

Stewart, D. D., & Stasser, G. (1993, May). *Information sampling in collective recall groups versus decision making groups.* Paper presented at the 65th annual meeting of the Midwest Psychological Association, Chicago.

Stogdill, R. (1948). Personal factors associated with leadership. *Journal of Psychology, 25,* 35–71.

Stone, J., Aronson, E., Crain, A. L., Winslow, M. P., & Fried, C. B. (1994). Inducing hypocrisy as a means of encouraging young adults to use condoms. *Personality and Social Psychology Bulletin, 20,* 116–128.

Stoner, J. (1961). *A comparison of individual and group decisions, including risk.* Master's thesis, MIT, School of Industrial Management, Cambridge.

Storms, M. (1973). Videotape and the attribution process: Reversing actor's and observer's points of view. *Journal of Personality and Social Psychology, 27,* 165–175.

Strack, F., Martin, L., & Stepper, S. (1988). Inhibiting and facilitating conditions of the human smile: A nonobtrusive test of the facial feedback hypothesis. *Journal of Personality and Social Psychology, 54,* 768–777.

Strauman, T. J., & Higgins, E. T. (1987). Automatic activation of self-discrepancies and emotional syndromes: When cognitive structures influence affect. *Journal of Personality and Social Psychology, 53,* 1004–1014.

Strauss, M. A., & Gelles, R. J. (1986). Societal change and change in family violence from 1975 to 1985 as revealed by two national surveys. *Journal of Marriage and the Family, 48,* 465–479.

Strauss, M. A., Gelles, R. J., & Steinmetz, S. K. (1980). *Behind closed doors.* Garden City, NY: Anchor Books.

Streufert, S., & Streufert, S. C. (1986). The development of internation conflict. In S. Worchel & W. G. Austin (Eds.), *The psychology of intergroup relations.* Chicago: Nelson-Hall.

Strom, P., & Buck, R. (1979). Staring and participants' sex: Physiological and subjective reactions. *Personality and Social Psychology Bulletin, 5,* 114–117.

Strong, S. R., Hills, H. J., Kilmartin, C. T., DeVries, H., Lanier, K., Nelson, B. N., Strickland, D., & Meyer, C. W. (1988). The dynamic relations among interpersonal behaviors: A test of complementarity and anticomplementarity. *Journal of Personality and Social Psychology, 54,* 798–810.

Stryphek, B. J., & Snyder, M. (1982). On the self-perpetuating nature of stereotypes about women and men. *Journal of Experimental Social Psychology, 18,* 277–291.

Sugarman, D. B., Aldarondo, E., & Boney-McCoy, S. (1996). Risk marker analysis of husband to wife violence: A continuum of aggression. *Journal of Applied Social Psychology, 26,* 313–337.

Suh, E., Diener, E., & Fujita, F. (1996). Events and subjective well-being: Only recent events matter. *Journal of Personality and Social Psychology, 70,* 1080–1090.

Sullivan, D. S., & Deiker, T. E. (1973). Subject-experimenter perceptions of ethical issues in human research. *American Psychologist, 28,* 587–591.

Suls, J., Gaes, G., & Gastorf, J. (1979). Evaluating a sex-related ability: Comparison with same-, opposite-, and combined-sex norms. *Journal of Research in Personality, 13,* 294–304.

Suls, J., & Wills, T. A. (Eds.). (1990). *Social comparison: Contemporary theory and research.* Hillsdale, NJ: Erlbaum.

Summers, A. (1986). *Goddess: The secret lives of Marilyn Monroe.* New York: New American Library.

Sumner, W. (1906). *Folkways.* Boston: Ginn.

Sweeney, P. D., Anderson, K., & Bailey, S. (1986). Attributional style in depression: A meta-analytic review. *Journal of Personality and Social Psychology, 50,* 974–991.

Sweeney, P. D., & Gruber, K. L. (1984). Selective exposure: Voter information preferences and the Watergate affair. *Journal of Personality and Social Psychology, 46,* 1208–1221.

Swenson, O. (1987). *The perilous path of cultism.* Caronport, SK: Briercrest Books.

Swinth, R. L. (1976). A decision process model for predicting job preferences. *Journal of Applied Psychology, 61,* 242–245.

Tagiuri, R., Blake, R., & Bruner, J. (1953). Some determinants of the perception of positive and negative feelings in others. *Journal of Abnormal and Social Psychology, 48,* 585–592.

Tajfel, H. (1970). Experiments in intergroup discrimination. *Scientific American, 223*(2), 96–102.

Tajfel, H., & Turner, J. C. (1986). The social identity theory of intergroup behavior. In S. Worchel & W. G. Austin (Eds.), *The psychology of intergroup relations.* Chicago: Nelson-Hall.

Takata, T., (1992, June). *Self-deprecative social comparison in Japan.* Paper presented at the International Conference on Emotion and Culture, Eugene, OR.

Tannenbaum, P. H., Greenberg, B. S., & Silverman, F. R. (1962). Candidate images. In S. Kraus (Ed.), *The great debates* (pp. 271–288). Bloomington: Indiana University Press.

Tannenbaum, P. H., & Zillman, D. (1975). Emotional arousal in the facilitation of aggression through communication. In L. Berkowitz (Ed.), *Advances in experimental social psychology* (Vol. 8). New York: Academic Press.

Taormina, R. J., & Messick, D. M. (1983). Deservingness for foreign aid: Effects of need, similarity, and estimated effectiveness. *Journal of Applied Social Psychology, 13,* 371–391.

Tatum J., & Kushner, B. (1980). *They call me assassin.* New York: Avon Books.

Taylor, D. A., Gould, R. J., & Brounstein, P. J. (1981). Effects of personalistic self-disclosure. *Personality and Social Psychology Bulletin, 7,* 487–492.

Taylor, D. M., Wright, S. C., & Porter, L. E. (1994). Dimensions of perceived discrimination: The personal/group discrimination discrepancy. In M. P. Zanna & J. M. Olson (Eds.), *The psychology of prejudice: The Ontario symposium* (Vol. 7, pp. 233–235). Mahwah, NJ: Erlbaum.

Taylor, S. E., & Fiske, S. T. (1975). Point of view and perceptions of causality. *Journal of Personality and Social Psychology, 32,* 439–445.

Taylor, S. E., & Fiske, S. T. (1978). Salience, attention and attribution: Top-of-the-head phenomena. In L. Berkowitz (Ed.), *Advances in experimental social psychology* (Vol. 11). New York: Academic Press.

Taylor, S. E., Fiske, S. T., Etcoff, N. L., & Ruderman, A. J. (1978). Categorical bases of person memory and stereotyping. *Journal of Personality and Social Psychology, 36,* 778–793.

Taylor, S. L., O'Neal, E. C., Langley, T., & Butcher, A. H. (1991). Anger arousal, deindividuation, and aggression. *Aggressive Behavior, 17,* 193–206.

Taylor, S. P., & Gammon, C. B. (1975). Effects of type and dose of alcohol on human physical aggression. *Journal of Personality and Social Psychology, 32,* 169–175.

Taylor, S. P., Gammon, C. B., & Capasso, D. R. (1976). Aggression as a function of the interaction of alcohol and threat. *Journal of Personality and Social Psychology, 34,* 938–941.

Tec, N. (1986). *When light pierced the darkness: Christian rescue of Jews in Nazi-occupied Poland.* New York: Oxford University Press.

Tedeschi, J. T. (1974). *Perspectives on social power.* Chicago: Aldine.

Tedeschi, J. T. (1979). Frustration, fantasy, aggression, and the exercise of coercive power. *Perceptual and Motor Skills, 48,* 215–219.

Tedeschi, J. T., Schlenker, B. R., & Bonoma, T. V. (1971). Cognitive dissonance: Private rationalization or public spectacle? *American Psychologist, 26,* 685–695.

Tedeschi, J. T., Smith, R. O., & Brown, R. C. (1974). A reinterpretation of research on aggression. *Psychology Bulletin, 81,* 540–563.

Teger, A. (1980). *Too much invested to quit.* New York: Pergamon.

Temple, M. T., & Leigh, B. C. (1992). Alcohol consumption and unsafe sexual behavior in discrete events. *Journal of Sex Research, 29,* 207–219.

Tennen, H., & Eller, S. J. (1977). Attributional components of learned helplessness and facilitation. *Journal of Personality and Social Psychology, 35,* 265–271.

Tennen, H., & Herzberger, S. (1987). Depression, self-esteem, and the absence of self-protective attributional biases. *Journal of Personality and Social Psychology, 52,* 72–80.

Terman, L. (1904). A preliminary study in the psychology and pedagogy of leadership. *Pedagogical Seminary, 4,* 413–451.

Tesser, A. (1978). Self-generated attitude change. In L. Berkowitz (Ed.), *Advances in experimental social psychology* (Vol. 11, pp. 289–338). New York: Academic Press.

Tesser, A. (1988). Toward a self-evaluation maintenance model of social behavior. In L. Berkowitz (Ed.), *Advances in experimental social psychology* (Vol. 21, pp. 181–227). New York: Academic Press.

Tesser, A. (1993). The importance of heritability in psychological research: The case of attitudes. *Psychological Review, 100,* 129–142.

Tesser, A., Millar, M., & Moore, J. (1988). Some affective consequences of social comparison and reflection processes: The pain and pleasure of being close. *Journal of Personality and Social Psychology, 54,* 49–61.

Tesser, A., & Smith, J. (1980). Some effects of task relevance and friendship on helping: You don't always help the one you like. *Journal of Experimental Social Psychology, 16,* 582–590.

Tetlock, P. E., Skitka, L., & Boettger, R. (1989). Social and cognitive strategies for coping with accountability: Conformity, complexity, and bolstering. *Journal of Personality and Social Psychology, 57,* 632–640.

t'Hart, P. (1988, July). *Groupthink: Observations toward a theory.* Paper presented at the meeting of the International Society of Political Psychology, Meadowlands, NJ.

t'Hart, P., & Kroon, M. (1989, June). *Groupthink in context.* Paper presented at the meeting of the International Society of Political Psychology, Tel Aviv, Israel.

Thibaut, J. W. (1968). The development of contractual norms in bargaining replication and variation. *Journal of Conflict Resolution, 12,* 102–112.

Thibaut, J. W., & Kelley, H. H. (1959). *The social psychology of groups.* New York: Wiley.

Thompson, E. P., Roman, R. J., Moskowitz, G. B., Chaiken, S., & Bargh, J. A. (1994). Accuracy motivation attenuates covert priming: The systematic reprocessing of social information. *Journal of Personality and Social Psychology, 66,* 474–489.

Thompson, W. C., Cowan, C. L., & Rosenhan, D. L. (1980). Focus of attention mediates the impact of negative effect on altruism. *Journal of Personality and Social Psychology, 39,* 291–300.

Thornton, B., & Moore, S. (1993). Physical attractiveness contrast effects: Implications for self-esteem and evolution of the social self. *Personality and Social Psychology Bulletin, 19,* 474–480.

Thornton, J. W., & Jacobs, P. D. (1971). Learned helplessness in human subjects. *Journal of Experimental Psychology, 87*(3), 367–372.

Thurstone, L. L., & Chave, E. J. (1929). *The measurement of attitudes.* Chicago: University of Chicago Press.

Tice, D. M., Butler, J. L., Muraven, M. B., & Stillwell, A. M. (1995). When modesty prevails: Differential favorability of self-presentation to friends and strangers. *Journal of Personality and Social Psychology, 69,* 1120–1138.

Tidwell, M. O., Reis, H. T., and Shaver, P. R. (1996). Attachment, attractiveness and social interaction. *Journal of Personality and Social Psychology, 71,* 729–745.

Tilker, H. A. (1970). Socially responsible behavior as a function of observer responsibility and victim feedback. *Journal of Personality and Social Psychology, 4,* 95–100.

Tougas, F., & Veilleux, F. (1988). The influence of identification, collective relative deprivation, and procedure of implementation on women's response to affirmative action: A causal modeling approach. *Canadian Journal of Behavioural Science, 20,* 15–28.

Touhey, J. C. (1972). Comparison of two dimensions of attitude similarity on heterosexual attraction. *Journal of Personality and Social Psychology, 23,* 8–10.

Townsend, J. M. (1995). Sex without emotional involvement: An evolutionary interpretation of sex differences. *Archives of Sexual Behavior, 24*(2), 173–206.

Tracey, T. J. (1994). An examination of the complementarity of interpersonal behavior. *Journal of Personality and Social Psychology, 67,* 864–878.

Travis, L. E. (1925). The effect of a small audience upon eye-hand coordination. *Journal of Abnormal and Social Psychology, 20,* 142–146.

Treas, J. (1977). Family support systems for the aged: Some social and demographic considerations. *Gerontologist, 17,* 486–491.

Triandis, H. (1975). Cultural training, cognitive complexity, and interpersonal attitudes. In R. Brislin, S. Bochner, & W. Lonner (Eds.), *Cross-cultural perspectives on learning.* Beverly Hills, CA: Sage.

Triandis, H. (1994). *Culture and social behavior.* New York: McGraw-Hill.

Triplett, N. (1897). The dynamogenic factors in pacemaking and competition. *American Journal of Psychology, 9,* 507–533.

Trope, Y., Cohen, O., & Moaz, Y. (1988). The perceptual and inferential effects of situational inducements on dispositional attribution. *Journal of Personality and Social Psychology, 55,* 165–177.

Tucker, J. A., Vucinish, R. E., & Sobell, M. S. (1981). Alcohol consumption as a self-handicapping strategy. *Journal of Abnormal Psychology, 90,* 220–230.

Tucker, P., & Aron, A. (1993). Passionate love and marital satisfaction at key transition points in the family life cycle. *Journal of Social and Clinical Psychology, 12,* 135–147.

Tuckman, B. W. (1965). Developmental sequence in small groups. *Psychological Bulletin, 63,* 384–399.

Turner, C. W., & Berkowitz, L. (1972). Identification with film aggressor (covert role taking) and reactions to film violence. *Journal of Personality and Social Psychology, 21,* 256–264.

Turner, J. C. (1987). *Rediscovering the social group: A self-categorization theory.* Oxford, England: Blackwell.

Tversky, A., & Kahneman, D. (1973). Availability: A heuristic for judging frequency and probability. *Cognitive Psychology, 5,* 207–232.

Uleman, J. S., Hon, A., Roman, R. J., & Moscowitz, G. B. (1996). On-line evidence for spontaneous trait inferences at encoding. *Personality and Social Psychology Bulletin, 22,* 377–394.

Uleman, J. S., Newman, L. S., & Moskowitz, G. B. (1996). People as flexible interpreters: Evidence and issues form spontaneous trait inference. In M. P. Zanna (Ed.), *Advances in experimental social psychology* (Vol. 28, pp. 211–279). Boston: Academic Press.

Underwood, B., Berenson, J. F., Berenson, R. J., Cheng, K. K., Wilson, D., Kulik, J., Moore, B. S., & Wenzel, G. (1977). Attention, negative affect, and altruism: An ecological validation. *Personality and Social Psychology Bulletin, 3,* 51–53.

United States Holocaust Memorial Council. (1989). *Night of pogroms: "Kristallnacht."* Washington, DC: U.S. Government Printing Office.

Van Hook, E., & Higgins, E. T. (1988). Self-related problems beyond the self-concept: Motivational consequences of discrepant self-guides. *Journal of Personality and Social Psychology, 55*, 625–633.

Veitch, R., & Griffitt, W. (1976). Good news, bad news: Affective and interpersonal effects. *Journal of Applied Social Psychology, 6*, 69–75.

Vidmar, N., & Rokeach, M. (1974). Archie Bunker's bigotry: A study in selective perception and exposure. *Journal of Communication, 24*, 36–47.

Viney, W. (1989). The cyclops and the twelve-eyed toad: William James and the unity-disunity problem in psychology. *American Psychologist, 44*, 1261–1265.

Vinokur, A., Burnstein, E., Sechrest, L., & Wortman, P. M. (1985). Group decision making by experts: A group problem solving approach. *Journal of Personality and Social Psychology, 49*, 70–84.

Von Baeyer, C. L., Sherk, D. L., & Zanna, M. P. (1981). Impression management in the job interview: When the female applicant meets the male (chauvinist) interviewer. *Personality and Social Psychology Bulletin, 7*, 45–51.

Wagner, C. C., Kiesler, D. J., & Schmidt, J. A. (1995). Assessing the interpersonal transaction cycle: Convergence of action and reaction interpersonal circumplex measures. *Journal of Personality and Social Psychology, 69*, 938–949.

Wagner, H. L., MacDonald, C. J., & Manstead, A. S. R. (1986). Communication of individual emotions by spontaneous facial expressions. *Journal of Personality and Social Psychology, 50*, 737–743.

Walker, L. E. (1989). Psychology and violence against women. *American Psychology, 44*, 695–702.

Wallach, M., Kogan, N., & Bem, D. (1962). Group influence on individual risk taking. *Journal of Abnormal and Social Psychology, 65*, 75–86.

Walster, E., Aronson, V., Abrahams, D., & Rottman, L. (1966). The importance of physical attractiveness in dating behavior. *Journal of Personality and Social Psychology, 4*, 508–516.

Walster, E., Berscheid, E., & Walster, G. W. (1978). *Equity: Theory and research.* Boston, MA: Allyn and Bacon.

Walster, E., & Walster, G. W. (1969). The matching hypothesis. *Journal of Personality and Social Psychology, 6*, 248–253.

Walster, E., & Walster, G. W. (1978). *Love.* Reading, MA: Addison-Wesley.

Walters, P. S., & Lindskold, S. (1982). *Intensity of conflict and response to conciliation.* Unpublished manuscript. Ohio University, Athens, OH.

Walters, R., & Willows, D. (1968). Imitation behavior of disturbed children following exposure to aggressive and nonaggressive models. *Child Development, 39*, 79–91.

Watson, R. I. (1973). Investigation into deindividuation using a cross-cultural survey technique. *Journal of Personality and Social Psychology, 25*, 342–345.

Watson, D., & Clark, L. A. (1984). Negative affectivity: The disposition to experience aversive emotional states. *Psychological Bulletin, 96*, 465–490.

Watzlawick, P., Beavin, J. H., & Jackson, D. D. (1967). *Pragmatics of human communication: A study of interactional patterns, pathologies, and paradoxes.* New York: Norton.

Weaver, G. (1994). Understanding and coping with cross-cultural adjustment stress. In G. Weaver (Ed.), *Culture, communication, and conflict: Reading in intercultural relations.* Needham Heights, MA: Simon and Schuster.

Webb, W., & Worchel, S. (1986). Trust and distrust. In S. Worchel & W. G. Austin (Eds.), *The psychology of intergroup relations.* Chicago: Nelson-Hall.

Weber, M. (1946). The sociology of charismatic authority. Reprinted in H. H. Gerth & C. W. Mills (Trans. and Eds.), *From Max Weber: Essay in sociology* (pp. 245–252). New York: Oxford University Press. (Originally published in 1921.)

Wegner, D. M. (1992). You can't always think what you want: Problems in the suppression of unwanted thoughts. In M. P. Zanna (Ed.), *Advances in experimental social psychology* (Vol. 25, pp. 193–225). Boston: Academic Press.

Wegner, D. M., & Gold, D. B. (1995). Fanning old flames: Emotional and cognitive effects of suppressing thoughts of a past relationship. *Journal of Personality and Social Psychology, 68*, 782–791.

Wegner, D. M., & Pennebaker, J. W. (1993). Changing our minds: An introduction to mental control. In D. M. Wegner & J. W. Pennebaker (Eds.), *Handbook of mental control* (pp. 1–12). Englewood Cliffs, NJ: Prentice-Hall.

Wegner, D. M., Schneider, D. J., Carter, S. R., III, & White, L. (1987). Paradoxical effects of thought suppression. *Journal of Personality and Social Psychology, 53*, 5–13.

Weigel, R. H., Loomis, J. W., & Soja, M. J. (1980). Race relations on prime time television. *Journal of Personality and Social Psychology, 39*, 884–893.

Weigel, R. H., & Newman, L. S. (1976). Increasing attitude-behavior correspondence by broadening the scope of the behavioral measure. *Journal of Personality and Social Psychology, 33*, 793–802.

Weiger, W. A., & Bear, D. M. (1988). An approach to the neurology of aggression. *Journal of Psychiatric Research, 22*, 85–98.

Weiner, B. (1985). An attributional theory of achievement motivation and emotion. *Psychological Review, 92*, 548–573.

Weiner, B. (1986). *An attribution theory of motivation and emotion.* New York: Springer-Verlag.

Weiner, B., Frieze, I., Kukla, A., Reed, L., Rest, B., & Rosenbaum, R. M. (1971). *Perceiving the causes of success and failure.* Morristown, NJ: General Learning Press.

Weiner, B., Perry, R. P., & Magnusson, J. (1988). An attributional analysis of reactions to stigmas. *Journal of Personality and Social Psychology, 55*, 738–748.

Weinstein, N. D. (1980). Unrealistic optimism about future life events. *Journal of Personality and Social Psychology, 39*, 806–820.

Wells, G. L., & Petty, R. E. (1980). The effects of overt head-movements on persuasion, compatibility, and incompatibility of responses. *Journal of Basic and Applied Social Psychology, 1,* 219–230.

Werner, G., & Latané, B. (1974). Interaction motivates attraction: Rats are fond of fondling. *Journal of Personality and Social Psychology, 29,* 328–334.

West, S. G., Gunn, S. P., & Chernicky, P. (1975). Ubiquitous Watergate: An attributional analysis. *Journal of Personality and Social Psychology, 32,* 55–65.

West, S. G., & Wicklund, R. A. (1980). *A primer of social psychological theories.* Pacific Grove, Calif.: Brooks/Cole.

Wheeler, L. (1966). Toward a theory of behavioral contagion. *Psychological Review, 73,* 179–192.

Wheeler, L., & Koestner, R. (1984). Performance evaluation: On choosing to know the related attributes of others when we know their performance. *Journal of Experimental Social Psychology, 20,* 263–271.

Wheeler, L., Koestner, R., & Driver, R. E. (1982). Related attributes in the choice of comparison others: It's there, but it isn't all there is. *Journal of Experimental Social Psychology, 18,* 489–500.

Whitcher, S. J., & Fisher, J. D. (1979). Multidimensional reaction to therapeutic touch in a hospital setting. *Journal of Personality and Social Psychology, 37,* 87–96.

White, G. L. (1980). Physical attractiveness and courtship progress. *Journal of Personality and Social Psychology, 39,* 660–668.

White, G. L. (1981). A model of romantic jealousy. *Motivation and Emotion, 5,* 295–310.

White, G. L., Fishbein, S., & Rutstein, J. (1981). Passionate love and the misattribution of arousal. *Journal of Personality and Social Psychology, 41,* 56–62.

White, M. (1975). Interpersonal distance as affected by room size, status, and sex. *Journal of Social Psychology, 95,* 241–249.

White, R. K. (1984). *Fearful warriors: A psychological profile of U.S.-Soviet relations.* New York: Free Press.

White, T. H. (1961). *The making of the President, 1960.* New York: Atheneum.

Whitely, B. E., Jr. (1990). The relationship of heterosexuals' attributions for the causes of homosexuality to attitudes toward lesbians and gay men. *Personality and Social Psychology Bulletin, 16,* 369–377.

Whitely, B. E., Jr. (1993). Reliability and aspects of the construct validity of Sternberg's triangular love scale. *Journal of Social and Personal Relationships, 10,* 475–480.

Whyte, W., Jr. (1956). *The organization man.* New York: Simon and Schuster.

Wicker, A. W. (1969). Attitude versus actions: The relationship of verbal and overt behavioral responses to attitude objects. *Journal of Social Issues, 25*(4), 41–78.

Wicklund, R. A., & Brehm, J. W. (1976). *Perspectives on cognitive dissonance.* Hillsdale, NJ: Erlbaum.

Wicklund, R. A., & Frey, D. (1980). Self-awareness theory: When the self makes a difference. In D. M. Wegner & R. R. Vallacher (Eds.), *The self in social psychology* (pp. 31–54). New York: Oxford University Press.

Wiggins, J. S. (1979). A psychological taxonomy of trait-descriptive terms: The interpersonal domain. *Journal of Personality and Social Psychology, 37,* 395–412.

Wilder, D. A. (1977). Perception of groups, size of opposition, and social influence. *Journal of Experimental Social Psychology, 13,* 253–268.

Wilke, H., & Van Knippenberg, A. (1988). Group performance. In M. Hewstone, W. Stroebe, J. Codol, & G. Stephenson (Eds.), *Introduction to social psychology.* Oxford, England: Basil Blackwell.

Wilkinson, G. S. (1990). Food sharing in vampire bats. *Scientific American,* 76–82.

Williams, K., Harkins, S., & Latané, B. (1981). Identifiability as a deterrent to social loafing: Two cheering experiments. *Journal of Personality and Social Psychology, 40,* 303–311.

Wills, T. A. (1981). Downward comparison principles in social psychology. *Psychological Bulletin, 90,* 245–271.

Wilson, T. D., & Lassiter, G. D. (1982). Increasing intrinsic interest with superfluous extrinsic constraints. *Journal of Personality and Social Psychology, 42,* 811–819.

Winch, R. (1958). *Mate-selection: A study of complementary needs.* New York: Harper and Row.

Winkler, J., & Taylor, S. E. (1979). Preference, expectation, and attributional bias: Two field studies. *Journal of Applied Social Psychology, 2,* 183–197.

Winter, D. G. (1987). Leader appeal, leader performance, and the motive profiles of leaders and followers: A study of American presidents and elections. *Journal of Personality and Social Psychology, 52,* 196–202.

Winter, L., & Uleman, J. S. (1984). When are social judgments made? Evidence for the spontaneousness of trait inferences. *Journal of Personality and Social Psychology, 47,* 237–252.

Wolfgang, M. E., & Fenacuti, F. (1967). *The subculture of violence.* London, England: Tavistock.

Wood, J. V., Giordano-Beach, M., Taylor, K. L., Michela, J. L., & Gaus, V. (1994). Strategies of social comparison among people with low self-esteem: Self-protection and self-enhancement. *Journal of Personality and Social Psychology, 67,* 713–730.

Wood, W. (1987). Meta-analytic review of sex differences in group performance. *Psychological Bulletin, 102,* 53–71.

Wood, W., Pool, G. J., Leck, K., & Purvis, D. (1996). Self-definition, defensive processing, and influence: The normative impact of majority and minority groups. *Journal of Personality and Social Psychology, 71,* 1181–1193.

Wood, W., Wong, F. Y., & Chachere, J. G. (1991). Effects of media violence on viewers' aggression in unconstrained social interaction. *Psychological Bulletin, 109,* 371–383.

Worchel, S. (1974). The effect of three types of arbitrary thwarting on the instigation to aggression. *Journal of Personality, 42,* 300–318.

Worchel, S. (1984). The darker side of helping: The social dynamics of helping and cooperation. In E. Staub et al. (Eds.), *The development and maintenance of prosocial behavior.* New York: Plenum.

Worchel, S. (1986). The role of cooperation in reducing intergroup conflict. In S. Worchel & W. G. Austin (Eds.), *The psychology of intergroup relations* (pp. 153–176). Chicago: Nelson-Hall.

Worchel, S. (1998). A developmental view of the search for group identity. In S. Worchel, F. Morales, D. Paez, & J. Deschamps (Eds.), *Social identity: International perspectives.* London, England: Sage.

Worchel, S., & Andreoli, V. (1978). Facilitation of social interaction through deindividuation of the target. *Journal of Personality and Social Psychology, 36,* 549–557.

Worchel, S., Andreoli, V., & Folger, R. (1977). Intergroup cooperation and intergroup attraction: The effect of previous interaction and outcome of combined effort. *Journal of Experimental Social Psychology, 13,* 131–140.

Worchel, S., Coutant-Sassic, D., & Grossman, M. (1991). A model of group development and independence. In S. Worchel, W. Wood, & J. Simpson (Eds.), *Group process and productivity.* Newbury Park, CA: Sage.

Worchel, S., Coutant-Sassic, D., & Grossman, M. (1992). A developmental approach to group dynamics: A model and illustrative research. In S. Worchel, W. Wood, & J. A. Simpson, (Eds.), *Group process and productivity.* Newbury Park, CA: Sage.

Worchel, S., Coutant-Sassic, D., & Wong, F. (1993). Toward a more balanced view of conflict: There is a positive side. In S. Worchel & J. Simpson (Eds.), *Conflict between people and groups.* Chicago: Nelson-Hall.

Worchel, S., Hart, D., & Buttermeyer, J. (1989, April). *Is social loafing a group phenomenon?* Paper presented at the Southwestern Psychological Association Meeting, Houston, TX.

Worchel, S., Wong, F., & Skeltema, K. (1989). Improving intergroup relations: Comparative effects of anticipated cooperation and helping in attraction for an aid-giver. *Social Psychology Quarterly, 52,* 213–219.

Word, C. H., Zanna, M. P., & Cooper, J. (1974). The nonverbal mediation of self-fulfilling prophesies in interracial interaction. *Journal of Experimental Social Psychology, 10,* 109–120.

Worth, L. T., & Mackie, D. M. (1987). Cognitive mediation of positive affect in persuasion. *Social Cognition, 5,* 76–94.

Wright, P., & Crawford, A. (1971). Agreement and friendship: A close look and some second thoughts. *Representative Research in Social Psychology, 2,* 52–69.

Yamaguchi, S. (1990). *Personality and cognitive correlates of collectivism among Japanese: Validation of Collectivism Scale.* Paper presented at the 22nd International Congress of Applied Psychology, Kyoto, Japan.

Yamaguchi, S. (1994). Collectivism among the Japanese: A perspective from the self. In Kim et al. (Eds.), *Individualism and collectivism: Theory, methods, and applications.* Thousand Oaks, CA: Sage.

Yost, J. H., & Weary, G. (1996). Depression and the correspondent inference bias: Evidence for more effortful cognitive processing. *Personality and Social Psychology Bulletin, 22,* 192–200.

Younger, J. C., Walker, L., & Arrowood, A. J. (1977). Postdecision dissonance at the fair. *Personality and Social Psychology Bulletin, 3,* 284–287.

Yousif, Y., & Korte, C. (1995). Urbanization, culture, and helpfulness: Cross-cultural studies in England and Sudan. *Journal of Cross-Cultural Psychology, 26,* 474–489.

Yu, A., & Yang, K. (1994). The nature of achievement motivation in collectivist societies. In Kim et al. (Eds.), *Individualism and collectivism: Theory, methods, and applications.* Thousand Oaks, CA: Sage.

Zajonc, R. B. (1965). Social facilitation. *Science, 149,* 269–274.

Zajonc, R. B. (1968). Attitudinal effects of mere exposure. *Journal of Personality and Social Psychology, 9,* (Monograph suppl., No. 2, Pt. 2), 1–27.

Zajonc, R. B. (1972). *Animal social behavior.* Morristown, NJ: General Learning Press.

Zajonc, R. B. (1980). Feeling and thinking: Preferences need no inferences. *American Psychologist, 35,* 151–175.

Zajonc, R. B. (1989). Styles of explanation in social psychology. *European Journal of Social Psychology, 19,* 345–368.

Zanna, M. P., & Cooper, J. (1974). Dissonance and the pill: An attribution approach to studying the arousal properties of dissonance. *Journal of Personality and Social Psychology, 29,* 703–709.

Zanna, M. P., Goethals, G. R., & Hill, J. (1975). Evaluating a sex-related ability: Social comparison with similar others and standard setters. *Journal of Experimental Social Psychology, 11,* 86–93.

Zanna, M. P., Kiesler, C. A., & Pilkonis, P. A. (1970). Positive and negative attitudinal affect established by classical conditioning. *Journal of Personality and Social Psychology, 14,* 321–328.

Zanna, M. P., Olson, J. M., & Fazio, R. H. (1980). Attitude-behavior consistency: An individual difference perspective. *Journal of Personality and Social Psychology, 38,* 432–440.

Zanna, M. P., & Rempel, J. K. (1988). Attitudes: A new look at an old concept. In D. Bar-Tal & A. W. Kruglanski (Eds.), *The social psychology of knowledge.* (pp. 315–334). Cambridge, England: Cambridge University Press.

Zelditch, M. (1955). Role differentiation in the nuclear family: A comparative study. In T. Parsons & R. Bales (Eds.), *Family, socialization and interaction process.* Glencoe, IL: Free Press.

Zillmann, D. (1971). Excitation transfer in communication-mediated aggressive behavior. *Journal of Experimental Social Psychology, 7,* 419–434.

Zillmann, D. (1978). *Hostility and aggression.* Hillsdale, NJ: Erlbaum.

Zillmann, D. (1983). Transfer of excitation in emotional behavior. In J. T. Cacioppo & R. E. Petty (eds.), *Social psychophysiology: A sourcebook.* New York: Guilford.

Zillmann, D. (1984). *Connections between sex and aggression.* Hillsdale, NJ: Erlbaum.

Zillmann, D. (1994). Cognition-excitation interdependencies in the escalation of anger and angry aggression. In M. Potegal & J. F. Knutson (Eds.), *The dynamics of aggression: Biological and social processes in dyads and groups* (pp. 45–72). Hillsdale, NJ: Erlbaum.

Zillmann, D. (1996). Sequential dependencies in emotional experience and behavior. In R. D. Kavanaugh, B. Zimmerberg, & S. Fein (Eds.), *Emotion: Interdisciplinary perspectives* (pp. 243–272). Mahwah, NJ: Erlbaum.

Zillmann, D., & Bryant, J. (1988). Pornography's impact on sexual satisfaction. *Journal of Applied Social Psychology, 18,* 438–453.

Zillmann, D., Bryant, J., Carveth, R. A. (1981). The effect of erotica featuring sadomasochism and bestiality on motivated intermale aggression. *Personality and Social Psychology Bulletin, 7,* 153–159.

Zillmann, D., Bryant, J., Comisky, P. W., & Medoff, N. J. (1981). Excitation and hedonic valence in the effect of erotica on motivated intermale aggression. *European Journal of Social Psychology, 11,* 233–252.

Zillmann, D., & Johnson, R. C. (1973). Maternal aggressiveness perpetuated by exposure to aggressive films and reduced by exposure to nonaggressive films. *Journal of Research in Personality, 7,* 261–276.

Zimbardo, P. (1970). The human choice: Individuation, reason, and order versus individuation, impulse, and chaos. *Nebraska Symposium on Motivation.* Lincoln: University of Nebraska Press.

Zuckerman, M., Amidon, M. D., Bishop, S. E., & Pomerantz, S. D. (1982). Face and tone of voice in the communication of deception. *Journal of Personality and Social Psychology, 43,* 347–357.

Zuckerman, M., DePaulo, B., & Rosenthal, R. (1981). Verbal and nonverbal communication of deception. In L. Berkowitz (Ed.), *Advances in experimental social psychology* (Vol. 14, pp. 1–59). New York: Academic Press.

Zukier, H. (1982). The role of the correlation and the dispersion of predictor variables in the use of nondiagnostic information. *Journal of Personality and Social Psychology, 43,* 1163–1175.

Zukier, H., & Pepitone, A. (1984). Social roles and strategies in prediction: Some determinants of the use of base-rate information. *Journal of Personality and Social Psychology, 47,* 349–360.

Author Index

Subject Index

PHOTO CREDITS

CHAPTER 1
Page 4   © UPI/Corbis-Bettmann
Page 7   © Lawrence Migdale: Tony Stone Images
Page 9   © Bob Thomason: Tony Stone Images
Page 10   © UPI/Corbis-Bettmann
Page 13   © Clark Jones: Impact Visuals

CHAPTER 2
Page 35   © AP/Wide World
Page 47   © Mark Pokempner: Tony Stone Images
Page 48   © UPI/Corbis-Bettmann
Page 51   © Michael O'Leary: Tony Stone Images
Page 54   © Agence France Presse/Corbis-Bettmann
Page 57   © William Cochrane: Impact Visuals

CHAPTER 3
Page 65   © Larry Williams: St. Louis Post-Dispatch
Page 66   © Rich LaSalle: Tony Stone Images
Page 70   © Brian Drake: SportsChrome USA
Page 81   © Alan Levenson: Tony Stone Images
Page 83   © Joseph Sohm: Tony Stone Images
Page 89   © Frank Siteman: Tony Stone Images

CHAPTER 4
Page 95   © Courtesy of Kansas City Museum, Kansas City, Missouri
Page 113 © Jonathan Nourak: Tony Stone Images
Page 117 © David Harry Stewart: Tony Stone Images
Page 119 © Leland Bobbe: Tony Stone Images

CHAPTER 5
Page 125 © Courtesy of Department of Psychology, University of Connecticut
Page 126 © (Authors Daughters)
Page 128 © Kent Reno: Jeroboam
Page 131 © Robert E. Daemmrich: Tony Stone Images
Page 137 © Stewart Cohen: Tony Stone Images
Page 142 © Courtesy of the American Lung Association
Page 146 © David Young Wolff: Tony Stone Images

CHAPTER 6
Page 158 © AP/Wide World Photos
Page 160 © Jon Riley: Tony Stone Images
Page 166 © Rex Ziak: Tony Stone Images
Page 171 © Suzanne Arms: Jeroboam
Page 176 © AP/Wide World
Page 184 © Agence France Presse/Corbis-Bettmann

CHAPTER 7
Page 193 © Courtesy of the U.S. Holocaust Memorial Museum
Page 197 © Jane Scherr: Jeroboam
Page 211 © Paul Damien: Tony Stone Images
Page 213 © Robert Galbraith
Page 219 © Nick Smee: Tony Stone Images

CHAPTER 8
Page 228 © Photofest
Page 233 © Donna Day: Tony Stone Images
Page 257 © Andy Sacks: Tony Stone Images
Page 263 © T. Firak: Photri

CHAPTER 9
Page 270 © Detroit Free Press
Page 278 © AP/Wide World
Page 284 © Robert Fox: Impact Visuals
Page 287 © AP/Wide World
Page 295 © Cindy Reiman: Impact Visuals
Page 298 © Don Smetzer: Tony Stone Images

CHAPTER 10
Page 303 © UPI/Corbis-Bettmann
Page 311 © Roberto Thoni/Corbis-Bettmann
Page 314 © Cathlyn Melloan: Tony Stone Images
Page 320 © Cleo Freelance: Jeroboam
Page 326 © Photofest
Page 332 © AP/Wide World

CHAPTER 11
Page 338 © AP/Wide World
Page 349 © AP/Wide World
Page 356 © Agence France Presse/Corbis-Bettmann
Page 369 © UPI/Corbis-Bettmann
Page 374 © Robert Daemmrich: Tony Stone Images
Page 377 © Jim West

CHAPTER 12
Page 383 © Courtesy of the West Virginia Division of Culture and History
Page 388 © Mark Ludak: Impact Visuals
Page 391 © AP/Wide World
Page 398 © AP/Wide World
Page 403 © Stuart McCall: Tony Stone Images
Page 407 © UPI/Corbis-Bettmann

CHAPTER 13
Page 413 © Thor Heyerdahl: Rand McNally Publishers
Page 416 © Kaluzny/Thatcher: Tony Stone Images
Page 422 © AP/Wide World
Page 426 © Photofest
Page 428 © Rhoda Sidney: PhotoEdit

CHAPTER 14
Page 436 © Yva Momatiuk and John Eastcott: National Geographic Image Collection
Page 443 © George Mobley: National Geographic Image Collection
Page 446 © Glen Allison: Tony Stone Images
Page 453 © James P. Blair: National Geographic Image Collection
Page 455 © James P. Blair: National Geographic Image Collection
Page 458 © AP/Wide World